THE TIMES
1000
1996

Times Books, London
77-85 Fulham Palace Road,
Hammersmith, London W6 8JB

This edition first published by Times Books 1995

© Times Books 1995

All rights reserved. No part of this publication may
be reproduced, stored in a retrieval system, or
transmitted, in any form or by any means, electronic,
mechanical, photocopying or otherwise without the
prior written permission of the publisher.

Compiled by FT Extel

Edited by Martin Barrow, City News Editor, *The Times*

Design: Ivan Dodd and Ian Smith
Editorial/typesetting: Cicely Oliver

Printed and bound in Great Britain by The Bath Press

ISBN 0 7230 0753 5

THE TIMES
1000
1996

The Definitive Reference to Business Today

TIMES BOOKS

THE TIMES 2000

FOR THE PERSONAL COMPUTER

DATABASES

TOP 1000 UK Companies

TOP 1000 European Companies

TOP 100 USA Companies

TOP 100 Japanese Companies

TOP 50 UK Investment Trusts

TOP 25 UK Banks

TOP 25 European Banks (excl. UK)

TOP 15 UK Life Assurance Companies

TOP 25 UK Property Companies

TOP 25 UK Building Societies

TOP 15 UK Non-Life Insurance Companies

Information on companies in the Top 1000 listings includes:

COMPANY DATA
- Company name
- Registration number
- Full board of Directors
- Full address, telephone and fax number
- Business summary
- Names of Auditors, Solicitors and Bankers
- Sector of Business
- Period end date

FINANCIAL DATA
- Turnover
- Net profit before interest and tax
- Net profit after tax
- Total assets
- Capital employed
- Price: earnings ratio
- Debt: capital ratio
- Return on capital employed
- Equity market capitalisation
- Number of employees
- Turnover per employee
- Profit per employee
- Net profit as % of turnover
- Mid market price at balance date
- Earnings per share
- Dividends per share
- Gross dividend yield
- Dividend cover

FUNCTIONS INCLUDE:

- Rank companies by selected criteria
- View companies individually on screen, or in tabulated form with other companies
- Create personalised mailing lists
- Compare latest and previous year's performance company by company
- Create and save customised tables and paste them into other Windows applications
- Undertake unique searches for information using the following search criteria: country • business sector • P&L and balance sheet items • shares, dividends and earnings data • directors • associates • town • county • telephone area code • postcode • keywords from business summaries.

THE TIMES 2000 Runs under Microsoft Windows 3.1 Minimum recommended equipment IBM compatible 386 PC with VGA screen and 4MB RAM RRP £110.00 inc. VAT. ISBN 0 7230 0720 9
TIMES BOOKS, London

*For further information please contact: Juliet Felton,
HarperCollins Publishers 77-85 Fulham Palace Road London W6 8JB
Tel: 0181 307 4158 (direct line) Fax: 0181 307 4753*

CONTENTS

	page
Introduction	*7*
Compilation	*11*
The World's top 50 industrial companies	*12*
The UK's top 1000: introduction	*14*
The UK's top 100: analysis	*15*
The UK's top 50 profit makers	*40*
The UK's top 50 investment trusts	*41*
The UK's top 1000	*42*
Europe's top 1000: introduction	*62*
Europe's top 100: analysis	*63*
Europe's top 50 profit makers	*88*
Europe's top 50 market capitalisation	*89*
Europe's top 1000	*90*
North America's top 100	*110*
Japan's top 100	*112*
Australia, New Zealand & Southeast Asia's top 100	*114*
Index	*116*

Books for Business

Published by
Thorsons
A Division of HarperCollins*Publishers*

MINDSTORE
THE ULTIMATE
MENTAL FITNESS
PROGRAMME
Jack Black
£12.99 hb £6.99 pb
£11.99 inc VAT
Audio

SHE WHO DARES WINS
A WOMAN'S GUIDE
TO PROFESSIONAL
& PERSONAL SUCCESS
Eileen Gillibrand &
Jenny Mosley
Foreword by Anita Roddick
£7.99 pb

"I have no doubt that large numbers of people are finding his approach and techniques helpful, and that has to be a good thing" *Sir John Harvey Jones*

'*She Who Dares Wins* helps women to develop an awareness of their own potential...one of the few self-help books written by women for women' *Anita Roddick*

MIND OPENERS FOR MANAGERS
John O'Keefe
£5.99 pb

TRAINING WITH NLP
Joseph O'Connor & John Seymour
£9.99 pb

Thorsons Business Series Titles

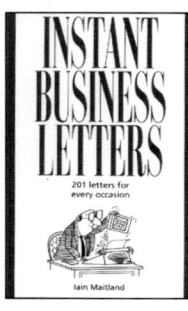

COPING WITH CHANGE AT WORK
Susan Jones
£6.99 pb

INSTANT BUSINESS LETTERS
Iain Maitland
£6.99 pb

THE PUBLIC SPEAKERS SOURCE BOOK
Prochnow & Prochnow
£8.99 pb

SURVIVING THE MEDIA
Diana Mather
£7.99 pb

Available from all good bookshops or alternatively for Access and Visa card holders call HarperCollins 24 hour telephone ordering service. Tel (0181) 307 4052

INTRODUCTION

WHAT IS THE BEST WAY to value a company? How can the size of a business be accurately measured? So many criteria are used every day as business people go about their routine – turnover, profit, market capitalisation, net assets, employment. All serve a useful purpose in helping to define a company: but can any single measure be taken, above all others, to establish beyond all argument the size of a business?

THIS WAS THE PROBLEM laid before a team of researchers at FT Extel as the first major review of *The Times 1000* got underway in late 1994. With the development of ever-more comprehensive databases providing instant access to the accounts of companies from around the world, it was apparent that Britain's premier corporate handbook was due for a fresh approach.

The aim was to make *The Times 1000* more relevant than ever to the needs of industry, to researchers and to students. There was a determination to make available a wider range of information, introducing some of the elements of on-line databases, in a format that retained the publication's clear and concise style.

At the heart of the revision was the first significant change to the way companies have been rated by *The Times 1000*. Until this edition the main tables were compiled according to company turnover. When the publication was originally conceived this measure had alluring advantages over other criteria. It was relatively simple to compile; it was a figure provided by the companies themselves; and it would be universally understood by readers from all walks of life.

It also had disadvantages. The most obvious was that financial companies – including banks, building societies and insurers – and property companies were excluded from the list of Britain's biggest companies because they had no obvious measure of turnover.

Secondly, the application of turnover as a measure of size was inclined to be biased in favour of agencies and traders, whose billings could be substantial even though the companies were relatively small. Thus a commodities trader, which bought and sold goods that were never delivered and made a profit on the margin, might appear larger than a substantial industrial company. So, too, would an advertising agency that booked air time on behalf of a client.

There was an understandable reluctance to jettison a definition that had served the publication well over so many years before establishing an alternative way of measuring companies that was itself free of inconsistencies. If turnover had inherent weaknesses, so, too, did other measures. Pre-tax profits could become losses one year without affecting the underlying size of the business; market capitalisation did not cover the many privately owned companies or subsidiaries of foreign-based corporations that make up a substantial part of the tables; numbers of employees favoured more labour-intensive businesses and discriminated against new, high-technology ventures.

The answer lies in a formula specifically devised by FT Extel for *The Times 1000* which, we believe, addresses most of the disadvantages of the previous rankings and creates a new-look table that is a more accurate reflection of what business in Britain and Europe is all about.

The formula is a measure of capital employed, a term that in itself conceals many arguments over what should and should not be included. For the record, the FT Extel formula comprises shareholders' funds plus long-term debt plus inter-group payables plus deferred liabilities minus technical reserves.

OTHER SIGNIFICANT CHANGES have been implemented in this year's edition with the aim of enhancing the information provided.

New analysis sections have been compiled, tracking return on capital employed, sales revenue and profitability for each of the 100 top British and European companies over the past five years, with a summary of each company's main areas of activity, ownership structure and origins. The charts provide an historic context against which the latest financial statistics can be assessed.

The main tables of the UK's top 1000 and Europe's top 1000 companies also have a new look. Financial information is now published on single pages and is focussed on key data for the most recent full financial year. Further detailed company information is included in the enhanced index which follows the traditional company tables. This gives the full company title, the names of senior directors and the full address of each business listed, providing an invaluable reference section.

Finally, the growing importance to the financial world of Australia and Southeast Asia is reflected in a new table listing the region's 100 top companies.

\multicolumn{3}{c}{THE WORLD'S TOP 10 INDUSTRIAL COMPANIES}
RANK	**COMPANY NAME**	**CAPITAL EMPLOYED £000**
1	Nippon Telegraph & Telephone Corpn JAP	73,301,390
2	General Motors Corpn USA	69,250,761
3	Tokyo Electric Power Co. JAP	69,116,782
4	General Electric Co. USA	63,826,150
5	Ford Motor Co. USA	53,481,472
6	Royal Dutch/Shell UK/NLD	50,207,000
7	Electricite de France FRA	45,015,779
8	Toyota Motor Corpn JAP	44,772,301
9	Exxon Corpn USA	38,767,659
10	Matsushita Electric Industrial Co. JAP	35,779,829

THESE SIGNIFICANT REVISIONS to *The Times 1000* this year ensure prominent changes at the top of each table.

Heading this year's list of the world's top 50 industrial companies is Nippon Telegraph and Telephone, Japan's leading telecommunications company, which boasts capital employed of £73.3 billion, more than four times the size of British Telecommunications, which enters the list in 46th place. General Motors, of the United States, is ranked second, with capital employed of £69.25 billion. Britain has four entries in the world's top 50, headed by Royal Dutch/Shell, jointly owned by Dutch interests, and ranked sixth with capital employed of £50.2 billion.

It is interesting that in the 1995 edition of *The Times 1000*, when tables were based on sales, the top five places were all Japanese companies – namely ITOCHU, Sumitomo, Mitsubishi, Marubeni and Mitsui – with General Motors lagging in sixth place. Measured by capital employed just four of the top companies are Japanese and four are American, and ITOCHU, one of Japan's formidable sogo sosha industrial trading giants, is relegated to 37th place.

INTRODUCTION

Europe's top 1000 has also undergone significant change, not least because of the introduction of companies from the financial sector. The largest company is the European Investment Bank, the principal financial entity of the the European Union, followed by the French banking group Societe Generale. Generally, French companies are better represented in the top 1000 as a result of the changes and, indeed, occupy five of the top ten places. But Britain continues to be the principal contributor, accounting for approximately one-third of all companies.

EUROPE'S TOP 10 COMPANIES

RANK	COMPANY NAME	CAPITAL EMPLOYED £000
1	European Investment Bank LUX	63,315,557
2	Societe Generale FRA	53,924,867
3	Royal Dutch/Shell1 UK/NLD	50,207,000
4	Electricite de France FRA	45,015,779
5	Cie de Suez FRA	29,817,951
6	Daimler-Benz GER	27,502,680
7	Siemens GER	25,449,826
8	France Telecom FRA	25,167,605
9	Credit Lyonnais FRA	24,648,708
10	British Gas UK	24,639,000

In the UK itself, the largest company is British Gas, the privatised utility, with capital employed of £24.64 billion. At some distance follows British Petroleum, whose capital employed totals £20.78 billion. There is also strong financial flavour to the top companies, with HSBC Holdings, parent company of the Midland Bank, placed third and with four other banks placed in the top ten.

THE UK'S TOP 10 COMPANIES

RANK	COMPANY NAME	CAPITAL EMPLOYED £000
1	British Gas	24,639,000
2	British Petroleum Company	20,777,000
3	HSBC Holdings	20,637,000
4	Shell Transport and Trading Company[1]	20,082,800
5	Abbey National	17,545,000
6	British Telecommunications	16,392,000
7	Hanson	14,832,000
8	National Westminster Bank	13,186,000
9	Barclays	11,562,000
10	Salomon Brothers Europe	11,086,900

NOTES: [1]Based on 40% of Royal Dutch Shell Group.

The highest placed property group is Land Securities, occupying 22nd position with capital employed of £5.10 billion. The company also heads up the property sector table, measured by total properties, with a value of £5.17 billion. MEPC is placed second, with total properties of £3.35 billion and British Land is third, with total properties of £1.98 billion.

The Halifax, Britain's largest building society, enters the table in 23rd place, with capital employed of £4.97 billion, and will advance further next year when the merger with the Leeds Permanent is taken into account. This may also be the final time the Halifax, with total assets of £72.15 billion, heads the building society table, for the Leeds merger represents the first stage in the combined entity's eventual flotation on the stock market, following in the footsteps of the Abbey National. This would leave the Nationwide, with total assets of £35.3 billion, as the top building society. Further mergers are anticipated in this sector: Abbey National has already taken over National & Provincial, which is ranked ninth with total assets of £13.26 billion ,and Cheltenham & Gloucester, placed sixth with total assets of £19.4 billion is now a subsidiary of Lloyds Bank.

In UK banking HSBC Holdings, domiciled in Britain since the acquisition of Midland Bank, is the dominant player, with capital employed of £20.64 billion. Abbey National, the building society-turned bank, is second with capital employed of £17.5 billion, followed by National Westminster, whose capital employed totals £13.2 billion. In fourth place is Barclays Bank, with capital employed of £11.56 billion.

In Europe the largest banks are from France, led by Societe Generale, with capital employed of £53.9 billion and Credit Lyonnais, with capital employed of £24.6 billion. Deutsche Bank, with capital employed of £21.8 billion, is followed by Britain's HSBC.

Martin Barrow, City News Editor, *The Times*

HarperCollins BusinessBooks

REENGINEERING MANAGEMENT

THE MANDATE FOR NEW LEADERSHIP
James Champy
Reengineering is the business revolution of the '90s. James Champy, a founder of CSC Index, the management consultancy firm that pioneered the development and practice of reengineering, shows how to put these ground-breaking theories into practice.

HARDBACK £17.99

THE REENGINEERING REVOLUTION

THE HANDBOOK
Michael Hammer and Steven A. Stanton
Practical guidance on the nuts and bolts of reengineering.
'In this brilliant and readable handbook, the father of reengineering explains what's gone wrong – and how to set it right'
Tom Peters

HARDBACK £18.00

THE DISCIPLINE OF MARKET LEADERS

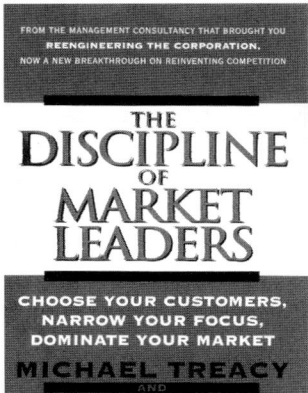

Michael Treacy and Fred Wiersema
From CSC Index comes a new breakthrough on reinventing competition. This shows how successful companies – market leaders – excel at delivering one type of value to their chosen customer.

HARDBACK £16.99

THE END OF THE NATION STATE

THE RISE OF REGIONAL ECONOMIES
Kenichi Ohmae
Offers a vision of the future that nobody involved in business can afford to ignore.
'Ken Ohmae is the best writer in the world at summarizing and forecasting the fast-paced changes in international business'
Philip H. Knight, Chairman and CEO, Nike, Inc.

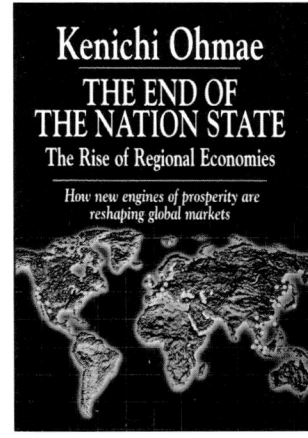

HARDBACK £16.99

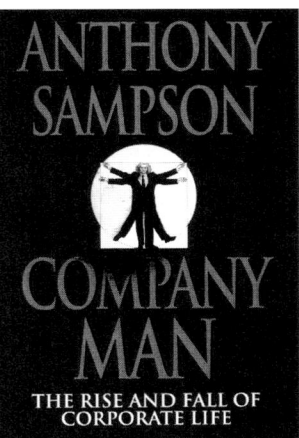

COMPANY MAN

THE RISE AND FALL OF CORPORATE LIFE
Anthony Sampson
Tells the dramatic story of the *Company Man*, the dominant species of the 20th century.
'A comprehensive and entertaining guide'
Sunday Telegraph

HARDBACK £20.00

All titles are available from good bookshops
OR 24 hour Telephone Ordering Service
for Access/Visa Cardholders
Tel: Glasgow 0141 772 2281
or London 0181 307 4052
Please quote Department 81K

HarperCollinsPublishers

BUSINESS REFERENCE FROM THE
TIMES BOOKS
RANGE

The Times Guide To The New British State
The Government Machine in the 1990s

Michael Dynes and David Walker

The first book to take the lid off the way Britain in the 1990s is really governed and to chart the new Whitehall.

£9.99 Hardback

The Times Guide To World Organisations
Their role and reach in the New World Order

Richard Owen

The first book to explore the changing roles of international organisations and the questions facing them.

£16.99 Hardback

NEW FOR JANUARY 1996

The Times Atlas Of The World
9th Comprehensive Edition
"Without doubt, the finest reference atlas ever produced."
Lord Shackleton, former president of the RGS.
£85.00 Hardback

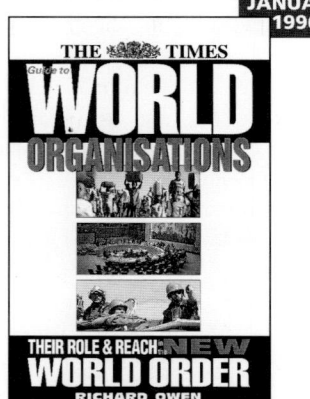

The Times Guide To The European Parliament June 1994
Robert Morgan
A unique and essential guide to the European Parliament after the June 1994 elections.
£25.00 Hardback

The Times Atlas Of The World
7th Concise Edition
Contains new and stunning mapping of unrivalled accuracy.
£40.00 Hardback Slipcased

The Times Guide To The Single European Market
Britain in a Europe without Frontiers
Richard Owen and Michael Dynes
A comprehensive handbook
£8.99 Paperback

COMPILATION

Please read these notes before consulting the tables.

FT Extel is responsible for all the tabulations in *The Times 1000*. For any queries regarding the figures in the tables, readers should either telephone 0171 825 8000 or write to FT Extel, Fitzroy House, 13-17 Epworth Street, London EC2A 4DL. Data in the book is sourced from FT Extel's Structured Database.

FT Extel and Times Books are grateful for the assistance given by many companies in supplying copies of their accounts directly to them.

The rankings in this year's tables are not directly comparable with those in previous editions since the rankings are now based on Capital Employed (*see* below for definition) rather than Turnover. This means that it is now possible to include most financial sector companies together with commercial and industrial sector companies within the main tables. Some mutual insurance companies are, however, excluded by this new ranking criterion. A further consequence of this change is that there are no comparative rankings shown in this edition of the book although they will appear in future editions.

Company accounting data shown in the tables is the latest available from annual reports and accounts at the date of going to press. Details of presidents, chairmen, chief executives, managing directors and finance directors are based on the latest available information at the same date. Only the principal position is shown where more than one is held.

Preliminary figures have not been used anywhere in the book. Where a company has reported figures for an accounting period of other than one year then, where appropriate, the figures have been converted to an annualised basis for comparative purposes. Where available, consolidated accounts have been used.

Fluctuations in exchange rates can lead to a misrepresentation of the relative growth rates of companies when international comparisons are made. The exchange rate used to convert foreign currency values to pounds sterling varies and is as close as possible to that obtaining at the year-end of each company.

In order to avoid overloading the tables with notes which apply generally, the following are definitions of the principal items which appear in the book:

1. Capital Employed: Shareholders' funds plus long-term loans (where separately disclosed) plus intra-group payables plus deferred liabilities less (for insurance companies) technical reserves.

2. Exchange Rates: As at each company's relevant financial period end.

3. Market Capitalisation: Total market capitalisation of each company's share capital at the latest balance sheet date.

4. Number of Employees: Where possible the average full-time equivalent number of employees during the latest accounting period. Otherwise, if disclosed by the company, the number of employees as at the latest period.

5. Profit Before Tax: Profit before deducting the tax charged. This data is also shown graphically for the leading companies.

6. Profit Before Interest and Tax (PBIT): Profit before taxation and interest payable.

7. Turnover: Invoiced value of goods sold excluding sales taxes (such as VAT) and other duties. If a company does not disclose a turnover figure because of the nature of its business, as is the case with many financial sector companies for example, an alternative figure is provided. For insurance companies it will show the sum of life business and general business net premium income. For other companies it will show the sum of investment income, interest income and other income.

8. Total Assets: This gives the total of all the company's assets at the balance sheet date.

9. Return on Capital Employed: Latest profit before tax plus latest finance charges divided by the previous year capital employed, expressed as a percentage. This has been rounded up to the nearest whole percentage.

10. L as a prefix denotes a loss.

Abbreviations
G: Governor; *P:* President; *CH:* Chairman; *CE:* Chief Executive; *MD:* Managing Director; *JMD:* Joint Managing Director; *FD:* Finance Director

Country Codes
ANT Netherlands Antilles; AUS Australia; AUT Austria; BEL Belgium; BER Bermuda; CAN Canada; CHI China; DNK Denmark; FIN Finland; FRA France; GER Germany; HKG Hong Kong; IDN Indonesia; IRL Republic of Ireland; ITA Italy; JAP Japan; KOR South Korea; LIE Liechtenstein; LUX Luxembourg; MAL Malaysia; NLD Netherlands; NOR Norway; NZL New Zealand; POR Portugal; SIN Singapore; SPA Spain; SWE Sweden; SWI Switzerland; THA Thailand; TWN Taiwan; UK United Kingdom; USA United States of America; VEN Venezuela.

THE WORLD'S TOP 50 INDUSTRIAL COMPANIES

THE TRADE WAR between America and Japan is far from settled. The watchdog World Trade Organisation (WTO) may have opened for business with the qualified blessing of the two economic superpowers, but the flashpoints that dogged the General Agreement of Tariffs and Trade, the WTO's predecessor body, live on.

Routine meetings between American and Japanese trade representatives may culminate in handshakes but behind the diplomatic smiles there is real tension. In the approach to the next US presidential election trade is likely to become a key campaign issue, with the Republicans pledging a much tougher stand on the question of sanctions than President Clinton has been able to.

It would not be difficult to convince the American public that free trade has so little to offer. The North American Free Trade Agreement, which lifted trade restrictions with Mexico in particular, has inflated imports and leeched jobs across the Rio Grande, starting a new depression in Texas. With anti-Japanese sentiment in America never too far from the surface, it is easy to see how a tougher trade policy can be translated into votes.

The automotive industry, in which America vests much industrial pride, could again become the main battleground as Japan seeks to lift its share of foreign markets to offset the impact of its sluggish domestic economy. Electronics and communications also present pitfalls for the negotiators charged with keeping the two nations at bay.

Japan believes it cannot afford to make concessions. The country has effectively been in recession since 1990, two years longer than the oil shock slowdown of the 1970s, and there appears to be no sign of an imminent recovery. The unemployment rate, officially put at three per cent, is acknowledged to be nearer five to six per cent; equity and property prices, by which Japan customarily measures its economic wealth, have fallen by 60 per cent from their peak at the end of 1989. Businesses have been failing at the rate of 18,000 a year and there is an estimated 40 trillion yen (£294 million) worth of bad debt in the financial sector. A strong yen has made exports difficult to sustain.

Japan's image as a strong, wealth-creating economy is increasingly being challenged by individual investors, too. The additional household wealth accumulated during the boom years has all been wiped out, leaving 15 per cent of households with negative equity. Deflation is now eroding wealth created in earlier years.

America's economic situation must seem benign by comparison. The US was on target for economic growth of between 1.5 and 2 per cent in 1995 and of 2.5 per cent in 1996. Employment has generally stabilised and consumer expenditure has recovered from the weak point of the recession. But analysts are far from unanimous in their belief that full economic health has been restored.

Jobs are still being lost in some regions and sectors of industry, personal incomes are flat and price-cutting is widespread as a means of enticing customers back into the market, which has the effect of sustaining sales but squeezing profit margins. A large trade deficit suggests cutbacks and closures implemented during the recession have impaired the ability of American companies to respond quickly to pick-ups in demand in certain sectors of the economy. A gradual slide back into recession cannot be ruled out altogether.

So, the stakes are high for a successful resolution to the trade dispute for both sides, with America and Japan desperately needing to keep international markets open to their goods and services, yet reluctant to give further ground within their domestic markets.

ALTHOUGH AMERICAN MANUFACTURERS have made much progress in enhancing competitiveness and regaining market share since the 1970s, Japan's persistent advantage on the world stage is difficult to overcome. Our table of the world's top industrial companies (opposite) confirms the absolute domination by Japanese and American companies, who account for no less than 30 of the 50 largest companies, as measured by capital employed. Each country has four companies in the top ten.

The world's largest company is Nippon Telegraph and Telephone Corporation, with capital employed of £73.3 billion. America's General Motors, the largest auto manufacturer in the world and with interests in aerospace and information technology, is second, with capital employed of £69.25 billion. They are followed by Tokyo Electric Power (£69.12 billion) and two American companies, General Electric (£63.8 billion) and Ford Motor Co. (£53.48 billion).

Royal Dutch/Shell, the Anglo-Dutch oil and gas company, represents Britain's highest entry, placed sixth with capital employed of £50 billion. Three other British companies secure places in the top 50. British Gas is ranked 19th, with capital employed of £24.6 billion; British Petroleum is 28th, with capital employed of £20.78 billion; and British Telecommunications is 46th, with capital employed of £16.39 billion, barely one-quarter of the size of its Japanese counterpart.

Europe has a total of 16 companies in the top 50. The leading French company is Electricite de France which, placed seventh with capital employed of £45 billion, is the highest-ranked state-owned corporation in the world. Other French companies include France Telecom (ranked 18th, with capital employed of £25.1 billion), SNCF, the railway and shipping combine (22nd, £22.4 billion), which are both also state-owned, and Elf Aquitaine, which is 23rd with capital employed of £22.25 billion.

The five German companies in the top 50 are headed by Daimler-Benz, which is 16th with capital employed of £27.5 billion, and Siemens, 17th with capital employed of £25.5 billion. Volkswagen emerges as Europe's largest auto manufacturer, placed 25th with capital employed of £21.9 billion and Veba is ranked 33rd with capital employed of £19.47 billion.

Other European companies include Spain's Telefonica de Espana, (34th, with capital employed of £18.45 billion) and, from Italy, IRI-Istituto per la Ricostruzione Industriale (38th, £17.24 billion) and ENI-Ente Nazionale Idrocarburi, the state oil and gas combine (47th, £16.3 billion).

Hydro-Quebec, of Canada, is ranked 21st, with capital employed of £22.4 billion, while Latin America's largest company, Petroleos de Venezuela, is 29th, just one place behind British Petroleum, with capital employed of £20.44 billion. Korea Electric Power claims 50th place, with capital employed of £15.1 billion, a testimony to the growing industrial strength of Korea and other economies of Southeast Asia.

DESPITE THE PHENOMENAL GROWTH in the sectors of electronics and information technology, the provision of energy is still the driving force behind the world's largest corporations, with oil, gas and electricity the main business of 18 of the top 50 companies. The communications industry accounts for eight companies, while transport manufacture and distribution retains its traditional importance to the global economy with seven entries. Significantly, just one retail group earns a place among the elite top 50: Sears Roebuck, of America, with capital employed of £16.5 billion, is ranked 45th.

THE WORLD'S TOP 50 INDUSTRIAL COMPANIES

RANK	COMPANY NAME	HEADQUARTERS	SECTOR	CAPITAL EMPLOYED £000	YEAR END
1	Nippon Telegraph & Telephone Corpn	JAP	Communications	73,301,390	31/03/94
2	General Motors Corpn	USA	Transport – Manufacture & Distribution	69,250,761	31/12/94
3	Tokyo Electric Power Co.	JAP	Electricity	69,116,782	31/03/94
4	General Electric Co.	USA	Electricals	63,826,150	31/12/94
5	Ford Motor Co.	USA	Transport – Manufacture & Distribution	53,481,472	31/12/93
6	Royal Dutch/Shell	UK/NLD	Oil, Gas & Nuclear Fuels	50,207,000	31/12/94
7	Electricite de France	FRA	Electricity	45,015,779	31/12/93
8	Toyota Motor Corpn	JAP	Transport – Manufacture & Distribution	44,772,301	30/06/94
9	Exxon Corpn	USA	Oil, Gas & Nuclear Fuels	38,767,659	31/12/94
10	Matsushita Electric Industrial Co.	JAP	Electronics	35,779,829	31/03/94
11	Hitachi	JAP	Electronics	34,595,155	31/03/94
12	Kansai Electric Power Co.	JAP	Electricity	32,643,090	31/03/94
13	Chubu Electric Power Co.	JAP	Electricity	29,155,757	31/03/94
14	Nissan Motor Co.	JAP	Transport – Manufacture & Distribution	28,424,453	31/03/94
15	AT&T Corpn	USA	Communications	27,745,609	31/12/94
16	Daimler-Benz	GER	Transport – Manufacture & Distribution	27,502,680	31/12/94
17	Siemens	GER	Electricals	25,449,826	30/09/94
18	France Telecom	FRA	Communications	25,167,605	31/12/93
19	British Gas	UK	Oil, Gas & Nuclear Fuels	24,639,000	31/12/94
20	International Business Machines Corpn	USA	Communications	24,201,348	31/12/94
21	Hydro-Quebec	CAN	Electricity	22,417,289	31/12/93
22	SNCF	FRA	Transport Services	22,415,742	31/12/94
23	Ste Elf Aquitaine	FRA	Oil, Gas & Nuclear Fuels	22,252,167	31/12/93
24	Mitsubishi Corpn	JAP	Soga Sosha	22,127,893	31/03/94
25	Volkswagen	GER	Transport – Manufacture & Distribution	21,922,476	31/12/94
26	Philip Morris Cos	USA	Food Manufacturing	21,297,539	31/12/94
27	RWE	GER	Electricity	20,837,346	30/06/94
28	British Petroleum Company	UK	Oil, Gas & Nuclear Fuels	20,777,000	31/12/94
29	Petroleos de Venezuela	VEN	Oil, Gas & Nuclear Fuels	20,445,899	31/12/93
30	East Jap Railway Co.	JAP	Transport Services	20,433,682	31/03/94
31	Fiat	ITA	Transport – Manufacture & Distribution	20,040,540	31/12/93
32	Mitsui & Co.	JAP	Soga Sosha	19,717,390	31/03/94
33	Veba	GER	Oil, Gas & Nuclear Fuels	19,473,111	31/12/94
34	Telefonica de Espana	SPA	Communications	18,451,800	31/12/94
35	GTE Corpn	USA	Communications	17,832,535	31/12/94
36	Nippon Steel Corpn	JAP	Metal & Metal Forming	17,815,667	31/03/94
37	ITOCHU Corpn	JAP	Soga Sosha	17,454,848	31/03/94
38	IRI-Istituto per la Ricostruzione Industriale	ITA	Other Financial	17,239,434	31/12/93
39	E.I. Du Pont De Nemours & Co.	USA	Oil, Gas & Nuclear Fuels	17,147,002	31/12/93
40	BellSouth Corpn	USA	Communications	17,084,949	31/12/94
41	Toshiba Corpn	JAP	Electronics	17,047,979	31/03/94
42	Tohoku Electric Power Co.	JAP	Electricity	16,852,838	31/03/94
43	Sony Corpn	JAP	Electronics	16,842,722	31/03/94
44	Mobil Corpn	USA	Oil, Gas & Nuclear Fuels	16,677,531	31/12/94
45	Sears Roebuck and Co.	USA	Stores	16,529,883	31/12/94
46	British Telecommunications	UK	Communications	16,392,000	31/03/95
47	ENI-Ente Nazionale Idrocarburi	ITA	Oil, Gas & Nuclear Fuels	16,317,210	31/12/93
48	Kyushu Electric Power Co.	JAP	Electricity	16,151,497	31/03/93
49	Marubeni Corpn	JAP	Soga Sosha	15,709,176	31/03/94
50	Korea Electric Power	KOR	Electricity	15,108,393	31/12/93

THE UK'S TOP 1000: INTRODUCTION

ENERGY AND FINANCIAL SERVICES, the two mainstays of the UK economy, dominate the ranking of Britain's top companies, with traditional manufacturing businesses continuing to be overshadowed.

British Gas emerges as Britain's biggest company, comfortably ahead of British Petroleum, HSBC Holdings, parent company of Midland Bank, and Shell Transport and Trading. With capital employed of over £24.6 billion, British Gas retains a formidable stronghold on its market of gas supply, despite the emergence of rival suppliers, and is developing interests overseas in oil and gas production.

BP is Britain's second largest company – but only just – with capital employed of £20.8 billion, followed by HSBC with £20.6 billion and Shell with £20.08 billion. All three have strong international interests, with BP earning substantial revenues in North America and, increasingly, South America, while HSBC still earns 40 per cent of revenues in Hong Kong and Shell shares in Royal Dutch Shell's global portfolio of petroleum assets.

THE INCLUSION OF FINANCIAL COMPANIES in *The Times 1000* for the first time has a dramatic impact on the constitution of the list. In addition to HSBC, Abbey National, National Westminster, Barclays and Salomon Brothers (Europe) all earn places in the top ten. No less than 14 of the top 50 companies operate in banking or insurance.

Abbey National, the former building society, with capital employed of £17.5 billion, is ranked ahead of National Westminster Bank and Barclays, with capital employed of £13.19 billion and £11.56 billion respectively.

BP still lays claim to the highest turnover at £33.12 billion, followed by Shell at £24.77 billion. They are followed by HSBC at £13.97 billion and British Telecom at £13.89 billion. British Gas, with turnover of just under £9.7 billion would have been ranked ninth under the book's previous ranking criteria.

Among the top ten companies only Hanson, ranked seventh, is involved in manufacturing and, ironically, the company has also decided that energy represents a sensible way forward by acquiring Eastern Group, the electricity distribution business. B.A.T Industries is ranked seven places lower, although its inclusion among the leading companies owes much to its financial services subsidiaries, Allied Dunbar and Eagle Star. In any case, its tobacco manufacturing interests are all located outside Britain, mainly in America, Germany and Brazil. Grand Metropolitan, the beverages and food company, and Imperial Chemical Industries, are ranked 16th and 17th respectively.

MEASURED BY STOCK MARKET VALUE the biggest company is British Telecom, with a price tag of £24.38 billion, followed closely by BP at £23.4 billion and Shell at £23.08 billion. Once again, British Gas, at £13.6 billion, trails behind the leaders, not helped by adverse investor sentiment in the City over fears of tighter regulatory controls and greater competition. HSBC's stock market value is £18.4 billion.

HSBC is also Britain's most profitable company, earning pre-tax profits of £3.17 billion before tax in the last financial year, with British Telecom second at £2.66 billion and Shell third at £2.65 billion. BP earned £2.28 billion, while Barclays, Glaxo Wellcome and B.A.T Industries all earned £1.8 billion.

THE DUBIOUS HONOUR of incurring the highest loss goes to Fisons, the pharmaceuticals group with a £463.7 million deficit after restructuring costs and write-offs. Eurotunnel, now fully operational but saddled with a massive debt burden, incurred losses of £386.9 million while Central Transport Rental Group, formerly Tiphook, lost £331.1 million. However, there are relatively few examples of the extreme losses incurred by many companies in the depths of the recession, and the profits performance of UK plc has generally stabilised.

THE BIGGEST EMPLOYER is the Post Office with a workforce of 193,196 – an indication of the sensitivities surrounding attempts to privatise the organisation. British Telecom is next, with 148,900 employees despite a significant reduction in the workforce since privatisation. British Rail's workforce of 128,414, the third largest in Britain, will also undergo substantial change as the privatisation of the railway network proceeds. BTR is fourth, employing 124,491.

At the other end of the scale a number of companies, mainly active in investment or property, employ a minimum number of staff in relation to the relatively large scale of their assets. Thus Greycoat, one of the country's premier property companies, has a staff of only 34 and Burford Holdings employs 23. But few can match Bourne End which, with capital employed of almost £145 million, has just one full-time member of staff.

IN STORES Tesco, ranked 32nd overall, emerges as the largest retailer, with capital employed of £4.09 billion, ahead of Marks and Spencer (36th, £3.95 billion) and J. Sainsbury (38th, £3.7 billion). Measured by turnover, Sainsbury recorded record sales of £10.6 billion and Tesco £10.1 billion. Marks and Spencer's sales were £6.54 billion.

A CURRENT FEATURE of corporate life is the revival of activity in mergers and acquisitions. After several years of relative quiet in M&A, when the recession dampened corporate ambitions, a number of multi-million takeover bids have taken place, with activity mainly focussed on the sectors of electricity, building societies and pharmaceuticals.

Glaxo's bid for Wellcome, which established Britain's largest pharmaceuticals company, was worth £9.1 billion, while Financiere Richemont's offer for outstanding shares in Rothman's International valued the company at £4.15 billion. In the electricity sector Hanson's agreed bid for Eastern Group was worth £2.5 billion. Trafalgar House bid £1.2 billion for Northern Electric. Scottish Power bid £1 billion for Manweb and America's Southern made a £1 billion bid for South Western Electricity.

In the sector of building societies, which is rapidly declining in numbers because of takeovers and conversions to plc status, Lloyds Bank acquired Cheltenham & Gloucester, Abbey National acquired National & Provincial for £1.35 billion and Halifax absorbed the Leeds, with the intention of subsequently converting the merged entity into a bank.

British merchant banks were also under siege, with Dresdner Bank acquiring Kleinwort Benson for £1 million, and Swiss Bank Corporation taking over S.G. Warburg for £860 million. America's Merrill Lynch purchased Smith New Court, the stockbroker, for £526.3 million.

THE UK'S TOP 100: ANALYSIS

1 British Gas

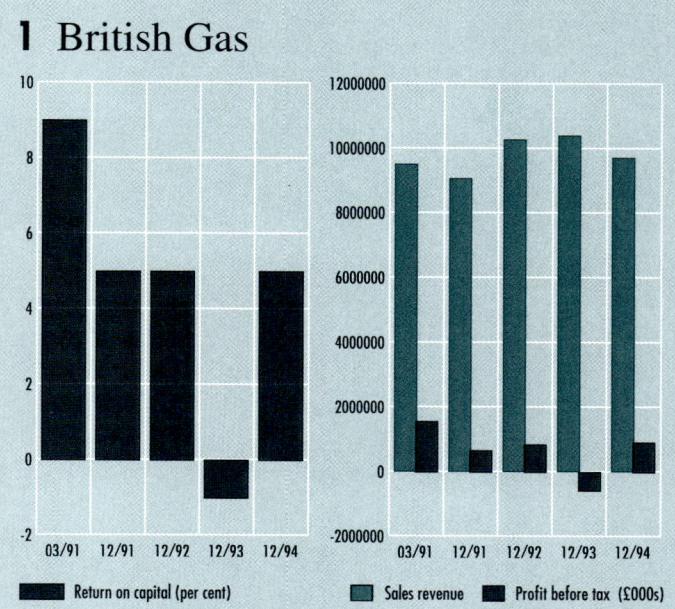

The group's principal business is the transmission, distribution and supply of gas in the United Kingdom, supported by a range of services to customers, and the marketing of gas appliances. The group has operations exploring for and producing oil and gas and is also active in the overseas gas supply market. In December 1993 the group reorganised its domestic activities into five new businesses: public gas supply, contract trading, transportation and storage, servicing and installation, and retailing. British Gas was privatised in 1986, obtaining a stock market listing through a public offer of shares.

2 British Petroleum Company

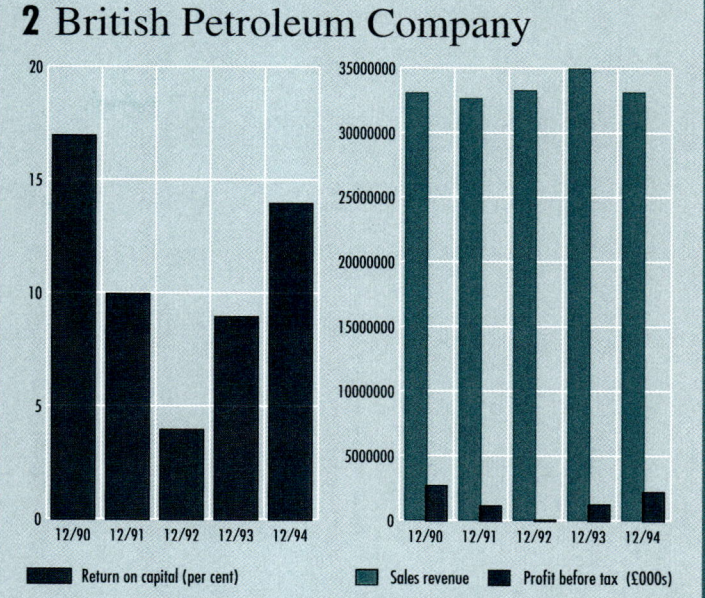

The group's principal activities are oil and gas exploration, oil refining, marketing, supply and transportation, and chemical manufacturing and marketing. BP produced an average of 1.3 million barrels of oil per day in 1994, with an average refinery throughput of 1.7 million barrels per day. Principal sources of crude oil are the UK and North America, with substantial reserves in Colombia. The company was established in 1909. Its name was changed from Anglo-Persian Oil to Anglo-Iranian Oil and subsequently to British Petroleum in 1954. The UK government acquired a controlling interest in 1914. The company was privatised through four public share offers between 1977-87.

3 HSBC Holdings

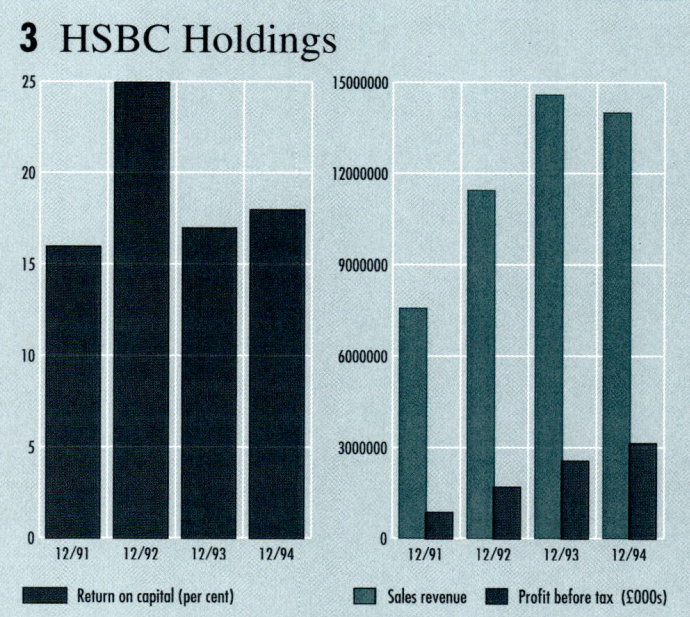

Through subsidiary and associated undertakings, the group provides financial services, including commercial, investment and private banking and insurance. The company owns Midland Bank, which was acquired in 1992 to become part of an international network of some 3,000 offices in 65 countries across Europe, the Asia Pacific region and the Middle East. HSBC became the holding company of the Hongkong and Shanghai Banking Corporation by way of a scheme of arrangement in 1991 and is now domiciled in London. Other wholly-owned subsidiaries include Samuel Montagu and America's Marine Midland Bank, both formerly part of the Midland group.

4 Shell Transport and Trading

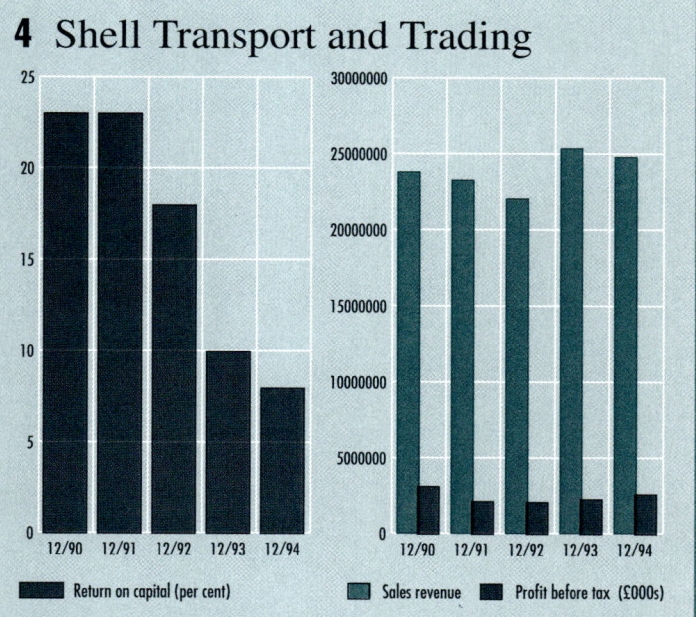

Shell is engaged in exploration, production, refining and marketing of oil and gas, coal mining and processing, and the production of chemicals. In conjunction with Royal Dutch Petroleum, a Netherlands company, Shell owns, directly or indirectly, investments in the numerous companies that constitute the Royal Dutch/Shell Group. Royal Dutch has a 60 per cent interest in the group and Shell 40 per cent. Shell's principal investments are its direct holdings in The Shell Petroleum Company, Shell Petroleum NV and Shell Petroleum Inc. The company supplied an average of 7.5 million barrels of oil per day in 1994 and processed 3.5 million barrels per day in its own refineries.

THE UK'S TOP 100: ANALYSIS   5-8

5 Abbey National

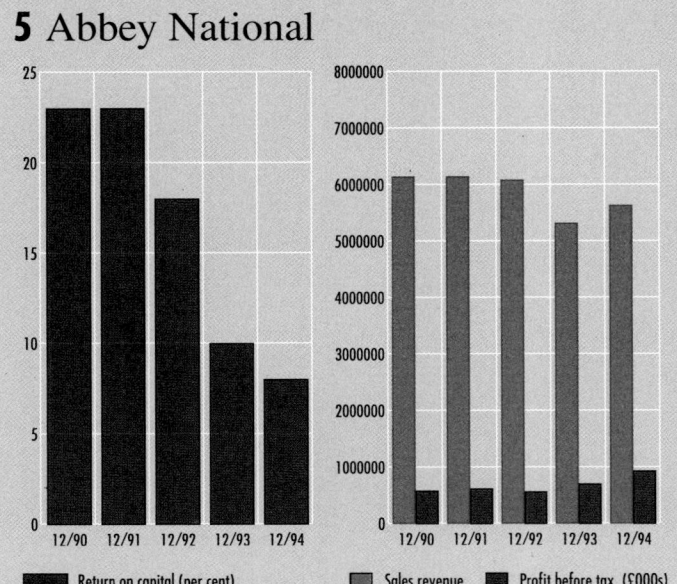

The group's principal activity is the provision of personal financial services, particularly those associated with mortgages and the residential property market. The business includes UK retail banking, life assurance and treasury operations. Established as a building society in 1944, the conversion to a public limited company took place in 1989 in tandem with a public offer of shares and a stock market listing in London. Acquisitions since flotation include Scottish Mutual Assurance for £288 million and HMC Group for £58 million. In April 1995 the company announced it sought to re-open merger talks with National & Provincial Building Society.

6 British Telecommunications

Alongside its traditional business of providing telephone services for residential and commercial customers, primarily in Britain but increasingly overseas, BT is developing interests in information technology, mobile telecommunications, satellite and multi-media. Formerly part of a single entity with the Post Office, the company reorganised as a statutory corporation in 1984 and subsequently privatised through a public offer of shares in three tranches. It acquired a 20 per cent interest in America's MCI in 1994, investing a total of $4.3 billion. The two companies then formed Concert, a $1 billion joint venture to provide global communications for multinational customers.

7 Hanson

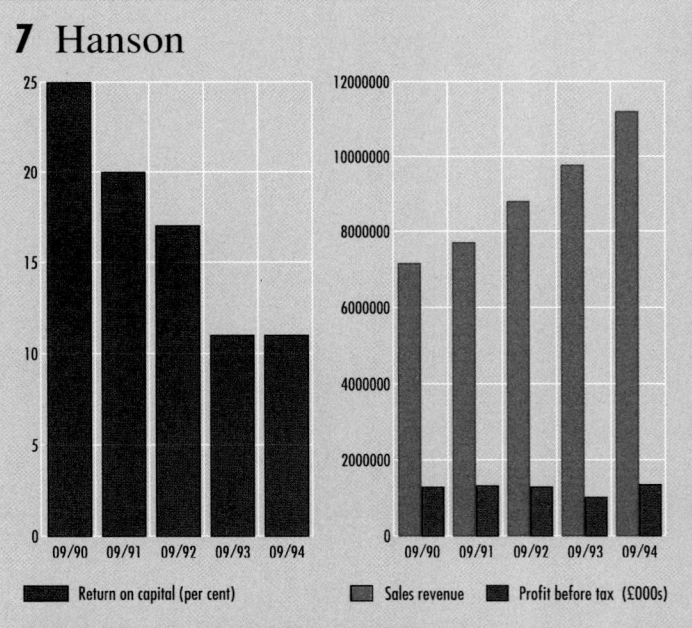

The company acts as an industrial management company for a group engaged in coal mining, chemicals and other industrial products, tobacco, propane, other consumer products, aggregates, forest products and building materials. Subsidiaries in the industrial sector include Peabody (coal mining), Quantum Chemical Co., and Grove Worldwide Co. (cranes). In consumer products Hanson owns Imperial Tobacco, whose brands include Regal, Embassy, Lambert & Butler and St Bruno. Building products subsidiaries take in ARC (aggregates, concrete products and waste management), Cavenham Forest Industries, London Brick and Jacuzzi.

8 National Westminster Bank

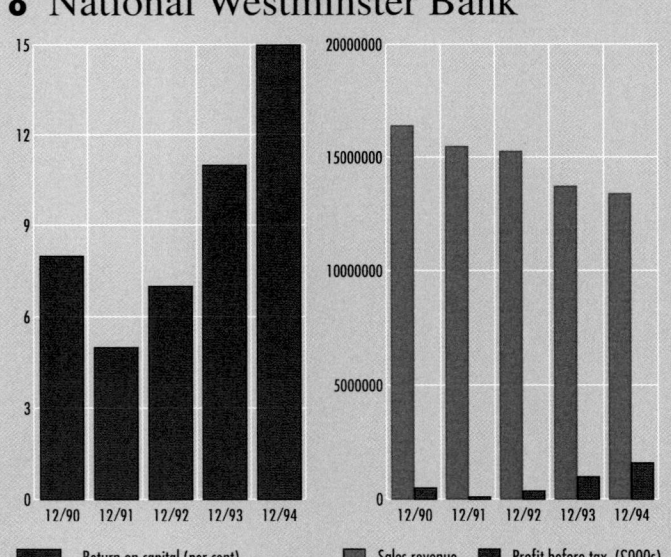

The bank and its subsidiaries provide banking and financial services through offices and branches in the UK and overseas. Activities comprise the UK branch business, US retail operations, international businesses and NatWest Markets. Subsidiaries include Ulster Bank, Coutts & Co., and Lombard North Central. In March 1994 the $500 million acquisition of Citizens First Bancorp of New Jersey was announced, followed in June 1994 by the $300 million purchase of Central Jersey Bancorp. National Westminster Bank was formed in 1968 through the merger of National Provincial Bank (established 1833) and Westminster Bank (established 1836).

9-12 THE UK'S TOP 100: ANALYSIS

9 Barclays

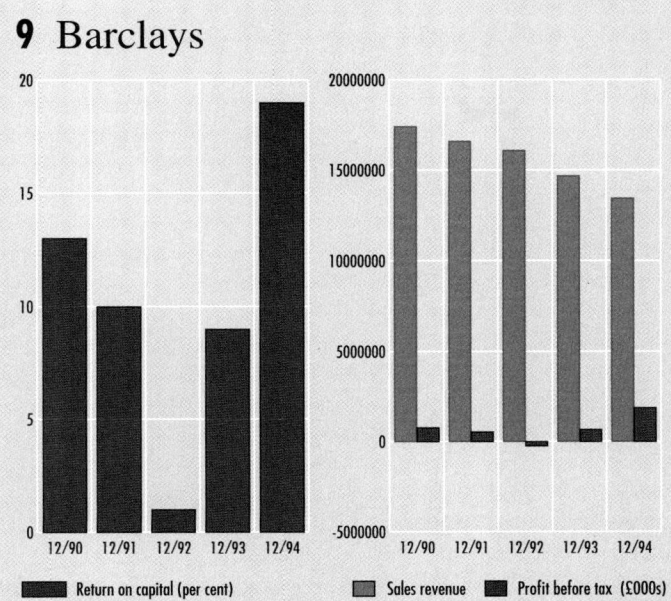

Barclays' principal businesses are the UK retail bank and BZW, its international investment bank. A range of commercial and investment banking, insurance and related services is provided through 2,400 UK branches, with a further 1,000 offices overseas in 77 countries. UK banking services include Barclaycard and a leasing and factoring group. Barclays Financial Services, embracing Barclays Life, conducts pensions, life and general insurance and trustee activities. Corporate and Institutional Banking Services, established in 1994, serves large corporate and institutional customers. The European Retail Banking Group operates in France, Spain, Portugal and Germany.

10 Salomon Brothers Europe

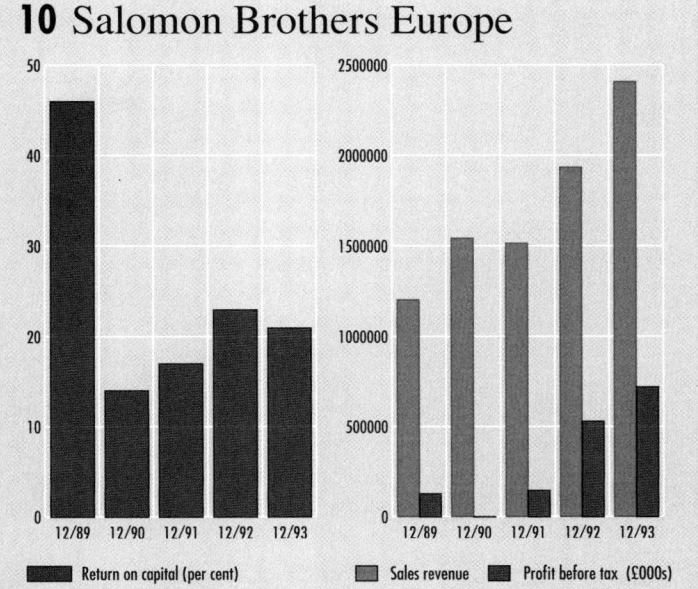

The group, which is wholly owned by Salomon Inc. (USA), conducts business in securities, mortgage lending and asset management. Subsidiaries comprise Salomon Brothers International (financial services), Salomon Brothers UK (gilt edged market maker), Salomon Brothers UK Equity (equity market maker), The Mortgage Corporation Group and The Residential Mortgage Company. The company was incorporated in 1981 and was formerly known as Phibro UK and Phibro-Salomon.

11 Eurotunnel Group

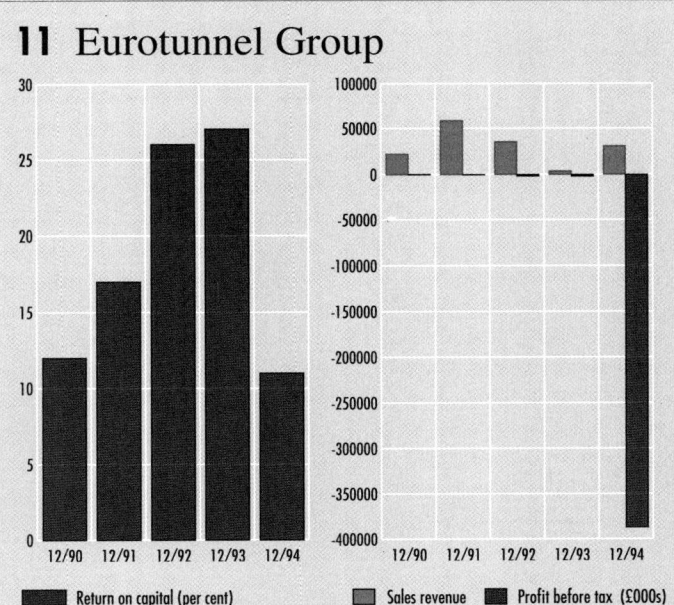

Eurotunnel PLC, Eurotunnel SA and their subsidiaries collectively make up the Eurotunnel Group, which operates the Channel tunnel rail link between Britain and France under the terms of a concession that expires in the year 2052. The concession agreement provides that revenues and costs shall be shared equally between the UK and French companies. Eurotunnel was incorporated in 1985 to design, finance, construct and subsequently operate the fixed rail link. Its shares were introduced to the stock exchange in London and Paris in 1987. The project was formally opened in 1994.

12 News International

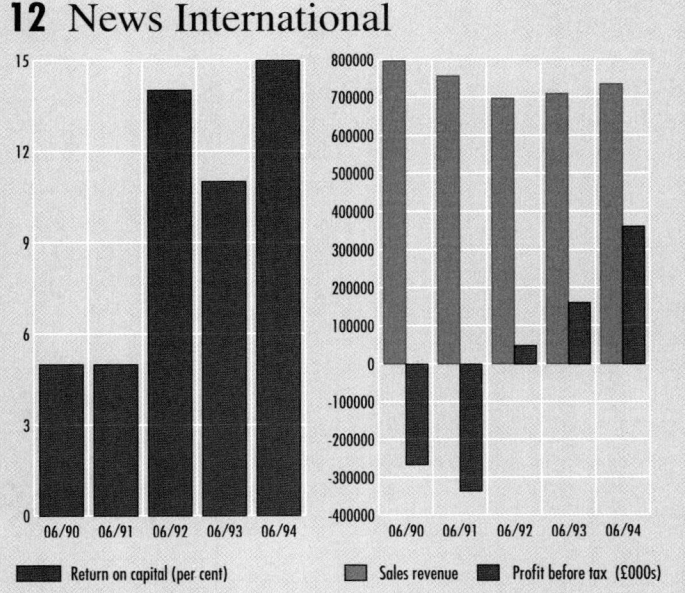

The group's principal activity is the printing and publishing of national newspapers in the UK, including *The Times*, *Sunday Times*, *The Sun*, *News of the World*, and *Today*. The Times Supplements also publishes *The Times Educational Supplement*, *The Times Higher Education Supplement*, *The Times Scottish Education Supplement* and *The Times Literary Supplement*. Other activities include satellite broadcasting (the group holds a 40 per cent interest in British Sky Broadcasting), publishing, warehousing, transportation, development and sale of conditional access software and provision of financial services to other areas of The News Corporation, of which the group is a subsidiary.

THE UK'S TOP 100: ANALYSIS   13-16

13 Nuclear Electric

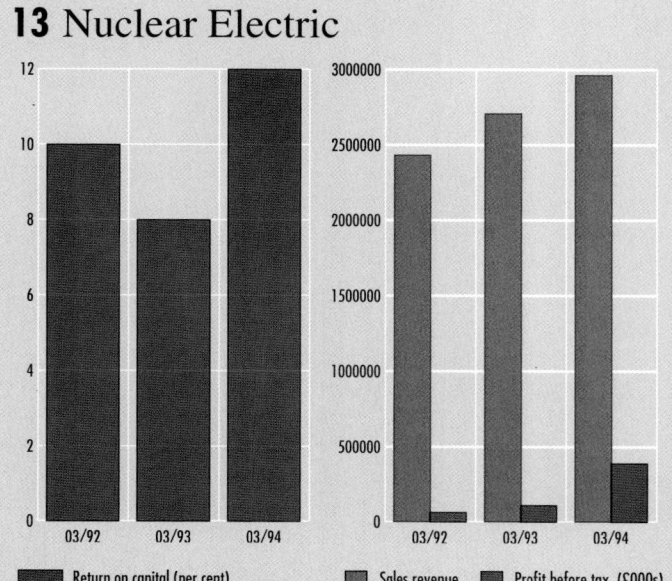

Activities are focussed on the generation and supply of electricity, and include uranium exploration and mining and insurance. The company operates five advanced gas cooled reactor power stations (Dungeness B, Hartlepool, Heysham 1 and 2, and Hinkley Point B), six Magnox stations (Bradwell, Dungeness A, Hinkley Point A, Oldbury, Sizewell A and Wyfla) and one hydro power station (Maentwrog). A pressurised water reactor exists at Sizewell B. Two Magnox stations at Berkeley and Trawsfynydd are decommissioning. In May 1994 the Government outlined proposals for the privatisation of Nuclear Electric and Scottish Nuclear as a single company.

14 B.A.T Industries

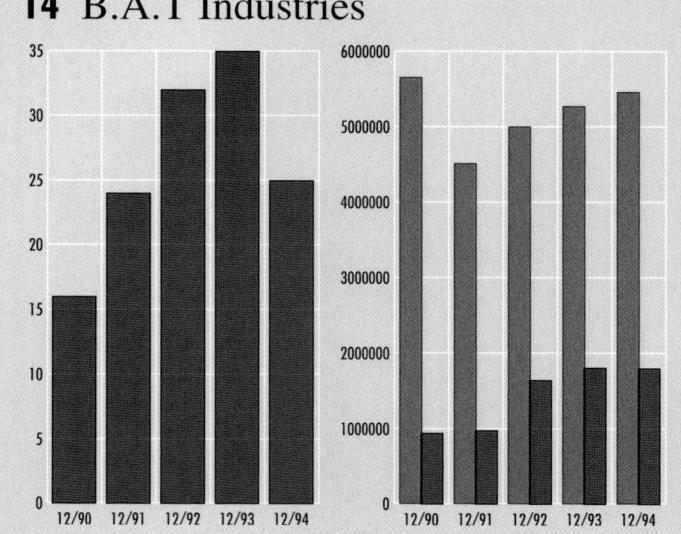

The group is the world's most international cigarette manufacturer operating through Brown & Williamson in America, British-American Tobacco (with production facilities in 45 countries), BAT Cigarettenfabriken in Germany, and Souza Cruz in Brazil. In financial services group subsidiaries provide personal financial and insurance services in the UK and North America. Principal operating companies are Farmers Group, a general insurer in the US that owns three life insurance companies; Eagle Star, a UK insurer acting in 30 countries through direct brokers and intermediaries; and Allied-Dunbar, a life assurance and pensions company.

15 Lloyds Bank

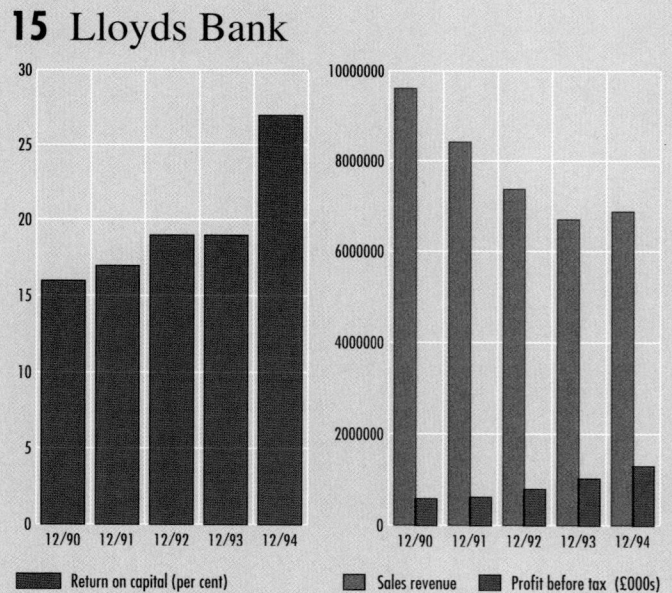

The group provides a comprehensive range of banking and financial services through branches and offices in the UK and overseas. The core UK retail banking business is complemented by activities in corporate banking and treasury, while life assurance and other financial services are provided through Lloyds Abbey Life, in which the bank has a 62 per cent interest. Lloyds also has interests in credit factoring and private banking. In April 1994 the bank announced the acquisition of Cheltenham and Gloucester Building Society for £1.8 billion, subject to the approval of the respective shareholders and members, and of regulatory authorities.

16 Grand Metropolitan

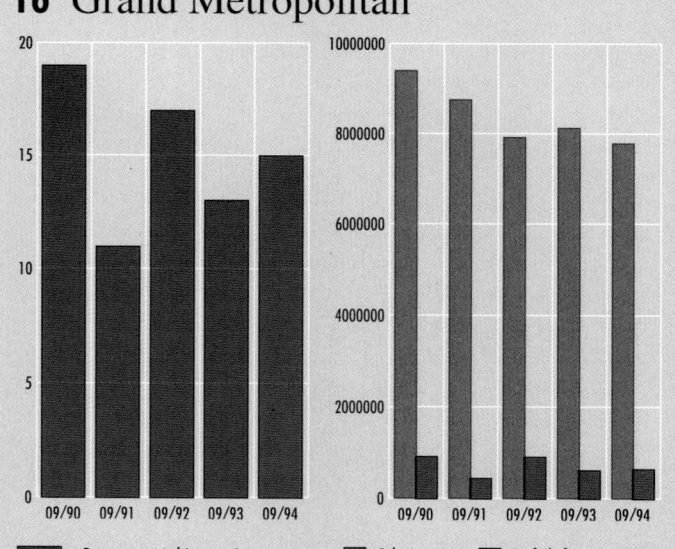

The group is international, specialising in branded foods and drinks businesses. Branded foods companies include Haagen-Dazs ice creams, yoghurts and desserts; Pillsbury ready-to-bake dough products; and Green Giant frozen and canned vegetables. In January 1995 Pillsbury agreed to acquire Pet Inc, the US branded food company, for £1.7 billion. Retailing companies include Burger King fast food outlets and Pearle eye care products. International Distillers & Vintners embraces interests in drinks and owns five of the top 20 spirits brands in the world. Grand Metropolitan was incorporated in 1934 and floated on the stock market in 1961.

17-20 THE UK'S TOP 100: ANALYSIS

17 Imperial Chemical Industries

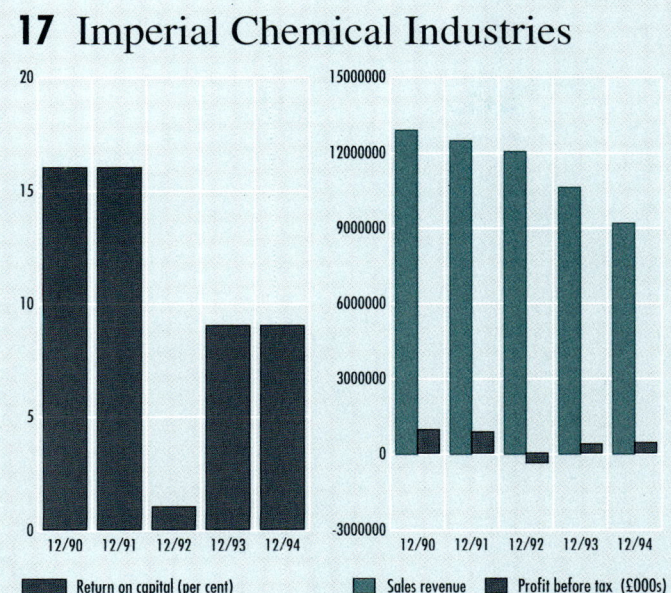

Return on capital (per cent) | Sales revenue | Profit before tax (£000s)

Principal activities are research, manufacture and sales of paints, explosives and industrial chemicals. In the UK subsidiaries comprise ICI Chemicals & Polymers (chemicals, plastics and fertilisers) and Tioxide Group (titanium dioxide pigments). Deutsche ICI, in Germany, makes chlorine, caustic soda, speciality paints and polyurethanes. North American subsidiaries produce acrylics, films, paints, composites, polyurethanes, industrial explosives and initiating systems. ICI also operates in South Africa, Australia, China, Japan, Pakistan and Taiwan, sometimes in partnership with local industrial groups. In June 1993 the bioscience activities were demerged into a new company, Zeneca.

18 Cable and Wireless

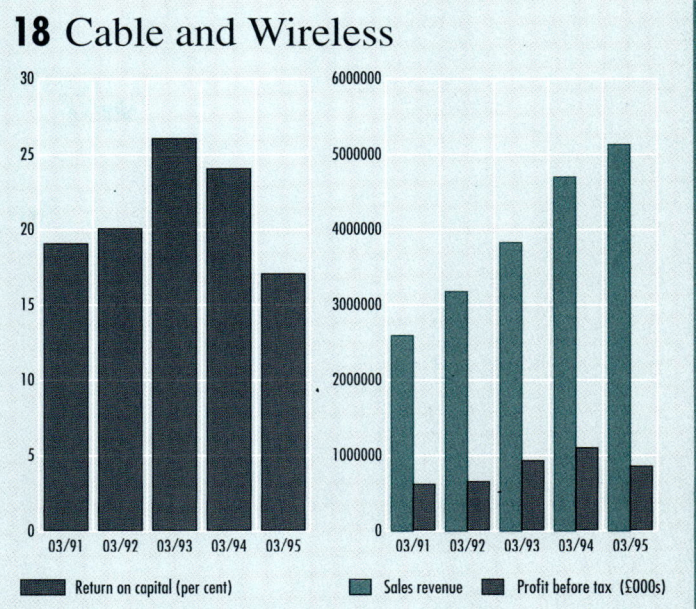

Return on capital (per cent) | Sales revenue | Profit before tax (£000s)

The international telecommunications group provides business and domestic users services that include telephone, fascimile, telex and data transmission. Operations are located in 50 countries. In the UK subsidiaries include Mercury Communications (80 per cent owned). Overseas investments include Hong Kong Telecom (57.5 per cent owned). Other activities include submarine cable systems and communications facilities management. In February 1995 Germany's Veba acquired a 10.5 per cent interest in the company as part of a joint venture agreement to develop telecommunications services in the European outside Britain.

19 Glaxo Wellcome

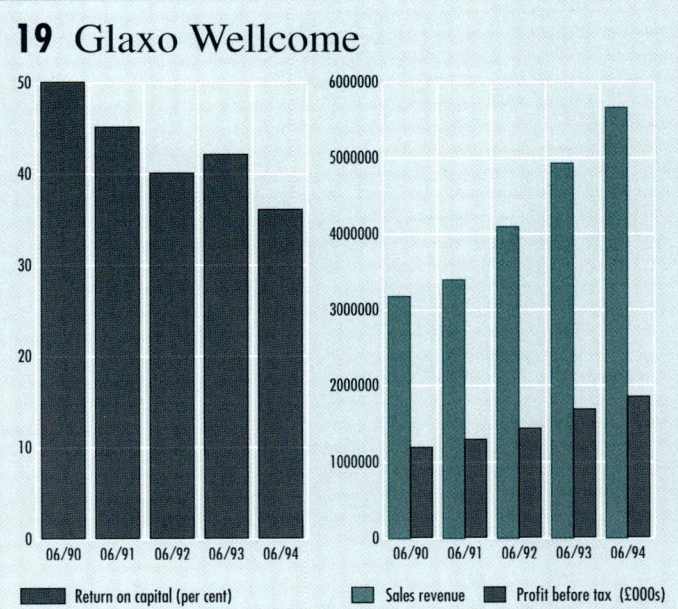

Return on capital (per cent) | Sales revenue | Profit before tax (£000s)

The group conducts research into and develops, manufactures and markets ethical pharmaceuticals around the world. Trademarks include the anti-ulcerant drug Zantac, the respiratory products Ventolin and Becotide, Zinnat antibiotics, Zofran for chemotherapy and the migraine treatment Imigran. In January 1995 Glaxo announced the terms of an £8.9 billion takeover bid for Wellcome, the pharmaceuticals group whose leading products are Retrovir, for the treatment of Aids, and the anti-viral Zovirax. The bid was declared unconditional in March 1995. In the same year Glaxo announced the acquisition of Affymax, a Dutch-based drug discovery company, for US$485 million.

20 British Airways

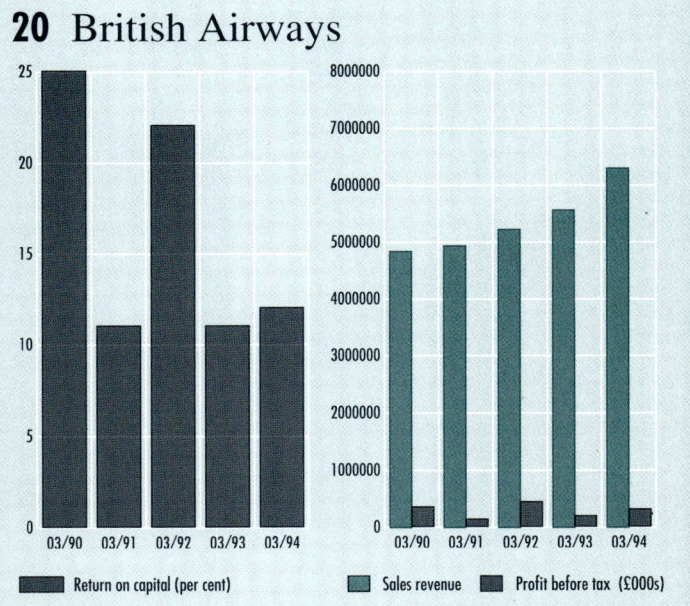

Return on capital (per cent) | Sales revenue | Profit before tax (£000s)

The main activities are the operation of international and domestic scheduled and charter air services for passengers, freight and mail, and ancillary services. Formed through the merger of British Overseas Aircraft Corporation (BOAC) and British European Airways (BEA), the company has expanded to become one of the world's largest and most profitable airlines. Acquisitions since privatisation in 1987 have included British Caledonian and Davies & Newman (Dan-Air). The company also has a 24.6 per cent interest in USAir, 25 per cent of Qantas Airways in Australia, 49.9 per cent of Deutsche BA and 49.9 per cent of TAT European Airlines in France.

THE UK'S TOP 100: ANALYSIS   21-24

21 Guinness

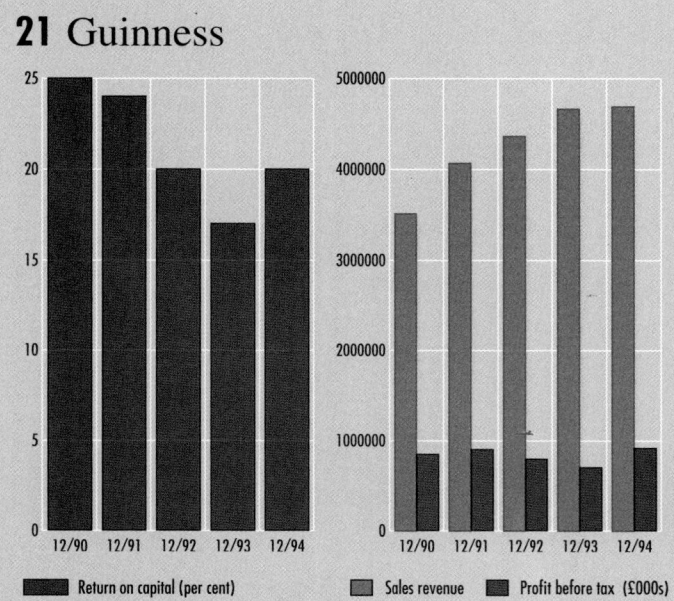

The distilling and marketing of Scotch whisky, gin and other spirits, and the brewing and marketing of beer are the group's principal businesses. Activities in spirits are mainly conducted through United Distillers and in brewing through Guinness Brewing Worldwide. Brands include Bell's, Dewar's, Johnnie Walker, Old Parr and White Horse Scotch whisky and Guinness stout beer. The company also has a 34 per cent interest in Moet Hennessy, the wines and spirits company of the French drinks and luxury goods group LVMH. In turn, LVMH holds a 20 per cent interest in Guinness. The company was formed to acquire a brewery business originally founded in 1859.

22 Land Securities

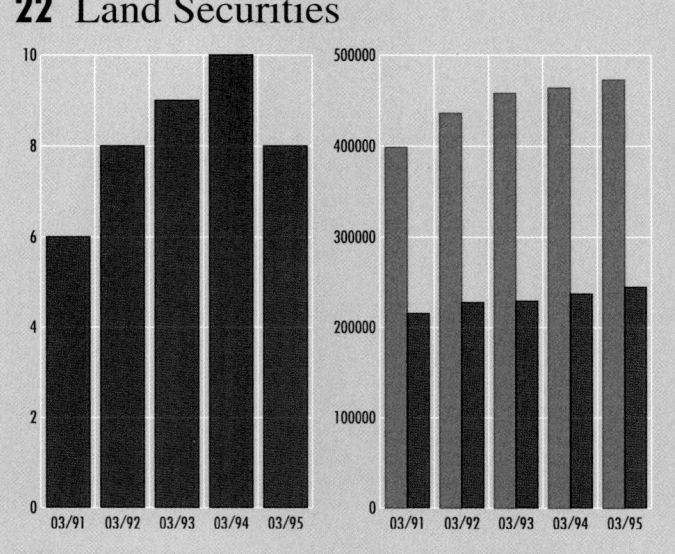

The business of the group is property investment and development of offices, shops, out-of-town retail, food superstores, industrial and warehouse premises, together with the management of its properties. The group's properties have been valued at in excess of £5 billion, with shops and offices in London, including the West End, Victoria and the City, accounting for about one-half of the total value of the portfolio. The company was formed in 1955 to acquire a business of the same name, registered in 1931, under a Scheme of Reconstruction.

23 Halifax Building Society

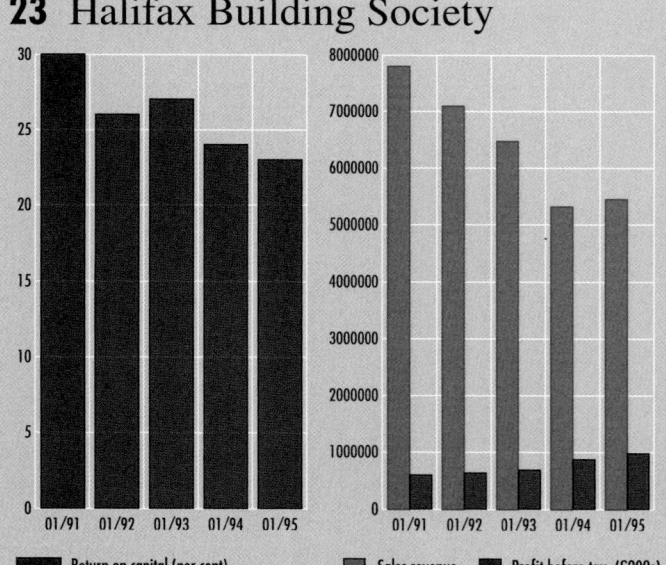

The group is the country's largest holder of personal savings, the largest provider of home mortgages and a significant lender to housing associations. The building society has 12 million savings and investment accounts and more than 1.8 million borrowers, 700 branches and around 1,300 agencies. Other activities include Halifax Financial Services, providing life assurance, pensions and unit trust investments; Halifax Property Services, the UK's largest estate agency; Colleys Professional Services, one of the largest firms of valuers; and a retail banking operation in Spain. In 1995 the Halifax and the Leeds Permanent Building Society proposed a merger and eventual flotation on the stock market.

24 Bass

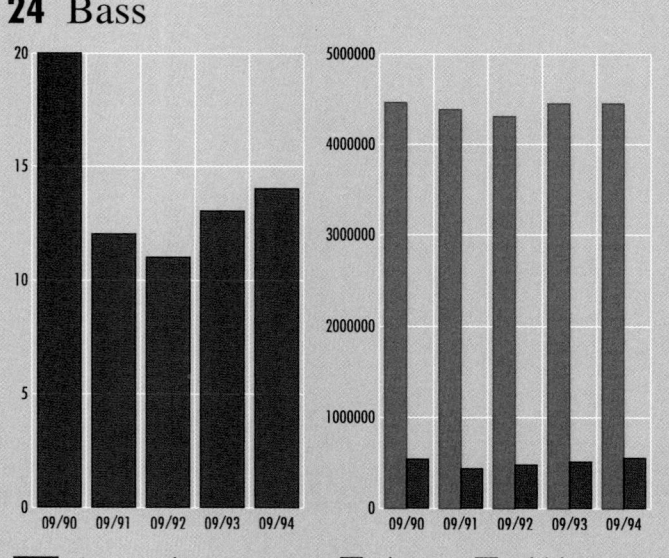

Brewing, and ownership and management of pubs are the principal activities. Bass also has interests in hotels, restaurants, bingo clubs, holiday centres, betting shops and bowling centres. Subsidiaries include Bass Taverns and Toby Restaurants (pubs); Coral Racing and Gala Leisure (leisure); Holiday Corporation and Holiday Inns Inc. (US hotels); Bass Brewers; and Britannia Soft Drinks (50 per cent owned) and Britvic Soft Drinks (90 per cent owned by Britannia). In 1995 the soft drinks business was expanded with the £103 million acquisition of Robinsons from Unilever. The company was formed in 1967 for the merger of Bass, Mitchells & Butlers, and Charrington United Breweries.

25-28 THE UK'S TOP 100: ANALYSIS

25 RTZ Corporation

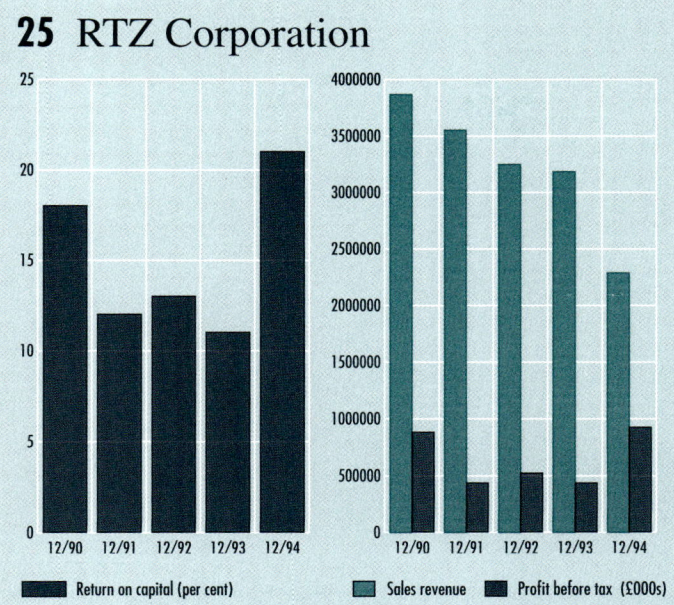

The group concentrates on large, high quality mineral deposits. Mining interests include copper, gold, iron ore, aluminium, zinc and silver in metals; coal and uranium in energy; and borax, titanium dioxide feedstock, diamonds and zinc in other minerals. Resources are located predominantly in North America and Australasia as well as Europe, southern Africa and South America. Subsidiaries in the UK include Borex Consolidated, Anglesey Aluminium and RTZ Finance. In America the company owns Kennecott Corporation, Nerco Inc., Cordero Mining, US Borax and US Silica. In Australia RTZ holds a 49 per cent interest in CRA? and in South Africa a 38.9 per cent interest in Palabora Mining.

26 BTR

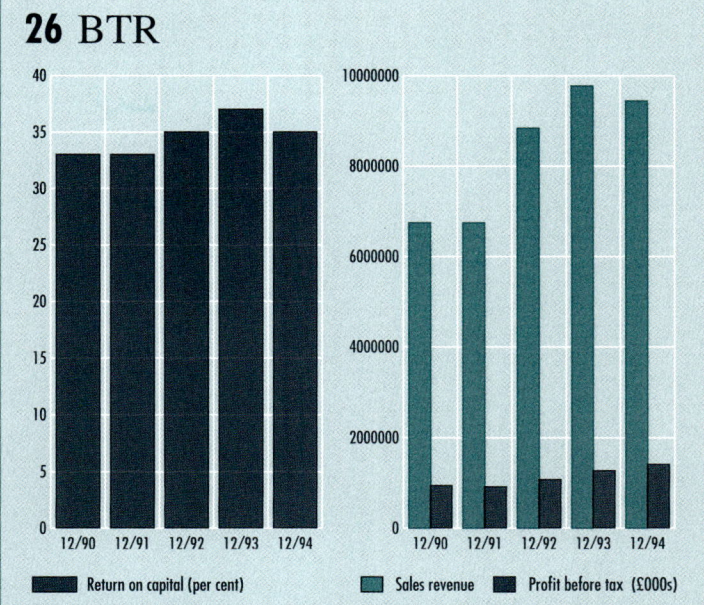

The international holding company has subsidiaries in industrial, construction, transportation, control and electrical systems, and consumer related divisions. The industrial division manufactures products including automated systems, plastics, batteries, motors and air filtration systems. The transportation division provides components for the automotive and aerospace industries. BTR manufactures and distributes fibreglass laminates, insulation, tiles and metal components. The controls and electrical division supplies sensors, transformers, avionics, switchgear, valves, semiconductors and instrumentation. Consumer-related products include packaging, sports goods and carpets.

27 British Steel

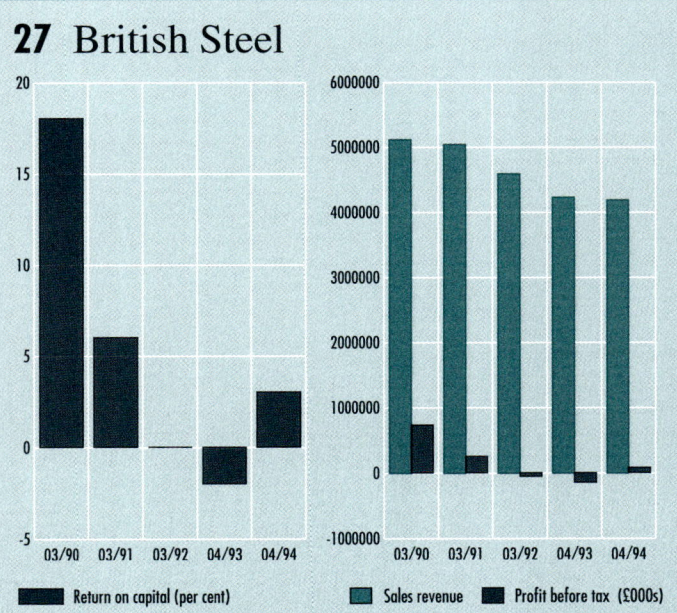

The principal activities of the company are the manufacture and distribution of steel in the United Kingdom and overseas. The company was formed in 1988, succeeding the state-owned British Steel Corporation, and its shares were floated on the stock market in London later that year. In 1992 the company merged virtually all of its stainless steel manufacturing and distribution interests with Avesta AB, of Sweden, to form Avesta Sheffield AB. Tuscaloosa Steel Corporation, an American subsidiary, is developing the company's first wholly owned steelmaking operation outside the UK, with start-up planned for late 1996.

28 Allied Domecq

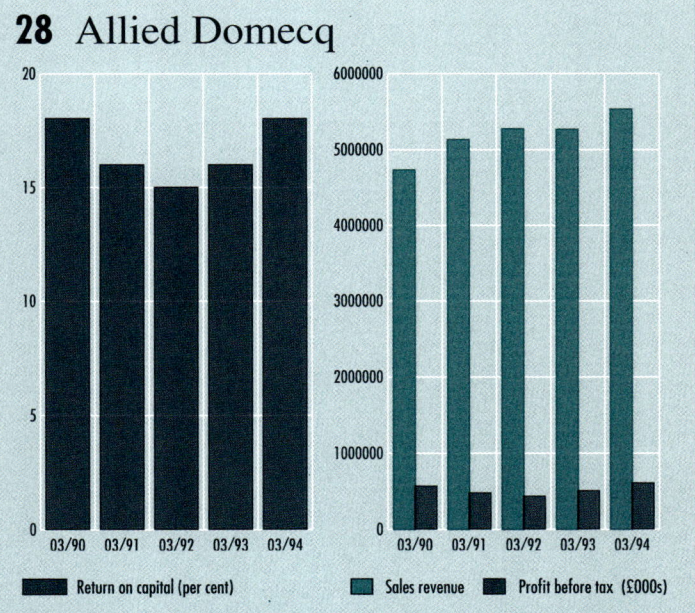

The main activities are production, marketing and selling of spirits and wine, operation of pubs, brewing and manufacture of food. In 1994 the group, formerly Allied-Lyons, acquired control of Pedro Domecq Group of Spain, for £739.2 million, and two core business sectors were established through Allied Domecq Spirits & Wine and Allied Domecq Retail. The spirits and wine sector includes Hiram Walker, Allied Distillers, James Burrough, Harveys of Bristol and Pedro Domecq. Retail companies include Ansells Retail, Ind Coope Retail, Ind Coope-Taylor Walker, the Tetley Pub Company and Victoria Wine. The group owns a 50 per cent of Carlsberg-Tetley, a joint venture in brewing.

THE UK'S TOP 100: ANALYSIS   29-32

29 Royal Bank of Scotland Group

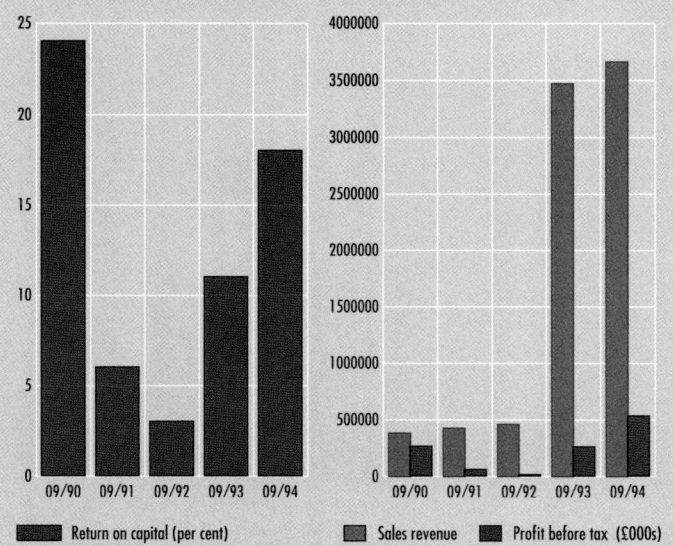

The group provides banking, insurance and other financial services. The branch banking division offers banking and related financial services to personal customers, with a branch network throughout the UK, while the corporate and institutional banking division serves the largest corporate and institutional clients. The operations division provides a range of services to the UK banking business, including credit card services. Direct Line Insurance provides motor and household insurance in the UK. In America the group owns Citizens Financial Group, which is engaged in personal and corporate banking through branches in Massachusetts, Connecticut and Rhode Island.

30 Commercial Union

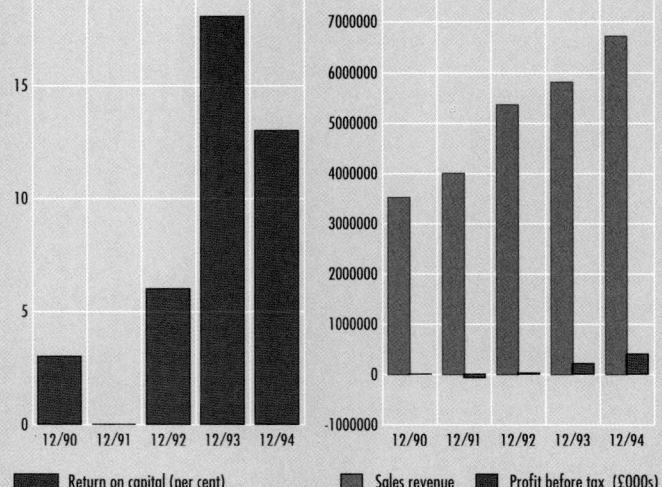

Principal activities comprise all classes of general insurance and life assurance, other than industrial life, in the UK, continental Europe, North America and elsewhere. The company provides financial services related to the core business of insurance, including unit trust and investment management, banking, stockbroking, private client investment management, trustee services and personal equity plans. The group also invests in stocks, shares, properties, mortgages and loans, and trades in property. In 1994 the company agreed to acquire Groupe Victoire, the French insurance company, from Compagnie de Suez for FFr 12.5 billion, partly funded through a rights issue of new shares, raising £322 million.

31 P & O

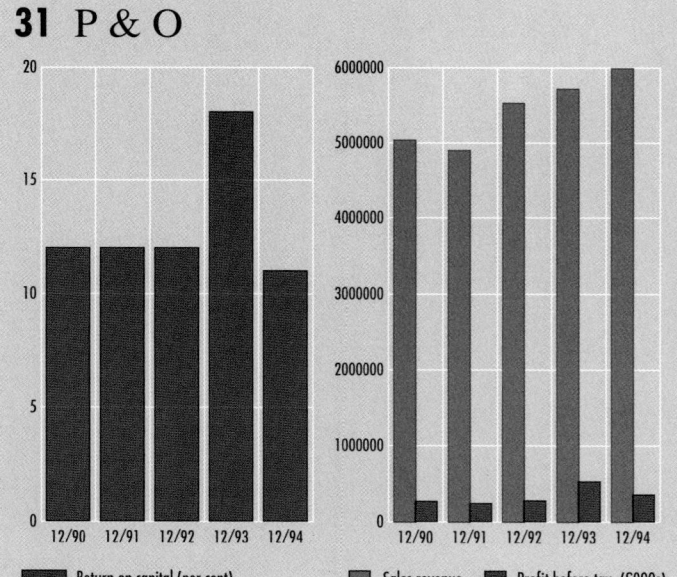

Subsidiaries include Princess Cruises, Swan Hellenic and P&O European Ferries. Luxury liners include the *Oriana*, which entered service in 1995, and the *Sun Princess*, scheduled for delivery in 1996. The housebuilding, construction and development division, in Britain and North America, owns companies trading under the Bovis name and Laing Estates. Interests in the service sector span transport, container and bulk shipping, port services, catering and holidays. The group has investments in property. P&O was established in 1840 by Royal Charter; a Supplemental Charter obtained in 1966 provides that P&O must remain under the control of 'citizens of the United Kingdom and colonies'.

32 Tesco

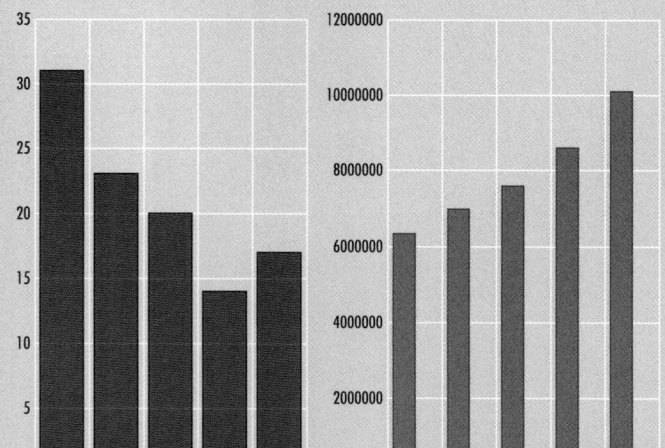

The main business of the group is the operation of food superstores and associated activities within the UK and France. The group significantly increased the number of retail outlets in the UK with the takeover of William Low for £247.4 million in November 1994. A further development was the launch of the Tesco Metro stores in prime high street locations. In continental Europe the group acquired Etablissement Catteau, of France, for £258.3 million in 1993. In addition, Tesco has an investment in Global TH, a Hungarian food retailing company.

33-36 THE UK'S TOP 100: ANALYSIS

33 National Power

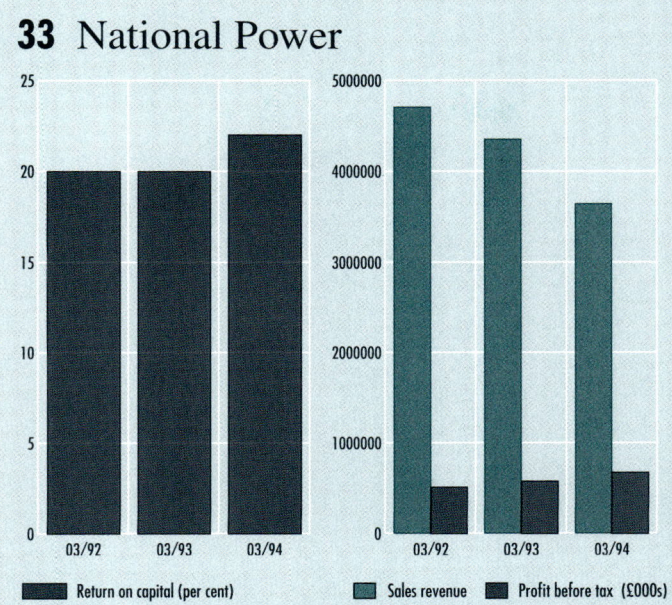

The company's principal activity is the generation and sale of electricity, principally in England and Wales but increasingly overseas. The company has 23 power stations in England and Wales, fuelled mainly by coal, gas and oil, with a capacity of approximately 22,300 MW. National Power's international business has secured interests in power generation projects in the United States, Portugal, Pakistan and Spain. The Government sold approximately 60 per cent of the shares in National Power in 1991, selling the balance via another share offer in 1995.

34 General Electric Company

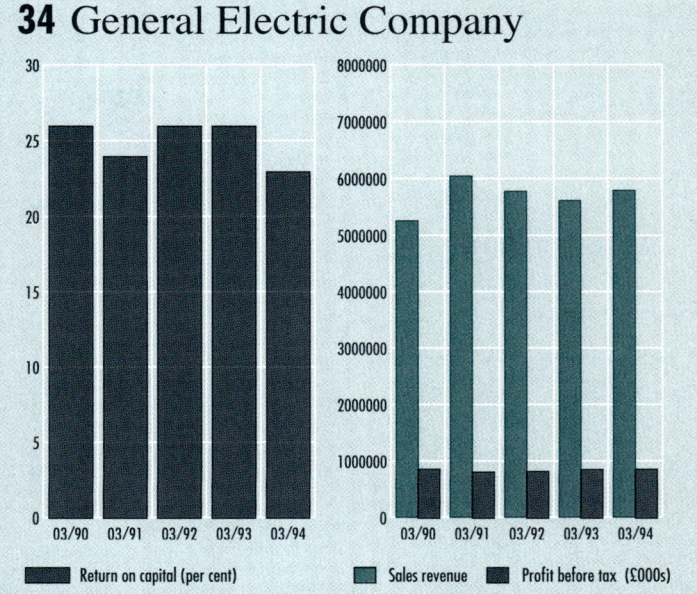

GEC comprises 10 sectors: electronic systems (including GEC Marconi and Yarrow Shipbuilders) supplies radar, flight and navigation systems, combat/weapon systems; electronic components (GEC Plessey Semiconductors); office equipment and printing (A.B. Dick, Videojet Systems International); power systems (GEC Alsthom, 50 per cent); medical equipment (Picker International); consumer goods (Hotpoint, Creda, Xpelair, Redring Electric); distribution and trading; electronic metrology; industrial apparatus; and telecommunications (GPT Holdings, 60 per cent). Registered in 1900, the company merged with English Electric in 1968 and subsequently acquired Plessey.

35 Forte

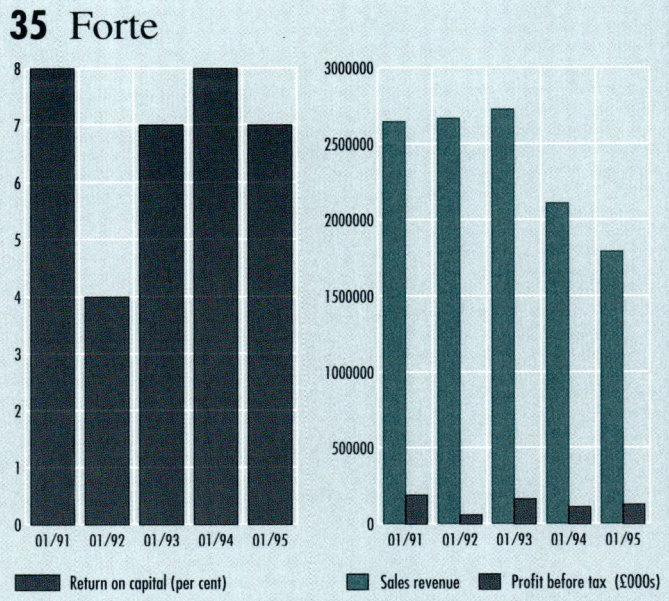

The group operates a branded network of hotels and a range of restaurants. Brands comprise Exclusive Hotels of the World, Forte Grand, Forte Heritage, Forte Agip, Forte Travelodge, Happy Eater, Little Chef, Welcome Break, Relais and Harvester Restaurants. Other subsidiaries include Lillywhites, the sports equipment and clothing retailer, and Puritan Maid, which manufactures and distributes food products. Forte also holds a substantial interest in The Savoy Hotel group and retains a 25 per cent interest in Alpha Airports Group. In November 1994 the company completed the £217 million acquisition of Societe des Hotels Meridien from Air France.

36 Marks and Spencer

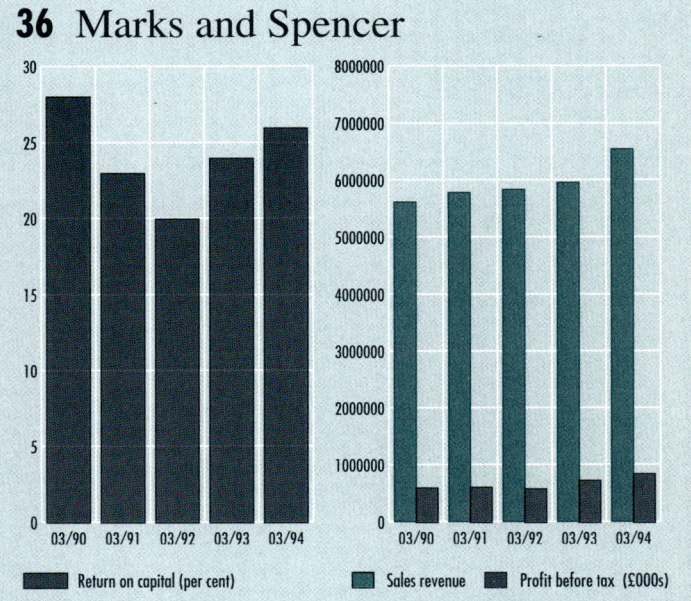

The principal activities are retailing (clothing, home furnishings, food and wine), and financial activities (financial services including Chargecard, Budgetcard, personal loans and the management of unit trusts, treasury and insurance). Retailing activities are primarily located in the United Kingdom and Ireland but expansion is progressing in continental Europe (France, Spain, Belgium, Holland, Greece and Austria) and the Far East. In America the company owns Brooks Brothers Inc. and Kings Super Markets Inc., both acquired in 1988 for $750 million and $110 million respectively. Marks & Spencer was formed to acquire a business registered in 1903.

THE UK'S TOP 100: ANALYSIS   37-40

37 Esso UK

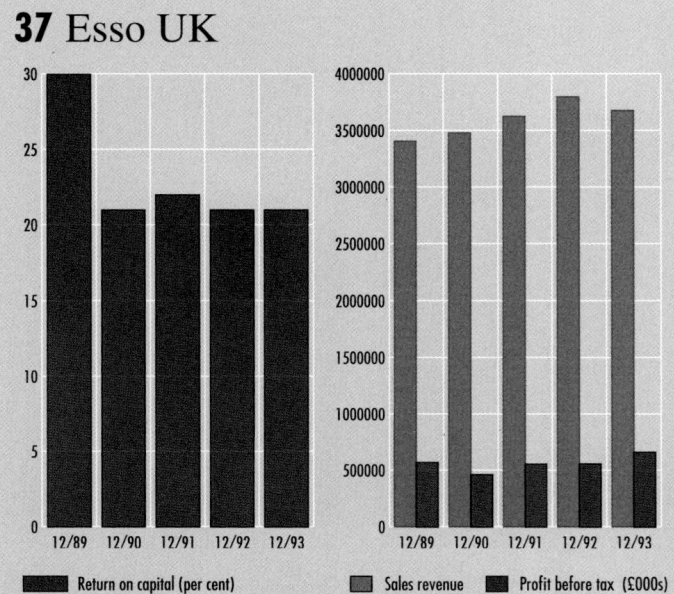

The principal activities of the group are the exploration for, production transportation and sale of crude oil, natural gas and natural gas liquids and the refining, distribution and marketing of petroleum products in the UK. The company was formed in 1982 to acquire the business and assets of Esso Exploration and Production UK and Esso Petroleum. The ultimate holding company is Exxon Corporation of the US. Subsidiaries generally trade under the Esso Banner but also include Dart Oil, Cleveland Petroleum, Redline Oil Services, Quadrant Gas, Saygas and Manchester Airport Storage and Hydrant Co.

38 J. Sainsbury

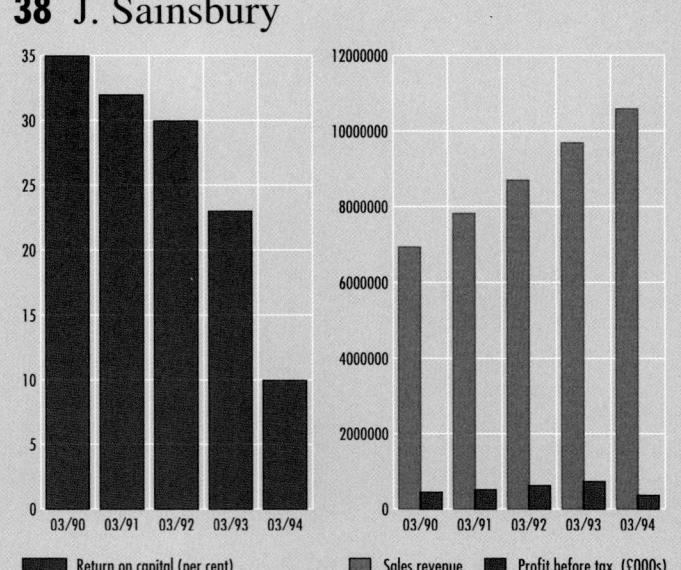

The principal activity of the company is the retail distribution of food and household goods through Sainsbury supermarkets. The company also owns Homebase, the retailer of home improvement products, and Savacentre, the discount food retailer. In America Sainsbury owns Shaw Supermarkets and, since November 1994, an interest in Giant Food Inc., a supermarket chain based in Washington DC. In January 1995 the company agreed to acquire, through its Homebase subsidiary, Texas Homecare Group from Ladbroke for £290 million. In July 1994 Sainsbury was outbid by Tesco after offering £210 million for the William Low supermarket group.

39 Great Universal Stores

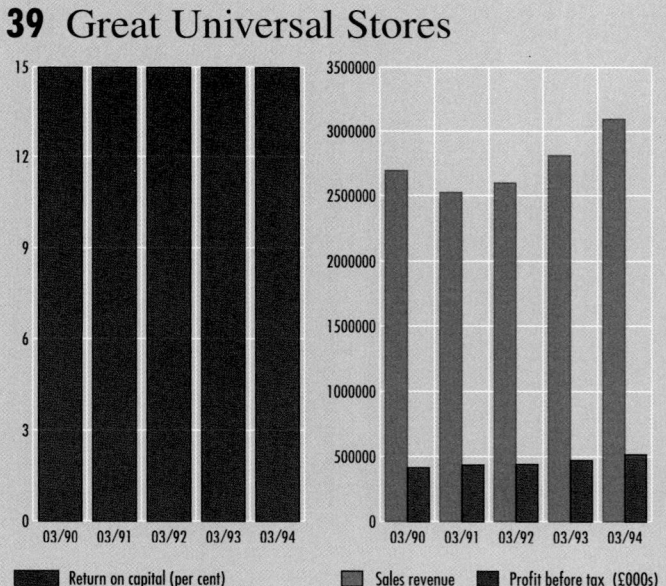

The company's activities include catalogue home shopping, consumer and corporate finance, banking, business information services, property overseas retailing and Burberry products and retailing. The company also has operations in Canada, South Africa, Austria, the Netherlands, Sweden and Switzerland. The main home shopping trading titles are Great Universal, Choice, Family Album, Fashion Extra, Kit, Marshall Wood and Kays. In addition to G.U.S. Catalogue Order, subsidiaries include Family Hampers, White Arrow Express, The Scotch House and Lewis Stores (South Africa). The company was formed to acquire the mail order business of Universal Stores, established in 1900.

40 Standard Chartered

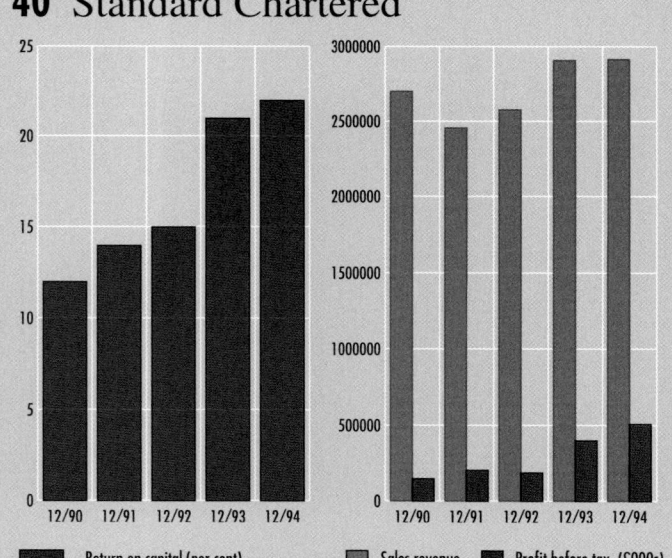

The company is engaged in banking and the provision of financial services. Activities include personal banking, with a branch network in many African, Asian and Middle Eastern countries; priority and private banking; credit cards; mortgages in major Asian markets; consumer finance; corporate banking; institutional banking; trade finance; custody services; treasury; capital markets; investment banking; stockbroking; merchant banking; bullion and commodities; and problem country debt management. The company was incorporated in 1969 to acquire the business of Standard Bank and Chartered Bank.

41-44 THE UK'S TOP 100: ANALYSIS

41 MEPC

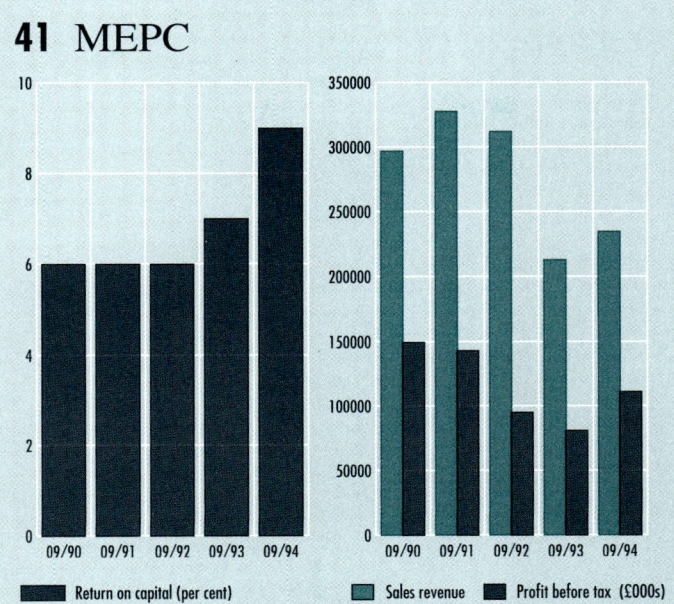

The group's business is property investment, management, development and trading. Assets are held mainly in the UK, with further investments in mainland Europe, America and Australia. Property mainly comprises offices and shops, with some interests in industrial and residential property. In the UK subsidiaries include a number of companies trading under the MEPC banner, Castelcourt Investments, English Property Corporation, Escort Property Investments, Lansdown Estates, The Oldham Estate Co., Manchester Commercial Buildings and Metropolitant Surplus Railway Lands. Incorporated in 1946, the company was formerly the Metropolitan Estate and Property Corporation.

42 British Aerospace

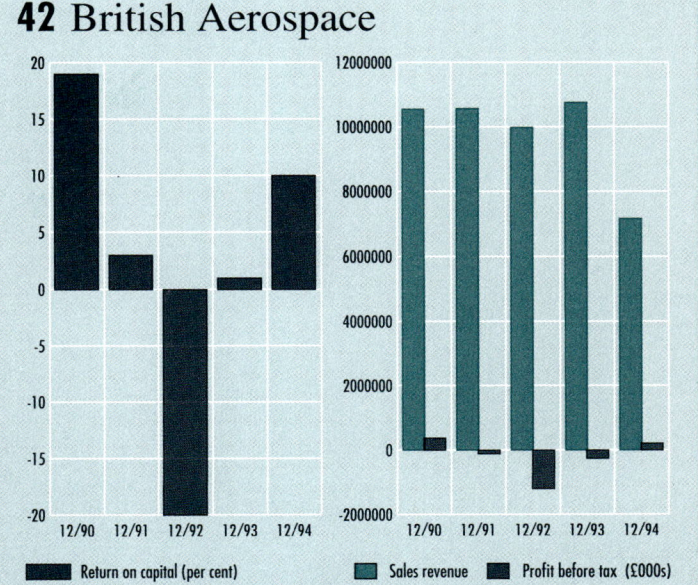

The group has two principal activities: defence, comprising military aircraft, guided weapons, ordnance and electronic systems; and commercial aerospace, comprising the design and production of wings for the Airbus Industrie range of jet airliners and the manufacture of the RJ series of regional jet airliners and the Jetstream series of turboprop aircraft. The group is also engaged in property activities through its Arlington subsidiary. Other group subsidiaries include Avro International Aerospace (commercial aerospace) and Royal Ordnance (manufacture of ammunition and weapon systems). In March 1994 the group completed the sale of Rover Group to BMW for £800 million.

43 BAA

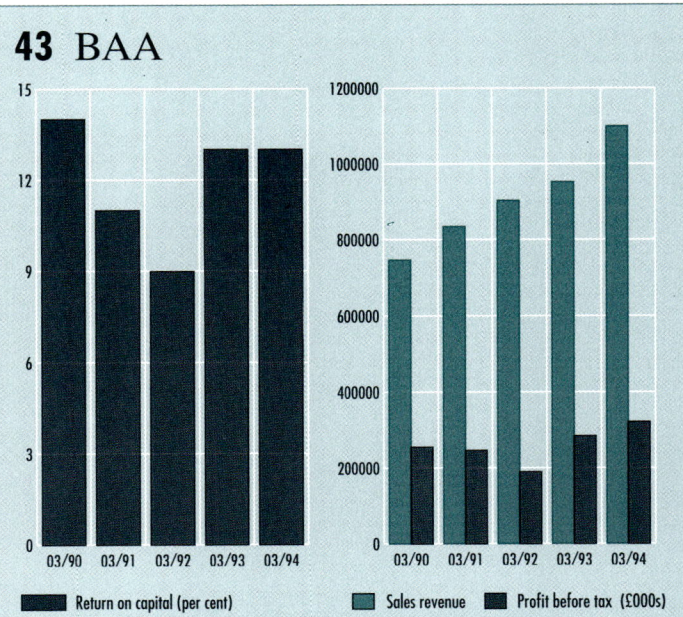

The provision and management of airport facilities in the UK and overseas is the main business of the group, which also has interests in property investment and development. The group owns and operates Heathrow, Gatwick and Stansted airports; regional airports include Glasgow, Edinburgh, Aberdeen and Southampton. It is also the master concessionaire at Pittsburgh in the United States. Property interests are principally held through Lynton, which was acquired in 1988 for £222 million, and BAA Hotels. The group was formerly the British Airports Authority, privatised in 1987 through a public offer of shares. The UK airports handle over 82 million passengers each year.

44 Woolwich Building Society

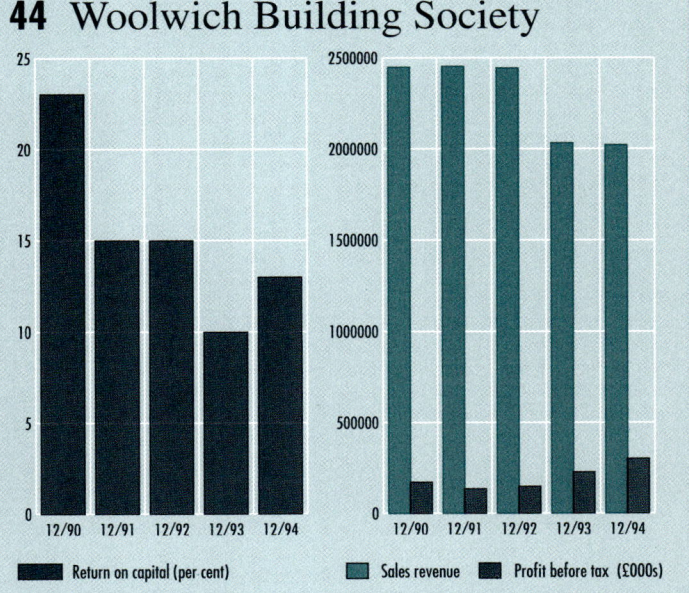

The principal activities are the provision of financial services related to the residential housing market, retail savings and investment, life assurance, personal banking and property services. The building society also has interests in rented housing, residential and commercial estate agency, property development and management, and survey and valuation services. There are mortgage lending subsidiaries in France and Italy. The building society was established in 1847 and was formerly known as the Woolwich Equitable. Mergers took place with Gateway Building Society in 1988 and Town & Country Building Society in 1992.

THE UK'S TOP 100: ANALYSIS   45-48

45 Unilever

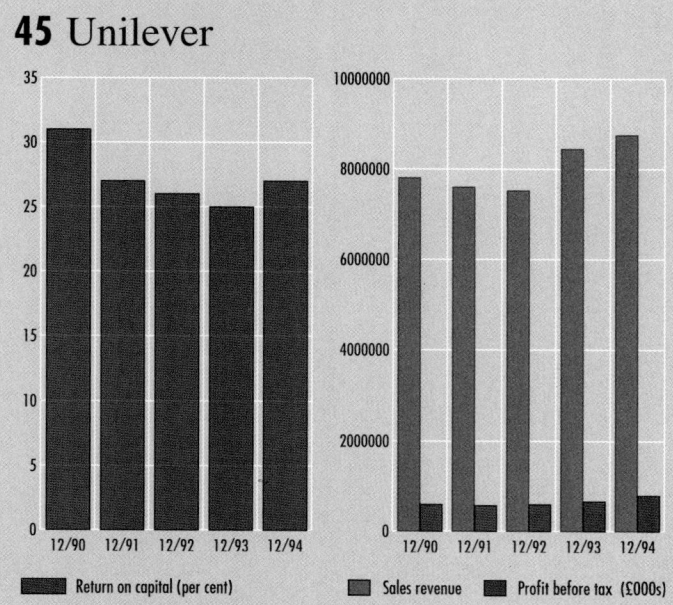

The greater part of the group's business is in branded consumer goods, primarily foods, detergents and personal products. Its other major activity is in speciality chemicals. UK subsidiaries include Lever Brothers, Birds Eye Walls, Brooke Bond Foods, Calvin Klein Cosmetics, Chesebrough-Ponds, Elida Gibbs, Elizabeth Arden, John West Foods, Lipton and Rimmel International. In 1995 the group acquired the Colman's mustards and dry sauces business for £250 million. Lever Brothers was incorporated in 1894 and Unilever in 1927; these companies were amalgamated in 1937 under a scheme that granted Unilever control of interests in the British Empire and the Dutch-based Unilever NV control of all other interests.

46 Ladbroke Group

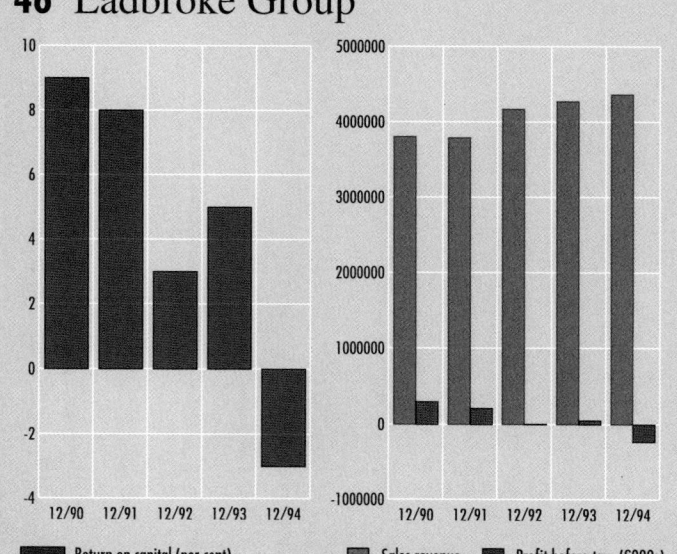

The group is involved in hotels, betting and gaming, and property. The group owns Hilton International (hotels), which operates in 47 countries in Europe, Asia, the Middle East and the Far East. US hotels are operated through Hilton International Co. Betting and gaming activities include Ladbroke Racing, Ladbroke Racing Corporation (USA) and Tierce Ladbroke (Belgium), operating betting shops and race track betting, and Vernons Pools. In property the group is involved in both investment and trading in the UK and overseas. In January 1995 Ladbroke agreed the sale of its retailing activities, Texas Homecare Group, to Homebase, a subsidiary of J. Sainsbury, for £290 million.

47 Bank of Scotland

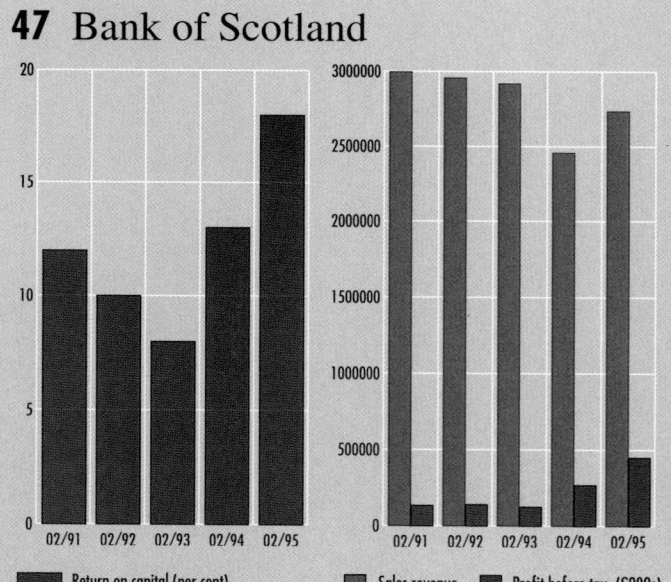

The group provides a range of financial services in the UK and overseas. Subsidiaries include NWS Bank (personal finance and banking services, including Equity Bank in Eire). British Linen Bank (merchant banking, property, investment and fund management), Kellock Holdings (debt factoring) and Countrywide Banking Corporation in New Zealand (including United Bank). Associated companies include Automobile Association Financial Services (50 per cent owned), NFU Mutual Finance (64 per cent) and Owen Owen Finance (50 per cent). The Bank of Scotland was constituted by Act of Parliament in 1695. British Linen Bank was transferred to the bank under the Bank of Scotland Order 1970.

48 Alliance & Leicester Building Society

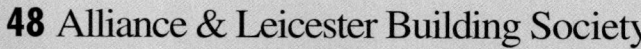
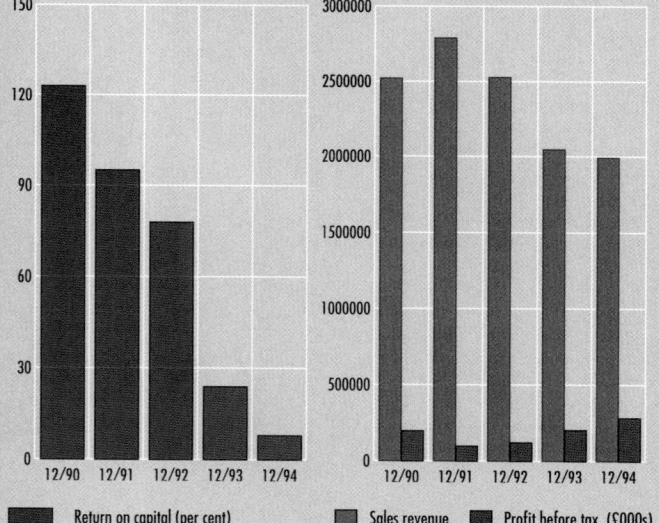

The building society's main business is the provision of financial services, principally related to the residential property market, residential and commercial estate agency and property development and management. The company also owns Girobank, which acts as a bank trading with branches of the Post Office. It was formed in 1985 through the merger of Alliance Building Society (incorporated in 1879) and Leicester Building Society (incorporated in 1875). In 1996 the building society will launch its own life and unit trust companies, ending the tie as an appointed representative of Scottish Amicable.

49-52 THE UK'S TOP 100: ANALYSIS

49 SmithKline Beecham

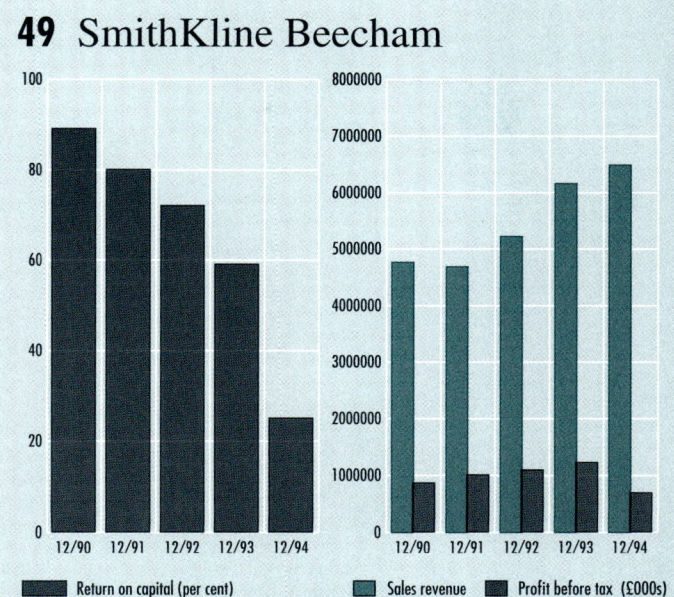

The group's activities comprise development, manufacture and marketing of pharmaceuticals, over-the-counter medicines, healthcare products and clinical laboratory testing services. Formed through the merger of Beecham Group (UK) and SmithKline Beckman (US) in 1989, the UK now accounts for less than 20 per cent of turnover, with North America and continental Europe the principal markets. In 1994 the group acquired Diversified Pharmaceuticals Inc., a US prescription drug benefit management business, for $2.3 billion, and Sterling Winthrop Inc., supplier of over-the-counter medicines, for $2.93 billion. The worldwide health business was sold to Pfizer Inc. for $1.45 billion.

50 TSB Group

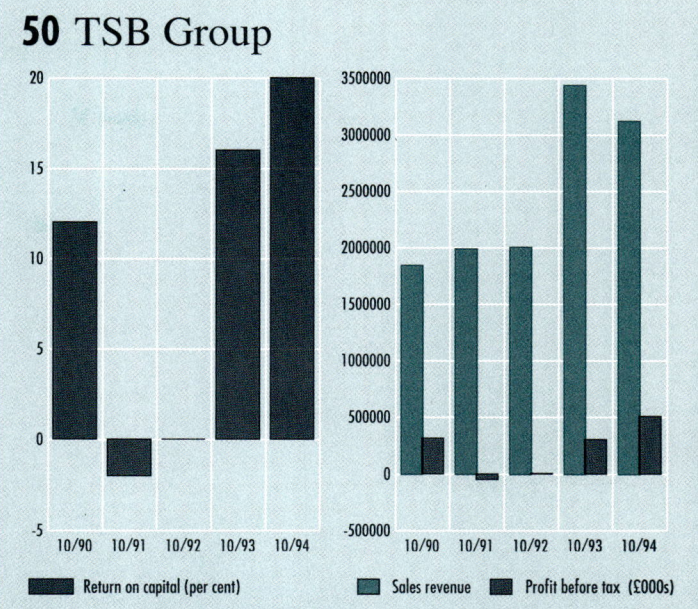

TSB is a holding company for a group providing banking, insurance and investment services. Banking and related activities are provided by TSB Bank, TSB Bank Channel Islands and TSB Bank Scotland. Other subsidiaries include TSB Life, TSB Pensions, TSB General Insurance, TSB Unit Trusts and TSB Property Services (estate agencies). The group also owns Hill Samuel (corporate and merchant banking, asset management and investment services); Mortgage Express (mortgage services) and United Dominions Trust (consumer credit, leasing and related services). In America the group owns Investment Advisors Inc., and Atlanta Capital Management.

51 Severn Trent

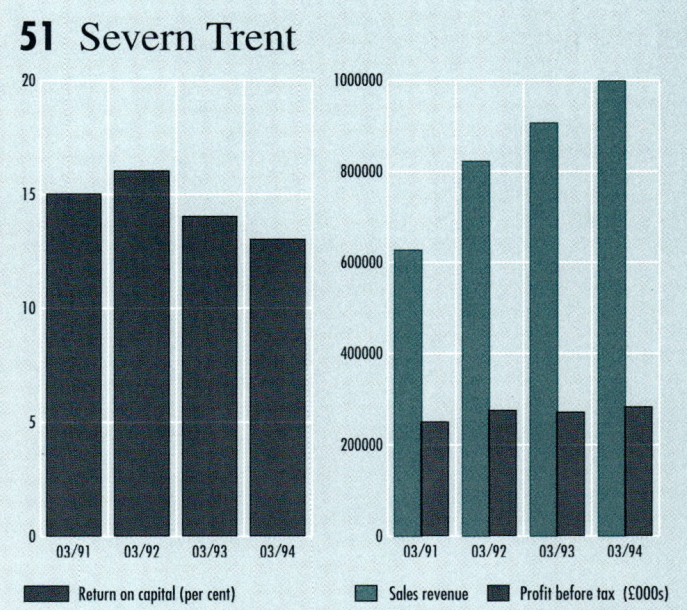

The company is engaged in the supply of water, the treatment and disposal of sewage, and waste management. The company was formerly a regional water authority, privatised in 1989 when its shares were listed on the London Stock Exchange. The water supply business covers the East Midlands and North Wales. In 1993 East Worcester Water, a statutory water company, was acquired for £33.8 million. Interests in waste management have been developed around the Biffa group of companies, purchased in 1991 for £212 million. Overseas activities include a 49 per cent interest in Mexico's Industrials del Agua, and the US water treatment companies ST Environmental Services and AM-Tex Corporation.

52 North West Water Group

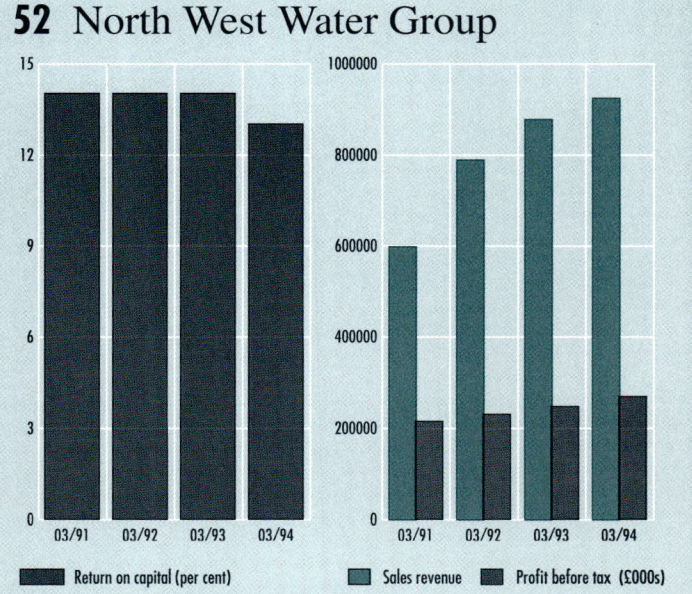

The group is engaged in the planning, design, engineering, manufacture, construction and operation of water and waste water systems in the UK and overseas. The main subsidiary provides water supply and sewerage services in the North West of England, subject to formal quality and economic regulations under the provisions of the Water Industry Act 1991. The group also has process equipment, instrumentation and contracting subsidiaries based in North America, Germany, the UK and Ireland. In 1994 the group established a partnership with Bechtel Corporation, of America, to expand water and waste management operations internationally.

THE UK'S TOP 100: ANALYSIS   53-56

53 British Railways Board

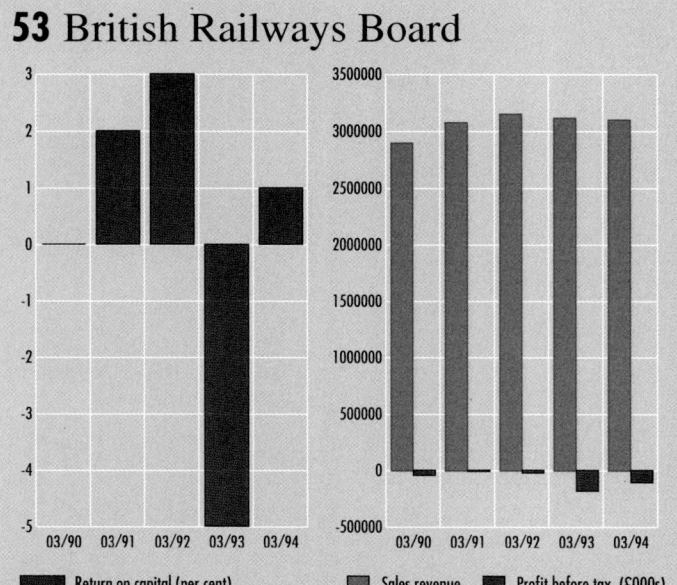

The Board is responsible for the provision of railway services in the UK and for associated services and facilities. Principal business sectors comprise InterCity, Network SouthEast, Regional Railways, Trainload Freight, Railfreight Distribution and Parcels. As part of the move to privatise the public rail system Railtrack, a separate government-owned company, was established to own and manage track and other infrastructure assets previously held by the Board. Private companies have been invited to apply for franchises to run a number of activities, including Gatwick Express and three rolling stock leasing companies.

54 BOC Group

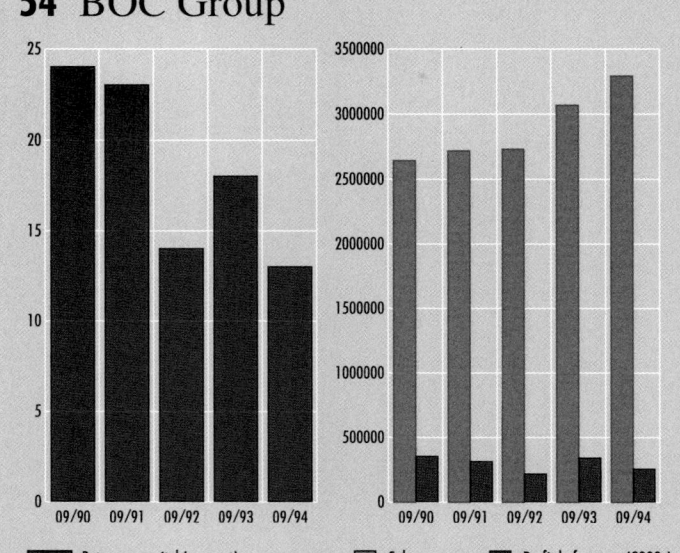

BOC is a holding company for a worldwide network of businesses engaged in the production and supply of industrial gasses and related products; healthcare (including pharmaceutical products, medical systems, medical devices and speciality products); and vacuum technology and distribution services. Although based in the UK, the main source of turnover by market is the US, followed by the Asia Pacific region. Incorporated in 1886, the name changed from Brin's Oxygen Company to the British Oxygen Company in 1906 and to BOC International in 1975. The present name was adopted in 1982.

55 Rank Xerox

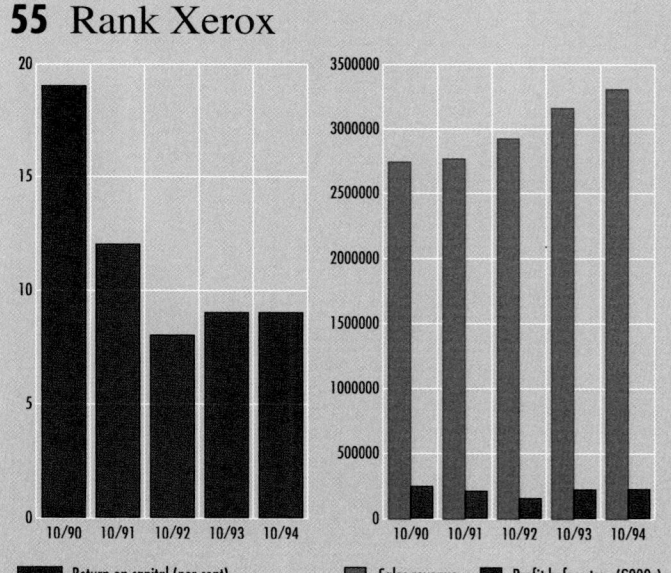

Principal activities are research, development, manufacture and maintenance of document processing systems and equipment, supported by a portfolio of document services, and financial activity through leasing operations. Rank Xerox was incorporated in 1956 to develop the European activities of Xerox Corporation (USA) in partnership with Rank Organisation (UK). Subsidiaries currently trade in Britain and Ireland, Austria, Belgium, Denmark, Finland, France, Germany, Greece, Hong Kong, Italy, Kenya, the Netherlands, Nigeria, Norway, Portugal, Spain, Sweden, Switzerland, Russia and Turkey. A 50 per cent interest is held in Fuji Xerox (Japan). Xerox Corporation is the ultimate holding company.

56 ZENECA Group

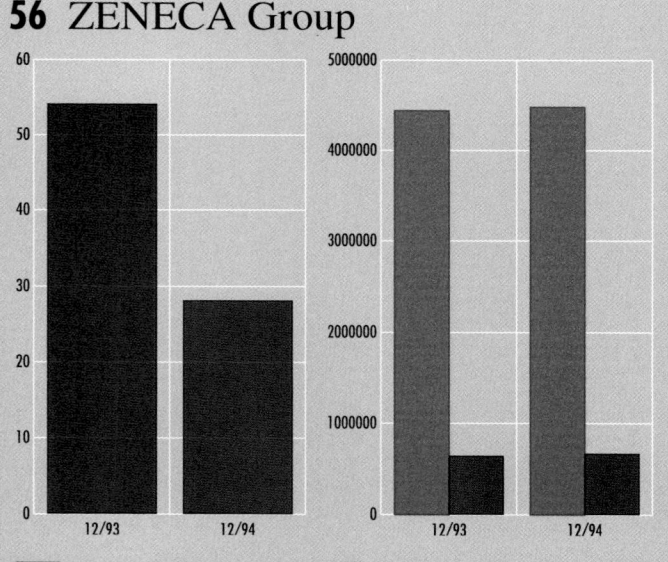

Subsidiaries are engaged in the research, manufacture and supply of pharmaceutical and agrichemical products, processing of seeds, speciality chemicals and related products. The company supplies products for therapeutic areas including cardiovascular, infectious, central nervous system and cancer. The agrichemicals businesses supply seeds and products for crop treatment, including herbicides, insecticides and fungicides. The company also manufactures organic chemicals, coatings and bio products. Zeneca was formed in 1992 following an internal reorganisation of Imperial Chemical Industries, with ICI shareholders receiving new Zeneca shares.

57-60   THE UK'S TOP 100: ANALYSIS

57 Whitbread

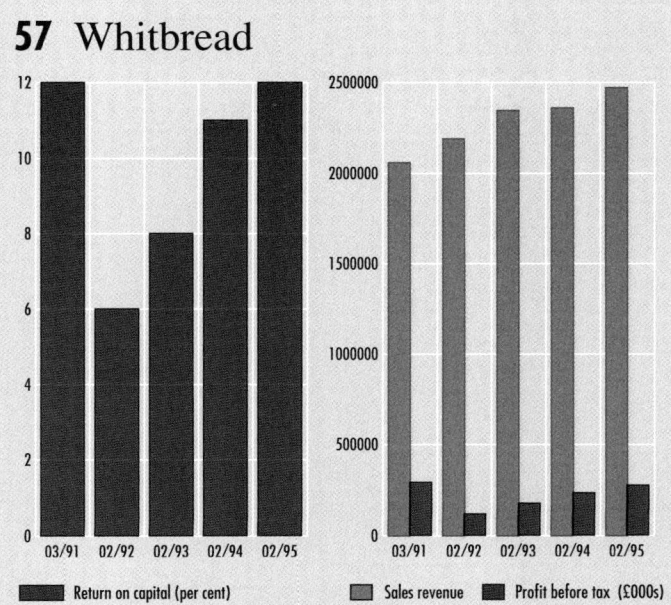

The business of the group includes brewing, leisure, restaurants and the management of pubs. Whitbread Beer Company, which embraces brewing activities, holds a range of brands in the UK that include Heineken, Stella Artois, Boddington's, Murphy's Irish Stout and Flowers Original. Whitbread Pub Partnerships is a leading franchised pub retailer, and Whitbread Inns operates the company's branded pubs, which include Brewers Fayre, Hogshead, Tut 'n' Shives and Beer Engines. Whitbread Restaurants & Leisure operates through Beefeater Restaurant & Pub, T.G.I. Friday's, Pizza Hut, Country Club Hotel Group and Thresher.

58 London Regional Transport

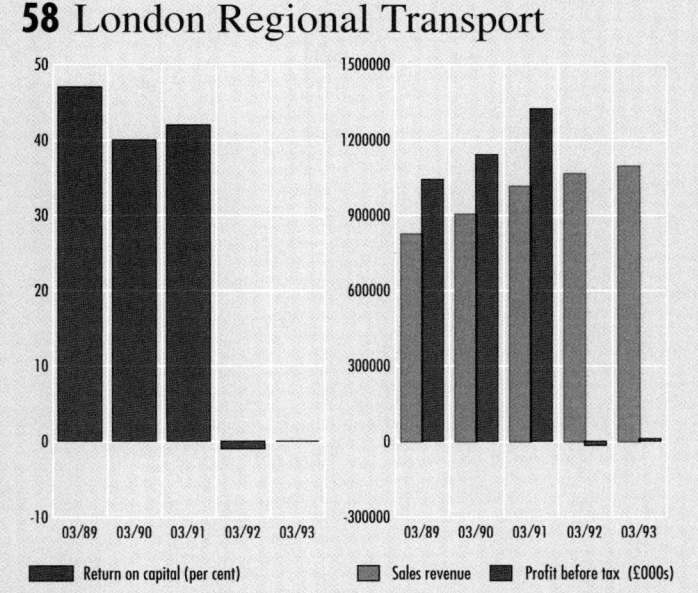

The corporation is responsible for the provision of public transport in Greater London, subject to financial objectives and principles set by the Secretary of State for Transport. Subsidiaries include London Underground, the underground railway network and Victoria Coach Station. Bus operations have been privatised and other activities, notably support services, will be transferred to the public sector. The corporation was established under the London Regional Transport Act 1944. The London Passenger Transport Board, a predecessor company, was created in 1933 to unify control of transport services.

59 Conoco (UK)

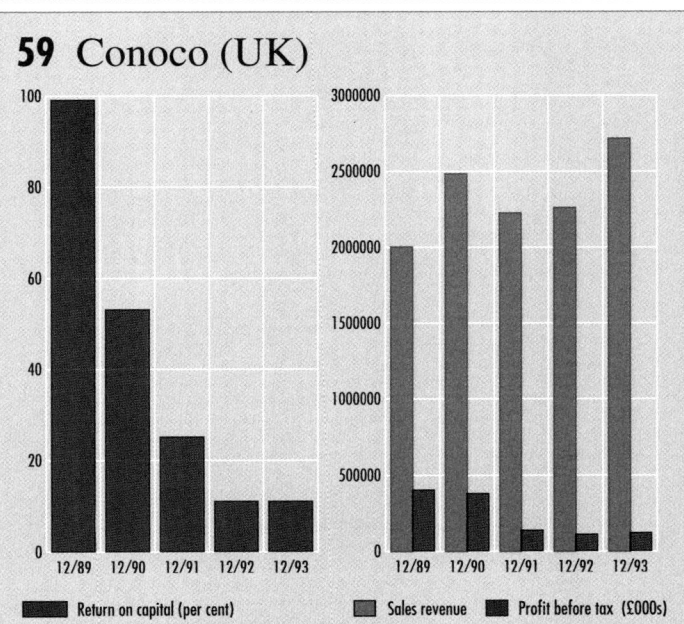

The company is engaged in acquisition, discovery, development, production, refining, marketing and sale of crude oil, natural gas, natural gas liquids and refined products, supported by supply, trading and transportation services. The company is also active in the manufacturing of chemicals, printing and electronics. Incorporated in 1953, it was formerly known as Jet Petroleum and Continental Oil. The ultimate holding company is E.I. Du Pont de Nemours, of America. In the UK subsidiaries include BT & D Technologies, Du Pont (UK), Mersey Oil and Vertoil Separation Systems. The company also owns 50 per cent of Kinetica, which is involved in the marketing of natural gas.

60 Thames Water

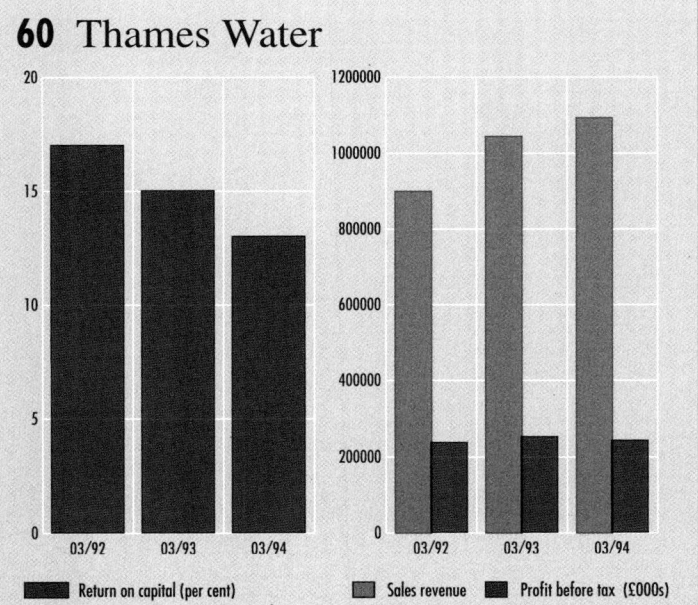

Main activities are the supply of water to residential and commercial customers, principally in the London region; water abstraction and treatment; and sewerage services. The company also engages in the development and manufacture of products for the treatment of water, waste water and industrial process fluids and the provision of underground waste management and urban environmental services. Thames has a growing international business, involved in water and waste water process design and contracting, and the marketing of technical management services. Incorporated in 1989, the company assumed most of the business of the former Thames Water Authority.

THE UK'S TOP 100: ANALYSIS   61-64

61 3i Group

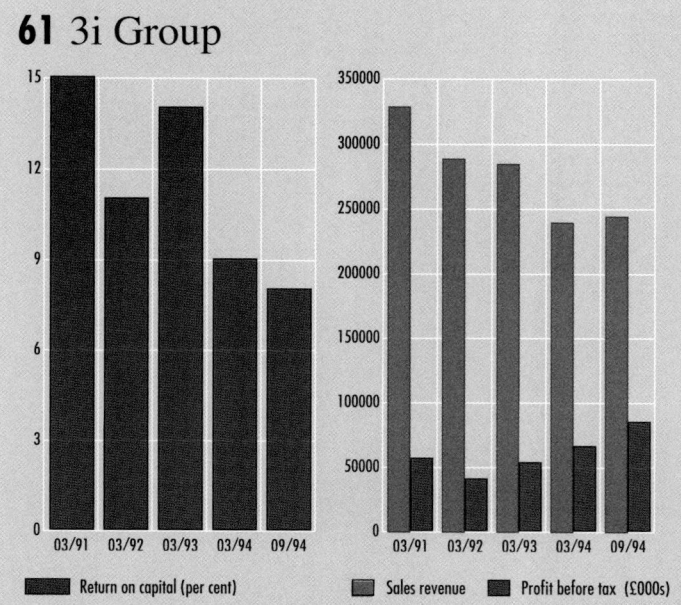

The company specialises in investment in small and medium-sized businesses that do not have ready access to the capital markets. It is managed in a way that satisfies Inland Revenue approval as an investment trust. The company, formerly named Investors In Industry, was floated on the London Stock Exchange in 1994 when its major shareholders, comprising the Bank of England, Bank of Scotland, Barclays Bank, Lloyds Bank, Midland Bank, Royal Bank of Scotland and National Westminster Bank reduced their holdings through the sale of shares.

62 LASMO

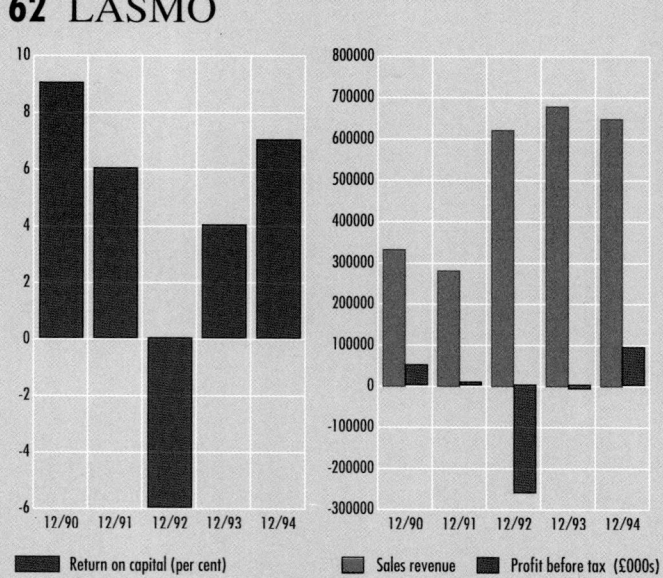

The company is a substantial oil and gas exploration and production company whose reserves and producing assets are concentrated primarily in the UK and Indonesia, which are regarded as core areas. Additional interests are held in exploration and development projects in other countries, including Algeria, Canada, Colombia, Gabon, Indonesia, Italy, Libya, Pakistan, Vietnam and Yemen. The company's shares are listed in London, New York and Toronto. In 1991 Lasmo acquired Ultramar, a rival oil and gas company, for £1.1 billion after a hostile takeover bid. In 1994 the company survived a hostile bid by Enterprise Oil.

63 National Grid Holding

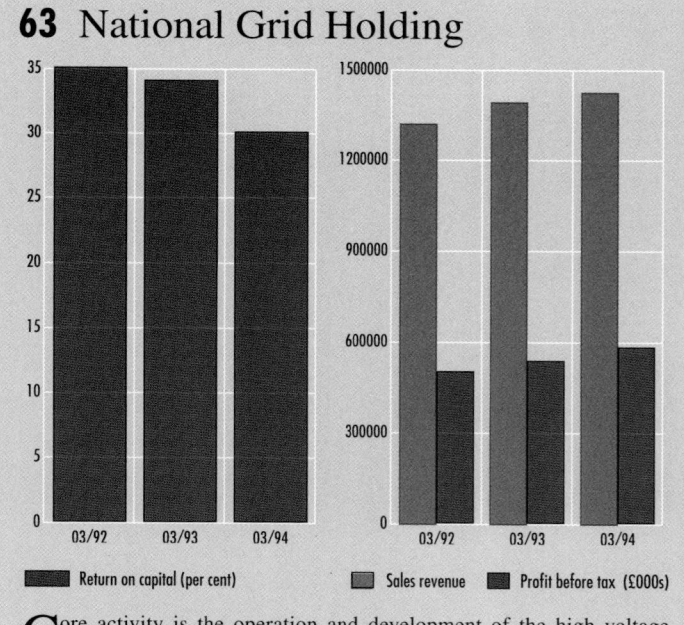

Core activity is the operation and development of the high voltage transmission system in England and Wales, offering connection to the system to generators and suppliers of electricity. The transmission business, including real-time control of the transmission system and the daily instruction of generating stations, is linked to the company's other licensed activities; administration of the pool settlement system; production of ancillary services to ensure the stability and security of the transmission system; and use of interconnection assets for the purpose of electricity trading with Scotland and France. Energis, a subsidiary, provides telecommunications services.

64 Redland

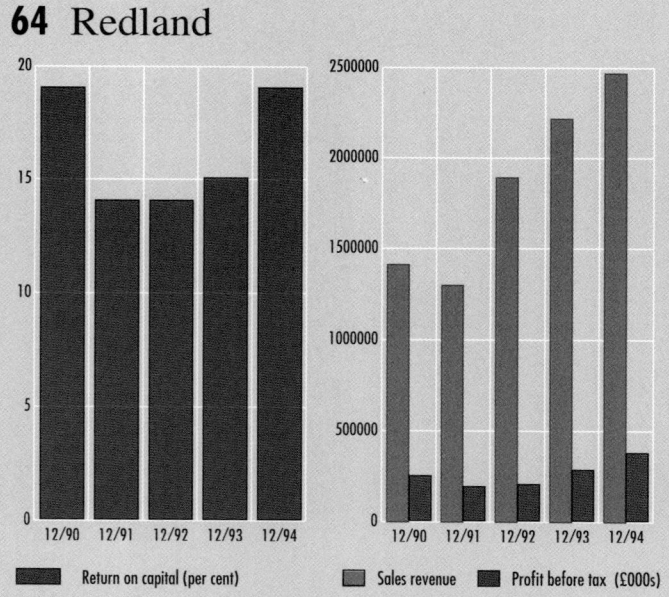

Principally engaged in production of materials for the construction industry, main products are roof tiles, construction aggregates and clay bricks, processed largely from the group's reserves of raw materials. Operations are located in 35 countries. UK subsidiaries include Redland Aggregates (quarrying, road surfacing materials, concrete and magnesia products); Redland Bricks; Redland Distribution; Redland of Northern Ireland; Redland Readymix; Redland Rooftiles and Redland Technologies. The UK accounts for one-fifth of turnover, with Germany making the greatest contribution.

65 PowerGen

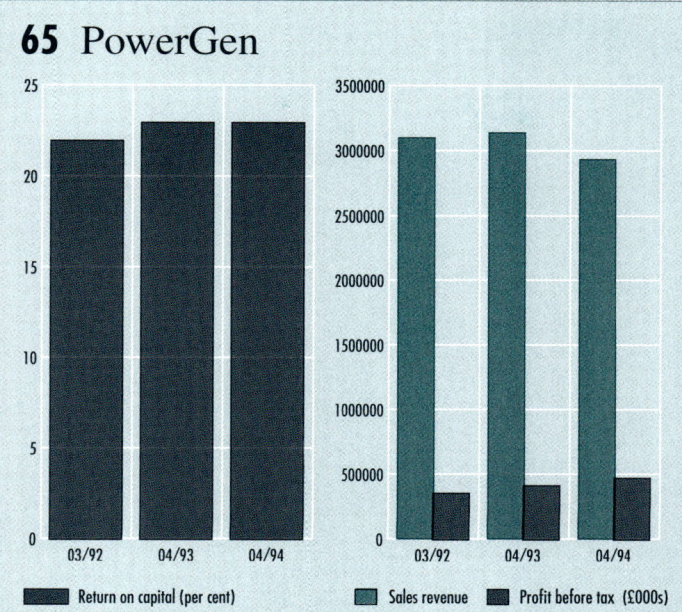

The company's principal activity is the generation and sale of electricity. PowerGen was incorporated in 1989 to continue part of the business carried out by the Central Electricity Generating Board, and was privatised through a public share offer, with the first tranche sold in 1991 and the balance in 1995. The company provides approximately one-quarter of the electricity required in Britain. Increased output from nuclear power stations and the arrival of new entrants to the market have encouraged the company to seek business overseas and it now has activities in Indonesia, Germany and Portugal. PowerGen also has interests in gas production in the southern gas basin of the North Sea.

66 Rank Organisation

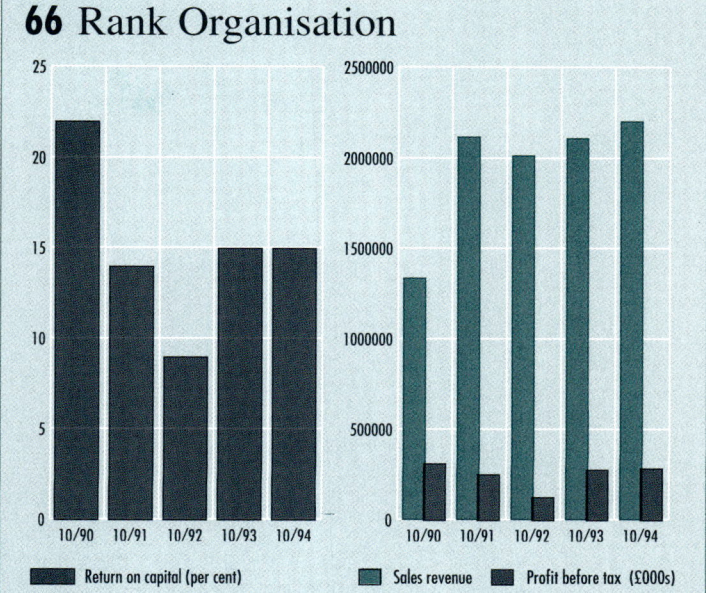

The group supplies products and services to the film and television industries, owns holiday businesses and operates organised leisure facilities in the UK and overseas. The group has an investment in the Rank Xerox companies owned jointly with Xerox Corporation and has a joint investment with MCA in the Universal Studios motion picture theme park in Orlando, Florida. Subsidiaries include Odeon Cinemas, Pinewood Studios, Rank Film Distributors, Rank Video Services (film sector); Butlin's; Haven Leisure, Shearings and Warner Holidays (holiday sector); Top Rank, Rank Amusements and Grosvenor Clubs (recreation); and Hard Rock Cafe, Rank Leisure and Resorts USA (leisure).

67 General Accident

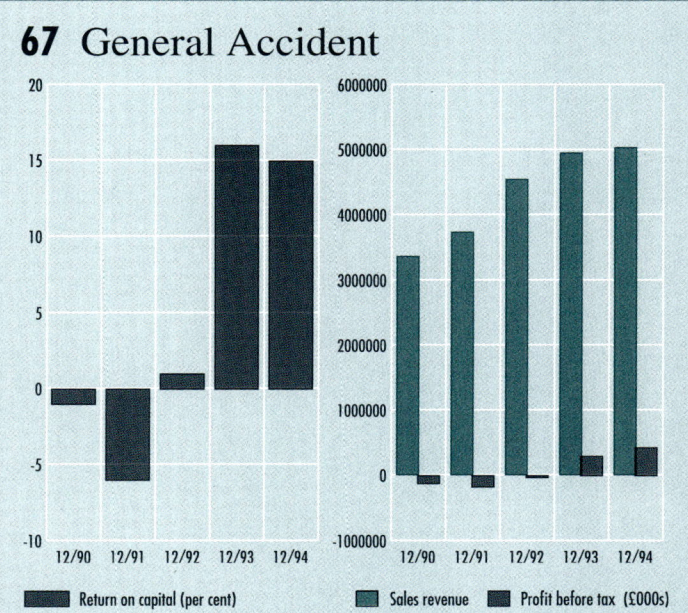

General Accident is the holding company of the General Accident Group, whose principal activity is insurance of all classes, other than industrial life, and financial services. UK subsidiaries include General Accident Fire and Life Assurance Corporation and General Accident Life Assurance. GA Property Services owns one of the largest estate agency businesses in the UK. General Accident Direct was established to provide mortgage-related creditor insurance. There are subsidiaries, wholly- or partly-owned, in the United States, Australia, Belgium, Brazil, Canada, Kenya, Malaysia, New Zealand, Norway, Puerto Rico, South Africa and Zimbabwe.

68 British Land Company

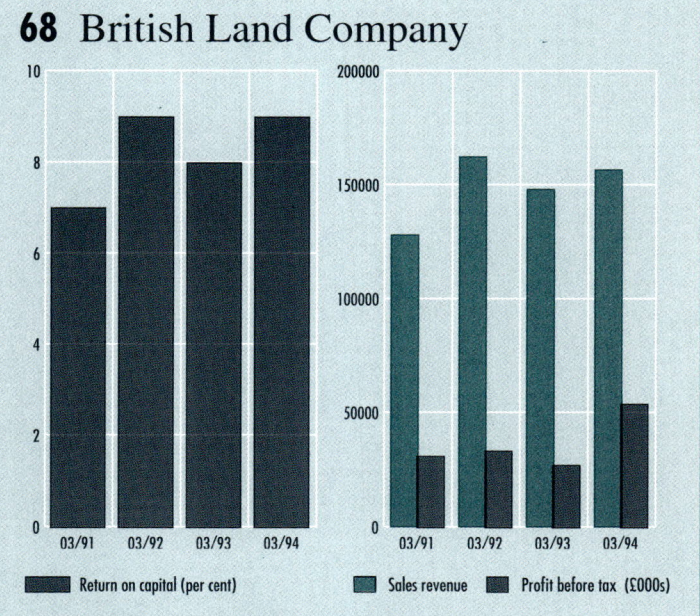

The group operates in property investment and development, finance and investment. Revenue is derived from rental income, property trading, fees and commission. Since 1988, the company has invested £1.8 billion in the purchase of property. This includes funds invested through British Land Quantum Property Fund, a partnership established in 1993 with George Soros. In 1994 Mr Soros's interest in was bought out by British Land for £142 million. In 1995 British Land acquired Stanhope Properties and a 50 per cent interest in the Broadgate development in the City of London, with pre-emption rights over the remaining 50 per cent.

THE UK'S TOP 100: ANALYSIS   69-72

69 Sun Alliance Group

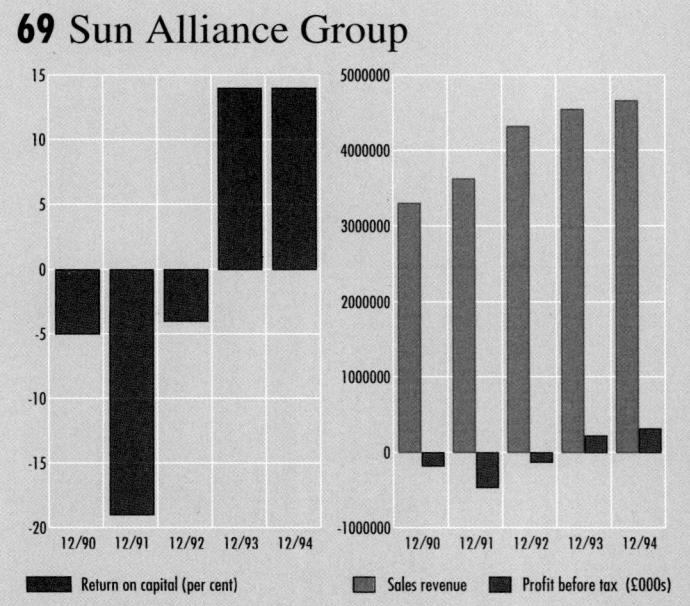

The principal activity is the transaction in the UK and overseas of all major classes of insurance business and the provision of related financial services. Business sectors comprise Sun Alliance UK, whose subsidiaries include Swinton Insurance and Bradford Pennine Insurance; Sun Alliance International (which manages UK-written commercial risks); Sun Alliance Overseas; Sun Alliance Life (which has a shareholding in Woolwich Life); investment (with holdings of fixed interest securities and equities); and property (with investments in the UK and overseas). In the United States the company has businesses under the management of Chubb.

70 Pilkington

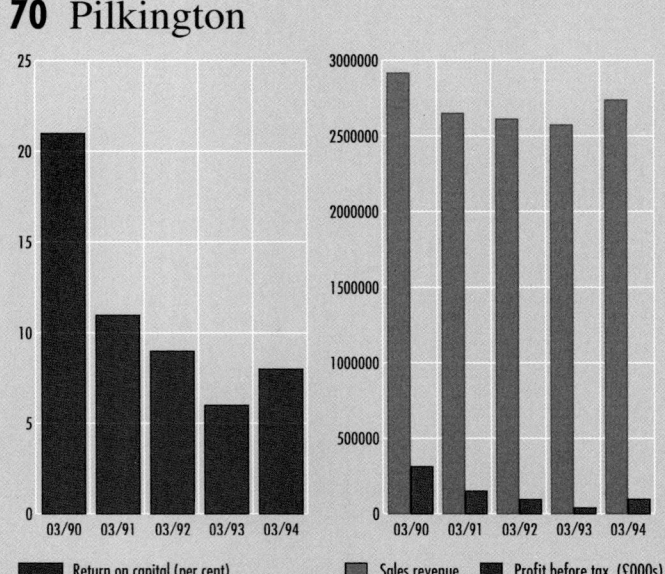

The group, a worldwide manufacturer and distributor of flat and safety glass, operates in the building, transportation and electronics markets. British and European subsidiaries include Pilkington Glass; Triplex; Flachglas (Germany); EOM (Austria); Pilkington Floatglas, Pilkington Bilglas (Sweden); Lamino OY and OY Lahden (Finland); Vitrage Isolants de L'Ouest (France); Pilkington Danmark (Denmark); Pilkington Aerospace (aircraft transparencies); and subsidiaries in Australia, Zimbabwe, Argentina, Brazil and New Zealand. In America the group owns Libby-Owens-Ford and Libby-Nippon Holdings (in the US) and LN Safety Glass (Mexico, 40 per cent).

71 Associated British Foods

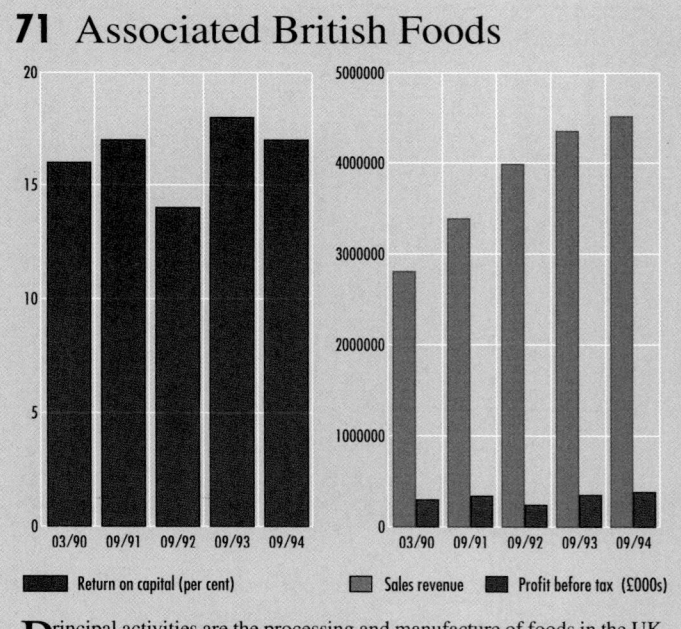

Principal activities are the processing and manufacture of foods in the UK, Europe and Australia, and food and textile retailing in the UK and Ireland. UK subsidiaries include AB Ingredients, ABR Foods, AB Technology, Allied Bakeries, Allied Foods, Allied Grain, Allied Mills, British Sugar, Burtons Gold Medal Biscuits, Crazy Prices, Eastbow Securities, Fishers Agricultural Holdings, Jacksons of Picadilly, Primark Stores, The Ryvita Company, Stewarts Supermarkets, and R. Twinning & Co. There are also subsidiaries in Australia, the US, New Zealand, France, Ireland and Poland. Wittington Investments, the ultimate holding company, owns 50.9 per cent of the shares.

72 Royal Insurance Holdings

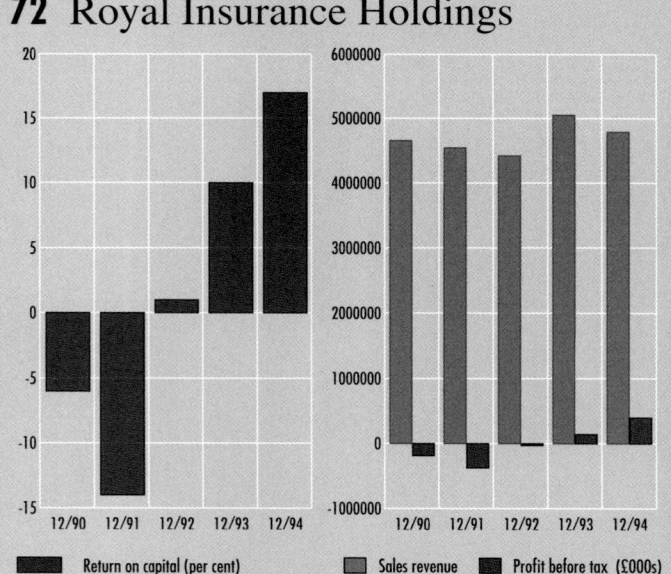

The group is the parent company of a worldwide insurance group of more than 120 subsidiary companies, transacting business in more than 90 countries and employing in excess of 20,000 staff. There are two principal subsidiaries. Royal Insurance Plc provides general insurance, overseas life insurance, estate agency services and investment services, and its businesses include Royal Insurance Property Services and Royal Insurance Asset Management. Royal Life Holdings provides life insurance through companies in the UK and the Isle of Man. More than half of the group's general insurance premiums are now generated outside the UK. Royal Insurance was established in 1845.

THE UK'S TOP 100: ANALYSIS

73 Ford Motor Co.

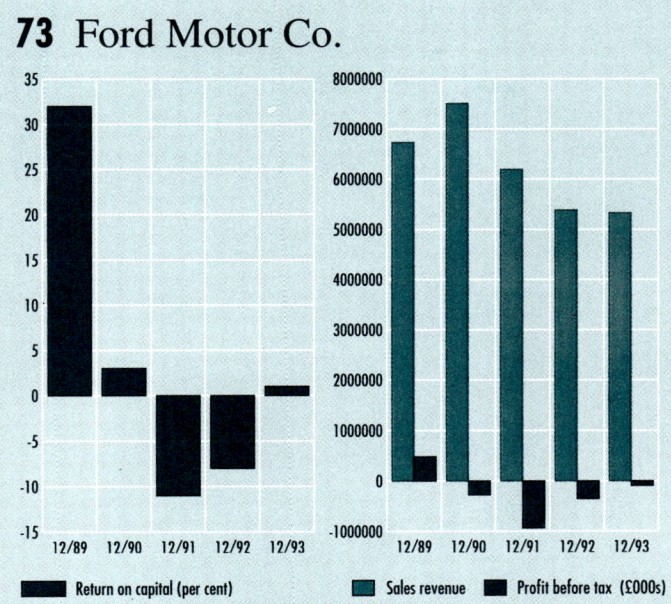

The principal activities of the group are the manufacture and sale of motor vehicles, and its finance operations. Ford's range of vehicles includes the Mondeo, Escort, Fiesta, Scorpio/Granada, Maverick and Probe. The company's principal market is the UK, followed by Germany, Spain and France. Incorporated in 1928, the ultimate holding company is Ford Motor Co (USA). Subsidiaries include Jaguar, which was acquired in 1989 for £1.38 billion, and Acona, a financial services company based in the Netherlands that was also acquired for £125 million, also in 1989. Ford has a 48 per cent interest in Iveco Ford Truck, a manufacturer of commercial vehicles.

74 Enterprise Oil

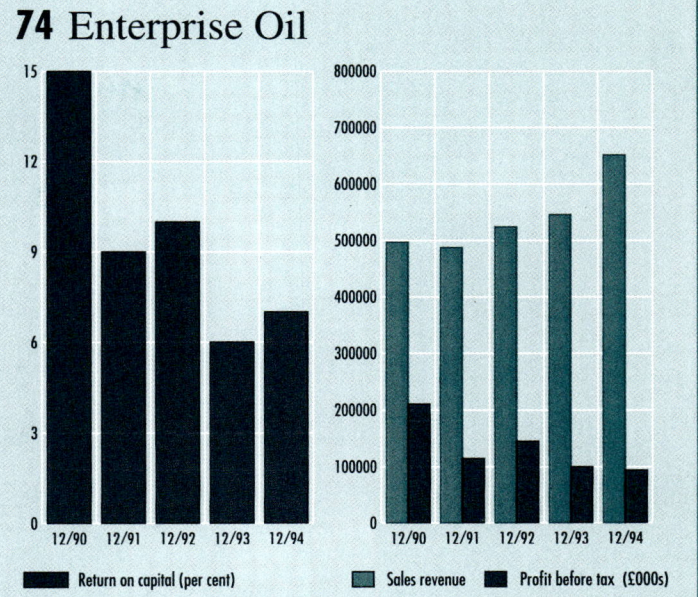

The company is engaged in oil and gas exploration and production. The international portfolio of exploration acreage embraces 17 countries, mainly in Northwest Europe, Italy, the Black Sea, Australia and Southeast Asia. Enterprise was incorporated in 1982 to assume ownership of certain offshore oil interests of British Gas, then preparing for privatisation. Enterprise shares began trading in 1984. Its operations were expanded through the purchase of the upstream oil and gas operations of Imperial Chemicals Industries. Some North Sea assets were transferred to a joint venture with France's Elf Aquitaine in 1991. In 1994 the company launched an unsuccessful takeover bid for Lasmo.

75 Post Office

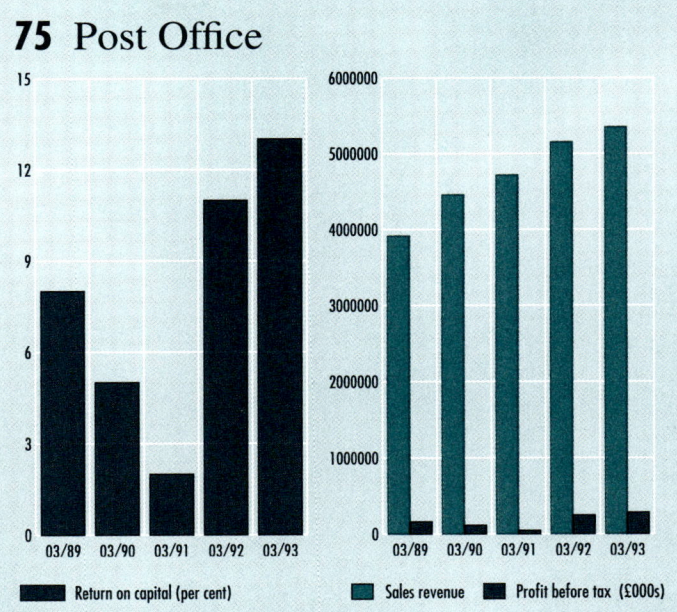

The group comprises the Post Office Corporation and its wholly-owned subsidiary, Post Office Counters. The Corporation comprises Royal Mail, Parcelforce, corporate services and a holding company function. Other subsidiaries include Post Office Finance (loans) and Subscription Services (television licensing). The Post Office ceased to be a government department in 1969, when postal, telecommunications, giro and remittance services were transferred to a new public authority. The British Telecommunications Act (1981) separated the functions of the Post Office, making it solely responsible for post office services and National Girobank. Girobank was sold in 1990.

76 British Nuclear Fuels

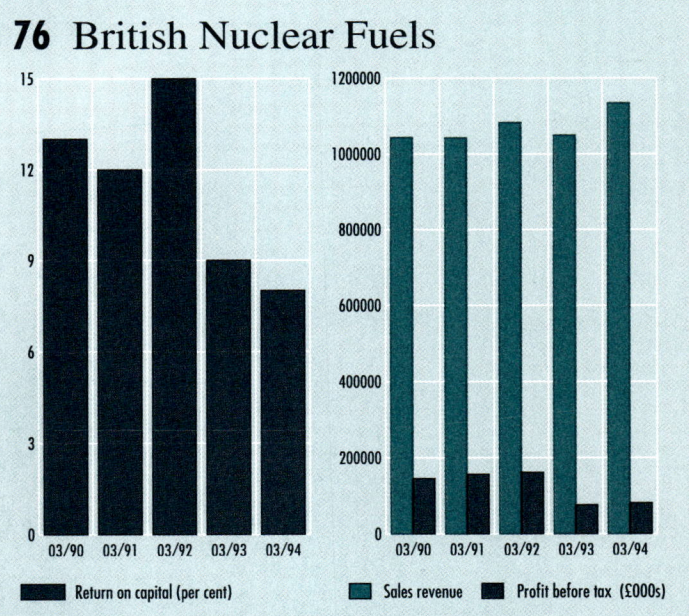

Principal activities include the conversion and enrichment of uranium, the manufacture and supply of uranium and platinum-based fuels; the provision of related fuel cycle services for nuclear power stations; and the reprocessing of nuclear fuel after use, including waste treatment and storage. The company also supplies electricity from the Calder Hall and Chapelcross nuclear power stations. Other activities include research, development and the design and construction of plant and equipment associated with the company's main business. The company has a 42.5 per cent interest in UK Nirex, which provides disposal services for low- and intermediate-level waste.

THE UK'S TOP 100: ANALYSIS   77-80

77 Anglian Water

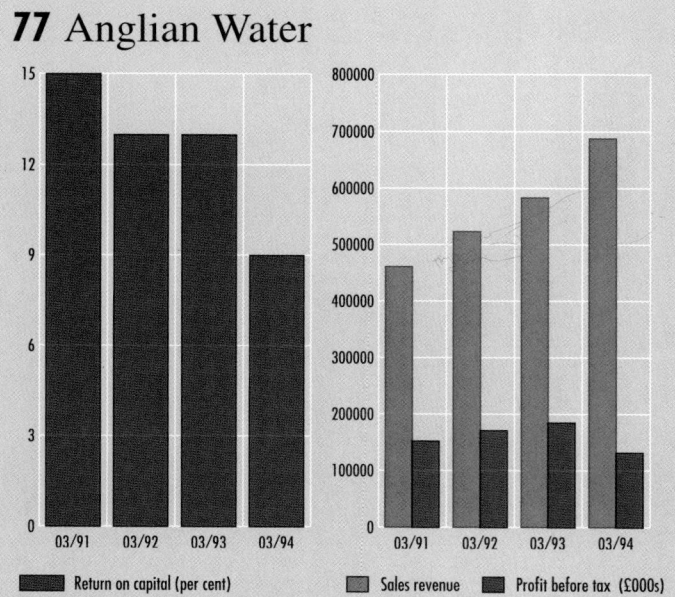

The company's main business is water supply and distribution, sewerage and sewerage treatment and disposal, principally operating in the region between the Thames and the Humber. Anglian succeeded the former regional water authority, which had responsibility for water, sewerage, environmental, land drainage and sea defence functions. The company's shares were listed on the stock market in 1989. The company has developed an international process engineering business whose activities are conducted mainly through the Purac group of companies, with operations in the UK, North America, Norway, Germany, Sweden, Australia and Poland.

78 Argyll Group

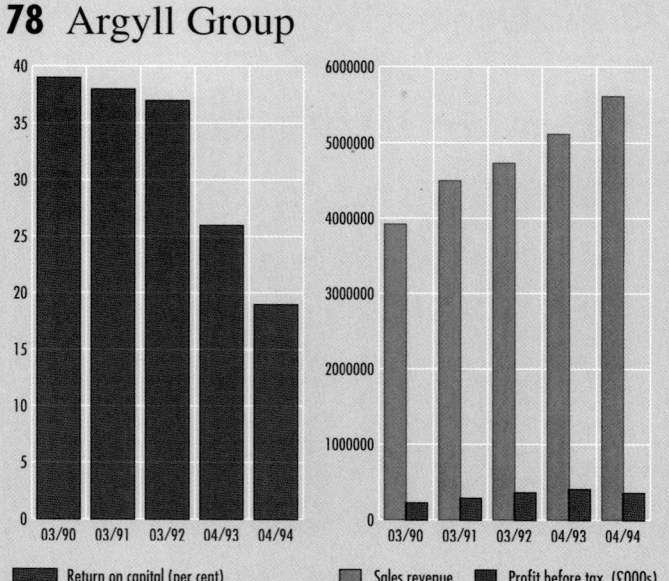

The company is engaged in food retailing and wholesaling in the UK, principally trading under the Safeway name. The company also has a regional supermarket chain in Northern England and Scotland trading as Presto. A discount business, Lo-Cost, has been discontinued through disposals and closure. The company was established in its current form in 1983 through the merger of Argyll Foods and Amalgamated Distilled Products. Argyll is a member of a three-strong European retailing alliance with Koninlijke Ahold, of the Netherlands, and Groupe Casino, of France, established in 1989 to pool resources and expertise in purchasing, distribution and marketing.

79 Cadbury Schweppes

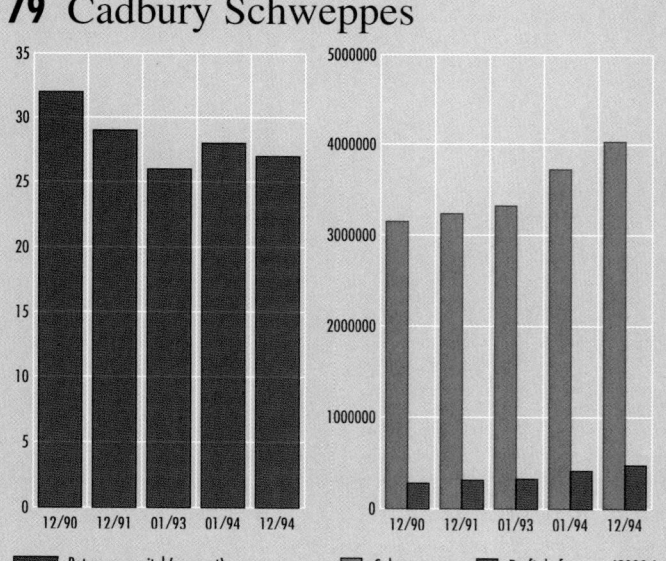

Companies in the group are principally engaged in the manufacture and sale of branded confectionery, licensed, catering and grocery trades in many countries throughout the world. In the UK subsidiaries include Cadbury, Coca-Cola & Schweppes Beverages (51 per cent owned, Sodastream and Trebor Bassett. In continental Europe, which typically accounts for almost one-quarter of group turnover, subsidiaries trade in France, Spain, Belgium, the Netherlands, Portugal and Germany. There are also businesses in Canada, the US, Mexico and Argentina. In March 1995 the company acquired the outstanding 77 per cent of Dr Pepper/Seven Up, not already owned, for $1.71 billion.

80 Scottish & Newcastle

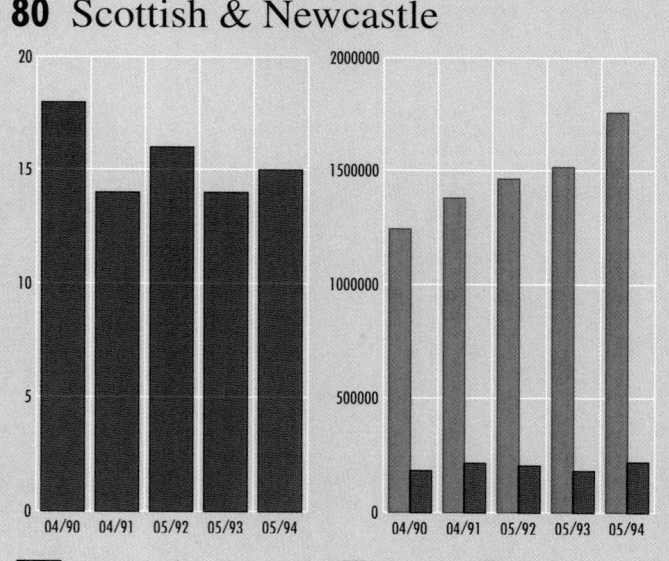

The company's beer division produces and packages ales and lagers which are marketed throughout the UK. It also imports and exports premium brands and is a supplier to the take-home sector. S&N's beers include Kestrel, McEwan's, Younger's, Newcastle Brown Ale, Tartan Special, Theakston's, Beck's Bier, Coors Extra Gold and Gillespie's. The leisure division owns Center Parcs, which has holiday villages throughout Europe specialising in short breaks, and Holiday Club Pontin's, offering family holidays in Britain. The retail division operates the company's tied estate of managed and tenanted pubs. In May 1995 the acquisition was announced of Courage, the UK brewer, from Fosters for £425 million.

81-84 THE UK'S TOP 100: ANALYSIS

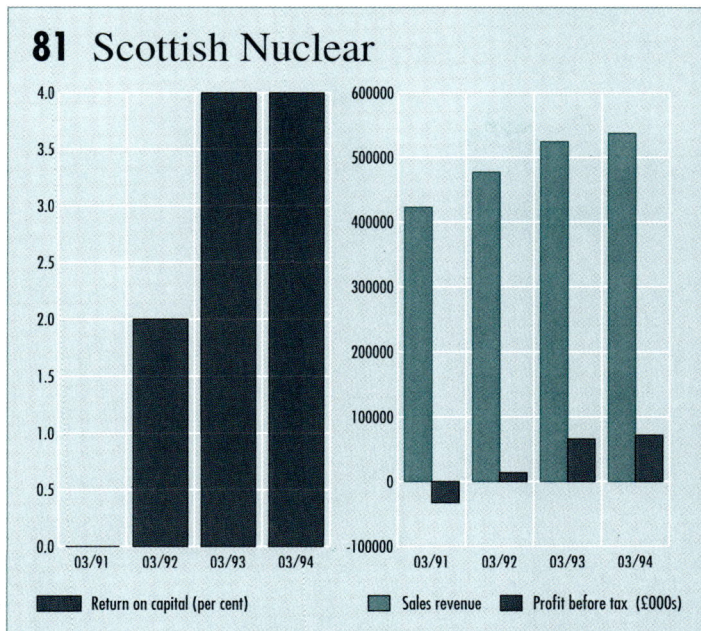

81 Scottish Nuclear

The company owns and operates the advanced gas-cooled reactor (AGR) nuclear power stations at Hunterston on the Firth of Clyde and at Torness on the east coast of Scotland. It is also responsible for the decommissioning of Hunterston A, the magnox power station. The company was established in 1990 when the nuclear activities of the South of Scotland Electricity Company and land at Stake Ness, Banffshire, belonging to the North of Scotland Hydro-Electric Board were vested in the company. In 1995 the government published proposals for the privatisation of Scottish Nuclear and the larger Nuclear Electric as a single entity.

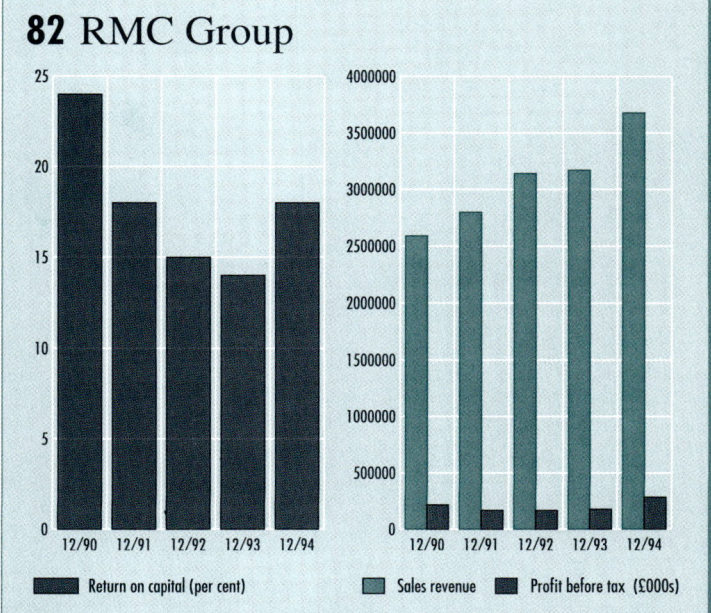

82 RMC Group

The group is mainly engaged in the production and supply of materials for use in the construction industry. In the UK activities are organised into divisions operating in sand, gravel and readymix, and roadstone products; building products; management and services; retail (including Great Mills' builders' merchants and DIY); merchanting; leisure; and waste management. The company also has operations in Germany, Austria, Belgium, the Czech Republic, France, Hungary, the Netherlands, Israel, Ireland, Spain and the US. The company was registered in 1930 and was formerly called Ready Mixed Concrete.

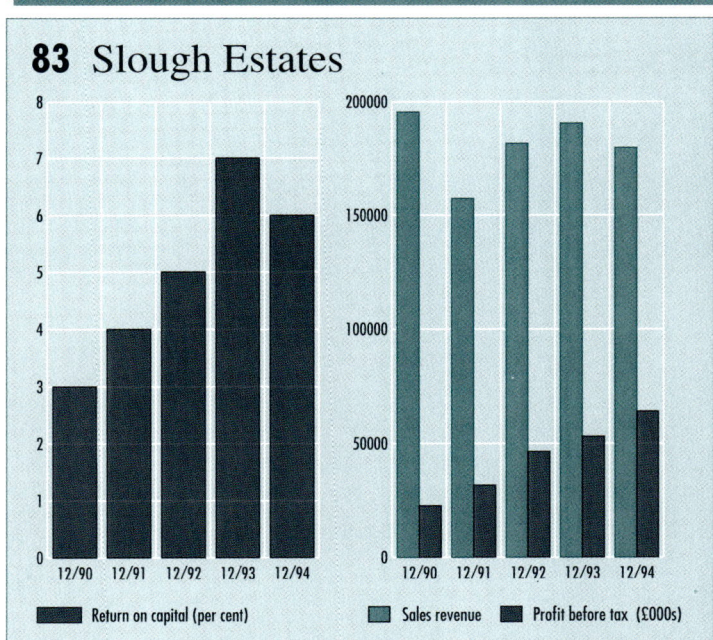

83 Slough Estates

The company owns properties with a portfolio value of £1.8 billion in the UK, Canada, the US, Australia, Belgium, France and Germany. The group is one of the largest owners and developers of industrial estates in Europe and, together with its substantial portfolio of office and retail developments, manages 31 million square feet of space occupied by some 2,400 tenants. There is also a utilities services division, called Slough Heat & Power, to provide utility services both on and off the company's properties. The company was founded in 1920 with the purchase of a trading estate at Slough, Buckinghamshire.

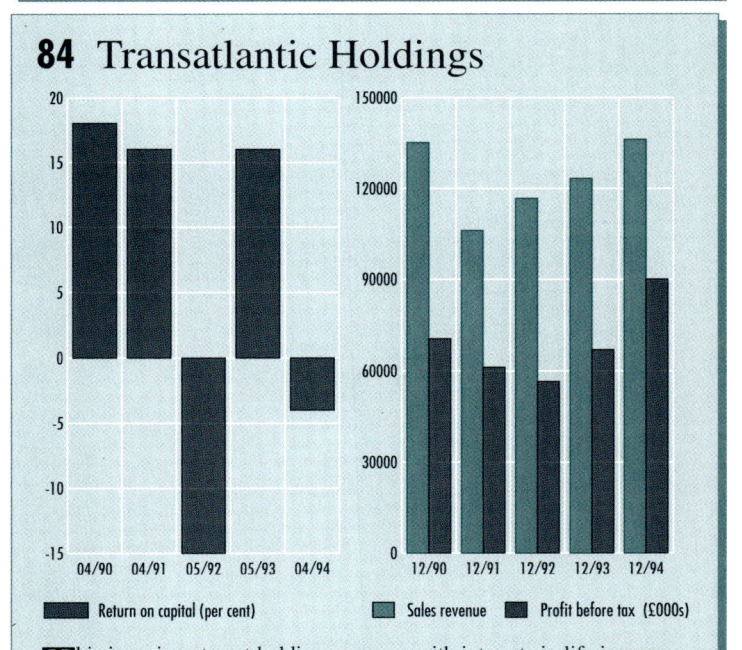

84 Transatlantic Holdings

This is an investment holding company with interests in life insurance, property and financial services, predominantly in the UK. The company owns 50 per cent of Sun Life Holdings, which in turn owns Sun Life Corporation, the life insurer. The principal subsidiaries are capital shopping centres, whose shares are listed separately on the London Stock Exchange, and Capital & Counties, both engaged in property investment, management and development. Transatlantic's ultimate holding company is Liblife Controlling Corporation (Proprietary) Ltd (South Africa). Union des Assurances de Paris is a substantial shareholder.

THE UK'S TOP 100: ANALYSIS   85-88

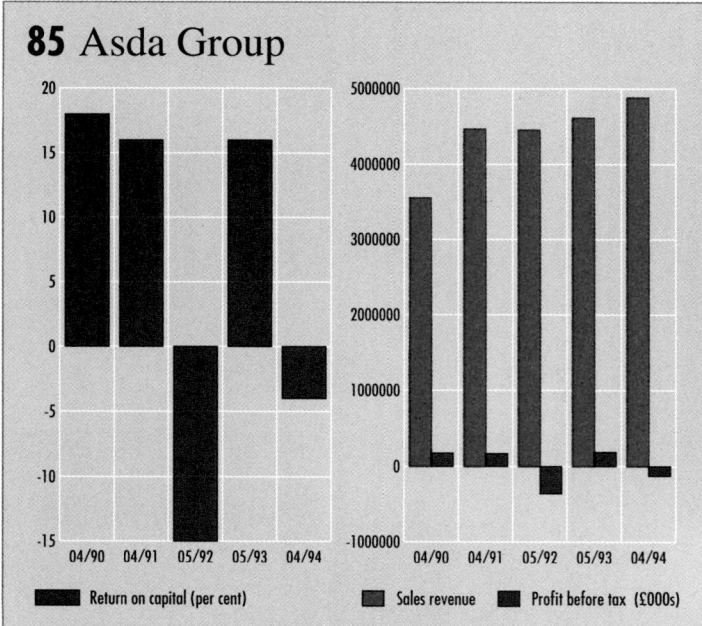

85 Asda Group

The principal activities are the retailing of food and clothing, home and leisure products, and property development. Subsidiaries comprise Asda Stores, Gazeley Properties (property development) and McLagan Investments (property investment). The company also has a 20 per cent interest in The George Davies Partnership. The company was formed through the merger of Associated Dairies and Allied Retailers; the name changed from Associated Dairies to Asda-MFI Group in 1985 and to Asda Group in 1988. In 1989 the company paid £704 million for 60 Gateway superstores.

86 Boots Company

The company's main business is the retailing of chemists' merchandise, autoparts, do-it-yourself, opticians' and children's products; and property investment, development and management. Subsidiaries include Boots The Chemists (retail chemists), Halfords (retailing of car parts, accessories, and bicycles and car servicing); and AG Stanley (retailer of decorative products and interior furnishings). The company also jointly owns Do It All, the supplier of DIY goods, in partnership with WH Smith. In March 1995 Boots agreed to sell its pharmaceuticals manufacturing activities to BASF, of Germany, for £840 million. Boots was originally incorporated in 1888.

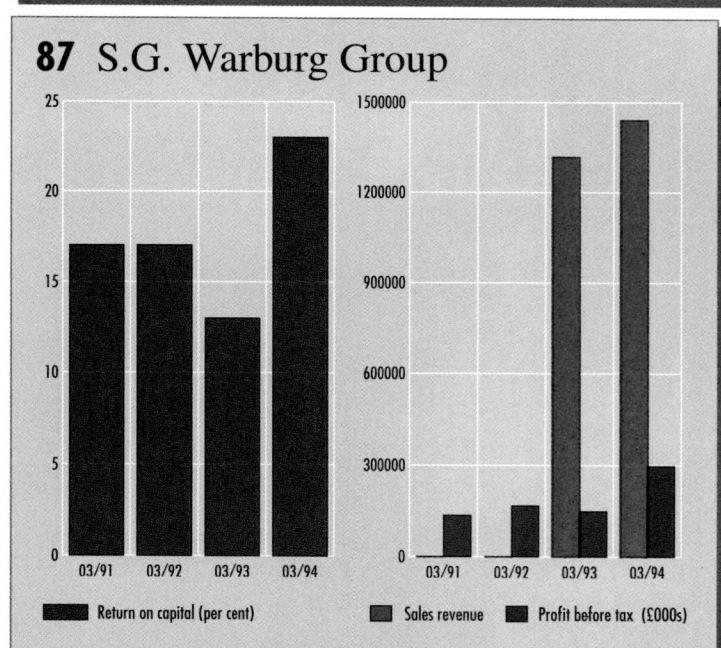

87 S.G. Warburg Group

The group is a investment banking firm, serving corporations, investors and governments, providing equity and fixed interest financing; merger, acquisition and restructuring execution; securities distribution and trading; company and economic research; specialist financing, such as leasing, banking and project finance; and securities custody and administration services. In May 1995 the group announced the sale of the investment banking business to Swiss Bank Corporation for £860 million. As part of the transaction Mercury Asset Management, the investment management services subsidiary of S.G. Warburg, became an independent company with its own London stock market listing.

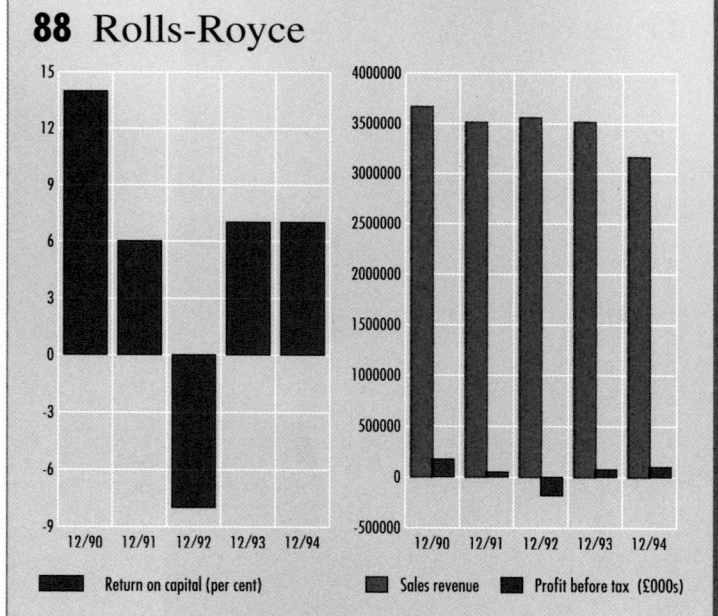

88 Rolls-Royce

The company operates through two main units, the Aerospace group, which specialises in gas turbines for civil and military aircraft; and the Industrial Power group, which designs, constructs and installs complete power generation, transmission and distribution systems and major equipment for marine propulsion, oil and gas pumping and defence markets. The restructured company was privatised and floated on the stock market in 1987. Its articles of association state that the company should remain under UK control. In November 1994 the company acquired Allison Engine Company, of the United States, for $525 million.

89-92 THE UK'S TOP 100: ANALYSIS

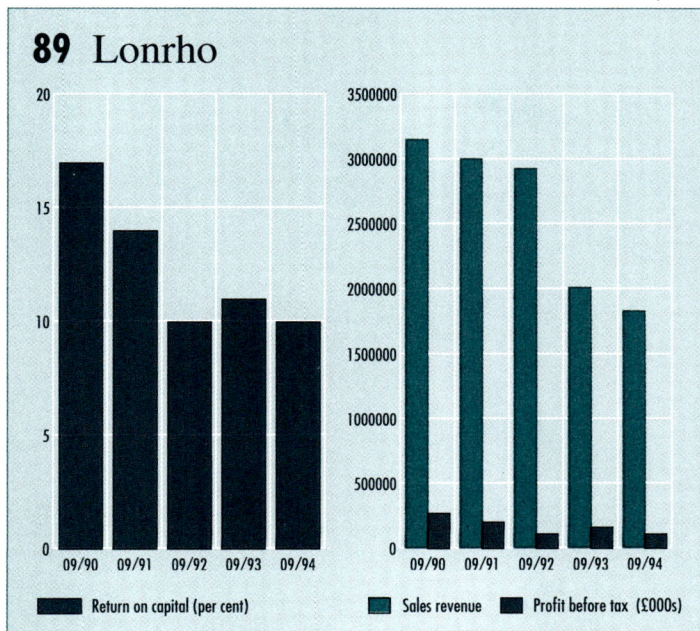

89 Lonrho

The group comprises four core activities: mining and refining, hotels, agriculture and general trade. The mining division includes Ashanti Goldfields and Lonrho's platinum mines, among the largest in the world and the lowest cost producers. The Lonrho Hotel group consists of more than 7,000 rooms in 26 hotels and lodges and is organised into three divisions: Metropole Hotels in the UK, Princess Hotels in North America and an African hotels division. Lonrho is the largest commercial food producer in Africa, where its farming and ranching activities are carried out on one million acres of land in 11 countries. General trade encompasses motor and equipment distribution and manufacturing.

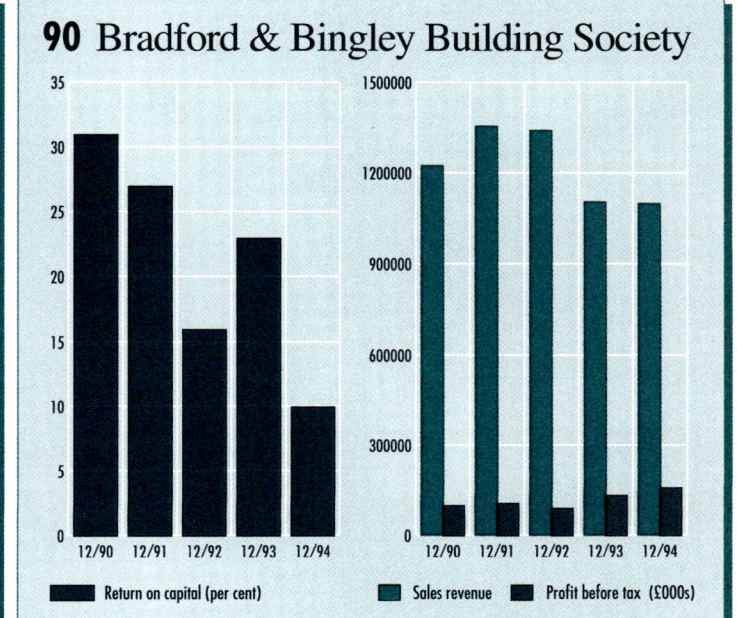

90 Bradford & Bingley Building Society

The company is engaged in the provision of finance for home purchase and improvements, commercial loans, savings and investment accounts, insurance services, the management of personal equity plans and the provision of independent financial advice on a range of products regulated under the Financial Services Act, including life assurance, unit trusts and personal pensions. It also has interests in two savings and loans and financial services companies in Germany. The building society was formed in 1964 through the merger of Bradford Equitable Building Society and Bingley Building Society, both of which were established in 1851.

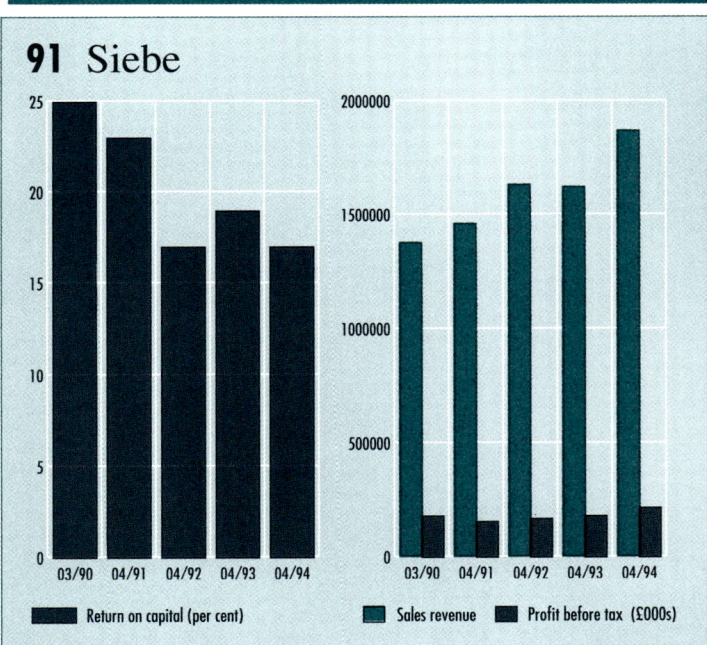

91 Siebe

The company designs and manufactures control devices and process control systems, high technology compressed air and pneumatic equipment, transfer and filtration equipment for gases and liquids, valves, automotive components and lubricators, specialist mechanical engineering, safety and lift support products. Although based in the UK the company typically generates a larger share of turnover and profits from both the US and continental Europe. In 1990 the company acquired The Foxboro Co., of America, for £356.7 million. Siebe was established in 1920 and was formerly known as Siebe Gorman.

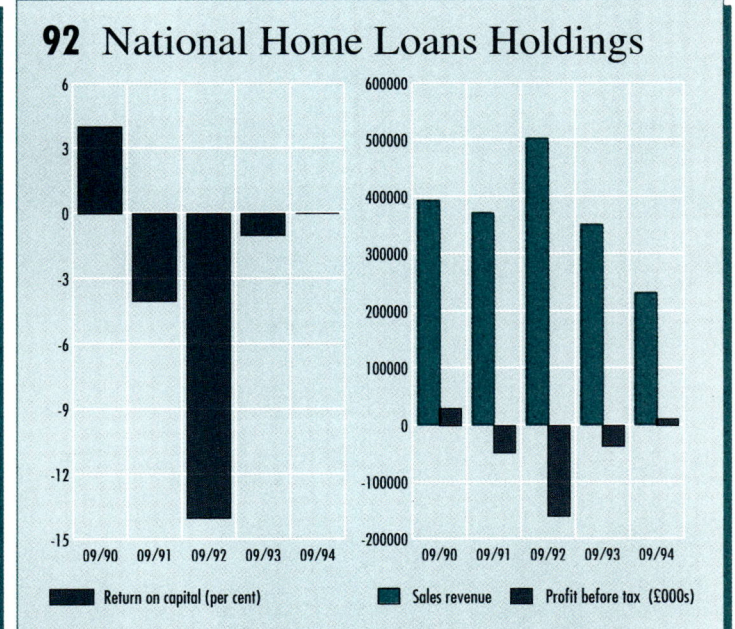

92 National Home Loans Holdings

Established in 1989 as the successor company to National Home Loans Corporation, the company operates a residential mortgage business. Business prospered in the late 1980s, but suffered from the downturn in the property market. When a capital reorganisation was implemented in 1995, raising £50.3 million through a rights issue, there was an accumulated deficit of £141.7 million. Interests in The National Mortgage Bank and J&J Securities were sold. The restructured company has returned to the mortgage market, launching a new subsidiary, Homeloans Direct. National Home Loans has also acquired a residential mortgage book from a European bank for £25.7 million.

THE UK'S TOP 100: ANALYSIS

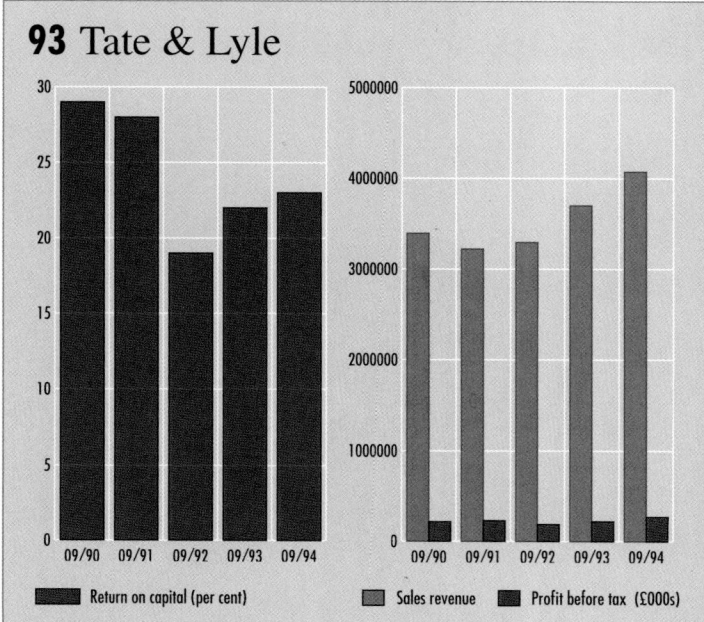

93 Tate & Lyle

The company's worldwide operations span sweetener and starch production, animal feed and bulk storage. Activities in North America, which comprise the major part of group businesses, include the subsidiaries A.E. Staley (cereal sweeteners and starches) in the US and Redpath Industries (sugar refining) in Canada. In the UK subsidiaries include Tate & Lyle Industries, Tate & Lyle International Finance, Tunnel Refineries and Greenwich Distilleries. The company was incorporated in 1903 and was formerly known as Henry Tate & Sons.

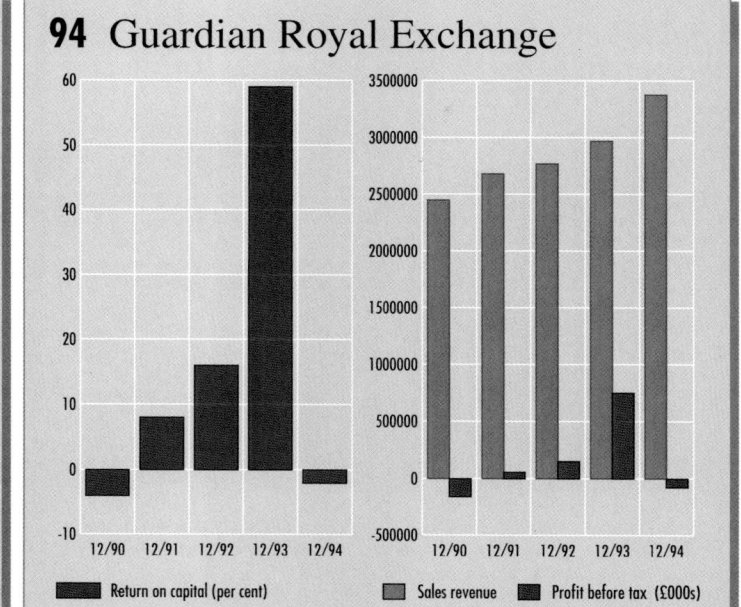

94 Guardian Royal Exchange

The company carries on insurance, financial services and investment business in the UK and throughout the world, with more than five million customers in over 50 countries. Business sectors comprise general insurance, with principal operations based in the UK, Ireland, continental Europe, the US and Canada, Asia and South Africa; life assurance, principally located in the UK, Ireland, Germany, France and a number of other territories; and corporate investment, which manages the investment of group funds with equities exposure focussed on the UK and German markets.

95 Nationwide Building Society

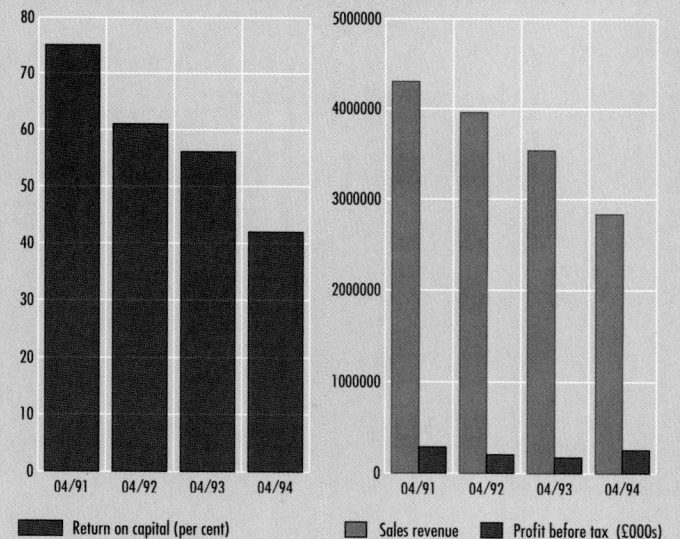

The building society provides a comprehensive and integrated range of personal financial and housing services. Activities include mortgage acquisition and management; housing development; independent financial advice; estate agency; BES fund management; surveying; syndicated lending; and property rental. Incorporated in 1875, the building society achieved its present structure as a result of the amalgamation of a number of societies over a long period. In 1987 its name changed from Anglia Building Society to Nationwide Anglia Building Society and in 1991 to Nationwide.

96 Arjo Wiggins Appleton

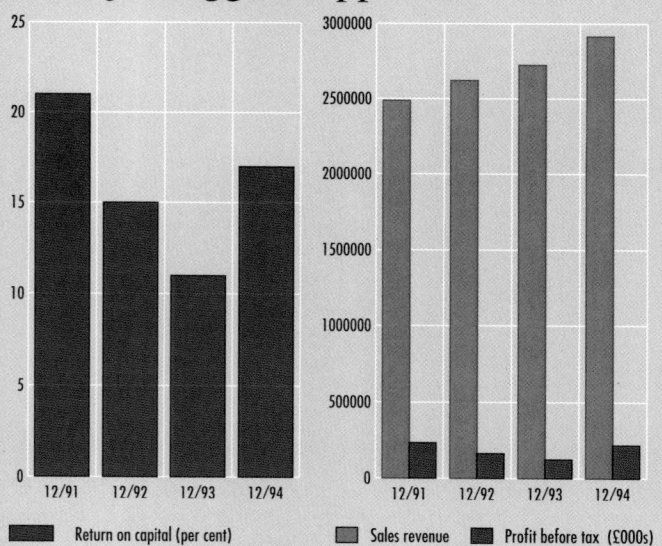

The group is principally engaged in the manufacture and distribution of carbonless, thermal, fine, coated and speciality papers and the manufacture of pulp. It has substantial operations throughout Europe and in North America. The group's present structure was put in place in 1990 through the merger of Britain's Wiggins Teape Appleton and France's Arjomari Europe. As a result of the merger Arjomari-Prioux, Saint Louis and Worms et Cie own 40.15 per cent of the company. Wiggins Teape Appleton itself was formed through the merger of Wiggins Teape, of Britain, and America's Appleton Inc., two former subsidiaries of BAT Industries, in 1989.

97-100   THE UK'S TOP 100: ANALYSIS

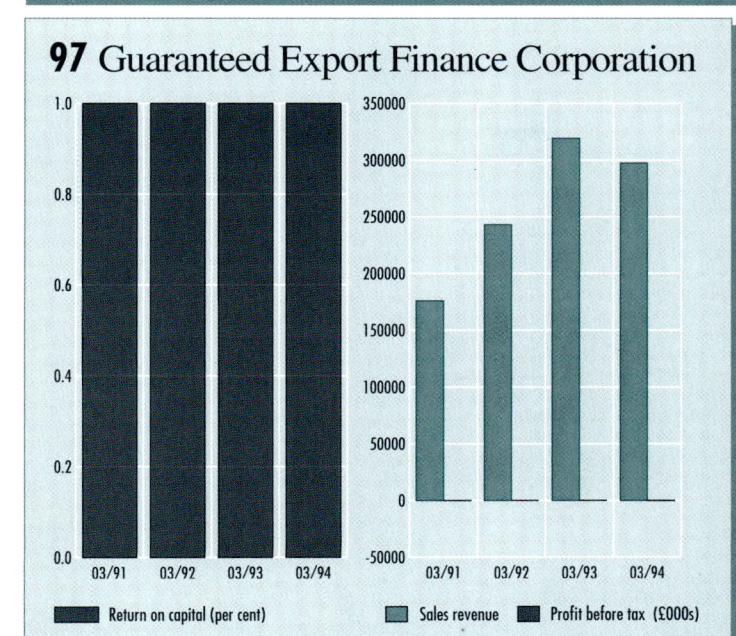

97 Guaranteed Export Finance Corporation

Return on capital (per cent)   **Sales revenue**   **Profit before tax (£000s)**

The company was established for the purpose of participating in loans supported or guaranteed by the Secretary of State for Trade and Industry, acting by the Exports Credit Guaranteed Department (ECGD). The company raises funds for this purpose from the banks and through the capital markets. ECGD has entered into support arrangements in respect of each lending transaction to which the company is committed. The ultimate holding company is First Securitisation Co.

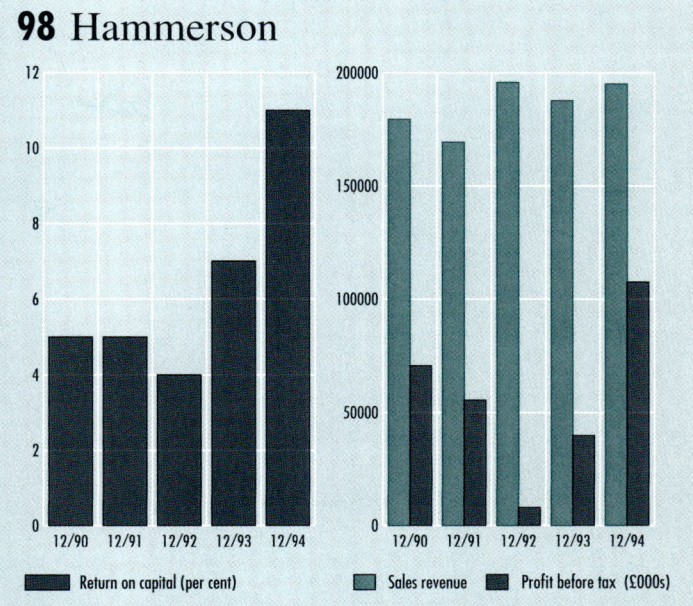

98 Hammerson

Return on capital (per cent)   **Sales revenue**   **Profit before tax (£000s)**

The group's main business is property investment and development and it holds a portfolio of retail and office properties in the UK, Germany, France, the Netherlands, Spain, the US and Canada. In 1994 the company withdrew from Australasia with the sale of Hammerson Australia to Australian Mutual Provident for £251 million. Subsequent investment has been biased towards Europe, to France in particular. The company was incorporated in 1931 under the Industrial and Provident Societies Act and was formerly the Associated Co-operative Investment Trust, changing later to Associated City Investment Trust. In 1989 Hammerson survived a hostile takeover bid by Rodamco Land.

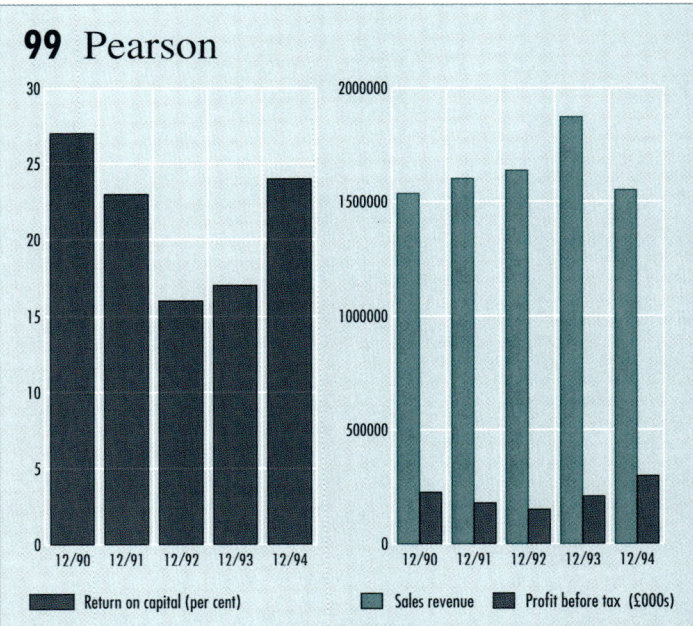

99 Pearson

Return on capital (per cent)   **Sales revenue**   **Profit before tax (£000s)**

Activities span information, education and entertainment. The company owns The Financial Times Group and Westminster Press, a regional newspaper group, and a range of on-line databases, news and research services. Subsidiaries include Addison-Wesley (educational, professional and general interest publishing), and Longman (professional and educational books). The company owns Penguin, the publisher; The Tussauds Group (including Madame Tussaud's, London Planetaurium, Chessington, World of Adventures, Alton Towers), and Pearson Television (including Thames Television). Pearson also has a 50 per cent interest in merchant bank Lazard Brothers.

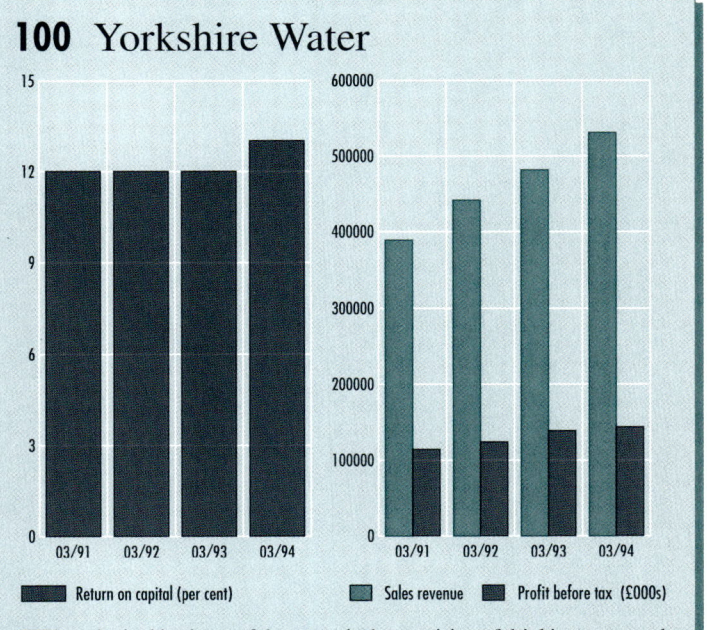

100 Yorkshire Water

Return on capital (per cent)   **Sales revenue**   **Profit before tax (£000s)**

The principal business of the group is the provision of drinking water and waste water to the Yorkshire region by a wholly owned subsidiary, Yorkshire Water Services. Most non-core businesses are managed by YW Enterprises. Major areas of activity are the treatment of liquid and hazardous wastes, analytical laboratory services and specialist water treatment chemicals. Yorkshire Water also has associated interests in regional property development. The company was incorporated in 1989 to continue the business of the former Yorkshire Water Authority, other than the part of the business vested in the National Rivers Authority.

THE UK'S TOP 50 PROFIT MAKERS

RANK	RANK IN EUROPE TOP 1000	COMPANY NAME	PROFIT BEFORE TAX Latest year £000	Previous year £000	Change in profit £000
1	17	HSBC Holdings	3,166,000	2,584,000	582,000
2	28	British Telecommunications	2,662,000	2,756,000	-94,000
3	n/a	Shell Transport and Trading Company	2,650,800	2,314,800	336,000
4	16	British Petroleum Company	2,281,000	1,302,000	979,000
5	46	Barclays	1,859,000	661,000	1,198,000
6	93	Glaxo Wellcome[1]	1,840,000	1,675,000	165,000
7	71	B.A.T Industries	1,802,000	1,809,000	-7,000
8	40	National Westminster Bank	1,592,000	989,000	603,000
9	121	BTR	1,412,000	1,274,000	138,000
10	32	Hanson	1,346,000	1,016,000	330,000
11	81	Lloyds Bank	1,304,000	1,031,000	273,000
12	111	Halifax Building Society	975,100	865,800	109,300
13	24	Abbey National	932,000	704,000	228,000
14	117	RTZ Corporation	922,000	435,000	487,000
15	10	British Gas	918,000	L569,000	1,487,000
16	101	Guinness	915,000	702,000	213,000
17	143	General Electric Company	866,000	863,000	3,000
18	146	Marks and Spencer	851,500	736,500	115,000
19	89	Cable and Wireless	844,100	1,088,300	-244,200
20	52	Unilever	792,000	663,000	129,000
21	48	Salomon Brothers Europe	719,700	531,400	188,300
22	190	SmithKline Beecham	691,000	1,220,000	-529,000
23	140	National Power	677,000	580,000	97,000
24	150	Esso UK	663,800	560,300	103,500
25	221	ZENECA Group	659,000	633,000	26,000
26	84	Grand Metropolitan	654,000	625,000	29,000
27	125	Allied Domecq	606,000	505,000	101,000
28	392	Prudential Corporation	603,000	589,000	14,000
29	237	National Grid Holding	579,500	533,200	46,300
30	115	Bass	552,000	508,000	44,000
31	139	Tesco	551,000	435,000	116,000
32	130	Royal Bank of Scotland Group	532,000	258,000	274,000
33	160	Great Universal Stores	518,900	475,000	43,900
34	170	Standard Chartered	510,000	401,000	109,000
35	566	Reuters Holdings	510,000	440,000	70,000
36	191	TSB Group	504,000	301,000	203,000
37	272	Cadbury Schweppes	478,500	416,300	62,200
38	242	PowerGen	476,000	418,127	57,873
39	184	Bank of Scotland	450,000	269,000	181,000
40	249	General Accident	428,300	294,900	133,400
41	299	Boots Company	415,900	405,200	10,700
42	87	Imperial Chemical Industries	408,000	360,000	48,000
43	131	Commercial Union	402,000	211,000	191,000
44	259	Royal Insurance Holdings	401,000	143,000	258,000
45	66	Nuclear Electric	392,000	109,000	283,000
46	258	Associated British Foods	382,000	349,259	32,741
47	239	Redland	373,000	278,900	94,100
48	157	J. Sainsbury	368,800	732,800	-364,000
49	605	Vodafone Group	363,330	322,473	40,857
50	271	Argyll Group	361,800	410,551	-48,751

NOTES: n/a – not applicable. UK part of a multinational group, part incorporated in the UK and part the Netherlands, which features in the Europe 1000 table in its entirety. [1]Figures do not reflect merger with Wellcome PLC.

THE UK'S TOP 50 INVESTMENT TRUSTS

RANK	COMPANY NAME	TOTAL ASSETS Latest year £000	TOTAL ASSETS Previous year £000	PROFIT BEFORE INTEREST & TAX Latest year £000	PROFIT BEFORE INTEREST & TAX Previous Year £000	EQUITY MKT CAPITAL £000
1	Foreign & Colonial Investment Trust	1,694,380	1,784,280	50,495	50,921	1,430,851
2	Edinburgh Investment Trust	1,180,766	1,238,395	54,969	54,883	860,263
3	Scottish Mortgage & Trust	1,099,148	1,073,698	38,346	32,258	789,977
4	Witan Investment Company	1,079,720	1,145,160	37,576	35,568	863,197
5	Alliance Trust	1,003,515	1,141,769	37,473	36,993	1,154,992
6	Scottish Investment Trust	804,721	845,220	27,557	24,887	551,310
7	British Investment Trust	797,063	695,747	35,439	29,524	763,620
8	Govett Oriental Investment Trust	792,199	830,168	10,333	8,297	593,285
9	Electra Investment Trust	790,790	713,197	26,352	25,553	550,352
10	British Assets Trust	748,590	787,068	35,717	35,851	360,960
11	Fleming Far Eastern Investment Trust	689,109	516,122	8,322	6,849	459,813
12	Scottish Eastern Investment Trust	670,893	749,218	22,328	19,266	475,200
13	Anglo & Overseas Trust	610,898	629,036	15,713	15,802	480,982
14	Fleming Japanese Investment Trust	539,149	308,299	2,312	1,598	456,601
15	Murray International Trust	533,166	603,198	24,036	25,002	399,383
16	RIT Capital Partners	531,614	485,579	10,102	8,845	314,415
17	Monks Investment Trust	507,409	457,814	13,959	15,016	404,254
18	Templeton Emerging Markets Investment Trust	506,515	257,698	3,936	2,710	110,982
19	Scottish American Investment Company	497,902	514,002	17,606	16,178	344,356
20	Foreign & Colonial Pacific Investment Trust	495,409	526,972	12,121	9,353	336,209
21	Mercury World Mining Trust	483,691	n/a	4,703	n/a	398,114
22	Kleinwort European Privatisation Investment Trust	478,889	n/a	6,364	n/a	385,000
23	Fleming Mercantile Investment Trust	460,349	550,054	13,375	13,072	382,948
24	Fleming Overseas Investment Trust	451,888	439,106	8,921	9,416	376,601
25	TR Smaller Companies Investment Trust	417,672	358,173	11,601	12,481	342,144
26	Edinburgh Dragon Trust	394,981	240,942	3,587	1,212	298,999
27	Govett Strategic Investment Trust	380,256	402,697	18,464	19,212	239,507
28	Scottish National Trust	372,641	384,334	20,009	20,734	363,014
29	Second Alliance Trust	342,055	323,475	10,949	10,489	355,296
30	Merchants Trust	335,709	384,632	19,001	16,413	354,915
31	TR City of London Trust	330,350	314,490	15,722	13,682	285,038
32	Bankers Investment Trust	329,374	327,407	11,189	10,816	286,974
33	Securities Trust of Scotland	328,566	340,040	18,198	17,826	260,824
34	Dunedin Income Growth Investment Trust	309,810	372,709	19,591	19,905	203,149
35	Dunedin Worldwide Investment Trust	298,664	326,706	5,103	8,588	256,108
36	Murray Income Trust	297,380	272,647	12,565	11,448	274,875
37	Murray Smaller Markets Trust	295,744	216,745	5,568	5,172	258,436
38	M & G Income Investment Trust	285,817	352,669	15,622	13,753	307,602
39	Throgmorton Trust	280,863	314,580	16,527	22,007	224,809
40	Fleming American Investment Trust	276,383	297,699	5,257	4,370	409,360
41	London Insurance Market Investment Trust	270,863	n/a	10,170	n/a	266,000
42	TR Technology	269,229	226,755	5,103	4,358	244,678
43	American Trust	264,241	227,410	6,821	6,078	201,184
44	Fleming Continental European Investment Trust	249,409	187,098	3,295	3,622	219,341
45	English & Scottish Investors	248,609	281,728	7,226	6,346	170,726
46	Kleinwort Overseas Investment Trust	244,466	273,411	4,295	4,583	214,634
47	Kleinwort Charter Investment Trust	235,593	233,094	6,444	7,011	217,264
48	Temple Bar Investment Trust	228,617	255,296	12,677	12,414	199,570
49	Baring Tribune Investment Trust	219,550	245,123	6,057	5,817	164,000
50	Foreign & Colonial Smaller Companies	219,452	152,119	4,991	4,205	190,051

NOTES: n/a – not available. Figures shown are from first accounts available since quotation.

THE UK'S TOP 1000 — 1-50

RANK	COMPANY NAME (Sector)	CAPITAL EMPLOYED £000	TURNOVER £000	PRE-TAX PROFIT £000	NUMBER OF EMPLOYEES	EQUITY MKT CAPITAL £000
1	British Gas (Oil, Gas & Nuclear Fuels)	24,639,000	9,698,000	918,000	69,971	13,622,000
2	British Petroleum Company (Oil, Gas & Nuclear Fuels)	20,777,000	33,116,000	2,281,000	66,550	23,420,000
3	HSBC Holdings (Banks)	20,637,000	13,975,000	3,166,000	106,861	18,424,000
4	Shell Transport and Trading Company[1] (Oil, Gas & Nuclear Fuels)	20,082,800	24,771,600	2,650,800	n/a	23,078,000
5	Abbey National (Banks)	17,545,000	5,621,000	932,000	16,703	5,649,000
6	British Telecommunications (Communications)	16,392,000	13,893,000	2,662,000	148,900	24,379,000
7	Hanson (Conglomerates)	14,832,000	11,199,000	1,346,000	74,000	11,911,000
8	National Westminster Bank (Banks)	13,186,000	13,345,000	1,592,000	97,000	8,820,000
9	Barclays (Banks)	11,562,000	13,429,000	1,859,000	95,700	9,982,000
10	Salomon Brothers Europe (Other Financial)	11,086,900	2,406,300	719,700	1,024	†
11	Eurotunnel Group[2] (Transport Services)	9,604,644	30,598	L386,887	2,302	2,524,169
12	News International (Media)	8,425,900	733,500	360,900	4,001	1,575,204
13	Nuclear Electric (Electricity)	8,425,000	2,962,000	392,000	10,728	†
14	B.A.T Industries (Tobacco)	7,975,000	5,456,000	1,802,000	83,619	13,298,000
15	Lloyds Bank (Banks)	6,652,000	6,863,000	1,304,000	62,120	7,166,000
16	Grand Metropolitan (Brewers & Distillers)	6,508,000	7,780,000	654,000	53,674	8,512,000
17	Imperial Chemical Industries (Chemicals)	6,289,000	9,189,000	408,000	67,500	5,422,000
18	Cable and Wireless (Communications)	6,126,100	5,132,800	844,100	41,124	8,518,000
19	Glaxo Wellcome§ (Health & Household)	5,731,000	5,656,000	1,840,000	47,189	16,589,000
20	British Airways (Transport Services)	5,614,000	6,303,000	301,000	53,060	3,905,000
21	Guinness (Brewers & Distillers)	5,428,000	4,690,000	915,000	23,774	9,081,000
22	Land Securities (Property)	5,104,500	472,600	244,700	551	3,029,382
23	Halifax Building Society (Other Financial)	4,969,900	5,444,700	975,100	n/a	†
24	Bass (Brewers & Distillers)	4,873,000	4,452,000	552,000	75,845	4,503,000
25	RTZ Corporation (Mines)	4,759,000	2,288,000	922,000	19,080	8,831,000
26	BTR (Conglomerates)	4,694,000	9,444,000	1,412,000	124,491	10,659,000
27	British Steel (Metal & Metal Forming)	4,498,000	4,191,000	80,000	41,300	3,239,000
28	Allied Domecq (Brewers & Distillers)	4,496,000	5,526,000	606,000	38,946	5,581,000
29	Royal Bank of Scotland Group (Banks)	4,434,000	3,661,000	532,000	22,496	3,322,000
30	Commercial Union (Insurance, Life/Non-life)	4,425,000	6,717,000	402,000	9,589	3,357,100
31	P & O (Transport Services)	4,417,600	5,989,600	349,500	61,467	4,031,758
32	Tesco (Stores)	4,094,000	10,101,000	551,000	71,467	5,186,775
33	National Power (Electricity)	4,083,000	3,641,000	677,000	6,955	5,445,000
34	General Electric Company (Electronics)	4,033,000	5,791,000	866,000	86,121	8,115,000
35	Forte (Hotels & Leisure)	4,017,000	1,789,000	127,000	36,000	2,236,000
36	Marks and Spencer (Stores)	3,952,400	6,541,200	851,500	62,120	11,910,561
37	Esso UK (Oil, Gas & Nuclear Fuels)	3,809,000	3,674,600	663,800	4,158	†
38	J. Sainsbury (Food Wholesaling & Retailing)	3,698,900	10,583,200	368,800	82,345	7,496,765
39	Great Universal Stores (Stores)	3,692,400	3,094,300	518,900	n/a	6,099,983
40	Standard Chartered (Banks)	3,412,000	2,913,000	510,000	28,734	2,804,000
41	MEPC (Property)	3,364,600	234,300	111,200	n/a	1,808,141
42	British Aerospace (Aerospace)	3,317,000	7,153,000	211,000	56,400	2,126,000
43	BAA (Transport Services)	3,302,100	1,097,800	322,400	8,171	4,837,558
44	Woolwich Building Society (Other Financial)	3,291,700	2,020,400	302,700	8,390	†
45	Unilever (Food Manufacturing)	3,290,000	8,750,000	792,000	n/a	9,432,000
46	Ladbroke Group (Hotels & Leisure)	3,282,400	4,360,700	L229,800	55,248	1,989,680
47	Bank of Scotland (Banks)	3,230,000	2,735,000	450,000	15,258	2,618,600
48	Alliance & Leicester Building Society (Other Financial)	3,153,900	1,990,900	284,000	n/a	†
49	SmithKline Beecham (Health & Household)	3,141,000	6,492,000	691,000	52,300	6,246,950
50	TSB Group (Banks)	3,125,000	3,122,000	504,000	26,860	3,453,000

NOTES: [1]Based on 40% of Royal Dutch/Shell Group. [2]Eurotunnel PLC/Eurotunnel SA units. §Figures do not reflect merger with Wellcome PLC. n/a – not available. †Market capitalisation not available. Figure not disclosed or company unquoted, government controlled, a nationalised industry, a subsidiary or newly quoted.

51-100 THE UK'S TOP 1000

RANK	COMPANY NAME (Sector)	CAPITAL EMPLOYED £000	TURNOVER £000	PRE-TAX PROFIT £000	NUMBER OF EMPLOYEES	EQUITY MKT CAPITAL £000
51	Severn Trent (Water)	2,957,300	998,000	281,400	10,783	1,870,451
52	North West Water Group (Water)	2,867,100	924,200	269,000	8,013	2,070,237
53	British Railways Board (Transport Services)	2,830,500	3,100,500	L108,400	128,414	†
54	BOC Group (Chemicals)	2,806,400	3,292,300	253,100	39,390	3,304,679
55	Rank Xerox (Electronics)	2,798,000	3,309,000	221,000	23,139	†
56	ZENECA Group (Health & Household)	2,759,000	4,480,000	659,000	30,800	8,315,000
57	Whitbread (Brewers & Distillers)	2,648,100	2,471,800	275,400	49,306	2,585,046
58	London Regional Transport (Transport Services)	2,642,900	1,096,100	10,300	40,139	†
59	Conoco (UK) (Oil, Gas & Nuclear Fuels)	2,622,300	2,714,800	117,700	8,896	†
60	Thames Water (Water)	2,605,600	1,093,200	241,700	10,141	1,922,649
61	3i Group (Investment Trusts)	2,557,674	244,233	84,255	589	1,907,547
62	LASMO (Oil, Gas & Nuclear Fuels)	2,526,000	648,000	92,000	1,440	1,419,000
63	National Grid Holding (Electricity)	2,501,000	1,425,000	579,500	5,127	†
64	Redland (Building Materials & Services)	2,493,600	2,468,800	373,000	21,545	2,382,800
65	PowerGen (Electricity)	2,462,000	2,932,000	476,000	4,782	3,358,000
66	Rank Organisation (Hotels & Leisure)	2,405,000	2,199,400	284,000	39,743	3,683,549
67	General Accident (Insurance, Life/Non-life)	2,398,200	5,026,700	428,300	11,510	2,287,941
68	British Land Company (Property)	2,368,000	156,500	53,900	295	1,485,569
69	Sun Alliance Group (Insurance, Life/Non-life)	2,307,100	4,657,800	315,500	16,987	2,335,866
70	Pilkington (Other Industrial Materials & Products)	2,301,000	2,737,400	97,800	41,100	1,310,360
71	Associated British Foods (Food Manufacturing)	2,301,000	4,513,000	382,000	50,241	2,528,000
72	Royal Insurance Holdings (Insurance, Life/Non-life)	2,295,000	4,785,000	401,000	13,224	1,816,000
73	Ford Motor Co. (Transport – Manufacture & Distribution)	2,256,000	5,327,000	L92,000	32,500	†
74	Enterprise Oil (Oil, Gas & Nuclear Fuels)	2,214,300	651,300	93,900	623	1,929,945
75	Post Office (Communications)	2,198,000	5,345,000	283,000	193,163	†
76	British Nuclear Fuels (Oil, Gas & Nuclear Fuels)	2,181,000	1,133,000	81,000	15,476	†
77	Anglian Water (Water)	2,171,600	687,900	132,200	6,031	1,424,222
78	Argyll Group (Food Wholesaling & Retailing)	2,148,800	5,607,700	361,800	67,323	3,269,205
79	Cadbury Schweppes (Food Manufacturing)	2,145,800	4,029,600	478,500	40,506	3,594,109
80	Scottish & Newcastle (Brewers & Distillers)	2,078,400	1,759,800	221,800	36,830	2,790,118
81	Scottish Nuclear (Electricity)	2,066,000	537,000	72,000	2,060	†
82	RMC Group (Building Materials & Services)	2,023,300	3,678,000	283,300	27,371	1,844,610
83	Slough Estates (Property)	1,970,100	179,400	64,000	427	1,090,921
84	Transatlantic Holdings (Property)	1,942,900	136,200	90,100	10,230	1,064,787
85	Asda Group (Stores)	1,927,900	4,882,200	L125,900	70,515	1,608,768
86	Boots Company (Stores)	1,912,900	4,167,100	415,900	80,099	4,830,017
87	S.G. Warburg Group (Merchant Banks)	1,857,400	1,441,800	297,000	n/a	1,686,530
88	Rolls-Royce (Aerospace)	1,846,000	3,163,000	101,000	43,500	2,195,000
89	Lonrho (Conglomerates)	1,840,000	1,824,000	112,000	100,113	1,018,000
90	Bradford & Bingley Building Society (Other Financial)	1,833,700	1,097,900	159,900	n/a	†
91	Siebe (Engineering – General)	1,818,000	1,863,500	217,200	29,938	2,355,412
92	National Home Loans Holdings (Other Financial)	1,811,900	231,100	11,400	n/a	61,062
93	Tate & Lyle (Food Manufacturing)	1,764,000	4,074,000	273,800	15,640	1,937,708
94	Guardian Royal Exchange (Insurance, Life/Non-life)	1,736,000	3,375,000	L75,000	7,325	1,451,000
95	Nationwide Building Society (Other Financial)	1,725,300	2,837,200	252,700	n/a	†
96	Arjo Wiggins Appleton (Packaging, Paper & Printing)	1,706,400	2,915,100	217,100	18,466	1,938,268
97	Guaranteed Export Finance Corporation (Other Financial)	1,700,283	297,504	L236	n/a	†
98	Hammerson (Property)	1,675,700	195,100	107,500	381	982,497
99	Pearson (Media)	1,644,800	1,550,100	297,800	17,215	3,068,312
100	Yorkshire Water (Water)	1,584,200	530,600	143,500	4,768	1,065,784

NOTES: n/a – not available. †Market capitalisation not available. Figure not disclosed or company unquoted, government controlled, a nationalised industry, a subsidiary or newly quoted.

THE UK'S TOP 1000   101-150

RANK	COMPANY NAME (Sector)	CAPITAL EMPLOYED £000	TURNOVER £000	PRE-TAX PROFIT £000	NUMBER OF EMPLOYEES	EQUITY MKT CAPITAL £000
101	Kingfisher (Stores)	1,579,300	4,887,700	244,200	43,741	2,956,627
102	Foreign & Colonial Investment Trust (Investment Trusts)	1,554,145	48,283	35,100	n/a	1,430,851
103	Tarmac (Building Materials & Services)	1,545,000	2,510,300	107,200	20,571	1,101,248
104	Leeds Permanent Building Society[3] (Other Financial)	1,534,900	1,589,800	245,800	n/a	†
105	Blue Circle Industries (Building Materials & Services)	1,506,400	1,779,800	184,400	19,690	2,214,459
106	Welsh Water (Water)	1,489,800	512,100	144,200	6,600	898,061
107	Trafalgar House (Property)	1,486,000	3,763,500	45,600	33,153	1,378,899
108	IBM United Kingdom Holdings (Electronics)	1,437,300	4,057,100	L174,100	14,708	†
109	Amerada Hess (Oil, Gas & Nuclear Fuels)	1,435,475	485,270	39,684	626	†
110	South West Water (Water)	1,418,600	251,600	93,000	3,060	622,399
111	Reckitt & Colman (Health & Household)	1,409,870	2,078,950	160,210	18,700	2,206,677
112	Lloyds Abbey Life (Insurance, Life/Non-life)	1,396,500	1,205,600	315,600	10,297	2,296,059
113	Lucas Industries (Engineering – General)	1,353,800	2,487,900	L129,700	45,731	1,487,500
114	Hillsdown Holdings (Food Manufacturing)	1,335,300	4,261,600	172,300	40,473	1,242,289
115	Coats Viyella (Textiles)	1,327,900	2,588,500	105,100	76,208	1,326,542
116	Sears (Stores)	1,294,200	2,143,700	153,800	42,783	1,494,958
117	GKN (Engineering – General)	1,290,500	2,470,200	200,300	32,520	2,038,829
118	Prudential Corporation (Insurance, Life/Non-life)	1,289,000	8,271,000	603,000	20,786	6,015,000
119	THORN EMI (Hotels & Leisure)	1,276,700	4,292,100	326,500	41,423	4,689,853
120	Burmah Castrol (Oil, Gas & Nuclear Fuels)	1,267,700	2,934,400	243,500	21,866	1,628,370
121	Britannia Building Society (Other Financial)	1,237,400	771,500	100,700	2,711	†
122	United Biscuits (Holdings) (Food Manufacturing)	1,235,300	2,998,200	133,800	39,691	1,723,277
123	Cheltenham & Gloucester Building Society[4] (Other Financial)	1,230,100	1,374,800	219,200	n/a	†
124	Reed International[5] (Media)	1,154,500	1,517,500	310,000	n/a	4,492,000
125	T & N (Engineering – General)	1,130,600	1,936,100	10,700	42,805	857,815
126	Southern Water (Water)	1,127,000	347,700	127,500	3,476	958,238
127	Scottish Power (Electricity)	1,118,400	1,568,600	351,100	8,560	2,622,069
128	Greenalls Group (Hotels & Leisure)	1,116,948	708,707	73,622	15,316	861,635
129	Bank of England (Banks)	1,116,400	225,900	123,700	3,194	†
130	Great Portland Estates (Property)	1,115,000	97,100	53,100	74	559,748
131	Burton Group (Stores)	1,110,800	1,909,600	41,100	37,337	889,900
132	Chevron UK (Oil, Gas & Nuclear Fuels)	1,099,136	1,023,097	90,585	2,624	†
133	Tomkins (Engineering – General)	1,087,900	3,245,100	257,100	45,496	2,991,300
134	Scottish Mortgage & Trust (Investment Trusts)	1,066,173	41,583	23,796	n/a	789,977
135	Waste Management International (Miscellaneous)	1,059,258	1,115,653	165,157	17,274	1,357,805
136	John Lewis Partnership (Stores)	1,058,500	2,183,900	58,700	38,800	2,706
137	Associated British Ports Holdings (Transport Services)	1,056,200	228,300	80,300	2,253	1,027,498
138	Nortel (Communications)	1,054,100	693,200	L310,400	8,172	†
139	Southern Electric (Electricity)	1,053,500	1,780,200	222,000	7,391	1,596,514
140	Inchcape (Transport – Manufacture & Distribution)	1,051,400	6,101,600	228,400	40,118	2,252,604
141	Edinburgh Investment Trust (Investment Trusts)	1,043,235	57,492	38,122	n/a	860,263
142	Courage (Brewers & Distillers)	1,041,393	1,310,195	L269,438	5,369	†
143	Mirror Group (Media)	1,033,600	462,900	189,300	2,915	537,303
144	Granada Group (Media)	1,020,700	2,097,700	265,400	42,878	3,275,600
145	Wessex Water (Water)	1,016,800	217,200	103,300	1,852	835,711
146	Northumbrian Water Group (Water)	1,015,500	298,600	62,800	3,314	588,963
147	REXAM (Packaging, Paper & Printing)	1,009,000	2,342,000	226,000	27,900	2,177,000
148	Hambros (Banks)	993,800	755,200	90,500	7,916	501,015
149	Witan Investment Company (Investment Trusts)	990,633	41,355	29,313	n/a	863,197
150	Northern Rock Building Society (Other Financial)	972,300	660,100	117,600	2,003	†

NOTES: [3]Merger with Halifax Building Society effective 1/8/95. [4]Business expected to be integrated with that of Lloyds Bank PLC. [5]Based on 50% Reed/Elsevier Group.
n/a – not available. †Market capitalisation not available. Figure not disclosed or company unquoted, government controlled, a nationalised industry, a subsidiary or newly quoted.

151-200 THE UK'S TOP 1000

RANK	COMPANY NAME (Sector)	CAPITAL EMPLOYED £000	TURNOVER £000	PRE-TAX PROFIT £000	NUMBER OF EMPLOYEES	EQUITY MKT CAPITAL £000
151	Alliance Trust (Investment Trusts)	958,802	39,369	36,508	n/a	1,154,992
152	London Electricity (Electricity)	935,200	1,308,400	186,500	5,532	1,150,589
153	Texaco (Oil, Gas & Nuclear Fuels)	929,039	3,832,496	L758	3,039	†
154	BICC (Engineering – General)	928,000	3,674,000	131,000	35,708	1,287,000
155	Vauxhall Motors (Transport – Manufacture & Distribution)	923,100	3,100,900	185,100	10,554	†
156	Thomson Corporation (Media)	918,400	508,100	120,300	8,763	†
157	National & Provincial Building Society[6] (Other Financial)	918,300	983,000	134,000	n/a	†
158	Eastern Group (Electricity)	918,000	1,846,300	176,800	7,003	1,424,229
159	Littlewoods Organisation (Stores)	913,482	2,395,316	117,210	28,603	†
160	BPB Industries (Building Materials & Services)	897,400	1,150,800	107,700	11,292	1,404,480
161	Scottish Hydro-Electric (Electricity)	894,500	792,400	164,200	3,552	1,193,509
162	International General Electric (USA) (Other Financial)	888,172	769,692	35,452	5,845	†
163	Isosceles (Food Wholesaling & Retailing)	885,200	3,059,310	L52,930	46,057	†
164	Yorkshire Electricity Group (Electricity)	880,500	1,307,900	149,000	5,764	1,114,423
165	East Midlands Electricity (Electricity)	875,100	1,444,500	51,200	7,590	1,351,619
166	Wolseley (Building Materials & Services)	873,181	3,254,082	202,343	19,073	2,266,442
167	Harrisons & Crosfield (Chemicals)	866,900	2,110,000	236,700	25,404	979,404
168	Stockholm & Edinburgh Investments (Property)	864,400	321,200	L77,400	2,555	†
169	Brixton Estate (Property)	858,709	70,021	32,578	69	400,802
170	Schroders (Merchant Banks)	840,700	1,038,400	195,400	3,380	1,472,325
171	Pepsico Finance (UK) (Other Financial)	840,248	125,984	68,111	4,751	†
172	English China Clays (Chemicals)	837,000	1,040,800	93,000	8,788	1,120,579
173	Cookson Group (Other Industrial Materials & Products)	834,300	1,428,500	51,100	12,230	1,291,560
174	NFC (Transport Services)	830,600	2,034,900	105,600	33,989	1,254,066
175	Williams Holdings (Building Materials & Services)	829,200	1,393,100	200,300	15,538	2,163,128
176	NORWEB (Electricity)	828,600	1,470,600	178,300	8,255	955,295
177	Courtaulds (Chemicals)	811,700	1,995,300	121,600	19,500	1,759,799
178	Midlands Electricity (Electricity)	791,700	1,415,500	195,400	6,207	1,159,703
179	Scottish Investment Trust (Investment Trusts)	783,096	29,833	18,123	n/a	551,310
180	Gallaher (Tobacco)	781,100	5,059,900	337,600	23,732	†
181	NFU Mutual Insurance Society (Insurance, Life/Non-life)	777,800	479,050	60,130	2,200	†
182	Reuters Holdings (Media)	774,000	2,309,000	510,000	12,718	7,798,368
183	Co-operative Wholesale Society (Food Wholesaling & Retailing)	772,400	3,111,500	17,200	n/a	†
184	Robert Fleming Holdings (Merchant Banks)	771,803	572,570	209,922	2,554	†
185	British Investment Trust (Investment Trusts)	765,971	45,328	27,095	133	763,620
186	TI Group (Engineering – General)	762,700	1,420,200	153,000	22,600	1,787,760
187	Caradon (Building Materials & Services)	756,200	1,989,900	201,200	26,714	1,703,336
188	Carlsberg-Tetley (Brewers & Distillers)	754,000	1,025,600	76,200	5,012	†
189	Taylor Woodrow (Contracting, Construction)	751,500	1,146,300	50,800	8,206	492,498
190	Kleinwort Benson Group (Banks)	746,700	765,700	97,000	2,892	737,713
191	Daily Mail and General Trust (Media)	743,000	778,800	92,100	8,492	965,900
192	Govett Oriental Investment Trust (Investment Trusts)	741,728	13,590	5,251	n/a	593,285
193	Electra Investment Trust (Investment Trusts)	740,751	39,084	19,481	71	550,352
194	George Wimpey (Contracting, Construction)	734,400	1,687,500	45,100	11,347	461,989
195	British Assets Trust (Investment Trusts)	732,803	38,034	26,793	n/a	360,960
196	Signet Group (Miscellaneous)	729,170	987,960	L85,437	14,840	123,747
197	BBA Group (Engineering – General)	728,600	1,380,000	63,900	17,778	813,800
198	Nissan (UK) (Transport – Manufacture & Distribution)	717,068	1,325,858	2,108	5,287	†
199	Vodafone Group (Communications)	706,046	850,529	363,330	31,170	6,064,064
200	Saur (UK) (Water)	705,831	106,294	21,262	1,426	†

NOTES: [6]On 10/7/95 the Society and Abbey National PLC announced agreement had been reached on terms of recommended merger. n/a – not available. †Market capitalisation not available. Figure not disclosed or company unquoted, government controlled, a nationalised industry, a subsidiary or newly quoted.

THE UK'S TOP 1000 — 201-250

RANK	COMPANY NAME (Sector)	CAPITAL EMPLOYED £000	TURNOVER £000	PRE-TAX PROFIT £000	NUMBER OF EMPLOYEES	EQUITY MKT CAPITAL £000
201	Fleming Far Eastern Investment Trust (Investment Trusts)	677,663	11,889	3,485	n/a	459,813
202	South Western Electricity (Electricity)	663,200	899,600	116,800	5,400	696,652
203	Scottish Eastern Investment Trust (Investment Trusts)	660,442	23,937	13,488	n/a	475,200
204	Peel Holdings (Property)	647,879	73,040	10,191	393	439,539
205	Bristol and West Building Society (Other Financial)	646,700	658,400	57,100	2,605	†
206	SEEBOARD (Electricity)	644,300	1,218,100	131,700	5,339	840,467
207	Laporte (Chemicals)	640,700	964,500	123,500	7,108	1,371,370
208	BHP – Hamilton Oil Great Britain (Oil, Gas & Nuclear Fuels)	633,984	90,388	L5,242	n/a	†
209	Manweb (Electricity)	626,300	929,600	126,300	4,604	744,330
210	Carlton Communications (Media)	608,329	1,404,696	190,231	8,451	2,305,922
211	Caledonia Investments (Other Financial)	604,100	51,000	45,200	1,028	531,800
212	ANZ Holdings (UK) (Banks)	603,852	513,341	138,421	6,599	†
213	Bardon Group (Mines)	603,600	331,700	19,500	2,659	214,010
214	W.H. Smith Group (Stores)	600,200	2,441,600	83,400	30,506	1,328,076
215	Chelsfield (Property)	598,430	52,873	10,202	197	250,979
216	Northern Foods (Food Manufacturing)	593,600	2,048,600	157,200	29,709	1,053,472
217	Northern Electric (Electricity)	591,000	1,030,500	128,700	4,714	835,426
218	Anglo & Overseas Trust (Investment Trusts)	574,032	17,732	11,438	n/a	480,982
219	Vaux Group (Brewers & Distillers)	558,873	243,503	29,273	6,090	346,757
220	IMI (Engineering – General)	552,000	1,161,200	50,300	17,186	1,031,959
221	Racal Electronics (Communications)	549,242	916,091	26,380	11,779	659,110
222	Seagram Holdings (Brewers & Distillers)	542,845	806,007	124,587	3,129	†
223	Dixons Group (Stores)	538,700	1,921,400	L165,200	12,020	976,800
224	Fleming Japanese Investment Trust (Investment Trusts)	535,567	4,677	522	n/a	456,601
225	London Merchant Securities (Property)	534,411	37,468	22,281	61	260,658
226	Rothschilds Continuation (Merchant Banks)	528,528	361,617	52,018	953	†
227	Central Transport Rental Group (Transport Services)	517,700	292,200	L331,100	951	35,429
228	Dalgety (Food Manufacturing)	517,000	4,955,300	120,100	16,609	955,504
229	Smith & Nephew (Health & Household)	511,400	964,600	L5,500	12,223	1,835,227
230	Wm. Morrison Supermarkets (Stores)	507,406	1,779,370	116,073	23,200	1,128,458
231	Birmingham Midshires Building Society (Other Financial)	501,300	367,700	52,100	1,516	†
232	Manchester Airport (Transport Services)	500,471	182,097	16,614	2,105	†
233	Monks Investment Trust, (Investment Trusts)	499,011	15,468	7,873	n/a	404,254
234	Murray International Trust (Investment Trusts)	497,643	26,124	20,934	n/a	399,383
235	Johnson Matthey (Metal & Metal Forming)	487,500	1,955,000	65,400	6,287	1,004,805
236	David S. Smith (Holdings) (Packaging, Paper & Printing)	481,500	782,800	42,200	8,113	858,162
237	Unigate (Food Manufacturing)	478,600	1,980,000	102,400	27,283	905,223
238	RIT Capital Partners (Investment Trusts)	478,263	12,933	8,169	n/a	314,415
239	Rugby Group (Building Materials & Services)	477,800	1,010,600	76,100	9,523	782,774
240	Automotive Financial Grp. Hldgs. (Transport – Manufacture & Distribution)	474,712	419,910	11,053	2,515	†
241	Fisons (Health & Household)	473,100	1,289,000	L463,700	11,863	760,217
242	United News & Media (Media)	470,688	1,013,430	138,023	13,333	1,151,330
243	Home Housing Association (Property)	467,287	50,222	12,515	691	†
244	Storehouse (Stores)	464,900	1,028,592	61,391	19,086	958,916
245	Sedgwick Group (Insurance, Brokers)	463,500	888,700	94,400	15,538	819,150
246	Burford Holdings (Property)	462,885	1,231	14,711	23	273,494
247	Clydesdale Bank (Banks)	462,585	511,671	110,666	n/a	†
248	Kleinwort European Privatisation Investment Trust (Investment Trusts)	460,973	10,580	6,316	n/a	385,000
249	Scottish American Investment Company (Other Financial)	459,250	20,303	13,825	n/a	344,356
250	Willis Corroon Group (Insurance, Brokers)	459,100	671,300	5,600	11,393	573,945

NOTES: n/a – not available. †Market capitalisation not available. Figure not disclosed or company unquoted, government controlled, a nationalised industry, a subsidiary or newly quoted.

251-300   THE UK'S TOP 1000

RANK	COMPANY NAME (Sector)	CAPITAL EMPLOYED £000	TURNOVER £000	PRE-TAX PROFIT £000	NUMBER OF EMPLOYEES	EQUITY MKT CAPITAL £000
251	Walkers Smiths Snack Foods (Food Manufacturing)	458,797	298,470	33,126	4,612	†
252	Marubeni UK (Commodities Trading)	456,136	551,113	L2,145	121	†
253	Templeton Emerging Markets Investment Trust (Investment Trusts)	454,651	9,920	3,936	n/a	110,982
254	ICL (Electronics)	454,500	2,623,500	23,400	25,157	†
255	Legal & General Group (Insurance, Life/Non-life)	449,000	2,427,800	164,900	7,306	2,117,672
256	Sony United Kingdom (Electronics)	447,315	1,442,449	37,297	3,677	†
257	Mercury World Mining Trust (Investment Trusts)	447,289	9,745	4,267	n/a	398,114
258	Lep Group (Transport Services)	446,559	1,420,632	L15,570	9,114	64,555
259	Fleming Overseas Investment Trust (Investment Trusts)	445,940	11,603	8,909	n/a	376,601
260	Kwik Save Group (Food Wholesaling & Retailing)	444,600	2,800,000	135,600	22,502	994,880
261	Fleming Mercantile Investment Trust (Investment Trusts)	442,152	14,597	13,070	n/a	382,948
262	Stakis (Hotels & Leisure)	441,952	145,885	20,151	5,622	425,064
263	Morgan Crucible Company (Other Industrial Materials & Products)	440,500	795,100	72,600	12,573	744,501
264	BET (Miscellaneous)	436,500	1,942,075	90,512	100,493	1,014,475
265	Charter (Building Materials & Services)	436,400	891,053	73,000	14,875	674,143
266	Costain Group (Contracting, Construction)	435,700	1,143,100	68,700	11,593	65,594
267	Telegraph (Media)	432,211	252,076	45,042	1,075	512,864
268	Christian Salvesen (Food Wholesaling & Retailing)	431,600	558,000	74,100	11,572	723,279
269	Foreign & Colonial Pacific Investment Trust (Investment Trusts)	430,735	14,802	8,669	n/a	336,209
270	MAI (Other Financial)	429,800	709,700	87,900	5,091	962,800
271	E.D.S. International (Business Services)	427,054	253,945	11,621	3,920	†
272	Barings¶ (Banks)	425,171	684,607	100,103	3,179	71,613
273	Kodak (Engineering – Instrument)	425,100	1,109,600	84,800	7,809	†
274	Delta (Electricals)	422,900	898,600	65,100	13,384	652,327
275	Marley (Building Materials & Services)	422,600	666,800	58,700	9,554	378,600
276	Honda Motor Europe (Transport – Manufacture & Distribution)	421,868	1,939,984	L19,784	1,839	†
277	South Wales Electricity (Electricity)	421,200	605,400	104,000	3,350	586,274
278	Cowie Group (Transport – Manufacture & Distribution)	419,034	934,161	43,607	4,377	323,441
279	Yorkshire Bank (Banks)	418,611	491,917	137,336	6,324	†
280	De La Rue (Packaging, Paper & Printing)	413,000	592,700	129,800	7,743	1,935,741
281	Co-operative Retail Services (Food Wholesaling & Retailing)	412,380	1,270,788	26,656	n/a	†
282	Yorkshire Building Society (Other Financial)	407,012	432,957	78,850	1,615	†
283	Wassall (Other Industrial Materials & Products)	405,895	638,745	21,926	7,730	549,592
284	Meyer International (Building Materials & Services)	403,200	1,192,900	41,600	8,588	384,708
285	Robert Stephen Holdings (Textiles)	399,300	494,100	17,500	5,414	†
286	E D & F Man Group (Miscellaneous)	397,700	219,900	66,700	3,401	†
287	Edinburgh Dragon Trust (Investment Trusts)	393,186	5,950	233	n/a	298,999
288	TR Smaller Companies Investment Trust (Investment Trusts)	391,066	13,444	9,188	n/a	342,144
289	Mobil Oil Co. (Oil, Gas & Nuclear Fuels)	389,480	1,196,476	L5,736	1,705	†
290	Vickers (Engineering – General)	387,000	727,200	44,800	9,118	575,923
291	AMEC (Contracting, Construction)	382,200	1,962,400	20,000	21,175	266,394
292	Courtaulds Textiles (Textiles)	382,100	1,053,200	47,300	24,000	463,296
293	Procter & Gamble (Health & Household)	381,467	1,377,102	104,147	5,636	†
294	Greycoat (Property)	377,200	38,300	L40,000	34	155,611
295	Wolverhampton & Dudley Breweries, (Brewers & Distillers)	375,965	231,448	38,298	10,044	365,107
296	Civil Aviation Authority (Transport Services)	373,982	494,747	24,611	7,754	†
297	Videotron Holdings (Media)	372,921	37,572	L5,995	644	†
298	Cathay International Holdings (Property)	372,822	5,941	469	1,169	120,762
299	Household International (UK) (Banks)	369,301	203,557	8,594	1,620	†
300	Sand Aire Investments (Insurance, Life/Non-life)	368,200	337,800	27,800	2,080	†

NOTES: ¶Now acquired by Internationale Nederlanden Groep NV. n/a – not available. †Market capitalisation not available. Figure not disclosed or company unquoted, government controlled, a nationalised industry, a subsidiary or newly quoted.

THE UK'S TOP 1000 — 301-350

RANK	COMPANY NAME (Sector)	CAPITAL EMPLOYED £000	TURNOVER £000	PRE-TAX PROFIT £000	NUMBER OF EMPLOYEES	EQUITY MKT CAPITAL £000
301	Kellogg Co. of Great Britain (Food Manufacturing)	366,991	589,228	89,310	2,831	†
302	Clyde Petroleum (Oil, Gas & Nuclear Fuels)	365,953	116,583	13,617	137	155,126
303	Ocean Group (Transport Services)	365,900	1,026,100	19,900	11,800	433,400
304	Laird Group (Other Industrial Materials & Products)	365,500	733,900	47,700	11,018	488,289
305	Scottish National Trust (Investment Trusts)	365,176	21,908	17,509	n/a	363,014
306	Bunzl (Packaging, Paper & Printing)	364,300	1,622,200	L4,900	8,116	734,200
307	Govett Strategic Investment Trust (Investment Trusts)	362,094	20,280	8,457	n/a	239,507
308	House of Fraser (Stores)	361,000	754,700	28,000	9,587	400,652
309	Gestetner Holdings (Electronics)	358,800	996,185	12,138	10,614	232,570
310	Albright & Wilson (Chemicals)	357,577	609,245	58,279	4,255	†
311	VSEL[7] (Engineering – General)	356,020	832,941	60,941	7,329	591,123
312	Provident Financial (Other Financial)	352,828	445,258	81,149	44,270	732,996
313	Sony Music Entertainment (UK) Group (Health & Household)	352,655	721,615	7,114	2,345	†
314	Digital Equipment Co. (Electronics)	347,646	809,449	L97,427	5,728	†
315	Lex Service (Transport – Manufacture & Distribution)	345,700	1,399,593	41,714	6,598	286,397
316	Northern Ireland Electricity (Electricity)	344,900	481,900	74,900	3,536	540,010
317	FKI (Engineering – General)	339,961	794,477	52,265	11,221	878,667
318	Scapa Group (Textiles)	339,900	391,700	48,500	6,536	491,644
319	NYNEX CableComms Group[8] (Media)	338,501	41,015	L95,144	1,919	†
320	Securicor Group (Business Services)	338,420	800,275	80,560	43,508	910,065
321	Camellia (Agriculture)	337,610	191,992	21,615	73,336	53,125
322	British Vita (Chemicals)	336,557	768,996	49,510	9,417	498,765
323	Hazlewood Foods (Food Manufacturing)	335,913	799,982	48,053	10,113	336,773
324	Halliburton Holdings (Contracting, Construction)	335,662	543,257	L10,327	6,524	†
325	TeleWest Communications (Communications)	335,599	40,338	L36,572	2,036	1,450,499
326	Second Alliance Trust (Investment Trusts)	335,388	11,534	10,921	n/a	355,296
327	Hardy Oil & Gas (Oil, Gas & Nuclear Fuels)	330,753	60,604	5,223	128	173,945
328	Norsk Hydro (UK) (Chemicals)	329,708	359,335	2,890	1,862	†
329	Coventry Building Society (Other Financial)	329,443	221,616	40,093	828	†
330	Frogmore Estates (Property)	329,319	66,876	16,449	104	208,446
331	Hewlett-Packard (Electronics)	328,227	1,313,989	66,764	5,003	†
332	Bilton (Property)	327,786	25,636	18,568	164	220,554
333	Portman Building Society (Other Financial)	327,600	229,200	29,200	1,156	†
334	Smiths Industries (Aerospace)	323,000	759,300	117,200	10,983	1,411,404
335	Greene King (Brewers & Distillers)	322,989	146,102	20,434	2,641	204,140
336	Minerva (Property)	318,634	22,806	10,929	18	†
337	Merchants Trust (Investment Trusts)	317,964	20,575	15,556	n/a	354,915
338	Summit Group (Business Services)	314,487	52,521	L18,385	343	†
339	Close Brothers Group (Merchant Banks)	311,717	115,880	33,055	445	214,786
340	Transport Development Group (Transport Services)	306,925	496,479	33,866	8,894	308,651
341	Chesterfield Properties (Property)	306,705	33,420	37,376	381	145,972
342	Bankers Investment Trust (Investment Trusts)	305,895	12,753	8,568	n/a	286,974
343	Haslemere Estates (Property)	304,137	44,043	36,051	n/a	†
344	Iceland Group (Food Wholesaling & Retailing)	303,600	1,301,700	70,200	16,161	508,210
345	Monument Oil and Gas (Oil, Gas & Nuclear Fuels)	303,155	25,724	7,636	39	425,864
346	Argos (Stores)	302,530	1,257,404	100,226	14,347	1,053,160
347	Next (Stores)	301,800	652,900	107,400	10,735	951,392
348	Securities Trust of Scotland (Investment Trusts)	297,977	19,383	14,084	n/a	260,824
349	TR City of London Trust (Investment Trusts)	295,862	16,600	13,314	n/a	285,038
350	Camas (Building Materials & Services)	291,983	449,907	19,200	4,733	228,925

NOTES: [7]Offer by The General Electric Company PLC became unconditional on 30/6/95. [8]NYNEX CableComms Group PLC/NYNEX CableComms Group Inc units.
n/a – not available. †Market capitalisation not available. Figure not disclosed or company unquoted, government controlled, a nationalised industry, a subsidiary or newly quoted.

351-400 THE UK'S TOP 1000

RANK	COMPANY NAME (Sector)	CAPITAL EMPLOYED £000	TURNOVER £000	PRE-TAX PROFIT £000	NUMBER OF EMPLOYEES	EQUITY MKT CAPITAL £000
351	Dunedin Worldwide Investment Trust (Investment Trusts)	291,586	8,055	2,740	n/a	256,108
352	Dawson International (Textiles)	288,049	443,137	L95,448	9,285	224,710
353	Daejan Holdings (Property)	285,077	27,075	19,457	146	278,325
354	Merck Sharp & Dohme (Holdings) (Health & Household)	284,687	291,278	10,697	2,385	†
355	Pfizer Group (Health & Household)	284,224	170,895	41,689	2,716	†
356	Kimberly-Clark (Packaging, Paper & Printing)	282,744	286,408	L10,835	3,042	†
357	Southend Property Holdings (Property)	280,925	22,248	5,032	36	85,986
358	D.C. Thomson & Co. (Media)	280,879	94,686	70,953	2,068	†
359	General Foods (Food Manufacturing)	280,722	364,550	16,639	3,347	†
360	M & G Income Investment Trust (Investment Trusts)	279,584	16,972	15,622	n/a	307,602
361	PSIT (Property)	278,763	23,610	12,048	44	187,503
362	Murray Smaller Markets Trust (Investment Trusts)	277,992	6,609	3,706	n/a	258,436
363	3M UK Holdings (Chemicals)	276,653	617,539	8,276	5,012	†
364	Security Services (Business Services)	275,941	772,520	58,422	42,935	836,369
365	Glynwed International (Metal & Metal Forming)	275,200	1,008,325	66,015	11,026	696,724
366	Pillar Property Investments (Property)	274,513	13,412	803	6	†
367	Hepworth (Building Materials & Services)	274,100	695,900	75,500	9,105	760,439
368	Toys 'R' Us Holdings (Miscellaneous)	272,018	252,604	20,644	2,702	†
369	Dairy Crest (Food Manufacturing)	271,900	997,700	2,800	6,708	†
370	Exxon Chemical (Chemicals)	270,691	456,229	25,355	1,654	†
371	National Parking Corporation (Transport Services)	270,588	265,277	50,482	4,018	494,235
372	Murray Income Trust (Investment Trusts)	269,831	13,882	12,191	n/a	274,875
373	Fleming American Investment Trust (Investment Trusts)	268,529	6,954	2,873	n/a	409,360
374	Throgmorton Trust (Investment Trusts)	267,943	14,889	10,167	119	224,809
375	London Insurance Market Investment Trust (Investment Trusts)	267,597	12,582	10,170	n/a	266,000
376	Ibstock (Building Materials & Services)	266,831	235,451	L18,717	3,175	197,812
377	AT&T (UK) Holdings (Electronics)	265,625	460,308	10,237	6,082	†
378	Linpac Group (Packaging, Paper & Printing)	264,362	592,830	24,317	7,430	†
379	Wilson Bowden (Contracting, Construction)	263,400	241,700	37,100	892	303,662
380	Argent Group (Property)	262,610	17,986	2,700	23	143,276
381	TR Technology (Investment Trusts)	262,511	7,048	5,088	n/a	244,678
382	WPP Group (Media)	261,000	1,426,900	85,300	19,198	788,906
383	APV (Engineering – General)	258,600	874,600	L18,200	9,552	155,160
384	American Trust (Investment Trusts)	258,096	7,518	6,821	n/a	201,184
385	Wilson (Connolly) Holdings (Contracting, Construction)	257,993	315,971	38,200	862	305,226
386	H.J. Heinz Co. (Food Manufacturing)	257,636	501,537	34,510	3,278	†
387	Marston, Thompson & Evershed (Brewers & Distillers)	257,155	142,765	23,252	4,014	254,428
388	C. & J. Clark (Miscellaneous)	256,332	655,314	20,761	17,913	†
389	Hunting (Oil, Gas & Nuclear Fuels)	256,200	1,125,700	28,500	13,588	170,570
390	Paterson Zochonis (Health & Household)	256,101	266,583	28,135	4,377	243,181
391	Compaq Computer Group (Electronics)	255,952	690,662	13,113	1,130	†
392	Boddington Group (Food Wholesaling & Retailing)	255,810	273,569	30,284	8,609	310,109
393	Baker Hughes (Oil, Gas & Nuclear Fuels)	255,634	298,124	1,980	2,384	†
394	EMAP (Media)	254,900	547,100	63,900	6,789	826,900
395	Booker (Food Wholesaling & Retailing)	254,100	3,722,300	69,800	21,049	893,199
396	Hoops (Food Manufacturing)	254,064	1,539,172	L12,703	5,758	†
397	Bryant Group (Contracting, Construction)	253,500	391,700	36,500	897	415,348
398	Bowthorpe (Electronics)	252,650	417,639	65,898	6,324	540,464
399	Jarvis Hotels (Hotels & Leisure)	252,219	63,344	2,452	2,420	†
400	Black & Decker International (Electricals)	251,629	398,955	30,344	5,439	†

NOTES: n/a – not available. †Market capitalisation not available. Figure not disclosed or company unquoted, government controlled, a nationalised industry, a subsidiary or newly quoted.

THE UK'S TOP 1000　　401-450

RANK	COMPANY NAME (Sector)	CAPITAL EMPLOYED £000	TURNOVER £000	PRE-TAX PROFIT £000	NUMBER OF EMPLOYEES	EQUITY MKT CAPITAL £000
401	Digital Equipment Scotland (Electronics)	250,833	648,374	L2,648	1,478	†
402	Smith New Court (Other Financial)	250,300	142,422	97,333	1,293	407,573
403	John Laing (Contracting, Construction)	249,500	1,160,700	23,800	8,475	200,930
404	Phillips Petroleum Co. United Kingdom (Oil, Gas & Nuclear Fuels)	248,417	608,921	15,257	663	†
405	Norcros (Building Materials & Services)	246,600	377,986	17,112	6,692	335,444
406	English & Scottish Investors (Investment Trusts)	246,306	8,613	5,095	n/a	170,726
407	First Leisure Corporation (Hotels & Leisure)	245,100	141,800	37,500	3,704	423,144
408	Evans of Leeds (Property)	244,833	25,002	9,739	56	134,572
409	TNT Europe (Transport Services)	242,919	430,965	2,199	8,705	†
410	Kleinwort Overseas Investment Trust (Investment Trusts)	241,601	5,839	3,828	n/a	214,634
411	Dunedin Income Growth Investment Trust (Other Financial)	241,179	20,583	11,265	n/a	203,149
412	Cargill (Commodities Trading)	240,821	1,362,511	36,196	5,845	†
413	Lawson Mardon Packaging (Packaging, Paper & Printing)	240,606	462,679	15,935	5,445	†
414	Hickson International (Chemicals)	239,800	393,100	19,200	2,848	219,700
415	Takare (Health & Household)	239,644	90,002	21,060	7,690	275,864
416	Hitachi Europe (Electronics)	237,336	750,419	18,295	602	†
417	Fleming Continental European Investment Trust (Investment Trusts)	235,396	4,782	2,504	n/a	219,341
418	Unitech (Electronics)	234,184	302,345	19,774	5,745	218,504
419	Tops Estates (Property)	233,654	14,344	2,367	20	105,506
420	J. Bibby & Sons (Agriculture)	233,578	764,584	L10,719	7,298	87,513
421	Premier Oil (Oil, Gas & Nuclear Fuels)	232,400	48,900	9,200	149	138,092
422	Amstrad (Electronics)	232,324	238,945	L19,939	787	165,682
423	Barratt Developments (Contracting, Construction)	231,800	498,900	35,200	2,300	355,299
424	Kleinwort Charter Investment Trust (Investment Trusts)	230,031	7,660	4,843	n/a	217,264
425	Panasonic UK (Electricals)	229,943	633,117	22,121	742	†
426	Roche Products (Health & Household)	229,853	315,461	14,646	2,305	†
427	Union Texas Petroleum (Oil, Gas & Nuclear Fuels)	228,657	140,527	L42,101	31	†
428	Yattendon Investment Trust (Packaging, Paper & Printing)	228,052	79,541	113	3,651	†
429	John Mowlem & Company (Contracting, Construction)	228,000	1,342,000	L124,200	12,285	176,326
430	St James's Place Capital (Other Financial)	225,500	32,400	81,100	78	306,895
431	Gillette Industries (Health & Household)	223,784	361,114	L52,126	3,378	†
432	Beazer Homes (Contracting, Construction)	223,700	328,766	45,159	1,979	401,602
433	Allied London Properties (Property)	223,542	32,390	10,598	74	111,003
434	Town Centre Securities (Property)	223,071	20,003	8,807	135	126,631
435	Automated Security (Holdings) (Electronics)	222,781	160,775	11,789	3,230	87,287
436	Croda International (Chemicals)	222,500	423,000	42,800	4,053	512,420
437	Alfred McAlpine (Contracting, Construction)	222,154	791,339	9,128	4,941	122,591
438	Temple Bar Investment Trust (Investment Trusts)	221,887	13,652	10,051	n/a	199,570
439	A. & J. Mucklow Group (Property)	219,793	20,527	10,103	29	173,802
440	Persimmon (Contracting, Construction)	219,378	206,228	25,206	802	236,013
441	Lawrie Group (Agriculture)	218,600	190,109	21,814	73,325	32,357
442	Powell Duffryn (Transport Services)	218,400	622,800	33,400	8,115	407,080
443	Edrington Holdings (Brewers & Distillers)	217,396	101,658	37,472	844	†
444	Mercury Asset Management Group (Other Financial)	217,151	221,451	109,543	637	1,369,862
445	Emerson Developments (Holdings) (Property)	216,414	54,367	5,185	450	†
446	Minet Group (Insurance, Brokers)	216,388	180,613	2,641	2,651	†
447	Schlumberger (Engineering – Instrument)	216,187	329,479	17,936	3,594	†
448	Baring Tribune Investment Trust (Investment Trusts)	215,685	6,853	3,797	n/a	164,000
449	Calor Group (Oil, Gas & Nuclear Fuels)	214,300	271,900	48,800	1,871	456,600
450	Chubb Security (Electronics)	212,825	700,975	77,140	18,735	847,655

NOTES: n/a – not available. †Market capitalisation not available. Figure not disclosed or company unquoted, government controlled, a nationalised industry, a subsidiary or newly quoted.

451-500 — THE UK'S TOP 1000

RANK	COMPANY NAME (Sector)	CAPITAL EMPLOYED £000	TURNOVER £000	PRE-TAX PROFIT £000	NUMBER OF EMPLOYEES	EQUITY MKT CAPITAL £000
451	Rolls-Royce Power Engineering (Engineering – General)	212,500	738,700	5,600	14,211	2,237
452	Allied Colloids Group (Chemicals)	211,389	326,788	45,946	2,884	650,728
453	PHH Europe (Transport Services)	210,495	933,142	8,240	805	†
454	Amersham International (Health & Household)	208,700	324,200	43,500	3,397	479,548
455	Antofagasta Holdings (Mines)	205,096	86,711	23,061	1,315	323,775
456	Mersey Docks and Harbour Company (Transport Services)	205,001	129,891	33,586	1,805	355,663
457	Berkeley Group (Contracting, Construction)	203,743	228,106	39,531	506	358,490
458	Cummins UK (Engineering – General)	201,998	595,548	40,785	5,005	†
459	Inco Europe (Metal & Metal Forming)	201,761	534,990	13,864	2,621	†
460	Co-operative Insurance Society (Insurance, Life/Non-life)	201,000	1,542,400	44,100	n/a	†
461	Scancem Group (Building Materials & Services)	199,681	355,484	11,863	2,340	†
462	Electric and General Investment Company (Investment Trusts)	199,167	5,337	3,905	n/a	172,746
463	General Cable (Communications)	198,478	21,119	L18,319	268	†
464	Lloyds Chemists (Health & Household)	198,419	939,741	58,322	14,710	363,699
465	International Stock Exchange of UK and Rep. of Ireland (Other Financial)	198,240	207,135	18,865	1,070	†
466	Eli Lilly Group (Health & Household)	197,793	258,424	L37,029	2,116	†
467	River and Mercantile Trust (Investment Trusts)	196,344	15,512	12,342	21	197,056
468	Wates City of London Properties (Property)	196,111	7,339	L456	29	142,826
469	Rentokil Group (Health & Household)	196,000	719,600	177,000	30,830	2,239,957
470	Brunner Investment Trust (Investment Trusts)	195,937	7,087	4,826	n/a	150,274
471	MFI Furniture Group (Health & Household)	194,900	648,736	86,380	7,134	826,635
472	London & Edinburgh Insurance Group (Insurance, Life/Non-life)	194,893	459,128	L28,622	1,569	†
473	Foreign & Colonial Smaller Companies (Investment Trusts)	194,667	5,985	3,043	n/a	190,051
474	Scottish Metropolitan Property (Property)	193,336	17,360	11,330	26	83,532
475	Superior Oil (UK) (Oil, Gas & Nuclear Fuels)	191,836	76,021	21,928	n/a	†
476	MD Foods (Food Manufacturing)	190,948	327,515	L10,098	2,994	†
477	Mayne Nickless Europe (Miscellaneous)	190,603	330,312	L9,023	9,331	†
478	BTP (Chemicals)	190,086	289,830	30,309	2,799	429,576
479	CLS Holdings (Property)	189,523	15,910	L2,322	18	97,085
480	Matheson & Co. (Miscellaneous)	188,830	68,372	5,993	885	†
481	Archer Daniels Midland International (Food Manufacturing)	188,559	396,081	13,635	879	†
482	Asprey (Miscellaneous)	188,252	187,569	25,449	1,258	296,141
483	Coca-Cola Holdings (United Kingdom) (Food Manufacturing)	187,701	94,814	54,044	314	†
484	M & G Recovery Investment Trust (Investment Trusts)	186,472	6,833	6,068	n/a	45,594
485	Hays (Business Services)	186,356	631,902	87,809	7,711	404,859
486	Air Products (Chemicals)	185,705	245,630	L7,139	2,253	†
487	Courts (Health & Household)	185,418	258,556	22,129	3,871	207,337
488	Wickes (Building Materials & Services)	185,276	733,585	30,129	5,594	338,253
489	TT Group (Electronics)	184,849	390,886	35,049	6,903	417,511
490	Del Monte Foods International (Food Manufacturing)	184,343	226,809	3,112	5,112	†
491	Drayton Far Eastern Trust (Investment Trusts)	183,318	3,184	1,276	n/a	164,125
492	Development Securities (Property)	182,797	17,952	L4,676	53	55,185
493	Weir Group (Engineering – General)	182,282	475,523	30,549	6,913	551,156
494	Scott Paper (UK) (Packaging, Paper & Printing)	182,142	301,599	26,059	2,116	†
495	Electrocomponents (Electronics)	180,700	396,500	72,700	2,646	1,121,662
496	McKechnie (Engineering – General)	180,392	419,979	35,341	6,692	467,407
497	G.T. Japan Investment Trust (Investment Trusts)	179,882	2,694	1,565	n/a	167,207
498	Wyn-Ro Properties (Property)	179,485	21,195	L52,009	n/a	†
499	Skipton Building Society (Other Financial)	178,599	225,221	17,427	1,053	†
500	Felixstowe Dock and Railway Co. (Transport Services)	178,560	81,319	17,285	1,838	†

NOTES: n/a – not available. †Market capitalisation not available. Figure not disclosed or company unquoted, government controlled, a nationalised industry, a subsidiary or newly quoted.

THE UK'S TOP 1000 — 501-550

RANK	COMPANY NAME (Sector)	CAPITAL EMPLOYED £000	TURNOVER £000	PRE-TAX PROFIT £000	NUMBER OF EMPLOYEES	EQUITY MKT CAPITAL £000
501	Singer & Friedlander Group (Merchant Banks)	178,546	86,210	34,420	266	167,071
502	Wembley (Hotels & Leisure)	178,005	150,522	L65,711	3,779	53,052
503	William Grant & Sons (Brewers & Distillers)	177,702	214,441	22,146	1,009	†
504	Diversified Agency Services (Media)	177,597	327,082	L2,560	1,348	†
505	William Baird (Textiles)	177,422	534,327	25,146	16,428	241,187
506	Waterford Wedgwood UK (Miscellaneous)	174,300	289,900	13,600	6,124	†
507	Wereldhave Property Corporation (Property)	173,085	16,386	6,490	50	†
508	Molins (Engineering – General)	172,770	223,860	23,620	2,786	168,959
509	Senior Engineering Group (Engineering – General)	172,153	393,600	18,110	56,250	246,981
510	Travis Perkins (Building Materials & Services)	171,952	466,525	38,911	3,753	294,152
511	Five Arrows Chile Investment Trust (Investment Trusts)	171,556	5,679	3,302	n/a	19,646
512	Geest (Food Wholesaling & Retailing)	171,000	675,700	12,800	7,484	126,419
513	Asda Property Holdings (Property)	169,875	27,034	8,312	37	103,143
514	Fleming Emerging Markets Investment Trust (Investment Trusts)	168,295	2,560	L413	n/a	155,647
515	Fine Art Developments (Packaging, Paper & Printing)	168,129	317,175	38,059	4,930	271,327
516	Cobham (Aerospace)	167,800	211,400	22,800	34,720	253,353
517	Hartwell Holdings (Transport – Manufacture & Distribution)	167,547	773,764	19,516	3,327	†
518	Thornton Asian Emerging Markets Investment Trust (Investment Trusts)	167,534	3,498	1,411	n/a	105,174
519	British Empire Securities and General Trust (Investment Trusts)	167,475	5,907	1,705	n/a	124,723
520	Goodyear Great Britain (Other Industrial Materials & Products)	167,395	432,506	7,673	5,238	†
521	AAH[9] (Health & Household)	166,300	1,598,900	42,000	9,937	398,542
522	Mansfield Brewery (Brewers & Distillers)	164,541	119,099	14,123	3,569	128,259
523	Airtours (Transport Services)	164,496	971,742	75,762	6,337	511,851
524	M & G Group (Other Financial)	163,982	1,163,135	61,039	775	692,409
525	Warner Estate Holdings (Property)	159,435	19,927	7,241	59	107,462
526	AEA Technology (Engineering – General)	159,200	415,200	L46,900	9,195	†
527	United Technologies Holdings (Engineering – General)	159,135	302,627	8,202	n/a	†
528	Overseas Investment Trust (Investment Trusts)	159,050	3,124	2,012	n/a	134,848
529	Western United Investment Co. (Food Manufacturing)	158,700	1,147,100	L32,800	12,586	†
530	UniChem (Health & Household)	158,340	1,324,658	44,011	5,535	460,789
531	Mitsui & Co. UK (Commodities Trading)	158,227	16,155,250	6,736	142	†
532	Berisford (Food Wholesaling & Retailing)	158,200	157,500	L3,200	2,827	286,698
533	Sphere Investment Trust (Investment Trusts)	157,946	8,648	7,431	5	153,453
534	Christies International (Miscellaneous)	157,129	167,879	16,372	1,517	309,838
535	British Air Transport (Holdings) (Transport Services)	156,372	358,706	L2,822	2,221	†
536	Marshalls (Building Materials & Services)	156,328	191,496	20,432	2,517	156,175
537	Compass Group (Food Wholesaling & Retailing)	155,800	903,055	54,799	36,492	758,742
538	Low & Bonar (Packaging, Paper & Printing)	155,130	420,926	44,091	4,318	393,614
539	Davis Service Group (Miscellaneous)	154,873	322,197	25,422	17,190	245,660
540	Leeds & Holbeck Building Society (Other Financial)	154,395	182,555	13,971	697	†
541	J.C. Bamford Excavators (Engineering – General)	153,641	201,440	8,987	904	†
542	Hewden Stuart (Contracting, Construction)	152,877	259,984	34,791	3,863	335,193
543	Bellway (Contracting, Construction)	152,598	201,284	27,984	731	296,500
544	Farnell Electronics (Electronics)	152,458	514,174	59,172	4,165	725,100
545	Spring Ram Corporation (Building Materials & Services)	152,400	256,600	3,300	3,697	179,086
546	UK Paper (Packaging, Paper & Printing)	152,200	245,000	L8,700	1,715	†
547	Lewis Trust Group (Miscellaneous)	151,343	248,218	33,045	3,890	†
548	Raine (Contracting, Construction)	151,192	456,453	13,138	3,534	138,137
549	Biwater (Contracting, Construction)	151,000	259,400	29,600	3,725	†
550	Guardian Media Group (Media)	150,518	253,492	11,669	3,762	†

NOTES: [9]Now ultimately held by Franz Haniel & Cie GmbH through acquisition by Gehe AG. n/a – not available. †Market capitalisation not available. Figure not disclosed or company unquoted, government controlled, a nationalised industry, a subsidiary or newly quoted.

551-600 — THE UK'S TOP 1000

RANK	COMPANY NAME (Sector)	CAPITAL EMPLOYED £000	TURNOVER £000	PRE-TAX PROFIT £000	NUMBER OF EMPLOYEES	EQUITY MKT CAPITAL £000
551	Edinburgh New Tiger Trust (Investment Trusts)	149,707	3,181	2,650	n/a	127,400
552	Nurdin & Peacock (Food Wholesaling & Retailing)	149,661	1,540,340	16,520	6,801	207,779
553	TR Pacific Investment Trust (Investment Trusts)	149,594	2,756	904	n/a	147,408
554	Young and Co's Brewery (Brewers & Distillers)	149,238	71,173	5,097	n/a	65,786
555	Sema Group (Business Services)	146,878	596,111	29,518	8,156	379,940
556	TR Property Investment Trust (Investment Trusts)	146,826	9,291	5,399	n/a	100,475
557	Grainger Trust (Property)	146,669	21,144	5,651	27	51,473
558	Foreign & Colonial Emerging Mkts. Investment Trust (Investment Trusts)	146,443	2,583	L810	n/a	134,761
559	Intermediate Capital Group (Other Financial)	145,914	20,059	14,628	16	104,533
560	Bourne End Properties (Property)	144,879	4,536	L55	1	44,516
561	Mitsubishi Electric UK (Electronics)	144,642	407,278	L9,477	2,089	†
562	Monarch Holdings (Transport Services)	144,501	305,070	19,257	2,062	†
563	ASW Holdings (Metal & Metal Forming)	143,900	464,300	4,200	2,332	144,570
564	Midland Independent Newspapers (Media)	143,836	89,529	12,687	1,749	155,792
565	Law Debenture Corporation (Investment Trusts)	143,651	12,592	7,108	60	166,002
566	Spirax-Sarco Engineering (Engineering – General)	143,600	217,875	34,559	3,503	350,028
567	Cattles (Other Financial)	143,351	230,144	16,656	1,679	196,819
568	Stena Offshore (Engineering – General)	143,007	180,299	10,630	775	†
569	Derwent Valley Holdings (Property)	142,735	12,113	6,360	12	75,165
570	Ecclesiastical Insurance Group (Insurance, Life/Non-life)	142,704	116,574	13,813	673	†
571	Howden Group (Engineering – General)	142,590	373,356	27,570	5,028	266,223
572	Foreign & Colonial Eurotrust (Investment Trusts)	141,888	4,692	1,477	n/a	138,924
573	James Finlay (Agriculture)	141,538	184,387	13,787	32,902	72,627
574	Cooper (Great Britain) (Engineering – General)	140,406	290,277	L11,221	3,031	†
575	London Forfaiting Company (Other Financial)	139,292	1,032,077	16,054	105	163,372
576	Stanley Leisure Organisation (Hotels & Leisure)	138,909	265,155	12,356	3,480	164,189
577	Heywood Williams Group (Building Materials & Services)	138,450	519,640	33,117	6,154	257,145
578	Staveley Industries (Engineering – General)	138,400	338,900	8,600	5,080	194,977
579	Kwik-Fit Holdings (Transport – Manufacture & Distribution)	138,400	297,600	29,300	3,973	250,166
580	Graham Group (Building Materials & Services)	138,215	418,834	18,869	2,968	198,325
581	Rohm and Haas (UK) (Chemicals)	137,695	229,169	34,548	554	†
582	Thwaites [Daniel] (Brewers & Distillers)	137,520	77,146	6,573	n/a	55,825
583	Body Shop International (Health & Household)	137,200	219,700	33,500	31,110	336,010
584	C.E. Heath (Insurance, Life/Non-life)	136,111	175,084	3,841	3,315	243,969
585	Chelsea Building Society (Other Financial)	135,300	182,100	18,100	645	†
586	Allders (Stores)	135,135	671,674	25,433	5,425	227,792
587	Ecclesiastical Insurance Office (Insurance, Life/Non-life)	134,995	116,574	15,005	660	3,608
588	Medeva (Health & Household)	134,700	239,600	64,200	2,149	455,303
589	Trinity International Holdings (Media)	134,599	161,840	22,507	3,958	223,645
590	Bradford Property Trust (Property)	134,483	48,634	30,737	79	261,425
591	Linton Park (Agriculture)	134,206	164,927	12,776	20,759	56,086
592	Majedie Investments (Investment Trusts)	133,837	4,754	3,637	9	14,540
593	Hertz (UK) (Transport Services)	133,833	160,859	12,856	1,602	†
594	Capital and Regional Properties (Property)	133,771	8,172	4,145	40	62,465
595	CPC (United Kingdom) (Food Manufacturing)	133,169	253,362	19,696	1,454	†
596	Morland & Co. (Brewers & Distillers)	133,114	57,098	9,677	1,207	105,594
597	First National Finance Corporation (Other Financial)	132,991	174,918	1,319	1,047	176,049
598	Nacanco (Holdings) (Metal & Metal Forming)	131,974	221,406	5,752	498	†
599	Tibbett & Britten Group (Transport Services)	131,638	463,950	26,858	12,180	313,819
600	First Choice Holidays (Transport Services)	131,100	821,800	16,300	3,314	231,793

NOTES: n/a – not available. †Market capitalisation not available. Figure not disclosed or company unquoted, government controlled, a nationalised industry, a subsidiary or newly quoted.

THE UK'S TOP 1000 — 601-650

RANK	COMPANY NAME (Sector)	CAPITAL EMPLOYED £000	TURNOVER £000	PRE-TAX PROFIT £000	NUMBER OF EMPLOYEES	EQUITY MKT CAPITAL £000
601	Mount Isa Holdings (UK) (Metal & Metal Forming)	130,726	241,125	5,351	961	†
602	Fleming Claverhouse Investment Trust (Investment Trusts)	130,370	7,300	4,575	n/a	112,255
603	Bridon (Metal & Metal Forming)	130,100	315,700	L22,700	3,510	89,735
604	B.S.G. International (Transport – Manufacture & Distribution)	130,096	573,868	10,550	6,805	165,483
605	Shepherd Building Group (Building Materials & Services)	129,600	300,400	15,500	3,670	†
606	Crest Nicholson (Contracting, Construction)	129,560	249,091	11,076	1,061	83,178
607	Scholl (Health & Household)	129,520	171,914	16,682	1,786	122,540
608	M & G Dual Trust (Investment Trusts)	129,205	5,162	5,162	n/a	127,972
609	Fenwick (Stores)	129,174	175,423	19,952	1,902	†
610	London and Manchester Group (Insurance, Life/Non-life)	128,436	332,466	38,900	n/a	374,879
611	EIS Group (Engineering – General)	128,417	253,181	16,209	6,113	174,168
612	Cilva Holdings (Transport Services)	127,639	362,546	L89,661	4,090	†
613	Gerrard & National Holdings (Banks)	126,859	272,084	25,031	641	158,360
614	Royal Doulton (Health & Household)	126,805	221,984	3,039	7,248	140,255
615	N. Brown Group (Miscellaneous)	126,258	208,164	26,488	1,777	343,168
616	London Park Hotels (Hotels & Leisure)	126,125	11,916	1,392	283	†
617	Warner Lambert (UK) (Health & Household)	125,860	207,914	L8,246	1,991	†
618	British-Borneo Petroleum Syndicate, (Oil, Gas & Nuclear Fuels)	125,740	31,857	10,393	34	99,895
619	Acco Europe (Miscellaneous)	125,588	211,619	12,172	2,894	†
620	Ingersoll-Rand Holdings (Engineering – General)	125,306	178,180	15,387	2,271	†
621	Maersk Co. (Transport Services)	124,689	135,865	3,874	1,104	†
622	Watmoughs (Holdings) (Packaging, Paper & Printing)	124,602	179,907	20,082	2,184	278,413
623	McDonald's Restaurants (Food Wholesaling & Retailing)	124,548	585,653	19,677	26,956	†
624	Leigh Interests (Miscellaneous)	124,134	113,184	9,891	1,813	134,370
625	Pacific Assets Trust (Investment Trusts)	124,057	2,544	596	n/a	112,154
626	Continental UK Group Holdings (Other Industrial Materials & Products)	123,329	328,213	5,212	3,800	†
627	INVESCO (Other Financial)	123,042	178,587	39,293	1,384	430,955
628	Laura Ashley Holdings (Textiles)	122,321	300,387	3,028	4,430	180,878
629	Louis Dreyfus & Co. (Commodities Trading)	122,043	3,335,738	2,053	140	†
630	Goal Petroleum (Oil, Gas & Nuclear Fuels)	121,930	43,701	2,791	21	85,832
631	Westminster Health Care Holdings (Health & Household)	121,814	50,370	11,231	4,998	172,386
632	Cyanamid (UK) Holdings (Health & Household)	121,387	255,192	20,389	2,136	†
633	British Printing Co. (Packaging, Paper & Printing)	120,882	317,592	2,747	5,311	†
634	Bloor Holdings (Contracting, Construction)	120,529	141,722	10,791	572	†
635	St. Ives (Packaging, Paper & Printing)	119,619	237,014	22,259	3,135	211,083
636	Schroder Split Fund (Investment Trusts)	119,353	6,063	5,913	n/a	123,263
637	Sun Life Corporation (Insurance, Life/Non-life)	119,300	2,285,400	66,400	3,332	†
638	Newarthill (Contracting, Construction)	118,993	263,694	3,842	2,239	39,440
639	Britannic Assurance (Insurance, Life/Non-life)	118,475	411,618	33,084	4,569	752,767
640	Fleming International High Income Investment Trust (Investment Trusts)	118,075	5,964	5,120	n/a	121,331
641	Gan Minster Insurance Co. (Insurance, Life/Non-life)	118,059	244,063	4,089	847	†
642	Astec (BSR) (Electronics)	117,868	312,178	21,036	10,895	261,231
643	Marlowe Holdings (Electricals)	117,751	523,527	22,696	3,028	†
644	John Menzies (Stores)	117,300	1,231,600	34,400	11,896	354,131
645	Hartstone Group (Textiles)	117,132	363,887	L70,712	4,190	64,692
646	Derbyshire Building Society (Other Financial)	116,622	125,209	21,439	549	†
647	HTR Japanese Smaller Companies Trust (Investment Trusts)	115,838	1,248	831	n/a	114,098
648	Bristol-Myers Squibb Holdings (Health & Household)	115,747	370,105	49,265	2,459	†
649	Redrow Group (Contracting, Construction)	115,547	188,318	19,216	850	249,919
650	Photo-Me International (Engineering – General)	115,054	172,356	13,944	2,427	186,905

NOTES: n/a – not available. †Market capitalisation not available. Figure not disclosed or company unquoted, government controlled, a nationalised industry, a subsidiary or newly quoted.

651-700 — THE UK'S TOP 1000

RANK	COMPANY NAME (Sector)	CAPITAL EMPLOYED £000	TURNOVER £000	PRE-TAX PROFIT £000	NUMBER OF EMPLOYEES	EQUITY MKT CAPITAL £000
651	Avon Rubber (Other Industrial Materials & Products)	114,510	280,247	8,548	5,774	155,328
652	Fleming Income & Capital Investment Trust (Investment Trusts)	114,472	6,795	5,693	n/a	93,708
653	Macmillan (Media)	114,302	219,414	15,336	1,977	†
654	Guinness Peat Group (Other Financial)	113,559	59,655	8,415	807	115,585
655	Central European Growth Fund (Investment Trusts)	113,394	5,075	2,778	n/a	108,725
656	Midland & Scottish Resources (Oil, Gas & Nuclear Fuels)	113,017	65,250	L48,297	114	4,674
657	SP Tyres UK (Other Industrial Materials & Products)	112,898	232,836	4,790	3,500	†
658	H.P. Bulmer Holdings (Brewers & Distillers)	112,820	254,577	3,881	1,395	233,250
659	Ryder System Holdings (UK) (Transport Services)	112,622	245,266	L12,893	2,547	†
660	Fuller, Smith & Turner (Brewers & Distillers)	112,557	82,541	8,018	1,443	89,151
661	Duracell Holdings (UK) (Miscellaneous)	112,389	135,405	5,612	796	†
662	Raglan Estates (Property)	112,036	9,215	2,129	6	†
663	Latin American Investment Trust (Investment Trusts)	112,020	3,263	L349	n/a	94,448
664	McCarthy & Stone (Contracting, Construction)	112,000	71,200	4,200	414	81,417
665	Sterling-Winthrop Group (Chemicals)	111,972	64,317	20,695	186	†
666	United Friendly Group (Insurance, Life/Non-life)	111,895	329,105	47,619	4,011	376,337
667	Meggitt (Aerospace)	111,860	359,735	23,280	6,529	162,455
668	Allied Textile Companies (Textiles)	111,735	168,286	17,028	3,088	172,940
669	General Consolidated Investment Trust (Investment Trusts)	111,674	6,956	6,168	6	111,656
670	Bernard Matthews (Food Manufacturing)	111,490	283,526	18,618	5,049	141,246
671	Weetabix (Food Manufacturing)	111,122	218,702	28,526	2,481	†
672	Fidelity European Values (Investment Trusts)	110,923	2,586	563	n/a	79,712
673	Taylor Clark (Property)	110,404	24,387	6,503	928	†
674	Warnford Investments (Property)	110,359	11,394	6,953	17	83,712
675	UGC (Transport – Manufacture & Distribution)	110,321	714,053	24,887	3,603	†
676	Sharp Electronics (UK) (Electronics)	110,001	257,000	3,407	1,401	†
677	Aberforth Smaller Companies Trust (Other Financial)	109,433	4,643	2,860	n/a	93,976
678	CP Holdings (Conglomerates)	109,169	235,748	24,112	2,820	†
679	River Plate & General Investment Trust (Investment Trusts)	108,482	7,214	6,432	n/a	58,075
680	Dresser (Holdings) (Contracting, Construction)	108,062	262,604	L4,415	3,360	†
681	National Semiconductor (UK) (Electronics)	107,971	402,356	12,187	1,691	†
682	Sumitomo Corporation (UK) (Commodities Trading)	107,887	13,260,160	6,117	147	†
683	Stylo (Miscellaneous)	107,753	116,480	2,552	3,608	56,987
684	Gartmore Emerging Pacific Investment Trust (Other Financial)	107,629	2,580	177	n/a	85,935
685	Govett & Co. (Other Financial)	107,599	11,213	35,942	n/a	153,692
686	Sidlaw Group (Packaging, Paper & Printing)	107,391	289,374	14,710	2,709	15,593
687	Huntingdon International Holdings (Research & Development)	106,886	162,489	L71,147	3,634	58,142
688	Abtrust New Dawn Investment Trust (Investment Trusts)	106,745	1,916	893	n/a	86,131
689	Danka Business Systems (Electronics)	106,362	347,218	31,999	5,945	765,407
690	Bristol Water Holdings (Water)	106,167	59,936	8,012	771	69,846
691	Cheshire Building Society (Other Financial)	105,438	105,280	18,431	522	†
692	Y.J. Lovell (Holdings) (Contracting, Construction)	104,664	250,577	4,164	1,536	25,757
693	Dow Corning (Other Industrial Materials & Products)	104,570	182,627	5,899	648	†
694	Community Hospitals Group (Health & Household)	104,522	57,595	7,744	n/a	76,606
695	Pitney Bowes Holdings (Miscellaneous)	103,994	148,563	24,784	2,054	†
696	Colaingrove (Hotels & Leisure)	103,646	81,831	5,945	958	†
697	Independent Television News (Media)	103,408	83,350	20,219	719	†
698	Trafford Park Estates (Property)	103,379	11,523	5,839	34	63,762
699	City Site Estates (Property)	103,379	10,171	2,070	11	9,544
700	Pioneer Concrete Holdings (Building Materials & Services)	103,313	182,187	12,862	994	†

NOTES: n/a – not available. †Market capitalisation not available. Figure not disclosed or company unquoted, government controlled, a nationalised industry, a subsidiary or newly quoted.

THE UK'S TOP 1000 — 701-750

RANK	COMPANY NAME (Sector)	CAPITAL EMPLOYED £000	TURNOVER £000	PRE-TAX PROFIT £000	NUMBER OF EMPLOYEES	EQUITY MKT CAPITAL £000
701	Interpublic (Media)	102,746	1,290,639	L640	2,305	†
702	Shires Investment (Investment Trusts)	102,713	7,869	5,558	n/a	74,684
703	Britton Group (Other Industrial Materials & Products)	102,665	121,367	10,675	978	161,253
704	Wace Group (Packaging, Paper & Printing)	102,504	323,543	23,055	4,503	230,555
705	Honeywell (Electronics)	102,316	230,939	16,878	2,568	†
706	West Bromwich Building Society (Other Financial)	102,258	99,012	17,234	603	†
707	Helical Bar (Property)	102,179	24,982	6,578	19	106,902
708	Mercury Keystone Investment Trust (Investment Trusts)	102,101	4,573	2,602	n/a	84,389
709	Ellis & Everard (Chemicals)	102,100	426,100	15,900	1,854	188,073
710	Intel Corporation (UK) (Electronics)	102,012	566,695	49,388	485	†
711	Westbury (Contracting, Construction)	101,960	152,082	8,314	460	143,533
712	Canon (UK) (Engineering – Instrument)	101,101	416,821	21,086	2,595	†
713	J.D. Wetherspoon (Hotels & Leisure)	100,614	46,600	6,477	1,101	12,771
714	Principality Building Society (Other Financial)	100,597	99,881	19,016	532	†
715	Gartmore Shared Equity Trust (Investment Trusts)	100,272	3,383	2,490	n/a	71,844
716	Hemingway Properties (Property)	100,016	5,677	L837	10	46,645
717	Chelsea Land (Property)	99,987	17,524	L2,962	282	†
718	Shanks & McEwan Group (Miscellaneous)	99,404	119,535	L6,055	1,318	147,352
719	Wagon Industrial Holdings (Engineering – General)	98,857	279,930	15,581	4,021	255,950
720	Cater Allen Holdings (Other Financial)	98,641	552,375	17,150	355	138,514
721	USDC Investment Trust (Investment Trusts)	98,601	2,874	2,268	n/a	85,018
722	Moorgate Smaller Companies Income Trust (Investment Trusts)	97,969	4,607	3,984	n/a	91,586
723	Adwest Group (Engineering – General)	97,926	147,922	11,415	2,438	131,518
724	Bunge & Co. (Commodities Trading)	97,841	200,548	1,200	449	†
725	Stagecoach Holdings (Transport Services)	97,825	191,034	18,922	13,481	239,831
726	NSM (Mines)	97,362	111,904	2,123	1,238	41,478
727	McKay Securities (Property)	97,245	10,026	3,004	22	47,486
728	TR European Growth Trust (Investment Trusts)	96,973	2,188	1,476	n/a	92,330
729	Life Sciences International (Engineering – Instrument)	96,657	178,173	28,470	2,190	230,653
730	Tennants Consolidated (Chemicals)	96,182	120,078	12,295	782	†
731	Bullough (Engineering – General)	94,777	284,017	17,558	4,351	179,030
732	Andrew Weir & Co. (Transport Services)	94,711	246,636	3,555	1,025	†
733	Fleming Enterprise Investment Trust (Investment Trusts)	94,422	4,680	2,631	n/a	76,200
734	Co-Steel (UK) (Metal & Metal Forming)	94,372	210,974	4,186	1,078	†
735	Britannia Hotels (Hotels & Leisure)	94,279	30,309	5,717	1,113	†
736	Dawsongroup (Transport – Manufacture & Distribution)	94,247	61,329	11,207	363	120,361
737	United Glass Group (Other Industrial Materials & Products)	94,045	171,649	10,398	2,103	†
738	John Waddington (Packaging, Paper & Printing)	92,770	236,056	8,067	3,587	196,676
739	TR Far East Income Trust (Investment Trusts)	92,733	5,406	4,054	n/a	81,369
740	Kelt Energy (Oil, Gas & Nuclear Fuels)	92,197	35,510	6,725	319	42,831
741	Blagden Industries (Other Industrial Materials & Products)	92,192	224,295	L5,595	2,178	74,577
742	Murray Ventures (Investment Trusts)	92,046	4,631	4,317	n/a	81,162
743	Savoy Hotel (Hotels & Leisure)	91,904	92,057	4,230	2,811	261,264
744	Johnson Group Cleaners (Health & Household)	91,689	166,761	14,104	6,535	128,695
745	Carclo Engineering Group (Engineering – General)	91,654	152,543	12,930	2,613	155,741
746	Tanjong (Hotels & Leisure)	91,600	295,100	56,700	n/a	825,967
747	Burtonwood Brewery (Brewers & Distillers)	91,097	50,563	3,070	956	37,506
748	Bush Boake Allen Holdings (UK) (Miscellaneous)	91,044	179,704	10,542	1,724	†
749	Borden (UK) (Chemicals)	91,010	178,979	9,095	2,491	†
750	CrestaCare (Health & Household)	90,695	36,437	6,026	3,302	58,973

NOTES: n/a – not available. †Market capitalisation not available. Figure not disclosed or company unquoted, government controlled, a nationalised industry, a subsidiary or newly quoted.

751-800   THE UK'S TOP 1000

RANK	COMPANY NAME (Sector)	CAPITAL EMPLOYED £000	TURNOVER £000	PRE-TAX PROFIT £000	NUMBER OF EMPLOYEES	EQUITY MKT CAPITAL £000
751	Murray International Holdings (Metal & Metal Forming)	90,605	213,808	L1,771	3,109	†
752	Fenner (Engineering – General)	90,535	200,812	8,152	3,776	76,734
753	London International Group (Health & Household)	90,300	396,600	L175,100	8,532	338,332
754	Fidelity Japanese Values (Investment Trusts)	90,106	1,487	476	n/a	87,373
755	Watts, Blake, Bearne & Co. (Mines)	90,091	76,273	7,935	1,066	111,283
756	Independent Insurance Group (Insurance, Life/Non-life)	90,056	187,117	23,013	1,002	119,626
757	Readicut International (Textiles)	89,970	238,265	20,915	3,725	197,164
758	Dow Chemical Co. (Chemicals)	89,889	281,726	4,418	601	†
759	Henlys Group (Transport – Manufacture & Distribution)	89,586	389,869	16,118	2,508	129,771
760	Goode Durrant (Transport Services)	89,536	100,764	10,613	856	101,057
761	Maritime Transport Services (Transport Services)	89,254	21,072	20,597	328	†
762	Diploma (Electronics)	89,200	191,500	25,000	1,422	252,232
763	Hoare Govett Smaller Companies Index Investment Trust (Investment Trusts)	89,114	979	547	n/a	69,124
764	British Polythene Industries (Chemicals)	89,110	212,402	15,388	2,514	186,577
765	Prowting (Contracting, Construction)	88,839	60,057	4,118	292	58,138
766	Finning Holdings (Engineering – General)	88,692	173,304	11,906	874	†
767	Cadogan Estates (Miscellaneous)	88,610	39,934	7,904	919	†
768	Yorkshire Chemicals (Chemicals)	88,215	119,795	14,383	1,076	163,392
769	Rutland Trust (Other Financial)	87,745	100,454	10,939	1,009	65,664
770	Newcastle Building Society (Other Financial)	87,704	92,350	13,894	518	†
771	Securum Industrial Holdings (Transport Services)	87,526	204,044	L4,445	6,447	†
772	Field Group (Packaging, Paper & Printing)	87,417	154,563	8,953	2,114	151,987
773	J. Saville Gordon Group (Other Industrial Materials & Products)	87,287	33,028	5,605	186	66,603
774	Dencora (Property)	87,268	29,631	1,584	65	41,755
775	Inoco (Property)	87,069	13,119	853	36	21,684
776	Pall Europe (Other Industrial Materials & Products)	86,675	120,481	22,471	1,434	†
777	Hambro Countrywide (Property)	86,558	106,478	L3,856	3,977	133,995
778	Kraft Foods (Food Manufacturing)	86,441	225,750	17,327	719	†
779	Argus Press (Media)	86,201	96,446	L11,786	1,573	†
780	BZW Convertible Investment Trust (Investment Trusts)	86,129	7,021	5,000	n/a	73,948
781	G.D. Searle & Co. (Health & Household)	85,288	117,090	24,086	958	†
782	Yule Catto & Co. (Chemicals)	85,135	241,485	28,513	2,466	277,244
783	Candover Investments (Other Financial)	85,030	10,711	4,855	21	75,648
784	Bentalls (Stores)	85,024	78,912	1,746	1,116	49,887
785	Fyffes Group (Food Wholesaling & Retailing)	85,002	245,272	9,256	823	†
786	Bridgewater Paper Co. (Packaging, Paper & Printing)	84,907	94,291	L1,827	610	†
787	McCain Foods (GB) (Food Manufacturing)	84,887	227,218	22,518	2,052	†
788	Kenning Motor Group (Transport – Manufacture & Distribution)	84,860	112,151	2,532	1,186	846
789	Yeoman Investment Trust (Investment Trusts)	84,727	5,047	4,564	n/a	86,468
790	Exco (Other Financial)	84,721	234,387	43,528	1,742	19,583
791	Bond Holdings (Aerospace)	84,527	77,409	8,039	742	†
792	Baillie Gifford Japan Trust (Investment Trusts)	84,416	608	L316	n/a	77,886
793	MJ Gleeson Group (Contracting, Construction)	84,409	174,025	8,907	1,568	89,549
794	John Wood Group (Oil, Gas & Nuclear Fuels)	84,319	241,972	19,101	3,154	†
795	Aberforth Split Level Trust (Investment Trusts)	84,091	2,738	2,389	n/a	36,000
796	Tullett & Tokyo Forex International (Other Financial)	83,873	237,847	23,356	1,947	†
797	New Throgmorton Trust (1983) (Investment Trusts)	83,536	4,368	2,269	n/a	†
798	Bodycote International (Engineering – General)	83,527	75,018	11,821	16,490	153,634
799	Thomas Tait and Sons (Packaging, Paper & Printing)	83,488	109,976	12,363	537	†
800	CEF Holdings (Electricals)	83,478	430,166	15,737	4,140	†

NOTES: n/a – not available. †Market capitalisation not available. Figure not disclosed or company unquoted, government controlled, a nationalised industry, a subsidiary or newly quoted.

THE UK'S TOP 1000　　801-850

RANK	COMPANY NAME (Sector)	CAPITAL EMPLOYED £000	TURNOVER £000	PRE-TAX PROFIT £000	NUMBER OF EMPLOYEES	EQUITY MKT CAPITAL £000
801	Abbott Laboratories (Health & Household)	82,886	154,473	38,784	868	†
802	IBC Vehicles (Transport – Manufacture & Distribution)	82,477	638,871	9,284	2,370	†
803	Jersey Electricity Co. (Electricity)	82,420	39,335	4,905	481	15,714
804	Renold (Engineering – General)	82,200	130,000	6,000	2,610	95,001
805	Miller Group (Contracting, Construction)	82,128	357,574	L11,854	2,287	†
806	Pavilion Services Group (Hotels & Leisure)	82,095	118,158	L15,656	1,311	†
807	Caparo Group (Engineering – General)	81,603	343,349	26,252	3,193	†
808	Kenwake (Transport Services)	81,529	309,437	L7,948	588	†
809	BBC Enterprises (Media)	81,500	238,876	13,580	1,163	†
810	Daewoo UK (Textiles)	81,457	335,687	1,163	65	†
811	Countryside Properties (Contracting, Construction)	81,361	149,145	8,238	463	96,990
812	St. Modwen Properties (Property)	81,223	30,899	13,207	n/a	58,614
813	Edinburgh Small Companies Trust (Investment Trusts)	81,142	1,814	486	n/a	68,395
814	Brunner Mond Holdings (Chemicals)	80,629	132,967	14,175	1,509	†
815	Etam (Stores)	80,600	220,268	14,014	5,540	131,956
816	Fleming Indian Investment Trust (Investment Trusts)	80,592	2,288	1,318	n/a	80,640
817	Brake Bros (Food Wholesaling & Retailing)	80,344	402,243	23,541	3,533	233,233
818	Beta Global Emerging Markets Investment Trust (Investment Trusts)	80,336	1,185	L1,119	n/a	78,196
819	Newman Tonks Group (Building Materials & Services)	80,277	257,638	15,777	4,765	209,054
820	Baxi Partnership (Engineering – General)	80,231	75,752	5,554	1,152	†
821	Selective Assets Trust (Investment Trusts)	80,076	1,839	166	n/a	41,399
822	Holliday Chemical Holdings (Chemicals)	79,805	132,873	19,277	1,279	210,954
823	Dana Holdings (Transport – Manufacture & Distribution)	79,788	199,580	3,015	2,870	†
824	Eurotherm (Electronics)	79,200	168,000	26,100	2,088	337,564
825	Polaroid (UK) (Health & Household)	79,185	219,353	13,727	1,414	†
826	Tilbury Douglas (Contracting, Construction)	78,800	406,333	15,159	3,549	191,794
827	Micro Focus Group (Electronics)	78,757	89,885	8,723	751	119,652
828	CLM Insurance Fund (Investment Trusts)	78,699	3,378	1,443	n/a	82,765
829	Virgin Retail Group (Stores)	78,573	22,539	32,134	83	†
830	TLG (Electricals)	78,490	328,802	11,370	4,288	256,426
831	Perkins Foods (Food Manufacturing)	78,051	382,128	15,713	1,923	106,600
832	Foreign & Colonial Enterprise Trust (Investment Trusts)	78,004	2,458	1,356	n/a	66,302
833	Remploy (Miscellaneous)	77,952	126,707	L84,176	10,229	†
834	Mid Kent Holdings (Water)	77,887	35,994	7,513	n/a	67,620
835	Hardys & Hansons (Brewers & Distillers)	77,759	32,705	7,724	685	53,068
836	Tandem Computers (Electronics)	77,734	107,441	L24,595	270	†
837	John Wyeth & Brother (Health & Household)	77,715	134,801	8,088	1,287	†
838	TBI (Property)	77,680	3,323	22,496	13	44,566
839	Triplex Lloyd (Engineering – General)	77,651	169,952	L2,916	3,652	95,755
840	Drayton English & International Trust (Investment Trusts)	77,602	3,740	2,319	n/a	67,056
841	IKEA (Property)	77,359	165,864	5,157	794	†
842	Shaftesbury (Property)	76,941	6,875	2,350	11	49,132
843	Sherwood Group (Textiles)	76,624	152,645	18,456	3,385	93,023
844	Ivory & Sime Enterprise Capital (Investment Trusts)	76,598	2,459	L124	n/a	33,565
845	George Williamson & Co. (Commodities Trading)	76,555	46,105	9,390	27,471	†
846	Babcock International Group (Engineering – General)	76,366	805,235	L41,232	10,980	200,857
847	Powerscreen International (Engineering – General)	75,722	122,450	24,563	628	219,342
848	Polypipe (Building Materials & Services)	75,400	145,400	20,600	2,055	210,053
849	Martin Currie Pacific Trust (Investment Trusts)	75,201	1,416	549	n/a	61,432
850	Emess (Electricals)	75,100	145,100	6,400	1,939	75,271

NOTES: n/a – not available. †Market capitalisation not available. Figure not disclosed or company unquoted, government controlled, a nationalised industry, a subsidiary or newly quoted.

851-900 — THE UK'S TOP 1000

RANK	COMPANY NAME (Sector)	CAPITAL EMPLOYED £000	TURNOVER £000	PRE-TAX PROFIT £000	NUMBER OF EMPLOYEES	EQUITY MKT CAPITAL £000
851	Assi Packaging (UK) (Packaging, Paper & Printing)	75,034	118,048	L9,851	1,665	†
852	Roadchef Holdings (Hotels & Leisure)	74,690	121,700	2,477	1,171	†
853	All England Lawn Tennis Ground (Hotels & Leisure)	74,392	3,032	2,032	14	†
854	Simon Engineering (Engineering – General)	74,271	386,116	L160,259	3,809	134,516
855	Israel Fund (Investment Trusts)	74,197	2,108	499	n/a	64,573
856	Reader's Digest Association (Packaging, Paper & Printing)	74,063	227,479	24,282	856	†
857	Hanover Acceptances (Food Wholesaling & Retailing)	73,531	209,354	2,997	1,433	†
858	Phillips-Imperial Petroleum (Oil, Gas & Nuclear Fuels)	73,341	430,334	6,597	n/a	†
859	Goldsborough Healthcare (Health & Household)	73,326	41,726	5,256	n/a	67,926
860	Sheffield Forgemasters (Metal & Metal Forming)	73,117	110,997	3,539	1,727	†
861	Bull Information Systems (Electronics)	73,098	239,308	10,609	1,891	†
862	Campbell's UK (Food Manufacturing)	73,094	166,809	7,332	1,991	†
863	Derby Trust (Investment Trusts)	72,760	3,081	2,676	n/a	66,143
864	US Smaller Companies Investment Trust (Investment Trusts)	72,754	914	538	n/a	62,661
865	Budgens (Stores)	72,341	277,212	5,270	4,752	43,936
866	Lowland Investment Company (Investment Trusts)	72,309	4,330	2,840	n/a	69,280
867	Vinten Group (Engineering – Instrument)	72,289	97,048	20,082	984	217,993
868	Bemrose Corporation (Packaging, Paper & Printing)	72,009	125,730	15,836	2,066	120,820
869	Hogg Robinson (Transport Services)	71,849	153,814	21,478	2,782	176,449
870	Iveco Ford Truck (Transport – Manufacture & Distribution)	71,755	251,614	L16,905	982	†
871	Eldridge, Pope & Co. (Brewers & Distillers)	71,609	42,146	2,643	1,271	33,143
872	Hobson (Commodities Trading)	71,600	173,700	L11,200	2,191	86,879
873	City Centre Restaurants (Hotels & Leisure)	71,179	95,175	12,642	3,589	155,666
874	Croudace Holdings (Property)	70,922	55,257	5,414	320	†
875	Cenargo International (Transport Services)	70,524	30,028	4,997	39	†
876	NEC Technologies (UK) (Electronics)	70,375	123,573	264	608	†
877	Watson & Philip (Food Wholesaling & Retailing)	70,263	440,570	10,644	5,968	164,200
878	Claverley Co. (Media)	70,153	128,918	8,641	1,764	†
879	Cray Electronics Holdings (Electronics)	69,952	271,718	26,168	3,362	407,617
880	Estates & Agency Holdings (Property)	69,702	338	1,102	5	25,993
881	Exeter Preferred Capital Investment Trust (Investment Trusts)	69,594	4,866	183	n/a	28,491
882	Engelhard (Metal & Metal Forming)	68,688	3,717,005	3,868	391	†
883	Capital Corpn (Hotels & Leisure)	68,643	51,315	23,210	264	137,943
884	Northington Group (Other Financial)	68,640	500,517	2,065	478	†
885	Gaymer Group Europe (Brewers & Distillers)	68,484	145,175	8,160	961	†
886	Value and Income Trust (Investment Trusts)	68,415	4,868	1,858	n/a	51,677
887	Bestway (Holdings) (Food Wholesaling & Retailing)	68,260	474,262	14,698	793	†
888	Kingsway Group (Building Materials & Services)	68,078	103,590	1,086	1,364	†
889	Suter (Engineering – General)	67,900	186,900	38,200	3,208	182,346
890	Finsbury Growth Trust (Investment Trusts)	67,817	2,499	1,427	n/a	53,590
891	Dobson Park Industries (Engineering – General)	67,682	99,973	10,510	1,646	102,094
892	Brunel Holdings (Building Materials & Services)	67,499	402,986	L71,457	4,031	37,101
893	James Walker Group (Engineering – General)	67,041	75,392	1,921	1,970	†
894	BI Group (Engineering – General)	66,735	123,734	7,185	2,169	76,091
895	Shepherd Neame (Brewers & Distillers)	66,706	43,098	5,022	786	35,730
896	Kunick (Health & Household)	66,457	95,152	8,980	1,711	73,390
897	Malvern UK Index Trust (Investment Trusts)	66,403	2,755	2,433	n/a	63,685
898	River & Mercantile Extra Income Trust (Investment Trusts)	66,387	5,027	3,961	n/a	40,877
899	Devro International (Food Manufacturing)	66,081	98,353	29,103	980	294,284
900	Vosper Thornycroft Holdings (Engineering – General)	65,951	239,224	21,516	2,639	235,974

NOTES: n/a – not available. †Market capitalisation not available. Figure not disclosed or company unquoted, government controlled, a nationalised industry, a subsidiary or newly quoted.

THE UK'S TOP 1000   901-950

RANK	COMPANY NAME (Sector)	CAPITAL EMPLOYED £000	TURNOVER £000	PRE-TAX PROFIT £000	NUMBER OF EMPLOYEES	EQUITY MKT CAPITAL £000
901	USM Texon (Engineering – General)	65,937	193,156	4,453	2,478	†
902	McDonnell Information Systems Group (Business Services)	65,931	148,911	7,157	1,772	101,000
903	Hall Engineering (Holdings) (Engineering – General)	65,856	154,819	870	1,459	47,338
904	Lancer Boss Group (Engineering – General)	65,391	192,386	L3,142	2,607	†
905	Ben Line Group (Transport Services)	65,192	17,095	L16,777	254	†
906	Vibroplant (Contracting, Construction)	65,145	71,076	2,796	1,182	42,117
907	M & G Second Dual Trust (Investment Trusts)	65,116	3,005	3,005	n/a	64,700
908	Johnson & Firth Brown (Metal & Metal Forming)	64,956	130,082	L4,391	2,178	60,035
909	Birse Group (Contracting, Construction)	64,919	351,343	L2,703	1,763	56,402
910	Higgs and Hill (Contracting, Construction)	64,759	262,204	1,226	1,203	55,596
911	Wates Building Group (Contracting, Construction)	64,707	189,024	282	992	†
912	Pendragon (Transport – Manufacture & Distribution)	64,559	388,886	9,621	1,904	97,123
913	Appleyard Group (Transport – Manufacture & Distribution)	64,518	560,456	8,110	2,481	75,056
914	London & Metropolitan (Property)	64,451	12,816	10,200	74	4,775
915	Smaller Companies Investment Trust (Investment Trusts)	64,280	2,894	1,949	n/a	60,895
916	Baring Emerging Europe Trust (Investment Trusts)	63,949	1,352	433	n/a	65,567
917	Save & Prosper Linked Investment Trust (Investment Trusts)	63,804	2,161	2,161	n/a	60,163
918	Moorfield Estates (Property)	63,792	6,757	1,260	5	20,172
919	Yorkshire Food Group (Food Manufacturing)	63,712	129,055	5,958	1,196	48,112
920	TVS Entertainment (Media)	63,300	236,100	13,600	543	†
921	Smurfit Corrugated (UK) (Packaging, Paper & Printing)	63,198	135,723	L331	1,390	†
922	MCIT (Investment Trusts)	63,167	4,446	3,331	n/a	58,650
923	Milk Products Holdings (Europe) (Food Manufacturing)	62,877	314,973	L302	499	†
924	Ex-Lands (Property)	62,866	5,162	1,278	112	31,691
925	Forth Ports (Transport Services)	62,830	33,092	9,616	519	138,000
926	Cleanaway (Miscellaneous)	62,789	113,570	13,949	1,445	†
927	Foreign & Colonial PEP Investment Trust (Investment Trusts)	62,731	2,716	2,363	n/a	63,997
928	Titaghur (Textiles)	62,523	22,138	L6,306	18,070	†
929	Plysu (Other Industrial Materials & Products)	62,508	88,785	5,429	1,590	109,927
930	Molyneux Estates (Property)	62,498	5,149	1,108	4	27,253
931	Dares Estates (Property)	62,252	5,074	L202	7	796
932	Fleming Geared Income & Assets Investment Trust (Investment Trusts)	62,231	4,004	3,750	n/a	25,763
933	Foreign & Colonial Special Utilities Investment Trust (Investment Trusts)	62,181	2,508	1,748	n/a	33,000
934	BSS Group (Other Industrial Materials & Products)	62,124	258,052	9,860	1,844	139,549
935	Alvis (Aerospace)	61,838	79,981	5,833	1,437	41,043
936	R.R. Donnelley (Packaging, Paper & Printing)	61,745	132,109	3,416	974	†
937	Ryan Group (Mines)	61,560	112,792	L7,347	1,191	†
938	Yorkshire-Tyne Tees Television Holdings (Media)	61,440	237,141	8,373	1,122	197,484
939	Oxford Instruments (Engineering – Instrument)	61,270	111,986	12,792	1,392	150,409
940	National Express Group (Transport Services)	61,198	170,009	15,236	1,458	116,443
941	Angerstein Underwriting Trust (Insurance, Life/Non-life)	60,940	1,451	1,043	n/a	66,150
942	Pantheon International Participations (Investment Trusts)	60,937	900	215	n/a	30,032
943	Herald Investment Trust (Investment Trusts)	60,847	1,220	538	n/a	59,150
944	Arnold Clark Automobiles (Transport – Manufacture & Distribution)	60,601	284,606	8,650	1,781	†
945	Dwyer Estates (Property)	60,309	5,837	1,415	29	25,142
946	HCG Lloyd's Investment Trust (Investment Trusts)	60,116	3,143	2,693	n/a	59,979
947	Investment Trust of Guernsey (Investment Trusts)	60,039	2,268	2,064	n/a	55,253
948	Grampian Holdings (Health & Household)	59,927	112,781	8,505	1,824	69,462
949	Cordiant (Media)	59,900	3,906,200	32,400	10,913	327,982
950	Fairey Group (Electronics)	59,749	145,079	25,786	2,143	325,118

NOTES: n/a – not available. †Market capitalisation not available. Figure not disclosed or company unquoted, government controlled, a nationalised industry, a subsidiary or newly quoted.

951-1000 — THE UK'S TOP 1000

RANK	COMPANY NAME (Sector)	CAPITAL EMPLOYED £000	TURNOVER £000	PRE-TAX PROFIT £000	NUMBER OF EMPLOYEES	EQUITY MKT CAPITAL £000
951	London American Growth Trust (Investment Trusts)	59,744	885	109	n/a	49,970
952	EFT Group (Other Financial)	59,733	9,284	3,354	72	23,767
953	First Philippine Investment Trust (Investment Trusts)	59,637	149	L336	n/a	44,501
954	London and St Lawrence Investment Company (Investment Trusts)	59,528	3,735	3,577	7	53,457
955	Mayflower Corporation (Transport – Manufacture & Distribution)	59,389	137,511	8,587	1,581	105,583
956	London & Associated Investment Trust (Property)	59,338	3,531	1,707	26	27,177
957	Foreign & Colonial German Investment Trust (Investment Trusts)	59,329	1,245	390	n/a	45,988
958	Tay Homes (Contracting, Construction)	59,309	85,135	6,233	420	50,292
959	Chrysalis Group (Hotels & Leisure)	59,212	69,995	L3,389	542	56,188
960	Halma (Engineering – General)	59,185	135,318	25,075	2,099	401,496
961	East German Investment Trust (Investment Trusts)	58,925	814	L873	n/a	44,930
962	Wyevale Garden Centres (Miscellaneous)	58,915	39,919	6,748	785	54,125
963	Premier Land (Property)	58,710	4,667	470	3	12,860
964	Eastern Counties Newspapers Group (Media)	58,574	116,396	7,593	1,885	†
965	O.C.S. Group (Miscellaneous)	58,250	227,488	11,107	34,006	†
966	Smurfit (Packaging, Paper & Printing)	58,080	69,059	L2,298	1,012	†
967	North Atlantic Smaller Companies Investment Trust (Investment Trusts)	58,044	1,287	184	n/a	22,449
968	Airlines of Britain Holdings (Transport Services)	57,997	460,513	L3,520	4,807	†
969	Shoprite Group (Miscellaneous)	57,890	163,961	5,079	n/a	129,493
970	Baltic (Other Financial)	57,830	12,049	7,790	21	30,567
971	Brazilian Smaller Companies Investment Trust (Investment Trusts)	57,786	1,507	452	7	49,993
972	BBW Partnership (Transport Services)	57,761	460,513	L3,520	4,807	†
973	Continental Assets Trust (Investment Trusts)	57,692	1,493	996	n/a	40,704
974	M C L Group (Transport – Manufacture & Distribution)	57,672	251,293	5,129	350	†
975	Brammer (Other Industrial Materials & Products)	57,357	140,795	8,282	1,236	158,584
976	Baxter Healthcare (Holdings) (Health & Household)	57,314	172,921	8,812	1,656	†
977	RHP Bearings (Engineering – General)	57,257	97,512	L9,656	2,862	†
978	Manders (Chemicals)	57,137	117,888	23,861	926	117,176
979	Toshiba (UK) (Electricals)	57,135	320,062	5,349	1,427	†
980	Scottish Asian Investment Co. (Investment Trusts)	57,130	1,224	162	n/a	40,500
981	Melton Medes (Other Industrial Materials & Products)	57,036	120,617	3,171	2,698	†
982	Scania (Great Britain) (Transport – Manufacture & Distribution)	56,782	182,906	3,377	432	†
983	I&S Optimum Income Trust (Investment Trusts)	56,750	3,154	2,711	n/a	59,984
984	Dartmoor Investment Trust (Investment Trusts)	56,612	5,711	3,493	n/a	32,281
985	Frost Group (Transport Services)	56,536	229,398	10,862	55	159,071
986	Trade Indemnity Group (Other Financial)	56,050	59,202	5,001	433	111,483
987	Whatman (Engineering – General)	56,040	76,945	10,726	927	89,481
988	Charles Wells (Brewers & Distillers)	55,943	81,029	3,147	1,278	†
989	South Staffordshire Water Holdings (Water)	55,714	56,344	12,037	704	89,728
990	Chloride Group (Electricals)	55,572	101,405	1,209	2,365	78,672
991	Warburtons (Food Manufacturing)	55,516	156,206	13,941	5,334	†
992	Concentric (Engineering – General)	55,378	127,952	10,242	1,919	102,776
993	Dewhirst Group (Textiles)	55,354	247,256	17,011	7,395	166,843
994	Amicable Smaller Enterprises Trust (Investment Trusts)	55,336	2,053	1,440	n/a	50,526
995	Wainhomes (Contracting, Construction)	55,335	69,401	6,218	263	100,211
996	Pepe Group (Textiles)	55,132	205,826	2,141	586	†
997	Scottish Value Trust (Investment Trusts)	54,970	2,142	1,384	n/a	55,856
998	Domino Printing Sciences (Packaging, Paper & Printing)	54,847	89,934	13,029	849	137,779
999	Thorntons (Food Manufacturing)	54,825	96,572	12,107	2,832	111,206
1000	Bristol Evening Post (Media)	54,784	59,475	5,079	n/a	49,525

NOTES: n/a – not available. †Market capitalisation not available. Figure not disclosed or company unquoted, government controlled, a nationalised industry, a subsidiary or newly quoted.

EUROPE'S TOP 1000: INTRODUCTION

BRITAIN OVERWHELMINGLY DOMINATES the list of Europe's top 1000 companies, accounting for one-third of all constituents. With 332 entries, and with shared ownership of a further five companies with interests from the Netherlands, France and America, Britain accounts for more companies than Germany and France combined.

Despite this significant presence, Britain has only modest representation among the largest companies. Royal Dutch/Shell, the Anglo-Dutch energy group, is ranked third while British Gas is tenth. British Petroleum and HSBC Holdings, the banking group that owns the Midland, are 16th and 17th respectively, rounding up the UK's presence in the top 20.

The European Investment Bank, headquartered in Luxembourg, emerges as Europe's top company with £63.3 billion of capital employed. The prominent position of the bank, the official financial institution of the European Union, reflects the growing importance of the administration of the European community in business affairs.

THERE IS A SURPRISINGLY Gallic flavour to the top of the table, with France occupying no less than five of the first ten entries. Societe Generale, the banking and financial group, is second behind the EIB, with capital employed of £53.9 billion. State-owned Electricite de France and France Telecom are ranked fourth and eighth respectively. Cie de Suez, the industrial and financial holding company, is fifth while Credit Lyonnais, the troubled banking giant which has necessitated huge state aid to remain in business, is listed ninth.

Another highly placed French company is SNCF, the state-owned railway company whose capital employed of £22.4 billion, earning 11th place, dwarfs British Rail's own capital employed of just £2.8 billion.

However, France has just 130 listed companies overall, considerably fewer than Britain and four fewer than Germany, which is indicative of the concentration of a large part of French industry into a relatively small number of state-owned or state-assisted enterprises.

Germany, with 134 companies in the top 1000, sees Daimler-Benz, its largest company, listed sixth in Europe, with Siemens seventh. There are six German companies in the top 20, including Volkswagen, the auto giant (13th), Deutsche Bank (14th), RWE, the electricity utility (15th), and Veba, the energy and telecommunications concern (20th).

Ranked by turnover, Royal Dutch/Shell leads the table by a considerable margin, with sales of £61.9 billion, followed by Daimler-Benz at £41.96 billion and Siemens at £33.8 billion. British Petroleum recorded turnover of £33.1 billion. Two Italian state-owned entities, ENI and IRI, follow, with turnover of £32.6 billion and £30.8 billion respectively.

THE TABLE OF EUROPE'S top profit makers (page 88) gives a clear insight into different corporate philosophies across the continent. In Britain, profit is the main benchmark and British companies dominate the table, occupying no less than eight of the top ten places. The most profitable is Royal Dutch/Shell, jointly owned by Dutch interests, with pre-tax profits of £6.6 billion. HSBC Holdings is second, lagging by a considerable margin with profits of £3.17 billion, followed by British Telecom at £2.66 billion.

By contrast, France has just four companies among the 50 most profitable, led by France Telecom, placed seventh, at £2.35 billion. Ten German companies are listed, led by Bayer, the chemicals company, placed 16th with profits of £1.3 billion. The mighty Daimler-Benz scrapes in 46th, with profits of £837 million. The performance of German companies will not be helped by the strong performance of the Deutschemark against other leading currencies, which has reduced competitiveness in international markets and resulted in foreign exchange losses.

EUROPE'S HEAVIEST LOSS-MAKER is IRI, whose broad-ranging state-owned interests accumulated a total deficit of £3.4 billion through trading losses and heavy provisions. Ferruzzi Finanziaria, also of Italy, saw losses mount to £1.17 billion. Fiat's losses totalled £582 million.

In France a number of enterprises also returned crippling losses, requiring state-aid to continue trading. Air France notched up a £1 billion loss and SNCF slumped £990.8 million into the red. In the electronics sector Cie de Machines Bull lost £593 million and Thomson £496.7 million. Michelin, the tyre and rubber group, returned a £434 million deficit, while Credit Lyonnais lost £473 million. Germany's biggest corporate disaster was Metallgesellschaft, which lost £1 billion, mainly as a result of ill-fated speculation on commodities markets.

In Britain, where recession struck much earlier than in the rest of Europe, large-scale losses were largely avoided. Notable exceptions were Fisons, the pharmaceuticals company, which lost £463.7 million, while the Anglo-French Eurotunnel incurred losses of £386.9 million.

THE HIGH STOCK MARKET VALUE of British companies is put into perspective in the table listing Europe's top 50 by market capitalisation (page 89). There are 22 British companies, compared with ten from Germany and six apiece from France and Switzerland. Royal Dutch/Shell commands a price of £60.3 million, the aggregate value of listings in London and Amsterdam. Roche Holdings, the Swiss pharmaceuticals manufacturer, is Europe's second most valuable company, worth £30.5 billion, and British Telecom is third, with a value of £24.4 billion. Food group Nestle, also of Switzerland, is valued at £23.8 billion.

Germany's largest company by stock market value is Allianz AG Holding, the insurer, placed seventh overall at £21.2 billion, with Daimler-Benz placed tenth at £16.1 billion. The leading French company is Elf Aquitaine, whose share listing in Paris values the oil and gas combine at £12.2 billion.

TWO GERMAN COMPANIES emerge as Europe's biggest employers. Siemens has a workforce of 393,900 while Daimler-Benz employs 341,905. Italy's IRI provides employment for 327,226. Europe's other leading employers include Fiat of Italy (256,600), Germany's Volkswagen (243,638) and Deutsche Bahn (249,870), and SNCF of France (221,003).

EUROPE'S TOP 100: ANALYSIS

1 European Investment Bank LUX

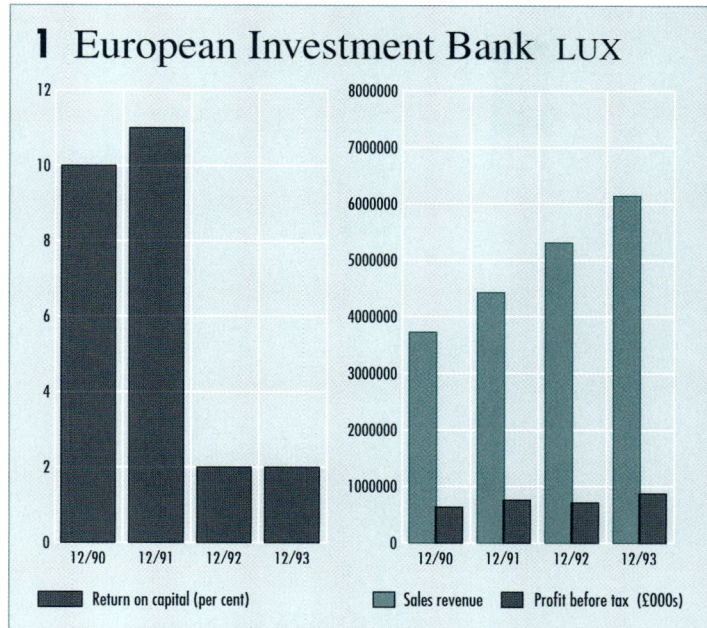

The task of the bank, the official financial institution of the European Union, is to contribute to the development, integration and economic and social cohesion of all member countries. It deploys banking resources to help finance capital projects. It also provides funding for projects in non-member countries with which the European Union has concluded economic and financial co-operation agreements. The bank grants loans and provides guarantees. In addition, it provides financing, principally outside the Union, under mandate and from member states' budgetary resources. The bank was established by the Treaty of Rome in 1957.

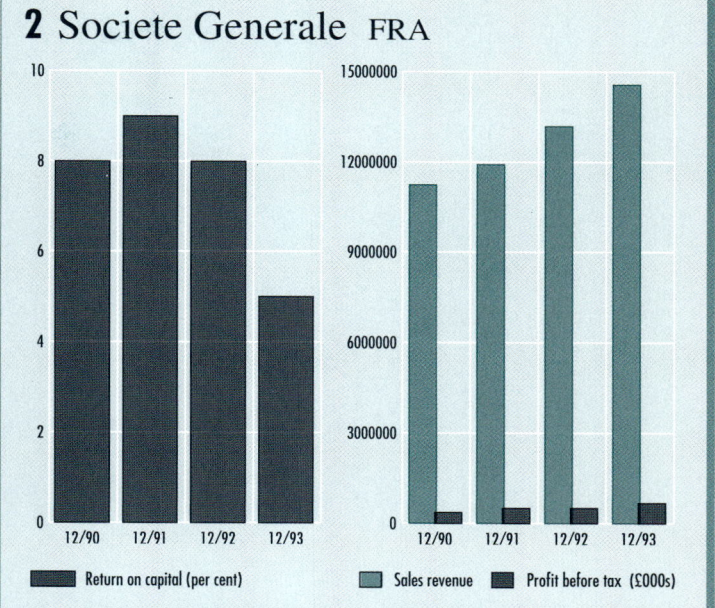

2 Societe Generale FRA

The company is a diversified banking and financial group. The business includes all types of banking, finance and credit operations including property and equipment leasing, long-term leasing, investments, portfolio management, capital equipment rental, industrial leasing, financial management, real estate, stock broking, export promotion, data processing, insurance, property development, venture capital, industry and commerce, services and management. It is represented in 63 countries. Established in 1864, the bank was nationalised in 1946 and reprivatised in 1987, when its shares were listed on the stock market in Paris. The bank is a member of the EBIC group of European banks.

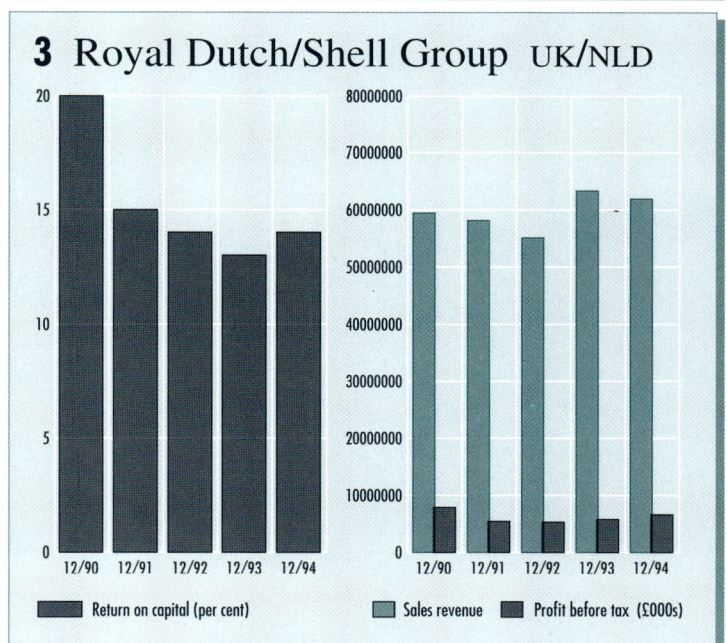

3 Royal Dutch/Shell Group UK/NLD

The company and Shell Transport and Trading, based in the UK, are holding companies who together own, directly or indirectly, investments in companies known collectively as the Royal Dutch/Shell Group and share net assets, dividends and investment income in the proportion of 60:40 respectively. The company's principal investments are its direct shareholdings in the Shell Petroleum Company (UK), Shell Petroleum NV, and Shell Petroleum Inc. (USA). These three companies own, directly or indirectly, interests in oil, natural gas, chemicals, coal and metals. Incorporated in 1890, Royal Dutch agreed to merge with Shell in 1907.

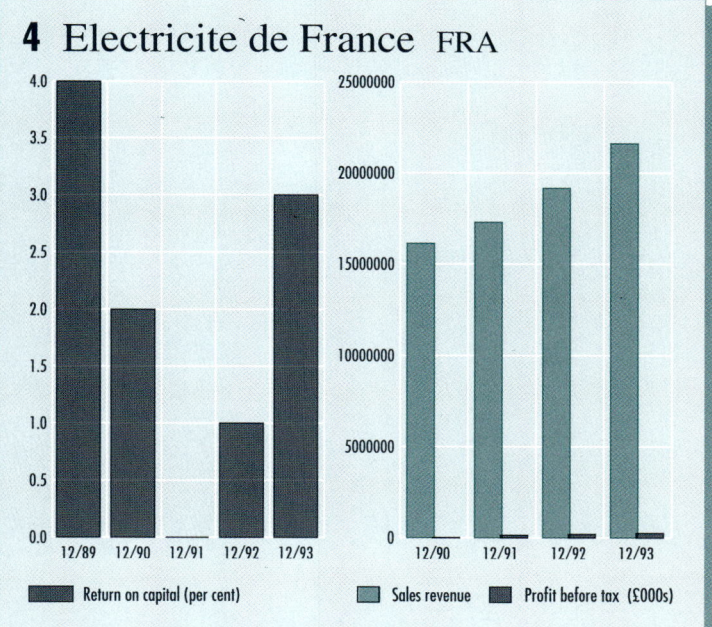

4 Electricite de France FRA

The company has a virtual monopoly on the transmission, distribution, import and export of electricity in France. However, it has no monopoly on generation, and private or publicly owned industry may produce electricity to supply its own needs, provided any excess is sold to EDF. In 1993 the company's output accounted for 20 per cent of that produced in western Europe. The company also operates hydro-electric power stations. It was created under the Nationalisation Law of 1946 and remains wholly owned by the French government, although plans exist to encourage private investment in EDF International, through which the company's foreign investments are held.

EUROPE'S TOP 100: ANALYSIS 5-8

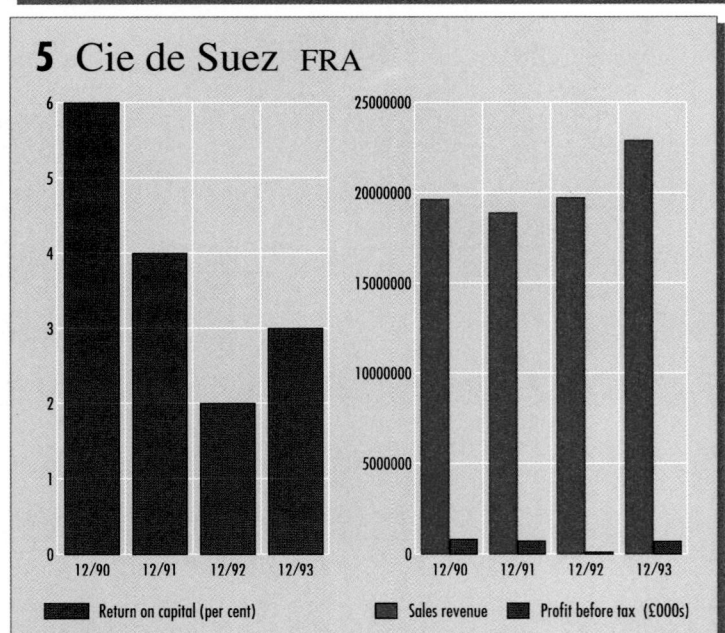

5 Cie de Suez FRA

The company is one of Europe's leading industrial and financial groups. The organisation is based around six main business units: Suez Investor (controlling stockholder), Banque Indosuez (merchant and investment banking), specialised financial subsidiaries, Credit Suez (real estate), and Ste Generale de Belgique (industry and services). The company sold its insurance company, Groupe Victoire, to Britain's Commercial Union for FFr12.5 billion in 1994. Cie de Suez was formed in 1858 by decree of the Viceroy of Egypt, and confirmed by the Sultan of Turkey, to construct and operate the Suez Canal. In 1958 the Egyptian government promulgated a law privatising the canal, backdated from 1956.

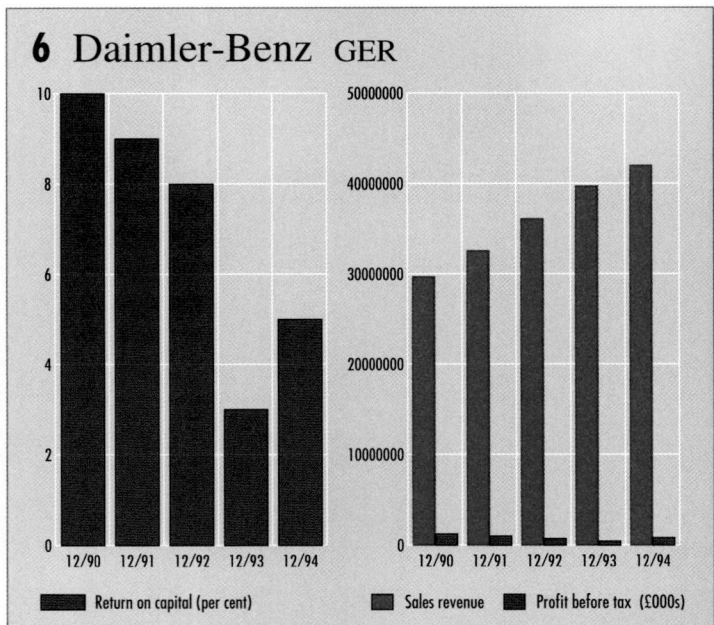

6 Daimler-Benz GER

The broad-ranging interests of Germany's largest industrial holding company are organised into four divisions. Mercedes-Benz manufactures passenger cars and commercial vehicles; AEG is engaged in heavy engineering, including rail systems, microelectronics, diesel engines and automation; Deutsche Aerospace manufactures aircraft and defence and civil systems; and Daimler-Benz Inter Services provides financial and marketing services and mobile communications. The company can trace its origins to 1890 but took its present shape through the acquisition of AEG, Dornier and MTU Motoren-und Turbinen in 1985 and a corporate reorganisation in 1990.

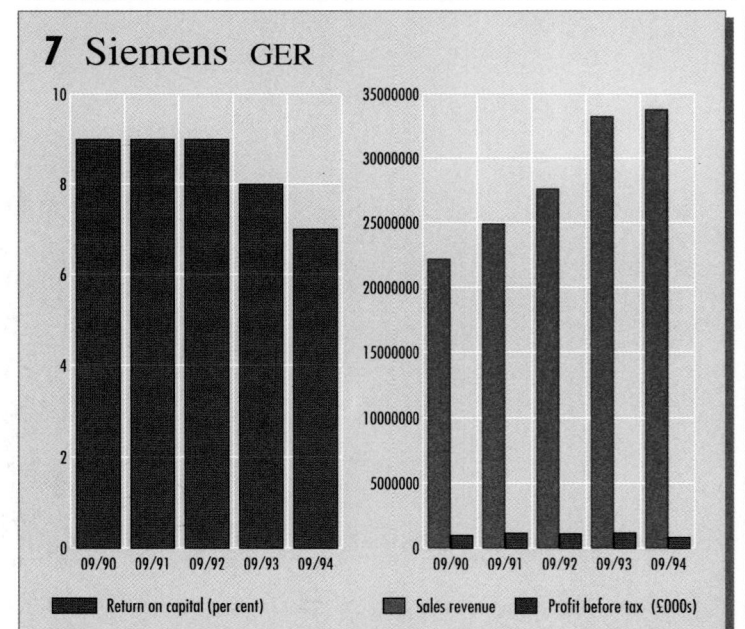

7 Siemens GER

The industrial holding company's extensive activities range from manufacturing power generation equipment to supplying washing machines and from railways to light bulbs. Established in Germany in 1847, it now has a world-wide presence, with sales exceeding DM84 billion a year. Group subsidiaries include Nixdorf, Bosch and Osram. In 1988 the company set up a joint venture with Britain's General Electric Company to execute the takeover of Plessey. Turnover by business sector is dominated by power generation, industry, communications and information systems. On a geographical basis Germany still accounts for about two-thirds of turnover, followed by the rest of Europe and the Americas.

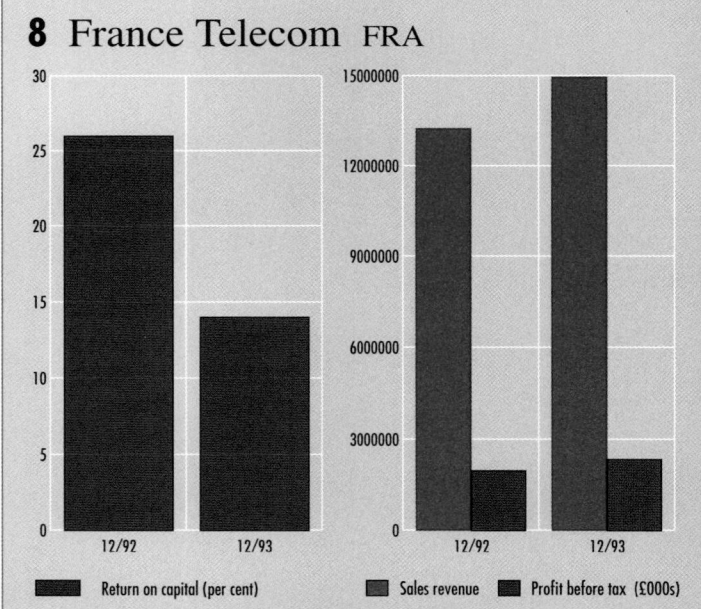

8 France Telecom FRA

The company supplies telecommunications equipment and services. Alongside its traditional business of providing telephone services for residential and commercial customers, the company is developing interests in information technology, mobile telecommunications, satellite and multi-media. Created in 1990 with the restructuring of the public postal and telecommunications sectors in France, the company is a state-owned entity, although the French government envisages reducing its shareholding to just over 50 per cent. In June 1995 the terms were announced of an alliance with America's Sprint Corp and Germany's Deutsche Telekom to develop business in Europe outside Germany and France.

EUROPE'S TOP 100: ANALYSIS

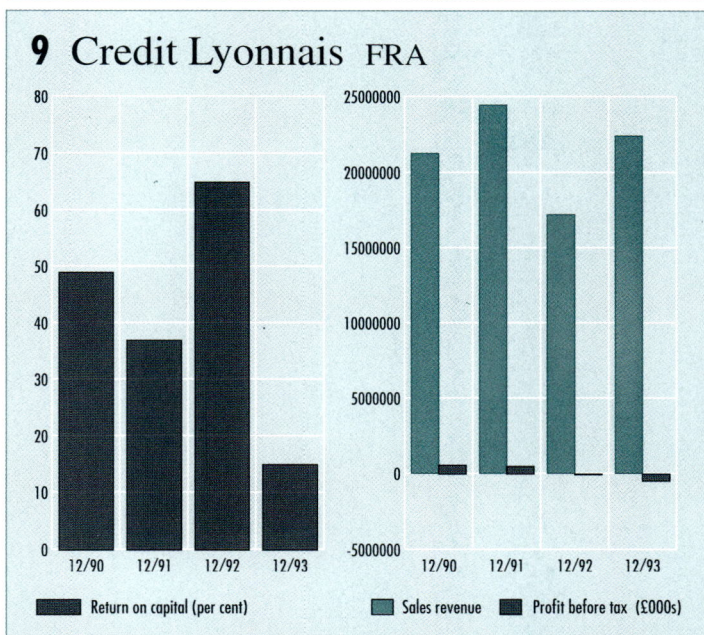

9 Credit Lyonnais FRA

The company is active in commercial banking (retail banking, corporate banking, leasing and factoring); capital markets (trading and stockbroking); equity investment (investment advisory services and venture capital activities); and asset management. Related products and services include comprise insurance and information technology. The bank has around 2,800 domestic branches, a further 962 in the rest of Europe and 864 elsewhere in the world. Established in 1863 and nationalised in 1982, the government still holds a majority stake. A rights issue in 1994 failed to alleviate financial problems and in 1995, after heavy losses, the government initiated a further financial restructuring and reorganisation.

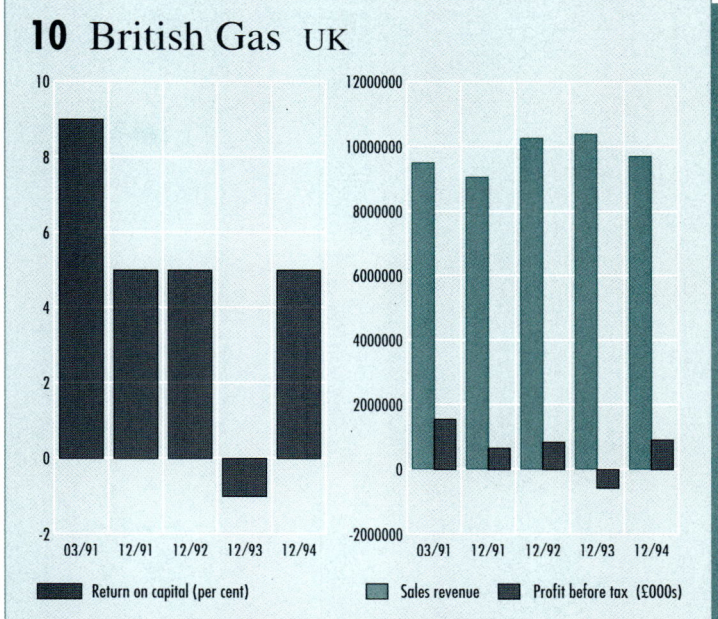

10 British Gas UK

The group's principal business is the transmission, distribution and supply of gas in the United Kingdom, supported by a range of services to customers, and the marketing of gas appliances. The group has operations exploring for and producing oil and gas and is also active in the overseas gas supply market. In December 1993 the group reorganised its domestic activities into five new businesses: public gas supply, contract trading, transportation and storage, servicing and installation, and retailing. British Gas was privatised in 1986, obtaining a stock market listing through a public offer of shares.

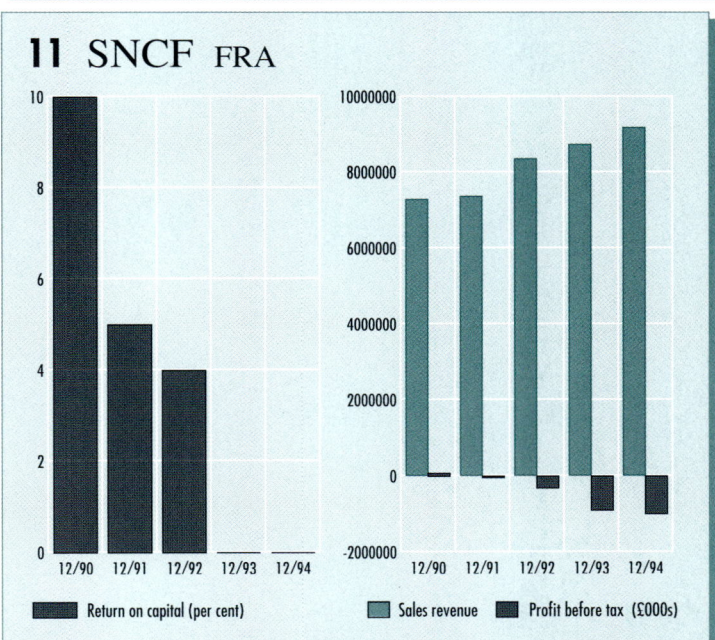

11 SNCF FRA

The group is the French national railways company, operating through five main business units: high speed and mainline passengers; Ile de France passengers (responsible for Paris and its suburbs); regional passengers; freight; and Sernam (parcels). Subsidiaries have interests in other sectors, such as road and maritime transport, coach services, tourism and hotels. The company is joint operator of Eurostar trains in the Channel Tunnel in conjunction with British Rail. SNCF was established in 1937 to consolidate all the privately-owned and government-operated railways into one company. In 1983 the company became a public entity and is now wholly owned by the French government.

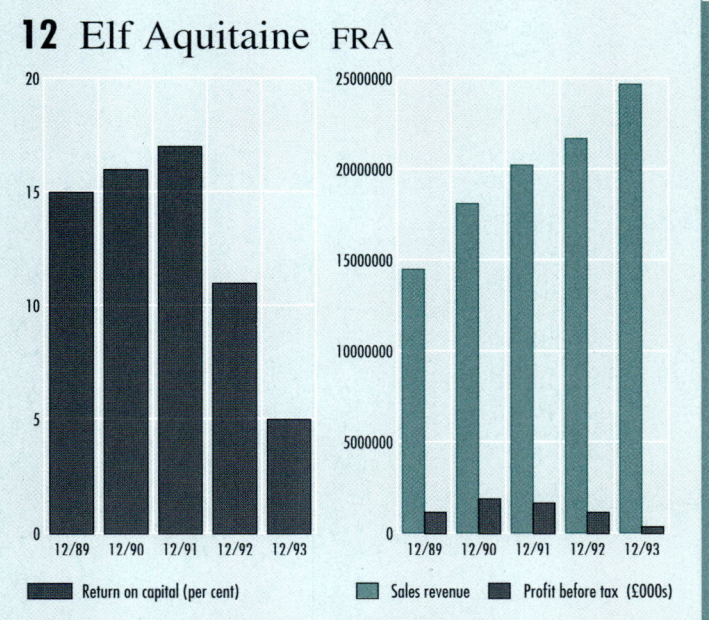

12 Elf Aquitaine FRA

France's largest industrial holding company is primarily involved in oil and gas exploration and production, refining and marketing, with interests in chemicals and pharmaceuticals. In 1994 the company was privatised, with an associated public offer of shares that was vastly oversubscribed. The French state retains a 13 per cent interest and the so-called stable group of investors, including Union des Assurances de Paris and Banque Nationale de Paris, holds 10.04 per cent. In 1993 the company acquired Yves St Laurent to expand its interests in perfumery and cosmetics.

EUROPE'S TOP 100: ANALYSIS 13-16

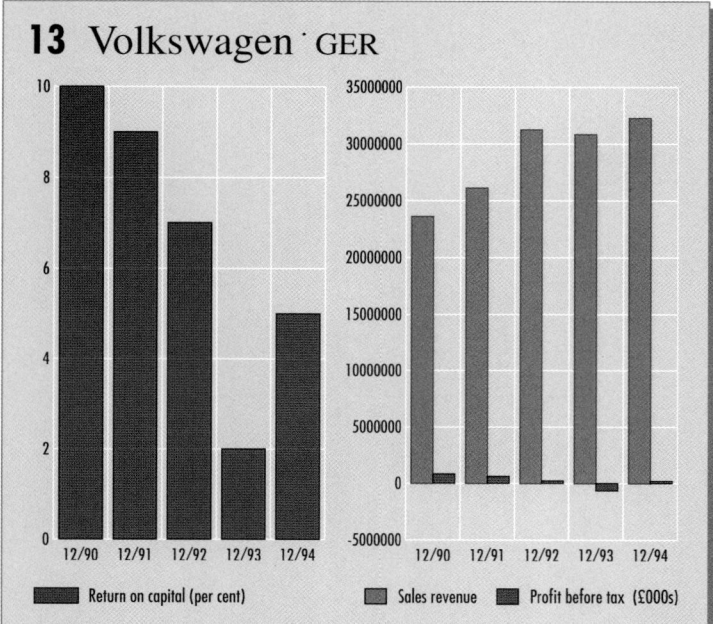

13 Volkswagen GER

The company produces passenger cars, mini-buses, vans, lorries, industrial motors and replacement parts under the Volkswagen, Audi, Seat and Skoda brands. Principal manufacturing plants in Germany are based at Wolfsburg, Hanover, Kassel, Emden, Salzgitter and Brunswick but activities are now spread across the European Union and eastern Europe, with extensive interests in Latin America. The original Volkswagen was established in 1937 to develop an affordable passenger car for lower income families and the company enjoyed prolonged success with the Beetle. Volkswagen is active in business information, car hire and leasing, and offers financial services through banking services.

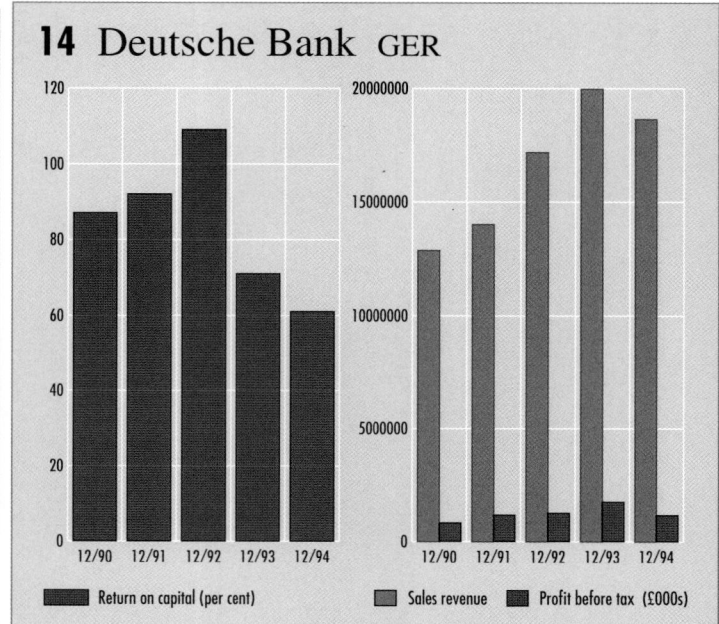

14 Deutsche Bank GER

The group is the largest of Germany's three leading banks. Activities include commercial, mortgage and investment banking, capital market and capital investment operation, instalment financing, leasing and consultancy as well as specialised services. There are 1,722 offices in Germany and 761 abroad. In 1989 Deutsche Bank acquired the share capital of Britain's Morgan Grenfell and London has become the centre of the group's European investment business. The group also has a substantial insurance operation and subsidiaries operating in research and consultancy. Deutsche Bank was established in 1870.

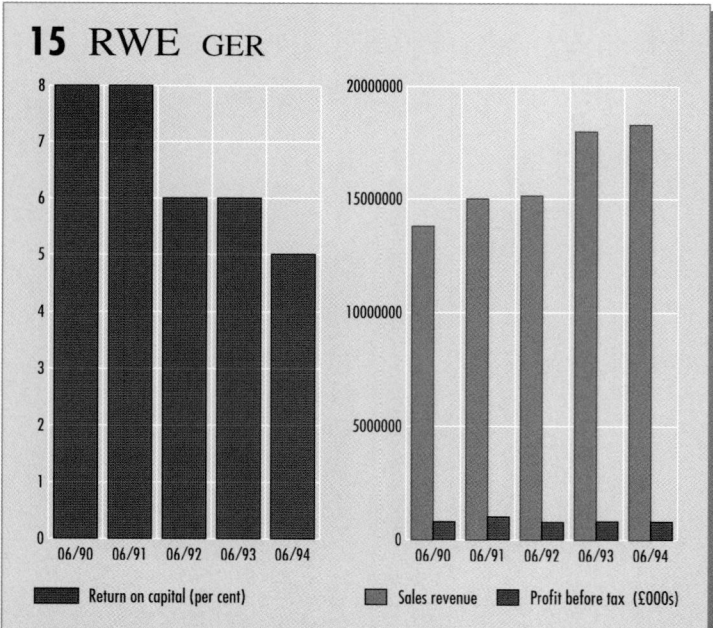

15 RWE GER

The company supplies industrial consumers and electricity utilities throughout Germany and neighbouring countries, operating through divisions in energy, oil and chemicals, mechanical and plant engineering, and mining and raw materials. The company was established in 1898 to distribute electricity to the city of Essen and group activities are still principally concentrated in Germany. German municipalities and public sector financial institutions hold a majority of the company's shares. In 1995 an alliance with AT&T, of America, was initiated with a view to providing basic phone services in Germany from 1998.

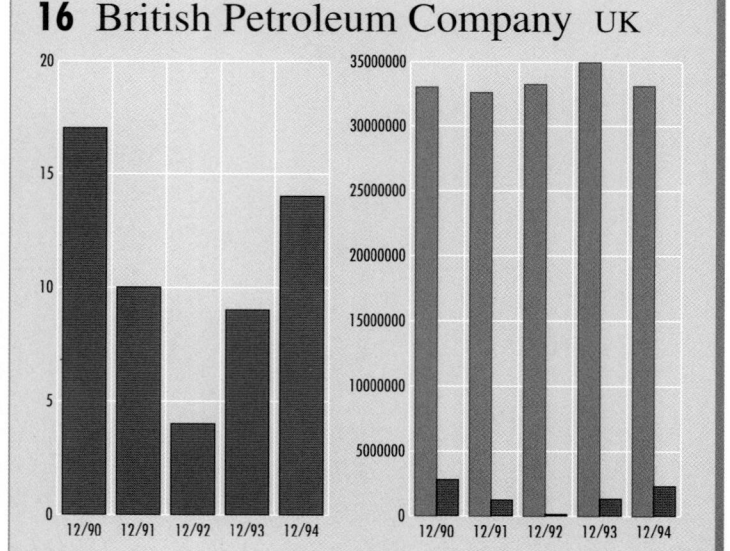

16 British Petroleum Company UK

The group's principal activities are oil and gas exploration, oil refining, marketing, supply and transportation, and chemical manufacturing and marketing. BP produced an average of 1.3 million barrels of oil per day in 1994, with an average refinery throughput of 1.7 million barrels per day. Principal sources of crude oil are the United Kingdom and North America, with substantial reserves being developed in Colombia. The company was established in 1909. Its name was changed from Anglo-Persian Oil to Anglo-Iranian Oil and subsequently to British Petroleum in 1954. The UK government acquired a controlling interest in 1914. The company was privatised through four public share offers between 1977-87.

17-20 EUROPE'S TOP 100: ANALYSIS

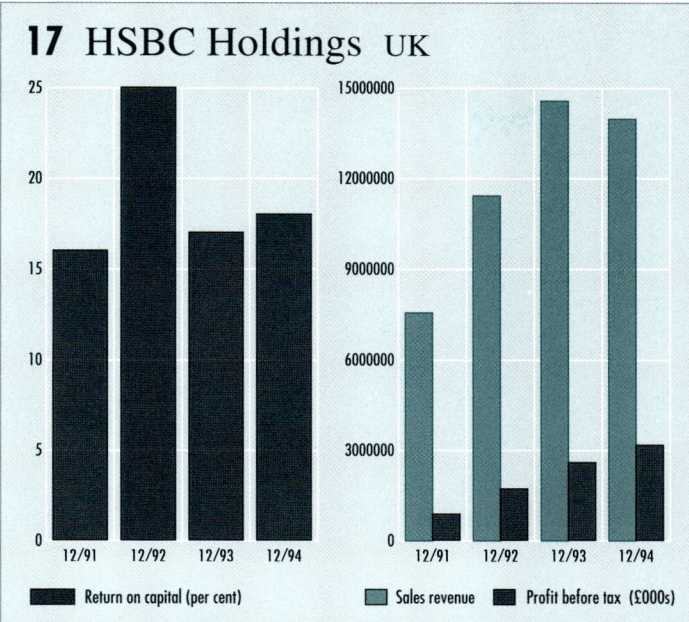

17 HSBC Holdings UK

Through subsidiary and associated undertakings, the group provides financial services, including commercial, investment and private banking and insurance. The company owns Midland Bank, which was acquired in 1992 to become part of an international network of some 3,000 offices in 65 countries across Europe, the Asia Pacific region and the Middle East. HSBC became the holding company of the Hongkong and Shanghai Banking Corporation by way of a scheme of arrangement in 1991 and is now domiciled in London. Other wholly-owned subsidiaries include Samuel Montagu and America's Marine Midland Bank, both formerly part of the Midland group.

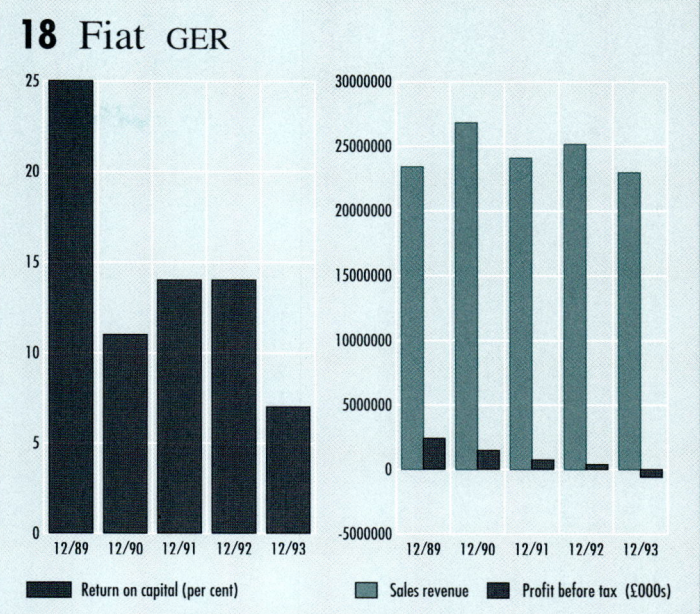

18 Fiat GER

Italy's largest private sector industrial group is active in 15 sectors: automobiles, commercial vehicles, agricultural and construction machinery, metallurgical products, automotive components, batteries, industrial components, production systems, aviation, rolling stock and railway systems, chemicals and fibres, civil engineering, publishing and communications, financial services and insurance. It is present in 66 countries worldwide through more than 1,000 companies. Automobiles continue be the single largest business sector, accounting for almost one-half of group turnover while on a geographical basis Europe, including Italy, accounts for almost 75 per cent of turnover.

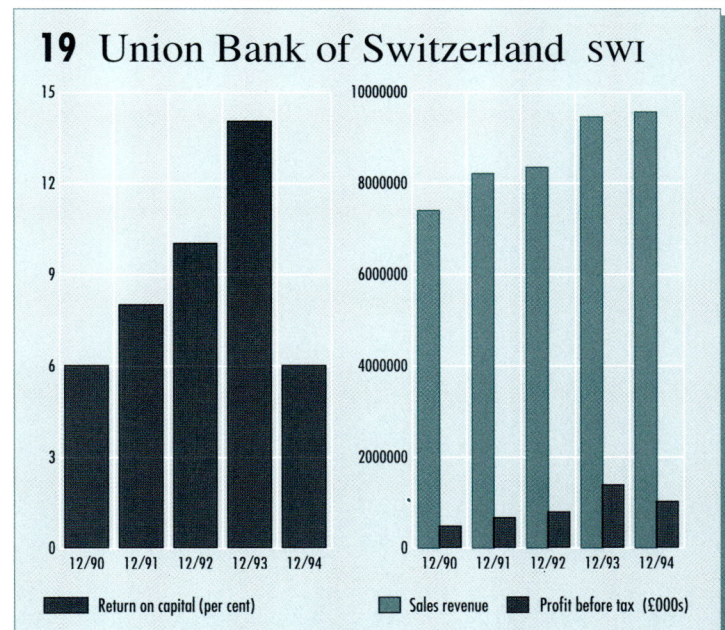

19 Union Bank of Switzerland SWI

The group's activities are organised into the divisions of corporate and institutional banking; retail banking and customer services; merchant banking and portfolio management; and primary market trading and risk management. There are some 335 branches and offices in Switzerland and more than 60 representative offices and subsidiaries abroad. Activities in the UK are based around the business that formerly traded as Philips and Drew. Union Bank was formed in 1912 through the merger of Bank of Winterthur (formed 1862) and Toggenburger Bank (founded 1863).

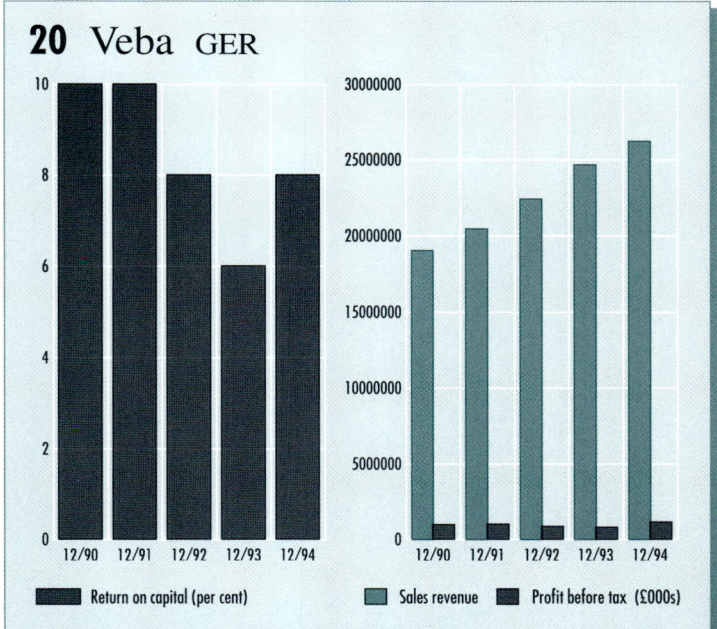

20 Veba GER

The company operates principally in electricity supply, oil and chemicals, with burgeoning interests in telecommunications. In 1994 it acquired a 10.5 per cent interest in Britain's Cable & Wireless, with whom a joint venture was established to develop a telecommunications business in the European Union, excluding Britain and Germany, and in Switzerland. The company was established in 1929, with the help of government investment, and was partly privatised in 1965. In 1987 the government sold its remaining 25.5 per cent interest. Although Veba is expanding its international operations the business is still predominantly based in Germany, which accounts for approximately three-quarters of group turnover.

EUROPE'S TOP 100: ANALYSIS 21-24

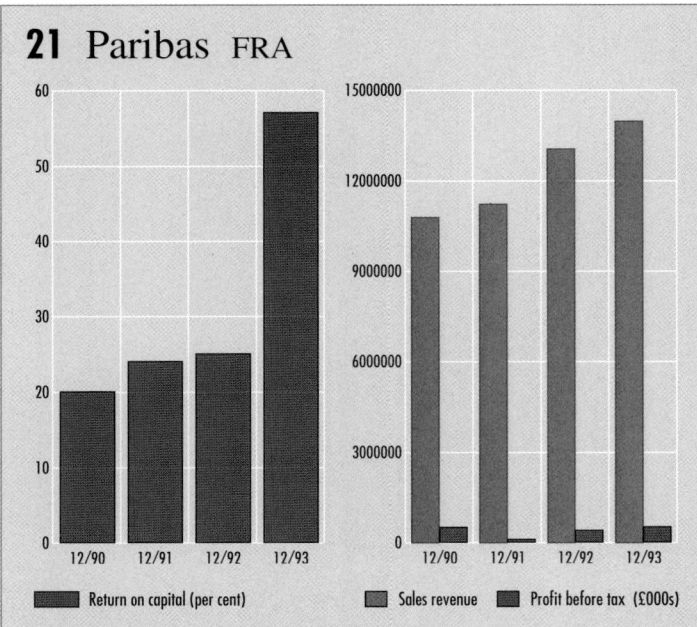

21 Paribas FRA

The group's business is organised into four areas: Banque Paribas (wholesale bank operating in corporate banking, capital markets, advisory services and asset management); Cie Bancaire (specialised financial services in the areas of business equipment, consumer lending, real estate lending and investment, life assurance and savings products, and real estate development); Credit du Nord (domestic retail banking) and Paribas Affaires Industrielles (equity investment portfolio). The bank, whose origins date back to 1872, was nationalised in 1982 through the transfer of its shares to the French state. It was reprivatised in 1987 through a public share offer.

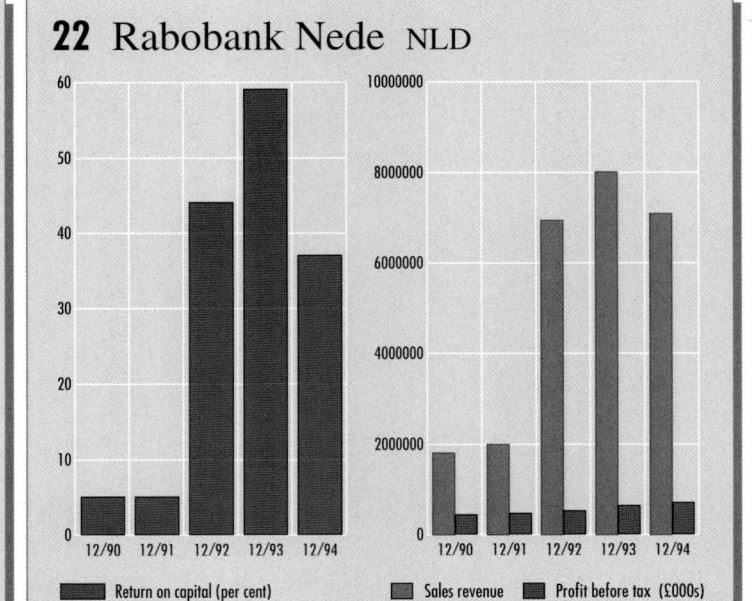

22 Rabobank Nede NLD

The group is a co-operative banking organisation. There are 744 local Rabobanks, all of which are co-operatives, with almost 2,000 branches throughout the Netherlands and 47 abroad. Members number approximately 650,000. In addition to its primary objective as a credit co-operative the group comprises specialist financial subsidiaries involved in factoring and leasing, ship mortgaging and insurance. Outside the Netherlands branches are located in Belgium, Singapore, Germany, Indonesia, Guernsey, Luxembourg, Switzerland, Hong Kong, Italy and Brazil.

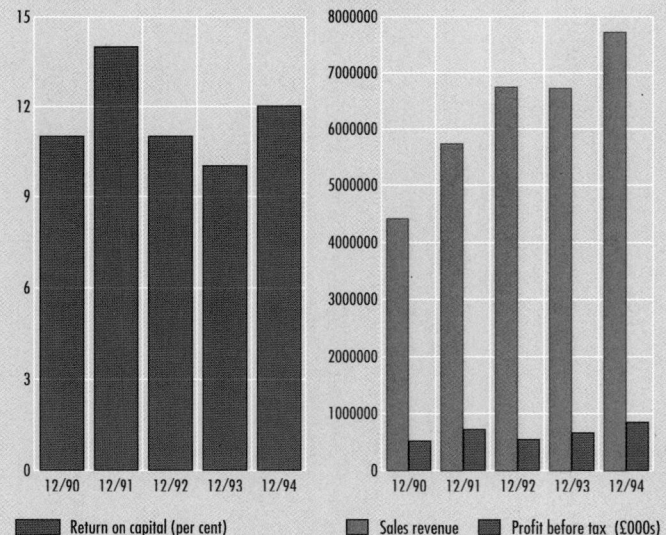

23 Telefonica de Espana SPA

The company's main business is to provide and operate international telecommunications services, including integrated business communications, mobile land and maritime services and high-speed data transmission. It is involved in design, manufacture and marketing of information services. The company was founded in 1924 by ITT and local investors to acquire existing private telephone companies in Spain. In 1944 ITT's shares were purchased by the government. The company's monopoly on telecommunications was withdrawn in 1987. In 1991 a new State Contract was signed, and the company assumed the management, under a monopoly agreement, of end-user services and transmission services.

24 Abbey National UK

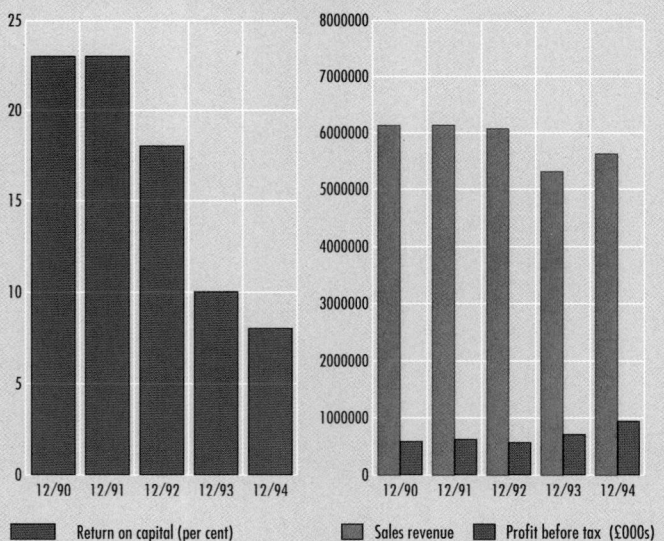

The group's principal activity is the provision of personal financial services, particularly those associated with mortgages and the residential property market. The business includes UK retail banking, life assurance and treasury operations. Established as a building society in 1944, the conversion to a public limited company took place in 1989 in tandem with a public offer of shares and a stock market listing in London. Acquisitions since flotation include Scottish Mutual Assurance for £288 million and HMC Group for £58 million. In April 1995 the company announced it sought to re-open merger talks with National & Provincial Building Society.

25-28 EUROPE'S TOP 100: ANALYSIS

25 Banque Nationale de Paris FRA

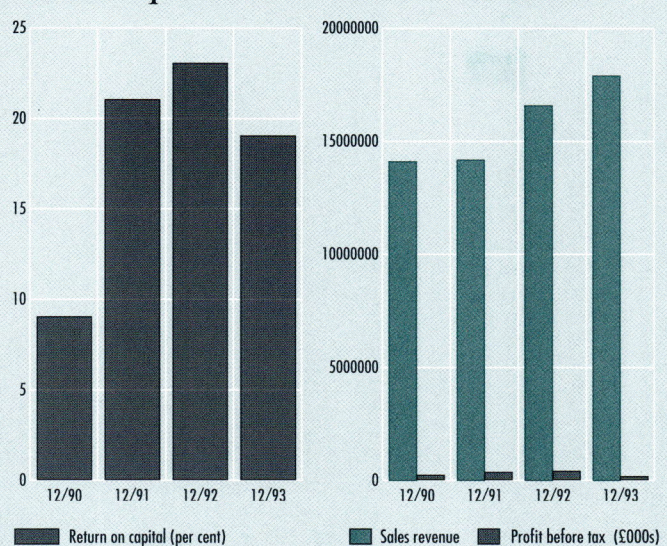

■ Return on capital (per cent) ■ Sales revenue ■ Profit before tax (£000s)

The bank provides retail banking services through 2,000 branches nationwide and a telematics network. A range of financial products and services is provided to 4.5 million consumers and one-third of France's small and medium-sized businesses. Its international network consists of 735 offices in 77 countries, covering services in four main areas: conventional banking, specialised finance (particularly in foreign trade), investment banking, and international and private banking. The bank has forged alliances with Germany's Dresdner Bank and Union des Assurances de Paris (UAP), France's biggest insurance company.

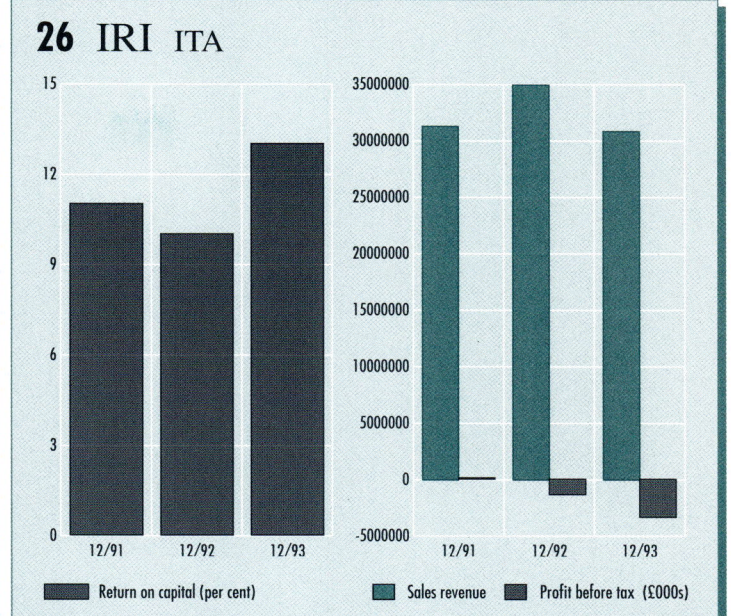

26 IRI ITA

■ Return on capital (per cent) ■ Sales revenue ■ Profit before tax (£000s)

Italy's largest industrial holding company is state-controlled but assets are being divested under the Italian government's privatisation programme. The group operates in the industrial and service sectors and in banking. Its main consolidated assets comprise Alitalia, the Italian flag-carrier airline; RAI, the television and radio entity; and Iritel, a telecommunications venture that is now part of the national telecommunications company Telecom Italia. Companies that have already been privatised include Ilva, the steel producer, and Banca Commerciale Italiana.

27 Swiss Bank Corporation SWI

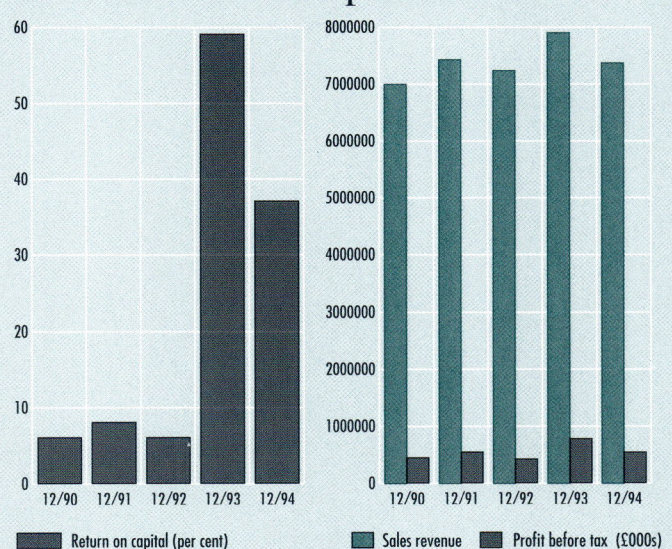

■ Return on capital (per cent) ■ Sales revenue ■ Profit before tax (£000s)

The group undertakes all forms of banking, with more than 300 branches in Switzerland and operations in London, New York, Chicago, Houston, Miami, San Francisco, Tokyo, Singapore and Bahrain. Subsidiaries are organised by sector, which comprise banks, finance and investment companies, services and real estate, and foreign banks. In May 1995 the group announced the acquisition of S.G. Warburg, the British merchant bank, for £860 million. The agreement excluded Mercury Asset Management, which was 75 per cent owned by Warburg. Swiss Bank Corporation was established in 1872.

28 British Telecommunications UK

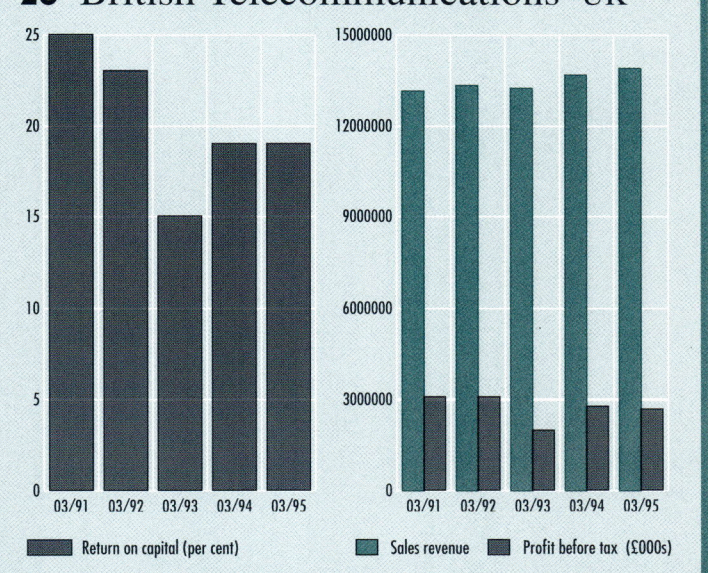

■ Return on capital (per cent) ■ Sales revenue ■ Profit before tax (£000s)

Alongside its traditional business of providing telephone services for residential and commercial customers, primarily in Britain but increasingly overseas, BT is developing interests in information technology, mobile telecommunications, satellite and multi-media. Formerly part of a single entity with the Post Office, the company reorganised as a statutory corporation in 1984 and subsequently privatised through a public offer of shares in three tranches. It acquired a 20 per cent interest in America's MCI in 1994, investing a total of $4.3 billion. The two companies then formed Concert, a $1 billion joint venture to provide global communications for multinational customers.

EUROPE'S TOP 100: ANALYSIS 29-32

29 Ente Nazionale Idrocarburi ITA

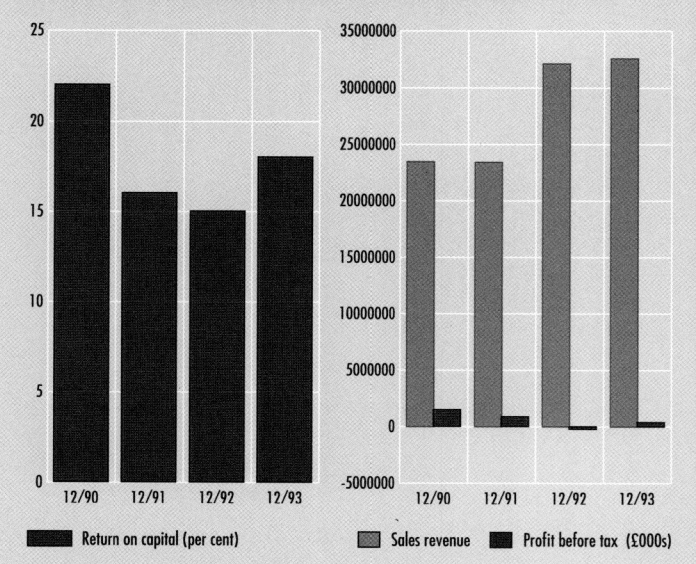

The company's main business is the exploitation of energy resources, principally oil, natural gas and nuclear fuels; crude oil refining; and the distribution of energy products in Italy. The company also has interests in coal mining and the manufacture of a broad range of chemicals and plastics. Subsidiaries in the machinery, manufacturing, engineering and services division are involved in infrastructure projects, including electrical power plants and urban transport. The main consolidated companies within the group include Agip and Enichem. Established in 1953, ENI is 100 per cent owned by the Italian government, which is committed to the company's eventual privatisation.

30 Instituto Mobiliare Italiano ITA

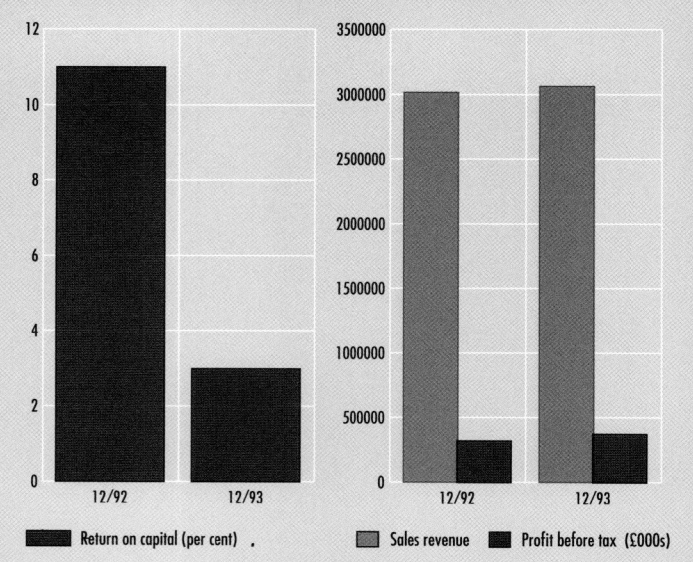

The group operates as an investment bank and offers a range of lending services to state and local entities and to industrial, commercial and service institutions. It also offers personal financial products and advisory services related primarily to individuals resident in Italy and conducts investment banking activities such as brokerage, market-making, underwriting and syndication of eurobonds and equities, foreign exchange and money market trading in Italy and abroad. Italy's ministry of the Treasury is a significant shareholder in IMI, which became a public limited company in 1990.

31 Instituto Nacional de Industria SPA

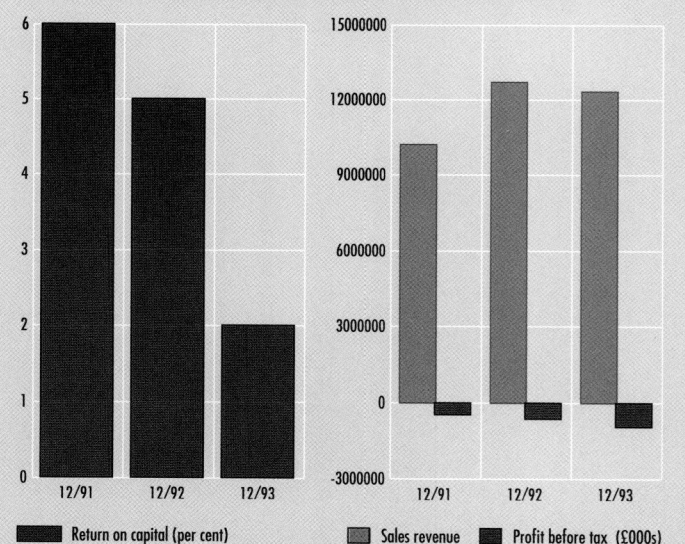

The company, a state-owned corporation, formed Teneo SA, its main subsidiary, to embrace holdings in 47 companies considered viable to compete against private sector entities. Teneo's activities span energy, transport, equipment industries, process industries and corporate services. Principal subsidiaries are CSI (50 per cent owned), and Sidenor (50 per cent) in iron and steel; Aesa Group, Astana and Barreras in naval construction; Santa Barbara and Bazan in defence; and Hunosa, Figaredo and Presur in mining. The company was established in 1941 and was converted from an autonomous government agency to a state corporation in 1989.

32 Hanson UK

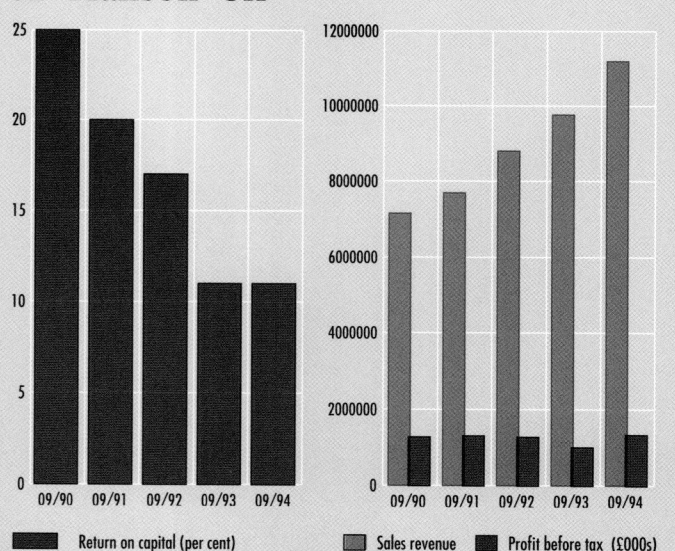

The company acts as an industrial management company for a group engaged in coal mining, chemicals and other industrial products, tobacco, propane, other consumer products, aggregates, forest products and building materials. Subsidiaries in the industrial sector include Peabody (coal mining), Quantum Chemical Co., and Grove Worldwide Co. (cranes). In consumer products Hanson owns Imperial Tobacco, whose brands include Regal, Embassy, Lambert & Butler and St Bruno. Building products subsidiaries take in ARC (aggregates, concrete products and waste management), Cavenham Forest Industries, London Brick and Jacuzzi.

33-36 EUROPE'S TOP 100: ANALYSIS

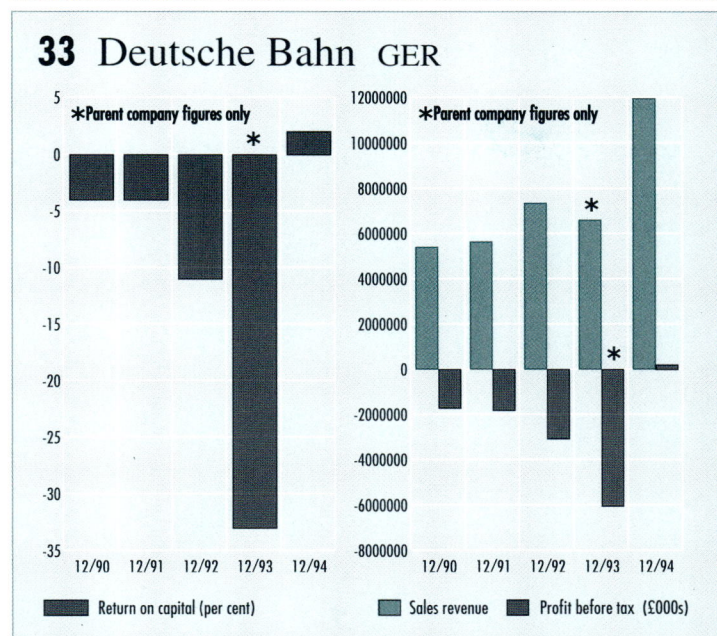

33 Deutsche Bahn GER

The company, which is state owned, operates freight and passenger rail services, including suburban and metropolitan transport systems, throughout Germany. The mainline network comprises 18,521 kilometres, and branch lines 8,252 kilometres. There are also interests in buses, travel agencies, advertising, telecommunications, quarrying, cleaning and housing. The company was established in 1949 and was formerly known as Deutsche Bundesbahn. A merger with the Deutsche Reichsbahn, railway company of the former East Germany, was initiated in 1991. Government subsidies are gradually being reduced.

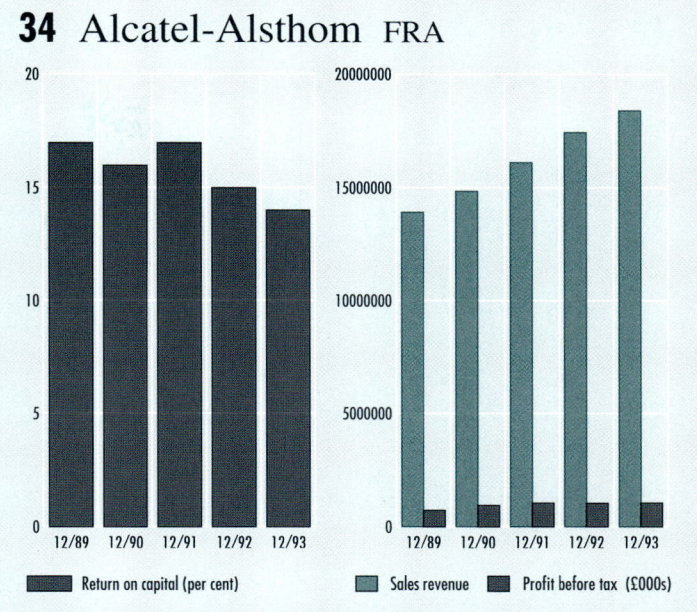

34 Alcatel-Alsthom FRA

The group has two main units. Alcatel provides communications systems for civil and military applications, including public telephone networks, mobile communications, radio transmission systems, railway signalling and space and defence systems. GEC Alsthom, a joint venture with Britain's GEC, has divisions operating in powerplants, power transmission and distribution, nuclear power reactors, transportation, robotics and marine equipment, and electrical engineering. There is a third unit, providing services in publishing, media, finance, data processing, general contracting and rental and leasing of consumer products. The French government offered its shares in the company to the public in 1987.

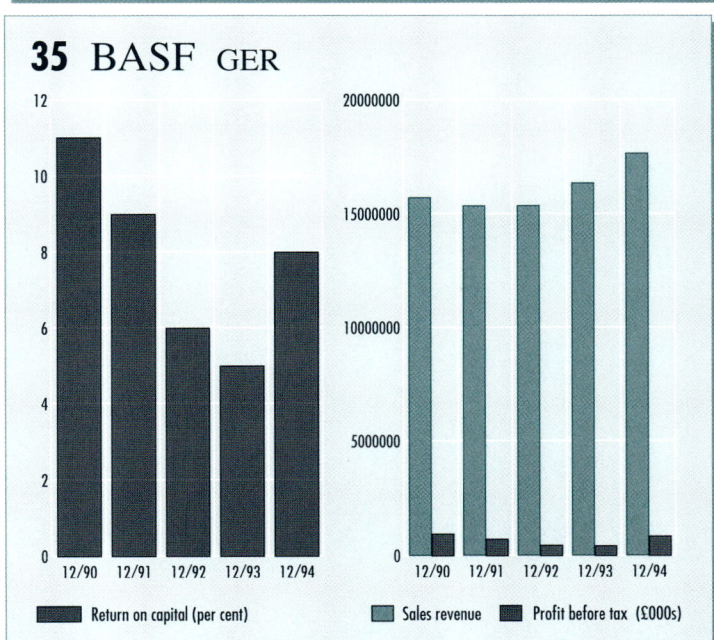

35 BASF GER

BASF, one of the largest chemical groups in the world, is engaged in a great number of activities through divisions in products for agriculture; oil and gas; plastics and fibres; chemicals; dyestuffs and finishing products; and consumer products. It also has interests in the sale of plant and equipment, electricity supply and the provision of rental services. Established in 1865, difficult market conditions in 1925 led to the amalgamation of the company and Germany's other foremost chemical companies into I.G. Farbenindustrie AG, which was dissolved in 1945. The company was reconstituted in its present form in 1952. The name was changed from Badische Anilin- & Soda-Fabrik in 1973.

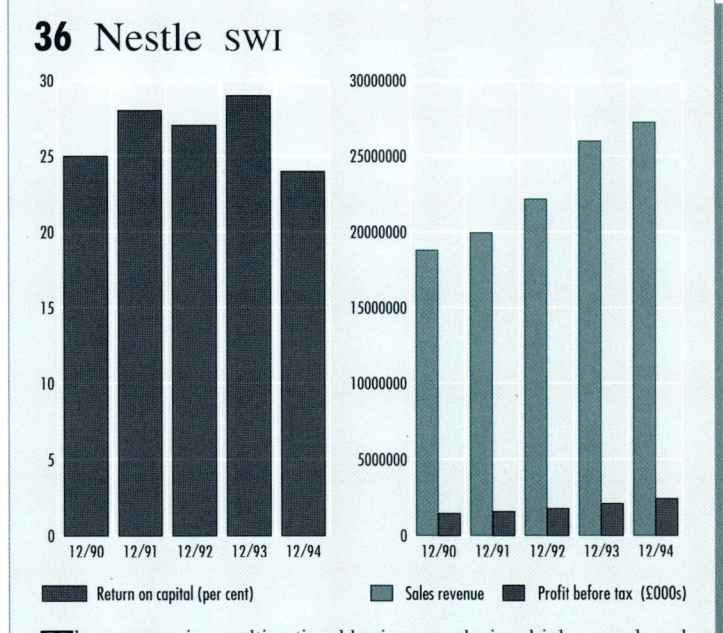

36 Nestle SWI

The company is a multi-national business producing drinks, cereals and milks, culinary products, chocolate and confectionery, and cosmetics. In 1988 the company acquired Britain's Rowntree chocolate and confectionery business and one year later a joint venture was established with the US group general Mills to produce breakfast cereals under the Nestle brand name. The company's origins can be traced back to the opening of the first European condensed milk factory in 1866. The group itself resulted from the merger of two companies, Anglo-Swiss Condensed Milk Co. and Farine Lectee Henry Nestle, in 1905.

EUROPE'S TOP 100: ANALYSIS   37-40

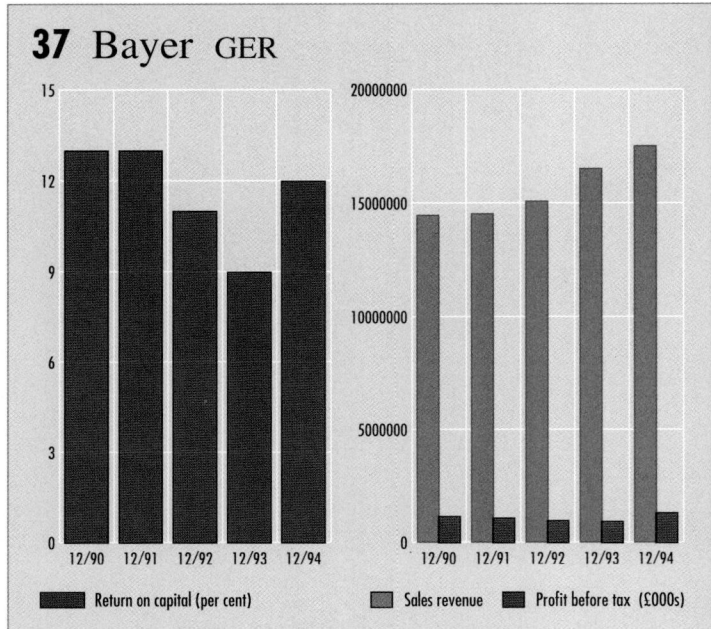

37 Bayer GER

The company is an international, broadly diversified chemicals and healthcare group with operations in some 150 countries. Its 21 business groups are organised in six divisions: polymers, organic products, industrial products, healthcare, agrochemicals and imaging technologies. A new division, speciality products, is established from January 1, 1996 to incorporate activities serving the paper and leather industries and the production of dyestuffs for paints and plastics. In 1994 the company acquired Sterling Winthrop's North American over-the-counter drugs business for $1 billion.

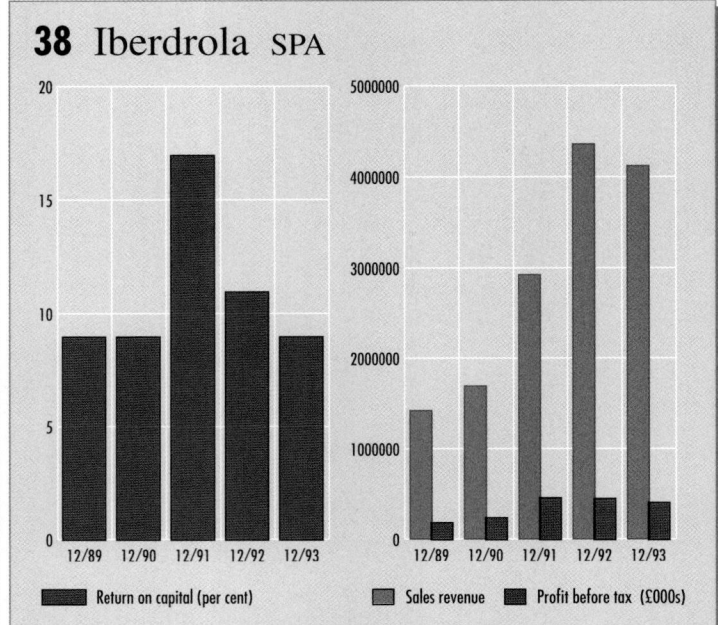

38 Iberdrola SPA

The company produces and distributes electricity in 15 autonomous communities in north-western Spain covering 204,134 sq kilometres, with more than eight million customers. The company has hydroelectric, nuclear, coal and gas-fired generating capacity. Other activities include engineering, information technology, property and insurance. Main consolidated subsidiaries are Hidroelectrica de Cataluna, Cia Electrica Coquense (54 per cent owned), Valores Mobiliarios y Energia and Iberdrola International. In 1992 the company acquired Hidroelectrica Espanola (Hidrola), which was subsequently renamed Iberdrola II.

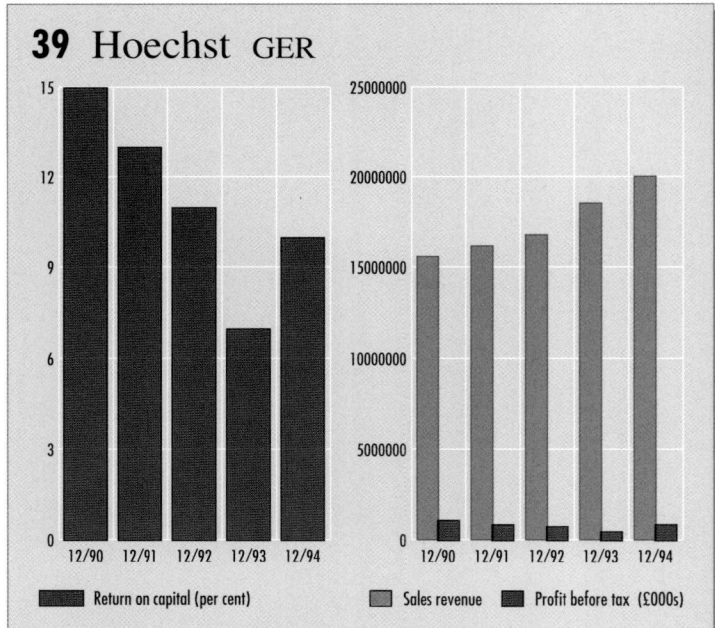

39 Hoechst GER

Pharmaceuticals play a growing role within Hoechst, whose pre-eminence in German manufacturing was based on its traditional strength in chemicals and fibres. Hoechst principally operates in chemicals and colour; fibres and polymers; and pharmaceuticals and cosmetics. The company has interests in engineering and technology, and in agriculture. In 1995 a controlling stake was acquired in Marion Merrell Dow for $7.15 billion, providing a powerful position in the US drugs market, and Dow Chemical's Latin American pharmaceuticals business was acquired for around $200 million. In 1994 the European viscose and acrylic fibre activities were merged in a joint venture with Britain's Courtaulds.

40 National Westminster Bank UK

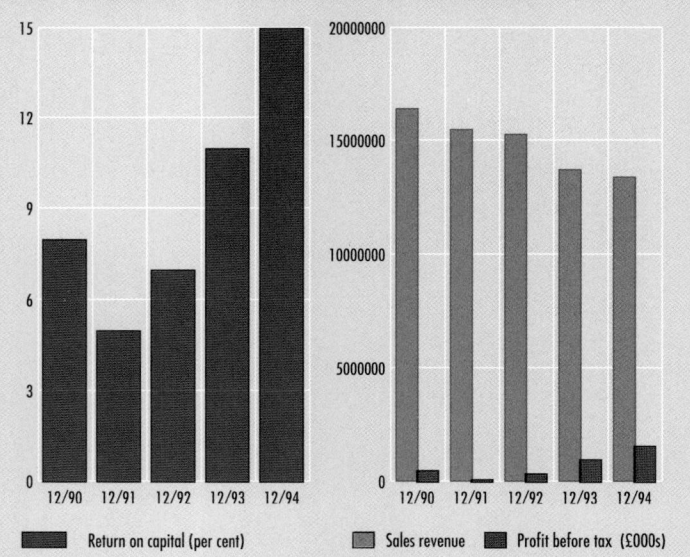

The bank and its subsidiaries provide a range of banking and financial services through offices and branches in the United Kingdom and overseas. Activities comprise the UK branch business, US retail operations, international businesses and NatWest Markets. Subsidiaries include Ulster Bank, Coutts & Co., and Lombard North Central. In March 1994 the $500 million acquisition of Citizens First Bancorp of New Jersey was announced, followed in June 1994 by the $300 million purchase of Central Jersey Bancorp. National Westminster Bank was formed in 1968 through the merger of National Provincial Bank (established 1833) and Westminster Bank (established 1836).

41-44 EUROPE'S TOP 100: ANALYSIS

41 Schweizerische Nationalbank SWI

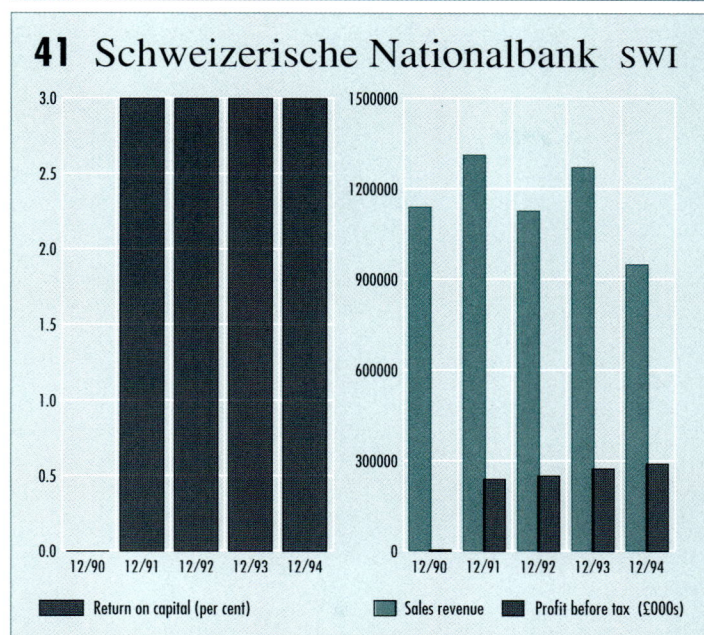

The bank carries out the main functions of a central bank with respect to money, foreign exchange and interest rates. Its network of agencies are managed by cantonal banks across Switzerland, with branches located in Aarau, Basle, Geneva, Lausanne, Lucerne, Lugano, Neichatel, and Saint-Gallen. Established in 1907, the bank's principal shareholders include the Canton of Berne and the Canton of Zurich, who receive and additional dividend each year of SFr0.80 per head of population.

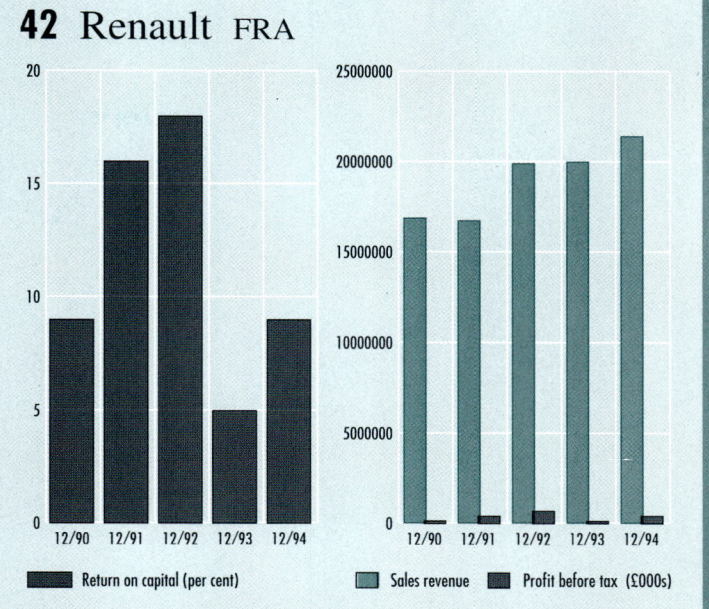

42 Renault FRA

The company's main activity is the design, production and sale of passenger and commercial vehicles in France and abroad, complemented by a range of financing and service operations related to the motor industry and road transport. The company was founded by Louis Renault in 1898, and was reformed and nationalised in 1945. A partial privatisation took place in 1994, valuing the company at FFr40 billion, with the state selling a 28 per cent interest. The introduction of private investors followed the failure of proposals to merger the automotive operations of Renault and Volvo AB after widespread opposition in both France and Sweden.

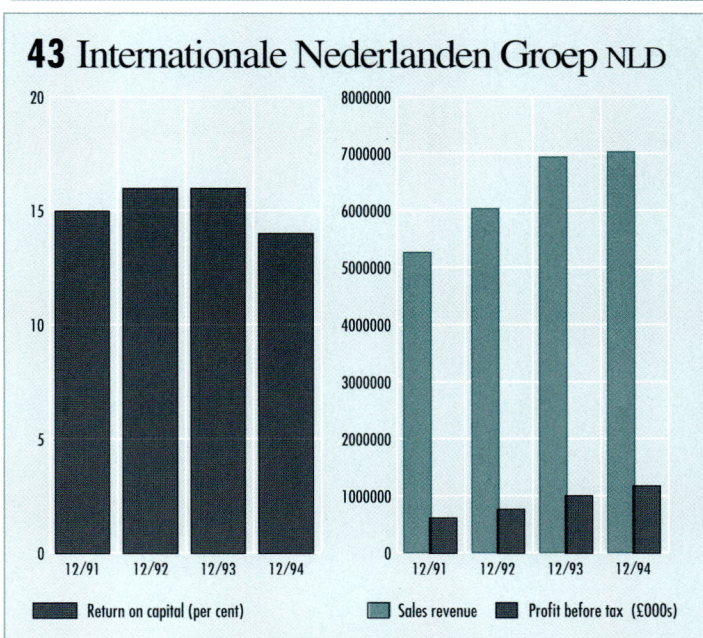

43 Internationale Nederlanden Groep NLD

Activities are divided among four management centres: ING Nederland (domestic banking and insurance activities); ING Financial Services International (international insurance activities and retail and commercial banking outside the Netherlands); ING Corporate and Capital Markets (with emphasis on emerging markets, treasury, trading and sales, investment banking and corporate finance); ING Asset Management (asset management and account management for institutional investors and international banking for high net worth individuals); and real estate. In 1995 ING acquired most of the business of Barings, the British merchant bank, from administrators for £660 million.

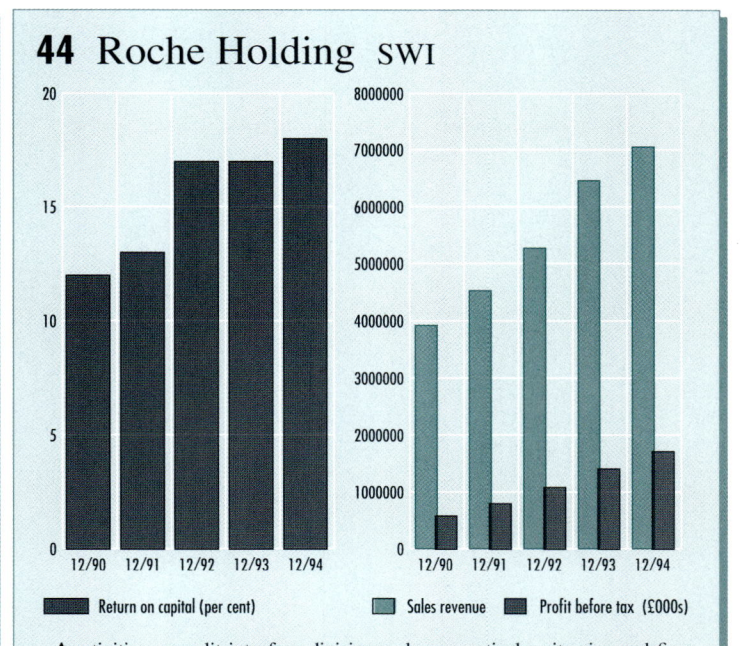

44 Roche Holding SWI

Activities are split into four divisions: pharmaceuticals; vitamins and fine chemicals; diagnostics; fragrances and flavourings. Until 1989 the company, formerly named F. Hoffman-La Roche, maintained a dual structure, with the Roche Group controlling subsidiaries in continental Europe, Scandinavia and Mediterranean countries, while the SAPAC Corporation (Canada) was the holding company for subsidiaries in the remaining regions, including the UK, North and South America, Asia and Oceania, and central and southern parts of Africa. Then a pure holding company was established to head the group, and all operational assets and liabilities were transferred to a new Swiss-based operating company.

EUROPE'S TOP 100: ANALYSIS   45-48

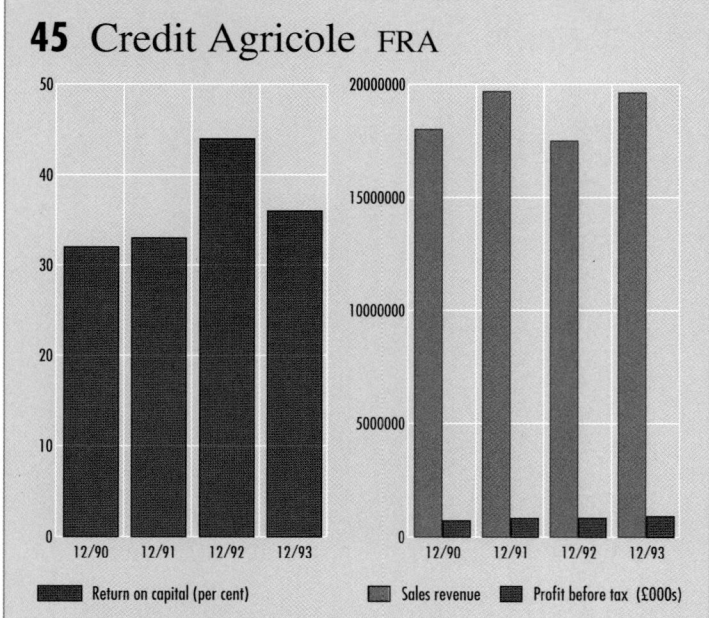

45 Credit Agricole FRA

The company is the leading banking institution for France's farming community. It has a three-tier structure, with 2,900 local branches grouped into 73 regional banks. The regional banks, in turn, own 91 per cent of the capital of Caisse Nationale de Credit Agricole, the central body and co-ordinating bank. The remaining nine per cent is held by current and former employees. The company is the largest bank in France in terms of market share. It has the largest retail banking network and is the leading bank for private individuals. It trades in 17 countries.

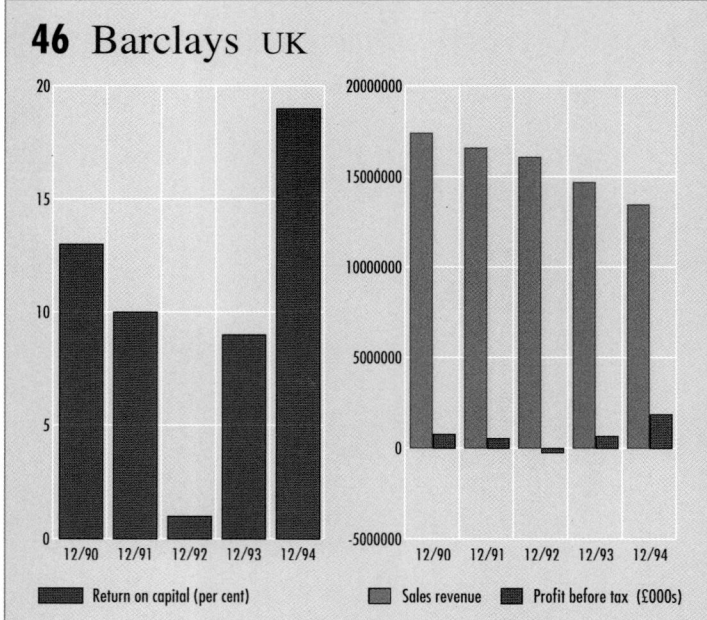

46 Barclays UK

Barclays' principal businesses are the UK retail bank and BZW, its international investment bank. A range of commercial and investment banking, insurance and related services is provided through 2,400 UK branches, with a further 1,000 offices overseas in 77 countries. UK banking services include Barclaycard and a leasing and factoring group. Barclays Financial Services, embracing Barclays Life, conducts pensions, life and general insurance and trustee activities. Corporate and Institutional Banking Services, established in 1994, serves large corporate and institutional customers. The European Retail Banking Group operates in France, Spain, Portugal and Germany.

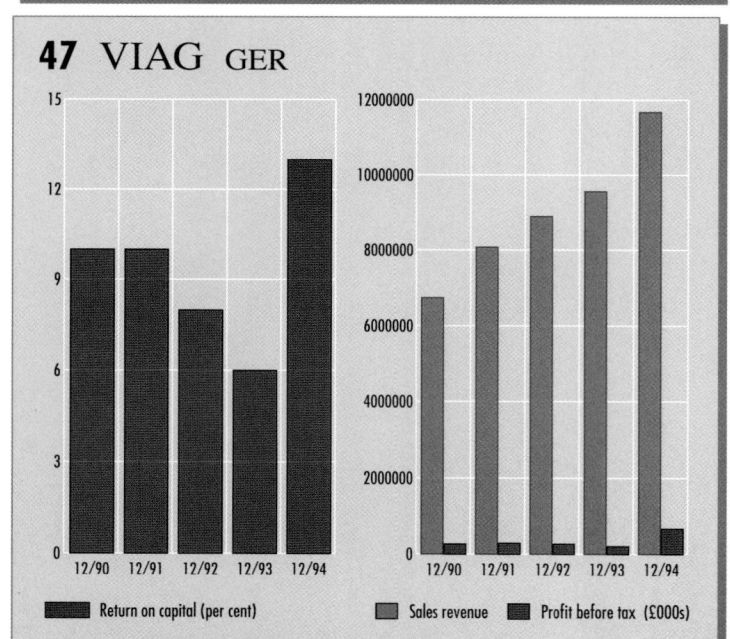

47 VIAG GER

Group activities are organised in eight divisions: energy (generation and distribution of electricity and the transport and distribution of gas); aluminium (production and processing of aluminium and aluminium products and metal trading); chemicals (manufacture of chemical and metallurgical products); metal packaging; trading and services (steel, raw materials, chemical and mechanical engineering products, and textiles); and transport and logistics. VIAG was established as a holding company for state-owned corporations in the energy, aluminium and chemicals sectors. In 1986 the government sold 40 per cent of its holding through a public share offer.

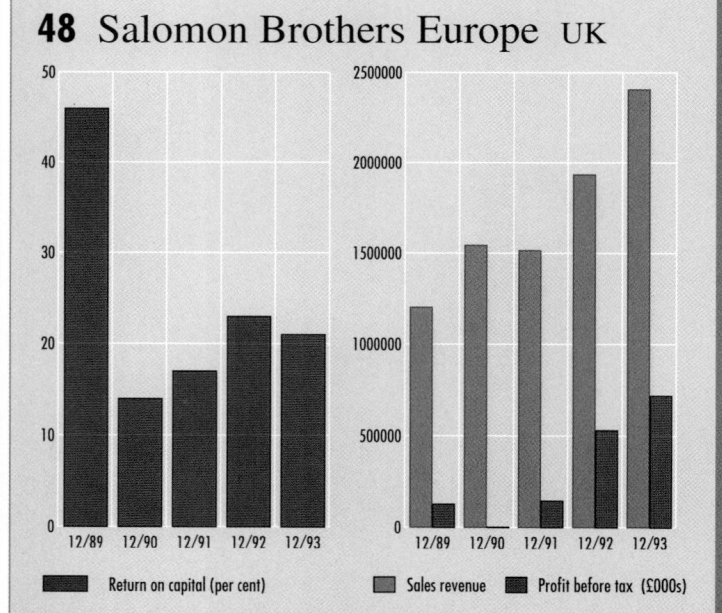

48 Salomon Brothers Europe UK

The group, which is wholly owned by Salomon Inc (USA), conducts business in securities, mortgage lending and asset management. Subsidiaries comprise Salomon Brothers International (financial services), Salomon Brothers UK (gilt edged market maker), Salomon Brothers UK Equity (equity market maker), The Mortgage Corporation Group and The Residential Mortgage Company. The company was incorporated in 1981 and was formerly known as Phibro UK and Phibro-Salomon.

EUROPE'S TOP 100: ANALYSIS

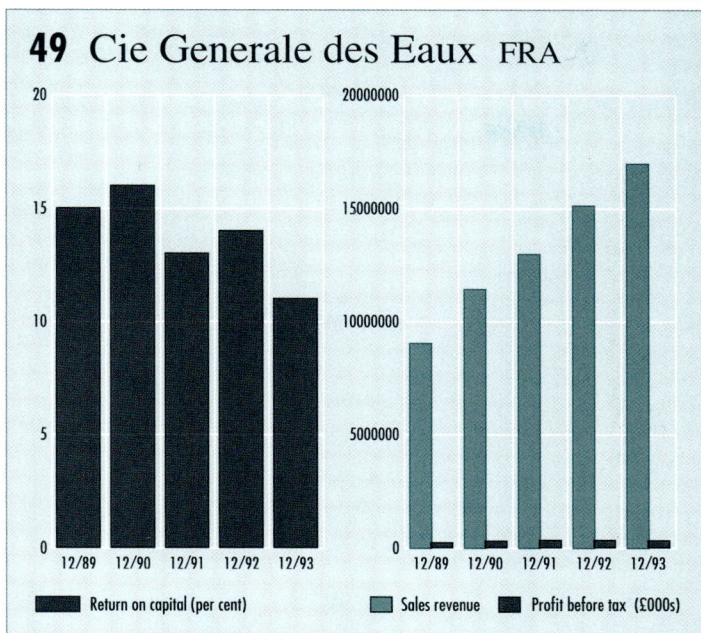

49 Cie Generale des Eaux FRA

The company treats, purifies and distributes water in Paris and elsewhere in France and abroad, and provides district heating, urban transport and public cleaning services. It is active in thermal energy, fuel trading, electrical contracting, waste management, communications, health, real estate, civil engineering and construction, and residential property. A UK subsidiary, General Utilities, holds interests in local water supply in Britain, with investments in South Staffordshire Water, Tendring Hundred Waterworks, Mid Kent Water and Folkestone and District Water. Interests in communications in Britain include investments in General Cable and GMC Talkland. The company was established in 1853.

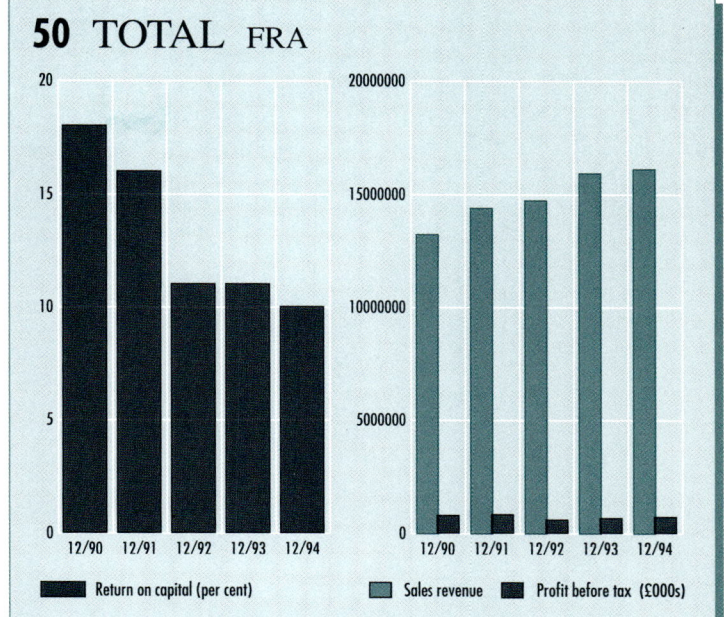

50 TOTAL FRA

The group is involved in all sectors of the oil and gas industry and has interests in chemicals, shipping, mining and solar energy. It holds onshore and offshore permits and interests in mainland Europe, the UK and Ireland, Africa, America, the Middle East and Far East, and Australia. The company was founded by 1924 on the initiative of the French state by a syndicate of industrialists and financiers as an oil exploration and production company. The TOTAL brand name was introduced in 1954. The company's name was changed from Cie Francaise des Petroles to Total Cie Francaise des Petroles in 1985 and to Total in 1991. The French government reduced its holding to 5.4 per cent from 31.7 per cent in 1992.

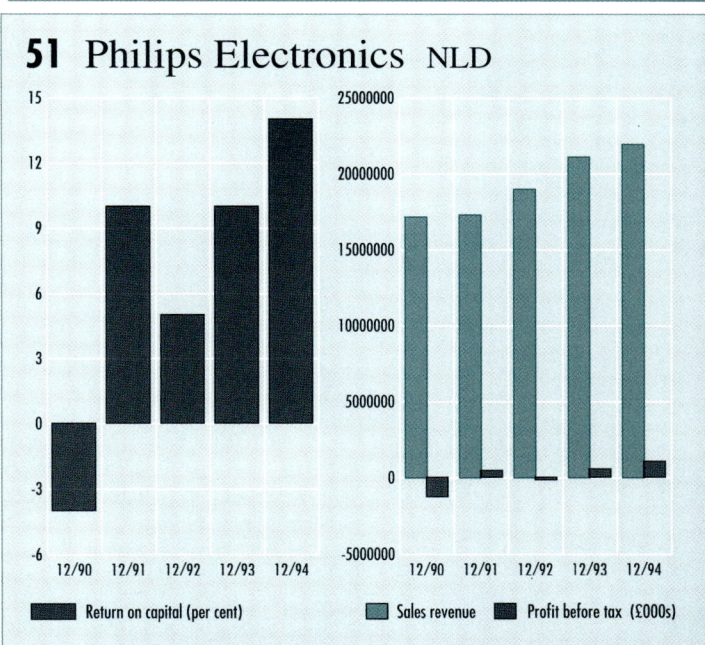

51 Philips Electronics NLD

The company's activities, organised in product divisions, are spread across the world. Products, systems and services are delivered in the fields of lighting, consumer electronics, music and film, multi-media, domestic appliances and personal care, components, semi conductors, communications systems, medical systems and industrial electronics. The company suffered losses in 1990 and 1992, during the course of a lengthy restructuring that included the sale of its defence unit and the disposal of the remaining 47 per cent interest in Whirlpool International. Philips holds 75 per cent of PolyGram, whose shares are listed separately in Amsterdam.

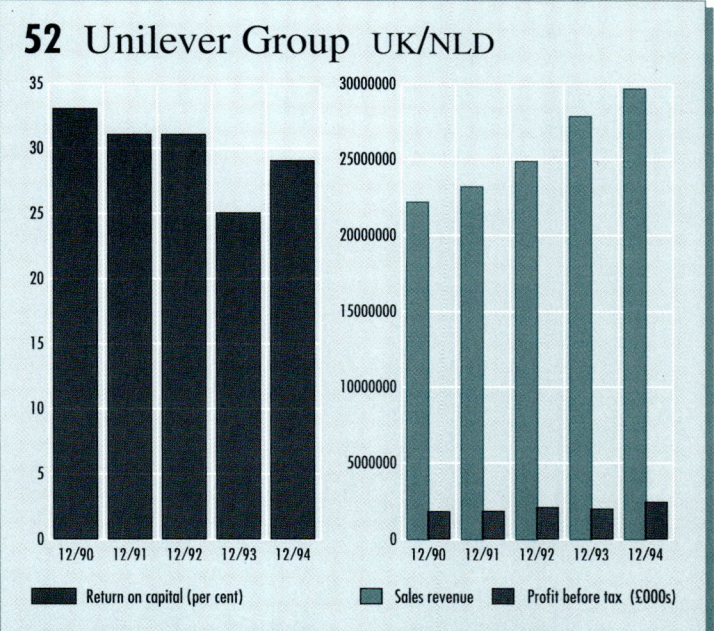

52 Unilever Group UK/NLD

The group's business comprises branded and packaged consumer goods and speciality chemicals. Product groups comprise foods (oil and dairy-based foods, beverages, snacks, meals and meal components); detergents (washing powders, soaps, domestic and industrial cleaning products and systems); personal products (personal and skin care products, toothpastes, hair care products, perfumes and deodorants); speciality chemicals (starches, speciality resins, adhesives, fragrances and flavours and medical diagnostics). In 1937 the company assumed control of assets owned by Lever Brothers and Unilever Ltd outside the then British Empire.

EUROPE'S TOP 100: ANALYSIS   53-56

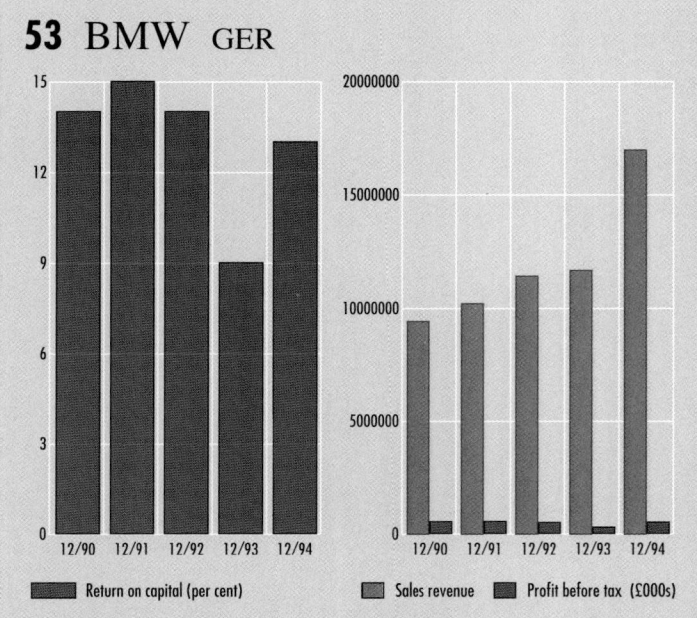

53 BMW GER

The company's main business is the manufacture, sale and leasing of cars and motorcycles. Other divisions operate in aircraft engine production, electronic systems and hardware production, and finance services. In January 1994 the company announced the acquisition of Rover Group Holdings, the British vehicle manufacturer, from British Aerospace for £800 million. Following the acquisition, BMW proposed to invest a further £800 million in Rover to upgrade manufacturing activities. Separately, BMW signed an agreement to supply components for Rolls-Royce Motors, a subsidiary of Vickers. In 1994 the enlarged BMW group sold 931,880 vehicles.

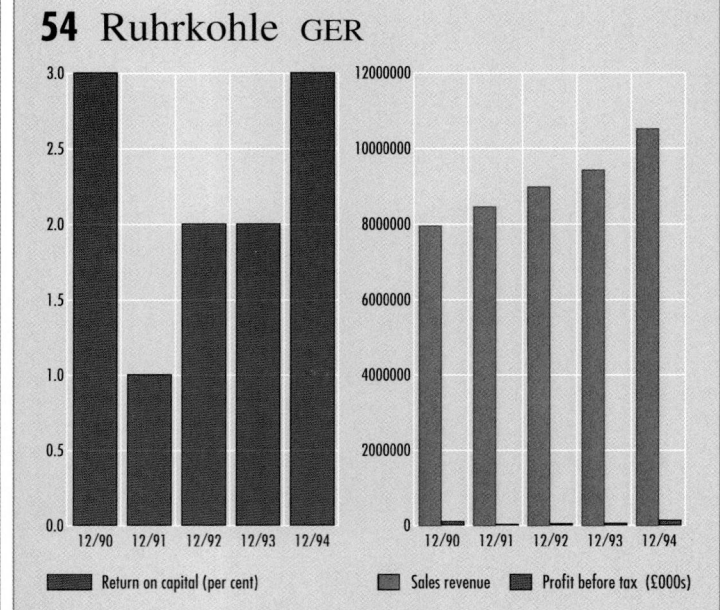

54 Ruhrkohle GER

The main activities of the company are mining and processing of coal and other minerals. The company also produces gas and supplies electricity and heating for residential and industrial use, and is involved in the manufacture of chemicals. In 1994 the company sold 44.5 million tonnes of coal. Veba, the industrial holding company, is a significant shareholder, owning an interest of more than 25 per cent. Ruhrkohle was established in 1968. UK subsidiaries include Isola Werke UK and MAS Electronics.

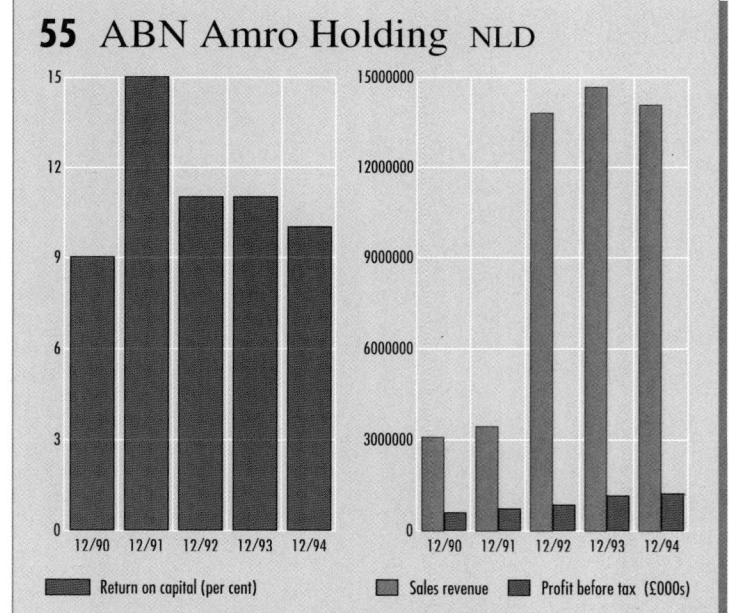

55 ABN Amro Holding NLD

The company is a holding company for the former Algemene Bank Nederland (ABN) and Amsterdam-Rotterdam Bank (AMRO) banking groups. It operates in the Netherlands and abroad, offering a range of banking services. There are around 1,330 domestic branches and more than 500 foreign branches. In the UK the company owns Hoare Govett, the merchant bank, acquired in 1992. In 1995 it was unsuccessful in an attempt to acquire Barings Securities. The merger of Algemene Bank Nederland and Amsterdam-Rotterdam Bank was finalised in September 1991.

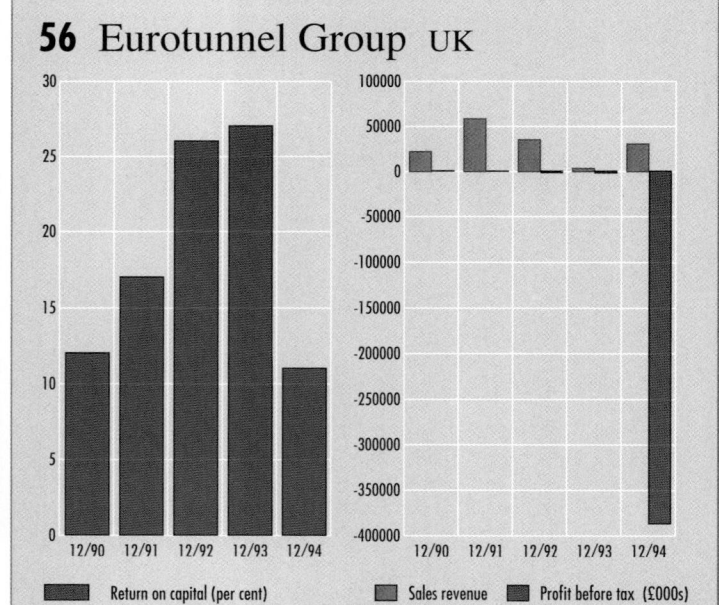

56 Eurotunnel Group UK

Eurotunnel PLC and Eurotunnel SA and their subsidiaries collectively make up the Eurotunnel Group, which operates the Channel tunnel rail link between Britain and France under the terms of a concession that expires in the year 2052. The concession agreement provides that revenues and costs shall be shared equally between the United Kingdom and French companies. Eurotunnel was incorporated in 1985 to design, finance, construct and subsequently operate the fixed rail link. Its shares were introduced to the stock exchange in London and Paris in 1987. The project was formally opened in 1994.

57-60 EUROPE'S TOP 100: ANALYSIS

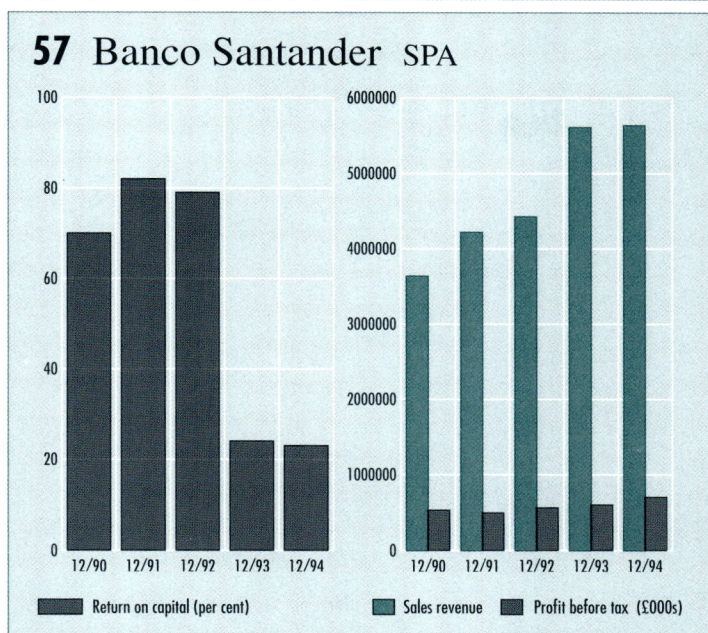

57 Banco Santander SPA

The bank's branch network covers the whole of Spain, the main areas of conceNtration being Andalucia, Castilla-Leon, Catalonia, Madrid, Valencia and Cantabria. The main business areas are retail banking, corporate banking, treasury and capital markets, and investment banking. Subsidiaries are also active in security investment, pension fund management, finance and real estate. The bank was established in 1857 to operate in the Santander region and has expanded through acquisition and merger. In 1984 it participated in the rescue of the Rumasa Group in collaboration with the Spanish Treasury.

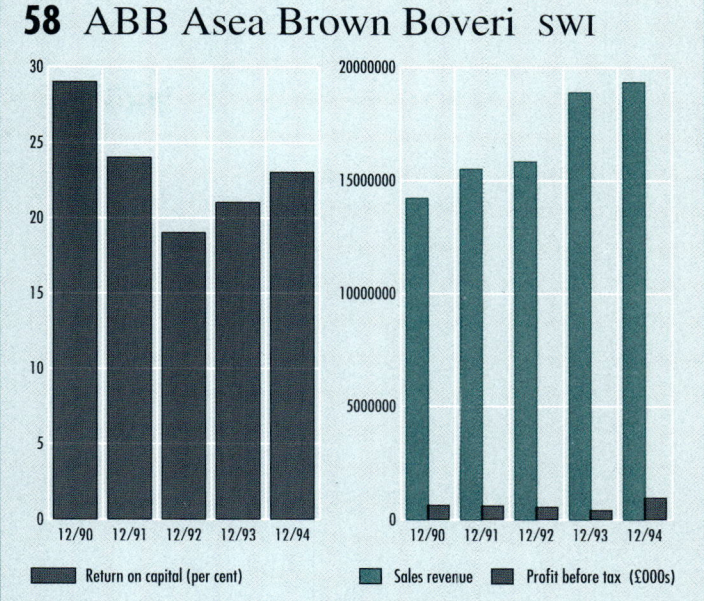

58 ABB Asea Brown Boveri SWI

This holding company is active in electric power generation, transmission and distribution, as well as industrial and building systems and rail transportation. With headquarters in Zurich, the company is jointly owned by Asea AB of Sweden, and BBC Brown Boveri, of Switzerland, whose worldwide engineering activities were merged to form ABB in 1988; their respective chairmen act as joint chairmen of the company. In March 1995 the company and Daimler-Benz announced plans to merge their rail activities in a joint venture, comprising 50 companies in ABB's transportation segment and the rail activities of the Daimler-Benz subsidiary, AEG.

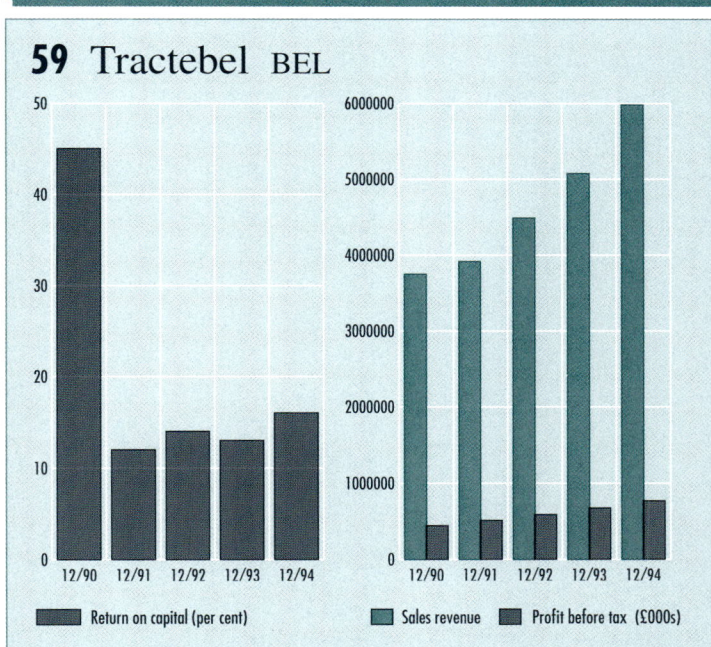

59 Tractebel BEL

The group is organised into seven operating units: Electricity in Belgium (through a 34 per cent interest in Electrabel); Gas in Belgium (through a 33 per cent interest in Distrigas); Electricity and Gas International (with investments outside Belgium held through Powerfin); Communications (cable TV, mobile telephony and computer services); Technical Installations and Services to the Community (through Fabricom, management of technical installations and waste); Real Estate (through Cie Immobiliere de Belgique); and engineering. The company was formed in 1986 through the merger of Tractionel and Electrobel.

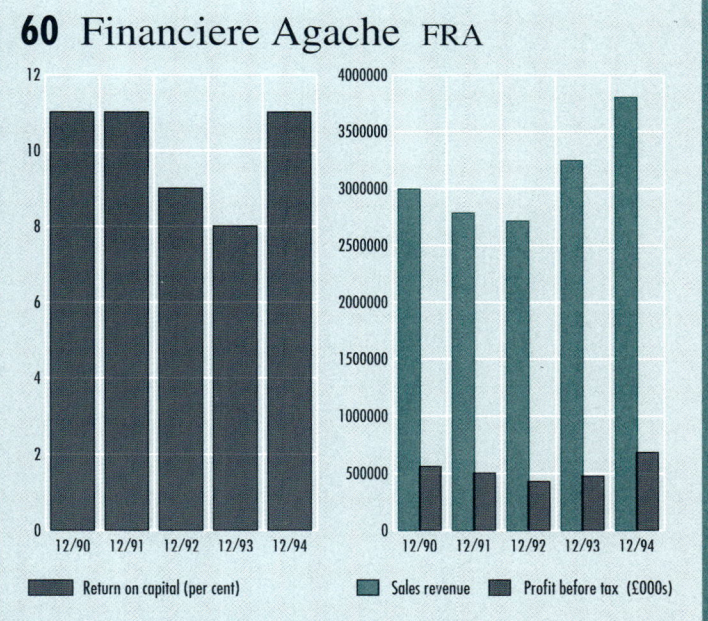

60 Financiere Agache FRA

The holding company's principal subsidiaries are LVMH (champagne and wine, cognac and spirits, luggage, leather goods, perfume and beauty products); Christian Dior (designer clothes and perfume); Celine (clothing, leather goods and accessories); Au Bon Marche (department store); Groupe George V and Sevres Participations et Gestion (property management). LVMH has a 20 per cent interest in Guinness, the British drinks group which, in turn, holds a 34 per cent stake in Moet & Hennesey, LVMH's wines and spirits company. Agache's controlling shareholder is Arnault et Associes.

EUROPE'S TOP 100: ANALYSIS 61-64

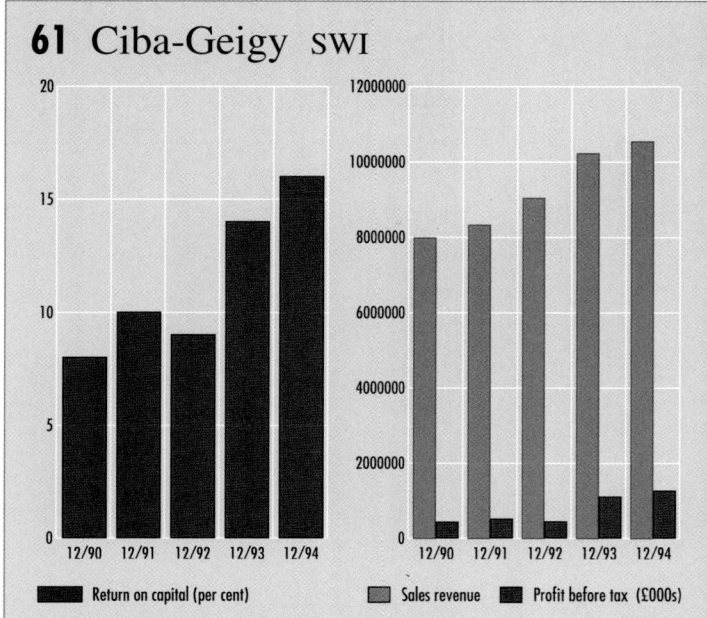

61 Ciba-Geigy SWI

Formed by the merger of Ciba and J.R. Geigy in 1970, the company operates in healthcare (including the production of drugs for heart and circulatory disorders, allergies and respiratory illnesses, and cancer, as well as over-the-counter medicines, diagnostic instruments and contact lenses); agriculture (including herbicides, veterinary products and seeds); and industry (dyestuffs and chemicals for textiles, paper and leather, additives, lubricants, pigments for paint, printing inks, plastics, fibres and adhesives, lightweight components for aviation and analytical instruments)

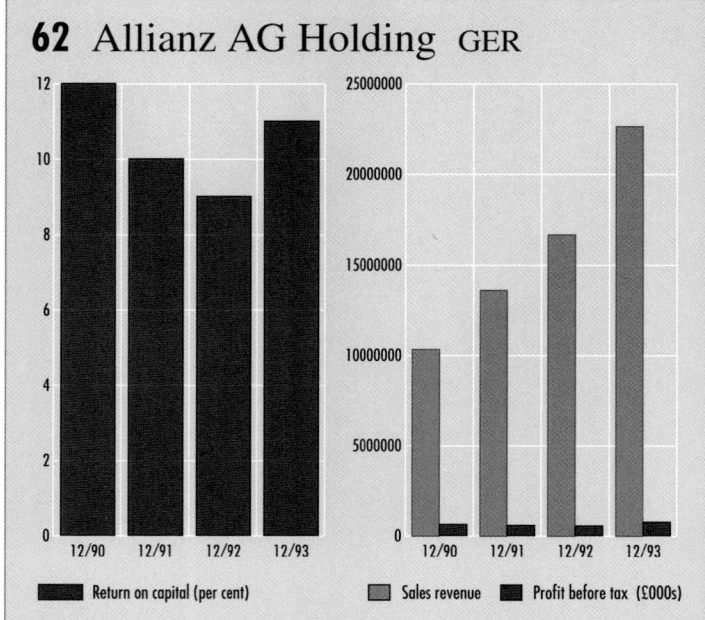

62 Allianz AG Holding GER

The group undertakes all major types of personal and commercial insurance and reinsurance. Domestic business is carried out through Allianz Versicherungs-AG (non-life business) and Allianz Lebensversicherung-AG (life business), while foreign business is carried out by subsidiaries or agents in the rest of Europe, North America, South America, Africa, Asia and Australia. The company was established in 1890; the name was changed from Allianz Versicherungs-AG to Allianz AG Holding in 1985. In the UK the company owns Cornhill Insurance.

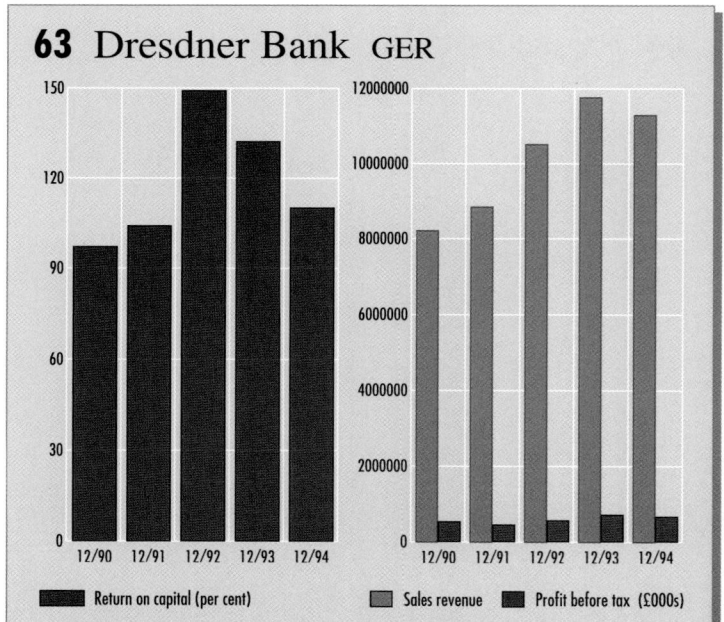

63 Dresdner Bank GER

The group is one of Germany's largest commercial banks, providing banking services and financial services to both corporate and private customers. In addition to the securities commission business, the bank is involved in portfolio management, administration of loans extended under public lending schemes, asset management, management of investment funds, brokerage of insurance policies, savings and loans contracts, and real estate. At the end of 1994 the bank had 1,583 branches in Germany and abroad. In 1995 Dresdner agreed to acquire Britain's Kleinwort Benson merchant banking group for £1 billion.

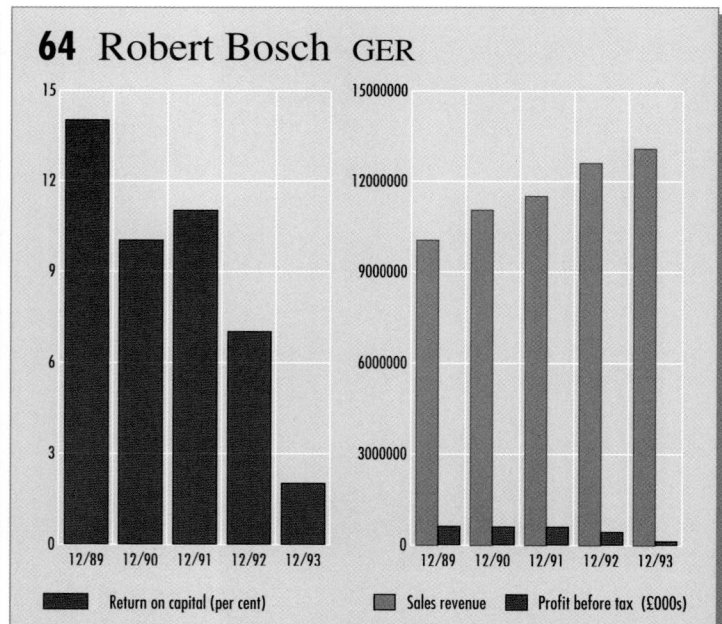

64 Robert Bosch GER

The engineering and industrial company's main divisions operate by product sector. Products include breaking systems, fuel injection equipment, semiconductors and electronic control units (automotive equipment division); traffic information and guidance systems, video and audio equipment, antennas, cable television technology, electronic medical equipment and satellite transmission systems (communications division); household appliances, electric power tools and heating system controls (consumer goods division); confectionery and beverages, packaging machines, industrial electronics (capital goods division). The company is closely controlled by the Robert Bosch Foundation.

EUROPE'S TOP 100: ANALYSIS

65 News International UK

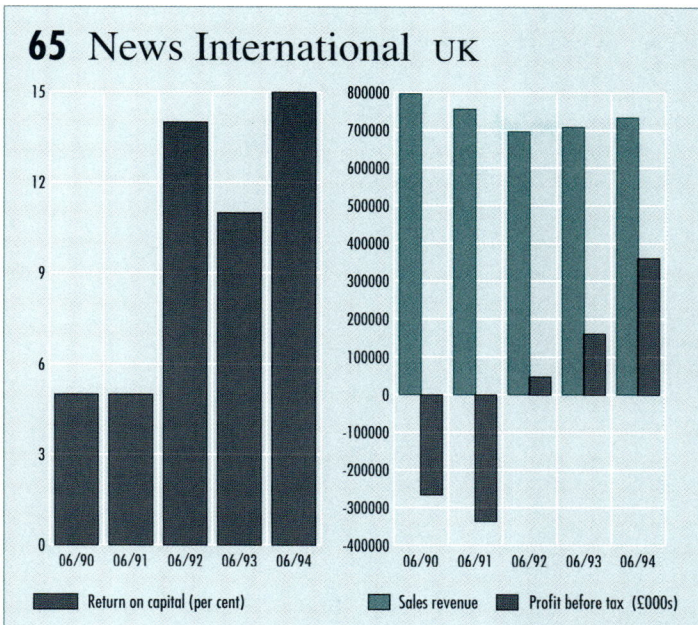

The group's principal activity is the printing and publishing of national newspapers in the UK. Titles include *The Times*, *Sunday Times*, *The Sun*, *News of the World*, and *Today*. The Times Supplements also publishes *The Times Educational Supplement*, *The Times Higher Education Supplement*, *The Times Scottish Education Supplement* and *The Times Literary Supplement*. Other activities include satellite broadcasting (the group holds a 40 per cent interest in British Sky Broadcasting), warehousing, transportation, development and sale of conditional access software and provision of financial services to other areas of The News Corporation, of which the group is a subsidiary.

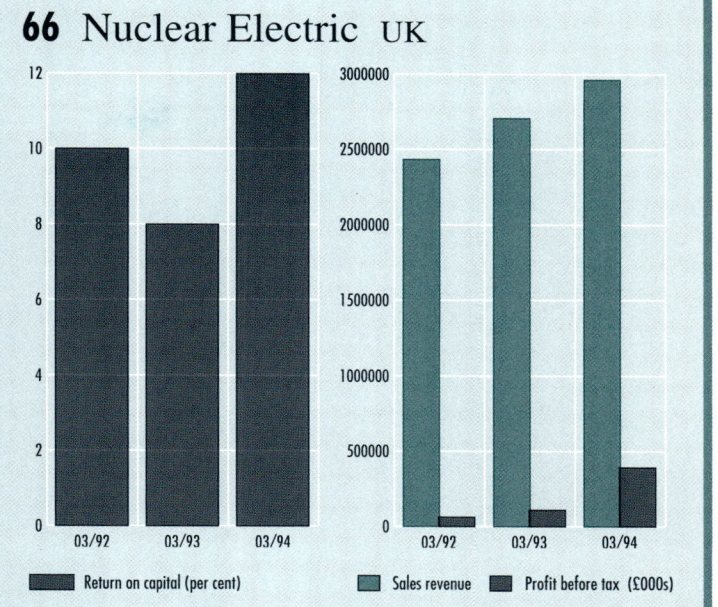

66 Nuclear Electric UK

Activities are focussed on the generation and supply of electricity, and include uranium exploration and mining and insurance. The company operates five advanced gas cooled reactor power stations (Dungeness B, Hartlepool, Heysham 1 and 2, and Hinkley Point B), six Magnox stations (Bradwell, Dungeness A, Hinkley Point A, Oldbury, Sizewell A and Wyfla) and one hydro power station (Maentwrog). A pressurised water reactor exists at Sizewell B. Two Magnox stations at Berkeley and Trawsfynydd are decommissioning. In May 1994 the Government outlined proposals for the privatisation of Nuclear Electric and Scottish Nuclear as a single company.

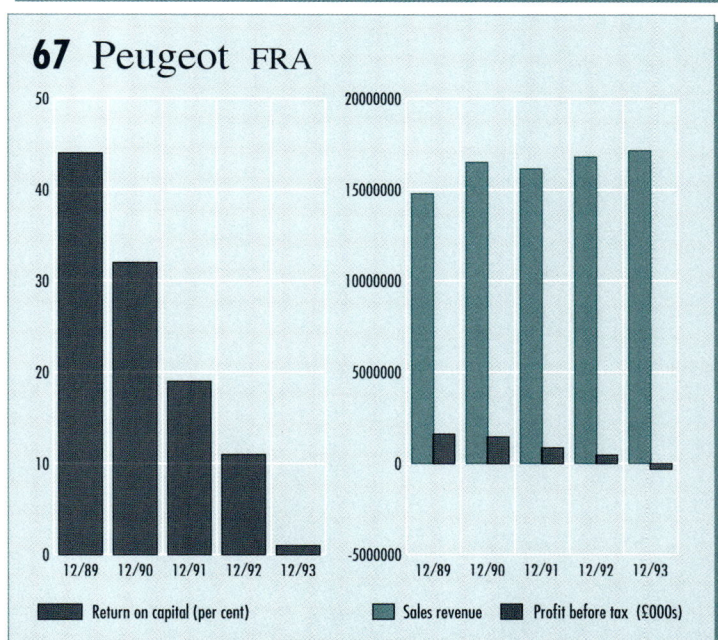

67 Peugeot FRA

The group operates as the holding company of the PSA Peugeot Citroen group, a diversified group of industrial, commercial, financial and services companies, the major constituents of which are Automobiles Peugeot and Automobiles Citroen, which are principally engaged in the manufacture and sale of motor vehicles. The original Peugeot was established in 1896. In 1976 the company merged with Citroen and in 1978 it acquired the major European automotive subsidiaries of Chrysler Corporation, shortly followed by the purchase of Chrysler's European financing and consumer credit subsidiaries. In 1989 the company sold its bicycle division.

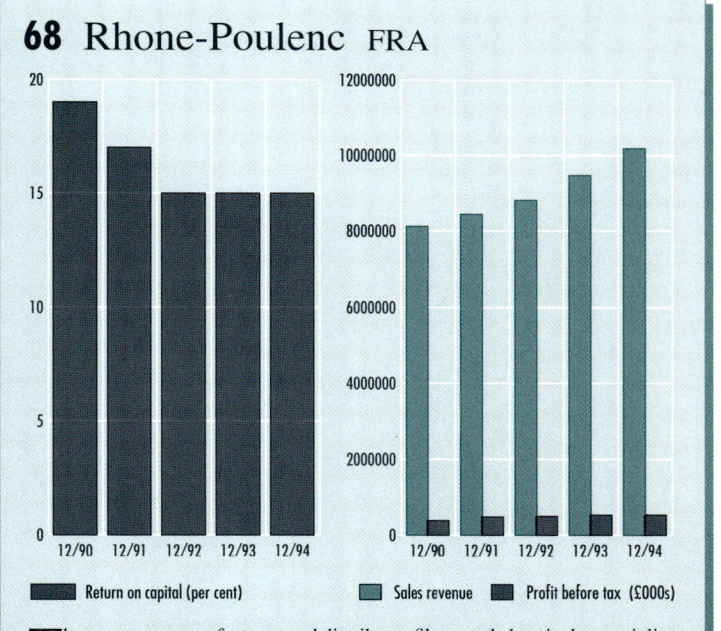

68 Rhone-Poulenc FRA

The company manufactures and distributes fibres and chemicals, speciality chemicals, agrichemicals, and organic and mineral intermediates. It operates in 140 countries. Established in 1961, the company was restructured in 1975 after a series of mergers and takeovers involving Progil, Pechiney and Saint-Gobain. It was nationalised in 1982 but shares were sold back to the public in 1993, with the French state relinquishing most of its holding. Rhone Poulenc's pharmaceuticals activities were merged with America's Rorer Group Inc. to form Rhone-Poulenc Rorer, whose shares were subsequently listed on the New York and Paris stock exchanges.

EUROPE'S TOP 100: ANALYSIS   69-72

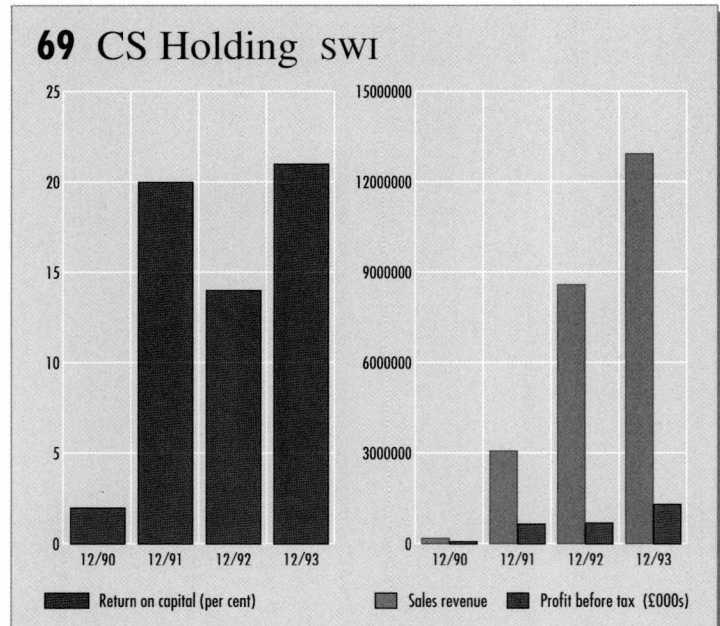

69 CS Holding SWI

Subsidiaries operate in commercial banking, life insurance, energy, industry and non-financial services. Principal subsidiaries comprise Credit Suisse, Swiss Volksbank, Leu Holdings, CS First Boston Group, Fides Informatik and CS Life. Established in 1982 as a sister company to Credit Suisse, it was transformed into the umbrella company for the entire group in 1989 via a share exchange. Swiss Volksbank, a retail banker, was acquired in 1993.

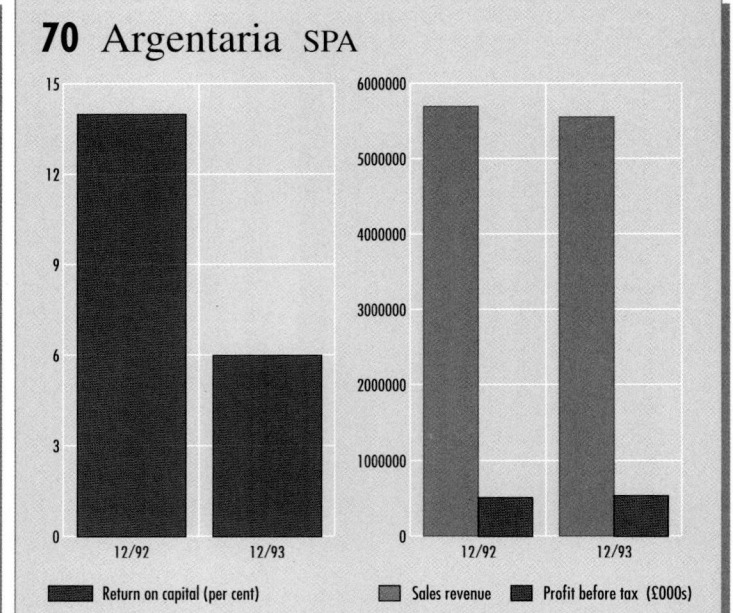

70 Argentaria SPA

The group's main activity is banking, although it also operates in the areas of investment, financial services, insurance and real estate management. In addition to a domestic network of 1,426 offices it is present in a further 28 countries through 87 offices. The group was set up as a result of the reorganisation of the government's principal holdings in credit institutions. In 1991 the government transferred to the company its holdings in Banco Exterior de Espana (BEX), Banco de Credito Industrial (BCI), Banco de Credito Local (BCL), and Banco de Credito Agricola (BCA). The group's were granted a listing on the Madrid stock exchange in 1993.

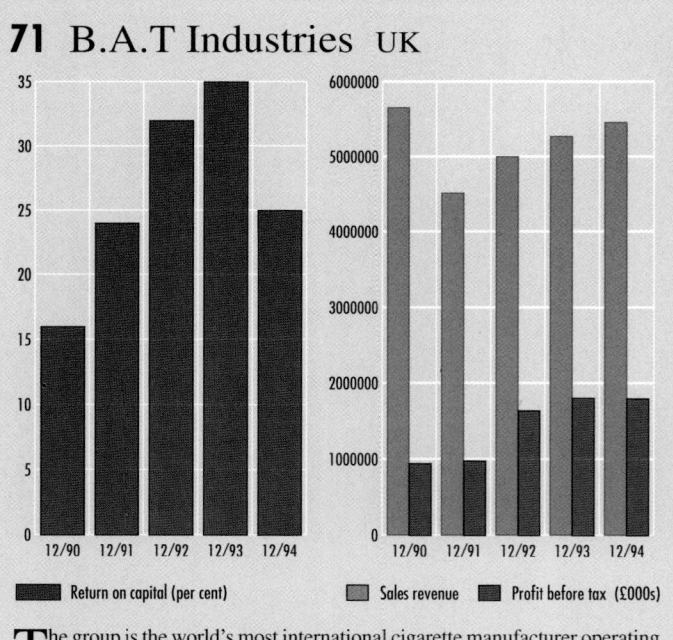

71 B.A.T Industries UK

The group is the world's most international cigarette manufacturer operating through Brown & Williamson in America, British-American Tobacco (with production facilities in 45 countries), BAT Cigarettenfabriken in Germany, and Souza Cruz in Brazil. In financial services group subsidiaries provide personal financial and insurance services in the United Kingdom and North America. Principal operating companies are Farmers Group, a general insurer in the United States that owns three life insurance companies; Eagle Star, a UK insurer acting in 30 countries through direct brokers and intermediaries; and Allied-Dunbar, a life assurance and pensions company.

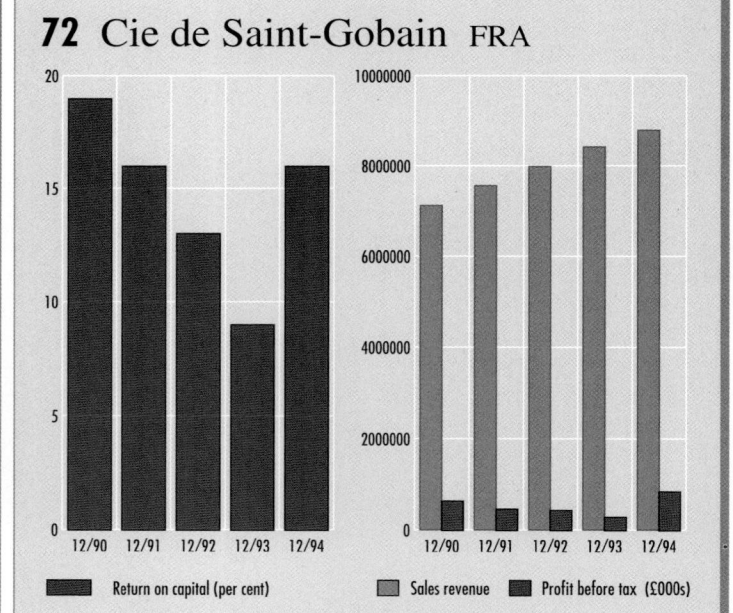

72 Cie de Saint-Gobain FRA

The company's activities are carried out through several divisions: flat glass, for construction and automobile markets; containers, used for food, perfume and pharmaceuticals; insulation; fibre reinforcements; pipe supplying equipment for water supply; building materials; industrial ceramics; abrasives, used for machining and polishing metals, wood and glass; and other activities, including finance and one service company. Saint Gobain was established in 1970 through the merger of Cie ce Saint-Gobain (established 1665) and Cie de Pont-a-Mousson (established 1854).

EUROPE'S TOP 100: ANALYSIS

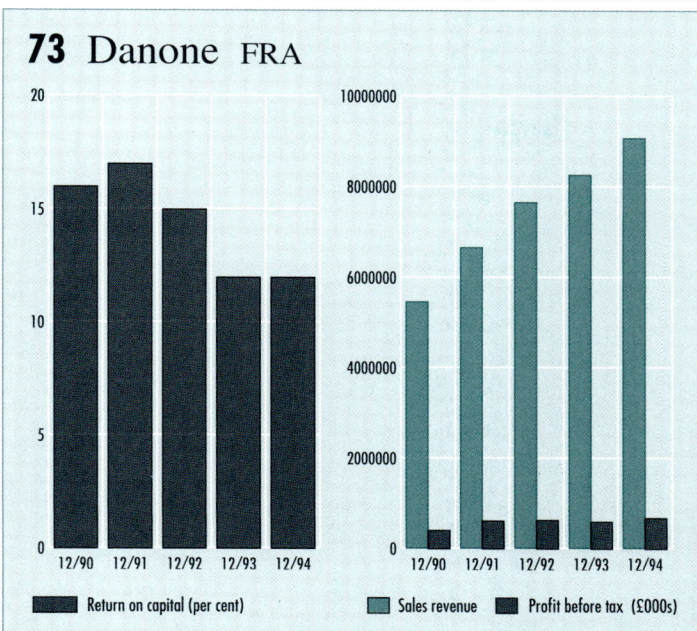

73 Danone FRA

The group is Europe's largest manufacturer of biscuits, the world's leading producer of dairy products and mineral water, Europe's leading bottle manufacturer and its second largest brewer and pasta manufacturer. Activities are conducted through seven divisions: dairy products (yoghurt, cheeses and desserts); grocery products and pasta (including ready-to-serve dishes, diet and infant food); biscuits (Jacobs and LV brands); beers (Kronenbourg and San Miguel); mineral water (Evian and Volvic); containers; and international (embracing businesses in the Americas, Africa and the Pacific). The company, established in 1899, was formerly known as BSN.

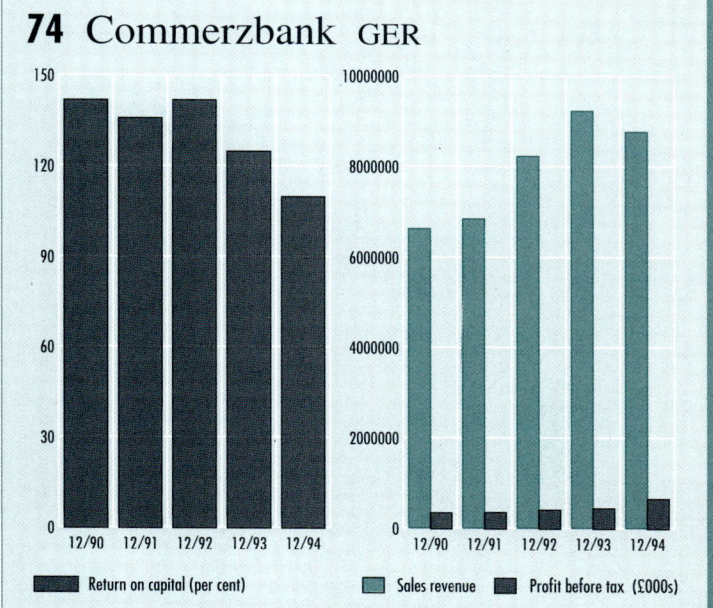

74 Commerzbank GER

One of Germany's three main banks, the company is active in all aspects of banking, occupying a major position in the securities business and in foreign financial transactions. It has more than 3.5 million customers and in excess of 1,000 branches. There are 27 representative offices outside Germany. Commerzbank was established in 1870. In 1952 its business was transferred to three new banks (Bankverein Westdeutschland, Commerz-und Credit-Bank and Commerz-und Disconto-Bank) who joined together again in 1958 to form the present structure of the bank. In 1995 the bank acquired Britain's Jupiter Tyndell asset management group.

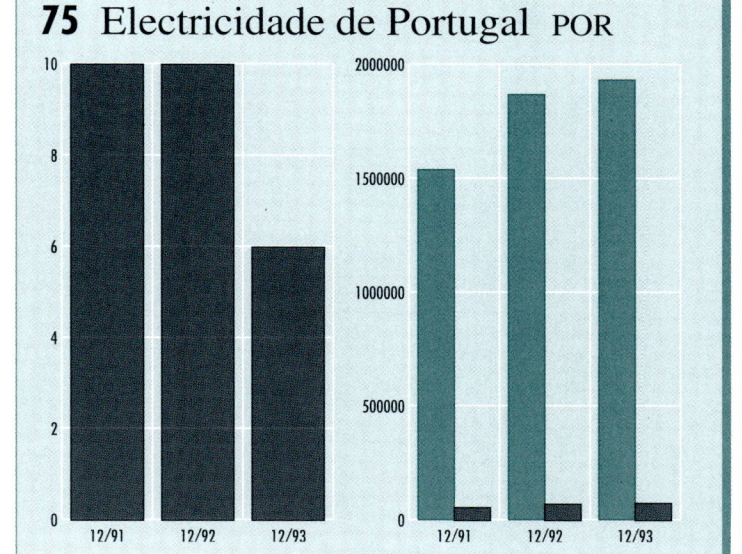

75 Electricidade de Portugal POR

The company is engaged in the generation, transmission and distribution of hydroelectric and thermoelectrical power in Portugal. Subsidiaries include Edinfor-Sistemas Informaticos; SPE-Sdade de Assistencia Technica Empresarial (Macau) and Edelpro-Imobiliaria Lda. The company is wholly owned by the Portuguese government, having been transformed into a state-controlled public limited company in 1991. At the end of 1993 total overall installed capacity was 7,282 MW, of which 3,727 MW was deployed in hydroelectric power stations and 3,555 MW in thermoelectric plants.

76 Empresa Nacional de Electricidad SPA

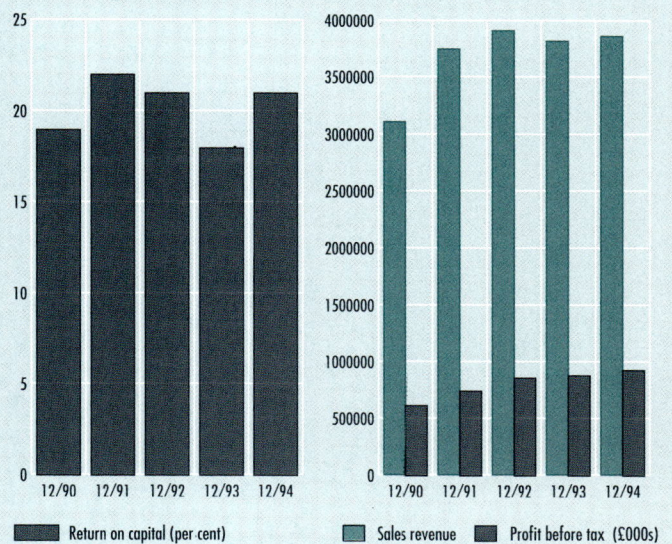

Involved in thermal, nuclear and hydro-electric energy production and in coal mining, the group has some 3.5 million customers. Established in 1944 the company's main shareholder is Teneo SA, the Spanish state-owned industrial holding company. The main subsidiaries are Empresa Nacional Hidroelectrica de Ribagorzana (91.4 per cent owned), Union Electrica de Canaria (99.7 per cent); Electricas Reunidas de Zaragoza (61.2 per cent), Gas y Electricidad (55.3 per cent), Empresa Nacional Carbonifera del Sur (86 per cent), Electra de Viesgo (87.6 per cent) and International Endesa BV (Netherlands). The company is actively investing in the newly-privatised utilities of Latin America.

EUROPE'S TOP 100: ANALYSIS 77-80

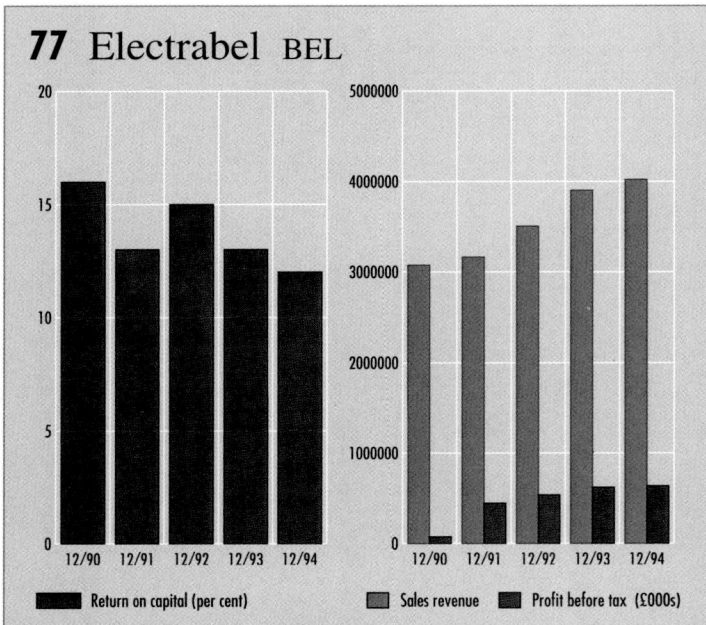

77 Electrabel BEL

The company is active in the fields of electricity generation and distribution, and the operation and management of networks for public utility services, including electricity, natural gas, cable television, steam and water. In 1994 the company provided about 86 per cent of Belgium's electricity needs and had more than three million cable television customers. The company's present structure is the result of a merger of EBES, Intercom and Unerg in 1990, under which Electrabel took over the electricity, gas and cable television interests of Powerfin and the broadcasting operations of Coditel. In consideration for the deals the company issued new shares.

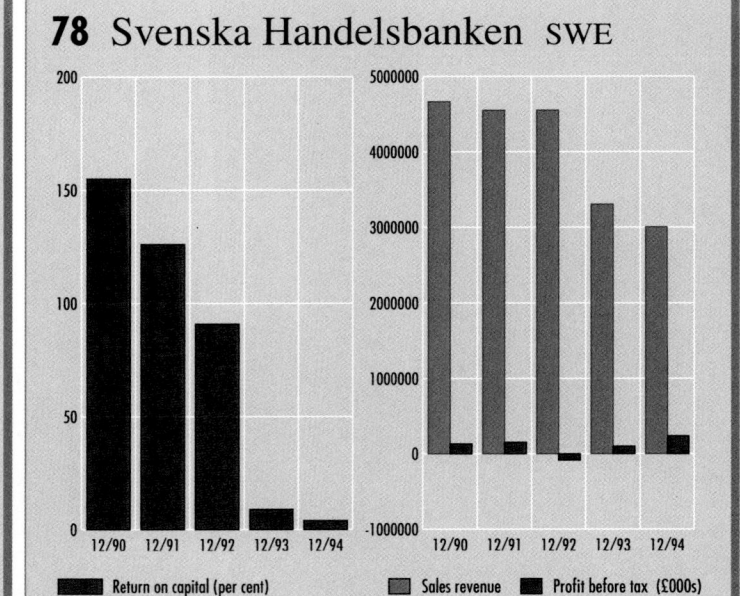

78 Svenska Handelsbanken SWE

The commercial bank's services include deposits, lending, mortgages, investment banking, leasing and life assurance. The group is active in equity trading, fund management, custodian services, foreign exchange and money market trading. Operations are strongly decentralised, with 487 branch offices in Sweden and branches in other Nordic countries. There are offices in Austria, China, France, Germany, Hong Kong, Japan, Luxembourg, Russia, Singapore, Spain, Switzerland, Taiwan, the UK and the US. Established in 1871, the bank's activities were largely confined to Stockholm until 1914, after which a number of regional banks were acquired during a period of rapid national expansion.

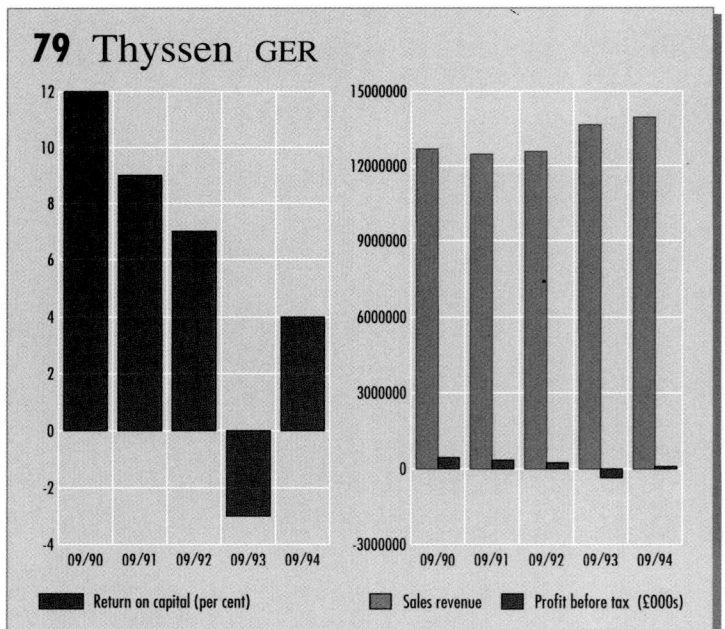

79 Thyssen GER

The company's main activities are the manufacture of capital goods, steel and steel products, with broad interests in trading and services. The capital goods and manufactured products division is involved in castings, mechanical engineering, lifts, polymers, stamping and frame and wheel and brake products, plastics, cement and ready-made building materials, refractories and ceramics. The steel division manufactures long, flat and precision strip and wire products. In trading and services Thyssen operates in recycling, building and construction products, fuels, logistica, project management and maintenance. Thyssen was established in 1953 and has operated as a holding company since 1983.

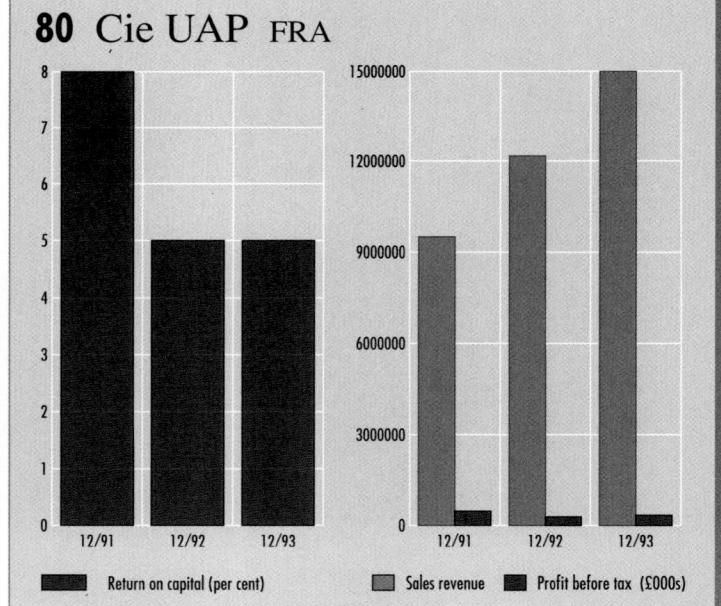

80 Cie UAP FRA

This is a holding company for a group that operates in three main business areas: insurance (including life, travel, accident, car and specialist insurance services such as aviation and space); banking (carried out by Worms, dealing principally with business clients, and IPPA, a savings bank in Belgium and Luxembourg); and finance and property (UIF and Simco, which together own 11,500 flats and 309,000 square metres of office and commercial property). The company was formerly known as Ste Centrale Union des Assurances de Paris. In 1995 the privatisation of 50.2 per cent of the company was launched, reducing the French government's interest to 3.8 per cent.

81-84 EUROPE'S TOP 100: ANALYSIS

81 Lloyds Bank UK

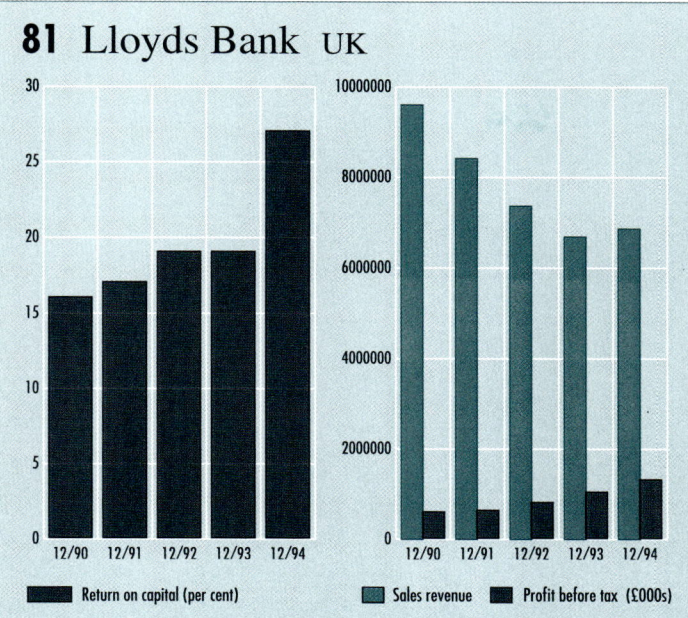

■ Return on capital (per cent) ■ Sales revenue ■ Profit before tax (£000s)

The group provides a comprehensive range of banking and financial services through branches and offices in the United Kingdom and overseas. The core UK retail banking business is complemented by activities in corporate banking and treasury, while life assurance and other financial services are provided through Lloyds Abbey Life, in which the bank has a 62 per cent interest. Lloyds also has interests in credit factoring and private banking. In April 1994 the bank announced the acquisition of Cheltenham and Gloucester Building Society for £1.8 billion, subject to the approval of the respective shareholders and members, and of regulatory authorities.

82 Zurich Insurance Co. SWI

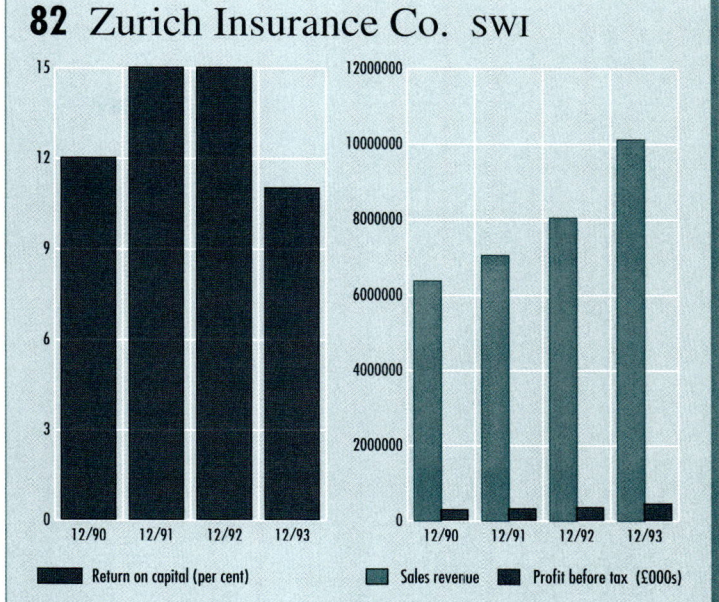

■ Return on capital (per cent) ■ Sales revenue ■ Profit before tax (£000s)

The group deals with all kinds of life and non-life insurance worldwide, including motor, general liability, accident and sickness, workers' compensation, fire, water damage, glass, burglary, marine, boiler and machinery, fidelity, surety and legal expenses. Non-life insurance includes direct general insurance and assumed reinsurance. In the UK businesses include Zurich Holdings (UK), Zurich Life (UK), Zurich International (UK) and Zurich Re (UK). In 1993 the company acquired part of the business of Municipal Mutual Insurance, which specialised in the provision of insurance services for local authorities in Britain.

83 Mannesmann GER

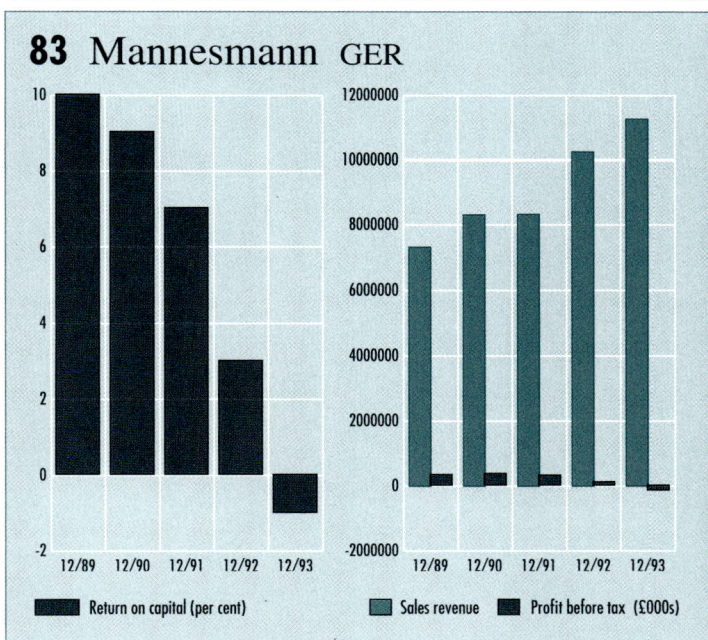

■ Return on capital (per cent) ■ Sales revenue ■ Profit before tax (£000s)

Main activities are the manufacture of machinery, plant, capital goods in the fields of electrical and electronic engineering, pipe and tubing, automotive technology, telecommunications, and the trading of its own and purchased products. Divisions are Mannesmann Demag, Mannesmann Demag Fordertechnik, Mannesmann Rexroth, Krauss-Maffei, Mannesmann Anlagenbau, VDO, Mannesmann Fichtel & Sachs, Mannesmann Hartmann & Braun, Mannesmann Mobilfunk, Mannesmannrohren-Werke and Mannesmann Handel. In 1952, following trading difficulties since the end of WWII, the company was split into three entities and Mannesmann emerged in its present form.

84 Grand Metropolitan UK

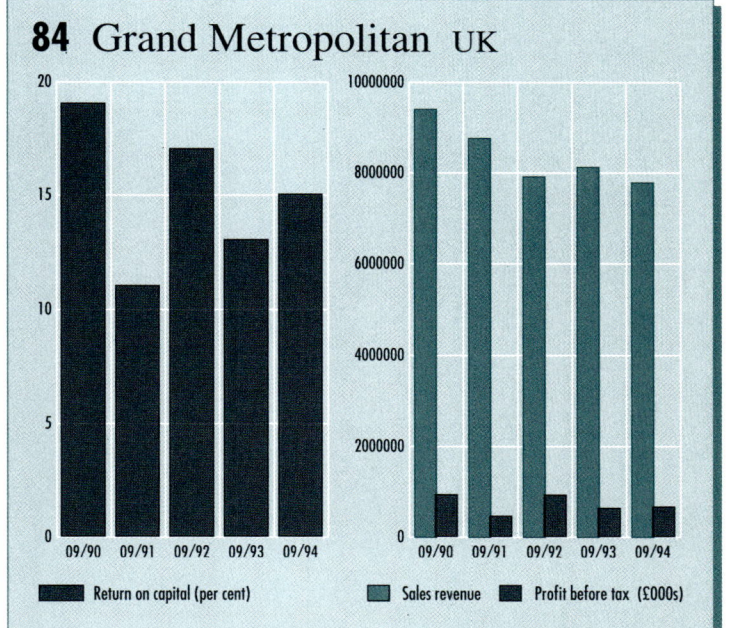

■ Return on capital (per cent) ■ Sales revenue ■ Profit before tax (£000s)

The group is international, specialising in branded foods and drinks businesses. Branded foods companies include Haagen-Dazs ice creams, yoghurts and desserts; Pillsbury ready-to-bake dough products; and Green Giant frozen and canned vegetables. In January 1995 Pillsbury agreed to acquire Pet Inc, the US branded food company, for £1.7 billion. Retailing companies include Burger King fast food outlets and Pearle eye care products. International Distillers & Vintners embraces interests in drinks and owns five of the top 20 spirits brands in the world, including Smirnoff, J&B Rare and Baileys. Grand Metropolitan was incorporated in 1934 and floated on the stock market in 1961.

EUROPE'S TOP 100: ANALYSIS   85-88

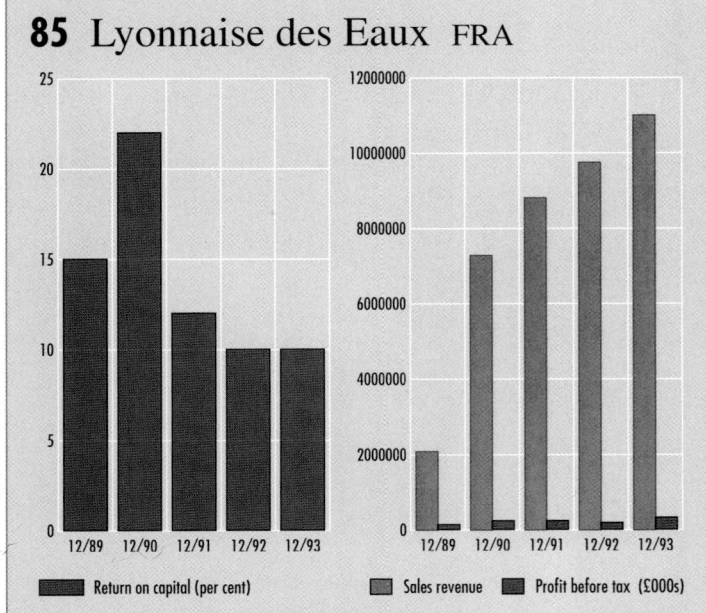

85 Lyonnaise des Eaux FRA

The company is a worldwide urban development and environmental services group. Services are divided into the areas of water supply, energy, waste management, urban construction and management, civil engineering and services in the community (including healthcare, television, financial services, funeral services and penal establishments). The company has significant investments in the UK water industry and in March 1995 it was announced that a cash offer would be made for all shares in Northumbrian Water, subject to regulatory approval. Lyonnais des Eaux already owns North East Water, a statutory water company operating in the same region.

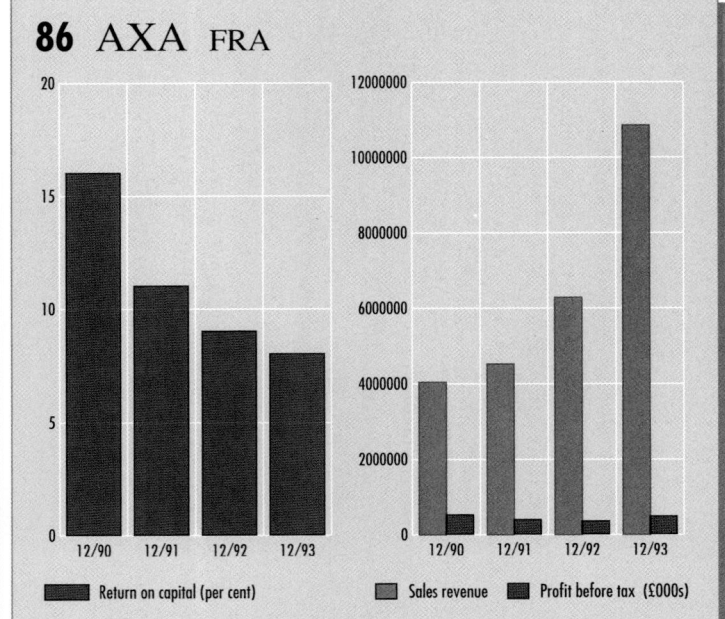

86 AXA FRA

The company operates in the sectors of insurance, reinsurance, banking and financial services, real estate, investment and portfolio management. Subsidiaries in the UK include Axa Equity & Law, Axa Equity & Law International, Axa Insurance, Axa Re (UK), and Axa Marine and Aviation. The company's origins date back to 1852. An agreement with Compagnie du Midi in 1988 resulted in Axa's insurance subsidiaries being merged with those of the company to form Axa-Midi Assurances. The company subsequently decided to concentrate on insurance and financial services, disposing of its industrial interests. The name was changed from Compagnie du Midi to Axa in 1991.

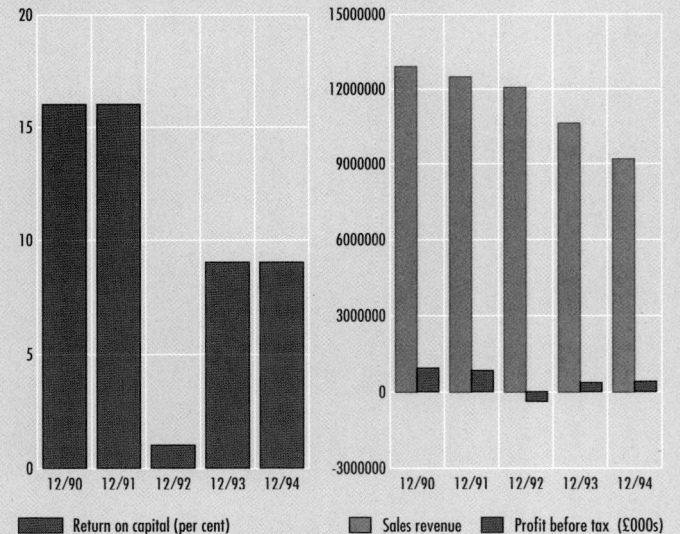

87 Imperial Chemical Industries UK

Principal activities are research, manufacture and sales of paints, explosives and industrial chemicals. In the UK subsidiaries comprise ICI Chemicals & Polymers (chemicals, plastics and fertilisers) and Tioxide Group (titanium dioxide pigments). Deutsche ICI, in Germany, makes chlorine, caustic soda, speciality paints and polyurethanes. North American subsidiaries produce acrylics, films, paints, composites, polyurethanes, industrial explosives and initiating systems. ICI also operates in South Africa, Australia, China, Japan, Pakistan and Taiwan, sometimes in partnership with local industrial groups. In June 1993 the bioscience activities were demerged into a new company, Zeneca.

88 Bayernwerk GER

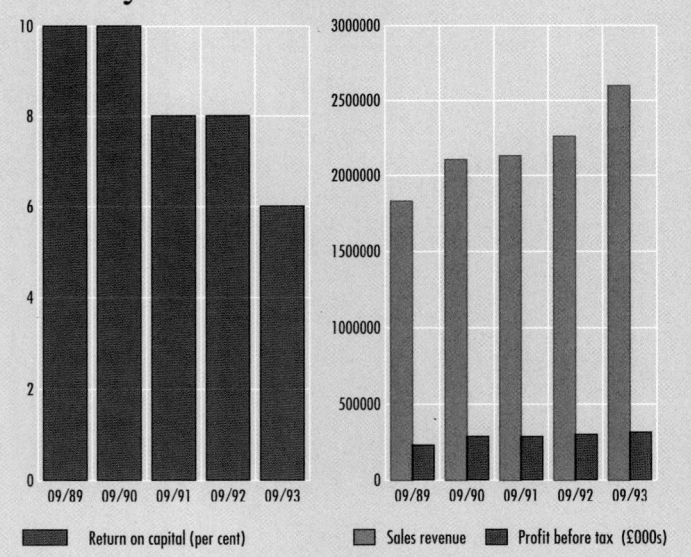

The company is engaged in the generation and and distribution of electricity as well as the supply of gas. Other activities include nuclear power and hydroelectric power. In 1995 the company merged with VIAG to form one of Germany's 10 largest industrial concerns. VIAG acquired 58 per cent of the company's capital from the state of Bavaria, while the state of Bavaria received a 25 per cent interest in VIAG. Certain investments in the energy sector were transferred to Bayernwerk from VIAG and VIAF moved its corporate headquarters to Munich from Bonn. Bayernwerk was established in 1921.

89 Cable and Wireless UK

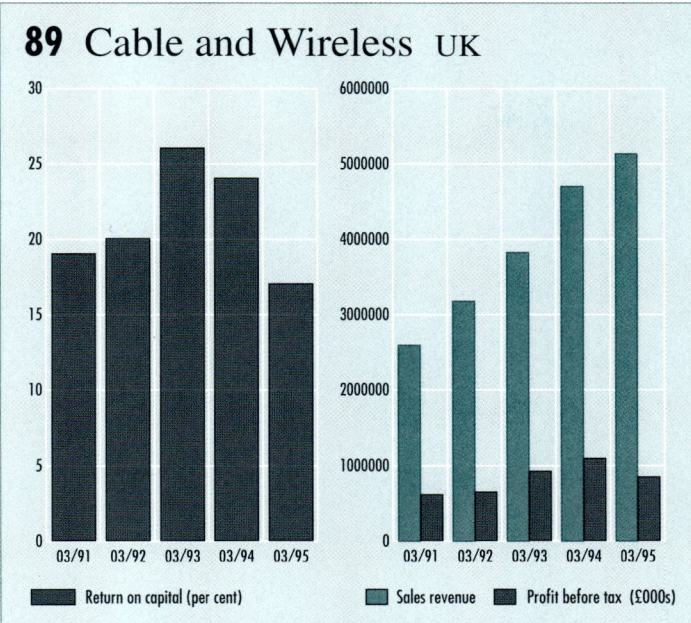

The international telecommunications group provides business and domestic users services that include telephone, fascimile, telex and data transmission. Operations are located in 50 countries. In the United Kingdom subsidiaries include Mercury Communications (80 per cent owned). Overseas investments include Hong Kong Telecom (57.5 per cent owned). Other activities include submarine cable systems and communications facilities management. In February 1995 Germany's Veba acquired a 10.5 per cent interest in the company as part of a joint venture agreement to develop telecommunications services in the European outside Britain.

90 Aegon NLD

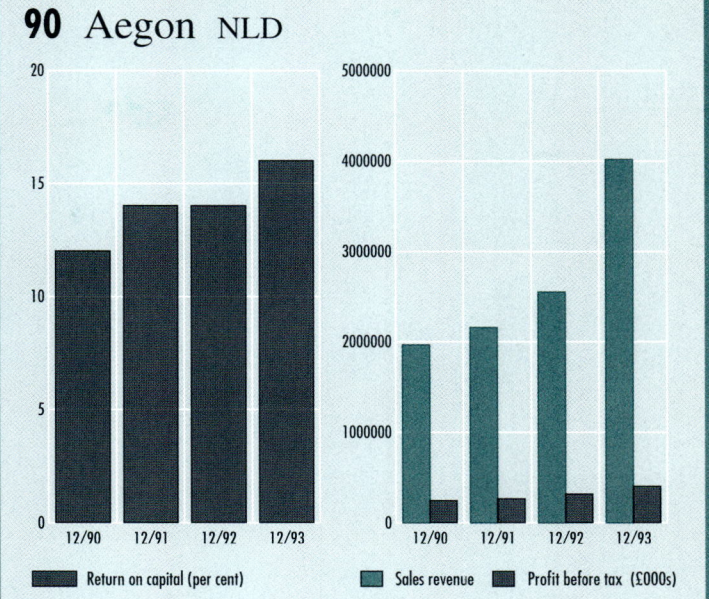

The company is an international insurance group offering a range of insurance and associated financial services, and is active in accident, health and other general insurance. The company is also engaged in a number of related non-insurance activities, mainly in the area of financial services. The most important markets are the Netherlands, North America and Europe. Subsidiaries in the UK include Scottish Equitable, Aegon Insurance Co. and Aegon Financial Services. Aegon was formed in 1969 through the merger of Eerste Nederlandsche and Nillmij. A further merger with AGO Holding took place in 1989.

91 Assurances Generales de France FRA

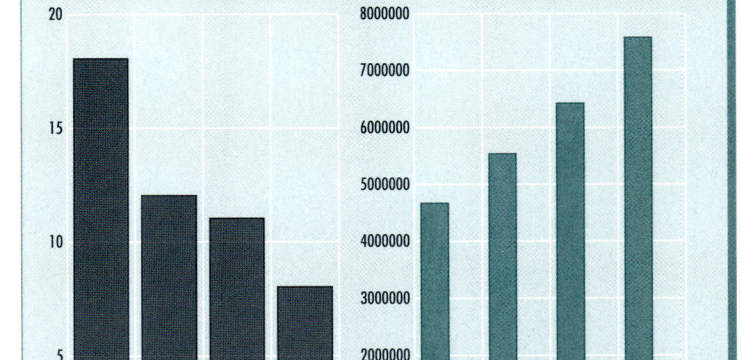

The group's core activities are life and non-life insurance and reinsurance. It is also involved in real estate management, banking and finance. The international network spans 23 countries worldwide, with Europe accounting for 65.3 per cent of premium income. Subsidiaries are organised in three business sectors, comprising insurance, reinsurance and brokerage; banking and finance; and investment and retail management. Established in 1968 the company's main shareholder is the French government, which is committed to its eventual privatisation.

92 Danske Bank DNK

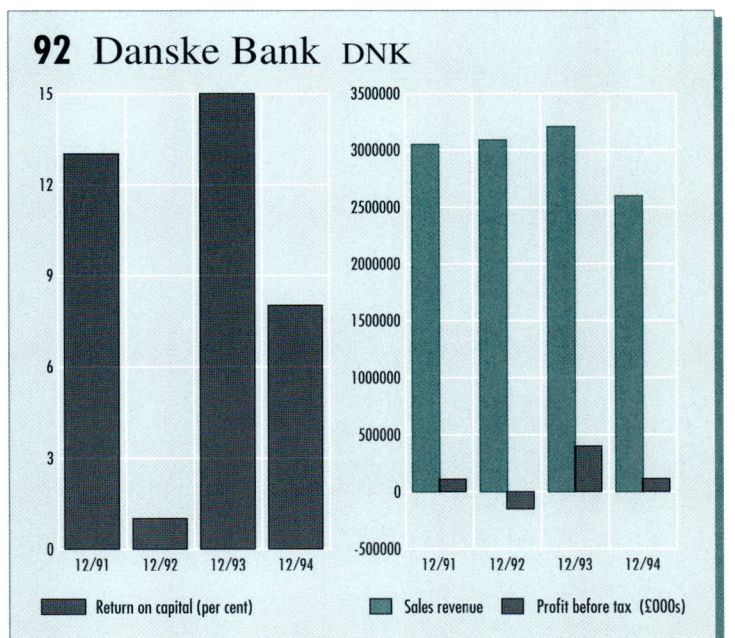

The bank serves approximately two million retail customers and a significant part of the Danish corporate sector. It also has a large number of corporate clients outside Denmark, particularly in northern Europe. There are branch offices in Luxembourg, London, New York, Hamburg, Singapore, Hong Kong and Frankfurt. The bank and its subsidiaries provide banking-related services such as insurance and residential mortgage finance. In accordance with Danish banking legislation, the insurance activities are not consolidated with the group. The bank was established in 1871. In 1990 it merged with Copenhagen Handelsbanken and with Provinsbanken.

EUROPE'S TOP 100: ANALYSIS   93-96

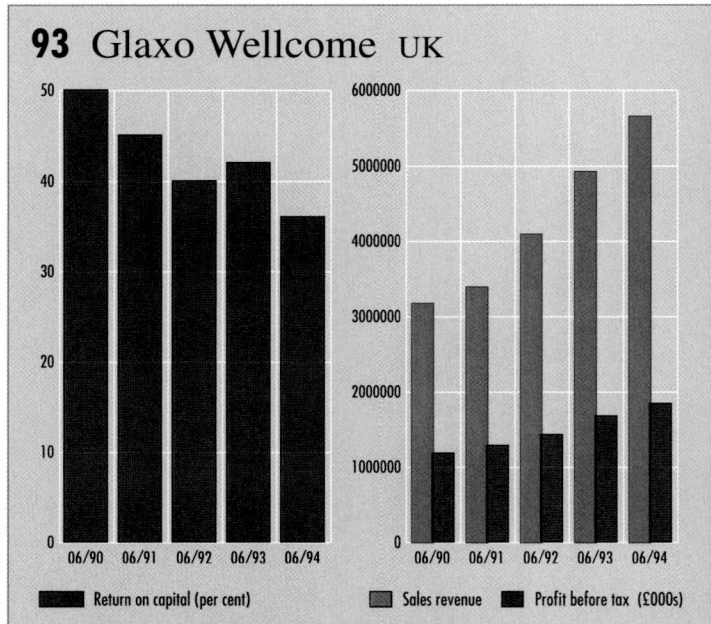

93 Glaxo Wellcome UK

The group conducts research into and develops, manufactures and markets ethical pharmaceuticals around the world. Trademarks include the anti-ulcerant drug Zantac, the respiratory products Ventolin and Becotide, Zinnat antibiotics, Zofran for chemotherapy and the migraine treatment Imigran. In January 1995 Glaxo announced the terms of an £8.9 billion takeover bid for Wellcome, the pharmaceuticals group whose leading products are Retrovir, for the treatment of Aids, and the anti-viral Zovirax. The bid was declared unconditional in March 1995. In the same year Glaxo announced the acquisition of Affymax, a Dutch-based drug discovery company, for US$485 million.

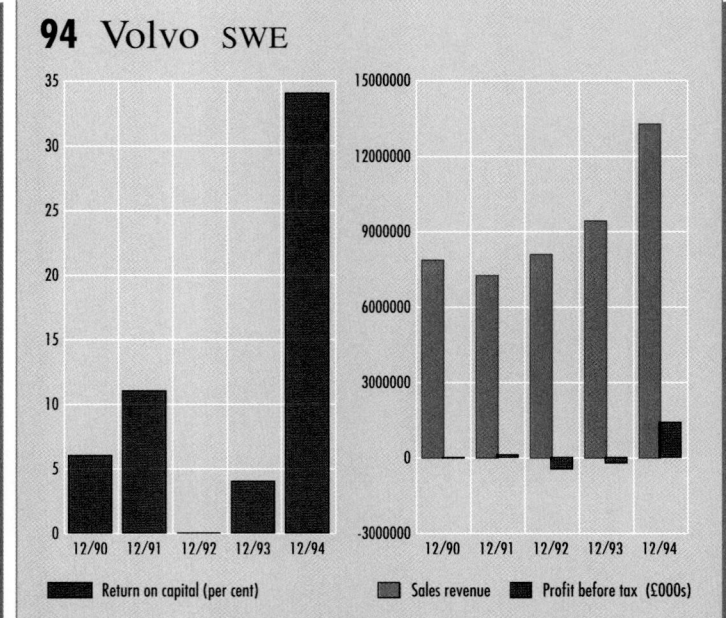

94 Volvo SWE

The group's main activity is the manufacture of cars, trucks and buses, including development and design, production, marketing and distribution of spare parts. About 90 per cent of total sales of vehicles are generated outside the home market of Sweden. The group also manufactures marine, industrial and aeroplane engines. The divestment of non-vehicle interests, including matches, tobacco, beverages, food, pharmaceuticals and investment banking, is currently underway. In 1994 plans to merge the automotive operations with Renault were aborted, in the face of opposition in Sweden and France. Existing cross-ownerships of joint ventures were dissolved and co-operation agreements were ended.

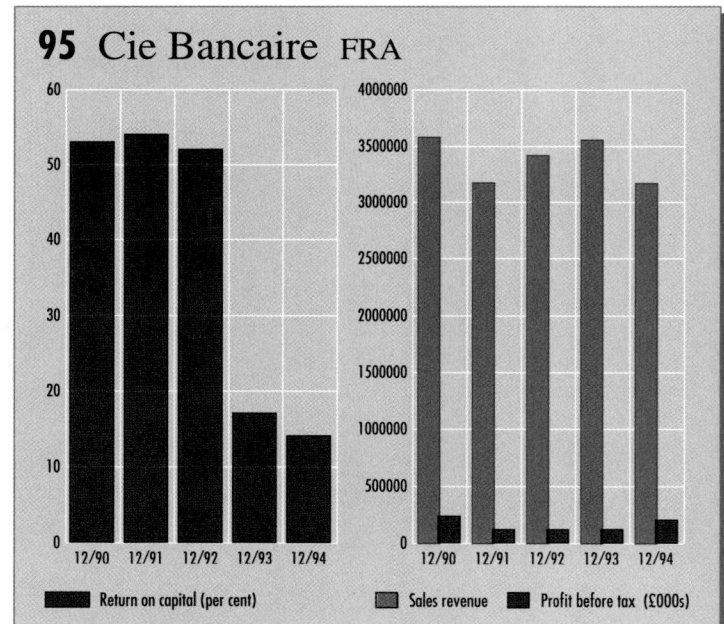

95 Cie Bancaire FRA

The group offers a range of financial services centred around five core activities, each headed by a main trading subsidiary: lease asset finance (through UFB Locabail); consumer credit (Cetelem); property finance and promotion (UCB and Sinvim); life assurance and investment management (Cardiff and Courtal). In 1995 the company sold UCB Home Loans, a mortgage lending business based in the UK, to the Nationwide Building Society for £85 million. Cie Bancaire was established in 1959. Cie Financiere de Paribas holds a 46.5 per cent interest; other shareholders include Credit Foncier de France, GPA Vie and Groupe Credit Lyonnais.

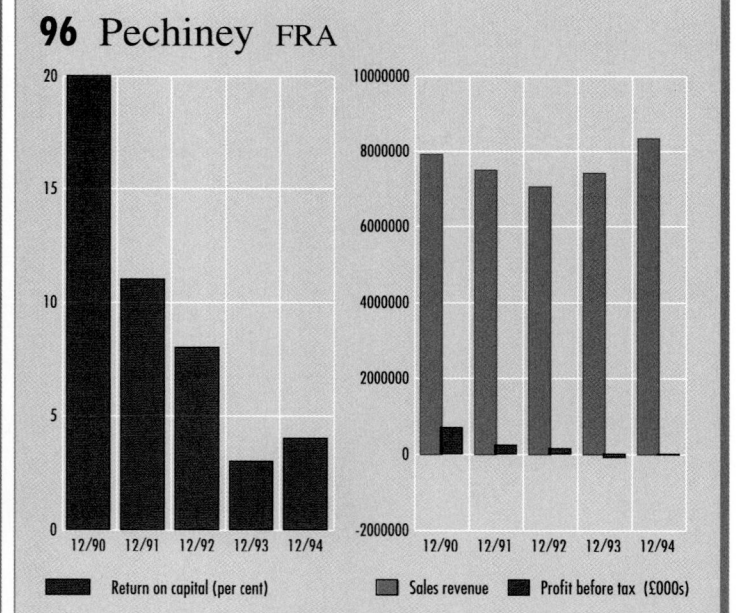

96 Pechiney FRA

Manufacturing activities comprise packaging (cans, flexible tubes and glass containers for the beverage, cosmetics and food markets); aluminium (rolled products for packaging, transportation, building and household appliances, speciality products and profiles for construction); turbine components (precision castings for jet aircraft and industrial gas turbine engines); and related industrial activities (carbon and graphite components and systems). The company, whose major shareholder is the French government, was established in 1972 through the merger of Cie Pechiney and Ugine Kuhlmann into Ste des Metaux et Alliages, which simultaneously changed its name to Pechiney Ugine Kuhlmann.

97-100   EUROPE'S TOP 100: ANALYSIS

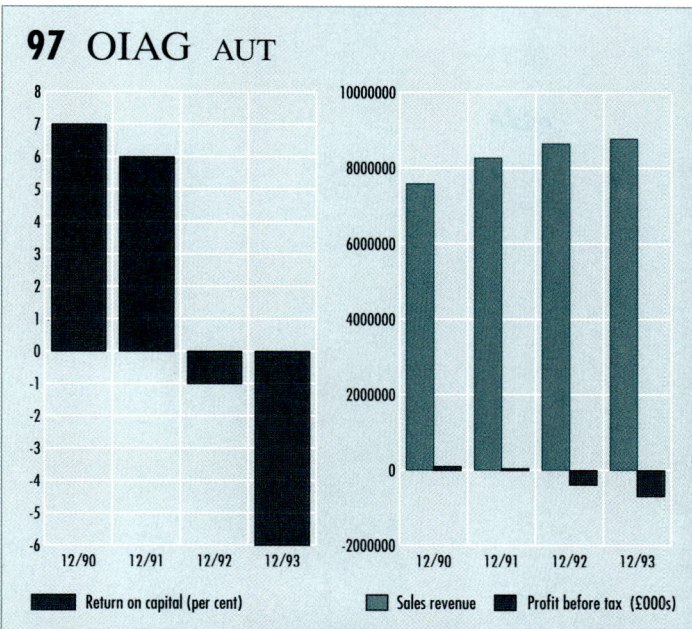

97 OIAG AUT

The company's principal activities are divided into three areas: production of steel, aluminium and technology. The steel division can be split into quality steel and special steel used in the manufacture of tubes, storage shelves, interior construction and castings for the manufacture of vehicles. Main subsidiaries include companies trading under the Voest-Alpine banner; Bohier-Uddeholm; Austria Mikro Systems International; Schoeller-Bieckmann; At&S Austria Technologie & Systemtechnik; Austria Metall; and Electro Bau. About one-half of group turnover is destined for the Austrian market.

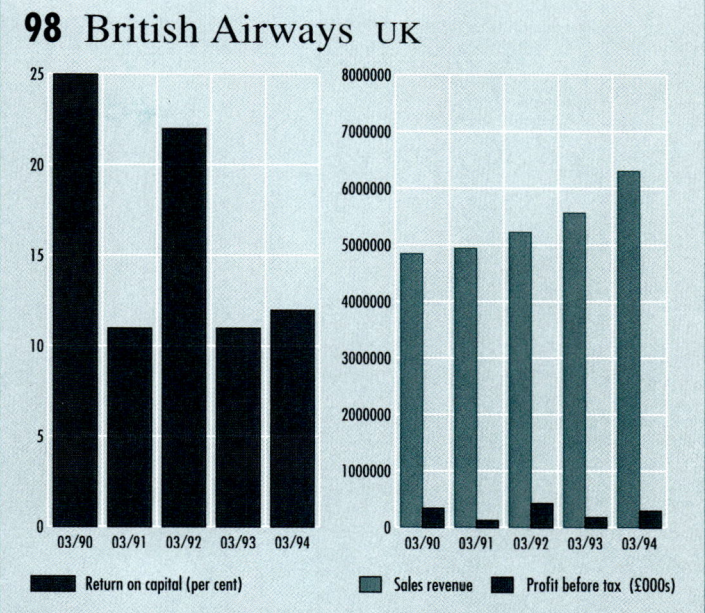

98 British Airways UK

The main activities are the operation of international and domestic scheduled and charter air services for passengers, freight and mail, and ancillary services. Formed through the merger of British Overseas Aircraft Corporation (BOAC) and British European Airways (BEA), the company has expanded to become one of the world's largest and most profitable airlines. Acquisitions since privatisation in 1987 have included British Caledonian and Davies & Newman (Dan-Air). The company also has a 24.6 per cent interest in USAir, 25 per cent of Qantas Airways in Australia, 49.9 per cent of Deutsche BA and 49.9 per cent of TAT European Airlines in France.

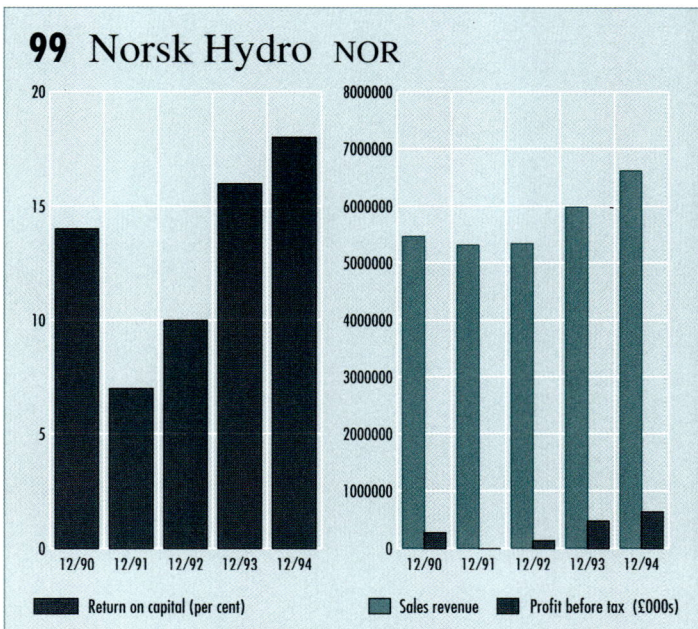

99 Norsk Hydro NOR

Activities are divided into the following business segments: agriculture (ammonia, mineral fertiliser, industrial chemicals and gases, and feedstuff blends); oil and gas (exploration, production, refining and marketing); light metals (aluminium and magnesium); and petrochemicals (vinyl chloride monomer, PVC and caustic soda). The company also has interests in salmon farming, pharmaceutical research, insurance and reinsurance. The company was established in 1905. The Norwegian government holds 51 per cent of the capital.

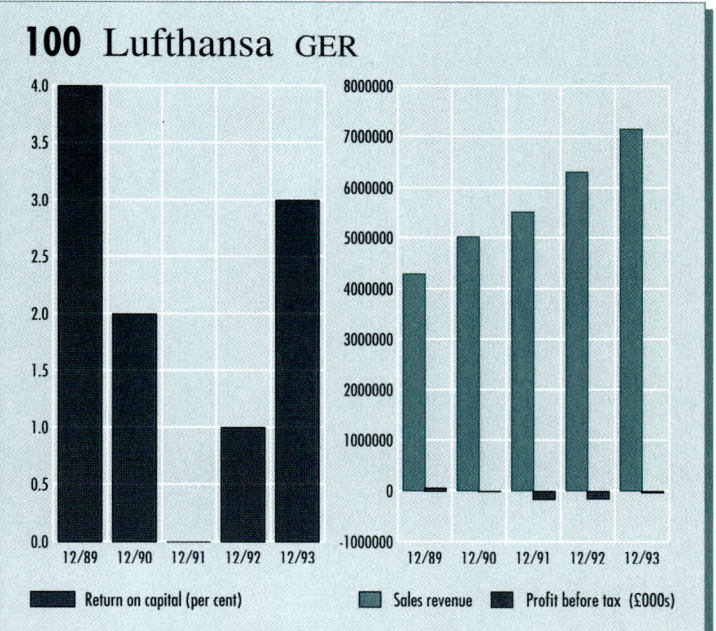

100 Lufthansa GER

Germany's flag carrying airline is active in the areas of passenger travel, freight, catering, travel services, hotels and finance. The company was formed in 1926 as the successor to Deutsche Aero Lloyd and Junkers Luftverkehr. The German government owns a 36 per cent shareholding but is committed to the full privatisation of the airline. In May 1995 Lufthansa formed an alliance with Scandinavian Airlines Systems to co-operate on passenger and freight services. An alliance with America's United Airlines came into effect in 1994 and there is also a co-operation agreement with Thai Airways International in the Asia Pacific region.

EUROPE'S TOP 50 PROFIT MAKERS

RANK	RANK IN EUROPE TOP 1000	COMPANY NAME	PROFIT BEFORE TAX Latest year £000	Previous year £000	Change in profit £000
1	3	Royal Dutch/Shell, UK/NLD	6,627,000	5,787,000	840,000
2	17	HSBC Holdings, UK	3,166,000	2,584,000	582,000
3	28	British Telecommunications, UK	2,662,000	2,756,000	-94,000
4	36	Nestle, SWI	2,421,996	2,096,610	325,386
5	52	Unilever Group, UK/NLD	2,384,718	1,941,383	443,335
6	8	France Telecom, FRA	2,350,945	1,976,494	374,451
7	16	British Petroleum Company, UK	2,281,000	1,302,000	979,000
8	46	Barclays, UK	1,859,000	661,000	1,198,000
9	93	Glaxo Wellcome§, UK	1,840,000	1,675,000	165,000
10	71	B.A.T Industries, UK	1,802,000	1,809,000	-7,000
11	44	Roche Holding, SWI	1,716,954	1,414,896	302,058
12	40	National Westminster Bank, UK	1,592,000	989,000	603,000
13	121	BTR, UK	1,412,000	1,274,000	138,000
14	94	AB Volvo, SWE	1,393,672	L224,002	1,617,674
15	32	Hanson, UK	1,346,000	1,016,000	330,000
16	37	Bayer, GER	1,327,634	947,732	379,902
17	69	CS Holding, SWI	1,317,830	695,767	622,063
18	81	Lloyds Bank, UK	1,304,000	1,031,000	273,000
19	61	Ciba-Geigy, SWI	1,253,778	1,097,063	156,715
20	55	ABN Amro Holding, NLD	1,209,000	1,136,000	73,000
21	43	Internationale Nederlanden Groep, NLD	1,183,372	1,011,944	171,428
22	20	Veba, GER	1,152,377	797,238	355,139
23	14	Deutsche Bank, GER	1,150,643	1,732,005	-581,362
24	113	Sandoz, SWI	1,082,656	990,517	92,139
25	103	Statoil-Den Norske Stats Oljeselskap, NOR	1,060,235	1,006,259	53,976
26	34	Alcatel-Alsthom Cie Generale d'Electricite, FRA	1,053,896	1,044,132	9,764
27	51	Philips Electronics, NLD	1,039,584	547,404	492,180
28	19	Union Bank of Switzerland, SWI	1,012,869	1,375,167	-362,298
29	111	Halifax Building Society, UK	975,100	865,800	109,300
30	58	ABB Asea Brown Boveri, SWI	942,204	397,763	544,441
31	24	Abbey National, UK	932,000	704,000	228,000
32	76	Empresa Nacional de Electricidad, ESP	931,210	883,500	47,710
33	117	RTZ Corporation, UK	922,000	435,000	487,000
34	45	Credit Agricole, FRA	920,933	847,465	73,468
35	10	British Gas, UK	918,000	L569,000	1,487,000
36	101	Guinness, UK	915,000	702,000	213,000
37	39	Hoechst, GER	890,599	493,996	396,603
38	1	European Investment Bank, LUX	876,159	715,171	160,988
39	143	General Electric Company, UK	866,000	863,000	3,000
40	72	Cie de Saint-Gobain, FRA	856,000	297,000	559,000
41	146	Marks and Spencer, UK	851,500	736,500	115,000
42	35	BASF, GER	851,210	425,795	425,415
43	89	Cable and Wireless, UK	844,100	1,088,300	-244,200
44	7	Siemens, GER	842,502	1,185,838	-343,336
45	23	Telefonica de Espana, ESP	840,100	656,700	183,400
46	6	Daimler-Benz, GER	837,381	454,943	382,438
47	717	Diehl GmbH & Co., GER	805,680	714,342	91,338
48	15	RWE, GER	795,259	805,145	-9,886
49	59	Tractebel, BEL	766,877	674,000	92,877
50	62	Allianz AG Holding, GER	749,650	535,577	214,073

NOTES: §Figures do not reflect merger with Wellcome PLC.

EUROPE'S TOP 50 MARKET CAPITALISATION

RANK	RANK IN EUROPE TOP 1000	COMPANY NAME	MARKET CAPITALISATION £000
1	3	Royal Dutch/Shell, UK/NLD	60,397,000
2	44	Roche Holding, SWI	30,510,570
3	28	British Telecommunications, UK	24,379,000
4	36	Nestle, SWI	23,828,000
5	16	British Petroleum Company, UK	23,420,000
6	52	Unilever Group, UK/NLD	21,340,000
7	62	Allianz AG Holding, GER	21,229,000
8	17	HSBC Holdings, UK	18,424,000
9	93	Glaxo Wellcome§, UK	16,589,000
10	6	Daimler-Benz, GER	16,120,000
11	55	ABN Amro Holding, NLD	15,233,000
12	7	Siemens, GER	14,233,000
13	14	Deutsche Bank, GER	14,081,000
14	19	Union Bank of Switzerland, SWI	14,015,000
15	10	British Gas, UK	13,622,000
16	113	Sandoz, SWI	13,596,000
17	71	B.A.T Industries, UK	13,298,000
18	107	Assicurazioni Generali, ITA	12,422,000
19	12	Ste Elf Aquitaine, FRA	12,254,000
20	32	Hanson, UK	11,911,000
21	146	Marks and Spencer, UK	11,910,561
22	61	Ciba-Geigy, SWI	11,200,000
23	43	Internationale Nederlanden Groep, NLD	11,085,000
24	20	Veba, GER	10,822,264
25	121	BTR, UK	10,659,000
26	37	Bayer, GER	10,374,000
27	332	AB Astra, SWE	10,148,000
28	69	CS Holding, SWI	10,098,000
29	46	Barclays, UK	9,982,000
30	49	Cie Generale des Eaux, FRA	9,242,000
31	101	Guinness, UK	9,081,000
32	255	Reed/Elsevier Group, UK/NLD	8,875,000
33	117	RTZ Corporation, UK	8,831,000
34	40	National Westminster Bank, UK	8,820,000
35	155	Moet Hennessy Louis Vuitton, FRA	8,674,000
36	89	Cable and Wireless, UK	8,518,000
37	84	Grand Metropolitan, UK	8,512,000
38	50	TOTAL, FRA	8,494,000
39	76	Empresa Nacional de Electricidad, SPA	8,361,000
40	221	ZENECA Group, UK	8,315,000
41	39	Hoechst, GER	8,172,000
42	143	General Electric Company, UK	8,115,000
43	35	BASF, GER	8,033,827
44	234	L' Oreal, FRA	8,016,061
45	566	Reuters Holdings, UK	7,798,368
46	171	Telefonaktiebolaget LM Ericsson, SWE	7,776,000
47	34	Alcatel-Alsthom Cie Generale d'Electricite, FRA	7,765,000
48	244	Munchener Ruckversicherungs-Ges, GER	7,548,712
49	157	J. Sainsbury, UK	7,496,765
50	63	Dresdner Bank, GER	7,444,000

NOTES: §Figure does not reflect merger with Wellcome PLC.

EUROPE'S TOP 1000 — 1-50

RANK	COMPANY NAME (Sector)	CAPITAL EMPLOYED £000	TURNOVER £000	PRE-TAX PROFIT £000	NUMBER OF EMPLOYEES	EQUITY MKT CAPITAL £000
1	European Investment Bank, LUX (Banks)	63,315,557	6,138,395	876,159	810	†
2	Societe Generale, FRA (Banks)	53,924,867	14,564,446	675,228	44,362	7,134,000
3	Royal Dutch/Shell[1], UK/NLD (Oil, Gas & Nuclear Fuels)	50,207,000	61,929,000	6,627,000	106,000	60,397,000
4	Electricite de France, FRA (Electricity)	45,015,779	21,596,220	250,093	118,146	†
5	Cie de Suez, FRA (Other Financial)	29,817,951	22,875,745	701,460	67,000	6,297,000
6	Daimler-Benz, GER (Transport – Manufacture & Distribution)	27,502,680	41,959,770	837,381	341,905	16,120,000
7	Siemens, GER (Electricals)	25,449,826	33,779,130	842,502	393,900	14,233,000
8	France Telecom, FRA (Communications)	25,167,605	14,940,290	2,350,945	154,548	†
9	Credit Lyonnais, FRA (Banks)	24,648,708	22,377,793	L473,718	71,398	847,000
10	British Gas, UK (Oil, Gas & Nuclear Fuels)	24,639,000	9,698,000	918,000	69,971	13,622,000
11	SNCF, FRA (Transport Services)	22,415,742	9,158,023	L990,849	221,003	†
12	Ste Elf Aquitaine, FRA (Oil, Gas & Nuclear Fuels)	22,252,167	24,665,220	376,081	94,300	12,254,000
13	Volkswagen, GER (Transport – Manufacture & Distribution)	21,922,476	32,270,010	185,861	243,638	5,652,000
14	Deutsche Bank, GER (Banks)	21,818,967	18,634,448	1,150,643	65,058	14,081,000
15	RWE, GER (Electricity)	20,837,346	18,295,330	795,259	117,958	7,097,000
16	British Petroleum Company, UK (Oil, Gas & Nuclear Fuels)	20,777,000	33,116,000	2,281,000	66,550	23,420,000
17	HSBC Holdings, UK (Banks)	20,637,000	13,975,000	3,166,000	106,861	18,424,000
18	Fiat, ITA (Transport – Manufacture & Distribution)	20,040,540	22,963,010	L582,535	256,600	5,502,000
19	Union Bank of Switzerland, SWI (Banks)	19,747,483	9,555,578	1,012,869	27,653	14,015,000
20	Veba, GER (Oil, Gas & Nuclear Fuels)	19,473,111	26,202,970	1,152,377	126,875	10,822,264
21	Cie Financiere de Paribas, FRA (Banks)	18,882,633	13,967,328	506,303	24,999	4,928,000
22	Rabobank Nede, NLD (Banks)	18,462,000	7,082,000	697,000	38,143	†
23	Telefonica de Espana, SPA (Communications)	18,451,800	7,727,200	840,100	103,938	7,094,000
24	Abbey National, UK (Banks)	17,545,000	5,621,000	932,000	16,703	5,649,000
25	Banque Nationale de Paris, FRA (Banks)	17,510,245	17,893,412	133,869	57,097	6,004,000
26	IRI-Istituto per la Ricostruzione Industriale, ITA (Other Financial)	17,239,434	30,834,330	L3,409,827	327,226	†
27	Swiss Bank Corpn, SWI (Banks)	16,997,656	7,367,800	533,919	23,334	6,584,000
28	British Telecommunications, UK (Communications)	16,392,000	13,893,000	2,662,000	148,900	24,379,000
29	ENI-Ente Nazionale Idrocarburi, ITA (Oil, Gas & Nuclear Fuels)	16,317,210	32,576,110	387,656	106,391	†
30	Istituto Mobiliare Italiano – IMI, ITA (Banks)	15,246,151	3,063,320	375,702	n/a	†
31	INI – Instituto Nacional de Industria, SPA (Engineering – General)	14,847,101	12,336,830	L941,938	129,380	†
32	Hanson, UK (Conglomerates)	14,832,000	11,199,000	1,346,000	74,000	11,911,000
33	Deutsche Bahn, GER (Transport Services)	14,246,600	11,931,100	202,500	249,870	†
34	Alcatel-Alsthom Cie Generale d'Electricite, FRA (Communications)	14,243,159	18,390,420	1,053,896	196,500	7,765,000
35	BASF, GER (Chemicals)	13,650,434	17,607,980	851,210	105,845	8,033,827
36	Nestle, SWI (Food Manufacturing)	13,588,942	27,194,990	2,421,996	212,687	23,828,000
37	Bayer, GER (Chemicals)	13,535,259	17,505,580	1,327,634	148,248	10,374,000
38	Iberdrola, SPA (Electricity)	13,241,947	4,118,647	414,117	15,861	4,284,000
39	Hoechst, GER (Chemicals)	13,192,990	20,012,080	890,599	169,760	8,172,000
40	National Westminster Bank, UK (Banks)	13,186,000	13,345,000	1,592,000	97,000	8,820,000
41	Schweizerische Nationalbank, SWI (Banks)	12,341,690	947,618	290,620	564	26,375
42	Renault, FRA (Transport – Manufacture & Distribution)	12,314,600	21,383,200	417,400	139,733	5,052,000
43	Internationale Nederlanden Groep, NLD (Insurance, Life/Non-life)	12,215,552	7,024,384	1,183,372	23,176	11,085,000
44	Roche Holding, SWI (Health & Household)	11,875,550	7,049,456	1,716,954	61,381	30,510,570
45	Credit Agricole, FRA (Banks)	11,570,112	19,629,086	920,933	72,561	†
46	Barclays, UK (Banks)	11,562,000	13,429,000	1,859,000	95,700	9,982,000
47	VIAG, GER (Metal & Metal Forming)	11,528,939	11,674,420	671,266	86,249	4,076,711
48	Salomon Brothers Europe, UK (Other Financial)	11,086,900	2,406,300	719,700	1,024	†
49	Cie Generale des Eaux, FRA (Water)	11,086,294	16,991,900	309,628	204,307	9,242,000
50	TOTAL, FRA (Oil, Gas & Nuclear Fuels)	11,035,900	16,124,900	701,000	41,803	8,494,000

NOTES: [1]Multinational group part incorporated in Great Britain and part in the Netherlands. n/a – not available. †Market capitalisation not available. Figure not disclosed or company unquoted, government controlled, a nationalised industry, a subsidiary or newly quoted.

51-100　　EUROPE'S TOP 1000

RANK	COMPANY NAME (Sector)	CAPITAL EMPLOYED £000	TURNOVER £000	PRE-TAX PROFIT £000	NUMBER OF EMPLOYEES	EQUITY MKT CAPITAL £000
51	Philips Electronics, NLD (Electronics)	10,965,413	21,919,340	1,039,584	249,759	6,380,000
52	Unilever Group[2], UK/NLD (Food Manufacturing)	10,718,996	29,688,550	2,384,718	304,000	21,340,000
53	BMW, GER (Transport – Manufacture & Distribution)	10,039,200	16,983,500	507,200	100,920	5,845,000
54	Ruhrkohle, GER (Mines)	10,022,634	10,515,281	128,228	111,150	†
55	ABN Amro Holding, NLD (Banks)	9,822,000	14,073,000	1,209,000	62,181	15,233,000
56	Eurotunnel Group[3], GBR/FRA (Transport Services)	9,604,644	30,598	L386,887	2,302	2,524,169
57	Banco Santander, SPA (Banks)	9,334,446	5,635,561	700,174	29,232	3,850,000
58	ABB Asea Brown Boveri, SWI (Electricity)	9,278,364	19,350,670	942,204	207,557	†
59	Tractebel, BEL (Electricity)	9,277,201	5,979,686	674,000	36,466	2,690,000
60	Financiere Agache, FRA (Miscellaneous)	9,058,974	3,802,908	681,606	21,296	466,000
61	Ciba-Geigy, SWI (Health & Household)	9,035,850	10,539,290	1,253,778	83,980	11,200,000
62	Allianz AG Holding, GER (Insurance, Life/Non-life)	8,723,035	22,643,700	749,650	69,859	21,229,000
63	Dresdner Bank, GER (Banks)	8,536,495	11,289,930	655,955	41,362	7,444,000
64	Robert Bosch, GER (Electricals)	8,446,680	13,072,170	113,535	164,506	†
65	News International, UK (Media)	8,425,900	733,500	360,900	4,001	1,575,204
66	Nuclear Electric, UK (Electricity)	8,425,000	2,962,000	392,000	10,728	†
67	Peugeot, FRA (Transport – Manufacture & Distribution)	8,319,680	17,107,840	L304,088	143,900	4,513,000
68	Rhone-Poulenc, FRA (Chemicals)	8,247,000	10,177,100	533,800	81,678	4,661,000
69	CS Holding, SWI (Banks)	8,209,996	12,919,613	1,317,830	n/a	10,098,000
70	Corporacion Bancaria de Espana SA Argentaria, SPA (Banks)	8,106,038	5,549,289	541,319	17,698	3,585,000
71	B.A.T. Industries, UK (Tobacco)	7,975,000	5,456,000	1,802,000	83,619	13,298,000
72	Cie de Saint-Gobain, FRA (Other Industrial Materials & Products)	7,804,000	8,784,000	856,000	89,613	5,886,000
73	Danone, FRA (Food Manufacturing)	7,643,304	9,058,714	686,184	68,181	6,251,000
74	Commerzbank, GER (Banks)	7,541,443	8,758,837	666,438	26,449	4,545,000
75	EDP – Electricidade de Portugal, POR (Electricity)	7,411,700	1,929,800	75,200	17,837	†
76	Empresa Nacional de Electricidad, SPA (Electricity)	7,244,065	3,858,981	883,500	16,140	8,361,000
77	Electrabel, BEL (Electricity)	7,133,104	4,020,588	635,543	17,290	6,227,000
78	Svenska Handelsbanken, SWE (Banks)	7,103,246	3,001,866	237,242	7,101	1,915,000
79	Thyssen, GER (Engineering – General)	6,996,809	13,954,660	97,946	131,863	3,607,405
80	Cie UAP, FRA (Insurance, Life/Non-life)	6,928,409	14,987,934	336,555	43,832	4,881,000
81	Lloyds Bank, UK (Banks)	6,652,000	6,863,000	1,304,000	62,120	7,166,000
82	Zurich Insurance Co., SWI (Insurance, Life/Non-life)	6,617,381	10,121,696	440,812	37,354	5,922,145
83	Mannesmann, GER (Engineering – General)	6,603,954	11,257,880	L151,609	131,422	6,373,000
84	Grand Metropolitan, UK (Brewers & Distillers)	6,508,000	7,780,000	654,000	53,674	8,512,000
85	Lyonnaise des Eaux, FRA (Contracting, Construction)	6,415,814	11,005,500	321,733	120,038	3,587,000
86	AXA, FRA (Insurance, Life/Non-life)	6,318,751	10,850,220	472,659	28,900	5,854,000
87	Imperial Chemical Industries, UK (Chemicals)	6,289,000	9,189,000	408,000	67,500	5,422,000
88	Bayernwerk, GER (Electricity)	6,148,340	2,597,034	310,509	9,790	†
89	Cable and Wireless, UK (Communications)	6,126,100	5,132,800	844,100	41,124	8,518,000
90	Aegon, NLD (Insurance, Life/Non-life)	6,085,824	4,018,360	403,917	18,734	3,708,000
91	Assurances Generales de France, FRA (Insurance, Life/Non-life)	5,959,653	7,578,077	240,447	21,779	3,402,000
92	Den Danske Bank, DNK (Banks)	5,798,779	2,598,996	114,213	15,498	1,845,547
93	Glaxo Wellcome§, UK (Health & Household)	5,731,000	5,656,000	1,840,000	47,189	16,589,000
94	AB Volvo, SWE (Transport – Manufacture & Distribution)	5,706,498	13,263,280	1,393,672	74,107	5,326,000
95	Cie Bancaire, FRA (Other Financial)	5,655,975	3,167,720	200,112	8,419	1,497,000
96	Pechiney, FRA (Metal & Metal Forming)	5,646,300	8,341,900	L17,200	58,234	536,000
97	OIAG, AUT (Metal & Metal Forming)	5,640,188	8,766,697	L689,005	62,293	†
98	British Airways, UK (Transport Services)	5,614,000	6,303,000	301,000	53,060	3,905,000
99	Norsk Hydro, NOR (Chemicals)	5,464,314	6,620,166	638;157	32,416	5,758,000
100	Deutsche Lufthansa, GER (Transport Services)	5,462,303	7,138,463	L28,454	60,514	2,854,639

NOTES: [2]Multinational group part incorporated in Great Britain and part in the Netherlands. [3]Eurotunnel PLC/Eurotunnel SA units. §Figures do not reflect merger with Wellcome PLC. n/a – not available. †Market capitalisation not available. Figure not disclosed or company unquoted, government controlled, a nationalised industry, a subsidiary or newly quoted.

EUROPE'S TOP 1000　　101-150

RANK	COMPANY NAME (Sector)	CAPITAL EMPLOYED £000	TURNOVER £000	PRE-TAX PROFIT £000	NUMBER OF EMPLOYEES	EQUITY MKT CAPITAL £000
101	Guinness, UK (Brewers & Distillers)	5,428,000	4,690,000	915,000	23,774	9,081,000
102	Ferruzzi Finanziaria, ITA (Chemicals)	5,365,620	9,598,366	L1,165,913	41,392	189,000
103	Statoil-Den Norske Stats Oljeselskap, NOR (Oil, Gas & Nuclear Fuels)	5,358,049	7,601,224	1,060,235	n/a	†
104	Autostrade Concessioni e Costruzioni Autostrade, ITA (Contracting, Construction)	5,291,822	1,038,743	101,429	8,323	†
105	Cie Nationale Air France, FRA (Transport Services)	5,262,621	6,488,372	L1,005,818	61,759	877,454
106	Bayerische Vereinsbank, GER (Banks)	5,144,743	9,512,763	401,959	20,247	4,050,000
107	Assicurazioni Generali, ITA (Insurance, Life/Non-life)	5,121,921	6,217,911	626,900	34,381	12,422,000
108	Land Securities, UK (Property)	5,104,500	472,600	244,700	551	3,029,382
109	Kredietbank, BEL (Banks)	5,027,130	4,229,128	313,957	11,646	1,963,000
110	Banca di Roma, ITA (Banks)	4,975,788	4,814,294	36,132	23,106	2,166,000
111	Halifax Building Society, UK (Other Financial)	4,969,900	5,444,700	975,100	n/a	†
112	Banco Bilbao Vizcaya, SPA (Banks)	4,962,751	5,344,225	562,133	28,543	3,603,000
113	Sandoz, SWI (Chemicals)	4,946,274	7,585,765	1,082,656	60,304	13,596,000
114	Michelin, FRA (Other Industrial Materials & Products)	4,879,273	7,446,081	L434,946	124,575	2,572,474
115	Bass, UK (Brewers & Distillers)	4,873,000	4,452,000	552,000	75,845	4,503,000
116	Montedison, ITA (Chemicals)	4,844,970	8,592,819	L290,426	32,774	812,000
117	RTZ Corporation, UK (Mines)	4,759,000	2,288,000	922,000	19,080	8,831,000
118	Vattenfall, SWE (Electricity)	4,751,861	1,837,437	434,491	9,071	†
119	Electrowatt, SWI (Electricity)	4,718,181	2,320,814	123,952	18,209	1,355,000
120	Banca Commerciale Italiana, ITA (Banks)	4,695,135	6,728,499	250,288	28,365	2,162,000
121	BTR, UK (Conglomerates)	4,694,000	9,444,000	1,412,000	124,491	10,659,000
122	Preussag, GER (Metal & Metal Forming)	4,612,966	9,267,708	166,961	66,783	275,557
123	Petrofina, BEL (Oil, Gas & Nuclear Fuels)	4,545,354	10,941,320	440,344	14,013	4,395,000
124	British Steel, UK (Metal & Metal Forming)	4,498,000	4,191,000	80,000	41,300	3,239,000
125	Allied Domecq, UK (Brewers & Distillers)	4,496,000	5,526,000	606,000	38,946	5,581,000
126	Ste Nationale de Credit a l'Industrie – SNCI, BEL (Other Financial)	4,483,846	821,298	18,242	1,029	113,000
127	Ste Generale de Belgique, BEL (Metal & Metal Forming)	4,475,813	3,003,934	68,639	18,371	3,130,000
128	Fried. Krupp AG Hoesch-Krupp, GER (Metal & Metal Forming)	4,465,567	8,218,994	35,882	72,673	1,835,000
129	Holderbank Financiere Glaris, SWI (Building Materials & Services)	4,436,347	3,804,959	297,065	37,523	976,751
130	Royal Bank of Scotland Group, UK (Banks)	4,434,000	3,661,000	532,000	22,496	3,322,000
131	Commercial Union, UK (Insurance, Life/Non-life)	4,425,000	6,717,000	402,000	9,589	3,357,100
132	P & O, UK (Transport Services)	4,417,600	5,989,600	349,500	61,467	4,031,758
133	Akzo Nobel, NLD (Chemicals)	4,316,181	7,983,088	592,046	70,400	5,241,000
134	IBM Deutschland, GER (Electronics)	4,269,958	5,208,015	365,356	23,682	†
135	Bayerische Hypotheken- und Wechsel-Bank, GER (Banks)	4,176,438	7,969,158	398,579	16,365	4,388,000
136	Migros-Genossenschafts-Bund, SWI (Food Wholesaling & Retailing)	4,149,871	7,469,019	204,711	74,827	†
137	Union Electrica-Fenosa, SPA (Electricity)	4,123,033	1,666,150	87,862	6,056	811,000
138	Stora Kopparbergs Bergslags, SWE (Packaging, Paper & Printing)	4,102,712	4,160,592	273,748	26,858	2,395,000
139	Tesco, UK (Stores)	4,094,000	10,101,000	551,000	71,467	5,186,775
140	National Power, UK (Electricity)	4,083,000	3,641,000	677,000	6,955	5,445,000
141	Schneider[4], FRA (Electronics)	4,056,931	6,631,934	148,103	91,458	2,347,000
142	Lafarge, FRA (Building Materials & Services)	4,050,636	3,579,647	291,501	30,572	3,720,000
143	General Electric Company, UK (Electronics)	4,033,000	5,791,000	866,000	86,121	8,115,000
144	Forte, UK (Hotels & Leisure)	4,017,000	1,789,000	127,000	36,000	2,236,000
145	Repsol, SPA (Oil, Gas & Nuclear Fuels)	3,955,345	11,225,760	633,568	19,739	6,069,000
146	Marks and Spencer, UK (Stores)	3,952,400	6,541,200	851,500	62,120	11,910,561
147	Istituto Bancario San Paolo di Torino, ITA (Banks)	3,893,995	6,549,704	297,991	20,704	2,779,000
148	Electrolux, SWE (Electricals)	3,870,566	9,190,506	532,264	109,500	2,378,000
149	De Beers Centenary, SWI (Mines)	3,836,010	423,792	372,402	n/a	†
150	Esso UK, UK (Oil, Gas & Nuclear Fuels)	3,809,000	3,674,600	663,800	4,158	†

NOTES: [4]Now a subsidiary of Spie-Batignolles (new name Schnieder SA). n/a – not available. †Market capitalisation not available. Figure not disclosed or company unquoted, government controlled, a nationalised industry, a subsidiary or newly quoted.

151-200 EUROPE'S TOP 1000

RANK	COMPANY NAME (Sector)	CAPITAL EMPLOYED £000	TURNOVER £000	PRE-TAX PROFIT £000	NUMBER OF EMPLOYEES	EQUITY MKT CAPITAL £000
151	Osterreichische Elektrizitatswirtschafts, AUT (Electricity)	3,807,195	1,117,500	86,785	5,164	557,529
152	MAN, GER (Transport – Manufacture & Distribution)	3,769,321	7,207,558	73,009	58,527	247,019
153	L'Air Liquide, FRA (Chemicals)	3,765,483	3,744,191	466,762	24,600	5,565,488
154	Gaz de France, FRA (Oil, Gas & Nuclear Fuels)	3,741,566	5,778,372	193,040	26,084	†
155	Moet Hennessy Louis Vuitton, FRA (Brewers & Distillers)	3,735,042	2,801,959	532,653	15,826	8,674,000
156	Solvay, BEL (Chemicals)	3,706,583	4,700,983	L121,305	41,314	2,534,000
157	J. Sainsbury, UK (Food Wholesaling & Retailing)	3,698,900	10,583,200	368,800	82,345	7,496,765
158	Rodamco, NLD (Property)	3,696,311	282,351	202,741	n/a	2,661,000
159	KLM Royal Dutch Airlines, NLD (Transport Services)	3,696,055	3,063,205	34,970	27,535	1,495,539
160	Great Universal Stores, UK (Stores)	3,692,400	3,094,300	518,900	n/a	6,099,983
161	Vereinigte Elektrizitatswerke Westfalen, GER (Electricity)	3,665,310	2,992,006	180,150	13,637	3,422,680
162	Unidanmark, DNK (Banks)	3,663,011	1,978,081	59,660	11,100	1,279,886
163	Robeco, NLD (Other Financial)	3,660,909	110,357	100,651	n/a	3,812,000
164	Thomson, FRA (Electronics)	3,646,099	7,940,982	L469,718	99,895	†
165	Banco Central Hispanoamericano, SPA (Banks)	3,606,408	6,764,888	425,797	34,426	2,574,000
166	Arbed, LUX (Metal & Metal Forming)	3,491,383	3,697,458	L134,822	25,145	476,000
167	Huhtamaki, FIN (Food Manufacturing)	3,473,826	5,394,590	264,299	11,145	622,604
168	Cie de Navigation Mixte, FRA (Food Manufacturing)	3,465,458	1,873,043	77,083	27,874	1,779,810
169	BNL-Banca Nazionale Del Lavoro, ITA (Banks)	3,455,790	7,576,328	82,077	25,600	†
170	Standard Chartered, UK (Banks)	3,412,000	2,913,000	510,000	28,734	2,804,000
171	Telefonaktiebolaget LM Ericsson, SWE (Communications)	3,391,140	7,024,861	477,378	74,096	7,776,000
172	Neste, FIN (Oil, Gas & Nuclear Fuels)	3,377,984	7,354,802	140,710	13,332	†
173	Lagardere Groupe, FRA (Oil, Gas & Nuclear Fuels)	3,365,075	6,350,033	177,606	41,904	565,000
174	MEPC, UK (Property)	3,364,600	234,300	111,200	n/a	1,808,141
175	Bonifiche Siele Finaziaria, ITA (Other Financial)	3,348,860	2,043,320	L1,072	7,385	163,000
176	British Aerospace, UK (Aerospace)	3,317,000	7,153,000	211,000	56,400	2,126,000
177	Telia, SWE (Communications)	3,312,125	3,143,888	251,453	32,807	†
178	BAA, UK (Transport Services)	3,302,100	1,097,800	322,400	8,171	4,837,558
179	Woolwich Building Society, UK (Other Financial)	3,291,700	2,020,400	302,700	8,390	†
180	Ladbroke Group, UK (Hotels & Leisure)	3,282,400	4,360,700	L229,800	55,248	1,989,680
181	Berliner Kraft- und Licht (BEWAG), GER (Electricity)	3,281,857	1,701,818	63,711	11,278	1,290,344
182	Eridania Beghin-Say, FRA (Food Manufacturing)	3,257,587	5,988,468	297,382	24,198	2,182,000
183	Matra-Hachette, FRA (Miscellaneous)	3,253,123	6,350,080	184,452	41,904	1,717,000
184	Bank of Scotland, UK (Banks)	3,230,000	2,735,000	450,000	15,258	2,618,600
185	Adam Opel, GER (Transport – Manufacture & Distribution)	3,207,768	9,262,695	L153,715	52,287	†
186	Repola, FIN (Other Industrial Materials & Products)	3,177,343	3,595,687	199,118	27,378	1,759,000
187	Cia Sevillana de Electricidad, SPA (Electricity)	3,173,934	1,338,968	83,993	5,999	985,000
188	Alliance & Leicester Building Society, UK (Other Financial)	3,153,900	1,990,900	284,000	n/a	†
189	Bertelsmann, GER (Media)	3,147,618	7,311,062	480,254	50,437	†
190	SmithKline Beecham, UK (Health & Household)	3,141,000	6,492,000	691,000	52,300	6,246,950
191	TSB Group, UK (Banks)	3,125,000	3,122,000	504,000	26,860	3,453,000
192	Ste Centrale du Gan, FRA (Insurance, Life/Non-life)	3,124,916	4,995,625	103,519	36,241	2,838,000
193	Aerospatiale Ste Nationale Industrielle, FRA (Aerospace)	3,119,994	5,981,763	L189,628	43,913	†
194	Accor, FRA (Hotels & Leisure)	3,105,228	3,424,956	124,694	143,740	1,599,000
195	Nederlandse Spoorwegen, NLD (Transport Services)	3,103,290	1,357,712	L16,537	27,914	†
196	Investor, SWE (Engineering – General)	3,087,015	2,660,891	34,762	27,372	2,458,000
197	Minorco, LUX (Mines)	3,086,418	2,006,838	233,944	17,668	3,391,000
198	Swissair, SWI (Transport Services)	3,074,083	2,635,661	38,375	25,026	761,000
199	Marine-Wendel, FRA (Investment Trusts)	3,058,589	3,336,117	237,454	34,754	352,000
200	Ing C. Olivetti & C., ITA (Electronics)	3,009,903	3,625,105	L179,180	n/a	1,047,000

NOTES: n/a – not available. †Market capitalisation not available. Figure not disclosed or company unquoted, government controlled, a nationalised industry, a subsidiary or newly quoted.

EUROPE'S TOP 1000 — 201-250

RANK	COMPANY NAME (Sector)	CAPITAL EMPLOYED £000	TURNOVER £000	PRE-TAX PROFIT £000	NUMBER OF EMPLOYEES	EQUITY MKT CAPITAL £000
201	SOVAC, FRA (Banks)	3,002,319	1,136,006	73,405	1,977	564,000
202	Fuerzas Electricas de Cataluna, – FECSA, SPA (Electricity)	2,992,004	1,135,108	54,754	3,669	848,000
203	Bayerische Landesbank Girozentrale, GER (Banks")	2,979,853	6,533,145	204,723	5,208	†
204	Severn Trent, UK (Water)	2,957,300	998,000	281,400	10,783	1,870,451
205	Italcementi, ITA (Building Materials & Services)	2,927,416	2,172,452	L79,868	20,220	535,000
206	CGIP-Cie Generale d'Industrie et de Participations, FRA (Miscellaneous)	2,909,672	3,291,031	222,742	34,293	866,968
207	De Nationale Investeringsbank, NLD (Other Financial)	2,897,551	349,697	53,219	358	493,596
208	North West Water Group, UK (Water)	2,867,100	924,200	269,000	8,013	2,070,237
209	Cie Financiere du Groupe Victoire, FRA (Insurance, Life/Non-life)	2,866,541	8,139,280	196,404	2,562	2,893,904
210	Teledanmark, DNK (Communications)	2,859,843	1,836,384	403,924	17,076	2,166,000
211	Winterthur Ste Suisse d'Assurances, SWI (Insurance, Life/Non-life)	2,858,980	6,653,306	230,835	20,500	3,317,711
212	Ruhrgas, GER (Oil, Gas & Nuclear Fuels)	2,832,973	5,777,025	524,966	11,126	†
213	British Railways Board, UK (Transport Services)	2,830,500	3,100,500	L108,400	128,414	†
214	Saint Louis, FRA (Food Manufacturing)	2,819,854	4,019,016	221,272	26,943	1,318,000
215	Henkel KGaA, GER (Health & Household)	2,809,462	5,582,920	235,121	40,590	1,540,000
216	BOC Group, UK (Chemicals)	2,806,400	3,292,300	253,100	39,390	3,304,679
217	DSM, NLD (Chemicals)	2,804,156	3,226,954	169,310	19,381	1,828,000
218	Rank Xerox, UK (Electronics)	2,798,000	3,309,000	221,000	23,139	†
219	SHV Holdings, NLD (Miscellaneous)	2,779,894	7,928,173	345,230	41,250	†
220	Cie Financiere Richemont, SWI (Tobacco)	2,760,700	3,665,100	476,000	n/a	6,472,800
221	ZENECA Group, UK (Health & Household)	2,759,000	4,480,000	659,000	30,800	8,315,000
222	Credito Italiano, ITA (Banks)	2,754,204	4,058,357	66,540	17,242	1,476,000
223	Carrefour, FRA (Stores)	2,746,066	16,072,560	398,574	90,300	6,793,000
224	Sydkraft, SWE (Electricity)	2,740,679	834,623	176,438	5,622	1,515,000
225	SCA – Svenska Cellulosa, SWE (Health & Household)	2,727,804	2,865,630	90,200	24,152	1,948,000
226	Bank Austria, AUT (Banks)	2,661,010	2,467,293	86,809	9,237	3,015,000
227	Pirelli, ITA (Other Industrial Materials & Products)	2,652,647	3,892,130	L21,377	42,132	1,284,000
228	Whitbread, UK (Brewers & Distillers)	2,648,100	2,471,800	275,400	49,306	2,585,046
229	London Regional Transport, UK (Transport Services)	2,642,900	1,096,100	10,300	40,139	†
230	Conoco (UK), UK (Oil, Gas & Nuclear Fuels)	2,622,300	2,714,800	117,700	8,896	†
231	Thames Water, UK (Water)	2,605,600	1,093,200	241,700	10,141	1,922,649
232	3i Group, UK (Investment Trusts)	2,557,674	244,233	84,255	589	1,907,547
233	Kymmene Corpn, FIN (Packaging, Paper & Printing)	2,531,289	2,372,159	L23,492	17,551	1,426,567
234	L'Oreal, FRA (Health & Household)	2,528,987	4,724,538	508,609	32,261	8,016,061
235	LASMO, UK (Oil, Gas & Nuclear Fuels)	2,526,000	648,000	92,000	1,440	1,419,000
236	Franz Haniel & Cie, GER (Miscellaneous)	2,521,844	9,830,327	132,318	35,720	†
237	National Grid Holding, UK (Electricity)	2,501,000	1,425,000	579,500	5,127	†
238	Enso-Gutzeit, FIN (Packaging, Paper & Printing)	2,498,204	1,522,558	7,146	14,071	1,178,253
239	Redland, UK (Building Materials & Services)	2,493,600	2,468,800	373,000	21,545	2,382,800
240	Ciments Francais, FRA (Building Materials & Services)	2,489,100	1,566,467	46,815	11,396	468,000
241	Swiss Reinsurance Co., SWI (Insurance, Life/Non-life)	2,486,944	8,996,822	280,361	26,364	4,512,000
242	PowerGen, UK (Electricity)	2,462,000	2,932,000	476,000	4,782	3,358,000
243	Schering, GER (Health & Household)	2,439,651	1,891,701	189,091	18,550	2,860,416
244	Munchener Ruckversicherungs-Ges, GER (Insurance, Life/Non-life)	2,437,947	10,386,375	251,919	17,325	7,548,712
245	OMV, AUT (Oil, Gas & Nuclear Fuels)	2,423,714	3,822,213	L252,678	10,696	1,461,955
246	Heineken Holding, NLD (Brewers & Distillers)	2,409,903	3,096,942	341,415	21,646	1,735,147
247	Ford-Werke, GER (Transport – Manufacture & Distribution)	2,407,388	8,530,711	L26,330	43,330	2,226,804
248	Rank Organisation, UK (Hotels & Leisure)	2,405,000	2,199,400	284,000	39,743	3,683,549
249	General Accident, UK (Insurance, Life/Non-life)	2,398,200	5,026,700	428,300	11,510	2,287,941
250	British Land Company, UK (Property)	2,368,000	156,500	53,900	295	1,485,569

NOTES: n/a – not available. †Market capitalisation not available. Figure not disclosed or company unquoted, government controlled, a nationalised industry, a subsidiary or newly quoted.

251-300 EUROPE'S TOP 1000

RANK	COMPANY NAME (Sector)	CAPITAL EMPLOYED £000	TURNOVER £000	PRE-TAX PROFIT £000	NUMBER OF EMPLOYEES	EQUITY MKT CAPITAL £000
251	NV Koninklijke KNP BT, NLD (Packaging, Paper & Printing)	2,349,627	4,725,940	133,004	27,636	1,982,000
252	Generale de Banque, BEL (Banks)	2,344,176	6,236,688	411,571	21,429	2,054,000
253	Nokia Corpn, FIN (Electronics)	2,317,194	3,791,037	586,049	28,043	7,049,420
254	Groupe Bruxelles Lambert, BEL (Other Financial)	2,314,948	12,073	25,686	70	1,683,000
255	Reed/Elsevier Group[5], GBR/NLD (Media)	2,309,000	3,035,000	620,000	26,900	8,875,000
256	Sun Alliance Group, UK (Insurance, Life/Non-life)	2,307,100	4,657,800	315,500	16,987	2,335,866
257	Pilkington, UK (Other Industrial Materials & Products)	2,301,000	2,737,400	97,800	41,100	1,310,360
258	Associated British Foods, UK (Food Manufacturing)	2,301,000	4,513,000	382,000	50,241	2,528,000
259	Royal Insurance Holdings, UK (Insurance, Life/Non-life)	2,295,000	4,785,000	401,000	13,224	1,816,000
260	SAS – Scandinavian Airlines System, SWE (Transport Services)	2,292,739	3,316,957	L41,714	37,330	†
261	Christiania Bank og Kreditkasse, NOR (Banks)	2,286,176	910,340	135,999	4,317	717,000
262	Ford Motor Co., UK (Transport – Manufacture & Distribution)	2,256,000	5,327,000	L92,000	32,500	†
263	Enterprise Oil, UK (Oil, Gas & Nuclear Fuels)	2,214,300	651,300	93,900	623	1,929,945
264	Post Office, UK (Communications)	2,198,000	5,345,000	283,000	193,163	†
265	Hoogovens, NLD (Metal & Metal Forming)	2,195,109	2,852,135	146,592	19,671	915,942
266	CarnaudMetalbox, FRA (Metal & Metal Forming)	2,185,576	2,863,247	153,514	31,100	1,773,000
267	British Nuclear Fuels, UK (Oil, Gas & Nuclear Fuels)	2,181,000	1,133,000	81,000	15,476	†
268	Anglian Water, UK (Water)	2,171,600	687,900	132,200	6,031	1,424,222
269	Pinault-Printemps-La Redoute, FRA (Stores)	2,159,248	7,446,325	137,163	50,586	2,386,000
270	Motor-Columbus, SWI (Engineering – General)	2,152,404	695,258	135,440	2,045	357,000
271	Argyll Group, UK (Food Wholesaling & Retailing)	2,148,800	5,607,700	361,800	67,323	3,269,205
272	Cadbury Schweppes, UK (Food Manufacturing)	2,145,800	4,029,600	478,500	40,506	3,594,109
273	Metallgesellschaft, GER (Engineering – General)	2,144,217	8,182,487	L1,013,270	27,409	826,000
274	Linde, GER (Engineering – General)	2,133,804	3,212,304	168,639	29,176	2,489,910
275	Bouygues, FRA (Contracting, Construction)	2,129,027	7,197,290	82,227	86,998	1,556,000
276	Aare-Tessin fur Elektrizitat, SWI (Electricity)	2,128,554	732,287	92,731	1,932	993,000
277	Creditanstalt-Bankverein, AUT (Banks)	2,110,435	2,969,460	106,177	9,000	1,833,000
278	Degussa, GER (Metal & Metal Forming)	2,101,515	5,516,508	111,667	27,259	1,728,562
279	Sidmar, BEL (Metal & Metal Forming)	2,093,952	1,593,951	L132,358	8,583	†
280	BBL-Banque Bruxelles Lambert, BEL (Banks)	2,083,517	4,409,735	172,985	n/a	1,656,000
281	Incentive, SWE (Engineering – General)	2,080,288	1,549,819	326,081	19,106	1,410,908
282	Scottish & Newcastle, UK (Brewers & Distillers)	2,078,400	1,759,800	221,800	36,830	2,790,118
283	Scottish Nuclear, UK (Electricity)	2,066,000	537,000	72,000	2,060	†
284	Karstadt, GER (Stores)	2,061,471	7,534,241	174,491	70,818	1,929,005
285	AMB, GER (Insurance, Life/Non-life)	2,057,764	4,386,272	59,643	19,106	2,447,406
286	Banco Popular Espanol, SPA (Banks)	2,051,228	1,736,579	419,815	12,069	2,196,000
287	Cockerill Sambre, BEL (Metal & Metal Forming)	2,043,574	2,838,909	L109,598	26,209	284,000
288	Allied Irish Banks, IRL (Banks)	2,034,349	1,875,968	333,792	15,105	1,784,325
289	Continental, GER (Other Industrial Materials & Products)	2,031,052	3,982,056	36,930	49,025	842,397
290	RMC Group, UK (Building Materials & Services)	2,023,300	3,678,000	283,300	27,371	1,844,610
291	Rolinco, NLD (Investment Trusts)	1,998,232	40,261	31,274	n/a	2,017,000
292	Slough Estates, UK (Property)	1,970,100	179,400	64,000	427	1,090,921
293	Sulzer, SWI (Engineering – General)	1,969,815	2,886,128	127,624	27,449	1,526,000
294	AB SKF, SWE (Metal & Metal Forming)	1,959,571	2,831,337	154,616	40,072	1,192,000
295	Transatlantic Holdings, UK (Property)	1,942,900	136,200	90,100	10,230	1,064,787
296	Esso, GER (Oil, Gas & Nuclear Fuels)	1,938,083	4,478,256	102,816	2,413	†
297	Asda Group, UK (Stores)	1,927,900	4,882,200	L125,900	70,515	1,608,768
298	Bremer Vulkan Verbund, GER (Transport – Manufacture & Distribution)	1,917,752	2,472,463	L73,652	25,445	568,092
299	Boots Company, UK (Stores)	1,912,900	4,167,100	415,900	80,099	4,830,017
300	Alusuisse-Lonza Holding, SWI (Metal & Metal Forming)	1,898,506	3,584,477	145,788	26,303	1,962,000

NOTES: [5]Multinational group part incorporated in Great Britain and part in the Netherlands. n/a – not available. †Market capitalisation not available. Figure not disclosed or company unquoted, government controlled, a nationalised industry, a subsidiary or newly quoted.

EUROPE'S TOP 1000   301-350

RANK	COMPANY NAME (Sector)	CAPITAL EMPLOYED £000	TURNOVER £000	PRE-TAX PROFIT £000	NUMBER OF EMPLOYEES	EQUITY MKT CAPITAL £000
301	IFI-Istituto Finanziario Industriale, ITA (Miscellaneous)	1,888,199	23,960	L100,695	n/a	†
302	Fortis Amev, NLD (Insurance, Life/Non-life)	1,877,529	22,707	204,936	n/a	1,945,796
303	S. G. Warburg Group, UK (Merchant Banks)	1,857,400	1,441,800	297,000	n/a	1,686,530
304	Rolls-Royce, UK (Aerospace)	1,846,000	3,163,000	101,000	43,500	2,195,000
305	Lonrho, UK (Conglomerates)	1,840,000	1,824,000	112,000	100,113	1,018,000
306	Bradford & Bingley Building Society, UK (Other Financial)	1,833,700	1,097,900	159,900	n/a	†
307	Otto Versand, GER (Stores)	1,824,988	6,675,866	265,710	37,668	†
308	Skanska, SWE (Contracting, Construction)	1,821,574	3,193,327	261,664	28,868	1,851,000
309	Siebe, UK (Engineering – General)	1,818,000	1,863,500	217,200	29,938	2,355,412
310	National Home Loans Holdings, UK (Other Financial)	1,811,900	231,100	11,400	n/a	61,062
311	Kon Ahold, NLD (Food Wholesaling & Retailing)	1,806,714	10,490,830	207,861	125,079	2,367,565
312	Baloise-Holding, SWI (Insurance, Life/Non-life)	1,793,006	3,001,611	90,197	9,475	1,174,170
313	Sandvik, SWE (Metal & Metal Forming)	1,775,231	2,150,329	324,294	27,581	2,814,000
314	Tate & Lyle, UK (Food Manufacturing)	1,764,000	4,074,000	273,800	15,640	1,937,708
315	Guardian Royal Exchange, UK (Insurance, Life/Non-life)	1,736,000	3,375,000	L75,000	7,325	1,451,000
316	BBC Brown Boveri, SWI (Engineering – General)	1,734,883	4,302	451,704	207,570	4,733,000
317	BHF-Bank (Berliner Handels- und Frankfurter Bank), GER (Banks)	1,733,608	1,776,851	123,935	3,108	1,277,000
318	Nationwide Building Society, UK (Other Financial)	1,725,300	2,837,200	252,700	n/a	†
319	Havas, FRA (Media)	1,717,738	4,112,183	202,568	18,628	2,366,492
320	Hochtief AG vorm. Gebr. Helfmann, GER (Contracting, Construction)	1,714,748	1,891,768	84,843	31,830	2,696,082
321	RWE-DEA, GER (Oil, Gas & Nuclear Fuels)	1,714,117	5,254,312	160,641	8,100	2,133,854
322	Sudzucker, GER (Food Manufacturing)	1,709,671	2,078,121	69,675	10,243	1,024,887
323	Arjo Wiggins Appleton, UK (Packaging, Paper & Printing)	1,706,400	2,915,100	217,100	18,466	1,938,268
324	Guaranteed Export Finance Corporation, UK (Other Financial)	1,700,283	297,504	L236	n/a	†
325	Charbonnages de France, FRA (Mines)	1,693,090	1,045,084	L343,292	18,714	†
326	Banque Cantonale Vaudoise, SWI (Banks)	1,682,186	487,291	36,181	1,778	327,995
327	Hammerson, UK (Property)	1,675,700	195,100	107,500	381	982,497
328	Fortis, BEL (Other Financial)	1,675,588	5,804	L5,116	32,127	1,913,184
329	Casino, Guichard-Perrachon et Cie, FRA (Stores)	1,665,424	7,412,199	89,850	45,326	1,320,000
330	CIR Cie Industriali Riunite, ITA (Miscellaneous)	1,656,852	286,033	24,097	71,289	486,000
331	Pearson, UK (Media)	1,644,800	1,550,100	297,800	17,215	3,068,312
332	AB Astra, SWE (Health & Household)	1,644,181	1,916,140	658,610	14,377	10,148,000
333	Isar-Amperwerke, GER (Electricity)	1,624,540	839,352	50,727	5,143	1,931,729
334	Carl-Zeiss-Stiftung, GER (Engineering – Instrument)	1,610,175	2,009,549	30,036	32,302	†
335	Energie-Versorgung Schwaben, GER (Electricity)	1,607,399	1,440,427	108,236	5,345	†
336	Philipp Holzmann, GER (Contracting, Construction)	1,596,257	4,671,756	89,272	43,264	1,541,505
337	Euro Disney, FRA (Hotels & Leisure)	1,588,563	496,846	L209,536	10,172	733,000
338	Yorkshire Water, UK (Water)	1,584,200	530,600	143,500	4,768	1,065,784
339	Pharmacia, SWE (Health & Household)	1,583,201	2,365,125	297,120	19,913	2,591,000
340	Kingfisher, UK (Stores)	1,579,300	4,887,700	244,200	43,741	2,956,627
341	Oerlikon-Buhrle Holding, SWI (Aerospace)	1,572,726	1,707,873	54,969	18,263	771,466
342	Sta Italiana per il Gas pA Italgas, ITA (Oil, Gas & Nuclear Fuels)	1,560,206	1,507,115	54,903	10,226	1,108,000
343	Delhaize Freres et Cie 'Le Lion', BEL (Food Wholesaling & Retailing)	1,556,663	7,046,564	31,867	82,200	1,331,000
344	AGIV-AG fur Industrie und Verkehrswesen, GER (Engineering – General)	1,556,624	3,625,649	76,144	41,155	800,000
345	Foreign & Colonial Investment Trust, UK (Investment Trusts)	1,554,145	48,283	35,100	n/a	1,430,851
346	Badenwerk, GER (Electricity)	1,554,079	1,194,488	51,050	4,201	†
347	Outokumpu, FIN (Metal & Metal Forming)	1,550,101	2,095,830	128,391	15,920	1,461,000
348	Tarmac, UK (Building Materials & Services)	1,545,000	2,510,300	107,200	20,571	1,101,248
349	Novo Nordisk, DNK (Health & Household)	1,541,564	1,250,121	191,778	12,448	2,277,478
350	Thyssen Industrie, GER (Metal & Metal Forming)	1,541,383	3,240,477	53,984	43,255	695,357

NOTES: n/a – not available. †Market capitalisation not available. Figure not disclosed or company unquoted, government controlled, a nationalised industry, a subsidiary or newly quoted.

351-400 EUROPE'S TOP 1000

RANK	COMPANY NAME (Sector)	CAPITAL EMPLOYED £000	TURNOVER £000	PRE-TAX PROFIT £000	NUMBER OF EMPLOYEES	EQUITY MKT CAPITAL £000
351	Leeds Permanent Building Society[6], UK (Other Financial)	1,534,900	1,589,800	245,800	n/a	†
352	ZF Friedrichshafen, GER (Transport – Manufacture & Distribution)	1,528,020	2,108,349	46,879	27,676	†
353	E. Merck, GER (Chemicals)	1,521,034	2,137,590	159,955	26,482	†
354	CCF-Credit Commercial de France, FRA (Banks)	1,509,516	7,278,342	195,981	n/a	1,567,000
355	Blue Circle Industries, UK (Building Materials & Services)	1,506,400	1,779,800	184,400	19,690	2,214,459
356	Assurantieconcern Stad Rotterdam, NLD (Insurance, Life/Non-life)	1,494,135	740,892	61,575	2,043	413,479
357	Welsh Water, UK (Water)	1,489,800	512,100	144,200	6,600	898,061
358	Trafalgar House, UK (Property)	1,486,000	3,763,500	45,600	33,153	1,378,899
359	Nordbanken, SWE (Banks)	1,475,676	2,976,422	306,169	7,582	†
360	Metsa-Serla, FIN (Packaging, Paper & Printing)	1,468,604	1,190,501	92,914	9,061	762,858
361	Banco Ambrosiano Veneto, ITA (Banks)	1,444,452	2,002,244	110,405	9,457	1,045,000
362	Kemira, FIN (Chemicals)	1,441,403	1,469,543	41,130	11,156	553,904
363	IBM United Kingdom Holdings, UK (Electronics)	1,437,300	4,057,100	L174,100	14,708	†
364	Amerada Hess, UK (Oil, Gas & Nuclear Fuels)	1,435,475	485,270	39,684	626	†
365	Skandia Insurance Co., SWE (Insurance, Life/Non-life)	1,420,993	2,365,021	L18,465	10,467	1,131,000
366	South West Water, UK (Water)	1,418,600	251,600	93,000	3,060	622,399
367	Reckitt & Colman, UK (Health & Household)	1,409,870	2,078,950	160,210	18,700	2,206,677
368	Kooperativa forbundet, SWE (Stores)	1,407,309	5,514,075	L14,040	33,606	†
369	Worms & Cie, FRA (Other Financial)	1,403,975	6,941	88,932	35,977	1,226,000
370	Lloyds Abbey Life, UK (Insurance, Life/Non-life)	1,396,500	1,205,600	315,600	10,297	2,296,059
371	Carlsberg, DNK (Brewers & Distillers)	1,390,320	1,719,070	133,510	17,481	1,964,000
372	Credit Foncier de France, FRA (Banks)	1,389,666	4,646,013	80,463	n/a	1,117,000
373	Kaufhof Holding, GER (Stores)	1,357,424	7,695,296	183,432	69,147	1,872,114
374	Kvaerner, NOR (Engineering – General)	1,356,794	2,423,956	112,900	24,145	1,293,000
375	Lucas Industries, UK (Engineering – General)	1,353,800	2,487,900	L129,700	45,731	1,487,500
376	Orkla, NOR (Health & Household)	1,343,470	1,927,735	146,018	16,873	1,120,000
377	Hillsdown Holdings, UK (Food Manufacturing)	1,335,300	4,261,600	172,300	40,473	1,242,289
378	Preussag Stahl, GER (Metal & Metal Forming)	1,333,429	2,394,982	L57,193	13,869	599,313
379	CLF – Credit Local de France, FRA (Other Financial)	1,328,653	3,214,624	223,860	n/a	1,628,000
380	Coats Viyella, UK (Textiles)	1,327,900	2,588,500	105,100	76,208	1,326,542
381	Promodes, FRA (Food Wholesaling & Retailing)	1,327,272	10,610,660	135,436	54,848	2,063,000
382	Banco Portugues do Atlantico, POR (Banks)	1,315,850	1,844,937	129,071	9,701	838,000
383	Saga Petroleum, NOR (Oil, Gas & Nuclear Fuels)	1,313,892	541,677	112,343	1,323	898,270
384	Corporacion Industrial y Financiera de Banesto, SPA (Miscellaneous)	1,309,345	1,558,289	L665,516	18,091	522,000
385	Pernod Ricard, FRA (Brewers & Distillers)	1,306,903	1,770,767	183,511	10,269	2,114,000
386	Mo och Domsjo, SWE (Packaging, Paper & Printing)	1,303,928	1,448,382	L38,068	11,414	1,027,000
387	ASEA, SWE (Engineering – General)	1,296,606	1,370	457,406	4[7]	4,245,784
388	Sears, UK (Stores)	1,294,200	2,143,700	153,800	42,783	1,494,958
389	Electrafina, BEL (Investment Trusts)	1,291,572	20,371	4,602	100	1,682,000
390	GKN, UK (Engineering – General)	1,290,500	2,470,200	200,300	32,520	2,038,829
391	Alcatel SEL, GER (Communications)	1,290,087	2,265,467	36,176	22,643	1,162,679
392	Prudential Corporation, UK (Insurance, Life/Non-life)	1,289,000	8,271,000	603,000	20,786	6,015,000
393	La Cie Immobiliere Phenix, FRA (Property)	1,285,931	561,821	L18,052	4,109	153,385
394	HEW-Hamburgische Electricitats-Werke, GER (Electricity)	1,284,927	1,105,714	67,597	5,710	866,895
395	CBR Cementbedrijven, BEL (Building Materials & Services)	1,276,759	1,036,140	107,838	11,654	1,095,511
396	THORN EMI, UK (Hotels & Leisure)	1,276,700	4,292,100	326,500	41,423	4,689,853
397	Burmah Castrol, UK (Oil, Gas & Nuclear Fuels)	1,267,700	2,934,400	243,500	21,866	1,628,370
398	Pargesa Holding, SWI (Other Financial)	1,244,852	18,805	73,455	n/a	1,156,896
399	Asko Deutsche Kaufhaus, GER (Stores)	1,241,603	7,553,929	179,704	65,906	1,455,677
400	SLR, SWI (Insurance, Life/Non-life)	1,237,554	4,206,763	648,306	7,187	94,200

NOTES: [6]Merger with Halifax Building Society effective 1/8/95. [7]Parent Company. n/a – not available. †Market capitalisation not available. Figure not disclosed or company unquoted, government controlled, a nationalised industry, a subsidiary or newly quoted.

EUROPE'S TOP 1000 — 401-450

RANK	COMPANY NAME (Sector)	CAPITAL EMPLOYED £000	TURNOVER £000	PRE-TAX PROFIT £000	NUMBER OF EMPLOYEES	EQUITY MKT CAPITAL £000
401	Britannia Building Society, UK (Other Financial)	1,237,400	771,500	100,700	2,711	†
402	United Biscuits (Holdings), UK (Food Manufacturing)	1,235,300	2,998,200	133,800	39,691	1,723,277
403	CEPSA-Cia Espanola de Petroleos, SPA (Oil, Gas & Nuclear Fuels)	1,233,532	3,171,545	92,146	8,655	1,033,000
404	Cheltenham & Gloucester Building Society[8], UK (Other Financial)	1,230,100	1,374,800	219,200	n/a	†
405	Saarbergwerke, GER (Mines)	1,219,391	1,798,454	L35,085	21,158	†
406	Albatros Investissement, FRA (Transport – Manufacture & Distribution)	1,218,599	2,918,366	L23,911	24,194	336,000
407	CKAG Colonia Konzern, GER (Insurance, Life/Non-life)	1,213,194	2,946,823	116,475	11,709	1,690,604
408	AGA, SWE (Chemicals)	1,210,300	1,067,400	146,900	10,546	1,392,000
409	Banco Comercial Portugues, POR (Banks)	1,206,895	1,145,804	113,637	4,480	1,087,000
410	Trelleborg, SWE (Metal & Metal Forming)	1,203,894	1,628,276	76,925	12,351	989,000
411	Berner Kantonalbank, SWI (Banks)	1,200,248	494,487	13,605	1,615	14,653
412	Compagnie Financiere Ottomane, LUX (Other Financial)	1,184,251	889,979	253,318	n/a	140,000
413	Autopistas, Concesionaria Espanola, SPA (Transport Services)	1,172,799	221,000	120,794	1,065	1,408,000
414	Banque Nationale de Belgique, BEL (Banks)	1,165,005	551,155	72,874	2,699	300,000
415	Valeo, FRA (Transport – Manufacture & Distribution)	1,160,039	2,380,354	93,991	25,000	2,189,000
416	Sparekassen Bikuben, DNK (Banks)	1,156,180	821,883	L105,550	5,210	370,436
417	Heidelberger Druckmaschinen, GER (Engineering – General)	1,155,072	1,303,558	88,111	12,000	†
418	Deutsche Babcock, GER (Engineering – General)	1,153,906	3,260,437	40,674	37,195	540,502
419	Danisco, DNK (Food Wholesaling & Retailing)	1,147,113	1,291,667	103,714	11,055	1,099,996
420	Unitas, FIN (Banks)	1,144,572	1,510,536	L141,581	9,191	793,000
421	Fondiaria, ITA (Insurance, Life/Non-life)	1,144,281	1,792,883	L217,514	5,592	1,261,000
422	Rautaruukki, FIN (Metal & Metal Forming)	1,139,829	956,435	52,131	9,444	616,140
423	SMH, SWI (Engineering – Instrument)	1,136,965	1,250,562	236,568	15,420	†
424	T & N, UK (Engineering – General)	1,130,600	1,936,100	10,700	42,805	857,815
425	Southern Water, UK (Water)	1,127,000	347,700	127,500	3,476	958,238
426	Bank of Ireland, IRL (Banks)	1,126,222	1,606,043	268,041	12,169	1,371,980
427	Sara Lee/DE, NLD (Food Manufacturing)	1,123,138	2,425,659	341,460	21,379	†
428	Cie CNP – Nationale a Portefeuille, BEL (Other Financial)	1,123,001	28,588	24,382	n/a	971,385
429	Scottish Power, UK (Electricity)	1,118,400	1,568,600	351,100	8,560	2,622,069
430	Greenalls Group, UK (Hotels & Leisure)	1,116,948	708,707	73,622	15,316	861,635
431	Bank of England, UK (Banks)	1,116,400	225,900	123,700	3,194	†
432	Great Portland Estates, UK (Property)	1,115,000	97,100	53,100	74	559,748
433	Burton Group, UK (Stores)	1,110,800	1,909,600	41,100	37,337	889,900
434	SNECMA, FRA (Aerospace)	1,110,268	2,301,679	L89,815	24,911	†
435	Chargeurs, FRA (Textiles)	1,109,900	1,159,049	56,013	9,743	970,000
436	Freudenberg & Co., GER (Other Industrial Materials & Products)	1,107,202	1,873,357	43,450	25,090	†
437	Legrand, FRA (Electricals)	1,105,436	1,174,355	93,403	18,200	1,609,845
438	Chevron U.K., UK (Oil, Gas & Nuclear Fuels)	1,099,136	1,023,097	90,585	2,624	†
439	Scor, FRA (Insurance, Life/Non-life)	1,097,804	1,106,102	32,664	1,076	378,000
440	Forsmarks Kraftgrupp, SWE (Oil, Gas & Nuclear Fuels)	1,091,707	362,473	8	820	†
441	Heidelberger Zement, GER (Building Materials & Services)	1,090,195	1,267,681	86,278	11,857	1,804,124
442	Tomkins, UK (Engineering – General)	1,087,900	3,245,100	257,100	45,496	2,991,300
443	EVN Energie-Versorgung Niederosterreich, AUT (Electricity)	1,085,102	597,561	43,640	2,884	387,556
444	Koninklijke Nedlloyd, NLD (Transport Services)	1,083,281	2,375,012	35,587	20,325	470,000
445	Kesko, FIN (Food Wholesaling & Retailing)	1,082,252	3,399,521	79,183	5,701	669,000
446	AS Potagua, DNK (Engineering – General)	1,081,332	1,357,585	51,214	14,872	137,047
447	FLS Industries, DNK (Engineering – General)	1,077,851	1,489,457	59,982	13,034	401,000
448	Espirito Santo Financial Holding, LUX (Banks)	1,076,646	1,412,592	142,354	n/a	255,000
449	Remy Cointreau, FRA (Brewers & Distillers)	1,072,278	752,796	38,683	3,611	729,655
450	Banca Nazionale dell'Agricoltura, ITA (Banks)	1,068,028	1,989,254	1,520	7,353	463,000

NOTES: [8]Business is expected to be integrated into that of Lloyds Bank PLC. n/a – not available. †Market capitalisation not available. Figure not disclosed or company unquoted, government controlled, a nationalised industry, a subsidiary or newly quoted.

451-500 EUROPE'S TOP 1000

RANK	COMPANY NAME (Sector)	CAPITAL EMPLOYED £000	TURNOVER £000	PRE-TAX PROFIT £000	NUMBER OF EMPLOYEES	EQUITY MKT CAPITAL £000
451	Scottish Mortgage & Trust, UK (Investment Trusts)	1,066,173	41,583	23,796	n/a	789,977
452	Coop Bank, SWI (Banks)	1,063,729	228,525	16,514	683	159,617
453	Beiersdorf, GER (Health & Household)	1,061,906	2,077,368	153,816	16,886	1,731,959
454	Waste Management International, UK (Miscellaneous)	1,059,258	1,115,653	165,157	17,274	1,357,805
455	John Lewis Partnership, UK (Stores)	1,058,500	2,183,900	58,700	38,800	2,706
456	Associated British Ports Holdings, UK (Transport Services)	1,056,200	228,300	80,300	2,253	1,027,498
457	Nortel, UK (Communications)	1,054,100	693,200	L310,400	8,172	†
458	Southern Electric, UK (Electricity)	1,053,500	1,780,200	222,000	7,391	1,596,514
459	Inchcape, UK (Transport – Manufacture & Distribution)	1,051,400	6,101,600	228,400	40,118	2,252,604
460	Schindler Holding, SWI (Engineering – General)	1,045,434	2,038,867	110,519	34,178	1,009,280
461	Bilfinger + Berger Bau, GER (Contracting, Construction)	1,043,372	2,101,616	72,593	46,260	1,329,752
462	Edinburgh Investment Trust, UK (Investment Trusts)	1,043,235	57,492	38,122	n/a	860,263
463	Courage, UK (Brewers & Distillers)	1,041,393	1,310,195	L269,438	5,369	†
464	CMB, BEL (Transport Services)	1,041,342	765,791	20,609	3,659	474,000
465	Kansallis Yhtyma, FIN (Banks)	1,040,918	1,552,646	L231,543	9,823	775,128
466	Mirror Group, UK (Media)	1,033,600	462,900	189,300	2,915	537,303
467	Neckarwerke Elektrizitatsversorgungs, GER (Electricity)	1,032,842	648,134	36,965	1,910	643,876
468	Fokker, NLD (Aerospace)	1,032,214	844,080	L291,838	9,621	228,307
469	An-Hyp (Caisse Hypothecaire Anversoise), BEL (Aerospace)	1,027,901	526,041	18,908	1,396	341,000
470	GTM-Entrepose, FRA (Contracting, Construction)	1,027,326	3,550,420	41,712	44,059	509,000
471	BIL GT Gruppe, LIE (Banks)	1,023,167	467,745	102,992	1,545	220,842
472	Eiffage, FRA (Contracting, Construction)	1,022,530	4,318,958	43,575	47,753	612,678
473	Granada Group, UK (Media)	1,020,700	2,097,700	265,400	42,878	3,275,600
474	Royale Belge, BEL (Insurance, Life/Non-life)	1,017,964	1,310,926	124,598	5,539	1,584,201
475	Wessex Water, UK (Water)	1,016,800	217,200	103,300	1,852	835,711
476	Cie des Machines Bull, FRA (Electronics)	1,016,036	3,323,202	L593,236	31,735	146,000
477	Northumbrian Water Group, UK (Water)	1,015,500	298,600	62,800	3,314	588,963
478	CRH, IRL (Building Materials & Services)	1,013,004	1,577,503	113,576	13,691	1,303,472
479	REXAM, UK (Packaging, Paper & Printing)	1,009,000	2,342,000	226,000	27,900	2,177,000
480	CANAL+, FRA (Media)	1,008,298	1,020,523	212,779	n/a	2,207,642
481	Almanij -Algemene Mij voor Nijverheidskrediet, BEL (Other Financial)	1,003,216	98,691	8,289	156	1,000,936
482	Hambros, UK (Banks)	993,800	755,200	90,500	7,916	501,015
483	Witan Investment Company, UK (Investment Trusts)	990,633	41,355	29,313	n/a	863,197
484	Bollore Technologies, FRA (Other Industrial Materials & Products)	978,996	2,918,639	L24,303	24,193	220,000
485	Aker, NOR (Contracting, Construction)	973,418	1,536,993	69,669	14,714	371,000
486	Northern Rock Building Society, UK (Other Financial)	972,300	660,100	117,600	2,003	†
487	Banca Popolare di Bergamo – Credito Varesino Scrl, ITA (Banks)	971,994	1,108,353	96,715	5,107	598,000
488	Gas Natural SDG, SPA (Oil, Gas & Nuclear Fuels)	969,287	804,382	127,269	4,128	1,500,000
489	IKB Deutsche Industriebank, GER (Banks)	965,544	1,588,383	78,845	1,047	856,970
490	Moeara Enim Petroleum Mij, NLD (Other Financial)	962,684	43,286	43,132	n/a	289,955
491	Alliance Trust, UK (Investment Trusts)	958,802	39,369	36,508	n/a	1,154,992
492	Hilti, LIE (Engineering – General)	953,357	964,468	86,727	11,490	331,346
493	Metra Corpn, FIN (Engineering – General)	946,811	1,269,885	78,303	11,676	504,894
494	J. Lauritzen Holding, DNK (Transport Services)	942,670	1,523,698	L6,043	14,500	273,243
495	Cap Gemini Sogeti, FRA (Business Services)	940,035	1,297,266	L39,154	20,900	812,622
496	London Electricity, UK (Electricity)	935,200	1,308,400	186,500	5,532	1,150,589
497	Texaco, UK (Oil, Gas & Nuclear Fuels)	929,039	3,832,496	L758	3,039	†
498	BICC, UK (Engineering – General)	928,000	3,674,000	131,000	35,708	1,287,000
499	SSAB Svenskt Stal, SWE (Metal & Metal Forming)	927,210	1,334,021	179,804	9,562	886,000
500	Credit National, FRA (Banks)	924,231	1,631,016	57,288	1,338	579,000

NOTES: n/a – not available. †Market capitalisation not available. Figure not disclosed or company unquoted, government controlled, a nationalised industry, a subsidiary or newly quoted.

EUROPE'S TOP 1000 — 501-550

RANK	COMPANY NAME (Sector)	CAPITAL EMPLOYED £000	TURNOVER £000	PRE-TAX PROFIT £000	NUMBER OF EMPLOYEES	EQUITY MKT CAPITAL £000
501	Vauxhall Motors, UK (Transport – Manufacture & Distribution)	923,100	3,100,900	185,100	10,554	†
502	Dassault Aviation, FRA (Aerospace)	922,420	1,563,650	45,120	12,426	521,491
503	Empresa Nacional Hidroelectrica del Ribagorzana, SPA (Electricity)	919,777	665,309	35,227	2,011	378,000
504	Thomson Corporation, UK (Media)	918,400	508,100	120,300	8,763	†
505	National & Provincial Building Society[9], UK (Other Financial)	918,300	983,000	134,000	n/a	†
506	Eastern Group, UK (Electricity)	918,000	1,846,300	176,800	7,003	1,424,229
507	A. Ahlstrom, FIN (Packaging, Paper & Printing)	917,290	1,361,969	47,613	13,479	†
508	VIB, NLD (Property)	913,509	105,692	51,408	51	651,735
509	Norske Skogindustrier, NOR (Packaging, Paper & Printing)	913,507	850,690	30,892	4,758	572,034
510	Littlewoods Organisation, UK (Stores)	913,482	2,395,316	117,210	28,603	†
511	Atlas Copco, SWE (Engineering – General)	910,478	1,602,945	111,916	18,247	1,499,000
512	NCC, SWE (Contracting, Construction)	910,317	1,492,555	14,837	14,905	468,000
513	Klockner-Werke, GER (Engineering – General)	897,729	1,651,487	13,942	19,722	462,489
514	BPB Industries, UK (Building Materials & Services)	897,400	1,150,800	107,700	11,292	1,404,480
515	NV Bekaert, BEL (Metal & Metal Forming)	894,513	1,046,166	32,361	11,015	1,014,195
516	Scottish Hydro-Electric, UK (Electricity)	894,500	792,400	164,200	3,552	1,193,509
517	PWA, GER (Packaging, Paper & Printing)	888,730	1,792,200	23,701	12,196	696,042
518	International General Electric (USA), UK (Other Financial)	888,172	769,692	35,452	5,845	†
519	Isosceles, UK (Food Wholesaling & Retailing)	885,200	3,059,310	L52,930	46,057	†
520	Yorkshire Electricity Group, UK (Electricity)	880,500	1,307,900	149,000	5,764	1,114,423
521	Euroc, SWE (Building Materials & Services)	877,521	1,123,923	74,568	8,487	785,264
522	East Midlands Electricity, UK (Electricity)	875,100	1,444,500	51,200	7,590	1,351,619
523	G. Haindl'sche Papierfabriken KGaA, GER (Packaging, Paper & Printing)	873,319	842,305	L20,803	4,559	†
524	Wolseley, UK (Building Materials & Services)	873,181	3,254,082	202,343	19,073	2,266,442
525	Harrisons & Crosfield, UK (Chemicals)	866,900	2,110,000	236,700	25,404	979,404
526	BK Vision, SWI (Other Financial)	864,838	27,605	7,327	n/a	904,806
527	Stockholm & Edinburgh Investments, UK (Property)	864,400	321,200	L77,400	2,555	†
528	Wereldhave, NLD (Investment Trusts)	861,763	82,211	39,578	131	536,834
529	Klockner-Humboldt-Deutz, GER (Engineering – General)	860,548	1,307,056	644	9,552	479,557
530	Brixton Estate, UK (Property)	858,709	70,021	32,578	69	400,802
531	Reemtsma Cigarettenfabriken, GER (Tobacco)	857,243	1,018,089	104,135	8,382	†
532	Mobil Oil, GER (Oil, Gas & Nuclear Fuels)	848,420	2,344,377	88,244	1,960	†
533	Schroders, UK (Merchant Banks)	840,700	1,038,400	195,400	3,380	1,472,325
534	Pepsico Finance (UK), UK (Other Financial)	840,248	125,984	68,111	4,751	†
535	Banco Espirito Santo e Comercial de Lisboa, POR (Banks)	838,620	1,000,137	114,440	6,426	703,000
536	English China Clays, UK (Chemicals)	837,000	1,040,800	93,000	8,788	1,120,579
537	Ugine, FRA (Metal & Metal Forming)	836,300	1,699,144	70,486	11,305	548,576
538	Cookson Group, UK (Other Industrial Materials & Products)	834,300	1,428,500	51,100	12,230	1,291,560
539	Club Mediterranee, FRA (Hotels & Leisure)	832,786	967,799	L21,078	8,744	438,825
540	Hafslund Nycomed, NOR (Health & Household)	832,646	541,652	147,229	4,037	1,341,000
541	NFC, UK (Transport Services)	830,600	2,034,900	105,600	33,989	1,254,066
542	Williams Holdings, UK (Building Materials & Services)	829,200	1,393,100	200,300	15,538	2,163,128
543	NORWEB, UK (Electricity)	828,600	1,470,600	178,300	8,255	955,295
544	Dragados y Construcciones, SPA (Contracting, Construction)	821,052	1,554,772	58,706	20,340	7,000
545	Banca Toscana, ITA (Banks)	820,940	1,153,396	88,497	4,558	378,000
546	Parmalat Finanziaria, ITA (Food Manufacturing)	819,620	1,197,573	48,233	9,558	†
547	Die Erste Osterreichische Spar-Casse-Bank, AUT (Banks)	818,703	849,781	26,006	3,536	152,000
548	Grundig, GER (Electronics)	813,916	1,441,946	L49,625	13,753	†
549	Courtaulds, UK (Chemicals)	811,700	1,995,300	121,600	19,500	1,759,799
550	SGS Holding, SWI (Business Services)	804,725	1,278,185	134,516	32,507	1,542,450

NOTES: [9] On 10/7/95 the Society and Abbey National PLC announced agreement had been reached on terms of recommended merger. n/a – not available. †Market capitalisation not available. Figure not disclosed or company unquoted, government controlled, a nationalised industry, a subsidiary or newly quoted.

551-600 EUROPE'S TOP 1000

RANK	COMPANY NAME (Sector)	CAPITAL EMPLOYED £000	TURNOVER £000	PRE-TAX PROFIT £000	NUMBER OF EMPLOYEES	EQUITY MKT CAPITAL £000
551	Feldschlosschen Holding, SWI (Brewers & Distillers)	797,908	426,374	14,813	3,182	298,035
552	Credit Foncier Vaudois, SWI (Banks)	797,504	332,507	17,004	533	141,985
553	Wacker-Chemie, GER (Chemicals)	795,431	1,311,686	83,339	13,137	†
554	Scac-Delmas-Vieljeux (SDV), FRA (Transport Services)	792,286	2,728,593	L34,474	22,201	338,287
555	Midlands Electricity, UK (Electricity)	791,700	1,415,500	195,400	6,207	1,159,703
556	L E Lundbergforetagen, SWE (Contracting, Construction)	791,610	204,209	29,477	520	495,824
557	Snia BPD, ITA (Chemicals)	791,442	942,331	9,972	9,377	442,000
558	Georg Fischer, SWI (Engineering – General)	790,271	1,019,561	37,284	10,160	486,000
559	Entreprise Miniere et Chimique, FRA (Chemicals)	785,869	1,741,453	L93,841	13,319	†
560	Rheinmetall Berlin, GER (Engineering – General)	784,910	1,146,027	18,834	13,342	314,573
561	Scottish Investment Trust, UK (Investment Trusts)	783,096	29,833	18,123	n/a	551,310
562	Hertie Waren-Und Kaufhaus, GER (Stores)	781,984	2,508,791	5,307	n/a	†
563	Gallaher, UK (Tobacco)	781,100	5,059,900	337,600	23,732	†
564	Fomento Construccion Y Contratas, SPA (Contracting, Construction)	778,384	1,908,702	106,809	31,659	1,174,000
565	NFU Mutual Insurance Society, UK (Insurance, Life/Non-life)	777,800	479,050	60,130	2,200	†
566	Reuters Holdings, UK (Media)	774,000	2,309,000	510,000	12,718	7,798,368
567	Co-operative Wholesale Society, UK (Food Wholesaling & Retailing)	772,400	3,111,500	17,200	n/a	†
568	Robert Fleming Holdings, UK (Merchant Banks)	771,803	572,570	209,922	2,554	†
569	British Investment Trust, UK (Investment Trusts)	765,971	45,328	27,095	133	763,620
570	Gemina-Generale Mobiliare Interessenze Azionarie, ITA (Other Financial)	763,166	447,055	128,510	12,834	824,000
571	TI Group, UK (Engineering – General)	762,700	1,420,200	153,000	22,600	1,787,760
572	Glaverbel, BEL (Other Industrial Materials & Products)	759,419	592,150	L9,038	9,670	464,582
573	Irish Permanent, IRL (Other Financial)	759,165	222,304	34,384	1,281	182,454
574	NV Nederlandse Gasunie, NLD (Oil, Gas & Nuclear Fuels)	758,083	5,857,724	41,898	n/a	†
575	Caradon, UK (Building Materials & Services)	756,200	1,989,900	201,200	26,714	1,703,336
576	Bergesen d.y., NOR (Transport Services)	755,697	250,940	9,926	2,429	884,000
577	Toro Assicurazioni, ITA (Insurance, Life/Non-life)	754,547	772,506	90,345	2,171	1,023,000
578	Carlsberg-Tetley, UK (Brewers & Distillers)	754,000	1,025,600	76,200	5,012	†
579	Taylor Woodrow, UK (Contracting, Construction)	751,500	1,146,300	50,800	8,206	492,498
580	Merkur Holding, SWI (Food Wholesaling & Retailing)	750,006	1,394,524	59,560	12,803	650,757
581	Benetton Group, ITA (Textiles)	748,312	1,158,108	147,258	5,895	1,715,000
582	Kleinwort Benson Group, UK (Banks)	746,700	765,700	97,000	2,892	737,713
583	Valenciana de Cementos Portland, SPA (Building Materials & Services)	744,611	377,528	36,066	3,904	1,174,000
584	Daily Mail and General Trust, UK (Media)	743,000	778,800	92,100	8,492	965,900
585	Pharma Vision 2000, SWI (Other Financial)	742,674	238,511	7,168	n/a	1,209,924
586	ICA Handlarnas AB, SWE (Stores)	742,193	3,418,004	58,095	12,745	†
587	SA Taittinger, FRA (Brewers & Distillers)	741,970	522,849	L2,438	7,292	206,392
588	Govett Oriental Investment Trust, UK (Investment Trusts)	741,728	13,590	5,251	n/a	593,285
589	Electra Investment Trust, UK (Investment Trusts)	740,751	39,084	19,481	71	550,352
590	Autopistas del Mare Nostrum, SPA (Transport Services)	738,939	131,315	52,820	611	546,000
591	GIB, BEL (Stores)	736,879	4,453,562	L45,971	47,772	849,703
592	Italmobiliare, ITA (Miscellaneous)	735,651	16,254	L5,394	n/a	291,000
593	BKW Energie, SWI (Electricity)	734,801	420,469	6,206	1,686	110,575
594	George Wimpey, UK (Contracting, Construction)	734,400	1,687,500	45,100	11,347	461,989
595	British Assets Trust, UK (Investment Trusts)	732,803	38,034	26,793	n/a	360,960
596	Sirti, ITA (Communications)	732,429	657,080	214,796	10,832	842,000
597	Signet Group, UK (Stores)	729,170	987,960	L85,437	14,840	123,747
598	BBA Group, UK (Engineering – General)	728,600	1,380,000	63,900	17,778	813,800
599	Ste Financiere Interbail, FRA (Property)	722,358	172,578	29,367	50	224,213
600	Victoria Holding, GER (Insurance, Life/Non-life)	718,435	2,873,157	36,606	12,179	1,530,928

NOTES: n/a – not available. †Market capitalisation not available. Figure not disclosed or company unquoted, government controlled, a nationalised industry, a subsidiary or newly quoted.

EUROPE'S TOP 1000 — 601-650

RANK	COMPANY NAME (Sector)	CAPITAL EMPLOYED £000	TURNOVER £000	PRE-TAX PROFIT £000	NUMBER OF EMPLOYEES	EQUITY MKT CAPITAL £000
601	Nissan (UK), UK (Transport – Manufacture & Distribution)	717,068	1,325,858	2,108	5,287	†
602	Landis & Gyr, SWI (Miscellaneous)	715,469	1,361,594	69,300	15,868	714,660
603	Ostasiatiske Kompagni (Det), DNK (Miscellaneous)	713,387	1,280,911	32,820	13,655	310,000
604	Hunter Douglas, ANT (Building Materials & Services)	710,846	2,082,478	90,357	10,848	491,271
605	Vodafone Group, UK (Communications)	706,046	850,529	363,330	31,170	6,064,064
606	Saur (UK), UK (Water)	705,831	106,294	21,262	1,426	†
607	Altana, GER (Health & Household)	702,007	1,146,242	78,327	10,068	1,063,362
608	Avesta Sheffield, SWE (Metal & Metal Forming)	701,598	1,432,900	133,172	7,881	998,000
609	Oce-van der Grinten, NLD (Electronics)	700,340	991,081	38,349	11,692	455,279
610	Zuger Kantonalbank, SWI (Banks)	695,800	201,242	8,998	434	134,899
611	Effjohn, FIN (Transport Services)	690,763	519,718	L15,578	7,565	96,000
612	EWE, GER (Electricity)	684,540	1,007,530	34,764	1,508	†
613	GAIC, ITA (Other Financial)	678,210	27	L238,566	9	372,000
614	D.N.L (Det Norske Luftfartselskap), NOR (Transport Services)	678,209	752,540	29,779	n/a	127,000
615	Baer Holding, SWI (Other Financial)	677,753	361,569	61,266	1,461	611,453
616	Fleming Far Eastern Investment Trust, UK (Investment Trusts)	677,663	11,889	3,485	n/a	459,813
617	FAG Kugelfischer Georg Schafer, GER (Engineering – General)	675,318	1,087,586	25,564	15,474	441,792
618	Hidroelectrica del Cantabrico, SPA (Electricity)	671,783	511,469	72,707	1,323	713,000
619	Liechtensteinische Landesbank, LIE (Banks)	671,087	225,737	31,465	368	593,924
620	Cerus – Compagnies Europeene Reunies, FRA (Other Financial)	666,903	71,992	L7,176	n/a	363,000
621	South Western Electricity, UK (Electricity)	663,200	899,600	116,800	5,400	696,652
622	Koninklijke Pakhoed, NLD (Transport Services)	661,762	490,764	52,184	5,047	498,936
623	Ascom Holding, SWI (Communications)	661,620	1,451,190	22,131	13,416	301,524
624	Esso Francaise, FRA (Oil, Gas & Nuclear Fuels)	661,190	3,871,665	81,416	3,024	1,020,592
625	Banco di Sardegna, ITA (Banks)	660,572	942,955	85,521	3,896	†
626	Scottish Eastern Investment Trust, UK (Investment Trusts)	660,442	23,937	13,488	n/a	475,200
627	Austrian Airlines Osterreichische Luftverkehrs, AUT (Transport Services)	657,300	593,068	L11,016	4,010	310,815
628	PORTUCEL, POR (Packaging, Paper & Printing)	655,920	103,638	L87,930	3,818	†
629	AS Th. Wessel & Vett, Magasin du Nord, DNK (Stores)	654,391	228,893	2,094	2,264	36,438
630	Stadtwerke Koln, GER (Electricity)	653,614	841,534	L13,511	7,898	†
631	Banque Generale du Luxembourg, LUX (Banks)	652,555	1,168,015	87,282	1,875	504,000
632	Buderus, GER (Engineering – General)	649,900	1,195,334	81,161	10,611	684,465
633	Galeries Lafayette, FRA (Stores)	648,639	3,472,708	24,736	33,453	356,294
634	Peel Holdings, UK (Property)	647,879	73,040	10,191	393	439,539
635	Bristol and West Building Society, UK (Other Financial)	646,700	658,400	57,100	2,605	†
636	Docks de France, FRA (Stores)	645,123	4,506,825	78,048	32,794	934,000
637	Kone, FIN (Engineering – General)	644,383	962,514	50,590	21,553	440,302
638	SEEBOARD, UK (Electricity)	644,300	1,218,100	131,700	5,339	840,467
639	Costa Crociere, ITA (Transport Services)	642,493	264,489	18,391	2,154	128,000
640	Laporte, UK (Chemicals)	640,700	964,500	123,500	7,108	1,371,370
641	Financiere et Industrielle Gaz et Eaux, FRA (Other Financial)	640,683	43,614	75,864	14	605,970
642	Bankinter, SPA (Banks)	638,087	1,014,728	139,840	2,057	1,021,000
643	Danzas Holding, SWI (Transport Services)	637,210	2,001,802	9,932	15,248	262,049
644	Finnair, FIN (Transport Services)	636,829	692,269	17,780	10,659	268,237
645	BHP – Hamilton Oil Great Britain, UK (Oil, Gas & Nuclear Fuels)	633,984	90,388	L5,242	n/a	†
646	Eurafrance, FRA (Other Financial)	632,060	32,513	38,675	4	767,594
647	Labinal, FRA (Engineering – General)	628,392	1,004,717	24,220	16,770	344,661
648	SIG Schweizerische Industrie-Ges Holding, SWI (Engineering – General)	628,211	802,648	48,516	7,438	352,662
649	Valmet, FIN (Engineering – General)	627,093	1,046,219	22,374	12,107	517,035
650	Manweb, UK (Electricity)	626,300	929,600	126,300	4,604	744,330

NOTES: n/a – not available. †Market capitalisation not available. Figure not disclosed or company unquoted, government controlled, a nationalised industry, a subsidiary or newly quoted.

651-700 EUROPE'S TOP 1000

RANK	COMPANY NAME (Sector)	CAPITAL EMPLOYED £000	TURNOVER £000	PRE-TAX PROFIT £000	NUMBER OF EMPLOYEES	EQUITY MKT CAPITAL £000
651	Axel Springer Verlag, GER (Media)	625,540	1,386,818	39,463	12,187	840,339
652	Sap, GER (Business Services)	619,566	738,259	184,383	4,596	2,577,697
653	Imetal, FRA (Building Materials & Services)	616,421	740,073	57,500	6,713	818,883
654	Carlton Communications, UK (Media)	608,329	1,404,696	190,231	8,451	2,305,922
655	Hapag-Lloyd, GER (Transport Services)	608,230	1,679,535	34,453	8,336	1,169,072
656	Societe Internationale Pirelli, SWI (Other Industrial Materials & Products)	606,968	4,763	L1,893	38,485	804,176
657	Caledonia Investments, UK (Other Financial)	604,100	51,000	45,200	1,028	531,800
658	ANZ Holdings (UK), UK (Banks)	603,852	513,341	138,421	6,599	†
659	Bardon Group, UK (Mines)	603,600	331,700	19,500	2,659	214,010
660	W.H. Smith Group, UK (Stores)	600,200	2,441,600	83,400	30,506	1,328,076
661	Biber Holding, SWI (Packaging, Paper & Printing)	599,009	338,022	L49,813	1,924	183,662
662	Energieversorgung Ostbayern, GER (Electricity)	598,489	874,001	85,348	2,352	503,268
663	Chelsfield, UK (Property)	598,430	52,873	10,202	197	250,979
664	Italcable Servizi Cablografici, ITA (Communications)	597,745	349,035	115,281	2,975	650,000
665	Vard, NOR (Transport Services)	597,555	594,134	36,352	4,889	49,764
666	UCB, BEL (Chemicals)	597,147	925,675	55,897	8,104	708,000
667	Heraeus Holding, GER (Metal & Metal Forming)	596,776	2,456,296	31,568	9,431	†
668	Northern Foods, UK (Food Manufacturing)	593,600	2,048,600	157,200	29,709	1,053,472
669	Stena Line, SWE (Transport Services)	592,230	801,076	42,717	8,352	214,050
670	Wienerberger Baustoffindustrie, AUT (Building Materials & Services)	591,567	694,098	47,769	4,803	957,199
671	Celsius Industries Corpn, SWE (Engineering – General)	591,552	983,506	60,282	15,598	397,000
672	Northern Electric, UK (Electricity)	591,000	1,030,500	128,700	4,714	835,426
673	Dyckerhoff & Widmann, GER (Contracting, Construction)	588,969	1,242,443	21,933	17,377	345,897
674	Amer Group, FIN (Miscellaneous)	587,998	843,081	34,170	5,360	241,000
675	Trygg-Hansa, SWE (Insurance, Life/Non-life)	587,497	665,477	145,661	2,462	568,000
676	Cia Logistica de Hidrocarburos CLH, SPA (Transport Services)	585,692	400,940	144,450	3,454	15,000
677	Cartiere Burgo, ITA (Packaging, Paper & Printing)	584,876	717,653	537	5,493	541,000
678	Ste Bic, FRA (Miscellaneous)	582,848	713,521	98,902	8,210	1,110,966
679	Asko, FIN (Health & Household)	582,158	857,138	27,588	8,700	204,388
680	La Rinascente, ITA (Stores)	580,348	2,091,585	67,222	14,835	719,000
681	Gotthard Bank, SWI (Banks)	579,808	393,532	29,492	842	556,315
682	Banco Portugues de Investimento, POR (Banks)	579,697	612,245	38,219	333	447,000
683	GIM-Generale Industrie Metallurgiche, ITA (Metal & Metal Forming)	577,094	1,400,381	L41,843	10,496	37,000
684	Koninklijke BolsWessanen, NLD (Food Manufacturing)	575,901	1,900,535	120,387	9,264	1,000,342
685	Anglo & Overseas Trust, UK (Investment Trusts)	574,032	17,732	11,438	n/a	480,982
686	Sefimeg, FRA (Property)	573,235	93,746	57,977	192	720,526
687	Banque Internationale a Luxembourg, LUX (Banks)	572,010	1,187,378	81,081	2,241	484,000
688	Bongrain, FRA (Food Manufacturing)	571,976	1,121,272	68,499	7,699	649,153
689	Vallehermoso, SPA (Property)	570,642	188,399	24,401	323	†
690	Strafor Facom, FRA (Engineering – General)	570,172	858,376	L38,974	12,021	313,176
691	Baden-Wurttembergische Bank, GER (Banks)	568,660	645,270	39,376	2,265	915,835
692	Synthelabo, FRA (Health & Household)	567,860	957,567	105,596	7,262	1,249,252
693	Tidnings AB Marieberg, SWE (Media)	566,819	651,742	35,355	7,737	357,247
694	Codan Forsikring, DNK (Insurance, Life/Non-life)	562,454	583,046	206	2,880	762,000
695	Rallye, FRA (Food Manufacturing)	559,080	376,524	13,043	4,043	316,959
696	Vaux Group, UK (Brewers & Distillers)	558,873	243,503	29,273	6,090	346,757
697	SAGEM, FRA (Electronics)	557,987	1,533,746	131,621	15,074	866,298
698	Rieter Holding, SWI (Engineering – General)	557,634	741,321	30,974	9,878	378,061
699	Svensk Interkontinental Lufttrafik AB – SILA, SWE (Transport Services)	556,428	10,518	72,066	5	478,866
700	Jelmoli Holding, SWI (Stores)	554,801	795,908	13,623	5,550	260,850

NOTES: n/a – not available. †Market capitalisation not available. Figure not disclosed or company unquoted, government controlled, a nationalised industry, a subsidiary or newly quoted.

EUROPE'S TOP 1000 — 701-750

RANK	COMPANY NAME (Sector)	CAPITAL EMPLOYED £000	TURNOVER £000	PRE-TAX PROFIT £000	NUMBER OF EMPLOYEES	EQUITY MKT CAPITAL £000
701	IMI, UK (Engineering – General)	552,000	1,161,200	50,300	17,186	1,031,959
702	Ares-Serono, SWI (Health & Household)	551,302	504,059	67,144	3,948	1,721,786
703	SEITA, FRA (Tobacco)	551,253	1,662,965	104,743	5,239	†
704	Soporcel, POR (Packaging, Paper & Printing)	550,627	168,096	L59,562	1,068	192,630
705	SEP – Samenwerkende Elektriciteits-Produktiebedrijven, NLD (Electricity)	550,570	2,153,600	14,062	443	†
706	Grosskraftwerk Mannheim, GER (Electricity)	550,172	337,094	138	1,393	†
707	Racal Electronics, UK (Communications)	549,242	916,091	26,380	11,779	659,110
708	Premafin Finanziaria, ITA (Property)	548,055	163,846	L110,335	n/a	238,000
709	Comptoirs Modernes, FRA (Stores)	543,991	3,036,120	79,243	18,820	822,000
710	Saipem, ITA (Contracting, Construction)	542,929	889,900	56,122	n/a	537,000
711	Seagram Holdings, UK (Brewers & Distillers)	542,845	806,007	124,587	3,129	†
712	AB Industrivarden, SWE (Other Industrial Materials & Products)	542,706	1,080,695	124,323	9,572	719,000
713	Europistas Concesionaria Espanola, SPA (Contracting, Construction)	541,330	57,111	30,140	322	261,000
714	Ebro Agricolas, Cia de Alimentacion, SPA (Food Manufacturing)	538,962	754,710	18,983	4,678	307,000
715	Dixons Group, UK (Stores)	538,700	1,921,400	L165,200	12,020	976,800
716	Fleming Japanese Investment Trust, UK (Investment Trusts)	535,567	4,677	522	n/a	456,601
717	Diehl, GER (Engineering – General)	534,737	1,214,852	805,680	14,795	†
718	London Merchant Securities, UK (Property)	534,411	37,468	22,281	61	260,658
719	Corporacion Financiera Alba, SPA (Other Financial)	534,324	28,152	19,475	32	474,000
720	Villeroy & Boch, GER (Health & Household)	533,857	670,464	L12,277	13,200	151,971
721	Tabacalera, SPA (Tobacco)	531,911	3,460,574	42,333	10,101	687,000
722	Sommer Allibert, FRA (Building Materials & Services)	528,897	1,151,820	44,526	12,365	497,454
723	Koninklijke Gist-Brocades, NLD (Food Manufacturing)	528,643	636,097	61,456	5,325	636,044
724	Rothschilds Continuation, UK (Merchant Banks)	528,528	361,617	52,018	953	†
725	Essilor International, FRA (Health & Household)	528,136	695,225	44,945	12,828	755,113
726	Bobst, SWI (Packaging, Paper & Printing)	527,499	503,137	34,081	4,844	143,597
727	Wella, GER (Health & Household)	527,179	1,156,248	72,787	16,350	728,008
728	Braun, GER (Electricals)	526,940	537,178	47,556	5,037	†
729	Gullspangs Kraft, SWE (Electricity)	519,417	278,934	55,643	1,035	448,389
730	Partek, FIN (Building Materials & Services)	518,840	774,652	L25,452	8,128	267,026
731	Central Transport Rental Group, UK (Transport Services)	517,700	292,200	L331,100	951	35,429
732	Dalgety, UK (Food Manufacturing)	517,000	4,955,300	120,100	16,609	955,504
733	Polar Corpn, FIN (Contracting, Construction)	514,743	315,309	L78,947	2,418	†
734	Cultor, FIN (Food Manufacturing)	512,263	740,521	56,322	5,276	397,861
735	Smith & Nephew, UK (Health & Household)	511,400	964,600	L5,500	12,223	1,835,227
736	Strabag, GER (Contracting, Construction)	510,479	1,711,689	34,099	21,253	407,408
737	Unicem, ITA (Building Materials & Services)	509,731	328,920	31,731	2,675	249,000
738	Finextel, FRA (Property)	507,915	152,938	24,268	21	129,377
739	COFIDE-Cia Finanziaria de Benedetti, ITA (Electronics)	507,812	104,828	L2,116	n/a	276,000
740	Cie d'Entreprises CFE, BEL (Contracting, Construction)	507,708	472,058	11,431	6,152	97,000
741	Wm. Morrison Supermarkets, UK (Stores)	507,406	1,779,370	116,073	23,200	1,128,458
742	Sdad General de Aguas de Barcelona, SPA (Water)	503,698	643,674	42,675	12,998	476,000
743	Birmingham Midshires Building Society, UK (Other Financial)	501,300	367,700	52,100	1,516	†
744	Manchester Airport, UK (Transport Services)	500,471	182,097	16,614	2,105	†
745	Monks Investment Trust,, UK (Investment Trusts)	499,011	15,468	7,873	n/a	404,254
746	Perstorp, SWE (Chemicals)	498,424	857,287	46,091	8,674	486,667
747	Murray International Trust, UK (Investment Trusts)	497,643	26,124	20,934	n/a	399,383
748	Dr Ing H.C.F Porsche, GER (Transport – Manufacture & Distribution)	495,428	932,169	L58,211	7,035	293,901
749	Koninklijke Van Ommeren, NLD (Transport Services)	494,647	349,605	28,305	3,497	257,233
750	Lille-Bonniere et Colombes, FRA (Property)	493,812	577,861	31,157	3,287	99,848

NOTES: n/a – not available. †Market capitalisation not available. Figure not disclosed or company unquoted, government controlled, a nationalised industry, a subsidiary or newly quoted.

751-800 EUROPE'S TOP 1000

RANK	COMPANY NAME (Sector)	CAPITAL EMPLOYED £000	TURNOVER £000	PRE-TAX PROFIT £000	NUMBER OF EMPLOYEES	EQUITY MKT CAPITAL £000
751	Corporacion Mapfre, SPA (Insurance, Life/Non-life)	492,989	864,942	46,601	5,251	904,000
752	Varta, GER (Other Industrial Materials & Products)	492,249	903,128	7,247	13,722	235,008
753	Intershop Holding, SWI (Property)	489,150	40,203	32,052	232	342,874
754	Danfoss, DNK (Engineering – Instrument)	488,959	829,918	30,868	13,290	†
755	Bau Holding, AUT (Contracting, Construction)	488,018	662,004	21,095	9,264	76,835
756	Johnson Matthey, UK (Metal & Metal Forming)	487,500	1,955,000	65,400	6,287	1,004,805
757	AG der Dillinger Huttenwerke, GER (Metal & Metal Forming)	487,006	679,619	L1,765	5,841	†
758	Spie-Batignolles[10], FRA (Contracting, Construction)	482,954	2,121,178	L19,695	31,143	253,806
759	Solvac, BEL (Investment Trusts)	482,810	4,102	L32,989	n/a	405,000
760	Dyckerhoff, GER (Building Materials & Services)	482,006	707,852	37,753	4,621	681,910
761	David S. Smith (Holdings), UK (Packaging, Paper & Printing)	481,500	782,800	42,200	8,113	858,162
762	Bilspedition, SWE (Transport Services)	479,683	1,362,017	L15,232	9,101	208,083
763	Unigate, UK (Food Manufacturing)	478,600	1,980,000	102,400	27,283	905,223
764	AVA Allgemeine Handelsgesellschaft der Verbraucher, GER (Stores)	478,541	2,728,567	64,289	n/a	1,016,819
765	RIT Capital Partners, UK (Investment Trusts)	478,263	12,933	8,169	n/a	314,415
766	Rugby Group, UK (Building Materials & Services)	477,800	1,010,600	76,100	9,523	782,774
767	Gambro, SWE (Health & Household)	477,620	766,965	82,750	8,889	900,000
768	Groupe Andre, FRA (Textiles)	476,891	1,147,240	29,724	11,854	471,992
769	Mahle, GER (Engineering – General)	476,316	781,018	3,472	13,534	†
770	Automotive Financial Grp. Hldgs., UK (Transport – Manufacture & Distribution)	474,712	419,910	11,053	2,515	†
771	Lech-Elektrizitatswerke, GER (Electricity)	474,327	554,788	22,732	1,804	558,818
772	Fisons, UK (Health & Household)	473,100	1,289,000	L463,700	11,863	760,217
773	United News & Media, UK (Media)	470,688	1,013,430	138,023	13,333	1,151,330
774	Gevaert, BEL (Investment Trusts)	469,953	36,659	59,572	n/a	712,513
775	Dyno Industrier, NOR (Chemicals)	468,546	771,263	28,921	7,329	469,678
776	Elkem, NOR (Metal & Metal Forming)	467,857	808,851	28,573	5,352	405,000
777	KBB-NV Koninklijke Bijenkorf Beheer, NLD (Stores)	467,498	1,596,358	70,236	23,721	426,859
778	Home Housing Association, UK (Property)	467,287	50,222	12,515	691	†
779	CEP Communication, FRA (Media)	467,165	647,187	43,960	11,190	688,055
780	Okobank Osuuspankkien Keskuspankki, FIN (Banks)	466,810	661,512	3,505	1,373	56,529
781	Von Roll, SWI (Engineering – General)	465,618	848,305	L198,194	7,614	262,000
782	AB Custos, SWE (Other Financial)	465,236	231,026	47,889	387	403,070
783	Storehouse, UK (Stores)	464,900	1,028,592	61,391	19,086	958,916
784	Credicom SA – Credit Commercial International, BEL (Property)	464,746	59,244	L2,439	1,680	23,220
785	Acciaierie e Ferriere Lombarde Falck, ITA (Metal & Metal Forming)	464,569	694,799	L21,579	3,839	114,000
786	Sedgwick Group, UK (Insurance, Brokers)	463,500	888,700	94,400	15,538	819,150
787	Burford Holdings, UK (Property)	462,885	1,231	14,711	23	273,494
788	Clydesdale Bank, UK (Banks)	462,585	511,671	110,666	n/a	†
789	Kleinwort European Privatisation Invst. Trst., UK (Investment Trusts)	460,973	10,580	6,316	n/a	385,000
790	Scottish American Investment Company, UK (Other Financial)	459,250	20,303	13,825	n/a	344,356
791	Willis Corroon Group, UK (Insurance, Brokers)	459,100	671,300	5,600	11,393	573,945
792	Vallourec, FRA (Metal & Metal Forming)	459,025	681,450	9,387	9,223	227,871
793	Walkers Smiths Snack Foods, UK (Food Manufacturing)	458,797	298,470	33,126	4,612	†
794	Marubeni UK, UK (Commodities Trading)	456,136	551,113	L2,145	121	†
795	Banco Espanol de Credito, SPA (Banks)	455,878	4,992,416	L2,993,992	15,720	†
796	Uralita, SPA (Building Materials & Services)	455,689	540,868	L38,593	6,993	303,000
797	Templeton Emerging Markets Investment Trust, UK (Investment Trusts)	454,651	9,920	3,936	n/a	110,982
798	ICL, UK (Electronics)	454,500	2,623,500	23,400	25,157	†
799	SIMCO, FRA (Property)	452,749	99,664	60,599	222	824,805
800	Stork, NLD (Engineering – General)	450,413	1,399,274	48,323	18,599	479,280

NOTES: [10]Name changed to Schneider SA. n/a – not available. †Market capitalisation not available. Figure not disclosed or company unquoted, government controlled, a nationalised industry, a subsidiary or newly quoted.

EUROPE'S TOP 1000　801-850

RANK	COMPANY NAME (Sector)	CAPITAL EMPLOYED £000	TURNOVER £000	PRE-TAX PROFIT £000	NUMBER OF EMPLOYEES	EQUITY MKT CAPITAL £000
801	DBV Holding, GER (Insurance, Life/Non-life)	450,224	1,150,774	41,233	3,635	605,911
802	Den Norske Bank, NOR (Banks)	450,069	1,651,682	92,088	6,079	353,000
803	Legal & General Group, UK (Insurance, Life/Non-life)	449,000	2,427,800	164,900	7,306	2,117,672
804	Cie des Gaz de Petrole Primagaz, FRA (Oil, Gas & Nuclear Fuels)	448,085	661,163	57,950	3,889	607,396
805	Sony United Kingdom, UK (Electronics)	447,315	1,442,449	37,297	3,677	†
806	Mercury World Mining Trust, UK (Investment Trusts)	447,289	9,745	4,267	n/a	398,114
807	Magneti Marelli, ITA (Engineering – General)	446,930	921,613	L16,611	7,905	263,000
808	Lep Group, UK (Transport Services)	446,559	1,420,632	L15,570	9,114	64,555
809	Fleming Overseas Investment Trust, UK (Investment Trusts)	445,940	11,603	8,909	n/a	376,601
810	EMS-Chemie Holding, SWI (Chemicals)	445,318	374,923	111,277	2,644	1,007,919
811	Kwik Save Group, UK (Food Wholesaling & Retailing)	444,600	2,800,000	135,600	22,502	994,880
812	Fleming Mercantile Investment Trust, UK (Investment Trusts)	442,152	14,597	13,070	n/a	382,948
813	Stakis, UK (Hotels & Leisure)	441,952	145,885	20,151	5,622	425,064
814	Morgan Crucible Company, UK (Other Industrial Materials & Products)	440,500	795,100	72,600	12,573	744,501
815	Topdanmark, DNK (Insurance, Life/Non-life)	440,199	307,773	11,889	2,781	237,164
816	Vicat, FRA (Building Materials & Services)	438,924	502,050	47,143	3,193	430,970
817	Milano Assicurazioni, ITA (Insurance, Life/Non-life)	438,589	571,593	L33,108	1,569	430,000
818	BET, UK (Miscellaneous)	436,500	1,942,075	90,512	100,493	1,014,475
819	Keramik Holding Laufen, SWI (Health & Household)	436,455	324,017	18,534	7,313	287,063
820	Charter, UK (Building Materials & Services)	436,400	891,053	73,000	14,875	674,143
821	Costain Group, UK (Contracting, Construction)	435,700	1,143,100	68,700	11,593	65,594
822	Siab AB, SWE (Contracting, Construction)	434,319	891,514	2,035	7,467	214,000
823	Telegraph, UK (Media)	432,211	252,076	45,042	1,075	512,864
824	Herlitz, GER (Miscellaneous)	432,000	473,260	28,233	4,753	268,811
825	GEA, GER (Engineering – General)	431,894	1,090,253	36,923	11,868	329,309
826	Christian Salvesen, UK (Food Wholesaling & Retailing)	431,600	558,000	74,100	11,572	723,279
827	Caltagirone, ITA (Building Materials & Services)	431,513	322,997	23,206	3,287	124,000
828	Foreign & Colonial Pacific Investment Trust, UK (Investment Trusts)	430,735	14,802	8,669	n/a	336,209
829	MAI, UK (Other Financial)	429,800	709,700	87,900	5,091	962,800
830	E.D.S. International, UK (Business Services)	427,054	253,945	11,621	3,920	†
831	CSM, NLD (Food Manufacturing)	426,949	939,056	89,217	5,075	935,000
832	Barings¶, UK (Banks)	425,171	684,607	100,103	3,179	71,613
833	Kodak, UK (Engineering – Instrument)	425,100	1,109,600	84,800	7,809	†
834	Colas, FRA (Contracting, Construction)	424,994	1,906,412	39,031	28,264	679,000
835	Flughafen Wien, AUT (Transport Services)	424,548	191,445	42,118	2,090	541,465
836	Groupe de la Cite, FRA (Media)	424,123	833,471	57,453	9,350	715,114
837	Jyske Bank, DNK (Banks)	423,008	487,486	10,820	2,732	286,614
838	Delta, UK (Electricals)	422,900	898,600	65,100	13,384	652,327
839	Marley, UK (Building Materials & Services)	422,600	666,800	58,700	9,554	378,600
840	Honda Motor Europe, UK (Transport – Manufacture & Distribution)	421,868	1,939,984	L19,784	1,839	†
841	South Wales Electricity, UK (Electricity)	421,200	605,400	104,000	3,350	586,274
842	Fresenius, GER (Health & Household)	420,145	824,400	48,692	7,807	587,505
843	Unibail, FRA (Property)	420,040	195,157	24,454	n/a	571,435
844	Rue Imperiale de Lyon, FRA (Property)	419,936	13,080	L790	50	260,870
845	Cowie Group, UK (Transport – Manufacture & Distribution)	419,034	934,161	43,607	4,377	323,441
846	Yorkshire Bank, UK (Banks)	418,611	491,917	137,336	6,324	†
847	Independent Newspapers, IRL (Media)	413,279	265,483	36,917	5,495	332,001
848	Manifattura Lane Gaetano Marzotto & Figli, ITA (Textiles)	413,042	822,130	45,764	11,625	248,000
849	SOPAF- Sta Partecipazioni Finanziarie, ITA (Other Financial)	413,025	54,160	21,969	n/a	196,000
850	De La Rue, UK (Packaging, Paper & Printing)	413,000	592,700	129,800	7,743	1,935,741

NOTES: ¶Now acquired by Internationale Nederlanden Groep NV. n/a – not available. †Market capitalisation not available. Figure not disclosed or company unquoted, government controlled, a nationalised industry, a subsidiary or newly quoted.

851-900   EUROPE'S TOP 1000

RANK	COMPANY NAME (Sector)	CAPITAL EMPLOYED £000	TURNOVER £000	PRE-TAX PROFIT £000	NUMBER OF EMPLOYEES	EQUITY MKT CAPITAL £000
851	Zurcher Ziegeleien Holding, SWI (Building Materials & Services)	412,981	320,848	31,272	2,204	239,328
852	Co-operative Retail Services, UK (Food Wholesaling & Retailing)	412,380	1,270,788	26,656	n/a	†
853	Saffa, ITA (Packaging, Paper & Printing)	411,730	296,022	L24,942	2,845	67,000
854	Vorwerk & Co., GER (Health & Household)	410,266	737,461	354,713	26,699	†
855	SA D'Ieteren, BEL (Transport – Manufacture & Distribution)	409,995	863,543	18,215	1,349	132,670
856	Klovern, SWE (Property)	408,767	58,315	936	55	81,331
857	Lenzing, AUT (Textiles)	407,421	500,672	L8,447	4,652	211,910
858	Yorkshire Building Society, UK (Other Financial)	407,012	432,957	78,850	1,615	†
859	Breda, ITA (Engineering – General)	406,391	424,774	L267,603	3,530	54,000
860	Wassall, UK (Other Industrial Materials & Products)	405,895	638,745	21,926	7,730	549,592
861	Meyer International, UK (Building Materials & Services)	403,200	1,192,900	41,600	8,588	384,708
862	Magazine zum Globus, SWI (Stores)	401,976	739,077	24,524	5,360	241,866
863	Robert Stephen Holdings, UK (Textiles)	399,300	494,100	17,500	5,414	†
864	Banco Pastor, SPA (Banks)	398,956	828,561	51,403	3,697	282,000
865	E D & F Man Group, UK (Miscellaneous)	397,700	219,900	66,700	3,401	†
866	Tessenderlo Chemie, BEL (Chemicals)	397,270	765,255	27,469	5,048	545,172
867	Nord Est, FRA (Packaging, Paper & Printing)	396,154	371,157	22,401	4,344	269,075
868	Hagemeyer, NLD (Health & Household)	393,690	1,698,970	75,012	8,360	779,973
869	Edinburgh Dragon Trust, UK (Investment Trusts)	393,186	5,950	233	n/a	298,999
870	Wilh. Wilhelmsen, NOR (Transport Services)	392,467	302,269	19,175	7,842	210,395
871	TR Smaller Companies Investment Trust, UK (Investment Trusts)	391,066	13,444	9,188	n/a	342,144
872	Attisholz Holding, SWI (Packaging, Paper & Printing)	390,977	244,217	7,456	1,523	172,298
873	Sodexho, FRA (Food Wholesaling & Retailing)	390,890	1,308,207	89,060	54,967	594,579
874	Editoriale L' Espresso, ITA (Media)	390,554	380,887	21,761	2,577	173,000
875	Seb, FRA (Electricals)	390,005	893,156	54,085	10,110	898,231
876	Energieversorgung Oberfranken, GER (Electricity)	389,749	473,994	25,717	1,754	443,907
877	Mobil Oil Co., UK (Oil, Gas & Nuclear Fuels)	389,480	1,196,476	L5,736	1,705	†
878	Bertrand Faure, FRA (Transport – Manufacture & Distribution)	387,788	1,257,015	10,451	n/a	356,462
879	Vickers, UK (Engineering – General)	387,000	727,200	44,800	9,118	575,923
880	Sophus Berendsen, DNK (Miscellaneous)	386,501	1,267,556	165,109	36,600	1,240,119
881	CGEA-Cie Generale d'Enterprises Automobiles, FRA (Miscellaneous)	386,473	1,002,817	30,580	26,494	334,207
882	Douglas Holding, GER (Health & Household)	385,909	1,218,957	87,391	13,550	401,440
883	Koninklijke Begemann Groep, NLD (Engineering – General)	385,330	795,979	4,635	8,770	50,999
884	Wunsche, GER (Miscellaneous)	384,713	564,107	19,668	935	196,007
885	Adia, SWI (Business Services)	384,157	1,405,878	L14,912	n/a	677,973
886	DMC-Dollfus-Mieg et Cie, FRA (Textiles)	382,902	938,966	12,352	9,990	279,000
887	Pirelli & C – Accomandita per Azioni, ITA (Other Financial)	382,834	66,627	24,458	103	333,000
888	AMEC, UK (Contracting, Construction)	382,200	1,962,400	20,000	21,175	266,394
889	Courtaulds Textiles, UK (Textiles)	382,100	1,053,200	47,300	24,000	463,296
890	Sika Finanz, SWI (Building Materials & Services)	381,871	587,177	34,808	6,743	450,689
891	Procter & Gamble, UK (Health & Household)	381,467	1,377,102	104,147	5,636	†
892	Acerinox, SPA (Metal & Metal Forming)	380,576	486,528	51,807	2,761	481,000
893	Walter Bau, GER (Contracting, Construction)	380,551	877,700	29,676	12,839	278,350
894	VNU (NV Verenigd Bezit), NLD (Media)	377,454	997,855	122,009	8,360	1,257,084
895	Greycoat, UK (Property)	377,200	38,300	L40,000	34	155,611
896	Radex-Heraklith Industriebeteiligungs, AUT (Building Materials & Services)	376,155	449,288	L16,778	5,268	166,065
897	Wolverhampton & Dudley Breweries, UK (Brewers & Distillers)	375,965	231,448	38,298	10,044	365,107
898	Kerry Group, IRL (Food Manufacturing)	375,309	858,681	34,171	6,375	420,646
899	ICB Shipping, SWE (Transport Services)	374,935	75,486	L3,847	12	166,993
900	Civil Aviation Authority, UK (Transport Services)	373,982	494,747	24,611	7,754	†

NOTES: n/a – not available. †Market capitalisation not available. Figure not disclosed or company unquoted, government controlled, a nationalised industry, a subsidiary or newly quoted.

EUROPE'S TOP 1000　　901–950

RANK	COMPANY NAME (Sector)	CAPITAL EMPLOYED £000	TURNOVER £000	PRE-TAX PROFIT £000	NUMBER OF EMPLOYEES	EQUITY MKT CAPITAL £000
901	Videotron Holdings, UK (Media)	372,921	37,572	L5,995	644	†
902	Cathay International Holdings, UK (Property)	372,822	5,941	469	1,169	120,762
903	Skibsaksjeselskapet Storli, NOR (Transport Services)	372,748	240,271	20,545	1,407	240,990
904	ECIA, FRA (Transport – Manufacture & Distribution)	372,517	805,921	41,010	9,669	306,687
905	Elektrizitats-AG Mitteldeutschland, GER (Electricity)	371,419	755,218	19,404	1,935	†
906	Household International (UK), UK (Banks)	369,301	203,557	8,594	1,620	†
907	IWKA, GER (Engineering – General)	368,907	680,154	37,977	8,087	326,950
908	Zanders Feinpapiere, GER (Packaging, Paper & Printing)	368,871	386,625	L14,873	3,261	234,557
909	Auxiliaire d'Entreprises et de Participations, FRA (Contracting, Construction)	368,684	2,613,793	L110,967	25,094	175,106
910	Sand Aire Investments, UK (Insurance, Life/Non-life)	368,200	337,800	27,800	2,080	†
911	Euro RSCG Worldwide, FRA (Media)	367,818	1,532,272	32,283	6,725	329,420
912	Hero, SWI (Food Manufacturing)	367,424	588,582	34,651	3,935	432,280
913	Kellogg Co. of Great Britain, UK (Food Manufacturing)	366,991	589,228	89,310	2,831	†
914	Osterreichische Brau-Beteiligungs, AUT (Brewers & Distillers)	366,377	557,100	23,952	6,093	309,352
915	Clyde Petroleum, UK (Oil, Gas & Nuclear Fuels)	365,953	116,583	13,617	137	155,126
916	Ocean Group, UK (Transport Services)	365,900	1,026,100	19,900	11,800	433,400
917	Laird Group, UK (Other Industrial Materials & Products)	365,500	733,900	47,700	11,018	488,289
918	Scottish National Trust, UK (Investment Trusts)	365,176	21,908	17,509	n/a	363,014
919	Bunzl, UK (Packaging, Paper & Printing)	364,300	1,622,200	L4,900	8,116	734,200
920	La Carbonique, FRA (Food Manufacturing)	362,863	849,211	66,671	6,383	345,112
921	Govett Strategic Investment Trust, UK (Investment Trusts)	362,094	20,280	8,457	n/a	239,507
922	Edeka Zentrale, GER (Miscellaneous)	361,679	5,457,218	15,389	726	†
923	House of Fraser, UK (Stores)	361,000	754,700	28,000	9,587	400,652
924	Koenig & Bauer, GER (Engineering – General)	360,007	515,029	L9,048	6,569	160,990
925	Steyrermuhl Papierfabriks, AUT (Packaging, Paper & Printing)	359,668	150,805	L29,655	700	177,800
926	Gestetner Holdings, UK (Electronics)	358,800	996,185	12,138	10,614	232,570
927	KSB, GER (Engineering – General)	357,608	814,118	14,756	13,910	252,995
928	Albright & Wilson, UK (Chemicals)	357,577	609,245	58,279	4,255	†
929	VSEL[11], UK (Engineering – General)	356,020	832,941	60,941	7,329	591,123
930	Portland Valderrivas, SPA (Contracting, Construction)	355,261	173,456	20,584	1,368	347,000
931	Ste Suisse de Ciment Portland, SWI (Building Materials & Services)	354,516	141,083	L12,506	1,291	150,068
932	Bank fur Oberosterreich und Salzburg, AUT (Banks)	354,001	298,664	12,823	1,656	270,308
933	Cia Assicuratrice Unipol, ITA (Insurance, Brokers)	353,188	520,994	39,138	1,747	377,000
934	Provident Financial, UK (Other Financial)	352,828	445,258	81,149	44,270	732,996
935	Sony Music Entertainment (UK) Group, UK (Health & Household)	352,655	721,615	7,114	2,345	†
936	Castorama Dubois Investissements SCA, FRA (Stores)	351,564	1,366,456	71,431	12,141	1,332,195
937	Berliner Elektro Holding, GER (Electronics)	351,411	331,024	31,808	3,914	80,588
938	H & M Hennes & Mauritz, SWE (Stores)	350,938	977,778	134,740	8,837	1,213,490
939	Brau und Brunnen, GER (Brewers & Distillers)	350,638	574,721	11,157	5,683	545,072
940	Standa, ITA (Stores)	348,520	1,940,847	13,199	14,158	436,000
941	Digital Equipment Co., UK (Electronics)	347,646	809,449	L97,427	5,728	†
942	Lex Service, UK (Transport – Manufacture & Distribution)	345,700	1,399,593	41,714	6,598	286,397
943	Leif Hoegh & Co., NOR (Transport Services)	345,105	259,753	13,915	1,250	255,143
944	Binding-Brauerei, GER (Brewers & Distillers)	344,980	707,298	26,520	3,529	251,852
945	Northern Ireland Electricity, UK (Electricity)	344,900	481,900	74,900	3,536	540,010
946	HBG Hollandsche Beton Groep, NLD (Contracting, Construction)	343,835	1,876,083	43,293	18,389	312,287
947	Metrovacesa – Inmobiliaria Metropolitano Vasco Central, SPA (Property)	343,567	86,420	22,192	161	523,628
948	Fromageries Bel, FRA (Food Manufacturing)	342,574	849,237	65,467	6,383	817,494
949	Zellweger Luwa, SWI (Engineering – General)	342,235	501,673	10,491	5,899	183,167
950	Hurlimann Holding, SWI (Brewers & Distillers)	342,078	92,135	4,247	606	140,824

NOTES: [11]Offer by The General Electric Company PLC became unconditional on 30/6/95. n/a – not available. †Market capitalisation not available. Figure not disclosed or company unquoted, government controlled, a nationalised industry, a subsidiary or newly quoted.

951-1000 — EUROPE'S TOP 1000

RANK	COMPANY NAME (Sector)	CAPITAL EMPLOYED £000	TURNOVER £000	PRE-TAX PROFIT £000	NUMBER OF EMPLOYEES	EQUITY MKT CAPITAL £000
951	Danieli & C. Officine Meccaniche, ITA (Engineering – General)	341,785	227,561	19,974	2,219	244,000
952	Maculan Holding, AUT (Engineering – General)	341,779	596,749	14,196	8,680	275,692
953	FKI, UK (Engineering – General)	339,961	794,477	52,265	11,221	878,667
954	Scapa Group, UK (Textiles)	339,900	391,700	48,500	6,536	491,644
955	Vorarlberger Kraftwerke, AUT (Electricity)	339,235	145,085	11,062	895	93,943
956	NYNEX CableComms Group[12], GBR/USA (Media)	338,501	41,015	L95,144	1,919	†
957	Securicor Group, UK (Business Services)	338,420	800,275	80,560	43,508	910,065
958	AB Catena, SWE (Transport – Manufacture & Distribution)	338,332	1,302,536	13,870	4,372	172,937
959	Camellia, UK (Agriculture)	337,610	191,992	21,615	73,336	53,125
960	British Vita, UK (Chemicals)	336,557	768,996	49,510	9,417	498,765
961	Hazlewood Foods, UK (Food Manufacturing)	335,913	799,982	48,053	10,113	336,773
962	Halliburton Holdings, UK (Contracting, Construction)	335,662	543,257	L10,327	6,524	†
963	TeleWest Communications, UK (Communications)	335,599	40,338	L36,572	2,036	1,450,499
964	Second Alliance Trust, UK (Investment Trusts)	335,388	11,534	10,921	n/a	355,296
965	Franco Tosi, ITA (Engineering – General)	335,347	92,410	11,006	883	151,000
966	Svedala Industri, SWE (Engineering – General)	334,807	880,214	49,440	8,958	352,000
967	Steyr-Daimler-Puch, AUT (Transport – Manufacture & Distribution)	334,637	596,435	L6,899	5,632	104,220
968	La Rochette, FRA (Packaging, Paper & Printing)	334,573	345,978	L22,339	3,121	91,173
969	Horten, GER (Stores)	333,224	1,138,423	19,722	11,261	431,340
970	Dragerwerk, GER (Engineering – Instrument)	332,371	548,294	12,730	7,844	69,204
971	SITA, FRA (Health & Household)	331,795	621,395	36,495	14,270	535,769
972	Pfalzwerke, GER (Electricity)	331,529	460,636	22,515	1,430	†
973	Hardy Oil & Gas, UK (Oil, Gas & Nuclear Fuels)	330,753	60,604	5,223	128	173,945
974	Esselte, SWE (Miscellaneous)	330,679	1,031,596	35,144	10,775	281,000
975	Harwanne, SWI (Other Industrial Materials & Products)	329,795	142,212	14,915	n/a	53,480
976	Norsk Hydro (UK), UK (Chemicals)	329,708	359,335	2,890	1,862	†
977	Lindt & Sprungli, SWI (Food Manufacturing)	329,687	412,939	23,087	4,218	331,043
978	Coventry Building Society, UK (Other Financial)	329,443	221,616	40,093	828	†
979	Frogmore Estates, UK (Property)	329,319	66,876	16,449	104	208,446
980	ISS-International Service System, DNK (Health & Household)	328,933	1,464,302	46,391	122,600	515,819
981	Forvaltnings AB Ratos, SWE (Other Financial)	328,357	1,286,964	17,274	9,675	168,000
982	Hewlett-Packard, UK (Electronics)	328,227	1,313,989	66,764	5,003	†
983	CGMF – Cie Generale Maritime et Financiere, FRA (Transport Services)	328,105	927,167	L64,629	6,629	†
984	Bilton, UK (Property)	327,786	25,636	18,568	164	220,554
985	Portman Building Society, UK (Other Financial)	327,600	229,200	29,200	1,156	†
986	Banco Atlantico, SPA (Banks)	326,829	605,024	23,381	3,270	298,000
987	Th. Goldschmidt, GER (Chemicals)	325,918	547,469	30,788	5,732	439,130
988	Kolbenschmidt, GER (Transport – Manufacture & Distribution)	325,276	499,118	2,223	7,255	204,556
989	NKT Holding, DNK (Electricals)	324,891	501,265	8,310	6,465	257,256
990	Dalmine, ITA (Metal & Metal Forming)	324,452	497,164	L18,349	4,367	174,000
991	NPM-Nederlandse Participatie Mij, NLD (Other Financial)	324,155	24,384	21,130	31	448,403
992	Graningeverkens, SWE (Electricity)	323,370	192,483	53,014	779	577,326
993	Smiths Industries, UK (Aerospace)	323,000	759,300	117,200	10,983	1,411,404
994	Greene King, UK (Brewers & Distillers)	322,989	146,102	20,434	2,641	204,140
995	ASSITALIA – Le Assicurazioni d'Italia, ITA (Insurance, Life/Non-life)	319,781	1,190,747	L66,847	2,719	607,000
996	Tampella, FIN (Engineering – General)	319,677	405,297	L25,075	4,447	172,301
997	Publicitas Holding, SWI (Media)	319,527	897,309	6,322	2,971	278,036
998	Luzerner Kantonalbank, SWI (Banks)	319,401	456,895	19,910	1,110	37,902
999	Minerva, UK (Property)	318,634	22,806	10,929	18	†
1000	Sampo Insurance, FIN (Insurance, Life/Non-life)	318,360	370,327	35,300	2,642	470,092

NOTES: [12] NYNEX CableComms Group PLC/NYNEX CableComms Group Inc. n/a – not available. †Market capitalisation not available. Figure not disclosed or company unquoted, government controlled, a nationalised industry, a subsidiary or newly quoted.

NORTH AMERICA'S TOP 100　　　　1-50

RANK	COMPANY NAME (Sector)	CAPITAL EMPLOYED £000	TURNOVER £000	PRE-TAX PROFIT £000	NUMBER OF EMPLOYEES	EQUITY MKT CAPITAL £000
1	General Motors Corpn, USA (Transport – Manufacture & Distribution)	69,250,761	98,056,610	5,439,193	693,000	28,642,000
2	General Electric Co. (USA CO), USA (Electricals)	63,826,150	38,623,200	5,750,244	221,000	60,536,000
3	Ford Motor Co., USA (Transport – Manufacture & Distribution)	53,481,472	72,425,510	2,586,793	322,213	18,230,000
4	Travelers Group, USA (Other Financial)	40,517,310	2,323,175	1,016,431	n/a	8,595,000
5	Exxon Corpn, USA (Oil, Gas & Nuclear Fuels)	38,767,659	73,011,370	5,081,520	86,000	48,228,000
6	AT&T Corpn, USA (Communications)	27,745,609	48,896,940	4,895,294	304,500	50,395,000
7	American Express Co., USA (Hotels & Leisure)	27,719,814	5,710,832	1,552,342	64,493	9,350,000
8	International Business Machines Corpn, USA (Communications)	24,201,348	41,707,010	3,356,642	n/a	27,611,000
9	Citicorp, USA (Banks)	22,795,140	20,348,221	3,002,421	82,600	11,726,000
10	Hydro-Quebec, CAN (Electricity)	22,417,289	3,613,875	728,038	21,028	†
11	Bankamerica Corpn, USA (Banks)	21,936,078	10,611,027	2,420,299	98,600	10,233,000
12	Philip Morris Cos Inc., USA (Food Manufacturing)	21,297,539	42,405,690	5,349,791	165,000	31,345,000
13	GTE Corpn, USA (Communications)	17,832,535	12,986,400	2,593,503	111,000	18,737,000
14	E.I. Du Pont De Nemours & Co., USA (Oil, Gas & Nuclear Fuels)	17,147,002	24,758,730	639,357	114,000	22,097,000
15	BellSouth Corpn, USA (Communications)	17,084,949	10,968,180	2,215,645	92,121	17,180,000
16	Mobil Corpn, USA (Oil, Gas & Nuclear Fuels)	16,677,531	43,468,360	2,394,904	58,500	21,324,000
17	Sears Roebuck and Co., USA (Stores)	16,529,883	35,525,710	1,114,757	n/a	11,399,164
18	Southern Co., USA (Electricity)	15,086,959	5,665,449	1,182,610	28,743	8,399,000
19	RJR Nabisco Holdings Corpn, USA (Tobacco)	15,071,270	10,005,460	895,322	68,000	6,310,000
20	Pacific Gas & Electric Co., USA (Electricity)	14,365,421	6,802,752	1,258,074	21,000	6,943,838
21	Amoco Corpn, USA (Oil, Gas & Nuclear Fuels)	13,899,009	19,180,720	1,621,997	43,205	18,759,000
22	Chevron Corpn, USA (Oil, Gas & Nuclear Fuels)	13,677,213	22,874,650	1,825,154	45,758	18,590,000
23	Entergy Corporation, USA (Electricity)	13,438,943	2,993,456	495,797	16,679	3,179,650
24	Texas Utilities Co., USA (Electricity)	13,375,554	3,626,923	462,790	10,859	4,619,311
25	BCE Inc, CAN (Communications)	13,118,252	10,291,160	1,034,340	116,000	6,360,000
26	Chemical Banking Corpn, USA (Banks)	13,060,655	8,293,620	1,406,852	41,567	6,115,000
27	NYNEX Corpn, USA (Communications)	12,867,114	8,664,500	713,848	70,600	9,950,000
28	Wal-Mart Stores Inc., USA (Stores)	12,686,332	44,908,920	2,461,740	n/a	33,107,000
29	Unicom Corpn, USA (Electricity)	12,295,256	4,097,923	449,793	n/a	3,288,055
30	SBC Communications Inc., USA (Communications)	12,291,978	7,565,306	1,584,752	58,800	15,719,000
31	Dow Chemical Co., USA (Chemicals)	11,936,083	13,032,630	1,336,146	53,700	11,912,000
32	NationsBank Corpn, USA (Banks)	11,875,776	6,879,426	1,328,768	57,463	8,972,000
33	Chrysler Corpn, USA (Transport – Manufacture & Distribution)	11,725,152	34,005,290	3,796,164	110,000	10,895,000
34	Salomon Inc., USA (Other Financial)	11,486,440	5,872,339	977,722	n/a	3,559,000
35	Texaco Inc., USA (Oil, Gas & Nuclear Fuels)	11,461,809	21,188,190	812,627	n/a	9,932,000
36	Pepsico Inc., USA (Food Manufacturing)	11,294,024	18,239,770	1,706,848	471,000	18,302,252
37	Atlantic Richfield Co., USA (Oil, Gas & Nuclear Fuels)	10,612,976	9,789,936	890,764	23,200	10,582,000
38	American International Group Inc., USA (Insurance, Life/Non-life)	10,407,630	10,219,489	1,735,928	n/a	18,758,193
39	U S West Inc., USA (Communications)	10,179,611	7,131,970	1,486,560	61,505	10,858,973
40	Procter & Gamble Co., USA (Health & Household)	10,078,216	20,213,250	2,232,425	n/a	25,270,000
41	J.P. Morgan & Co. Inc., USA (Other Financial)	9,909,236	7,678,930	1,188,336	17,055	6,830,000
42	Pacific Telesis Group, USA (Communications)	9,792,792	6,169,327	134,145	60,050	7,725,000
43	Public Service Enterprise Group Inc., USA (Electricity)	9,395,135	3,852,060	1,106,409	11,919	4,144,771
44	Merrill Lynch & Co. Inc., USA (Other Financial)	9,296,534	11,872,291	1,126,478	43,800	4,293,798
45	Bell Atlantic Corpn, USA (Communications)	9,238,991	8,980,174	1,489,034	72,300	13,870,000
46	USX Corpn, USA (Oil, Gas & Nuclear Fuels)	9,066,751	12,055,680	L159,506	44,903	5,697,000
47	Xerox Corpn, USA (Electronics)	8,952,715	11,242,140	L151,497	97,000	6,758,000
48	Peco Energy Co., USA (Electricity)	8,939,835	2,631,030	435,820	n/a	3,470,386
49	SCECorp, USA (Electricity)	8,829,658	5,433,789	786,581	17,074	4,186,042
50	International Paper Co., USA (Packaging, Paper & Printing)	8,821,989	9,745,007	432,359	70,000	6,066,000

NOTES: n/a – not available. †Government controlled.

51-100 NORTH AMERICA'S TOP 100

RANK	COMPANY NAME (Sector)	CAPITAL EMPLOYED £000	TURNOVER £000	PRE-TAX PROFIT £000	NUMBER OF EMPLOYEES	EQUITY MKT CAPITAL £000
51	American Electric Power Co. Inc, USA *(Electricity)*	8,664,319	3,516,357	403,792	20,007	4,630,525
52	Chase Manhattan Corpn, USA *(Banks)*	8,399,413	7,415,338	487,860	35,774	4,646,000
53	Occidental Petroleum Corpn, USA *(Chemicals)*	8,318,314	6,013,957	70,975	n/a	3,898,000
54	Merck & Co., Inc., USA *(Health & Household)*	8,290,708	7,006,363	2,104,272	47,500	30,408,000
55	AMR Corpn, USA *(Transport Services)*	8,191,587	10,555,390	L75,415	111,100	3,433,000
56	WMX Technologies Inc., USA *(Miscellaneous)*	8,173,369	6,574,799	898,036	74,400	8,288,980
57	Time Warner Inc., USA *(Media)*	8,109,301	4,815,854	57,952	n/a	8,516,000
58	Union Pacific Corpn, USA *(Transport Services)*	8,104,826	5,077,614	923,972	46,900	5,974,000
59	Boeing Co., USA *(Aerospace)*	7,896,452	14,275,660	744,257	119,400	10,240,000
60	Consolidated Edison Co. of New York Inc., USA *(Electricity)*	7,860,681	4,149,791	763,700	17,097	3,996,252
61	Textron Inc., USA *(Aerospace)*	7,766,142	4,182,035	409,114	53,000	2,756,000
62	Dominion Resources Inc., USA *(Electricity)*	7,680,154	2,924,349	422,722	10,789	3,967,134
63	Long Island Lighting Co., USA *(Electricity)*	7,544,939	1,922,739	312,897	5,947	1,469,588
64	Bankers Trust New York Corpn, USA *(Miscellaneous)*	7,292,427	4,873,806	565,843	14,529	2,763,000
65	Ameritech Corpn, USA *(Communications)*	7,267,370	8,184,543	1,133,901	63,594	14,231,000
66	Sprint Corpn, USA *(Communications)*	7,207,415	8,244,643	899,945	51,600	6,155,000
67	Duke Power Co., USA *(Electricity)*	7,176,786	2,922,925	674,516	17,052	4,992,177
68	Golden West Financial Corpn, USA *(Other Financial)*	7,014,695	1,274,491	305,251	n/a	1,685,183
69	FPL Group Inc., USA *(Electricity)*	6,977,809	3,530,927	537,840	12,135	4,188,744
70	Motorola Inc., USA *(Electronics)*	6,859,700	14,484,680	1,586,836	132,000	21,799,000
71	McDonald's Corpn, USA *(Food Wholesaling & Retailing)*	6,846,852	5,418,031	1,228,447	183,000	12,970,000
72	Detroit Edison Co., USA *(Electricity)*	6,776,285	2,372,702	550,488	8,819	3,215,121
73	Houston Industries Inc., USA *(Electricity)*	6,763,199	2,885,735	431,902	11,498	2,989,737
74	K Mart Corpn, USA *(Stores)*	6,691,560	22,777,030	L440,123	348,000	3,749,000
75	Pacificorp, USA *(Electricity)*	6,686,939	2,277,392	407,173	13,635	3,656,403
76	Morgan Stanley Group Inc., USA *(Merchant Banks)*	6,540,267	2,344,655	800,224	8,273	3,515,000
77	Hewlett-Packard Co., USA *(Electronics)*	6,450,878	16,421,790	1,592,173	98,400	15,296,000
78	Canadian Pacific, CAN *(Transport Services)*	6,302,530	3,349,686	342,026	36,200	3,251,981
79	J C Penney Co. Inc., USA *(Stores)*	6,203,022	13,055,650	1,036,289	193,000	5,929,000
80	Banc One Corpn, USA *(Banks)*	5,889,082	4,812,377	1,133,970	45,300	9,383,665
81	CSX Corpn, USA *(Transport Services)*	5,700,863	6,256,183	655,050	46,747	4,660,000
82	Aluminum Co. of America, USA *(Metal & Metal Forming)*	5,617,067	6,449,116	535,565	61,700	4,947,507
83	Central and South West Corpn, USA *(Electricity)*	5,552,574	2,359,091	384,826	8,055	2,757,000
84	Intel Corpn, USA *(Electronics)*	5,548,552	5,860,994	2,355,877	29,500	16,855,000
85	ITT Corpn, USA *(Insurance, Life/Non-life)*	5,508,470	15,380,000	819,789	110,000	3,750,000
86	Weyerhaeuser Co., USA *(Building Materials & Services)*	5,507,830	6,770,586	599,052	36,665	4,985,000
87	Norfolk Southern Corpn, USA *(Transport Services)*	5,487,824	2,983,082	683,049	27,168	5,158,972
88	Canadian Imperial Bank of Commerce, CAN *(Banks)*	5,454,712	5,379,081	708,041	40,807	3,138,000
89	Anheuser-Busch Cos Inc., USA *(Brewers & Distillers)*	5,429,915	8,942,473	1,111,566	42,622	8,367,000
90	Walt Disney Co., USA *(Hotels & Leisure)*	5,410,816	6,656,457	1,127,449	65,000	15,288,000
91	MCI Communications Corpn, USA *(Communications)*	5,402,129	7,955,922	697,420	36,235	6,389,000
92	Eastman Kodak Co., USA *(Engineering – Instrument)*	5,396,613	8,827,546	652,445	150,600	10,369,000
93	Tenneco Inc, USA *(Engineering – General)*	5,388,942	7,927,016	632,911	55,000	5,099,000
94	Cigna Corpn, USA *(Insurance, Life/Non-life)*	5,269,876	9,151,212	110,119	50,624	3,054,000
95	Seagram Co. Ltd, CAN *(Brewers & Distillers)*	5,265,904	4,146,325	419,233	n/a	6,746,000
96	Dayton Hudson Corpn, USA *(Stores)*	5,221,901	13,808,770	462,647	194,000	3,186,000
97	Champion International Corpn, USA *(Packaging, Paper & Printing)*	5,194,085	3,382,874	L106,015	25,300	1,011,571
98	Minnesota Mining & Manufacturing Co., USA *(Chemicals)*	5,184,856	9,356,767	1,336,109	85,166	14,322,000
99	Enron Corpn, USA *(Oil, Gas & Nuclear Fuels)*	5,097,728	5,320,732	312,188	n/a	4,882,571
100	United Technologies Corpn, USA *(Aerospace)*	5,088,527	13,544,430	700,630	171,500	4,949,000

NOTES: n/a – not available.

JAPAN'S TOP 100   1-50

RANK	COMPANY NAME (Sector)	CAPITAL EMPLOYED £000	TURNOVER £000	PRE-TAX PROFIT £000	NUMBER OF EMPLOYEES	EQUITY MKT CAPITAL £000
1	Nippon Telegraph & Telephone Corpn (Communications)	73,301,390	41,564,310	1,085,259	248,000	92,758,000
2	Tokyo Electric Power Co. Inc. (Electricity)	69,116,782	29,344,620	951,174	41,967	27,749,000
3	Toyota Motor Corpn (Transport – Manufacture & Distribution)	44,772,301	59,327,950	1,498,804	110,534	54,045,000
4	Dai-Ichi Kangyo Bank (Banks)	43,107,131	15,086,478	433,538	n/a	36,621,000
5	Matsushita Electric Industrial Co. (Electronics)	35,779,829	41,170,140	796,994	254,059	23,359,000
6	Hitachi (Electronics)	34,595,155	45,997,370	1,419,433	330,637	20,008,000
7	Kansai Electric Power Co. Inc. (Electricity)	32,643,090	14,742,540	640,110	26,205	17,785,000
8	Chubu Electric Power Co. Inc. (Electricity)	29,155,757	12,156,260	475,886	20,631	13,450,000
9	Nissan Motor Co. (Transport – Manufacture & Distribution)	28,424,453	36,056,320	L629,842	143,310	13,504,000
10	Mitsubishi Corpn (Soga Sosha)	22,127,893	107,384,300	235,096	13,959	11,287,000
11	East Japan Railway Co. (Transport Services)	20,433,682	14,565,510	748,332	79,679	12,718,000
12	Mitsui & Co. (Soga Sosha)	19,717,390	109,627,000	158,208	12,084	7,555,000
13	Mitsubishi Bank (Banks)	18,124,968	13,580,300	455,504	n/a	51,539,000
14	Nippon Steel Corpn (Metal & Metal Forming)	17,815,667	17,089,630	L371,369	n/a	14,542,000
15	ITOCHU Corpn (Soga Sosha)	17,454,848	104,066,000	53,349	7,434	6,494,000
16	Toshiba Corpn (Electronics)	17,047,979	28,784,270	560,593	175,000	15,527,000
17	Tohoku Electric Power Co. Inc. (Electricity)	16,852,838	8,350,896	463,038	14,081	9,074,000
18	Sony Corpn (Electronics)	16,842,722	23,207,650	635,007	130,000	14,333,000
19	Kyushu Electric Power Co. Inc. (Electricity)	16,151,497	6,033,260	416,110	13,755	7,941,000
20	Marubeni Corpn (Soga Sosha)	15,709,176	96,916,930	224,411	10,006	4,719,000
21	Nomura Securities Co. (Other Financial)	13,735,199	4,222,044	593,834	n/a	27,659,000
22	Fuji Bank (Banks)	13,730,736	16,143,383	398,426	n/a	41,020,000
23	Orient Corpn (Other Financial)	13,646,492	2,324,997	32,893	5,772	1,518,000
24	Sakura Bank (Banks)	12,955,998	13,989,655	371,077	22,355	26,730,000
25	NEC Corpn (Electronics)	12,760,072	22,250,840	156,076	147,910	10,703,000
26	Mitsui Fudosan Co. (Property)	12,652,778	8,092,205	90,917	10,531	6,146,000
27	ORIX Corpn (Other Financial)	12,372,925	1,999,233	212,769	6,731	1,522,000
28	Sumitomo Corpn (Soga Sosha)	12,168,144	105,668,500	156,915	n/a	6,971,000
29	NKK Corpn (Metal & Metal Forming)	11,707,876	11,050,840	L253,749	n/a	5,613,000
30	Mitsubishi Estate Co. (Property)	11,471,538	3,473,756	216,809	2,045	8,858,000
31	Mitsubishi Electric Corpn (Electronics)	11,350,697	19,302,390	444,229	111,053	8,149,000
32	Honda Motor Co. (Transport – Manufacture & Distribution)	10,873,765	24,009,440	291,454	91,300	10,533,000
33	Chugoku Electric Power Co. Inc. (Electricity)	10,422,185	4,684,193	284,145	10,957	6,034,000
34	Japan Airlines Co. (Transport Services)	10,300,375	7,810,709	L246,129	n/a	7,534,000
35	Nissho Iwai Corpn (Soga Sosha)	10,240,318	64,026,300	142,271	7,245	2,210,000
36	Fujitsu (Electronics)	10,156,080	20,000,000	L56,000	161,974	6,600,000
37	Sumitomo Metal Industries (Metal & Metal Forming)	9,997,165	7,600,600	L216,778	21,595	5,382,000
38	Industrial Bank of Japan (Banks)	9,619,583	15,731,284	282,814	n/a	46,401,000
39	Mitsubishi Heavy Industries (Engineering – General)	9,613,689	13,505,610	723,538	n/a	11,682,000
40	Nippon Oil Co. (Oil, Gas & Nuclear Fuels)	9,354,555	16,033,250	403,535	11,117	5,272,000
41	Kobe Steel (Metal & Metal Forming)	8,878,567	7,763,196	L45,903	n/a	4,926,000
42	Export-Import Bank of Japan (Banks)	8,726,066	2,845,897	265,584	n/a	†
43	Kawasaki Steel Corpn (Metal & Metal Forming)	8,702,970	7,366,094	L138,883	17,276	7,439,000
44	Fuji Photo Film Co. (Chemicals)	8,194,286	6,782,474	857,235	26,555	7,475,000
45	Canon Inc. (Electronics)	8,154,184	12,397,310	496,974	67,672	8,988,000
46	Tokyo Gas Co. (Oil, Gas & Nuclear Fuels)	8,099,698	5,040,600	251,530	n/a	9,487,000
47	Daiwa Securities Co. (Other Financial)	8,018,524	1,709,973	315,658	11,295	14,442,000
48	Nippon Shinpan Co. (Other Financial)	7,961,636	2,414,099	125,712	8,283	1,964,000
49	Hokuriku Electric Power Co. Inc. (Electricity)	7,728,342	2,829,661	120,298	5,545	3,682,000
50	Long-Term Credit Bank of Japan (Other Financial)	7,523,421	12,872,019	384,080	3,878	14,589,000

NOTES: n/a – not available. †Market capitalisation not available.

51-100　　　　　　　　　　　　　　　　　　　　　　　　　JAPAN'S TOP 100

RANK	COMPANY NAME (Sector)	CAPITAL EMPLOYED £000	TURNOVER £000	PRE-TAX PROFIT £000	NUMBER OF EMPLOYEES	EQUITY MKT CAPITAL £000
51	Ito-Yokado Co. (Stores)	7,482,514	17,739,860	1,142,601	33,629	15,594,000
52	Sanyo Electric Co. (Electronics)	7,446,667	10,595,170	180,395	58,417	7,303,000
53	Nippondenso Co. (Electricals)	7,427,898	9,055,721	594,353	55,901	11,636,000
54	Bank of Tokyo (Banks)	7,414,112	10,743,618	613,035	n/a	19,354,000
55	All Nippon Airways Co. (Transport Services)	7,212,918	5,327,877	L28,455	n/a	9,458,000
56	Sharp Corpn (Electronics)	7,025,558	9,262,054	344,144	42,883	11,959,000
57	Nikko Securities Co. (Other Financial)	6,984,425	1,533,013	L32,282	9,829	7,372,000
58	Kajima Corpn (Contracting, Construction)	6,772,892	12,273,610	80,226	n/a	5,584,000
59	Sekisui House (Contracting, Construction)	6,613,933	7,908,043	462,825	13,607	5,109,000
60	Asahi Glass Co. (Other Industrial Materials & Products)	6,606,631	7,414,670	137,521	9,354	9,240,000
61	Tokyu Corpn (Transport Services)	6,589,756	2,850,906	87,337	5,093	5,347,000
62	Shikoku Electric Power Co. Inc. (Electricity)	6,416,524	2,370,406	239,551	n/a	4,347,000
63	Sumitomo Trust & Banking Co. (Banks)	6,189,360	6,377,296	243,655	7,345	12,476,000
64	Hokkaido Electric Power Co. Inc. (Electricity)	6,022,315	2,491,756	179,404	6,437	3,266,000
65	Mitsubishi Trust and Banking Corpn (Banks)	5,961,072	6,216,310	282,814	6,782	12,465,000
66	Mitsubishi Motors Corpn (Transport – Manufacture & Distribution)	5,890,710	18,317,210	118,048	n/a	4,809,000
67	Nippon Yusen K.K. (Transport Services)	5,843,018	5,332,079	54,176	n/a	4,297,000
68	Bridgestone Corpn (Other Industrial Materials & Products)	5,808,686	9,661,222	432,596	87,332	7,790,000
69	Mazda Motor Corpn (Transport – Manufacture & Distribution)	5,765,401	13,601,180	L294,506	33,118	3,316,000
70	Taisei Corpn (Contracting, Construction)	5,721,351	11,242,670	612,023	n/a	4,004,000
71	Aplus Co. (Other Financial)	5,690,616	837,824	11,847	n/a	296,000
72	Dai Nippon Printing Co. (Packaging, Paper & Printing)	5,488,162	7,120,289	585,941	n/a	8,698,000
73	Japan Energy Corpn (Oil, Gas & Nuclear Fuels)	5,429,337	11,208,630	145,217	7,742	3,034,000
74	Osaka Gas Co. (Oil, Gas & Nuclear Fuels)	5,376,675	4,376,678	247,117	9,146	8,121,000
75	Asahi Breweries (Brewers & Distillers)	5,330,860	4,271,304	89,678	n/a	2,954,000
76	Kirin Brewery Co. (Brewers & Distillers)	5,124,536	5,214,795	544,804	8,242	7,484,000
77	Nichimen Corpn (Soga Sosha)	5,049,836	35,870,460	70,815	n/a	1,200,000
78	Matsushita Electric Works (Electricals)	5,037,095	6,161,003	223,196	29,345	4,805,000
79	Shimizu Corpn (Contracting, Construction)	5,008,225	14,325,390	399,905	12,139	4,598,000
80	Mitsubishi Chemical Corpn (Chemicals)	4,998,583	6,695,005	6,645	n/a	4,852,000
81	Sumitomo Electric Industries (Other Industrial Materials & Products)	4,992,239	6,846,787	344,480	39,355	6,965,000
82	Asahi Chemical Industry Co. (Chemicals)	4,988,841	7,157,390	118,024	28,447	6,354,000
83	Toray Industries Inc. (Textiles)	4,950,504	5,495,116	159,215	31,542	5,896,000
84	Ricoh Co. (Electronics)	4,853,751	6,018,763	159,128	n/a	3,493,000
85	Yamaichi Securities Co. (Other Financial)	4,782,293	1,228,773	76,639	n/a	6,727,000
86	Mitsui Trust & Banking Co. (Banks)	4,742,985	6,366,202	82,812	n/a	8,169,000
87	Komatsu (Engineering – General)	4,736,937	5,257,559	86,603	28,446	5,919,000
88	Kumagai Gumi Co. (Contracting, Construction)	4,734,173	5,675,692	103,211	n/a	1,946,000
89	Nichii Co. (Stores)	4,733,177	8,729,187	L33,488	20,241	2,705,000
90	Seiyu (Stores)	4,654,176	5,960,585	162,083	n/a	1,494,000
91	Daiwa Bank (Banks)	4,513,969	6,108,021	254,464	9,897	9,612,000
92	Tomen Corpn (Soga Sosha)	4,503,316	43,347,740	46,239	n/a	1,690,000
93	Takeda Chemical Industries (Chemicals)	4,374,258	3,443,108	444,787	15,781	6,812,000
94	Sumitomo Realty & Development Co. (Property)	4,289,113	2,134,948	46,860	n/a	1,927,000
95	Toppan Printing Co. (Packaging, Paper & Printing)	4,286,101	6,774,877	384,297	25,697	5,811,000
96	Daiei Inc. (Stores)	4,270,938	16,320,900	226,910	n/a	5,141,000
97	Kubota Corpn (Other Industrial Materials & Products)	4,202,291	6,088,342	169,651	n/a	6,070,000
98	Sumitomo Chemical Co. (Chemicals)	4,200,508	5,657,806	225,545	15,327	4,174,000
99	Mitsui O.S.K. Lines (Transport Services)	4,128,643	3,218,077	54,572	n/a	2,507,000
100	Hanwa Co. (Miscellaneous)	4,058,364	3,378,743	L708,744	1,324	1,417,000

NOTES: n/a – not available.

AUSTRALIA, NEW ZEALAND & SOUTHEAST ASIA'S TOP 100   1-50

RANK	COMPANY NAME (Sector)	CAPITAL EMPLOYED £000	TURNOVER £000	PRE-TAX PROFIT £000	NUMBER OF EMPLOYEES	EQUITY MKT CAPITAL £000
1	Korea Electric Power, KOR (Electricity)	15,108,393	6,310,829	608,686	30,142	6,631,499
2	News Corpn, AUS (Media)	10,663,326	4,640,141	504,291	n/a	7,331,242
3	Broken Hill Proprietary Co., AUS (Mines)	10,122,252	7,604,156	1,023,779	48,000	†
4	Swire Pacific, HKG (Transport Services)	9,391,802	4,013,671	704,017	n/a	3,866,101
5	Sun Hung Kai Properties, HKG (Property)	9,195,069	1,535,289	882,489	n/a	8,668,652
6	Wharf (Holdings), HKG (Property)	9,021,026	686,286	309,931	n/a	4,675,514
7	Hutchison Whampoa, HKG (Conglomerates)	7,321,267	2,542,348	862,956	n/a	9,361,000
8	Westpac Banking Corpn, AUS (Banks)	6,667,947	2,956,900	95,800	33,724	3,038,300
9	National Australia Bank, AUS (Banks)	6,015,000	4,522,100	841,000	n/a	6,845,100
10	Cheung Kong (Holdings), HKG (Property)	5,183,319	1,250,696	1,108,190	n/a	5,718,735
11	Tenaga Nasional, MAL (Electricity)	4,945,970	1,422,099	500,617	n/a	11,113,850
12	Australia and New Zealand Banking Group, AUS (Banks)	4,684,289	3,968,067	573,686	n/a	2,483,460
13	Jardine Matheson Holdings, BER/HKG (Conglomerates)	4,163,606	5,622,403	550,127	n/a	1,695,737
14	Fletcher Challenge, NZL (Building Materials & Services)	4,156,677	3,062,212	261,349	n/a	2,125,928
15	Commonwealth Bank Of Australia, AUS (Banks)	3,947,400	3,485,100	498,800	n/a	3,328,500
16	Henderson Land Development Co., HKG (Property)	3,856,962	860,712	646,315	n/a	4,849,463
17	Singapore Airlines, SIN (Transport Services)	3,727,900	2,594,932	362,585	24,377	4,741,280
18	CRA, AUS (Mines)	3,697,620	2,772,138	300,123	17,831	5,260,729
19	Bangkok Bank Public Co., THA (Banks)	3,386,700	2,334,600	662,900	n/a	5,245,700
20	Samsung Electronics Co., KOR (Electronics)	3,305,215	6,838,087	176,290	47,597	2,406,609
21	Hysan Development Co., HKG (Property)	3,140,756	137,896	101,439	n/a	1,271,371
22	Cathay Pacific Airways, HKG (Transport Services)	3,063,216	2,293,490	251,218	14,216	2,663,000
23	Hang Seng Bank, HKG (Banks)	2,970,771	1,566,635	714,888	n/a	8,855,997
24	Telekom Malaysia, MAL (Communications)	2,933,818	1,116,730	416,763	29,574	8,614,921
25	BTR Nylex, AUS (Engineering – General)	2,898,813	2,388,814	276,618	32,461	3,922,492
26	Development Bank of Singapore, SIN (Banks)	2,883,471	958,005	294,106	n/a	3,082,687
27	State Bank of New South Wales, AUS (Banks)	2,746,600	803,100	2,800	n/a	†
28	Hang Lung Development Co., HKG (Property)	2,664,685	335,594	207,942	n/a	1,234,668
29	Korean Air Lines, KOR (Transport Services)	2,651,993	2,264,875	29,077	n/a	789,069
30	New World Development Co., HKG (Property)	2,598,104	906,028	209,844	n/a	2,871,385
31	Hyundai Motor Co., KOR (Transport – Manufacture & Distribution)	2,558,675	6,021,707	59,155	41,409	1,257,000
32	Sino Land Co., HKG (Property)	2,521,861	315,616	147,990	n/a	1,331,526
33	Tsim Sha Tsui Properties, HKG (Other Financial)	2,458,473	323,078	145,144	n/a	672,951
34	Qantas Airways, AUS (Transport Services)	2,452,444	3,010,847	109,327	26,791	†
35	CSR, AUS (Building Materials & Services)	2,398,716	1,972,576	146,965	19,719	2,290,658
36	Coles Myer, AUS (Stores)	2,368,183	7,248,206	278,385	n/a	2,631,756
37	Foster's Brewing Group, AUS (Brewers & Distillers)	2,340,538	1,933,362	109,142	n/a	1,673,777
38	Daewoo Corpn, KOR (Engineering – General)	2,318,360	7,994,255	56,892	n/a	1,307,000
39	M.I.M. Holdings, AUS (Mines)	2,272,046	1,012,507	L59,763	n/a	1,242,475
40	Wheelock and Co., CHI/HKG (Miscellaneous)	2,144,357	169,267	132,469	n/a	3,854,490
41	Citic Pacific, HKG (Transport – Manufacture & Distribution)	2,126,419	996,203	190,247	n/a	4,034,892
42	Great Eagle Holdings, BER/HKG (Property)	2,093,525	153,772	78,443	n/a	823,992
43	Carter Holt Harvey, NZL (Packaging, Paper & Printing)	2,066,163	775,577	84,144	n/a	2,201,376
44	Boral, AUS (Conglomerates)	2,008,199	2,144,500	101,206	22,200	1,731,792
45	Kia Motors, KOR (Transport – Manufacture & Distribution)	2,002,864	3,448,792	15,649	n/a	1,290,506
46	Oversea-Chinese Banking Corpn, SIN (Banks)	1,970,400	1,024,000	330,000	n/a	†
47	LG Electronics Co., KOR (Electronics)	1,861,026	3,586,509	71,088	29,720	1,312,000
48	Western Mining Corpn Holdings, AUS (Mines)	1,852,960	692,464	58,655	n/a	3,348,622
49	Hopewell Holdings, HKG (Other Financial)	1,831,096	232,019	240,747	n/a	3,655,569
50	Amcor, AUS (Packaging, Paper & Printing)	1,819,562	2,095,063	194,877	18,100	2,569,544

NOTES: n/a – not available. †Market capitalisation not available or company is state controlled.

51-100 AUSTRALIA, NEW ZEALAND & SOUTHEAST ASIA'S TOP 100

RANK	COMPANY NAME (Sector)	CAPITAL EMPLOYED £000	TURNOVER £000	PRE-TAX PROFIT £000	NUMBER OF EMPLOYEES	EQUITY MKT CAPITAL £000
51	Chinese Estates Holdings, BER/HKG (Property)	1,791,361	193,775	107,834	n/a	812,456
52	United Industrial Corpn, SIN (Property)	1,777,817	132,979	52,509	n/a	753,423
53	Henderson Investment, HKG (Property)	1,737,065	110,106	109,575	n/a	1,279,176
54	Lai Sun Garment (International), HKG (Textiles)	1,700,781	404,378	105,652	n/a	300,896
55	Malaysian Airline System, MAL (Transport Services)	1,621,124	873,673	36,925	19,783	1,036,126
56	China Light & Power Co., HKG (Electricity)	1,581,658	1,323,945	391,569	6,375	6,420,000
57	Lai Sun Development Co., HKG (Property)	1,557,276	263,758	98,225	n/a	364,067
58	Hongkong and Shanghai Hotels, HKG (Hotels & Leisure)	1,550,155	150,427	43,569	5,540	798,000
59	Hongkong Electric Holdings, HKG (Electricity)	1,500,091	562,101	386,055	n/a	3,530,000
60	LG Chemical, KOR (Chemicals)	1,478,061	1,912,492	61,882	n/a	875,000
61	Pioneer International, AUS (Building Materials & Services)	1,472,819	2,277,232	91,279	1,645	1,199,164
62	Pacific Dunlop, AUS (Other Industrial Materials & Products)	1,415,389	2,737,751	162,929	47,071	2,160,033
63	Woodside Petroleum, AUS (Oil, Gas & Nuclear Fuels)	1,396,815	230,393	61,682	n/a	2,806,667
64	Thai Farmers Bank Public Co., THA (Banks)	1,382,500	1,330,100	377,000	16,363	†
65	Fraser & Neave, SIN (Brewers & Distillers)	1,367,182	888,175	123,568	n/a	1,779,848
66	Sime Darby, MAL (Other Financial)	1,318,702	1,712,072	204,435	n/a	2,574,925
67	Miramar Hotel & Investment Co., HKG (Hotels & Leisure)	1,311,659	94,208	6,514	n/a	1,102,416
68	Alcoa of Australia, AUS (Metal & Metal Forming)	1,307,724	1,001,373	267,594	n/a	†
69	Lion Nathan, NZL (Brewers & Distillers)	1,274,190	794,419	44,640	4,027	608,167
70	Hyundai Engineering & Construction, KOR (Contracting, Construction)	1,262,450	2,326,655	40,313	n/a	973,544
71	Hong Kong Telecommunications, HKG (Communications)	1,246,785	1,661,431	571,772	15,888	15,846,016
72	Regal Hotels International Holdings, BER/HKG (Hotels & Leisure)	1,246,097	151,199	28,097	n/a	398,660
73	Neptune Orient Lines, SIN (Transport Services)	1,220,555	789,617	40,344	n/a	834,906
74	Hanil Bank, KOR (Banks)	1,208,900	1,144,400	148,000	n/a	†
75	Korea First Bank, KOR (Banks)	1,208,500	1,304,300	129,000	n/a	†
76	Telecom Corpn of New Zealand, NZL (Communications)	1,174,052	779,768	51,558	n/a	2,368,839
77	Consolidated Electric Power Asia, HKG (Electricity)	1,142,092	67,691	24,300	n/a	1,349,903
78	Shinan Bank, KOR (Banks)	1,137,900	793,700	177,500	n/a	†
79	Santos, AUS (Oil, Gas & Nuclear Fuels)	1,129,450	311,247	128,077	1,526	912,079
80	Overseas Union Bank, SIN (Banks)	1,123,300	529,600	140,200	n/a	1,840,400
81	Bank of Western Australia, AUS (Banks)	1,092,400	398,300	35,600	3,462	†
82	Goodman Fielder, AUS (Food Manufacturing)	1,083,041	1,714,570	69,731	n/a	725,757
83	Hanwha Chemical Corpn, KOR (Chemicals)	1,078,837	860,495	L28,447	n/a	348,600
84	Daelim Industrial, KOR (Contracting, Construction)	1,070,770	1,308,500	12,233	n/a	296,411
85	Cho Hung Bank, KOR (Banks)	1,070,600	1,169,400	112,800	n/a	†
86	Siam Cement Public Co., THA (Building Materials & Services)	1,063,706	1,168,321	117,212	n/a	4,375,098
87	Malaysian International Shipping Corpn, MAL (Transport Services)	1,063,278	603,410	145,540	n/a	1,614,518
88	Ssangyong Cement, KOR (Building Materials & Services)	1,056,517	798,833	31,594	n/a	650,900
89	Daewoo Electronics, KOR (Electronics)	1,053,843	1,680,186	20,662	n/a	1,063,755
90	PT Indocement Tunggal Prakarsa, IDN (Building Materials & Services)	1,051,422	922,007	134,086	n/a	1,476,000
91	Brambles Industries, AUS (Miscellaneous)	1,036,537	1,218,377	L62,809	15,000	1,345,162
92	Lend Lease Corpn, AUS (Property)	1,030,400	641,687	107,705	5,172	1,318,405
93	Far Eastern Textile, TWN (Textiles)	963,832	514,391	29,362	n/a	1,361,000
94	North, AUS (Agriculture)	955,818	657,037	102,102	n/a	1,070,619
95	Seoul Bank, KOR (Banks)	953,100	1,036,000	11,900	n/a	†
96	Commercial Bank of Korea, KOR (Banks)	950,400	1,160,500	17,600	n/a	†
97	Burns Philp & Co., AUS (Food Manufacturing)	942,176	1,285,939	71,808	12,000	717,279
98	Bank of East Asia, HKG (Banks)	939,527	454,426	155,433	n/a	1,878,688
99	First Pacific Co., BER/HKG (Miscellaneous)	932,758	2,397,444	192,608	30,808	901,510
100	City Developments, SIN (Property)	907,793	317,183	84,025	n/a	2,031,828

NOTES: n/a – not available. †Market capitalisation not available or company is state controlled.

INDEX

Abbreviations: *G*: Governor; *P*: President; *CH*: Chairman; *CE*: Chief Executive; *MD*: Managing Director; *JMD*: Joint Managing Director; *FD*: Finance Director.

AAH PLC
76 South Park, Lincoln, LN5 8ES
Tel: 01522 546577
Fax: 01522 546212
CH: D. Kammerer 52

ABB Asea Brown Boveri Ltd
PO Box 8131, 8050 Zurich, Switzerland
Tel: +41 1 317 73 34
Fax: +41 1 317 79 58
CH: D. de Pury, P. Wallenberg 77, 88, 91

ABN Amro Holding NV
Foppingadreef 22, 1102 BS Amsterdam, The Netherlands
Tel: +31 20 628 98 98
CH: J.D. Hooglandt, P.J. Kalff 76, 88, 89, 91

AEA Technology
Harwell, Oxfordshire, OX11 0RA
Tel: 01235 435555
Fax: 01235 432859
CH: A. Claver 52

AG der Dillinger Huttenwerke
Postfach 15 80, 66763 Dillingen/Saar, Germany
Tel: +49 68 31 47-0
Fax: +49 472 212
CH: F. Mer, R. de Bonneville 105

AGA AB
181 81 Lidingo, Sweden
Tel: +46 8 731 10 00
Fax: +46 8 767 63 44
P: M. Storch, *CH*: S. Agrup 98

AGIV-AG fur Industrie und Verkehrswesen
Mainzer Landstrasse 41, 60329 Frankfurt am Main, Germany
Tel: +49 69 25 42-0
Fax: +49 69 2 54 23 47
CH: Dr H.C. Schroeder-Hohenwarth, Dr W. Graebner, U.G. Stark 96

AMB-Aachener und Munchener Beteiligungs AG
Aachneuer und Munchener Allee 9, 52074 Aachen, Germany
Tel: +49 2 41-4 61 01
Fax: +49 2 41-461-18 05
CH: Dr rer pol H. Kramer, Dr W. Kaske 95

AMEC PLC
Sandiway House, Hartford, Northwich, Cheshire, CW8 2YA
Tel: 01606 883885
Fax: 01606 883996
CH: Sir Alan Cockshaw, *FD*: S.G. Batey 47, 107

AMR Corpn
PO Box 619616, Dallas/Fort Worth Airport, Texas, 75261-9616, USA
Tel: +1 817 963-1234
CH: R.L. Crandall 111

ANZ Holdings (UK) PLC
Minerva House, Montague Close, London, SE1 9DH
Tel: 0171 378 2121
Fax: 0171 378 2378
No officers designated 46, 103

APV PLC
1 Lygon Place, London, SW1W 0JR
Tel: 0171 730 7244
Fax: 0171 730 2660
CH: Sir Peter Cazalet, *CE*: Dr Neil P.D. French 49

AS Potagua
Kalvebod Brygge 20, 1560 Copenhagen V, Denmark
Tel: +45 33 91 58 00
Fax: +45 33 91 17 50
CH: J. Munter, *MD*: F. Bjergvang 98

ASEA AB
Hamngatan 2, Box 7373, 103 91 Stockholm, Sweden
Tel: +46 8 613 65 60
Fax: +46 8 613 65 65
CH: C. Nicolin, P. Wallenberg, *MD*: K. Hogfelt 77, 88, 91, 97

ASSITALIA - Le Assicurazioni d'Italia SpA
Corso d'Italia 33, 00198 Rome, Italy
Tel: +39 6 84 831
Fax: +39 6 848 335 20
CH: S. Siglienti, *JMD*: G. Giannini, R. Pontremoli 109

ASW Holdings PLC
PO Box 207, St Mellons, Cardiff, CF3 0YJ
Tel: 01222 471333
Fax: 01222 795499
CH: G. Duncan, *CE*: Sir Alan G. Cox, *FD*: E.C. Townsend 53

AT&T (UK) Holdings Ltd
PO Box 5, Grosvenor House, Prospect Hill, Redditch, Worcestershire, B97 4DQ
Tel: 01527 64274
Fax: 01527 63360
No officers designated 49

AT&T Corpn
32 Avenue of the Americas, New York, NY, 10013-2412, USA
Tel: +1 212 387-5400
CH: R.E. Allen 13, 110

AVA Allgemeine Handelsgesellschaft der Verbraucher AG
Fuggerstrasse 11, 33689 Bielefeld, Germany
Tel: +49 52 05 94-01
Fax: +49 52 05 94-10 29
CH: Prof Dr G. Laule, K. Daudel 105

AXA
21-23 avenue Matignon, 75008 Paris, France
Tel: +33 1 40 75 57 00
Fax: +33 1 40 75 57 50
CH: C. Bebear 84, 91

Aare-Tessin AG fur Elektrizitat
Bahnhofquai 12, 4601 Olten, Switzerland
Tel: +41 62 31 71 11
Fax: +41 62 31 73 73
CH: Prof A. Pozzi, Dr W. Burgi, *MD*: Dr W. Burgi 95

Abbey National PLC
Abbey House, Baker Street, London, NW1 6XL
Tel: 0171 612 4000
Fax: 0171 612 4010
CH: The Lord Tugendhat, *CE*: P.G. Birch, *FD*: I. Harley 14, 16, 40, 42, 45, 68, 88, 90, 100

Abbott Laboratories Ltd
Queenborough, Kent, ME11 5EL
Tel: 01795 663371
Fax: 01795 667164
CH: D. Gibbons 58

Aberforth Smaller Companies Trust PLC
14 Melville Street, Edinburgh, EH3 7NS
Tel: 0131 220 0733
Fax: 0131 220 0735
CH: W.Y. Hughes 55

Aberforth Split Level Trust PLC
14 Melville Street, Edinburgh, EH3 7NS
Tel: 0131 220 0733
Fax: 0131 220 0735
CH: M.J. Walker 57

Abtrust New Dawn Investment Trust PLC
99 Charterhouse Street, London, EC1M 6AB
Tel: 0171 490 4466
Fax: 0171 490 4436
CH: R. Scott Brown 57

Acco Europe PLC
The Lodge, Harmondsworth Lane, Harmondsworth, West Drayton, Middlesex, UB7 0LQ
Tel: 0181 759 4822
Fax: 0181 897 2928
CH: G.J. Trussler 54

Accor
2 rue de la Mare-Neuve, 91021 Evry Cedex, France
Tel: +33 1 60 87 43 20
Fax: +33 1 60 77 04 58
CH: P. Dubrule, G. Pelisson 93

Acerinox SA
Santiago de Compostela 100, 28080 Madrid, Spain
Tel: +34 1 398 51 74
Fax: +34 1 398 51 95
CH: V. Munoz Cava 107

Adia SA
1261 Cheserex, Switzerland
Tel: +41 22 69 12 22
CH: H.-F. Lavanchy, K.J. Jacobs, *CE*: J.P. Bowmer 107

Adwest Group PLC
Woodley, Reading, Berkshire, RG5 4SN
Tel: 01734 697171
Fax: 01734 690121
CH: D.E. Filer, *CE*: G.R. Menzies, *FD*: R.S. Shearer 56

Aegon NV
Mariahoeveplein 50, PO Box 202, 2501 CE The Hague, The Netherlands
Tel: +31 70 3 44 32 10
Fax: +31 70 3 47 52 38
CH: G. van Schaik, K.J. Storm 85, 91

Aerospatiale Ste Nationale Industrielle
37 boulevard de Montmorency, 75781 Paris Cedex 16, France
Tel: +33 1 42 24 24 24
CH: L. Gallois, H. Martre, *JMD*: Y. Michot, C. Terrazzoni, M. Delaye 93

Agache [Financiere]
11 rue Francois 1er, 75008 Paris, France
Tel: +33 1 40 73 57 57
CH: J. Dromer, *MD*: R. Leon 77, 91

Aguas de Barcelona [Sdad General de] SA
Paseo de San Juan 39-43, 08009 Barcelona, Spain
Tel: +34 32 65 80 11
Fax: +34 32 65 11 36
CH: R. Fornesa Ribo, *JMD*: J.L. Jove Vintro, J. Vila Bassas, A. Ramiro Fernandez 104

Ahlstrom [A.] Oy
Etelaesplanadi 14, 00101 Helsinki, Finland
Tel: +358 0 503 911
Fax: +358 0 503 9709
P: K. Ahlstrom, *CH*: J. Gullichsen 100

Ahold NV [Kon]
Albert Heijnweg 1, 1507 AH Zaandam, The Netherlands
Tel: +31 75 59 91 11
Fax: +31 75 59 83 50
P: C.H. van der Hoeven, *CH*: J.H. Choufoer 96

Air France [Cie Nationale]
1 square Max Hymans, 75757 Paris Cedex 15, France
Tel: +33 1 43 23 81 81
Fax: +33 1 43 23 97 11
CH: C. Blanc 23, 62, 92

Air Liquide [L'] SA
75 Quai d'Orsay, 75321 Paris Cedex 07, France
Tel: +33 1 40 62 55 55
CH: J. Delorme, A. Joly, E. de Royere, *JMD*: E. de Royere, A. Joly 93

Air Products PLC
Hersham Place, Molesey Road, Walton-on-Thames, Surrey, KT12 4RZ
Tel: 01932 249200
Fax: 01932 249565
MD: G.P. Wyatt 51

Airlines of Britain Holdings PLC
Donington Hall, Castle Donington, Derby, DE74 2SB
Tel: 01332 810741
Fax: 01332 850301
CH: Sir Michael Bishop 61

Airtours PLC
Wavell House, Holcombe Road, Helmshore, Rossendale, Lancashire, BB4 4NB
Tel: 01706 240033
Fax: 01706 212144
CH: D. Crossland, *MD*: H.H. Collinson, *FD*: A.H. Coe 52

Aker AS
Fjordalleen 16, 0250 Oslo, Norway
Tel: +47 22-94 50 00
Fax: +47 22-94 50 16
P: T. Ruud, *CH*: G. Heiberg 99

Akzo Nobel NV
Velperweg 76, PO Box 9300, 6800 SB Arnhem, The Netherlands
Tel: +31 85 66 44 33
Fax: +31 85 66 32 50
CH: Ir F.H. Fentener van Vlissingen, C.J.A. van Lede 92

Alba [Corporacion Financiera] SA
Calle Castello 77, Floor 5, 28006 Madrid, Spain
Tel: +34 1 362 61 00
Fax: +34 1 575 67 37
CH: J. March Delgado 104

Albatros Investissement SA
Odet, 29500 Ergue-Gaberic, Quimper, France
Tel: +33 46 96 42 95
Fax: +33 46 96 40 81
CH: V. Bollore 98

Albright & Wilson PLC
210-222 Hagley Road West, Oldbury, Warley, West Midlands, B68 0NN
Tel: 0121 429 4942
Fax: 0121 420 5151
CH: Sir Christopher Benson, *CE*: Dr R. Paul, *FD*: M. Winstanley 48, 108

Alcatel SEL AG
Lorenzstrasse 10, 70435 Stuttgart, Germany
Tel: +49 7 11 8 21-0
Fax: +49 7 11 8 21-60 55
CH: E. Falk, Dr rer pol J. Holzer, *MD*: P. Landsberg 71, 97

Alcatel-Alsthom Cie Generale d'Electricite
54 rue La Boetie, 75382 Paris, Cedex 08, France
Tel: +33 1 42 56 15 61
P: F. de Laage de Meux, *CH*: S. Tchuruk, M. Vienot 71, 88, 90

Alcoa of Australia Ltd
530 Collins Street, Melbourne, Victoria, 3000, Australia
Tel: +61 3 270 6111
CH: Sir Arvi Parbo, *MD*: Robert F. Slagle 115

All England Lawn Tennis Ground Ltd (The)
Hill House, 1 Little New Street, London, EC4A 3TR
Tel: 0171 936 3000
Fax: 0171 583 8517
CH: J.A.H. Curry 59

All Nippon Airways Co. Ltd
PO Box 106, Kasumigaseki Building, 3-2-5 Kasumigaseki, Chiyoda-ku, Tokyo 100, Japan
Tel: +81 3 3592 3065
Fax: +81 3 3581 7084
P: Seiji Fukatsu, *CH*: Tokuji Wakasa, Takaya Sugiura 113

Allders PLC
Royal London House, Christchurch Road, Bournemouth, BH1 3LT
Tel: 01202 298289
Fax: 01202 298263
CH: J.H. Pattisson, *CE*: H.B. Lipsith, *FD*: A.D. Collyer 53

Alliance & Leicester Building Society
49 Park Lane, London, W1Y 4EQ
Tel: 0171 629 6661
Fax: 0171 408 1399
CH: S. EverardA, *CE*: P.R. White, *FD*: R.A. Pym 26

Alliance Trust PLC (The)
Meadow House, 64 Reform Street, Dundee, DD1 1TJ
Tel: 01382 201700
Fax: 01382 25133
CH: Sir Robert Smith, *JMD*: L. Bolton, G.R. Suggett 41, 45, 48, 99, 109

Allianz AG Holding
Koniginstrasse 28, Postfach 44 01 24, 80802 Munich, Germany
Tel: +49 89 3 80 00
Fax: +49 89 34 99 41
CH: Dr W. Schieren, Dr H. Schulte-Noelle 62, 78, 88, 89, 91

Allied Colloids Group PLC
Cleckheaton Road, Low Moor, Bradford, BD12 0JZ
Tel: 01274 671267
Fax: 01274 606499
CH: Sir Trevor Holdsworth, *CE*: D. Farrar, *FD*: G.S. Senior 51

Allied Domecq PLC
24 Portland Place, London, W1N 4BB
Tel: 0171 323 9000
Fax: 0171 323 1742
CH: M.C.J. Jackaman, *CE*: A.J. Hales, *FD*: J.A.F. Trigg 21, 40, 42, 92

Allied Irish Banks PLC
Bankcentre, Ballsbridge, Dublin 4, Ireland
Tel: +353 1 660 0311
Fax: +353 1 668 4502
CH: J.P. Culliton, *CE*: T.P. Mulcahy, *FD*: K.J. Kelly 95

Allied London Properties PLC
Allied House, 26 Manchester Square, London, W1A 2HU
Tel: 0171 486 6080
Fax: 0171 486 5428
CH: Sir Geoffrey Leigh, *MD*: H.T. Stanton, *FD*: F.P. Graham-Watson 50

Allied Textile Companies PLC
Allied House, Centre 27 Business Park, Bankwood Way, Birstall, West Yorkshire, WF17 9TB
Tel: 01924 443366
Fax: 01924 442525
CH: J.P. Honeysett, *CE*: J.R. Corrin 55

Almanij NV -Algemene Mij voor Nijverheidskrediet
Schoenmarkt 33, 2000 Antwerp, Belgium
Tel: +32 3 234 29 97
CH: L. Wauters, J. Huyghbaert, *MD*: F. Verdonck 99

Altana AG
Seedammweg 55, 61352 Bad Homburg vor der Hohe, Germany
Tel: +49 61 72 4 04 40
Fax: +49 61 72 4 04 338
CH: H. Weiss, K. Schweickart 102

Aluminum Co. of America
425 Sixth Avenue, Pittsburgh, Pennsylvania, 15219-1850, USA
Tel: +1 412 553 4545
Fax: +1 412 553 4498
CH: P.H. O'Neill 111

Alusuisse-Lonza Holding AG
Feldeggstrasse 4, PO Box 495, 8034 Zurich, Switzerland
Tel: +41 1 386 22 22
Fax: +41 1 386 25 85
CH: H.K. Jucker, T.M. Tschopp 95

Alvis PLC
215 Vauxhall Bridge Road, London, SW1V 1EN
Tel: 0171 821 8080
Fax: 0171 931 7433
CH: J.D. Robertshaw, *CE*: N.M. Prest, *FD*: S.R. Mitchell 60

Amcor Ltd
Southgate Tower East, 40 City Road, South Melbourne, Victoria 3205, Australia
Tel: +61 3 694 9000
Fax: +61 3 686 2924
CH: A.D. Lapthorne, *MD*: S.D.M. Wallis 114

Amer Group Ltd
Makelankatu 91, 00610 Helsinki, Finland
Tel: +358 0 757 71
Fax: +358 0 757 7200
P: S. Ahonen, *CH*: R. Taivalkoski, J. Harmala 103

Amerada Hess Ltd
33 Grosvenor Place, London, SW1X 7HY
Tel: 0171 823 2626
Fax: 0171 927 9799
CH: L. Hess, *MD*: W.S.H. Laidlaw 44, 97

American Electric Power Co. Inc.
1 Riverside Plaza, Columbus, Ohio 43215, USA
Tel: +1 614 223-1000
CH: Dr E.L. Draper Jr 111

American Express Co.
American Express Tower,

116

World Financial Center, New York, New York, 10285, USA
Tel: +1 212 640-2000
P: J.E. Stiefler, *CH:* H. Golub 110

American International Group Inc.
70 Pine Street, New York, New York, 10270, USA
Tel: +1 212 770-7000
P: T.R. Tizzio, *CH:* M.R. Greenberg 51

American Trust PLC
Donaldson House, 97 Haymarket Terrace, Edinburgh, EH12 5HD
Tel: 0131 313 1000
Fax: 0131 313 6300
CH: Lord Macfarlane of Bearsden 41, 49

Ameritech Corpn
30 South Wacker Drive, Chicago, Illinois, 60606, USA
Tel: +1 312 750-5000
CH: R.C. Notebaert 111

Amersham International PLC
Amersham Place, Little Chalfont, Buckinghamshire, HP7 9NA
Tel: 01494 544000
Fax: 01494 542266
CH: Sir Edwin Nixon, *CE:* W.M. Castell, *FD:* R.K. Stephenson 51

Amicable Smaller Enterprises Trust PLC
150 St Vincent Street, Glasgow, G2 5NQ
Tel: 0141 248 2323
Fax: 0141 221 3893
CH: H.W. Laughland 61

Amoco Corpn
200 East Randolph Drive, Chicago, Illinois, 60601-7125, USA
Tel: +1 312 856-6111
CH: H.L. Fuller 110

Amstrad PLC
Brentwood House, 169 Kings Road, Brentwood, Essex, CM14 4EF
Tel: 01277 228888
Fax: 01277 211350
CH: A.M. Sugar , *CE:* D.C.W. Rogers, *FD:* A.G. Dean 50

An-Hyp (Caisse Hypothecaire Anversoise)
Grotesteenweg 214, 2600 Antwerp, Belgium
Tel: +32 3 286 22 11
Fax: +32 3 286 25 32
CH: P. Vanderlinden, Baron C. de Villenfagne de Vogelsanck, *MD:* Baron C. de Villenfagne de Vogelsanck 99

Angerstein Underwriting Trust PLC
14th Floor, One Angel Court, Throgmorton Street, London, EC2R 7HJ
CH: A.R.W. Smithers 60

Anglian Water PLC
Anglian House, Ambury Road, Huntingdon, Cambridgeshire, PE18 6NZ
Tel: 01480 443000
Fax: 01480 443115
CH: R.M. Gourlay, *MD:* A.F. Smith, *FD:* C.J. Mellor 34, 43, 95

Anglo & Overseas Trust PLC
20 Finsbury Circus, London, EC2M 1NB
Tel: 0171 256 7500
Fax: 0171 826 0451
CH: Lord Wakehurst 41, 46, 103

Anheuser-Busch Cos Inc.
1 Busch Place, St Louis, Missouri, 63118, USA
Tel: +1 314 577-2000
CH: A.A. Busch III 111

Antofagasta Holdings PLC
Park House, 16 Finsbury Circus, London, EC2M 7AH
Tel: 0171 374 8091
Fax: 0171 628 3773
CH: A.A. Luksic, *MD:* P.J. Adeane 51

Aplus Co. Ltd
Midosuji Center Building, 6-6, Minami Kyuhoji-machi 3-chome, Chuo-ku, Osaka 541, Japan
Tel: +81 6 245 7771
Fax: +81 6 243 0468
P: Eigo Maeda, *CH:* Hirokazu Tada, *JMD:* Michio Koroyasu, Takeshi Takada, Yukio Tonomizu, Toshihiko Tabata, Masaharu Shirao 113

Appleyard Group PLC
Windsor House, Cornwall Road, Harrogate, North Yorkshire, HG1 2PW
Tel: 01423 531999
Fax: 01423 530949
CH: M.G. Williamson, *FD:* P.J. Chambers 60

Arbed SA
19 Avenue de la Liberte, 2930 Luxembourg
Tel: +352 4792-2360
Fax: +352 4792-2658
CH: E. Tesch, J. Kinsch 93

Archer Daniels Midland International Ltd
Church Manorway, Erith, Kent, DA8 1DL
Tel: 01322 443000
Fax: 01322 437536
CH: D.O. Andreas, *MD:* P.B. Mulhollem 51

Ares-Serono SA
PO Box 11, 1267 Vich-Coinsins, Switzerland
CH: H. Thierstein, *CE:* F. Bertarelli 104

Argent Group PLC
5 Albany Court, Piccadilly, London, W1V 9RB
Tel: 0171 734 3721
Fax: 0171 734 4474
CH: G.A.B. Steer, *CE:* M.I. Freeman, P.G. Freeman, *FD:* R.M. Millar 49

Argentaria [Corporacion Bancaria de Espana SA]
Paseo de Recoletos 10, 28001 Madrid, Spain
CH: F. Luzon Lopez 80, 91

Argos PLC
Avebury, 489-499 Avebury Boulevard, Saxon Gate West, Central Milton Keynes, MK9 2NW
Tel: 01908 600925
Fax: 01908 692301
CH: Sir Richard Lloyd, *CE:* M.J. Smith, *FD:* R.D. Stewart 48

Argus Press Ltd
Somerset Hse, London Rd, Redhill, Surrey, RH1 1LU
Tel: 01737 768611
Fax: 01737 760510
CH: C.D. Jakes 57

Argyll Group PLC
6 Millington Road, Hayes, Middlesex, UB3 4AY
Tel: 0181 848 8744
Fax: 0181 573 1865
CH: Sir Alistair Grant, *CE:* C.D. Smith 34, 40, 43 , 95

Arjo Wiggins Appleton PLC
Gateway House, Basing View, Basingstoke, Hampshire, RG21 2EE
Tel: 01256 723000
Fax: 01256 723723
CH: A.W.P. Stenham, *CE:* A. Soulas, *FD:* A. Charles 38, 43, 96

Asahi Breweries Ltd
23-1, Azumabashi 1-chome, Sumida-ku, Tokyo 130, Japan
Tel: +81 3 5608 5112
Fax: +81 3 5608 7111/5119
P: Yuzo Seto, *CH:* Hirotaro Higuchi, *JMD:* Yasuo Ogura, Daizaburo Yui, Shigeo Fukuchi, Kaoru Chihara, Hisashi Usuba, Hirofumi Tange, Teisuke Fukuda, Yasuo Matsui, Akira Tayama, Hiroshi Hasegawa, Akira Etoh, Minoru Tabuchi, Ryoji Igarashi 113

Asahi Chemical Industry Co. Ltd
Hibiya-Mitsui Building, 1-2 Yuraku-cho 1-chome, Chiyoda-ku Tokyo, Japan
Tel: +81 3 3507 2730
P: Reiichi Yumikura, *CH:* Nobuo Yamaguchi, *JMD:* Kazumoto Yamamoto, Yukio Sawabe, Keizo Sasao, Koji Namba, Takeo Chikaike, Minoru Makita, Hiroshi Oh-hama, Shigeo Katsuyama, Harurou Tabata, Shigeru Yonekawa, Yuji Tsuchiya, Hideo Ishikawa, Tetsuo Tokunaga 113

Asahi Glass Co. Ltd
1-2 Marunouchi 2-chome, Chiyoda-ku, Tokyo 100, Japan
Tel: +81 3 3218 5555
Fax: +81 3 3287 0772
P: Hiromichi Seya, *CH:* Jiro Furumoto 113

Ascom Holding AG
Belpstrasse 37, 3000 Bern 14, Switzerland
Tel: +41 31 999 11 11
Fax: +41 31 999 27 00
CH: Dr F. Wittlin, H-U. Schroder 102

Asda Group PLC
Asda House, Southbank, Great Wilson Street, Leeds, LS11 5AD
Tel: 0113 243 5435
Fax: 0113 241 8666
CH: P.J. Gillam, *CE:* A.J. Norman, *FD:* P.R. Cox 36, 43, 95

Asda Property Holdings PLC
58 Queen Anne Street, London, W1M 9LA
Tel: 0171 2241030
Fax: 0171 2240574
CH: E.W. Davidson, *MD:* A.D. Roscoe, *FD:* P.L. Huberman 52

Ashley [Laura] Holdings PLC
150 Bath Road, Maidenhead, Berkshire, SL6 4YS
Tel: 01628 39151
Fax: 01628 71122
CH: Lord Hooson, *CE:* Ann Iverson, *FD:* J. Walsh 54

Asko Deutsche Kaufhaus AG
Mainzer Strasse 180-184, 66121 Saarbrucken, Germany
Tel: +49 6 81 81 04-01
Fax: +49 6 81 81 04-261
CH: E. Conradi, K. Wiegandt 97

Asko Oy
Askonkatu 3, PO Box 45, 15101 Lahti, Finland
Tel: +358 18 815 11
Fax: +358 18 815 2600
CH: J. Ihamuotila, *CE:* J. Rytilahti 97, 103

Asprey PLC
165/169 New Bond Street, London, W1Y 0AR
Tel: 0171 493 6767
Fax: 0171 491 0384
CH: J.R. Asprey 51

Assi Packaging (UK) Ltd
Spencer House, 99 Dewhurst Road, Birchwood Centre, Warrington, WA3 7PG
Tel: 01925 827077
Fax: 01925 820921
CH: U.G. Kilander (Sweden) 59

Associated British Foods PLC
Weston Centre, Bowater House, 68 Knightsbridge, London, SW1X 7LR
Tel: 0171 589 6363
Fax: 0171 584 8560
CH: G.H. Weston 32, 40, 43, 95

Associated British Ports Holdings PLC
150 Holborn, London, EC1N 2LR
Tel: 0171 430 1177
Fax: 0171 430 1384
CH: Sir Keith Stuart, *FD:* C.W. Orange 44, 99

Assurances Generales de France [Ste Centrale des]
87 rue de Richelieu, 75113 Paris Cedex 02, France
Tel: +33 1 40341848
CH: M. Albert, A. Jeancourt-Galignani 85, 91

Assurantieconcern Stad Rotterdam
Weena 70, 3012 CM Rotterdam, The Netherlands
Tel: +31 10 401 7200
Fax: +31 10 412 5490
CH: J.M. Schroder, C.J. de Swart 97

Astec (BSR) PLC
High Street, Wollaston, Stourbridge, West Midlands, DY8 4PG
Tel: 01384 440044
Fax: 01384 440777
CE: D.N. Farr, *FD:* D.N. Farr 54

Astra [AB]
151 85 Sodertalje, Sweden
Tel: +46 8 553 260 00
Fax: +46 8 553 290 00
P: H. Mogren, *CH:* B. Berggren 89, 96

Atlantic Richfield Co.
515 South Flower Street, Los Angeles, CA, 90071, USA
Tel: +1 213 486-3511
CH: M.R. Bowlin 110

Atlas Copco AB
105 23 Stockholm, Sweden
Tel: +46 8 743 8000
Fax: +46 8 644 9045
P: M. Treschow, *CH:* P. Wallenberg 100

Attisholz Holding AG
4533 Riedholz, Switzerland
Tel: +41 65 21 51 11
Fax: +41 65 22 90 65
CH: T.D. Berg, *MD:* F. Berger 107

Australia and New Zealand Banking Group Ltd
Level 2, 100 Queen Street, Melbourne, Victoria 3000, Australia
Tel: +61 3 273 6141
Fax: +61 3 273 6142
CH: J.B. Gough, *CE:* D.P. Mercer 114

Austrian Airlines Osterreichische Luftverkehrs AG
Fontanastrasse 1, 1107 Vienna, Austria
Tel: +43 222 68 35 11-0
Fax: +43 222 68 65 26
CH: Dipl-Ing Dr R. Streicher 102

Automated Security (Holdings) PLC
The Clock House, The Campus, Hemel Hempstead, Herts, HP2 7TZ
Tel: 01442 60008
Fax: 01442 62129
CH: The Lord Lane of Horsell, *CE:* T. Dignum, *FD:* P. Bertram 50

Automotive Financial Group Holdings Ltd
Columbia Drive, Durrington, Worthing, West Sussex, BN13 3HD
Tel: 01903 68561
Fax: 01903 690100
No officers designated 46, 105

Autopistas del Mare Nostrum SA, Concesionaria del Estado
Martinez Cubells 5, 46002 Valencia, Spain
Tel: +34 6 337 20 02
CH: J.L. Ceron Ayuso 98, 101

Autopistas, Concesionaria Espanola SA
Plaza Gal la Placidia 1, 08006 Barcelona, Spain
Tel: +34 3 217 28 00
CH: J. Vilarasau Salat, *MD:* J.-M. Basanez Villaluenga 92

Autostrade Concessioni e Costruzioni Autostrade SpA
Via Alberto Bergamini 50, Rome, Italy
CH: G.E. Valori, *MD:* D. Cempella 92

Auxiliaire d'Entreprises et de Participations
2 rue de Laborde, 75008 Paris, France
CH: P. Luciani 108

Avesta Sheffield AB
Vasagatan 8-10, PO Box 16377, 103 27 Stockholm, Sweden
Tel: +46 8 613 36 00
Fax: +46 8 20 84 81
P: P. Molin, *CH:* J. McDowall 21, 102

Avon Rubber PLC
Bath Road, Melksham, Wiltshire, SN12 8AA
Tel: 0125 703101
Fax: 01225 707880
CH: The Rt Hon Lord Farnham, *CE:* S.J. Willcox 55

B.A.T Industries PLC
Windsor House, 50 Victoria Street, London, SW1H 0NL
Tel: 0171 222 7979
Fax: 0171 222 0122
CH: Sir Patrick Sheehy, *FD:* D.P. Allvey 18, 80, 88, 89, 91

B.S.G. International PLC
Seton House, Warwick Technology Park, Gallows Hill, Warwick, CV34 6DE
Tel: 01926 400 040
Fax: 01926 406 300
CH: M.C. Stoddart, *CE:* R.E.C. Marton, *FD:* A.D. Dawson 54

BAA PLC
130 Wilton Road, London, SW1V 1LQ
Tel: 0171 834 9449
Fax: 0171 932 6699
CH: Dr N.B. Smith, *CE:* Sir John Egan, *FD:* J.R.F. Wallis 25, 42, 93

BASF AG
Carl-Bosch Strasse 38, 67063 Ludwigshafen (Rhein), Germany
Tel: +49 6 21 6 00
Fax: +49 6 21 6 04 25 25
CH: M. Seefelder, H. Albers, J. Strube 36,71, 88, 90

BBA Group PLC
PO Box 20, Whitechapel Road, Cleckheaton, West Yorkshire, BD19 6HP
Tel: 01274 874444
Fax: 01274 869916
CH: V.E. Treves, *CE:* R. Quarta, *FD:* P.E. Clappison 45, 101

BBC Brown Boveri AG
5401 Baden, Switzerland
Tel: +41 56 75 77 00
Fax: +41 56 22 10 26
CH: D. de Pury 77, 96

BBC Enterprises Ltd
Woodlands, 80 Wood Lane, London, W12 0TT
Tel: 0181 576 2000
Fax: 0181 749 0538
CH: R. Phillis, *MD:* Dr J.A.G. Thomas 58

BBL-Banque Bruxelles Lambert SA
Avenue Marnix 24, 1050 Brussels
Tel: +32 2 547 21 11
Fax: +32 2 547 38 44
P: D. Cardon de Lichtbuer, *CH:* J. Moulaert 95

BBW Partnership Ltd (The)
Donington Hall, Castle Donington, Derby, DE74 2SB
CH: Sir Michael Bishop 61

BCE Inc.
1000 rue de LA Gauchetiere Ouest, Montreal, Quebec, Canada, H3B 4Y7
Tel: +1 514 397-7267
Fax: +1 514 397-7157
CH: L.R. Wilson 110

BET PLC
Stratton House, Piccadilly, London, W1X 6AS
Tel: 0171 629 8886
Fax: 0171 499 5118
CH: Sir Christopher Harding, *CE:* L.J. Clark, *FD:* K.F. Payne 47, 106

BHF-Bank (Berliner Handels- und Frankfurter Bank)
Bockenheimer Landstrasse 10, 60323 Frankfurt, Germany
Tel: +49 69 718-0
Fax: +49 69 718-2296
CH: Dr jur H.C. Schroeder-Hohenwarth, K. Subjetzki 96

BHP - Hamilton Oil Great Britain PLC
Devonshire House, Piccadilly, London, W1X 6AQ
Tel: 0171 499 9555
Fax: 0171 499 4784
CH: F.C. Hamilton 46, 102

BI Group PLC
Neville House, 42-46 Hagley Road, Edgbaston, Birmingham, B16 8PZ
Tel: 0121 456 1088
Fax: 0121 456 1407
CH: B.M. Sedghi, *FD:* S.H. Hayes 59

BICC PLC
Devonshire House, Mayfair Place, London, W1X 5FH
Tel: 0171 629 6622
Fax: 0171 409 0070
CH: Sir Robin Biggam, *CE:* A. Jones, *FD:* R.A. Henderson 45, 99

BIL GT Gruppe AG
Herrengasse 12, PO Box 85, 9490 Vaduz, Principality of Liechtenstein
Tel: +41 75 235 1122
Fax: +41 75 235 1522
CH: HSH Prince Philipp von und zu Liechtenstein 99

BK Vision AG
Egglirain 24, 8832 Wilen-Wollerau, Switzerland
Tel: +41 1 785 05 65
CH: M. Ebner 100

BKW - Beazer

BKW Energie AG
Viktoriaplatz 2, 3000 Bern 25,
Switzerland
Tel: +41 31 330 51 11
Fax: +41 31 330 56 36
CH: W. Stoffer, R. von Werdt   101

BNL-Banca Nazionale Del Lavoro SpA
Via Vittorio Veneto 119,
00187 Rome, Italy
Tel: +39 6 47021
Fax: +39 6 47026469
CH: M. Sarcinelli, *MD:* D. Croff   93

BOC Group PLC (The)
Chertsey Road, Windlesham, Surrey,
GU20 6HJ
Tel: 01276 477222
Fax: 0276 471333
CH: R.V. Giordano, *MD:* Dr D. Chatterji,
FD: A. Isaac   28, 43, 94

BPB Industries PLC
Langley Park Hse, Uxbridge Road,
Slough, SL3 6DU
Tel: 01753 573273
Fax: 01753 823397
CH: A.G. Turner, *CE:* J.-P. Cuny,
FD: P.E. Sydney-Smith   45, 100

BSS Group PLC (The)
Fleet House, Lee Circle, Leicester,
LE1 3QQ
Tel: 0116 262 3232
Fax: 0116 253 1343
CH: P. Hammersley, *CE:* P. Cooper   60

BTP PLC
Hayes Road, Cadishead, Manchester,
M30 5BX
Tel: 0161 775 3945
Fax: 0161 775 3970
CH: J.H.B. Ketteley, *CE:* S.J. Hannam,
FD: R.C. Martin   51

BTR Nylex PLC
15th Floor, 390 St Kilda Road,
Melbourne, Victoria 3004, Australia
Tel: +61 3 823 5700
Fax: +61 3 867 4103
CH: A.R. Jackson   114

BTR PLC
Silvertown House, Vincent Square,
London, SW1P 2PL
Tel: 0171 834 3848
Fax: 0171 834 3879
CH: N.C. Ireland, *CE:* I.C. Strachan,
MD: A.R. Jackson,
FD: Kathleen A. O'Donovan   14, 21, 40, 42, 88, 89, 92, 114

BZW Convertible Investment Trust PLC
Ebbgate House, 2 Swan Lane, London,
EC4R 3TS
Tel: 0171 623 2323
Fax: 0171 626 1879
CH: P. Birch   57

Babcock International Group PLC
Badminton Court, Church Street,
Amersham, Buckinghamshire, HP7 0DD
Tel: 01494 727296
Fax: 01494 721909
CH: Dr T.J. Parker, *CE:* N.R. Salmon,
FD: E.A.S. Porter   58

Baden-Württembergische Bank AG
Kleiner Schlossplatz 11,
70173 Stuttgart, Germany
Tel: +49 711 20 94-0
Fax: +49 711 20 94-5 66
CH: G. Mayer-Vorfelder   103

Badenwerk AG
Postfach 16 80, 76005 Karlsruhe,
Germany
Tel: +49 7 21 93 60
Fax: +49 7 21 9 36 26 89
CH: G. Mayer-Vorfelder   96

Baer Holding AG
Bahnhofstrasse 36, Postfach, 8010
Zurich, Switzerland
Tel: +41 1 228 57 47
Fax: +41 1 221 20 26
P: R.E. Baer, *CH:* H.J. Bar   102

Baillie Gifford Japan Trust PLC (The)
1 Rutland Court, Edinburgh, EH3 8EY
Tel: 0131 222 4000
CH: G.M. Murray   57

Baird [William] PLC
George House, 50 George Square,
Glasgow, G2 1RR
Tel: 0141 552 3456
Fax: 0141 553 1812
CH: T.D. Parr, *CE:* J.M. Green-Armytage,
FD: N.P.H. Webster   52

Baker Hughes Ltd
2nd Floor, Hammersley House,
5/8 Warwick Street, London, W1R 5RA
Tel: 0171 287 6585
MD: P.J. Woolley   49

Baloise-Holding
Aeschengraben 21, 4002 Basle,
Switzerland
Tel: +41 61 285 85 85
P: G. Balestra, *CH:* R. Schauble   96

Baltic PLC
25/26 Albemarle Street, London,
W1X 4AD
Tel: 0171 493 9899
Fax: 0171 491 8678
CH: M. Goddard   61

Bamford [J.C.] Excavators Ltd
Rocester, Uttoxeter, Staffs, ST14 5JP
Tel: 01889 590312
Fax: 01889 591144
CH: Sir Anthony Bamford   52

Banc One Corpn
100 East Broad Street, Columbus,
Ohio, 43271-0251, USA
Tel: +1 614 248-5944
P: D.L. McWhorter,
CH: J.B. McCoy   111

Banca Commerciale Italiana
Piazza della Scala 6, 20121 Milan, Italy
Tel: +39 2 88501
Fax: +39 2 885 030 26
CH: L. Adler, *JMD:* E. Beneduce,
E. Beneduce   69, 92

Banca Nazionale dell'Agricoltura SpA
Via Salaria 231, 00199 Rome, Italy
Tel: +39 6 85 881
Fax: +39 6 826 14 361
CH: P. Accorinti, *MD:* G. Greco   98

Banca Popolare di Bergamo - Credito Varesino Scrl
Piazza Vittorio Veneto 8, 24100
Bergamo, Italy
Tel: +39 35 392 111
Fax: +39 35 392 103
CH: E. Zanetti, *JMD:* G. Frigeri,
G. Cattaneo   99

Banca Toscana SpA
Via del Corso 6, 50122 Florence, Italy
CH: G. Bartolomei   100

Banca di Roma SpA
Via Marco Minghetti 17, 00187 Rome,
Italy
Tel: +39 6 67071
Fax: +39 6 6781929
CH: P. Capaldo   92

Bancaire [Cie]
5 avenue Kleber, 75116 Paris, France
Tel: +33 1 45 25 25 25
Fax: +33 1 40 67 50 76
CH: J.-Y. Haberer, M. Francois-Poncet,
A. Levy-Lang, F. Henrot   68, 86, 91

Banco Ambrosiano Veneto SpA
Contra S. Corona 25, 36100 Vicenza,
Italy
Tel: +39 444 519111
Fax: +39 444 519205
CH: G. Bazoli, *MD:* C. Salvatori   97

Banco Atlantico SA
Avda Diagonal 407 bis, Barcelona, Spain
Tel: +34 3 402 01 00
Fax: +34 3 218 83 17
CH: A.A. Saudi,
MD: A. Sanchez-Pedreno Martinez 109

Banco Bilbao Vizcaya SA
Plaza San Nicolas 4, 48005 Bilbao, Spain
Tel: +34 4 487 55 55
Fax: +34 4 423 21 32
CH: E. Ybarra y Churruca,
MD: P.L. Uriarte Santamarina   92

Banco Central Hispanoamericano SA
Alcala 49, 28014 Madrid, Spain
Tel: +34 1 532 8510

Fax: +34 1 532 76 59
CH: Alfonso Escamez Lopez,
J.M. Amusategui de la Cierva,
CE: A. Corcostegui   93

Banco Comercial Portugues
Rua Julio Dinis 705/719, 4000 Porto,
Portugal
Tel: +35 2 69 61 36
Fax: +35 2 69 95 12
CH: J.M. Jardim Goncalves   98

Banco Espanol de Credito SA
Paseo de la Castellana 7,
28046 Madrid, Spain
Tel: +34 1 338 23 49
Fax: +34 1 308 69 88
CH: A.S. Abad, *MD:* V. Menendez 105

Banco Espirito Santo e Comercial de Lisboa
Avenida da Liberdade 195,
1250 Lisbon, Portugal
Tel: +351 1 315 83 31
Fax: +351 1 57 49 24
CH: A.L. Roquette Ricciardi   100

Banco Pastor SA
Canton Pequeno 1, La Coruna, Spain
CH: V. Arias Mosquera,
J.M. Arias Mosquera   107

Banco Popular Espanol
Velazquez 34, 28001 Madrid, Spain
Tel: +34 1 520 70 00
Fax: +34 1 577 92 08
CH: L. Valls, L. Valls, *JMD:* I. Ayala,
R. Lacasa   95

Banco Portugues de Investimento SA
Rua Tenente Valadin 284, 4100 Porto,
Portugal
Tel: +351 6003731
Fax: +351 698787
P: A. Santos Silva,
CH: R. de Carvalho   97

Banco Portugues do Atlantico
Praca D Joao 1, 28, Oporto, Portugal
CH: J. dos Santos Oliveira   103

Banco Santander SA
Paseo de Pereda 9-12,
39004 Santander, Spain
Tel: +34 42 221 200
CH: E. Botin-Sanz de Sautuola y
Garcia de los Rios   77, 91

Banco di Sardegna SpA
Viale Bonaria, 09100 Cagliari, Italy
Tel: +39 70 600 71
CH: Prof L. Idda   102

Bangkok Bank Public Co. Ltd
333 Silom Road, P.O. Box 95 BMC,
Bangkok 100000, Thailand
Tel: +66 2 231 4333
CH: Prasit Kanchanawat,
Chatri Sophonpanich   114

Bank Austria AG
Vordere Zollamtsstrasse 13, 1030
Vienna, Austria
Tel: +43 1 711 91-0
Fax: +43 1 711 91-3230
CH: S. Sellitsch, G. Randa   94

Bank fur Oberosterreich und Salzburg
Hauptplatz 10-11, 4010 Linz, Austria
Tel: +43 732 28 02-0
Fax: +43 732 78 58 10
CH: Dr H. Treichl, Dr G. Schmidt-Chiari,
Dkfm Dr H. Bell   108

Bank of East Asia Ltd (The)
10 Des Voeux Road, Central, Hong Kong
Tel: +852 2 8423200
CH: Li Fook-wo   115

Bank of England
Threadneedle Street, London, EC2R 8AH
Tel: 0171 601 4444
G: E.A.J. George   30, 44, 98

Bank of Ireland (The Governor and Company of The)
Lower Baggot Street, Dublin 2, Ireland
Tel: +353 1 661 5933
Fax: +353 1 661 5671
CH: H.E. Kilroy, *CE:* P.J.A. Molloy   98

Bank of Scotland (Governor and Company of The)
PO Box 5, The Mound, Edinburgh,
EH1 1YZ
Tel: 0131 442 7777

Fax: 0131 243 5437
G: Sir Bruce Pattullo   22, 26, 30, 40, 42, 77, 92, 93

Bank of Tokyo Ltd (The)
3-2 Nihombashi Hongokucho 1-chome,
Chuo-ku, Tokyo 103, Japan
Tel: +81 3 3245 1111
P: Tasuku Takagaki, *CH:* Toyoo
Gyohten, *JMD:* Mitsukazu Ishikawa,
Eiichi Yoshimura, Taisuke Shimizu,
Tadashi Kurachi, Syushin Maekawa,
Shin Nakahara, Mamoru Hashimoto,
Tetsuo Shimura, Keishi Fujii, Ryuichi
Ohno, Kiyoshi Teramoto   113

Bank of Western Australia Ltd
108 St George's Terrace, GPO Box
E237 Perth, Western Australia, 6001,
Australia
Tel: +61 9 320 6206
CH: Ross Gregory Garnaut   115

Bankamerica Corpn
PO Box 37000, San Francisco, CA,
USA, 94137
Tel: +1 415 622-3456
CH: D. Coulter   110

Bankers Investment Trust PLC (The)
3 Finsbury Avenue, London, EC2M 2PA
Tel: 0171 638 5757
Fax: 0171 377 5742
CH: A.C. Barker   41, 48

Bankers Trust New York Corpn
280 Park Avenue, New York, NY,
10017, USA
Tel: +1 212 250-2500
P: E.B. Shanks Jr,
CH: C.S. Sanford Jr   111

Bankinter SA
Paseo de la Castellana 29, 28046 Madrid,
Spain
Tel: +34 1 339 75 00
Fax: +34 1 339 75 56
CH: J. Botin-Sanz de Sautuola y Garcia
de los Rios,
MD: J. Arena de la Mora   102

Banque Cantonale Vaudoise
Place Saint-Francois 14, PO Box 2172,
1002 Lausanne, Switzerland
Tel: +41 021 642 11 11
Fax: +41 021 642 11 22
P: J.-E. Treyvaud, *CH:* F. Pahud   96

Banque Generale du Luxembourg
14 rue Aldringen, 2951 Luxembourg
CH: M. Mart, A. Georges,
JMD: A. Georges, P. Meyers   102

Banque Internationale a Luxembourg
69 route d'Esch, 1470 Luxembourg
Tel: +352 4590-1
Fax: +352 4590-2010
CH: G. Thorn, J. Krier, *JMD:* J. Krier,
A. Roelants, F. Moes   103

Banque Nationale de Belgique
Boulevard de Berlaimont 5, 1000
Brussels, Belgium
Tel: +32 2 221 21 11
Fax: +32 2 217 17 65
G: A. Verplaetse   98

Banque Nationale de Paris
16 boulevard des Italiens, 75009 Paris,
France
CH: M. Pebereau   90

Barclays PLC
54 Lombard Street, London, EC3P 3AH
Tel: 0171 699 5000
Fax: 0171 929 0394
CH: A.R.F. Buxton, *CE:* J.M. Taylor,
FD: O.H.J. Stocken   17, 30, 74

Bardon Group PLC
Radcliffe House, Blenheim Court,
Lode Lane, Solihull, West Midlands,
B91 2AA
Tel: 0121 711 1717
Fax: 0121 711 1505
CH: F. Davies, *CE:* P.W.G. Tom,
FD: W. McGrath   46, 103

Baring Emerging Europe Trust PLC (The)
155 Bishopsgate, London, EC2M 3XY
Tel: 0171 628 6000
Fax: 0171 638 7928
CH: Sir William Ryrie   60

Baring Tribune Investment Trust PLC
155 Bishopsgate, London, EC2M 3XY
Tel: 0171 628 6000
Fax: 0171 214 1630
CH: M.J. Rivett-Carnac   41, 50

Barings PLC
8 Bishopsgate, London, EC2N 4AE
Tel: 0171 283 8833
Fax: 0171 283 2633
CH: M. Miles, O. van den Broek   47, 73, 76, 106

Barratt Developments PLC
Wingrove House, Ponteland Road,
Newcastle-upon-Tyne, NE5 3DP
Tel: 0191 286 6811
Fax: 0191 271 2242
CH: Sir Lawrence Barratt,
CE: F. Eaton   50

Bass PLC
20 North Audley Street, London,
W1Y 1WE
Tel: 0171 409 1919
Fax: 0171 409 8503
CH: I.M.G. Prosser,
FD: R.C. North   20, 40, 42, 92

Bau Holding AG
Ortenburger Strasse 27, A-9800
Spittal/Drau, Austria
Tel: +43 4762/620
Fax: +43 4762/49 62
CH: H. Schober, H.P. Haselsteiner   105

Baxi Partnership Ltd
Brownedge Road, Bamber Bridge,
Preston, Lancs, PR5 6SN
Tel: 01772 36201
Fax: 01772 315998
No officers designated   58

Baxter Healthcare (Holdings) Ltd
Caxton House, Thetford, Norfolk,
IP24 3SE
Tel: 01842 767000
Fax: 01842 767099
No officers designated   61

Bayer AG
Bayerwerk, 51368 Leverkusen, Germany
Tel: +49 214 301
Fax: +49 214 30 36 20
CH: Prof Dr H. Grunewald,
Prof Dr-Ing K. Hansen, H.J. Strenger,
Dr M. Schneider   62, 72, 88, 90

Bayerische Hypotheken - und Wechsel-Bank AG
Theatinerstrasse 11, 80333 Munich,
Germany
Tel: +49 89 92 44-0
Fax: +49 89 92 44-28 80
CH: Dr jur K. Gotte   92

Bayerische Landesbank Girozentrale
Brienner Strasse 20, 80333 Munich,
Germany
Tel: +49 89 2171-01
Fax: +49 89 2171-3579
CH: H. Schmidhuber, F. Neubauer   94

Bayerische Motoren Werke AG
Petuelring 130, 80788 Munich,
Germany
Tel: +49 89 38 20
Fax: +49 89 38 9 56 22
CH: E. von Kuenheim,
B. Pischetsrieder   25, 76, 91

Bayerische Vereinsbank AG
Kardinal-Faulhaber-Strasse 14, 80311
Munich, Germany
Tel: +49 89 21 32-1
Fax: +49 89 21 32 64 15
CH: Dr W. Premauer, Dr M. Hackl   92

Bayernwerk AG
Nymphenburger Strasse 39, 80335
Munich, Germany
Tel: +49 89 12 54-1
Fax: +49 89 12 54 37 06
CH: Dr J. Holzer, Dr O. Majewski   84, 91

Beazer Homes PLC
Beazer House, Lower Bristol Road,
Bath, Avon, BA2 3EY
Tel: 01225 428401
Fax: 01225 339279
CH: V.W. Benjamin, *CE:* D.M. Webb,
FD: D.J. Smith   50

Begemann - Britannia

Begemann Groep [Koninklijke] NV
Takkebijsters 3, 4817 BL Breda,
The Netherlands
Tel: +31 76 717 000
Fax: +31 76 717 007
CH: Ir W.H. Brouwer,
Ir A.H.C. Deleye 107

Beiersdorf AG
Unnastrasse 48, 20245 Hamburg,
Germany
Tel: +49 40 5 69 0
Fax: +49 40 569 34 34
CH: Dr W. Schieren, Dr R. Kunisch 99

Bekaert [NV] SA
Bekaertstraat 2, 8550 Zwevegem,
Belgium
Tel: +32 56 76 61 11
CH: Baron Velge, R. Decaluwe,
MD: Rafael Decaluwe 100

Bell Atlantic Corpn
1717 Arch Street, Philadelphia,
Pennsylvania, 19103, USA
Tel: +1 215 963-6000
CH: R.W. Smith 110

BellSouth Corpn
1155 Peachtree Street, NE, Atlanta,
Georgia, 30309-3610, USA
Tel: +1 404 249-2000
CH: J.L. Clendenin 13, 110

Bellway PLC
Seaton Burn House, Dudley Lane,
Seaton Burn, Newcastle upon Tyne,
NE13 6BE
Tel: 0191 217 0717
Fax: 0191 236 6230
CH: K. Bell, *MD:* H.C. Dawe 52

Bemrose Corporation PLC
North Bar House, Beverley, North
Humberside, HU17 8DG
Tel: 01482 867862
Fax: 01482 867864
CH: D.C. Wigglesworth,
CE: R. Booth, *FD:* R. Harrison 59

Ben Line Group Ltd
Suite 7, Bonnington Bond, 2 Anderson
Place, Edinburgh, EH6 5NP
Tel: 0131 555 5222
Fax: 0131 557 4742
CH: W.R.E. Thompson 60

Benetton Group SpA
Villa Minelli, 31050 Ponzano Veneto
(Treviso), Italy
Tel: +39 422 4491
Fax: +39 422 449586
CH: L. Benetton, M. Frenzel,
MD: C. Gilardi 101

Bentalls PLC
Anstee House, Wood Street,
Kingston upon Thames, Surrey, KT1 1TS
Tel: 0181 546 2002
Fax: 0181 549 6163
CH: L.E. Bentall, *CE:* F.G. Peacock,
FD: J.B. Ryan 57

Berendsen AS [Sophus]
1 Klausdalsbrovej, 2860 Soborg,
Denmark
Tel: +45 39 69 85 00
Fax: +45 39 69 73 00
P: H. Werdelin,
CH: R. Koch-Nielsen 107

Bergesen d.y. AS
Drammensveien 106, Oslo, Norway
Tel: +47 22 12 05 05
Fax: +47 22 12 05 00
CH: P.C.G. Sundt,
MD: M.S. Bergesen 101

Berisford PLC
1 Baker Street, London, W1M 1AA
Tel: 0171 312 2500
Fax: 0171 312 2501
CH: J.R. Sclater, *CE:* A.J. Bowkett,
FD: D. Mulhall 52

Berkeley Group PLC (The)
The Old House, 4 Heath Road,
Weybridge, Surrey, KT13 8TB
Tel: 01932 847222
Fax: 01932 858596
CH: G.J. Roper, *MD:* A.W. Pidgley,
FD: R.S.J.H. Lewis 51

Berliner Elektro Holding AG
Kurfurstendamm 36, 10719 Berlin,
Germany
Tel: +49 30 88 57 51-0
Fax: +49 30 882 54 92
CH: Prof Dr H. Welling,
Dr M.R. Bernau 108

**Berliner Kraft-und Licht
(BEWAG)-AG**
Stauffenbergstrasse 26, 10785 Berlin,
Germany
Tel: +49 30 267 12375
Fax: +49 30 267 12933
CH: Dr. W. Lamby 93

Berner Kantonalbank
Bundesgasse 6, 3001 Berne, Switzerland
Tel: +41 31 666 11 11
Fax: +41 31 666 60 50
CH: Dr jur M. Kopp 98

Bertelsmann AG
Carl-Bertelsmann-Strasse 270, Postfach
111, 33311 Gutersloh, Germany
Tel: +49 52 41 80-0
Fax: +49 52 41 7 51 66
CH: R. Mohn, Dr D. Vogel,
Dr M. Wossner 93

Bertrand Faure
276, rue Louis Bleriot,
92641 Boulogne Cedex, France
Tel: +33 1 45 62 40 22
Fax: +33 1 45 62 12 91
CH: P. Richier, D. Dewavrin,
JMD: A. Batteux, P. Douay 107

Bestway (Holdings) Ltd
Hobson House, 155 Gower Street,
London, WC1E 6BJ
Tel: 0181 961 2233
CH: M.A. Pervez 59

**Beta Global Emerging Markets
Investment Trust PLC**
3 Bolt Court, Fleet Street, London,
EC4A 3DQ
Tel: 0171 353 2066
Fax: 0171 353 2061
CH: P.A. Scott 58

Bibby [J.] & Sons PLC
16 Stratford Place, London, W1N 9AF
Tel: 0171 629 6243
Fax: 0171 409 0556
CH: R.M. Mansell-Jones,
FD: R. McGregor 50

Biber Holding AG
4562 Biberist, Switzerland
Tel: +41 65 34 32 11
Fax: +41 65 34 31 32
CH: T.D. Berg, C.R. Speiser 103

Bic [Ste]
8 Impasse des Cailloux,
92110 Clichy, France
CH: B. Bich, *CE:* B. Bich,
JMD: E. Buffard, C. Bich, F. Bich,
Marie-Aimee Bich-Dufour 103

Bilfinger + Berger Bau AG
Carl-Reiss-Platz 1-5, 68165
Mannheim, Germany
Tel: +49 6 21 4 59-0
Fax: +49 6 21 4 59-23 66
CH: J. Sarrazin, C. Roth 99

Bilspedition AB
Falkenbergsgata 3, 412 97
Gothenburg, Sweden
Tel: +46 31 83 40 00
Fax: +46 31 40 78 73
P: Hakan Larsson, H. Larsson,
CH: Hans Larsson 105

Bilton PLC
Bilton House, Uxbridge Road, Ealing,
W5 2TL
Tel: 0181 567 7777
Fax: 0181 840 0249
CH: H.D. Free 48, 109

Binding-Brauerei AG
Darmstadter Landstrasse 185,
60598 Frankfurt am Main, Germany
Tel: +49 69 60 65-0
Fax: +49 69 6 06 52 09
CH: Dr G. Sandler, K.P. Erbrich 108

**Birmingham Midshires Building
Society**
35-49 Lichfield Street,
Wolverhampton, WV1 1EL
Tel: 01902 710710
Fax: 01902 713412
CH: C.J. James, *CE:* M. Jackson,
46, 104

Birse Group PLC
Hill House, 1 Little New Street,
London, EC4A 3TR
Tel: 01652 633222
Fax: 01652 633360
CH: P.M. Birse, *FD:* M. Budden 60

Biwater Ltd
Biwater House, Station Approach,
Dorking, Surrey, RH4 1TZ
Tel: 01306 740740
Fax: 01306 885233
CH: A.E. White, *CE:* P.L. Robinson,
FD: C.R.J. Goscomb 52

Black & Decker International
Westpoint, The Grove, Slough,
Berkshire, SL1 1QQ
Tel: 01753 74277
Fax: 01753 79311
CH: C.B. Powell-Smith 49

Blagden Industries PLC
60 Gray's Inn Road, London, WC1X 8MJ
Tel: 0171 405 4275
Fax: 0171 405 4261
CH: D.W. Kendall, *CE:* R.J. Searle,
FD: D.J. Roache 56

Bloor Holdings Ltd
Ashby Road, Measham, Swadlincote,
Derbyshire, DE12 7JP
Tel: 01530 270100
Fax: 01530 273665
CH: J.S. Bloor 54

Blue Circle Industries PLC
84 Eccleston Square, London, SW1V 1PX
Tel: 0171 828 3456
Fax: 0171 245 8772
CH: Sir Peter Walters,
CE: K. Orrell-Jones,
FD: J.R.H. Loudon 44, 97

Bobst SA
50 route des Flumeaux,
1008 Prilly-Lausanne, Switzerland
Tel: +41 21 62 21 11
Fax: +41 21 24 11 70
CH: B. de Kalbermatten,
MD: P. Baroffio 104

Boddington Group PLC (The)
Queens Court, Winslow Road,
Alderley Edge, Cheshire, SK9 7RR
Tel: 01625 586656
Fax: 01625 586657
CH: H.V. Reed, *MD:* A. Smith,
FD: A.J. Garety 29, 49

Body Shop International PLC (The)
Watersmead, Littlehampton, West
Sussex, BN17 6LS
Tel: 01903 731500
Fax: 01903 726250
CH: T.G. Roddick, *CE:* Anita L.
Roddick, *MD:* E.G. Helyer 53

Bodycote International PLC
140 Kingsway, Manchester, M19 1BB
Tel: 0161 257 2345
Fax: 0161 257 2353
CH: J.C. Dwek, *MD:* J. Chesworth,
FD: R.M. Green 57

Boeing Co. (The)
7755 East Marginal Way South,
Seattle, Washington, 98108, USA
Tel: +1 206 655-2121
P: P.M. Condit, *CH:* F. Shrontz 111

Bollore Technologies SA
Odet, PO Box 607, 29500 Ergue
Gaberic, France
Tel: +33 1 46 96 44 33
Fax: +33 1 46 96 44 22
CH: V. Bollore 99

BolsWessanen [Koninklijke] NV
Prof E.M. Meijerslaan 2, 1183 AV
Amstelveen, The Netherlands
Tel: +31 20 5479547
CH: A.P.J.M.M. van der Stee,
A.M. Zondervan 103

Bond Holdings Ltd
Bourn Airfield, Bourn,
Cambridgeshire, CB3 7TQ
CH: K.H.H. Jones, *MD:* S.W. Bond 57

Bongrain SA
7 route de Dampierre, 78041
Guyancourt Cedex, PO Box 10, France
Tel: +33 1 30 48 12 00
Fax: +33 1 30 43 37 23
CH: C. Boutineau, *CE:* J.-N Bongrain 103

Bonifiche Siele Finaziaria SpA
Via Guido d' Arezzo 32, 00198 Rome,
Italy
Tel: +39 85 41 441
Fax: +39 6 84 50 384
CH: G. Monterastelli, *MD:* F. Maggi 93

Booker PLC
Portland House, Stag Place, London,
SW1E 5AY
Tel: 0171 828 9850
Fax: 0171 630 8029
CH: J.F. Taylor, *CE:* C.J. Bowen,
FD: J. Kitson 49

Boots Company PLC (The)
Nottingham, NG2 3AA
Tel: 0115 950 6111
Fax: 0115 959 2727
CH: Sir Michael Angus,
FD: D.A.R. Thompson 36, 40, 43, 95

Boral Ltd
20th Floor, Norwich House, 6-10
O'Connell Street, Sydney, New South
Wales, 2000, Australia
Tel: +61 2 232 8800
Fax: +61 2 233 6605
CH: James B Leslie,
MD: Anthony R Beng 114

Borden (UK) Ltd
St Christophers Works, North
Baddesley, Southampton, SO52 9ZB
Tel: 01703 732131
Fax: 01703 738656
No officers designated 56

Bosch [Robert] GmbH
Robert-Bosch-Platz 1, Gerlingen-
Schillerhohe, 70049 Stuttgart, Germany
Tel: +49 7 11 811-0
Fax: +49 7 11 811 66 30
CH: Dr M. Bierich, H. Scholl 64, 78, 91

Bourne End Properties PLC
5 Wigmore St, London, W1H 2LA
Tel: 0181 455 2440
Fax: 0181 458 7087
CH: D.J. Hughes, *CE:* L. Noe,
FD: I. Smith 14, 53

Bouygues SA
Challenger, 1 avenue Eugene-Freyssinet,
Guyancourt, 78061 Saint-Quentin-
Yvelines Cedex, France
Tel: +33 1 30 60 23 11
Fax: +33 1 30 60 31 40
CH: M. Bouygues 95

Bowthorpe PLC
Gatwick Road, Crawley, West Sussex,
RH10 2RZ
Tel: 01293 528888
Fax: 01293 541905
CH: H.A. Vice, *CE:* J.M. Westhead,
FD: C.M. McCarthy 49

**Bradford & Bingley Building
Society**
Crossflatts, Bingley, West Yorkshire,
BD16 2UA
Tel: 01274 555555
Tel: 01274 569116
CH: J.L. Mackinlay, *CE:* G.R. Lister,
FD: J.A.W. Smith 37, 43, 96

Bradford Property Trust PLC (The)
69 Market Street, Bradford, Yorkshire,
BD1 1NE
Tel: 01274 723181
Fax: 01274 395304
CH: P.C.T. Warner, *JMD:* D.G. Baker,
T.N. Watts, *FD:* N.A. Denby 53

Brake Bros PLC
Enterprise House, Godinton Road,
Ashford, Kent, TN23 1EU
Tel: 01233 637370
Fax: 01233 648200
CH: W.T. Brake, *CE:* F.R. Brake,
FD: M.J. Champion 58

Brambles Industries Ltd
Level 40, Gateway, 1 Macquarie Place,
Sydney New South Wales, 2000,
Australia
Tel: +61 2 256 5222
Fax: +61 2 256 5299
CH: A.W. Coates, *CE:* J.E. Fletcher,
FD: R.C. Milne 115

Brammer PLC
1 Tabley Court, Victoria Street,
Altrincham, Cheshire, WA14 1EZ
Tel: 0161 928 3363
Fax: 0161 941 5742
CH: H.M. Lang, *CE:* R.G. Ffoulkes-Jones,
FD: J.W. Cumming 61

Brau und Brunnen AG
Methfesselstrasse 28/48, 10965 Berlin,
Germany
Tel: +49 30 7 80 03-0
CH: Dr E. Martini 108

Braun AG
Postfach 11 20, Frankfurter Strasse 145,
61476 Kronberg (Taunus), Germany
Tel: +49 61 73 30-0
Fax: +49 61 73 30-28 75
CH: J. Lagarde, A. Livis 83, 104

**Brazilian Smaller Companies
Investment Trust PLC**
Exchange House, Primrose Street,
London, EC2A 2NY
Tel: 0171 628 1234
Fax: 0171 628 2281
CH: M.J. Hart 61

Breda
Piazza della Repubblica 32,
20124 Milan, Italy
Tel: +39 2 667 001
Fax: +39 2 670 0498
CH: A. Aiello, *MD:* L. Roth 107

Bremer Vulkan Verbund AG
Lindenstrasse 110, 28755 Bremen,
Germany
Tel: +49 421 668-0
Fax: +49 421 65 13 24
CH: Baron H.H. Thyssen-Bornemisza,
Dr-Ing Eh Dipl-Ing J. Schaffler,
Dr rer pol F. Hennemann 95

Bridgestone Corpn
10-1 Kyobashi 1-chome, Chuo-ku,
Tokyo 104, Japan
Tel: +81 3 3567 0111
Fax: +81 3 3535 2553
P: Yoichiro Kaizaki, *CH:* Kanichiro
Ishibashi 113

Bridgewater Paper Co. Ltd
North Road, Ellesmere Port, South
Wirrall, L6S 1AF
Tel: 0151 355 7272
Fax: 0151 355 2597
CH: A.M.J. Van Hattum 99

Bridon PLC
Carr Hill, Doncaster, South Yorkshire,
DN4 8DG
Tel: 01302 344010
Fax: 01302 320369
CH: J.B. Clayton, *CE:* R.J. Petersen,
FD: G.J. Beswick 54

Bristol Evening Post PLC (The)
Temple Way, Bristol
Tel: 0117 926 0080
Fax: 0117 927 9568
CH: S.G.G. Clarke, *CE:* A. Goode,
FD: K. Salder 61

Bristol Water Holdings PLC
PO Box 218, Bridgwater Road, Bristol,
BS99 7AU
Tel: 0117 966 5881
Fax: 0117 963 3755
CH: Sir John Vernon Wills,
MD: J.R. Browning, *FD:* A. Parsons 55

Bristol and West Building Society
The Bristol & West Building Society,
PO Box 27, Broad Quay, Bristol,
BS99 7AX
Tel: 0117 979 2222
Fax: 0117 929 3787
P: Sir John Wills,
CH: The Lord Armstrong of Ilminster,
CE: J.J. Burke 46, 102

Bristol-Myers Squibb Holdings Ltd
Swakeleys House, Milton Road,
Ickenham, Uxbridge, UB10 8NS
Tel: 018956 39911
Fax: 018956 36975
No officers designated 54

Britannia Building Society
PO Box 20, Britannia House, Leek,
Staffs, ST13 5RG
Tel: 01538 399399
Fax: 01538 399149
CH: C.A. MacLeod, *CE:* J.E. Heaps
44, 98

Britannia - Cadogan

Britannia Hotels Ltd
The Former Fire Station, London Road, Manchester, M1 2PH
Tel: 0161 2282288
Fax: 0161 2369154
No officers designated 56

Britannic Assurance PLC
Moor Green, Moseley, Birmingham, B13 8QF
Tel: 0121 449 4444
Fax: 0121 449 0456
CH: M.A.H. Willett, *FD:* D. Barnes 54

British Aerospace PLC
Warwick House, PO Box 87, Farnborough Aerospace Centre, Farnborough, Hampshire, GU14 6YU
Tel: 01252 373232
Fax: 01252 383825
CH: R.P. Bauman, *CE:* R.H. Evans, *FD:* R.D. Lapthorne 25, 42, 76, 93

British Air Transport (Holdings) Ltd
Cayzer House, 1 Thomas More Street, London, E1 9AR
No officers designated 52

British Airways PLC
Speedbird House, Heathrow Airport, Hounslow, Middlesex, TW6 2JA
Tel: 0181 759 5511
Fax: 0181 897 2439
CH: Sir Colin Marshall, *MD:* R.J. Ayling, *FD:* D.M. Stevens 19, 42, 87, 91

British Assets Trust PLC
One Charlotte Square, Edinburgh, EH2 4DZ
Tel: 0131 225 1357
Fax: 0131 225 2375
CH: W.R.E. Thomson 41, 45, 101

British Empire Securities and General Trust PLC
23 Cathedral Yard, Exeter, Devon, EX1 1HB
Tel: 01392 412122
Fax: 01392 53282
CH: W.G. Fossick 52

British Gas PLC
Rivermill Hse, 152 Grosvenor Road, London, SW1V 3JL
Tel: 0171 821 1444
Fax: 0171 821 8522
CH: R.V. Giordano, *CE:* C.H. Brown, *FD:* R.A. Gardner 13, 14, 15, 40, 42, 65, 90

British Investment Trust PLC (The)
Donaldson House, 97 Haymarket Terrace, Edinburgh, EH12 5HD
Tel: 0131 313 1000
Fax: 0131 313 6300
CH: M. Butler 41, 45, 101

British Land Company PLC (The)
10 Cornwall Terrace, Regents Park, London, NW1 4QP
Tel: 0171 486 4466
Fax: 0171 935 5552
CH: J.H. Ritblat 31, 43, 94

British Nuclear Fuels PLC
Risley, Warrington, Cheshire, WA3 6AS
Tel: 01925 832000
Fax: 01925 822711
CH: J.R.S. Guinness,
CE: L.N. Chamberlain,
FD: P.S. Phillips 33, 43, 95

British Petroleum Company PLC (The)
Britannic House, 1 Finsbury Circus, London, EC2M 7BA
Tel: 0171 496 4000
Fax: 0171 496 5656
CH: D.A.G. Simon, *CE:* E.J.P. Browne, *JMD:* S.J. Ahearne, R.F. Chase, Dr R. Stomberg, K.R. Seal, B.K. Sanderson 12, 15, 40, 42, 62, 66, 88-90

British Polythene Industries PLC
10 Foster Lane, London, EC2V 6HH
Tel: 0171 606 6130
Fax: 0171 600 0992
CH: C. McLatchie, *FD:* J. Langlands 57

British Printing Co. Ltd (The)
Rembrandt House, Whippendell Road, Watford, WD1 7PP
Tel: 01923 211311
CH: L. Allen, *CE:* P.J. Holloran,
FD: F.J. Brown 54

British Railways Board
Euston House, 24 Eversholt Street, PO Box 100, London, NW1 1DZ
Tel: 0171 928 5151
Fax: 0171 320 0008
CH: Sir Bob Reid, *CE:* J Welsby,
FD: J.J. Jerram 28, 43, 94

British Steel PLC
9 Albert Embankment, London, SE1 7SN
Tel: 0171 735 7654
Fax: 0171 587 1142
CH: B.S. Moffat,
FD: P.R. Hampton 21, 42, 92

British Telecommunications PLC
British Telecom Centre, 81 Newgate Street, London, EC1A 7AJ
Tel: 0171 356 5000
Fax: 0171 356 5520
CH: Sir Iain Vallance,
MD: M.L. Hepher, *FD:* R.P. Brace 12, 13, 16, 33, 40, 42, 69, 88-90

British Vita PLC
Oldham Road, Middleton, Manchester, M24 2DB
Tel: 0161 643 1133
Fax: 0161 653 5411
CH: R. McGee , *CE:* R.H. Sellers,
FD: K.R. Bhatt 48, 109

British-Borneo Petroleum Syndicate, PLC
8th Floor, East Wing, Bowater House, 68 Knightsbridge, London, SW1X 7JX
Tel: 0171 581 8822
Fax: 0171 584 8562
CH: Sir Robert Reid, *CE:* A.J. Gaynor, *FD:* W. Colvin 54

Britton Group PLC
1 Castle Lane, London, SW1E 6DN
Tel: 0171 931 9161
Fax: 0171 931 7481
CH: A.H. Westropp,
CE: R.G.W. Williams, *FD:* S.D. Beart 54

Brixton Estate PLC
22-24 Ely Place, London, EC1N 6TQ
Tel: 0171 400 4400
Fax: 0171 405 1630
CH: D.F. Gardner, *MD:* T.J. Nagle,
FD: S.J. Owen 45, 100

Broken Hill Proprietary Co. Ltd (The)
48th Floor, BHP Tower-Bourke Place, 600 Bourke Street, Melbourne, Victoria 3000, Australia
Tel: +61 3 609 3333
Fax: +61 3 609 3015
CH: B.T. Loton, *CE:* J.B. Prescott 114

Brown [N.] Group PLC
53 Dale Street, Manchester, M60 6ES
Tel: 0161 236 8256
Fax: 0161 238 2308
CH: Sir David Alliance, *CE:* J. Martin, *FD:* A. White 54

Brunel Holdings PLC
BM House, Avon Reach, Chippenham, Wiltshire, SN15 1EE
Tel: 01249 656263
Fax: 01249 656528
CH: J.M. Woolley, *CE:* T.C. Walker,
FD: A. Hicks 59

Brunner Investment Trust PLC (The)
10 Fenchurch Street, London, EC3M 3LB
Tel: 0171 623 8000
Fax: 0171 623 4069
CH: T.B.H. Brunner 51

Brunner Mond Holdings Ltd
Mond House, Winnington, Northwich, Cheshire, CW8 4DT
Tel: 01606 724000
Fax: 01606 781353
CH: E. Kinder, *MD:* S.R. Smith 58

Bryant Group PLC
Cranmore House, Cranmore Boulevard, Solihull, West Midlands, B90 4SD
Tel: 0121 711 1212
Fax: 0121 711 2610
CH: C.F.N. Hope, *CE:* A. MacKenzie 49

Buderus AG
Sophienstrasse 30-32, 35576 Wetzlar, Germany
Tel: +49 64 41 49 00
Fax: +49 64 41 49 12 00
CH: Dr H.J. Klein, Dr H.-U. Plaul 102

Budgens PLC
PO Box 9, Stonefield Way, South Ruislip, Middlesex, HA4 0JR
Tel: 0181 422 9511
Fax: 0181 423 2263
CH: C.T. Clague, *CE:* J.A. Von Spreckelsen, *FD:* G.L. Rigby 59

Bull Information Systems Ltd
Computer House, Great West Road, Brentford, Middlesex, TW3 9DH
Tel: 0181 568 9191
Fax: 0181 568 1581
CH: B. Long, *MD:* P.J. Crawford 59

Bullough PLC
21 The Crescent, Leatherhead, Surrey, KT22 8DY
Tel: 01372 379088
Fax: 01372 362007
CH: D.B. Battle, *CE:* G. Bond,
FD: R.J. Overend 56

Bulmer [H.P.] Holdings PLC
The Cider Mills, Plough Lane, Hereford, HR4 0LE
Tel: 01432 352000
Fax: 01432 352084
CH: J.E. Bulmer, *CE:* J.K. Rudgard,
FD: A.C. Flockhart 55

Bunge & Co. Ltd
Bunge House, PO Box 540, 15-25 Artillery Lane, London, E1 7HA
Tel: 0171 247 4444
Fax: 0171 375 2443
CH: G. Born Jnr 56

Bunzl PLC
110 Park Street, London, W1Y 3RB
Tel: 0171 495 4950
Fax: 0171 495 4953
CH: A.P. Dyer, *CE:* A.J. Habgood,
FD: D.M. Williams 48, 108

Burford Holdings PLC
20 Thayer Street, London, W1M 6DD
Tel: 0171 224 2240
Fax: 0171 224 1710
CH: N.W. Wray, *CE:* N.M. Leslau,
FD: J. Gleek 14, 46, 105

Burgo [Cartiere] SpA
Via Roma 26, 12039 Verzuolo, Cuneo, Italy
Tel: +39 175 280111
CH: L. Adler, *CE:* G. Lignana 103

Burmah Castrol PLC
George Hse, 50 George Square, Glasgow, G2 1RR
Tel: 01793 511521
Fax: 01793 513723
CH: L.M. Urquhart, *CE:* J.M. Fry,
FD: B. Hardy 44, 97

Burns Philp & Co. Ltd
7 Bridge Street, Sydney, New South Wales, 2000, Australia
Tel: +61 2 259 1111
Fax: +61 2 2513254
CH: Andrew Turnbull,
CE: Ian D. Clack 115

Burton Group PLC (The)
214 Oxford Street, London, W1N 9DF
Tel: 0171 636 8040
Fax: 0171 927 7806
CH: Sir John Hoskyns,
CE: J.L. Hoerner,
FD: A. Higginson 44, 98

Burtonwood Brewery PLC
Bold Lane, Burtonwood, Nr Warrington, Cheshire, WA5 4PJ
Tel: 01925 225131
Fax: 01925 229033
CH: J.G. Dutton-Forshaw,
MD: Lynne D'Arcy, *FD:* S.W. Kay 56

Bush Boake Allen Holdings (UK) Ltd
Blackhorse Lane, Walthamstow, London, E17 5QP
Tel: 0181 523 6000
Fax: 0181 531 7413
CH: J.W. Boyden 56

CANAL+
85/89 Quai Andre Citroen, 75015 Paris, France
Tel: +33 1 44 25 10 00
Fax: +33 1 44 25 12 34
No officers designated 64, 99

CBR Cementbedrijven NV [SA Cimenteries]
Chaussee de La Hulpe 185, 1170 Brussels, Belgium
Tel: +32 2 678 33 53
Fax: +32 2 678 33 55
CH: M. Nokin, J. Van Hove, P. Schuhmacher, *CE:* D. Fallon 97

CCF-Credit Commercial de France
103 avenue des Champs-Elysees, 75008 Paris, France
Tel: +33 1 40 70 70 40
Fax: +33 1 40 70 24 72
CH: G. Pallez, C. de Croisset 97

CEF Holdings Ltd
1 Station Road, Kenilworth, Warwickshire, CV8 1JJ
Tel: 01926 58126
Fax: 01926 50448
CH: R.H. Thorn 57

CEP Communication
20 Avenue Hoche, 75008 Paris, France
Tel: +33 1 44 95 56 00
CH: C. Bregou 105

CEPSA-Cia Espanola de Petroleos SA
Avenida de America 32, 28028 Madrid, Spain
Tel: +34 24 337 60 00
Fax: +34 24 225 41 16
CH: A. Escamez Lopez,
MD: E. Marin Garcia-Mansilla 98

CFE [Cie d'Entreprises] SA
Chaussee de La Hulpe 164, 1170 Brussels, Belgium
Tel: +32 2 661 12 11
Fax: +32 2 660 77 10
CH: Sir Walter Z. Vanden Avenne, H.L. Taverne, *JMD:* H.L. Taverne, J.-P. Coirbay, *FD:* J.-M. Lambert 104

CGEA-Cie Generale d'Enterprises Automobiles
163/169 avenue Georges Clemenceau, 92000 Nanterre, France
Tel: +33 1 46 69 70 00
Fax: +33 1 46 69 30 01
CH: C. Cans, B. Rouer, H. Proglio, *JMD:* J.-P. Couplan, Y.-M. Le Dore 107

CGIP-Cie Generale d'Industrie et de Participations
89 rue Taitbout, 75009 Paris, France
Tel: +33 1 42 85 30 00
Fax: +33 1 42 80 68 67
CH: P. Celier, J. Droulers,
E.-A. Seilliere 94

CGMF - Cie Generale Maritime et Financiere
22 quai Gallieni, 92158 Suresnes Cedex, France
Tel: +33 1 46 25 70 00
Fax: +33 1 46 25 78 00
CH: E. Giuily 109

CIR Cie Industriali Riunite SPA
Strada Volpiano 53, 10040 Leini, Turin, Italy
Tel: +39 11 998 06 68
CH: C. De Benedetti,
MD: R. De Benedetti 96

CKAG Colonia Konzern AG
Gereonsdriesch 9-11, 50670 Cologne, Germany
Tel: +49 221 148101
Fax: +49 221 148-32956
CH: Dipl-Kfm D. Wendelstadt, C. Kleyboldt 98

CLF - Credit Local de France
Tour Cristal, 7-11 quai Andre Citroen, PO Box 1002, 75901 Paris Cedex 15, France
Tel: +33 1 43 92 77 77
Fax: +33 1 43 92 70 00
CH: P. Richard 97

CLM Insurance Fund PLC
130 Fenchurch Street, London, EC3M 5EE
Tel: 0171 2837474

Fax: 0171 2837478
CH: The Rt. Hon. The Lord Rees,
CE: M.J. Wade 58

CLS Holdings PLC
65 High Street, Harpenden, Hertfordshire, AL5 2SW
CH: S.A. Mortstedt, *CE:* G.V. Hirsch 51

CMB SA
De Gerlachekaai 20, 2000 Antwerp, Belgium
Tel: +32 3 247 59 11
Fax: +32 3 248 09 06
CH: E. Davignon, *MD:* M. Saverys 99

CNP - Nationale a Portefeuille [Cie]
Eikenstraat 9, 2000 Antwerp, Belgium
CH: J. Dils, *MD:* G. Samyn 98

COFIDE-Cia Finanziaria de Benedetti SpA
Via Valeggio 41, 10129 Turin, Italy
Tel: +39 11 5517
CH: Carlo de Benedetti 104

CP Holdings Ltd
12 York Gate, London, NW1 4QS
Tel: 0171 486 0111
Fax: 0171 935 6852
CH: B.D. Schreier 55

CPC (United Kingdom) Ltd
Claygate House, Esher, Surrey, KT10 9PN
Tel: 01372 62181
Fax: 01372 68775
CH: P.W. Phillips, *MD:* I.M. Ramsay 53

CRA Ltd
33rd Floor, 55 Collins Street, Melbourne 3001, Australia
Tel: +61 3 283 3333
Fax: +61 3 2833707
CH: John A Uhrig,
CE: Leon A Davis 21, 114

CRH PLC
42 Fitzwilliam Square, Dublin 2, Ireland
Tel: +353 01 676 5144
Fax: +353 01 676 5013
CH: A.D. Barry, *CE:* D.J. Godson,
FD: H.P. Sheridan 99

CS Holding
Nuschelerstrasse 1, Postfach 669, 8021 Zurich, Switzerland
Tel: +41 1 212 16 16
Fax: +41 1 212 06 69
P: R.E. Gut, *CH:* R.E. Gut 80, 88, 89, 91

CSM NV
Nienoord 13, 1112 XE Diemen, Amsterdam, The Netherlands
Tel: +31 20 59 06 911
Fax: +31 20 69 51 942
CH: F.H. Fentener van Vlissingen, G.M.L. van Loon 106

CSR Ltd
Level 24, 1 O'Connell Street, Sydney, New South Wales, Australia
Tel: +61 2 235 8000
Fax: +61 2 235 8555
CH: Alan Coates,
MD: Geoffrey Kells 114

CSX Corpn
One James Center, 901 East Cary Street, Richmond, Virginia, 23219, USA
Tel: +1 804 782-1400
CH: J.W. Snow 111

Cable and Wireless PLC
124 Theobalds Road, London, WC1X 8RX
Tel: 0171 315 4000
Fax: 0171 315 5000
CH: The Rt Hon Lord Young of Graffham, *CE:* J.H. Ross,
FD: R.J. Olsen 19, 40, 42, 67, 85, 88, 89, 91

Cadbury Schweppes PLC
25 Berkeley Square, London, W1X 6HT
Tel: 0171 409 1313
Fax: 0171 830 5200
CH: N.D. Cadbury, *CE:* D.G. Wellings,
FD: D.J. Kappler 34, 40, 43, 95

Cadogan Estates Ltd
18 Cadogan Gardens, London, SW3 2RP
Tel: 0171 730 4567
Fax: 0171 730 5239

120

Caledonia - City

CH: Viscount Chelsea,
CE: S.A. Corbyn, *FD:* R.J. Grant 57
Caledonia Investments PLC
Cayzer House, 1 Thomas More Street,
London, E1 9AR
Tel: 0171 481 4343
Fax: 0171 488 0896
CH: P.N. Buckley,
FD: J.H. Cartwright 46, 103
Calor Group PLC
Appleton Park, Riding Court Road,
Datchet, Slough, SL3 9JG
Tel: 01753 40000
Fax: 01753 48121
CH: A.M. Davies,
CE: H.C.A. Robinson 50
Caltagirone SpA
Via Montello 10, 00184 Rome, Italy
Tel: +39 6 374 921
Fax: +39 6 372 8546
CH: E. Caltagirone 106
Camas PLC
Regent House, Rodney Road,
Cheltenham, Gloucestershire, GL50 1HX
Tel: 01242 227722
Fax: 01242 229050
CH: M.E. Warren, *CE:* A. L. Shearer,
FD: C.S. Bailey 48
Camellia PLC
3 Carlos Place, London, W1Y 5AE
Tel: 0171 629 5728
Fax: 0171 629 4484
CH: G. Fox, *MD:* D.M. Bacon 48, 109
Campbell's U.K. Ltd
Heathrow Boulevard, 284 Bath Road,
West Drayton, Middlesex, UB7 0DT
Tel: 0181 564 8686
Fax: 0181 564 8620
No officers designated 59
Canadian Imperial Bank of Commerce
Commerce Court, Toronto, Ontario,
M5L 1A2
Tel: +1 416 980-2211
CH: A.L. Flood 111
Canadian Pacific Ltd
PO Box 6042, Station Centre-ville,
Montreal, Quebec, H3C 3E4, Canada
P: D.P. O'Brien, *CE:* W.W. Stinson 111
Candover Investments PLC
20 Old Bailey, London, EC4M 7LN
Tel: 0171 489 9848
Fax: 0171 248 5483
CH: C.R.E. Brooke, *CE:* S.W. Curran 57
Canon (UK) Ltd
Canon House, Manor Road,
Wallington, Surrey, SM6 0AJ
Tel: 0181 773 3173
Fax: 0181 773 2156
MD: Y. Yamashita 56
Canon Inc
30-2 Shimomaruko 3-chome, Ohta-ku,
Tokyo 146, Japan
P: Hajime Mitarai, *CH:* Ryuzaburo
Kaku, *JMD:* Masahiro Tanaka, Giichi
Marushima, Yoshiaki Suguri, Ryozo
Hirako, Takashi Kitamura, Hajime
Katayama 112
Cap Gemini Sogeti SA
3 rue Malakoff, PO Box 206, 38005
Grenoble Cedex 1, France
Tel: +33 76 59 63 00
CH: S. Kampf 99
Caparo Group Ltd
Caparo Hse, 103 Baker Street, London,
W1M 1FD
Tel: 0171 486 1417
Fax: 0171 935 3242
CH: Dr Swraj Paul 58
Capital Corpn PLC
Interpark House, 7 Downstreet,
London, W1Y 7DS
Tel: 0171 495 0101
Fax: 0171 629 6440
CE: G. Nesbitt, *JMD:* D.W. Gray,
P. McNally, *FD:* N.C.L. Barker 59
Capital and Regional Properties PLC
22 Grosvenor Gardens, London,
SW1W 0DH
Tel: 0171 730 5565

Fax: 0171 730 0151
CH: M. Barber, *JMD:* X. Pullen,
R.M. Boyland, *FD:* Lynda S. Coral 53
Caradon PLC
Caradon House, 24 Queens Road,
Weybridge, Surrey, KT13 9UX
Tel: 01932 850850
Fax: 01932 823328
CH: A.P. Hichens 45, 101
Carbonique (La)
4 Rue d'Anjou, 75008 Paris, France
CH: Mrs P. Sauvin 108
Carclo Engineering Group PLC
Carclo House, PO Box 224, Fife Street,
Sheffield, S9 1YX
Tel: 0114 256 2162
Fax: 0114 261 9686
CH: J.W.D. Ewart, *CE:* I. Williamson 56
Cargill PLC
Knowle Hill Park, Fairmile Lane,
Cobham, Surrey, KT11 2PD
Tel: 01932 861000
Fax: 01932 861200
CH: R. Murray 50
Carl-Zeiss-Stiftung
89520 Heidenheim, Germany
Tel: +49 73 64 200
Fax: +49 73 64 68 08
CE: Prof Dr-Ing P. H. Grassmann,
H. Fahlbusch 96
Carlsberg AS
100 Vesterfaelledvej,
1799 Copenhagen V, Denmark
Tel: +45 33 27 33 27
Fax: +45 33 27 47 11
P: P.J. Svanholm, *CH:* P.C. Mattiessen,
MD: J.W. Werner 97
Carlsberg-Tetley PLC
2410 The Crescent, Birmingham
Business Park, Birmingham, B37 7YE
Tel: 0121 6060606
Fax: 0121 60604020
CH: M.C. Iuul 21, 45, 101
Carlton Communications PLC
15 St George Street, Hanover Square,
London, W1R 9DE
Tel: 0171 499 8050
Fax: 0171 895 9575
CH: M.P. Green, *MD:* June F. de
Moller, *FD:* B.A. Cragg 46, 103
CarnaudMetalbox
153 rue de Courcelles, 75017 Paris,
France
Tel: +33 1 44 15 68 00
Fax: +33 1 40 53 03 53
CH: E.-A. Seilliere, B.J. Hintz 95
Carrefour
5 avenue du General de Gaulle,
91005 Lisses, France
Tel: +33 1 60 86 96 52
Fax: +33 1 60 86 35 79
MD: J. Fournier, D. Bernard,
MD: J. Badin 94
Carter Holt Harvey Ltd
640 Great South Road, Manukau City,
Auckland, New Zealand
CH: W.J. Whineray, *CE:* D.W. Oskin 114
Casino, Guichard-Perrachon et Cie
24 rue de la Montat,
42008 Saint-Etienne Cedex 2, France
Tel: +33 77 45 31 31
Fax: +33 77 21 85 15
CH: J.-C. Naouri, A. Guichard 34, 96
Castorama Dubois Investissements SCA
Zone Industrielle,
59175 Templemars, France
Tel: +33 20 87 75 11
Fax: +33 20 87 75 97
No officers designated 108
Catena [AB]
Kampegatan 3, Box 500, 401 24
Gothenburg, Sweden
Tel: +46 31 80 16 00
Fax: +46 31 15 47 22
CH: M. Jansson, J. Palmstierna 109
Cater Allen Holdings PLC
20 Birchin Lane, London, EC3V 9DJ
Tel: 0171 623 2070
Fax: 0171 929 1641
CH: J.C. Barclay, *FD:* R.W. Lilley 56

Cathay International Holdings PLC
Brookdale House, Stonehill Business
Park, Angel Road, London, N18 3LD
Tel: 0181 807 1020
Fax: 0181 884 3528
CH: J.R.H. Buchanan,
CE: Wu Zhen Tao 47, 108
Cathay Pacific Airways Ltd
Swire House, 4th Floor, 9 Connaught
Road, Central, Hong Kong
Tel: +852 5-8425000
CH: Peter Sutch, *MD:* Rod Eddington,
FD: Victor Hughes 114
Cattles PLC
Haltemprice Court, 38 Springfield
Way, Anlaby, Hull, HU10 6RR
Tel: 01482 564422
Fax: 01482 564425
CH: P.H. Courtney, *CE:* J.E.G. Cran,
FD: G. Clappison 53
Celsius Industries Corpn
Celsiusgatan 10, 402 74 Gothenburg,
Sweden
Tel: +46 31 65 86 00
Fax: +46 31 51 61 05
P: A. Plyhm, *CH:* O. Lund 103
Cenargo International Ltd
12 Grosvenor Place, London, SW1X 7HH
Tel: 0171 2359801
Fax: 0171 2357463
CH: M.A.W.Hendry 59
Central European Growth Fund PLC (The)
Rolls House, 7 Rolls Building, Fetter
Lane, London, EC4A 1NH
CH: J.S. Fairbairn 55
Central Transport Rental Group PLC
123 Buckingham Palace Road,
London, SW1W 9TG
Tel: 0171 828 4000
Fax: 0171 396 7957
CH: I.M. Clubb,
CE: I.M. Clubb 14, 46, 104
Central and South West Corpn
1616 Woodall Rodgers Freeway,
PO Box 660164, Dallas, Texas,
75266-0164, USA
Tel: +1 214 777-1000
CE: E.R. Brooks 111
Cerus - Compagnies Europeene Reunies
21 avenue George V, 75008 Paris, France
Tel: +33 1 40 70 00 63
Fax: +33 1 47 20 06 97
CH: C. de Benedetti 102
Champion International Corpn
One Champion Plaza, Stamford,
Connecticut, 06921, USA
P: L.C. Heist, *CH:* A.C. Sigler 111
Charbonnages de France
65 avenue de Colmar,
92507 Rueil-Malmaison Cedex, France
Tel: +33 1 47 52 92 52
CH: B. Pache, J. Bouvet 96
Chargeurs
5 boulevard Malesherbes, 75008 Paris,
France
Tel: +33 1 49 24 40 00
Fax: +33 1 49 24 41 20
CH: J. Seydoux 98
Charter PLC
7 Hobart Place, London, SW1W 0HH
Tel: 0171 838 7000
Fax: 0171 259 5112
CH: Sir Michael Edwardes,
CE: J.W. Herbert,
FD: N.E. Robson 47, 106
Chase Manhattan Corpn (The)
1 Chase Manhattan Plaza, New York,
NY, 10081, USA
Tel: +1 212 552-2222
CH: T.G. Labrecque 111
Chelsea Building Society
Thirlestane Hall, Thirlestane Road,
Cheltenham, Gloucestershire, GL53 7AL
Tel: 01242 521391
Fax: 01242 571441
CH: M.G. Hart 53
Chelsea Land Ltd
18 Cadogen Gardens, London, SW3 2RP

Tel: 0171 730 4567
Fax: 0171 730 5239
CH: Viscount Chelsea,
CE: S.A. Corbyn, *FD:* R.J. Grant 56
Chelsfield PLC
67 Brook Street, London, W1Y 1YE
Tel: 0171 493 3977
Fax: 0171 491 9369
CH: E. Bernerd.
MD: W.N. Hugil 46, 103
Cheltenham & Gloucester Building Society
Barnett Way, Gloucester, GL4 7RL
Tel: 01452 372372
Fax: 01452 373955
CH: J.N. Bays, *CE:* A.H. Longhurst,
FD: D. Barnes 14, 18, 44, 83, 98
Chemical Banking Corpn
270 Park Avenue, New York,
New York, 10017-2036, USA
Tel: +1 212 270-6000
P: E.D. Miller, *CH:* W.V. Shipley 110
Cheshire Building Society
Castle Street, Macclesfield, SK11 6AH
Tel: 01625 613612
Fax: 01625 617246
CH: D.B. Jennings,
CE: J.D.P. Hughes 55
Chesterfield Properties PLC
38 Curzon Street, London, W1Y 8EY
Tel: 0171 465 0565
Fax: 0171 499 2018
CH: R.C. Wingate, *MD:* J.S. Gamble,
FD: D.P. Kiernan 48
Cheung Kong (Holdings) Ltd
China Building, 18th-22nd floors,
29 Queen's Road Central, Hong Kong
Tel: +852 2 526 6911
CH: Li Ka-shing 114
Chevron Corpn
225 Bush Street, San Francisco,
California, 94104, USA
Tel: +1 415 894-7700
CH: K.T. Derr 110
Chevron U.K. Ltd
2 Portman Street, London, W1H 0AN
Tel: 0171 487 8100
Fax: 0171 487 8905
No officers designated 98
China Light & Power Co. Ltd
147 Argyle Street, Kowloon, Hong Kong
CH: Sir Sidney Gordon,
MD: R.E. Sayers 115
Chinese Estates Holdings Ltd
Cedar House, 41 Cedar Avenue,
Hamilton HM12, Bermuda
CH: Joseph Lau, Luen-hung 115
Chloride Group PLC
Abford House, 15 Wilton Road,
London, SW1V 1LT
Tel: 0171 834 5500
Fax: 0171 630 0563
CH: R. Horrocks, *CE:* K.H. Hodgkinson,
FD: M.L. Vass 61
Cho Hung Bank
14, 1-Ga Nadaemonno, Chung-Gu, Seoul
Tel: +82 2 733 2000
Fax: +82 2 732 0835
P: Lee Chong Yeon, *JMD:* Woo Chan
Mok, Lee Chun Hun, Lee Kyoon Sup, Kim
Dong Yong, Jang Chull Hoon, Che Byung
Yun, Hur Jong Wook, Choe Nam Yong 115
Christiania Bank og Kreditkasse
Middelthunsgate 17, Majorstua, Oslo,
Norway
Tel: +47 22 48 50 00
CH: P. Ditlev-Simonsen, E. Norvik,
MD: B.A. Lenth 95
Christies International PLC
8 King Street, St James's, London,
SW1Y 6QT
Tel: 0171 839 9060
Fax: 0171 839 1611
CH: Sir Anthony Tennant,
CE: C.M. Davidge 52
Chrysalis Group PLC
The Chrysalis Building, Bramley Road,
London, W10 6SP
Tel: 0171 221 2213
Fax: 0171 221 6455
CH: C.N. Wright 61

Chrysler Corpn
12000 Chrysler Drive, Highland Park,
Michigan, 48288-0001, USA
Tel: +1 313 956-5741
P: R.A. Lutz, *CH:* R.J. Eaton 79, 110
Chubb Security PLC
Chubb House, Staines Road West,
Sunbury-on-Thames, Middlesex,
TW16 7AR
Tel: 01932 785588
Fax: 01932 787729
CH: Sir Ernest T. Harrison,
CE: D.J. Peacock, *FD:* J.A. Biles 32, 50
Chubu Electric Power Co. Inc.
1 Higashi-Shincho, Higashi-ku,
Nagoya 461-91, Japan
Tel: +81 052 951 8211
Fax: +81 052 962 4624
P: Kohei Abe, *CH:* Kamesaburo
Matsunaga, *JMD:* Hideo Ishida,
Hiroshi Owaki, Bunkai Kino, Hajime
Okada, Isao Koiso, Koichi Hasumi,
Youichi Kimura, Motohide Sato,
Masaaki Shiga 112
Chugoku Electric Power Co. Inc. (The)
4-33, Komachi Naka-ku, Hiroshima,
Japan
Tel: +81 82 241 0211
Fax: +81 82 242 8437
P: Koki Tada, *CH:* Ken-ichiro
Matsutani, *JMD:* Takao Nagamoto,
Koji Tsuda, Takahisa Yokoshige,
Takashi Furukawa, Kazunori Hiraoka,
Yukio Inoue, Kazuo Yoshida, Ken-ichi
Kaikawa, Koji Kisaka 112
Ciba-Geigy AG
Klybeckstrasse 141, 4002 Basle,
Switzerland
Tel: +41 61 696 111
Fax: +41 61 697 34 20
CH: Dr A. Krauer, H. Lippuner 78, 88,
89, 91
Cigna Corpn
One Liberty Place, 1650 Market Street,
Philadelphia, Pennsylvania,
19192-1550, USA
Tel: +1 215 761-1000
CH: W.H. Taylor 111
Cilva Holdings PLC
Avis House, Park Road, Bracknell,
Berks, RG12 2EW
Tel: 01344 426644
Fax: 01344 485616
CH: W.A. Cathcart 54
Ciments Francais
Tour Ariane, 5 place de la Pyramide,
Quartier Villon, 92088 Puteaux, Paris
La Defense, France
Tel: +33 1 42 91 75 00
Fax: +33 1 47 74 59 55
CH: B. Laplace, Y.R. Nanot 94
Citic Pacific Ltd
Level 35, Two Pacific Place,
88 Queensway, Hong Kong
CH: Larry Yung Chi Kin,
MD: Henry Fan Hung Ling 114
Citicorp
399 Park Avenue, New York,
10043, USA
Tel: +1 212 559-4822
CH: J.S. Reed 110
City Centre Restaurants PLC
122 Victoria Street, London,
SW1E 5LD
Tel: 0171 834 0585
Fax: 0171 630 6191
CH: B.W. Johnston,
CE: J.P.G. Naylor 59
City Developments Ltd
36 Robinson Road, 20-01 Cith House,
Singapore 0106
Tel: +65 2212266
Fax: +65 2232746
CH: Kwek Leng Beng 115
City Site Estates PLC
219 St Vincent Street, Glasgow, G2 5QY
Tel: 0141 248 2534
Fax: 0141 226 3321
CH: W.W.C. Syson,
MD: L.M. Goodman 55

Civil - D.N.L

Civil Aviation Authority
CAA House, 45-59 Kingsway, London, WC2B 6TE
Tel: 0171 379 7311
Fax: 0171 240 1153
CH: The Rt Hon C.J. Chataway,
MD: T. Murphy   47, 107

Clark [Arnold] Automobiles Ltd
43 Allison Street, Glasgow, G42 8NJ
Tel: 0141 424 4333
Fax: 0141 422 1803
CH: J.A. Clark, *MD:* W.G.P. Gall   60

Clark [C. & J.] Ltd
40 High Street, Street, Somerset, BA16 0YA
Tel: 01458 443131
Fax: 01458 447547
CH: R.A. Pedder, *MD:* M.J. Cotton,
FD: R.A. Mackay   49

Claverley Co.
51-53 Queen Street, Wolverhampton, West Midlands, WV1 3BU
Tel: 01902 313131
Fax: 01902 319721
CH: M.G.D. Graham   59

Cleanaway Ltd
The Drive, Warley, Brentwood, Essex, CM13 3BE
Tel: 01277 234567
Fax: 01277 230067
CH: P.A.M. Heath   60

Close Brothers Group PLC
12 Appold Street, London, EC2A 2AA
Tel: 0171 426 4000
Fax: 071 426 4044
CH: H.G. Ashton, *MD:* R.D. Kent   48

Club Mediterranee SA
25 rue Vivienne, Place de la Bourse, 75002 Paris, France
Tel: +33 1 42 61 85 00
Fax: +33 1 40 20 09 61
CH: G. Trigano, S. Trigano   100

Clyde Petroleum PLC
Apex Hse., 9 Haddington Place, Edinburgh, EH7 4AL
Tel: 0131 243 5317
Fax: 0131 243 5327
CH: J.M. Gourlay, *MD:* R.A. Franklin,
FD: P.S.J. Zatz   48, 108

Clydesdale Bank PLC
30 St Vincent Place, Glasgow, G1 2HL
Tel: 0141 248 7070
Fax: 0141 204 0828
CH: Rt. Hon Lord David Nickson 46, 105

Co-Steel (U.K.) Ltd
Sheerness, Kent, ME12 1TH
Tel: 01795 663333
Fax: 01795 666059
CH: W.J. Shields   56

Co-operative Insurance Society Ltd
Miller Street, Manchester, M60 0AL
Tel: 0161 832 8686
Fax: 0161 837 4048
CH: D.J. Wise   51

Co-operative Retail Services Ltd
29 Dantzic Street, Manchester, M4 4BA
Tel: 0161 832 8152
Fax: 0161 833 7355
CH: P. Rowbotham   47, 107

Co-operative Wholesale Society Ltd (The)
New Century House, Manchester, M60 4ES
Tel: 0161 834 1212
Fax: 0161 834 4507
CH: G.L. Fyfe, *CE:* D. Skinner,
FD: W.A. Prescott   45, 101

Coats Viyella PLC
28 Savile Row, London, W1X 2DD
Tel: 0171 734 4030
Fax: 0171 437 5166
CH: Sir David Alliance,
CE: N.C. Bain, *FD:* J. Phillips   44, 97

Cobham PLC
Brook Road, Wimborne, Dorset, BH21 2BJ
Tel: 01202 882020
Fax: 01202 840523
CH: M.J. Cobham, *CE:* G.F. Page,
FD: A.G. Irwin   52

Coca-Cola Holdings (United Kingdom) Ltd
1 Queen Caroline Street, London, W6 9HQ
Tel: 0181 237 3000
Fax: 0181 237 3700
No officers designated   34, 51

Cockerill Sambre
Chaussee de la Hulpe 187, 1170 Brussels, Belgium
Tel: +32 2 674 02 11
Fax: +32 2 660 36 40
P: J. Lecomte, *CH:* J. Gandois,
CE: P. Delaunois, P. Delaunois 95

Codan Forsikring
Codanhus, Gl. Kongevej 60, 1790 Copenhagen V, Denmark
Tel: +45 31 21 21 21
Fax: +45 31 21 21 22
CH: H. Christrup   103

Colaingrove Ltd
Normandy Court, 1 Wolsey Road, Hemel Hempstead, Hertfordshire, HP2 2TU
No officers designated   55

Colas SA
7 place Rene Clair, 92653 Boulogne-Billancourt Cedex, France
Tel: +33 1 47 61 75 00
Fax: +33 1 47 61 74 58
CH: A. Dupont   106

Coles Myer Ltd
800 Toorak Road, Tooronga, Victoria 3146, Australia
Tel: +61 3 829 3111
Fax: +61 3 829 6787
CH: Solomon Lew, *CE:* Peter T. Bartels,
FD: P. Bowman   114

Commercial Bank of Korea (The)
111-1, 2-Ga Namdaemunno, Chung-Gu, Seoul
Tel: +82 02 775 0050
Fax: +82 02 773 7903
P: Chung Jee Tae, *JMD:* Bae Chan Byung, Chang Soon Yong, Kim Myung Hwan, Kim Heun Gil, Koo Ja Yong, Ju Kwang Joon, Shin In Sik, Park Yung Sik, Joo Jung Seop   115

Commercial Union PLC
St Helen's, 1 Undershaft, London, EC3P 3DQ
Tel: 0171 283 7500
Fax: 0171 662 8140
CH: N.H. Baring, *CE:* J.G.T. Carter,
FD: P.J. Foster   22, 40, 42, 64, 92

Commerzbank AG
Neue Mainzer Strasse 32-36, 60311 Frankfurt am Main, Germany
Tel: +49 69 1 36 20
Fax: +49 69 28 53 89
CH: Dr W. Seipp,
M. Kohlhaussen   81, 91

Commonwealth Bank Of Australia
48 Martin Place, Sydney, New South Wales, 2000, Australia
Tel: +61 02 227 7111
Fax: +61 02 227 3317
CH: M.A. Besley,
MD: D.V. Murray   114

Community Hospitals Group PLC
Priory Terrace, 24 Bromham Road, Bedford, MK40 2QD
Tel: 01234 273473
Fax: 01234 325882
CH: Sir Peter Thompson,
CE: A.M. Dexter, *MD:* A. Pilgrim,
FD: D.G. Croker   55

Compagnie Financiere Ottomane SA
23 avenue de la Porte-Neuve, 2227 Luxembourg
CH: H. de Saint-Amand   98

Compaq Computer Group Ltd
43 Brook Street, London, W1Y 2BL
Tel: 0181 332 3000
Fax: 0181 332 1961
CH: A. Barth   49

Compass Group PLC
Queen's Wharf, Queen Caroline Street, London, W6 9RJ
Tel: 0181 741 8900

Fax: 081 741 3802
CH: J. Thomson   52

Comptoirs Modernes
1 place du Gue de Maulny, 72019 Le Mans, France
CH: R. Gouloumes, J.-C. Plassart,
MD: J.-P. Rudaux   104

Concentric PLC
Coleshill Road, Sutton Coldfield, West Midlands, B75 7AZ
Tel: 0121 378 4229
Fax: 0121 378 4941
CH: A.C. Firth   61

Conoco (U.K.) Ltd
Park House, 116 Park Street, London, W1Y 4NN
Tel: 0171 408 6000
Fax: 0171 408 6660
CH: R.L. Abel,
MD: G.E. Watkins   29, 43, 94

Consolidated Edison Co. of New York Inc.
4 Irving Place, New York, New York, 10003, USA
Tel: +1 212 460-4600
No officers designated   111

Consolidated Electric Power Asia Ltd
Cedar House, 41 Cedar Avenue, Hamilton HM12, Bermuda
CH: Gordon Ying Sheung Wu,
CE: Stewart W.G. Elliott   115

Continental AG
Vahrenwalder Strasse 9, 30165 Hanover, Germany
Tel: +49 511 938-01
Fax: +49 511 938 2766
CH: U. Weiss, H. von Grunberg 73, 95

Continental Assets Trust PLC
One Charlotte Square, Edinburgh, EH2 4DZ
Tel: 0131 225 1357
Fax: 0131 225 2375
CH: I.M. Dalziel   61

Continental U.K. Group Holdings Ltd
4-8 High Street, West Drayton, Middlesex, UB7 7DJ
Tel: 01895 445678
Fax: 01895 446595
No officers designated   54

Cookson Group PLC
130 Wood Street, London, EC2V 6EQ
Tel: 0171 606 4400
Fax: 0171 606 2851
CH: R. Malpas, *CE:* R.M. Oster,
JMD: S.L. Howard, D.L. Carcieri,
FD: I.S. Barr   45, 100

Coop Bank AG
Aeschenplatz 3, 4002 Basle, Switzerland
Tel: +41 61 286 21 21
Fax: +41 61 271 45 95
CH: Dr G. Metz, H. Walti   99

Cooper (Great Britain) Ltd
Callywhite Lane, Dronfield, Sheffield, South Yorkshire, S18 GX7
Tel: 01246 299100
Fax: 01246 290354
No officers designated   56

Cooperatieve Centrale Raiffeisen-Boerenleenbank BA (Rabobank Nederland)
Croeselaan 18, PO Box 17100, 3500 HG Utrecht, The Netherlands
Tel: +31 30 90 2804
Fax: +31 30 90 1976
CH: Drs R. Zijlstra, Drs H.H.F. Wijffels, W. Meijer   68, 90

Cordiant PLC
83/89 Whitfield Street, London, W1A 4XA
Tel: 0171 436 4000
Fax: 0171 436 1998
CE: R.L. Seelert, *FD:* Wendy Smyth 60

Corporacion Industrial y Financiera de Banesto SA
Paseo de la Castellana 7, 28046 Madrid, Spain
Tel: +34 1 388 10 00
CH: A. Saenz Abad   97

Corporacion Mapfre Cia Internacional de Reaseguros, SA
Ctr de Pozuelo de Alarcon a Majadahonda, Km 3800, 28220 Majadahonda (Madrid), Spain
CH: C. Alvarez Jimenez,
CE: J.M. Martinez Martinez 105

Costa Crociere SpA
Via Gabriele D'Annunzio 2, 16121 Genoa, Italy
Tel: +39 10 54 831
Fax: +39 10 5483 - 290
CH: N. Costa, *JMD:* F. Pellicari,
A. Rossi   102

Costain Group PLC
111 Westminster Bridge Road, London, SE1 7UE
Tel: 0171 705 8444
Fax: 0171 705 8599
CH: Sir Christopher Benson,
CE: P.J. Costain, *FD:* A. Lovell 47, 106

Countryside Properties PLC
Countryside House, The Warley Hill Business Park, The Drive, Brentwood, Essex, CM13 3AT
Tel: 01277 260000
Fax: 01277 690690
CH: A.H. Cherry, *JMD:* G.S. Cherry, R.S. Cherry   58

Courage Ltd
Ashby House, 1 Bridge Street, Staines, Middlesex, TW18 4TP
Tel: 01784 466199
Fax: 01784 468131
No officers designated   34, 44, 99

Courtaulds PLC
50 George Street, London, W1A 2BB
Tel: 0171 612 1000
Fax: 0171 612 1500
CH: Sir Christopher Hogg,
CE: S. Huismans, *FD:* H. Evans 45, 72, 100

Courtaulds Textiles PLC
13-14 Margaret Street, London, W1A 3DA
Tel: 0171 331 4500
Fax: 0171 331 4600
CH: J.D. Eccles, *CE:* N. Jarvis,
FD: Pippa Wicks   47, 107

Courts PLC
The Grange, 1 Central Road, Morden, Surrey, SM4 5RX
Tel: 0181 640 3322
Fax: 0181 528 7505
CH: P.C. Cohen, *CE:* B.J.R. Cohen,
FD: M.B. Hacker   51

Coventry Building Society
Economic House, PO Box 9, High Street, Coventry, CV1 7QN
Tel: 01203 555255
Fax: 01203 839310
CH: I.N. Smith,
CE: M.H. Ritchley   48, 109

Cowie Group PLC
Millfield House, Hylton Road, Sunderland, Tyne and Wear, SR4 7BA
Tel: 0191 514 4122
Fax: 0191 514 5148
CH: Sir James McKinnon,
CE: G.W. Hodgson,
FD: S.P. Lonsdale   47, 106

Cray Electronics Holdings PLC
55 High Street, Frimley, Surrey, GU16 5HJ
Tel: 01276 675888
Fax: 01276 678895
CH: R.M. Holland, *CE:* J.M. Richards,
FD: J.G.H. Harrison   59

Credicom SA - Credit Commercial International
Frankrijklei 115, 2000 Antwerp, Belgium
Tel: +32 3 239 59 40
CH: C. Vaturi,
MD: H. Van Zeveren   105

Credit Agricole
91-93 Boulevard Pasteur, 75015 Paris, France
Tel: +33 1 43 23 52 02
CH: Y. Barsalou   74, 88, 90

Credit Foncier Vaudois
Place Chauderon 8, PO Box 77, 1000 Lausanne 9, Switzerland
Tel: +41 21 341 61 11

Fax: +41 21 341 69 20
CH: D. Schmutz, *MD:* J.-C. Grangier 101

Credit Foncier de France
19 rue des Capucines, 75001 Paris, France
Tel: +33 1 42 44 80 00
G: J.-C. Colli   86, 97

Credit Lyonnais
18 rue de la Republique, 69002 Lyons, France
CH: J. Peyrelevade   62, 65, 86, 90

Credit National
45 rue Saint-Dominique, 75700 Paris, France
Tel: +33 1 45 50 90 01
Fax: +33 1 45 55 68 96
CH: E. Rodocanachi   99

Creditanstalt-Bankverein
Schottengasse 6, 1010 Vienna, PO Box 72, Austria
Tel: +43 1 531 31-0
Fax: +43 1 531 31 7566
CH: W. Fremuth, G. Schmidt-Chiari 95

Credito Italiano
Via Dante 1, 16121 Genoa, Italy
Tel: +39 10 28521
CH: L. Rondelli, E.G. Bruno 94

Crest Nicholson PLC
Crest House, 39 Thames Street, Weybridge, Surrey, KT13 8JL
Tel: 01932 847272
Fax: 01932 840150
CH: J. St Lawrence, *CE:* J. Callcutt,
FD: J.C. Littler   54

CrestaCare PLC
Saddle Mews Clinic, Groves Road, Douglas, Isle of Man, IM2 1HY
Tel: 01624 661666
Fax: 01624 661176
CH: Sir Matthew Goodwin,
CE: A. Taee,
FD: J. Ramsay   56

Croda International PLC
Cowick Hall, Snaith, Goole, North Humberside, DN14 9AA
Tel: 01405 860551
Fax: 01405 861767
CH: M.R. Valentine, *CE:* K.G.G. Hopkins,
FD: R.M.H. Heseltine   50

Croudace Holdings Ltd
Croudace House, Godstone Road, Caterham, Surrey, CR3 6XQ
Tel: 01883 46464
Fax: 01883 40166
CH: J.B. Ratcliffe, *CE:* A.J. Timms 59

Cultor Oy
Kyllikinportti 2, 00240 Helsinki, Finland
Tel: +358 0 134 411
Fax: +358 0 1344 1344
P: B. Mattsson, *CH:* E. Utter 104

Cummins UK Ltd
46/50 Coombe Road, New Malden, Surrey, KT3 4QL
Tel: 0181 9496171
Fax: 0181 949 5704
CH: K.G. Sanford   51

Custos [AB]
Norrlandsgatan 16, PO Box 1738, 111 87 Stockholm, Sweden
Tel: +46 8 679 6310
Fax: +46 8 611 5074
CH: B. Haak, *MD:* L. Oberg, *FD:* L. Elbing   105

Cyanamid (UK) Holdings PLC
Cyanamid House, Fareham Road, Gosport, Hampshire, PO13 0AS
Tel: 01329 224000
Fax: 01329 220213
No officers designated   54

D'Ieteren [SA] NV
50 rue du Mail, 1050 Brussels, Belgium
Tel: +32 2 536 51 11
CH: R. D'Ieteren   107

D.N.L (Det Norske Luftfartselskap) AS
Fornebuvn 40, 1330 Oslo Lufthavn, Oslo, Norway

DBV - Dow

Tel: +47 67 59 63 99
Fax: +47 67 58 08 20
CH: H. Norvik 102

DBV Holding AG
Frankfurter Strasse 50, 65189
Wiesbaden, Germany
Tel: +49 6 11 3 63 23 23
Fax: +49 6 11 3 63 3 59
CH: F. Bode, M. Broska 106

DMC-Dollfus-Mieg et Cie
10 avenue Ledru-Rollin, 75012 Paris, France
Tel: +33 1 49 28 10 00
Fax: +33 1 43 42 51 91
CH: J.R. Charlier, J. Boubal 107

DSM NV
Het Overloon 1, 6411 TE Heerlen, The Netherlands
Tel: +31 45 788111
Fax: +31 45 719753
CH: H.H.F. Wijffels 94

Daejan Holdings PLC
Freshwater House,
158-162 Shaftesbury Avenue, London, WC2H 8HR
Tel: 0171 836 1555
Fax: 0171 379 6365
CH: B.S.E. Freshwater 49

Daelim Industrial
1460-12 Susong-Dong, Chung-Gu, Seoul, Korea
Tel: +82 2 730 8221
Fax: +82 2 733 3664
P: Sung Ki Woong, Lee Chung Kook, *CH:* Lee Joon Yong, *JMD:* Kim Kwan Soo, Kim Jung Hwan, Choi Kye Shik, Han Gyoon Min, Kim Ho Sung, Kang Seok Min, Lim Hwi Ryun, Lee Kwang Soon, Lee Yong Koo, Oh Soon Mo, Kim Jun Soo, Kim Yong Hwan 115

Daewoo Corpn
541 5-Ga Namdaemunno, Chung-Gu, Seoul, Korea
Tel: +82 2 759 2114
Fax: +82 2 753 9489
P: Suh Hyung Seok, Chang Young Soo, Hong Soung Bu, Yoon Young Suk, Lee Yun Ki, *CH:* Kim Woo Choong, Kim Joon Sung, *JMD:* Yu Tae Chang, Jin Jae Soon, Han Yong Ho, Choi Dong Wook 114

Daewoo Electronics
541 5-Ga Namdaemunno, Chung-Gu, Seoul, Korea
Tel: +82 2 360 7114
P: Bae Soon Hoon, *JMD:* Nam Kwi Hyen, Jung Ju Ho, Park Woon Hee, Lee Seung Bok, Nam Hong 115

Daewoo UK Ltd
Templar House, 82 Northolt Road, South Harrow, Middlesex, HA2 0YL
Tel: 0181 864 5366
Fax: 0181 864 6070
No officers designated 58

Dai Nippon Printing Co. Ltd
1-1 Ichigaya Kagacho 1-Chome, Shinjuku-ku, Tokyo 162, Japan
Tel: +81 3 3266 2111
Fax: +81 3 3266 2119
CH: Yoshitoshi Kitajima, *JMD:* Michiji Sato, Yasuo Yamaji, Jitsuo Okauchi, Ryozo Kitami 113

Dai-Ichi Kangyo Bank Ltd (The)
1-5 Uchisaiwaicho 1-chome, Chiyoda-ku, Tokyo 100, Japan
Tel: +81 3 3596 1111
Fax: +81 3 3596 2585
P: Tadashi Okuda, *CH:* Kuniji Miyazaki, *JMD:* Akira Kanazawa, Masakuni Nishiyama, Hisao Kobayashi, Tsuneo Uchida, Tsuneto Chimura, Katsuhiko Kondo, Yoshiharu Mani, Hisashi Kanai, Kenji Tanaka, Akio Sato, Yasuo Noda, Hideo Kitahara, Mitsuo Hamamoto, Hisaaki Nakajima, Ichiro Fujita, Junichi Hamada 112

Daiei Inc. (The)
4-1-1, Minatojima Nakamachi, Chuo-ku, Kobe 650, Japan
Tel: +81 78 302 5001
Fax: +81 78 302 5572
P: Isao Nakauchi, *CH:* Isao Nakauchi,

JMD: Shohei Nomura, Kazumi Taguchi, Tadashi Inoue, Kazuo Kawa, Hiromitsu Kameyama, Hironao Seike, Juro Suetake, Takashi Endo, Hiroshi Tomonoh, Hiromasa Kohama 113

Daily Mail and General Trust PLC
Northcliffe House, 2 Derry St, London, W8 5TT
Tel: 0171 938 6000
Fax: 0171 938 4626
CH: The Rt Hon The Viscount Rothermere, *CE:* C.J.F. Sinclair, *FD:* J.P. Williams 45, 101

Daimler-Benz AG
70546 Stuttgart, Germany
Tel: +49 711 1 79 22 87
Fax: +49 711 1 79 41 09
CH: H. Kopper,
J.E. Schrempp 13, 64, 90

Dairy Crest Ltd
Dairy Crest House, Portsmouth Road, Surbiton, Surrey, KT6 5QL
Tel: 0181 398 4155
Fax: 0181 398 0705
CH: G.R. John, *CE:* W.J. Houliston, *FD:* D.A. Harding 49

Daiwa Bank Ltd (The)
2-1 Bingomachi 2-chome, Chuo-ku, Osaka 541, Japan
Tel: +81 6 271 1221
P: Akira Fujita, *CH:* Sumio Abekawa, *JMD:* Hiroshi Kondo, Shigeyoshi Genjida, Kaneyoshi Nishiyama, Toshiro Kawakami, Kazuya Sunahara, Tsunao Kimura, Hiroshi Nonoyama, Ikuhiro Katsuda, Koichi Kunisada, Hiroyuki Yamaji, Shiro Itoshima, Hisao Nagaoka 113

Daiwa Securities Co Ltd
6-4 Otemachi 2-chome, Chiyoda-ku, Tokyo 100, Japan
Tel: +81 3 3243 2111
Fax: +81 3 3241 9366
P: Motoo Esaka, *CH:* Yoshitoki Chino, Sadakane Doi, *JMD:* Noboru Sugitani, Minoru Mori, Kyoichiro Ohga, Masayuki Kanoh, Juro Konno, Tomoaki Kusuda, Nobuo Kurakazu, Tatsuhiko Kawakami, Masuo Nishizawa, Kenji Ebihara, Koji Yoneyama, Takeshi Shimamura, Seiki Makino, Isao Shibuya, Takeshi Nojima 112

Dalgety PLC
100 George Street, London, W1H 5RH
Tel: 0171 486 0200
Fax: 0171 486 2005
CH: M.E. Warren, *CE:* R.J. Clothier, *FD:* J.R. Martyn 46, 104

Dalmine SpA
1 Piazza Caduti VI Luglio 1944, 24044 Dalmine (BG), Italy
Tel: +39 35 560 111
Fax: +39 35 563381
CH: L. Girardin, *MD:* S. Noce 109

Dana Holdings Ltd
Great Eastern House, Greenbridge Road, Stratton St Margaret, Swindon, Wiltshire, SN3 3LB
Tel: 01793 513315
Fax: 01793 641942
No officers designated 58

Danfoss AS
6430 Nordborg, Denmark
Tel: +45 74 88 22 22
Fax: +45 74 49 09 49
CH: H. Agerley, *CE:* H. Petersen 105

Danieli & C. Officine Meccaniche SpA
Via Nazionale 41, 33042 Buttrio (UD), Italy
Tel: +39 432 5981
Fax: +39 432 598289
CH: Cecilia Danieli,
MD: G. Benedetti 109

Danisco AS
Langebrogade 1, PO Box 17, 1001 Copenhagen K, Denmark
Tel: +45 32 66 20 00
Fax: +45 32 66 21 75
CH: H. Schroeder, *CE:* P. Marcus 98

Danka Business Systems PLC
Masters House, 107 Hammersmith Road, London, W14 0QH

Tel: 0171 603 1515
Fax: 0171 603 8448
CH: M.A. Vaughan-Lee,
CE: D.M. Doyle, *FD:* D.C. Snell 55

Danone
7 rue de Teheran, 75008 Paris, France
Tel: +33 1 44 35 20 20
Fax: +33 1 42 25 67 16
CH: A. Riboud 81, 91

Danske Bank [Den] AS
2-12 Holmens Kanal, 1092 Copenhagen K, Denmark
Tel: +45 33 44 00 00
Fax: +45 31 18 58 73
CH: P.J. Svanholm 85, 91

Danzas Holding AG
Leimenstrasse 1, 4051 Basel, Switzerland
Tel: +41 61 268 77 77
Fax: +41 61 261 58 47
CH: P. Gross, *MD:* B. Menzinger 102

Dares Estates PLC
9 Chalfont Court, Lower Earley District Centre, Lower Earley, Reading, RG6 2SY
Tel: 01734 312777
Fax: 01734 314625
CH: E. Landau, *MD:* B. Tomlinson 60

Dartmoor Investment Trust PLC
23 Cathedral Yard, Exeter, Devon, EX1 1HB
Tel: 01392 412122
Fax: 01392 53282
CH: T.R.H. Kimber 61

Dassault Aviation
9 Rond-Point des Champs-Elysees, Marcel Dassault, 75008 Paris, France
CH: S. Dassault 100

Davis Service Group PLC (The)
34 Francis Grove, Wimbledon, London, SW19 4DY
Tel: 0181 543 6644
Fax: 0181 879 3998
CH: N.W. Benson, *CE:* J.C. Ivey,
FD: G.M. Boyle 52

Dawson International PLC
9 Charlotte Square, Edinburgh, EH2 4DR
Tel: 0131 220 1919
Fax: 0131 459 1786
CH: R.D. Finlay, *MD:* P. Forrest,
FD: G. Fairweather 49

Dawsongroup PLC
Delaware Drive, Tongwell, Milton Keynes, MK15 8JH
Tel: 01908 218111
Fax: 01908 218444
CH: T. Frendo, *CE:* M.J. Williams,
FD: C. Gear 56

Dayton Hudson Corpn
777 Nicollet Mall, Minneapolis, Minnesota, 55402, USA
Tel: +1 612 370-6948
P: S.E. Watson, *CH:* J.R. Ulrich 111

De Beers Centenary AG
Lucerne, Switzerland
CH: J.O. Thompson 92

De La Rue PLC
6 Agar Street, London, WC2N 4DE
Tel: 0171 836 8383
Fax: 0171 240 4224
CH: The Rt Hon The Earl of Limerick, *CE:* J.J.S. Marshall,
FD: L.G. Cullen 47, 106

Degussa AG
Weissfrauenstrasse 9, 60311 Frankfurt am Main, Germany
Tel: +49 69 2 18-01
Fax: +49 69 2 18-32 18
CH: H. Sihler, G. Becker 95

Del Monte Foods International Ltd
Del Monte House, London Road, Staines, Middlesex, TW18 4JD
Tel: 01784 447400
Fax: 01784 465301
No officers designated 51

Delhaize Freres et Cie 'Le Lion' [SA Ets]
Rue Osseghem 53, PO Box 60, Molenbeek-Saint-Jean, 1080 Brussels, Belgium
Tel: +32 2 412 21 11
Fax: +32 2 412 21 94

CH: G. Beckers, Gui de Vaucleroy,
MD: G. de Vaucleroy 96

Delta PLC
1 Kingsway, London, WC2B 6XF
Tel: 0171 836 3535
Fax: 0171 836 4511
CH: Sir Martin Jacomb,
CE: Dr R.A. Easton, *FD:* M. Gill 47, 106

Den Norske Bank
Torgalmenning 2, 5020 Bergen, Norway
Tel: +47 55 21 10 00
Fax: +47 55 21 11 50
CH: G. Heiberg, K. Willoch,
MD: F.A. Hvistendahl 106

Dencora PLC
Dencora House, Blyburgate, Beccles, Suffolk, NR34 9TQ
Tel: 01502 712729
Fax: 01502 716821
CH: J.H. Bushell, *JMD:* C.R. Holmes,
R.C. Youngs, *FD:* R.M. Morritt 57

Derby Trust PLC
Hesketh House, Portman Square, London, W1A 4SU
Tel: 0171 486 6351
Fax: 0171 935 3829
CH: Sir Michael Richardson 59

Derbyshire Building Society
Duffield Hall, Duffield, Derby, DE56 1AG
Tel: 01332 841000
Fax: 01332 840350
CH: A.M. West, *CE:* R.E. Hollick 54

Derwent Valley Holdings PLC
87 Wimpole Street, London, W1M 7DB
Tel: 0171 486 4848
Fax: 0171 465 8198
CH: J.C. Ivey, *MD:* J.D. Burns 53

Detroit Edison Co. (The)
2000 Second Avenue, Detroit, Michigan, 48226-1279, USA
Tel: +1 313 237-8000
P: A.F. Earley Jr, *CH:* J.E. Lobbia 111

Deutsche Babcock AG
Duisburger Strasse 375, 46049 Oberhausen, Germany
Tel: +49 2 08 83 30
Fax: +49 2 08 2 60 91
CH: H.L. Ewaldsen, F. Neuber,
H. Schmiedeknecht 98

Deutsche Bahn AG
Friedrich-Ebert-Anlage 43-45, 60327 Frankfurt am Main, Germany
Tel: +49 69 2651
Fax: +49 69 2656 480
CH: G. Sassmannshausen, H. Durr 62, 71, 90

Deutsche Bank AG
PO Box 10 06 01, Taunusanlage 12, 60262 Frankfurt am Main, Germany
Tel: +49 69 7 15 00
Fax: +49 69 71 50 42 25
CH: H.J. Abs, Dr F.W. Christians,
H. Kopper 62, 66, 88, 90

Development Bank of Singapore Ltd (The)
DBS Building, 6 Shenton Way, Singapore, 0106
Tel: + 65 2201111
Fax: + 65 2211306
P: Patrick Yeoh Khwai Hoh,
CH: Ngiam Tong Dow 114

Development Securities PLC
2 South Audley Street, Mayfair, London, W1Y 6AJ
Tel: 0171 491 8400
Fax: 0171 499 1053
CH: M.D. Wigley, *JMD:* M.H. Marx,
A.E. Bodie 51

Devro International PLC
Moodiesburn, Chryston, Glasgow, G69 0JE
Tel: 01236 872261
Fax: 01236 872557
CH: L.R. Allen, *CE:* Dr G.Y. Alexander,
FD: J.A. Neilson 59

Dewhirst Group PLC
Dewhirst House, Westgate, Driffield, North Humberside, YO25 7TH
Tel: 01377 252561
Fax: 01377 43814
CH: T.C. Dewhirst, *CE:* D. Witt 61

Die Erste Osterreichische Spar-Casse-Bank AG
Graben 21, 1010 Vienna, Austria
CH: Komm-Rat H. Schimetschek,
Dr K. Fuchs 100

Diehl GmbH & Co
Stephanstrasse 49, 90478 Nuremberg, Germany
Tel: +49 9 11/9 47-0
Fax: +49 9 11/9 47-34 29
CH: K. Diehl, T. Diehl 88, 104

Digital Equipment Co. Ltd
Enterprise House, 190 High Holborn, London, WC1V 7BE
Tel: 0171 831 8282
Fax: 0171 405 6477
CH: C.J. Conway 48, 108

Digital Equipment Scotland Ltd
Mosshill Industrial Estate, Ayr, KA6
Tel: 01292 266955
Fax: 01292 883198
No officers designated 50

Diploma PLC
20 Bunhill Row, London, EC1Y 8LP
Tel: 0171 638 0934
Fax: 0171 638 7651
CH: A.J.C. Thomas,
FD: A.M.R. Parkinson 57

Disney [Walt] Co. (The)
500 South Buena Vista Street, Burbank, California, 91521-7320, USA
Tel: +001 818 560-1000
P: S.P. Gold, *MD:* M.D. Eisner 111

Diversified Agency Services Ltd
12 Bishop's Bridge Road, London, W2 6AA
Tel: 0171 298 7000
Fax: 0171 724 8292
CH: M. Boase 52

Dixons Group PLC
29 Farm Street, London, W1X 7RD
Tel: 0171 499 3494
Fax: 0171 629 1410
CH: S. Kalms, *CE:* J. Clare,
FD: R.N. Shrager 46, 104

Dobson Park Industries PLC
Dobson Park House, Manchester Road, Ince, Wigan, WN2 2DX
Tel: 01942 31421
Fax: 01942 47058
CH: A. Kaye, *CE:* A. Buckmaster,
FD: A.C. Taylor 59

Docks de France
Zone Industrielle du Menneton 32-36, Avenue Charles-Bedaux, PO Box 1805, 37018 Tours Cedex, France
Tel: +33 47 77 77 77
Fax: +33 47 77 90 87
CH: M. Deroy, J. Dian,
MD: J.-F. Toulouse 102

Dominion Resources Inc.
Riverfront Plaza - West Tower, 901 East Byrd Street, Richmond, Virginia, 23219-4069, USA
P: T.L. Baucom, *CH:* T.E. Capps 111

Domino Printing Sciences PLC
Trafalgar Way, Bar Hill, Cambridge, CB3 8TU
Tel: 01954 781888
Fax: 01954 782713
CH: G.L. Dennis, *MD:* H.W. Whitesmith,
FD: I.R. Dye 61

Donnelley [R.R.] Ltd
The Printing Works, Boroughbridge Road, York, YO2 5SS
Tel: 01904 798241
Fax: 01904 791017
No officers designated 60

Douglas Holding AG
Kabeler Strasse 4, 58099 Hagen, Germany
Tel: +49 23 31 69 03 66
Fax: +49 23 31 69 06 90
CH: Dr G. Sandler, Dr J. Kreke 107

Dow Chemical Co. (The)
2030 Dow Center, Midland, Michigan, 48674, USA
Tel: +1 517 636-1463
P: W.S. Stavropoulos,
CH: F.P. Popoff 110

Dow - Entreprise

Dow Chemical Co. Ltd
Lakeside House, Stockley Park,
Uxbridge, Middlesex, UB11 1BE
Tel: 0181 848 8688
Fax: 0181 848 5400
No officers designated 57, 72

Dow Corning Ltd
Barry Plant, Cardiff Road, Barry,
Glamorgan, CF6 7YL
Tel: 01446 732350
Fax: 01446 747944
No officers designated

Dragados y Construcciones SA
Paseo de la Alameda de Osuna 50,
28042 Madrid, Spain
Tel: +34 1 583 30 00
Fax: +34 1 742 77 53
CH: A. Duran Tovar,
S. Foncillas Casaus 100

Dragerwerk AG
Moislinger Allee 53-55, 23542
Lubeck, Germany
Tel: +49 4 51 8 82 22 01
Fax: +49 4 51 8 82 39 44
CH: Prof Dr D. Feddersen,
Dr C. Drager 109

Drayton English & International Trust PLC
11 Devonshire Square, London,
EC2M 4YR
Tel: 0171 626 3434
Fax: 0171 623 3339
CH: Sir Michael Richardson 58

Drayton Far Eastern Trust PLC
11 Devonshire Square, London,
EC2M 4YR
Tel: 0171 626 3434
Fax: 0171 623 3339
CH: Sir Michael Richardson 51

Dresdner Bank AG
Jurgen-Ponto-Platz 1, 60301 Frankfurt am Main, Germany
Tel: +49 69 26 30
CH: Dr W. Roller 14, 69, 78, 89, 91

Dresser (Holdings) Ltd
197 Knightsbridge, London, SW7 1RJ
Tel: 0171 584 7065
Fax: 0171 548 9414
No officers designated 55

Dreyfus [Louis] & Co. Ltd
162 Queen Victoria Street, London,
EC4V 4BS
Tel: 0171 489 9489
Fax: 0171 489 9449
CH: R.E. Cornwell 54

Du Pont [E.I.] De Nemours & Co
1007 Market Street, Wilmington,
Delaware, 19898, USA
Tel: +1 302 774 1000
CH: E.S. Woolard Jr 13, 29, 110

Duke Power Co
422 South Church Street, PO Box
33189, Charlotte, North Carolina,
28242-0001, USA
Tel: +1 704 594-0887
P: R.B. Priory, *CH*: W.H. Grigg 111

Dunedin Income Growth Investment Trust/ Dunedin Worldwide Investment Trust PLC
Belsize House, West Ferry, Dundee,
DD5 1NF
Tel: 01382 778244
Fax: 01382 3152222
CH: W.D. Marr 41, 50

Duracell Holdings (UK) Ltd
Mallory House, Hazelwick Avenue,
Three Bridges, Crawley, West Sussex,
RH10 1FQ
Tel: 01293 611666
Fax: 01293 21697
No officers designated 55

Dwyer Estates PLC
40 Park Street, London, W1Y 3PF
Tel: 0171 629 666
Fax: 0171 493 5096
CH: G.N. Kennedy, *CE*: J. Esfandi,
FD: W.A. Oliver 60

Dyckerhoff & Widmann AG
Postfach 81 02 80, Erdinger
Landstrasse 1, 81902 Munich,
Germany
Tel: +49 89 92 55-1

Fax: +49 89 92 55 21 27
CH: I. Walter, H.-J. Wolff 103

Dyckerhoff AG
Biebricher Strasse 69, 65203
Wiesbaden, Germany
Tel: +49 6 11 67 60
Fax: +49 6 11 6 76 10 40
CH: P.C. von Harder 105

Dyno Industrier AS
Tollbugaten 22, PO Box 779 Sentrum,
0106 Oslo, Norway
Tel: +47 22 31 70 00
Fax: +47 22 31 78 56
P: A. Ingierd, *CH*: R. Halvorsen 105

E D & F Man Group PLC
Sugar Quay, Lower Thames Street,
London, EC3R 6DU
Tel: 0171 285 3000
Fax: 0171 621 0149
CH: M.J.C. Stone, *MD*: H.A. McGrath,
FD: S. Fink 47, 107

E.D.S. International Ltd
4 Roundwood Avenue, Stockley Park,
Uxbridge, Middx, UB11 1BQ
Tel: 0181 848 8989
Fax: 0181 756 0130
CH: J.A. Bateman 47, 106

ECIA-Equipements et Composants pour l'Industrie Automobile
25400 Audincourt (Doubs), France
CH: G. Nicolet 108

EDP - Electricidade de Portugal SA
Avenida Jose Malhoa, Lote A 13,
1000 Lisbon, Portugal
CH: J. Serrao da Silva Correia 91

EFT Group PLC
10 Snow Hill, London, EC1A 2AL
Tel: 0171 248 9133
Fax: 0171 236 3728
CH: H.M. Grossart, *MD*: J.E. Black 61

EIS Group PLC
6 Sloane Square, London, SW1W 8EE
Tel: 0171 730 9187
Fax: 0171 730 2271
CH: Sir Norman Wooding,
CE: P.J.K. Haslehurst 54

EMAP PLC
1 Lincoln Court, Lincoln Road,
Peterborough, Cambridgeshire, PE1 2RF
Tel: 01733 68900
Fax: 01733 349290
CH: Sir John Hoskyns, *CE*: R. Miller,
MD: T.D.G. Arculus, *FD*: D.J. Grigson 49

EMS-Chemie Holding AG
Selnaustrasse 16, 8039 Zurich,
Switzerland
Tel: +41 1 284 18 80
Fax: +41 1 284 18 99
CH: Dr C. Blocher 106

ENI-Ente Nazionale Idrocarburi
Piazzale Enrico Matteo 1,
00144 Rome, Italy
Tel: +39 6 59001
CH: L. Meanti, *MD*: F. Bernabe 12, 13, 62, 70, 90

EVN Energie-Versorgung Niederosterreich AG
Johann-Steinbock-Strasse 1,
2344 Maria Enzersdorf, Austria
Tel: +43 22 36 200-0
Fax: +43 22 36 200-2600
CH: S. Ludwig, Dr R. Gruber 98

EWE AG
Tirpitzstrasse 39, 26122 Oldenburg,
Germany
Tel: +49 4 41 8 03-0
Fax: +49 4 41 8 03-39 99
CH: G. Boekhoff 102

East German Investment Trust PLC (The)
3 Finsbury Avenue, London, EC2M 2PA
Tel: 0171 638 5757
Fax: 0171 377 5742
CH: Dr R.J. Escherich (Germany) 61

East Japan Railway Co. Ltd
6-5 Marunouchi 1-chome, Chiyoda-ku,
Tokyo 100, Japan
Tel: +81 3 3240 5663
P: Masatake Matsuda, *CH*: Shoji
Sumita, *JMD*: Shuichiro Rikimura,

Kozo Yoshida, Eiji Tomoura, Takuro
Yamamoto, Kazuhiko Suzuki,
Nobuyuki Sasaki, Yoshiharu
Takamutsa, Mutsutake Otsuka, Yukio
Fukunishi, Kiyomi Harayama 112

East Midlands Electricity PLC
398 Coppice Road, Arnold,
Nottingham, NG5 7HX
Tel: 0115 926 9711
Fax: 0115 920 9789
CH: A.N.R. Rudd, *CE*: N.B.M. Askew,
FD: R.J. Davies 27, 45, 100

Eastern Counties Newspapers Group Ltd
Prospect House, Rouen Road,
Norwich, NR1 1RE
Tel: 01603 628311
CH: T.J.A. Colman,
CE: G.H.C. Copeman 61

Eastern Group PLC
Wherstead Park, Wherstead, Ipswich,
Suffolk, IP9 2AQ
Tel: 01473 688688
Fax: 01473 601036
CH: J.C. Smith, *CE*: J.F. Devaney,
FD: E.E. Anstee 14, 45, 100

Eastman Kodak Co.
343 State Street, Rochester, New York,
14650, USA
Tel: +1 716 724-4000
CH: G.M. Fisher 111

Eaux [Cie Generale des]
52 rue d'Anjou, 75384 Paris Cedex 08,
France
Tel: +33 1 49 24 49 24
Fax: +33 1 49 24 69 99
CH: J-M. Messier, G. Dejouany,
JMD: J.-M. Messier, P.-L. Girardot,
J.-H. David 75, 89, 91

Ebro Agricolas, Cia de Alimentacion SA
C/ Balmes 103, 08008 Barcelona, Spain
Tel: +34 3 454 6800
Fax: +34 3 451 7298
CH: M. Guasch Molins 104

Ecclesiastical Insurance Group PLC/ Ecclesiastical Insurance Office PLC
Beaufort House, Brunswick Road,
Gloucester, GL1 1JZ
Tel: 01452 528533
Fax: 01452 423557
CH: M.R. Cornwall-Jones,
MD: B.V. Day 53

Edeka Zentrale AG
New-York-Ring 6, 22297 Hamburg,
Germany
Tel: +49 40/63 77-0
Fax: +49 40/63 77 22 31
CH: A. Nolte, H. Neuhaus 108

Edinburgh Dragon Trust PLC
Donaldson House, 97 Haymarket
Terrace, Edinburgh, EH12 5HD
Tel: 0131 313 1000
Fax: 0131 313 6300
CH: Sir Hugh Campbell Byatt 41, 47, 107

Edinburgh Investment Trust PLC (The)
Dunedin House, 25 Ravelston Terrace,
Edinburgh, EH4 3EX
Tel: 0131 315 2500
Fax: 0131 315 2222
CH: The Earl of Eglinton and Winton 41, 44, 99

Edinburgh New Tiger Trust PLC
Donaldson House, 97 Haymarket
Terrace, Edinburgh, EH12 5HD
Tel: 0131 313 1000
Fax: 0131 313 6300
CH: I.W. Bell 53

Edinburgh Small Companies Trust PLC
Donaldson House, 97 Haymarket
Terrace, Edinburgh, EH12 5HD
Tel: 0131 313 1000
Fax: 0131 313 6300
CH: A.D.M. MacDonald 58

Edrington Holdings Ltd
106 West Nile Street, Glasgow, G1 2QX
Tel: 0141 332 6525
Fax: 0141 332 6697
CH: J.J.G. Good 50

Emerson Developments (Holdings) Ltd
Emerson House, Heyes Lane,

Effjohn Oy AB
Bulevardi 1A, 00101 Helsinki, Finland
Tel: +358 0 180 45 10
Fax: +358 0 17 66 23
P: R.G. Ehrenrooth,
CH: J. Ihamuotila 102

Eiffage
2 rue de Laborde, 75008 Paris, France
Tel: +33 1 44 90 44 44
Fax: +33 44 90 44 90
CH: L. Lesne, J.-F. Roverato 99

Eldridge, Pope & Co. PLC
Weymouth Avenue, Dorchester, DT1 1QT
Tel: 01305 251251
Fax: 01305 251028
CH: C.J.R. Pope, *FD*: M.E.D. Davis 59

Electra Investment Trust PLC
65 Kingsway, London, WC2B 6QT
Tel: 0171 831 6464
Fax: 0171 404 5388
CH: F. Vinton, M.C. Stoddart 41, 45, 101

Electrabel
Boulevard du Regent 8, 1000 Brussels,
Belgium
Tel: +32 2 518 61 11
Fax: +32 2 518 64 00
CH: P. Cols, R. Neirynck, P. Bodson,
CE: J.-P. Hansen 77, 82, 91

Electrafina
24 avenue Marnix, 1050 Brussels,
Belgium
Tel: +32 2 547 21 11
Fax: +32 2 542 22 73
CH: A. Frere, *MD*: T. de Rudder 97

Electric & General Investment Company PLC
3 Finsbury Avenue, London, EC2M 2PA
Tel: 0171 638 5757
Fax: 0171 377 5742
CH: D.A. Acland 51

Electricite de France
2 rue Louis-Murat, 75384 Paris,
Cedex 08, France
Tel: + 33 1 40 42 22 22
CH: G. Menage, *MD*: F. Ailleret 13, 90

Electrocomponents PLC
21 Knightsbridge, London, SW1X 7LY
Tel: 0171 245 1277
Fax: 0171 235 4458
CH: R.C.G. Cotterill, *CE*: R.A. Lawson,
FD: R.C. Tomkinson 51

Electrolux AB
Lilla Essingen, 105 45 Stockholm,
Sweden
Tel: +46 8 738 6000
P: L. Johansson, *CH*: H. Werthen,
A. Scharp 92

Electrowatt SA
Bellerivestrasse 36, 8022 Zurich,
Switzerland
Tel: +41 1 385 22 11
Fax: +41 1 385 25 55
CH: A. Gugler, O.K. Ronner 92

Elektrizitats-AG Mitteldeutschland
Scheidemannplatz 1, EAM-Hochhaus,
34117 Kassel, Germany
Tel: +49 5 61 70 81
Fax: +49 5 61 708-200
CH: G. Bokel, U. Cahn von Seelen 108

Elf Aquitaine SA [Ste]
Tour Elf, 2 place de la Coupole,
La Defense 6 - 92400 Courbevoie, France
Tel: +33 1 47 44 45 46
CH: P. Jaffre 12, 13, 33, 62, 65, 89, 90

Elkem AS
Nydalsveien 28, N-0401 Oslo, Norway
Tel: +47 22 45 01 00
Fax: +47 22 45 01 55
P: O. Enger, *CH*: F.M. Jebsen,
FD: B. Haugen 105

Ellis & Everard PLC
46 Peckover Street, Bradford,
West Yorkshire, BD1 5BD
Tel: 01274 308052
Fax: 01274 737058
CH: J.F. Taylor, *MD*: P.S. Wood,
FD: J. Samuel 56

Alderley Edge, Cheshire, SK9 7LF
Tel: 01625 584531
Fax: 01625 585791
CH: P.E. Jones, *FD*: M.A. Schuler 50

Emess PLC
20 St James's Street, London,
SW1A 1HA
Tel: 0171 321 0127
Fax: 0171 925 2734
CH: M. Meyer, *FD*: D. Cutler 58

Empresa Nacional Hidroelectrica del Ribagorzana SA
Passeig de Gracia 132,
08008 Barcelona, Spain
Tel: +34 3 415 50 00
Fax: +34 3 415 7572
MD: C. Vazquez Fernandez-Victorio 81, 100

Empresa Nacional de Electricidad, SA
Principe de Vergara 187, 28002
Madrid, Spain
Tel: +34 1 563 09 23
Fax: +34 1 563 81 81
CH: F. Fuster Jaume 88, 89, 91

Energie-Versorgung Schwaben AG
Kriegsbergstrasse 32, 70174 Stuttgart,
Germany
Tel: +49 7 11 1 28-0
Fax: +49 7 11 1 28-21 80
CH: Dr G. Blaser, E. Hagenmeyer 96

Energieversorgung Oberfranken AG
Luitpoldplatz 5, 95444 Bayreuth,
Germany
Tel: +49 9 21 2 85-1
Fax: +49 9 21 2 85-25 65
CH: Dr O. Majewski 107

Energieversorgung Ostbayern AG
Prufeninger Strasse 20, 93049
Regensburg, Germany
Tel: +49 9 41 201-0
Fax: +49 941 201-399
CH: Dr O. Majewski 103

Engelhard Ltd
Engelhard House, 8 Throgmorton
Avenue, London, EC2N 2DL
Tel: 0171 588 4080
Fax: 0171 374 4632
No officers designated 59

English & Scottish Investors PLC
Gartmore House, 16-18 Monument
Street, London, EC3R 8AJ
Tel: 0171 782 2000/623 12
Fax: 0171 782 2075
CH: P.N. Buckley 41, 50

English China Clays PLC
1015 Arlington Business Park, Theale,
Reading, RG7 4SA
Tel: 01734 304010
Fax: 01734 309500
CH: L.M. Urquhart, *CE*: A.H. Teare,
FD: P. Drayton 45, 100

Enron Corpn
1400 Smith Street, Houston, Texas,
77002-7369, USA
Tel: +1 713 853-6161
P: R.D. Kinder, *CH*: K.L. Lay 111

Enso-Gutzeit Oy
Kanavaranta 1, 00160 Helsinki, Finland
Tel: +358 0 162 91
Fax: +358 0 162 9471
CH: J. Harmala, M. Louekoski 94

Entergy Corporation
PO Box 61005, New Orleans, Lousiana,
70161, USA
Tel: +1 800 292-9960
CH: E. Lupberger 110

Enterprise Oil PLC
Grand Buildings, Trafalgar Square,
London, WC2N 5EJ
Tel: 0171 925 4000
Fax: 0171 925 4321
CH: G.J. Hearne, *MD*: M.J. Pink,
FD: A.B. Shilston 30, 33, 43, 95

Entreprise Miniere et Chimique
62 rue Jeanne-d'Arc, 75641 Paris
Cedex 13, France
Tel: +33 1 44 06 52 00
Fax: +33 1 44 06 54 00
CH: C. de Torquat, R. Greif 101

Ericsson - Flughafen

Ericsson [Telefonaktiebolaget LM]
126 25 Stockholm, Sweden
Tel: +46 8 719 3444
P: L. Ramqvist, *CH:* B. Svedberg 89, 93

Eridania Beghin-Say
59239 Thumeries, France
CH: J.-M. Vernes, S. Meloni 93

Espirito Santo Financial Holding SA
37 Rue Notre-Dame, Luxembourg
Tel: +11-352/4797-3933
CH: R. Espirito Santo Silva Salgado 98

Espresso [Editoriale L'] SpA
Via Po 12, 00198 Rome, Italy
Tel: +39 6 84 781
Fax: +39 6 8443174
CH: C. Caracciolo,
MD: Giulia Maria Crespi Mozzoni 107

Esselte AB
Sundbybergsvagen 1, PO Box 1371,
171 27 Solna, Sweden
Tel: +46 08 27 27 60
Fax: +46 08 83 32 98
P: B. Lundquist, *CH:* R. Andersson 109

Essilor International SA
147, rue de Paris,
94227 Charenton le Pont, France
Tel: +33 1 49 77 42 24
CH: G. Cottet, *JMD:* X. Fontanet,
P. Alfroid 104

Esso AG
Kapstadtring 2, 22297 Hamburg, Germany
Tel: +49 40 63 93-0
Fax: +49 40 6393-3368
CH: T. Kohlmorgen, J.D. Siemer 92, 95

Esso SA Francaise
2 rue des Martinets, Rueil-Malmaison
(Hauts-de-Seine), France
Tel: +33 1 47 10 60 00
Fax: +33 1 47 10 66 03
CH: J. Verre 102

Esso UK PLC
Esso House, Victoria Street, London,
SW1E 5JW
Tel: 0171 834 6677
Fax: 0171 245 2556
CH: K.H. Taylor, *JMD:* P.J. Dingle,
D. Clayman, *FD:* J.I. Alcock 24, 40,
42, 92

Estates & Agency Holdings PLC
33 Ely Place, London, EC1N 6TD
Tel: 0171 831 8600
Fax: 0171 831 8921
CH: J.S.I. Rosefield,
FD: K.M. Loukes 59

Etam PLC
Jubilee House, 213 Oxford Street,
London, W1R 2AH
Tel: 0171 437 5655
Fax: 0171 734 0326
CH: S. Lewis, *MD:* N. Hollingworth,
FD: K.C. Miles 58

Eurafrance
12 avenue Percier, 75008 Paris, France
Tel: +33 1 44 13 01 11
CH: M. David-Weill 102

Euro Disney SCA
Immeuble Administratif, Route
Nationale 34, 77700 Chessy, Seine et
Marne, France
Tel: +33 1 64 74 40 00
CH: J. Taittinger, P. Bourguignon,
MD: S.B. Burke 96

Euro RSCG Worldwide
8 rue de l'Hotel de Ville, 92522
Neuilly-sur-Seine Cedex, France
Tel: +33 1 47 38 99 99
Fax: +33 1 47 47 12 23
CH: A. de Pouzilhac, A. de Pouzilhac,
JMD: J.-M. Goudard, J. Seguela,
P. Becouarn 108

Euroc AB
Annetorpsvagen 100, Box 60066, 216
10 Malmo, Sweden
Tel: +46 40 16 50 00
Fax: +46 40 15 96 10
P: S. Ohlsson, *CH:* M. Schorling,
CE: S. Ohlsson 100

European Investment Bank
100 Boulevard Konrad Adenauer,
L-2950 Luxembourg
Tel: +352 4379 1

Fax: +352 43 77 04
CH: Sir Brian Unwin 62, 63, 88, 90

Europistas Concesionaria Espanola SA
C/ Principe de Vergara 132,
28004 Madrid, Spain
Tel: +34 1 563 99 74
Fax: +34 1 562 63 36
CH: R. del Pino y Moreno, C. Boada
Vilallonga, *MD:* J. Prior Perna 104

Eurotherm PLC
Leonardslee, Lower Beeding,
Horsham, West Sussex, RH13 6PP
Tel: 01403 891665
Fax: 01403 891689
CH: Dr J.L. Leonard, *CE:* C.A. Hultman,
FD: R.M. Biddle 58

Eurotunnel Group
The Adelphi, John Adam Street,
London, WC2N 6JT
Tel: 0171 715 6789
Fax: 0171 715 6666
CH: Sir Alastair Morton, P. Ponsolle,
CE: G.-C. Chazot, *FD:* P.G. Corbett 14,
17, 42, 62, 76, 91

Evans of Leeds PLC
Millshaw, Ring Road, Beeston, Leeds,
LS11 8EG
Tel: 0113 271 1888
Fax: 0113 271 8487
CH: J.A.C. Humphries, *MD:* J.D. Bell,
FD: W.M. Gibson 50

Ex-Lands PLC (The)
25 City Road, London, EC1Y 1BQ
Tel: 0171 628 9371
Fax: 0171 638 9426
CH: D.C. Marshall, *CE:* R.A. Bourne,
G.A. Bourne, *FD:* A.F. Blurton 60

Exco PLC
Sherborne House, 119 Cannon Street,
London, EC4N 5AX
Tel: 0171 623 4040
Fax: 0171 283 8450
CH: C.M. Mosselmans, *CE:* P.J. Edge,
FD: K.M. Taylor 57

Exeter Preferred Capital Investment Trust PLC
23 Cathedral Yard, Exeter, Devon,
EX1 1HB
Tel: 01392 412122
Fax: 01392 53282
CH: T.R.H. Kimber 59

Export-Import Bank of Japan (The)
4-1 Ohtemachi 1-chome,
Chiyoda-ku, Tokyo 100, Japan
Tel: +81 3 3287 1221
Fax: +81 3 3287 9540
G: Hiroshi Yasuda 112

Exxon Chemical Ltd
PO Box 122, 4600 Parkway, Fareham,
Hampshire, PO15 7AP
CH: J.G. Holloway 49

Exxon Corpn
225 East John W Carpenter Freeway,
Irving, Texas, 75062-2298, USA
Tel: +1 214 444-1000
P: C.R. Sitter, *CH:* L.R. Raymond 13,
110

FAG Kugelfischer Georg Schafer AG
Georg-Schafer-Strasse 30,
97421 Schweinfurt, Germany
Tel: +49 97 21 91 0
Fax: +49 97 21 91 34 35
CH: O. Schafer, K.J. Neukirchen,
P.-J. Kreher 102

FKI PLC
West House, Kings Cross Road,
Halifax, West Yorkshire, HX1 1EB
Tel: 01422 330267
Fax: 01422 330084
CH: J. Whalley, *CE:* R.G. Beeston,
FD: E.J. Bowers 48, 109

FLS Industries AS
Vigerslev Alle 77, 2500 Valby,
Copenhagen, Denmark
Tel: +45 36 18 18 00
Fax: +45 36 30 44 41
P: B. Riisager, *CH:* C. Arnstedt 98

FPL Group Inc.
700 Universe Boulevard, Juno Beach,
Florida, 33408, USA
CH: J.L. Broadhead 111

Fairey Group PLC
Station Road, Egham, Surrey, TW20 9NP
Tel: 01784 470470
Fax: 01784 470848
CH: D.J. Kingsbury, *CE:* J.W. Poulter,
FD: M.A. Fay 60

Falck SpA [Acciaierie e Ferriere Lombarde]
48 Corso Venezia, 20121 Milan, Italy
Tel: +39 2 76 00 61 67
CH: A. Falck, *MD:* A. Colombo 105

Far Eastern Textile Ltd
36th Floor, 207 Tun Hwa South Road,
Sec 2, Taipei, Taiwan
Tel: +886 2 7338000
Fax: +886 2 7369934
CH: Xu Xudong 115

Farnell Electronics PLC
Farnell House, Forge Lane, Leeds,
LS12 2NE
Tel: 0113 279 0101
Fax: 0113 231 0048
CH: R.E. Hanwell, *CE:* H. Poulson,
FD: A.C. Fisher 52

Feldschlosschen Holding
4310 Rheinfelden, Switzerland
Tel: +41 61 835 09 11
Fax: +41 61 835 02 07
CH: Dr H.R. Haab 101

Felixstowe Dock and Railway Co.
Tomline House, The Dock, Felixstowe,
Suffolk, IP11 8SY
Tel: 01394 604500
Fax: 01394 604949
CH: C. Fok, *MD:* D.J. Harrington 51

Fenner PLC
Welton Hall, Welton, Brough, HU15 1PQ
Tel: 01482 668111
Fax: 01482 667597
CH: C.I. Cooke, *CE:* M.S. Abrahams,
FD: R. Perry 57

Fenwick Ltd
Elswick Court, 39 Northumberland
Street, Newcastle-upon-Tyne, NE99 1AR
Tel: 0191 232 5100
Fax: 0191 2611164
CH: J.J. Fenwick 54

Ferruzzi Finanziaria
Via XIII Giugno 8, 48100 Ravenna, Italy
Tel: +39 544 51 41 11
Fax: +39 544 356 92
CH: L. Lucchini, *MD:* E. Bondi 62, 92

Fiat SpA
Corso Marconi 10/20, 10125 Turin, Italy
Tel: +39 11 686 111
Fax: +39 11 686 3400
CH: C. Romiti 13, 62, 67, 90

Fidelity European Values PLC
Oakhill Avenue, 130 Tonbridge Road,
Hildenborough, Tonbridge, Kent,
TN11 9DZ
Tel: 01732 361144
Fax: 01732 838886
CH: Sir Charles Annand Fraser 55

Fidelity Japanese Values PLC
Oakhill Avenue, 130 Tonbridge Road,
Hildenborough, Tonbridge, Kent,
TN11 9DZ
Tel: 01732 361144
Fax: 01732 838886
CH: Sir Peter Parker 57

Field Group PLC
Misbourne House, Badminton Court,
Rectory Way, Old Amersham,
Buckinghamshire, HP7 0DD
Tel: 01494 433711
Fax: 01494 431138
CH: F.W. Knight, *CE:* K. Gilchrist,
FD: D.S.M. Nussbaum 57

Financiere Richemont AG [Cie]
Rigistrasse 2, 6300 Zug, Switzerland
Tel: +41 42 22 33 22
Fax: +41 42 21 71 38
CH: N. Senn, *MD:* J. Rupert 14, 94

Financiere et Industrielle Gaz et Eaux
3 rue Jacques Bingen, 75017 Paris,
France
Tel: +33 1 47 66 02 64
Fax: +33 1 47 66 84 41
CH: B. Roger 102

Fine Art Developments PLC
Dawson Lane, Dudley Hill, Bradford,
West Yorkshire, BD4 6HW
Tel: 01274 651188
Fax: 01274 687386
CH: K. Chapman, *MD:* D.A. Johnson 52

Finextel SA
37 rue de Rome, 75008 Paris, France
Tel: +33 1 42 93 26 26
Fax: +33 1 42 93 08 04
CH: A. de Montalivet 104

Finlay [James] PLC
Finlay House, 10/14 West Nile Street,
Glasgow, G1 2PP
Tel: 0141 204 1321
Fax: 0141 248 4751
CH: R.J.K. Muir 53

Finnair Oy
Dagmarinkatu 4, 00100 Helsinki, Finland
Tel: +358 90 818 81
P: A. Potila 102

Finning Holdings Ltd
Watling Street, Cannock, Staffordshire,
WS11 3LL
Tel: 01543 462551
Fax: 01543 573124
CH: J.F Shepard, *MD:* N.B. Lloyd 57

Finsbury Growth Trust PLC
Apex House, 9 Haddington place,
Edinburgh, EH7 4AL
CH: M.A.F. Reeve, *CE:* N. Browe,
FD: C. Hume 59

First Choice Holidays PLC
First Choice House, London Road,
Crawley, West Sussex, RH10 2GX
Tel: 01293 560777
Fax: 01293 539039
CH: M.F. Julien, *CE:* F.S.K. Baron,
FD: M.B. Heald 53

First Leisure Corporation PLC
7 Soho Street, London, W1V 5FA
Tel: 0171 437 9727
Fax: 0171 439 0088
CH: M.I. Grade, *CE:* J.O. Conlan,
FD: C.G. Coles 50

First National Finance Corporation PLC
St Alphage House, Fore Street,
London, EC2P 2HJ
Tel: 0171 638 2855
Fax: 0171 628 9963
CH: R.M. Mays-Smith,
FD: T.C.W. Ingram 53

First Pacific Co. Ltd
Cedar House, 41 Cedar Avenue,
Hamilton HM12, Bermuda
Tel: +809 295 2244
Fax: +809 292 8666
CH: Soedono Salim,
MD: Manuel V. Pangilinan 115

First Philippine Investment Trust PLC
Knightsbridge House,
197 Knightsbridge, London, SW7 1RB
Tel: 0171 412 0703
Fax: 0171 581 3857
CH: R. del Rosario Jnr 61

Fischer [Georg] AG
Amsler-Laffon-Strasse 9, 8201
Schaffhausen, Switzerland
Tel: +41 53 81 11 11
Fax: +41 53 25 57 38
P: M. Huber, *CH:* U. Bremi 101

Fisons PLC
Fison House, Princes Street, Ipswich,
Suffolk, IP1 1QH
Tel: 01473 232525
Fax: 01473 231540
CH: L.E. Linaker, *CE:* S. Wallis,
FD: D.R.L. Hankinson 14, 46, 62, 105

Five Arrows Chile Investment Trust Ltd
PO Box 242, St Peter Port House,
Sausmarez Street, St Peter Port,
Guernsey, GY1 3PH
Tel: 01481 713713
Fax: 01481 723965
CH: L. de Rothschild 52

Fleming American Investment Trust PLC
25 Copthall Avenue, London, EC2R 7DR
Tel: 0171 638 5858

Fax: 0171 588 7219
CH: I.O.S. Saunders 41, 49

Fleming Claverhouse Investment Trust PLC
25 Copthall Avenue, London, EC2R 7DR
Tel: 0171 638 5858
Fax: 0171 588 7219
CH: Lord Mark Fitzalan Howard 54

Fleming Continental European Investment Trust PLC
25 Copthall Avenue, London, EC2R 7DR
Tel: 0171 638 5858
Fax: 0171 588 7219
CH: Lord Mark Fitzalan Howard 41, 50

Fleming Emerging Markets Investment Trust PLC
25 Copthall Avenue, London, EC2R 7DR
Tel: 0171 638 5858
Fax: 0171 588 7219
CH: Sir John A. Thomson 52

Fleming Enterprise Investment Trust PLC
25 Copthall Avenue, London, EC2R 7DR
Tel: 0171 638 5858
Fax: 0171 588 7219
CH: V.P. Fleming 56

Fleming Far Eastern Investment Trust PLC
25 Copthall Avenue, London, EC2R 7DR
Tel: 0171 638 5858
Fax: 0171 628 0683
CH: Lord Mark Fitzalan Howard 41,
46, 102

Fleming Geared Income & Assets Investment Trust PLC
25 Copthall Avenue, London, EC2R 7DR
Tel: 0171 638 5858
Fax: 0171 588 7219
CH: J.D. Webster 60

Fleming Income & Capital Investment Trust PLC
25 Copthall Avenue, London, EC2R 7DR
Tel: 0171 638 5858
Fax: 0171 588 7219
CH: C.K.R. Nunneley 55

Fleming Indian Investment Trust PLC
25 Copthall Avenue, London, EC2R 7DR
Tel: 0171 638 5858
Fax: 0171 588 7219
CH: M.B. Cannan 58

Fleming International High Income Investment Trust PLC
25 Copthall Avenue, London, EC2R 7DR
Tel: 0171 638 5858
Fax: 0171 588 7219
CH: V.P. Fleming 54

Fleming Japanese Investment Trust PLC
25 Copthall Avenue, London, EC2R 7DR
Tel: 0171 638 5858
Fax: 0171 588 7219
CH: P.A.F. Gifford 41, 46, 104

Fleming Mercantile Investment Trust PLC
25 Copthall Avenue, London, EC2R 7DR
Tel: 0171 638 5858
Fax: 0171 588 7219
CH: S.L. Keswick 41, 47, 106

Fleming Overseas Investment Trust PLC
25 Copthall Avenue, London, EC2R 7DR
Tel: 0171 638 5858
Fax: 0171 588 7219
CH: Sir Philip Haddon-Cave 41, 47,
106

Fleming [Robert] Holdings Ltd
25 Copthall Avenue, London, EC2R 7DR
Tel: 0171 638 5858
Fax: 0171 588 7219
CH: R. Fleming, *CE:* P.J. Manser 45 101

Fletcher Challenge Ltd
Fletcher Challenge House,
810 Great South Road, Penrose,
Auckland, New Zealand
CH: Sir Ronald Trotter 114

Flughafen Wien AG
1300 Wien-Flughafen, Postfach 1, Austria
Tel: +43 1 711 10-0
Fax: +43 1 711 10-3001
CH: Dr W. Nolz 106

Fokker - Gleeson

Fokker [NV Koninklijke Nederlandse Vliegtuigenfabriek]
Hoogoorddreef 15,
1101 BA Amsterdam-Zuidoost,
The Netherlands
CH: J.E. Schrempp,
B.J.A. van Schaik 99

Fomento Construccion Y Contratas
c/ Balmes 36, 08007 Barcelona, Spain
Tel: +34 3 487 62 26
CH: G. Visedo Navarro,
MD: R. Montes Sanchez 101

Fondiaria SpA
Piazza della Liberta 6, 50129 Florence,
Italy
Tel: +39 55 47941
Fax: +39 55 476 026
CH: L.A. Molinari,
MD: A. Bianchi di Lavagna 98

Ford Motor Co.
The American Road, PO Box 1899,
Dearborn, Michigan, 48121-1899, USA
Tel: +1 313 322-3000
CH: A. Trotman 12, 13, 110

Ford Motor Co. Ltd
Eagle Way, Brentwood, Essex,
CM13 3BW
Tel: 01277 253000
Fax: 01277 211285
CH: I.G. McAllister 33, 43, 95

Ford-Werke AG
Henry-Ford Strasse 1, 50725 Cologne,
Germany
Tel: +49 221 90-1 75 26
Fax: +49 221 90-1 29 84
CH: R. Parry-Jones, A. Caspers 94

Foreign & Colonial Emerging Markets Investment Trust PLC
Orchard Brae House, 30 Queensferry
Road, Edinburgh, EH4 2HG
CH: G.M. Nissen 53

Foreign & Colonial Enterprise Trust PLC
8th Floor, Exchange House, Primrose
Street, London, EC2A 2NY
Tel: 0171 628 8000
Fax: 0171 628 8188
CH: J.R. Sclater 58

Foreign & Colonial Eurotrust PLC
8th Floor, Exchange House, Primrose
Street, London, EC2A 2NY
Tel: 0171 628 8000
Fax: 0171 628 8188
CH: T.G. Abell 53

Foreign & Colonial German Investment Trust PLC
PO Box 435, Owen House, 8 Bankhead
Crossway North, Edinburgh, EH11 4BR
Tel: 0131 556 8555
Fax: 0131 442 4924
CH: D.P. Thomson 61

Foreign & Colonial Investment Trust PLC
Foreign & Colonial Management Ltd,
Exchange House, Primrose Street,
London, EC2A 2NY
Tel: 0171 628 8000
Fax: 0171 628 8188
CH: J.R. Sclater, *MD:* M.J. Hart 41, 44, 96

Foreign & Colonial PEP Investment Trust PLC
8th Floor, Exchange House, Primrose
Street, London, EC2A 2NY
Tel: 0171 628 8000
Fax: 0171 628 8188
CH: G. Ross Russell 60

Foreign & Colonial Pacific Investment Trust PLC
8th Floor, Exchange House, Primrose
Street, London, EC2A 2NY
Tel: 0171 628 8000
Fax: 0171 628 8188
CH: A.J. Davis 41, 47 106

Foreign & Colonial Smaller Companies PLC
8th Floor, Exchange House, Primrose
Street, London, EC2A 2NY
Tel: 0171 628 8000
Fax: 0171 628 8188
CH: Sir Peter Hordern,
MD: A. Barker 41, 51

Foreign & Colonial Special Utilities Investment Trust PLC
8th Floor, Exchange House, Primrose
Street, London, EC2A 2NY
Tel: 0171 628 8000
Fax: 0171 628 8188
CH: A.E. Wheatley 60

Forsmarks Kraftgrupp AB
S-742 03 Osthammar, Sweden
Tel: +46 173 810 00
Fax: +46 173 551 16
CH: S. Nordin, *MD:* A. Lindfors 98

Forte PLC
166 High Holborn, London, WC1V 6TT
Tel: 0171 836 7744
Fax: 0171 240 9993
CH: The Hon Sir Rocco Forte,
FD: K. Hamill 23, 42, 92

Forth Ports PLC
Tower Place, Leith, Edinburgh, EH6 7DB
Tel: 0131 554 6473
Fax: 0131 553 7462
CH: W.A.C. Thomson,
CE: H.M. Thompson,
FD: W.W. Murray 60

Fortis AG
Boulevard Emile Jacqmain 53, 1000
Brussels, Belgium
Tel: +32 2 220 81 11
Fax: +32 2 220 80 92
CH: Viscount C. de Jonghe d'Ardoye,
M. Lippens, *MD:* V. Croes 96

Fortis Amev
Archimedeslaan 10, 3584 BA Utrecht,
The Netherlands
Tel: +31 30 579 111
Fax: +31 30 522394
CH: F. Roos, J.L.M. Bartelds 96

Foster's Brewing Group Ltd
One Garden Street, South Yarra,
Victoria, 3141, Australia
Tel: +61 3 828 2424
CH: N.R. Clark, *CE:* E.T. Kunkel 114

France Telecom
6 place d'Alleray,
75505 Paris Cedex 15, France
Tel: +33 1 44 44 22 22
Fax: +33 1 42 21 45 45
CH: M. Roulet 12, 13, 62, 64, 88, 90

Fraser & Neave Ltd
21-00 Alexandra Point, 438 Alexandra
Road, Singapore, 0511
Tel: +65 272 9488
Fax: +65 271 0811
CH: Dr Michael Fam 115

Fresenius AG
Borkenberg 14, 6370 Oberursel/Ts,
Germany
Tel: +49 61 71 60 24 85/2
Fax: +49 61 71 60 24 88
CH: Dr A. Stiefenhofer, Dr G. Krick 106

Freudenberg & Co
Bergstrasse, 69465 Weinheim, Germany
Tel: +49 6201 80-5807
Fax: +49 6201 80-3430
No officers designated 98

Frogmore Estates PLC
8 Manchester Square, London, W1A 2JZ
Tel: 0171 224 4343
Fax: 0171 935 6476
CH: D.J. Cope, *MD:* P. White,
FD: D.K. Wilmot 48, 109

Fromageries Bel
4 rue d'Anjou, 75008 Paris, France
Tel: +33 1 40 07 72 50
CH: R. Fievet, *MD:* B. Dufort 108

Frost Group PLC (The)
Walton Lodge, Walton Street,
Aylesbury, Buckinghamshire,
HP21 7QY
Tel: 01296 395551
Fax: 01296 26857
CH: R.J. Frost,
FD: J.W. Murgatroyd 61

Fuerzas Electricas de Cataluna, SA - FECSA
Avenida Parallel 51, 08004 Barcelona,
Spain
Tel: +34 3 4434469
CH: L. Magana Martinez,
MD: J. Zaforteza Delgado 94

Fuji Bank Ltd (The)
5-5, Otemachi 1-Chome, Chiyoda-ku,
Tokyo 100, Japan
Tel: +81 3 3216 2211
Fax: +81 3 3201 0527
P: Toru Hashimoto, *JMD:* Yoshihisa
Tomoda, Ritsuo Koakutsu, Tatsuro
Arita, Shunichi Itoga, Yasuyuki Hirota,
Hiromichi Tsuda, Tomohiro Kamio,
Hiroaki Etoh, Tosaku Harada, Hiroshi
Ohtani, Kazushi Hara, Toshiyuki
Ogura, Akio Tenmei 112

Fuji Photo Film Co. Ltd
26-30 Nishiazabu 2-chome, Minato-ku,
Tokyo 106, Japan
Tel: +81 3 3406 2111
P: Minoru Ohnishi, *JMD:* Masayuki
Muneyuki, Tsutomu Omura, Minoru
Sonoda, Akira Kumai, Kenichi Mori,
Osamu Inoue, Yasushi Oishi, Hiroshi
Ashizawa, Harushi Yagi 112

Fujitsu Ltd
6-1 Marunouchi 1-chome, Chiyoda-ku,
Tokyo 100, Japan
Tel: +81 3 3216 3211
Fax: +81 3 3216 9352
P: Tadashi Sekizawa, *CH:* Takuma
Yamamoto, *JMD:* Michio Naruto, Toshio
Hiraguri, Keizo Fukagawa, Masuo
Tanaka, Shigeo Muraoka, Iwao Katsuki,
Iwao Toda, Hikotaro Masunaga 112

Fuller, Smith & Turner PLC
Griffin Brewery, Chiswick Lane South,
Chiswick, London, W4 2QB
Tel: 0181 994 3691
Fax: 0181 995 0230
CH: A.G.F. Fuller, *MD:* M.J. Turner 55

Fyffes Group Ltd
12 York Gate, Regents Park, London,
NW1 4QJ
Tel: 0171 487 4472
Fax: 0171 487 3644
CH: A.J. Ellis 57

G.T. Japan Investment Trust PLC
Alban Gate, 14th Floor, 125 London
Wall, London, EC2Y 5AS
Tel: 0171 710 4567
Fax: 0171 710 4555
CH: W.T.J. Griffin 51

GAIC SpA
Via Cerva 28, Milan, Italy
Tel: +39 2 7600 9272
CH: L.J. Celesia 102

GEA AG
Dorstener Strasse 484, 44809 Bochum,
Germany
Tel: +49 2 34 980-0
Fax: +49 234 98 10 53
CH: O. Happel, *CE:* V. Hannemann 106

GIB SA
rue Neuve 111, 1000 Brussels, Belgium
CH: P. Scohier, D. du Monceau,
D: Count D. du Monceau de Bergendal 101

GIM-Generale Industrie Metallurgiche SpA
Borgo Pinti 97/99, Florence, Italy
Tel: +39 55 49741
Fax: +39 55 247067
CH: L. Orlando 103

GKN PLC
PO Box 55, Ipsley House, Ipsley
Church Lane, Redditch,
Worcestershire, B98 0TL
Tel: 01527 517715
Fax: 01527 517700
CH: Sir David Lees,
FD: D.J. Turner 44, 97

GTE Corpn
One Stamford Forum, Stamford,
Connecticut, 06904, USA
Tel: +1 203 965-2000
CH: C.R. Lee 13, 110

GTM-Entrepose
61 avenue Jules Quentin, 92000
Nanterre, France
Tel: +33 1 46 95 76 93
Fax: +33 1 46 95 75 75
CH: A. Jarrosson 99

Galeries Lafayette
40 boulevard Haussmann, Paris 9e, France
CH: M. Heilbronn, G. Meyer 102

Gallaher Ltd
Members Hill, Brooklands Road,
Weybridge, Surrey, KT13 0QU
Tel: 01932 859777
Fax: 01932 849119
CH: P.M. Wilson 45, 101

Gambro AB
Magistratsvagen 16, PO Box 10101,
220 10 Lund, Sweden
Tel: +46 46 16 90 00
Fax: +46 46 16 96 96
P: B. Lindqvist, *CH:* M. Lilius 105

Gan Minster Insurance Co. Ltd
Minster House, Arthur Street, London,
EC4R 9BJ
Tel: 0171 623 5280
Fax: 0171 623 5930
CH: A.P.D. Lancaster 54

Gan [Ste Centrale du]
2 rue Pillet-Will,
75448 Paris Cedex 09, France
Tel: +33 1 42 47 60 26
Fax: +33 1 42 47 58 65
CH: J.-J. Bonnaud, *JMD:* J.-J. Bonnaud,
G. de Chavanne 54, 93

Gartmore Emerging Pacific Investment Trust PLC
Gartmore House, 16-18 Monument
Street, London, EC3R 8AJ
Tel: 0171 782 2000/623 12
Fax: 0171 782 2075
CH: J.G. Curtis 55

Gartmore Shared Equity Trust PLC
Gartmore House, 16-18 Monument
Street, London, EC3R 8AJ
Tel: 0171 782 2000/623 12
Fax: 0171 782 2075
CH: R.N.A. Wood 56

Gas Natural SDG SA
Avenida Portal de l'Angel 22, 08002
Barcelona, Spain
Tel: +34 3 402 51 00
Fax: +34 3 402 58 70
CH: P. Duran Farell,
MD: J. Badosa Pages 99

Gaymer Group Europe Ltd (The)
Whitchurch Lane, Bristol, BS14 0JZ
Tel: 0127 5836100
Fax: 0127 836726
CH: M. Dowdall 59

Gaz de France
23 Philibert-Delorme, 75840 Paris
cedex 17, France
Tel: +33 1 47 54 29 05
CH: L. Le Floch-Prigent, P. Gadonneix 93

Geest PLC
White House Chambers, Spalding,
Lincs, PE11 2AL
Tel: 01775 761111
Fax: 01775 710445
CH: M. Dowdall, *CE:* D.A. Sugden 52

Gemina-Generale Mobiliare Interessenze Azionarie SpA
Via F. Turati 16/18, 20121 Milan, Italy
Tel: +39 2 63 791
Fax: +39 2 6379662
CH: G. Pesenti, *MD:* F. Vitali 101

General Accident PLC
Pitheavlis, Perth, Scotland, PH2 0NH
Tel: 01738 21202
Fax: 01738 21843
CH: The Rt Hon The Earl of Airlie,
CE: W.N. Robertson 31, 40, 43, 94

General Cable PLC
37 Old Queen Street, London, SW1H 9JA
Tel: 0171 393 2828
Fax: 0171 393 2800
CH: Sir Anthony Brian Cleaver,
MD: P.X. Galteau,
FD: D.J. Miller 51, 75

General Consolidated Investment Trust PLC
49 Hay's Mews, London, W1X 7RT
Tel: 0171 409 3419
Fax: 0171 493 7229
CH: Sir Mark Thomson 55

General Electric Co. (USA CO)
3135 Easton Turnpike, Fairfield,
Connecticut, 06431, USA
Tel: +1 203 373-2211
CH: J.F. Welch Jr 13, 110

General Electric Company PLC (The)
1 Stanhope Gate, London, W1A 1EH
Tel: 0171 493 8484
Fax: 0171 493 1974
CH: The Rt Hon Lord Prior,
MD: Lord Weinstock,
FD: D.B. Newlands 23, 40, 42, 48, 64, 88, 89, 92, 108

General Foods Ltd
Banbury, Oxfordshire, OX16 7QU
Tel: 01295 4433
Fax: 01295 59018
No officers designated 49

General Motors Corpn
3044 West Grand Boulevard, Detroit,
Michigan, 48202-3091, USA
Tel:
P: J.F. Smith Jr, *CH:* J.G. Smale 13, 110

Generale de Banque SA
Montagne du Parc 3, 1000 Brussels,
Belgium
Tel: +32 2 565 11 11
Fax: +32 2 565 42 22
CH: P.-E. Janssen, F. Chaffart,
JMD: F. Chaffart, A. Dirckx,
M.-Y. Blanpain, P. Catteau,
J.-J. Verdickt, A. Bergen, J. Tack 102

Generale de Belgique [Ste]
Rue Royale 30, 1000 Brussels,
Belgium
Tel: +32 2 507 02 11
Fax: +32 2 512 18 95
CH: E. Davignon, M. Lippens,
MD: G. Mestrallet 64, 92

Generali SpA [Assicurazioni]
Piazza Duca degli Abruzzi 2, 34132
Trieste, Italy
Tel: +39 40 67 11
Fax: +39 67 11 600
CH: E. Randone, A. Bernheim,
JMD: E. Coppola di Canzano, G. Gutty 89, 92

Gerrard & National Holdings PLC
33 Lombard Street, London,
EC3V 9BQ
Tel: 0171 623 9981
Fax: 0171 623 6173
CH: R.B. Williamson,
JMD: D.A. Brayshaw, A.S.R. Jones,
FD: R.J. Elkington 54

Gestetner Holdings PLC
66 Chiltern Street, London, W1M 2AP
Tel: 0171 465 1000
Fax: 0171 224 5742
CH: D. Thompson, *CE:* G. Melgaard,
FD: S. King 48, 108

Gevaert SA
Septestraat 27, 2640 Mortsel, Antwerp,
Belgium
Tel: +32 3 443 02 11
Fax: +32 3 440 04 78
CH: A. Leysen, *MD:* M. Francken 105

Gillette Industries PLC
Gillette Corner, Great West Road,
Isleworth, Middlesex, TW7 5NP
Tel: 0181 560 1224
Fax: 0181 847 6165
No officers designated 50

Gist-Brocades NV [Koninklijke]
Wateringseweg 1, 2611 XT Delft,
The Netherlands
Tel: +31 15-799111
CH: Drs G. van Schaik 104

Glaverbel SA
Chaussee de la Hulpe 166,
1170 Brussels, Belgium
Tel: +32 2 674 31 11
Fax: +32 2 672 44 62
CH: Y. Furukawa, L. Willame 101

Glaxo Wellcome PLC
Lansdowne House, Berkeley Square,
London, W1X 6BQ
Tel: 0171 493 4060
Fax: 0171 408 0228
CH: Sir Colin Corness,
FD: J.D. Coombe 14, 19, 40, 42, 86, 88, 89, 93

Gleeson [MJ] Group PLC
Haredon House, London Road, North
Cheam, Surrey, SM3 9BS
Tel: 0181 644 4321

Glynwed - Hazlewood

Fax: 0181 641 6110
CH: D.J. Gleeson, FD: C.W. McLellan   57

Glynwed International PLC
Headland House, New Coventry Road, Sheldon, Birmingham, B26 3AZ
Tel: 0121 742 2366
Fax: 0121 742 0403
CH: G. Davies, CE: B. Ralph,
FD: D.L. Milne   49

Goal Petroleum PLC
1 James Street, London, W1M 5HY
Tel: 0171 499 6060
Fax: 0171 491 3025
CH: R. Bexon, MD: D. Ritchie,
FD: K. Waters   54

Golden West Financial Corpn
1901 Harrison Street, Oakland, California, 94612, USA
CH: H.M. Sandler,
Marion O. Sandler   111

Goldsborough Healthcare PLC
Bridge House, Outwood Lane, Horsforth, Leeds, LS18 4UP
Tel: 0113 2591177
Fax: 0113 2390332
CH: Sir Brian Hill, CE: G. Smith,
FD: G.R. Stevens   59

Goldschmidt [Th.] AG
Goldschmidtstrasse 100, 45127 Essen, Germany
Tel: +49 201 173 23 65
Fax: +49 201 173 18 38
CH: G. Rossmy, H.-J. Kollmeier   109

Goode Durrant PLC
22 Buckingham Street, London, WC2N 6PU
Tel: 0171 782 0010
Fax: 0171 782 0995
CH: D.J. Kingsbury, CE: F.M. Waring,
FD: D.S. Thompson   57

Goodman Fielder Ltd
Grosvenor Place, Level 42, 225 George Street, Sydney, New South Wales, 2000, Australia
Tel: +61 02 258 4000
Fax: +61 02 251 5839
CH: D.S. Clarke, N.C. Lister   115

Goodyear Great Britain Ltd
Bushbury, Wolverhampton, West Midlands, WV10 6DH
Tel: 01902 22321
Fax: 01902 327562
CH: W.B. Hirsch, FD: R.M. Archer   52

Gotthard Bank
Viale S. Franscini 8, 6901 Lugano, Switzerland
Tel: +41 91 28 11 11
Fax: +41 91 23 94 87
P: L. Cereghetti, CH: C. Generali   103

Govett & Co. Ltd
Minden House, 6 Minden Place, St Helier, Jersey JE2 4WQ, Channel Islands
Tel: 01534 38578
Fax: 01534 26997
CH: A.I. Trueger   55

Govett Oriental Investment Trust PLC
Shackleton House, 4 Battle Bridge Lane, London, SE1 2HR
Tel: 0171 378 7979
Fax: 0171 638 3468
CH: M.R. Cornwall-Jones   41, 45, 101

Govett Strategic Investment Trust PLC
Shackleton House, 4 Battle Bridge Lane, London, SE1 2HR
Tel: 0171 378 7979
Fax: 0171 638 3468
No officers designated   41, 48, 108

Graham Group PLC
96 Leeds Road, Huddersfield, HD1 4RH
Tel: 01484 537366
Fax: 01484 430420
CH: G. Yardley, CE: I. Mills, FD: R. Elsmore   53

Grainger Trust PLC
Chaucer Buildings, 57 Grainger Street, Newcastle upon Tyne, NE1 5JE
Tel: 0191 261 1819
Fax: 0191 232 7874

CH: R.H. Dickinson,
MD: S. Dickinson   53

Grampian Holdings PLC
Stag House, Castlebank Street, Glasgow, Lanarkshire, G11 6DY
Tel: 0141 357 2000
Fax: 0141 334 8709
CH: W.Y. Hughes,
FD: D.C. McGibbon   60

Granada Group PLC
36 Golden Square, London, W1R 4AH
Tel: 0171 734 8080
Fax: 0171 494 2893
CH: A. Bernstein, CE: G. Robinson,
FD: H. Staunton   44, 99

Grand Metropolitan PLC
20 St James's Square, London, SW1Y 4RR
Tel: 0171 321 6000
Fax: 0171 321 6001
CH: Lord Sheppard, CE: G.J. Bull,
FD: G.M.N. Corbett   14, 18, 40, 42, 83, 89, 91

Graningeverkens AB
PO Box 7602, 103 94 Stockholm, Sweden
Tel: +46 8 614 48 30
Fax: +46 8 614 48 40
CH: L.-O. Hakansson,
MD: B. Kallstrand   109

Grant [William] & Sons Ltd
The Glenfiddich Distillery, Dufftown, Banffshire
Tel: 01340 820000
CH: A.G. Gordon, MD: G.G. Gordon   52

Great Eagle Holdings Ltd
Cedar House, 41 Cedar Avenue, Hamilton HM12, Bermuda
CH: Lo Ying Shek   114

Great Portland Estates PLC
Knighton House, 56 Mortimer Street, London, W1N 8BD
Tel: 0171 580 3040
Fax: 0171 631 5169
CH: R. Peskin, FD: J Whiteley   44, 98

Great Universal Stores PLC (The)
Universal House, Devonshire Street, Manchester, M60 1XA
Tel: 0161 273 8282
Fax: 0161 277 4056
CH: The Rt Hon Lord Wolfson of Marylebone   24, 40, 42, 93

Greenalls Group PLC (The)
Wilderspool House, Greenalls Avenue, Warrington, WA4 6RH
Tel: 01925 51234
Fax: 01925 413137
CH: A.G. Thomas,
MD: The Hon P.G. Greenall,
FD: A.G. Rothwell   44, 98

Greene King PLC
Westgate Brewery, Bury St Edmunds, Suffolk, IP33 1QT
Tel: 01284 763222
Fax: 01284 706502
CH: D. McCall, CE: T.J.W. Bridge,
FD: M.J. Shallow   48, 109

Greycoat PLC
9 Savoy Street, London, WC2E 7EG
Tel: 0171 379 1000
Fax: 0171 379 8717
CH: M.E. Beckett, MD: P.A. Thornton,
FD: M.A. Poole   14, 47, 107

Grosskraftwerk Mannheim AG
Aufeldstrasse 23, 68199 Mannheim, Germany
Tel: +49 6 21 86 80
Fax: +49 6 21 868 4410
CH: G. Widder   104

Groupe Andre SA
28 rue de Flandre, 75019 Paris, France
Tel: +33 1 44 72 30 01
Fax: +33 1 40 05 09 37
CH: J.-L. Descours, JMD: R. Cottard, J.-P. Rivat   105

Groupe Bruxelles Lambert SA
24 avenue Marnix, 1050 Brussels, Belgium
Tel: +32 2 547 21 11
Fax: +32 2 547 22 85
CH: A. Frere, JMD: G. Frere,
T. de Rudder, D. Bellens   95

Groupe Victoire [Cie Financiere du]
52 rue de la Victoire, 75009 Paris, France
Tel: +33 1 42 80 75 75
Fax: +33 1 42 80 70 57
CH: R. Gachet, P. Chareyre, G. Worms   22, 64, 94

Groupe de la Cite
20, avenue Hoche, 75008 Paris, France
Tel: +33 1 44 95 56 00
CH: C. Bregou   106

Grundig AG
Kurgartenstrasse 37, 90762 Furth/Bayern, Germany
Tel: +49 911 70 30
Fax: +49 911 70 96 87
CH: Dr C. Schwarz-Schilling,
P.D. Harmsen   100

Guaranteed Export Finance Corporation PLC
Fourth Floor, One Aldgate, London, EC3N 1RE
Tel: 0171 283 7101
Fax: 0171 621 2598
No officers designated   39, 43, 96

Guardian Media Group PLC
164 Deansgate, Manchester, M60 2RR
Tel: 0161 832 7200
Fax: 0161 832 5351
CH: H.J. Roche   52

Guardian Royal Exchange PLC
Royal Exchange, London, EC3V 3LS
Tel: 0171 283 7101
Fax: 0171 283 3587
CH: Lord Hambro,
CE: J.V.H. Robins   38, 43, 96

Guinness PLC
39 Portman Square, London, W1H 0EE
Tel: 0171 486 0288
Fax: 0171 486 0288
CH: A.A. Greener   20, 40, 42, 77, 88, 89, 92

Guinness Peat Group PLC
2nd Floor, 21-26 Garlick Hill, London, EC4V 2AU
Tel: 0171 236 0336
Fax: 0171 329 8870
CH: Sir Ron Brierley   55

Gullspangs Kraft AB
Stubbengatan 2, 701 16 Orebro, Sweden
Tel: +46 19 21 81 00
Fax: +46 19 26 24 23
CH: M. Storch, MD: O.G. Wikstrom   104

HCG Lloyd's Investment Trust PLC
30 Queen Anne's Gate, London, SW1H 9AL
Tel: 0171 222 2020
Fax: 0171 222 1823
CH: J.A. Morrell   60

HEW-Hamburgische Electricitats-Werke AG
Uberseering 12, 22297 Hamburg, Germany
Tel: +49 40 639 60
Fax: +49 40 30 68
CH: Senator Dr F. Vahrenholt,
M. Timm   97

HSBC Holdings PLC
10 Lower Thames Street, London, EC3R 6AE
Tel: 0171 260 0500
Fax: 0171 260 0501
CH: Sir William Purves,
CE: J.R.H. Bond, FD: R. Delbridge   14, 15, 40, 42, 62, 67, 88, 90

HTR Japanese Smaller Companies Trust PLC
3 Finsbury Avenue, London, EC2M 2PA
Tel: 0171 638 5757
Fax: 0171 377 5742
CH: A.D. Loehnis   54

Hafslund Nycomed AS
Slemdalsveien 37, PO Box 5010 Majorstua, 0301 Oslo, Norway
Tel: +47 2296 3400
Fax: +47 2296 3600
P: S. Aaser, CH: T. Mikalsen   100

Hagemeyer NV
Rijksweg 69, 1411 GE Naarden, The Netherlands
Tel: +31 2159 57611
Fax: +31 2159 47850
CH: F.O.J. Sickinghe, A.H. Land   107

Haindl'sche [G.] Papierfabriken KGaA
Georg-Haindl-Strasse 5, 86153 Augsburg, Germany
Tel: +49 821 31 09-0
Fax: +49 821 3 96 79
CH: G. Becker, CE: Dr C. Haindl   100

Halifax Building Society
Trinity Road, Halifax, West Yorkshire, HX1 2RG
Tel: 01422 333333
Fax: 01422 333000
CH: H.J. Foulds, CE: J.M. Blackburn,
FD: G.J. Folwell   14, 20, 40, 42,44, 88, 92, 97

Hall Engineering (Holdings) PLC
Harlescott Lane, Shrewsbury, SY1 3AS
Tel: 01743 235541
Fax: 01743 235010
CH: R.N.C. Hall, MD: J. Sword,
FD: A.M. Smith   60

Halliburton Holdings Ltd
150 The Broadway, Wimbledon, London, SW19
Tel: 0181 544 5000
Fax: 0181 544 6655
No officers designated   48, 109

Halma PLC
Misbourne Court, Rectory Way, Amersham, Buckinghamshire, HP7 0DE
Tel: 01494 721111
Fax: 01494 728032
CH: D.S. Barber, CE: D.S. Barber   61

Hambro Countrywide PLC
Queensgate, 1 Myrtle Road, Brentwood, Essex, CM14 5EG
Tel: 01277 264466
Fax: 01277 217916/215405
CH: C.H. Sporborg, MD: H.D. Hill,
FD: M.C. Nower   57

Hambros PLC
41 Tower Hill, London, EC3N 4HA
Tel: 0171 480 5000
Fax: 0171 702 4424
CH: The Rt Hon the Lord Hambro,
FD: C.B. Tilley   44, 99

Hammerson PLC
100 Park Lane, London, W1Y 4AR
Tel: 0171 629 9494
Fax: 0171 629 0498
CH: G. Maitland Smith,
CE: R.R. Spinney,
FD: S.R. Melliss   39, 43, 96

Hang Lung Development Co Ltd
25th Floor, Hanglung Centre, 2-20 Paterson St, Causeway Bay, Hong Kong
Tel: +852 7904111
CH: Ronnie C. Chan,
MD: Nelson Wai Leung Yuen   114

Hang Seng Bank Ltd
83 Des Voeux Road, Central, Hong Kong
Tel: +852 2 8255111
Fax: +852 2 8459301
CH: Dr Ho S.H., Sir Lee Quo-Wei   114

Haniel [Franz] & Cie GmbH
Franz-Haniel-Platz 1, 47119 Duisburg, Germany
Tel: +49 203-806-0
Fax: +49 203-806-204
CH: J.v. Haeften, Dr D. Schadt   52, 94

Hanil Bank
130, 2-Ga Namaemonno, Chung-Gu, Seoul, Korea
Tel: +82 2 771 2000
Fax: +82 2 775 3346
P: Yoon Soun Jung, JMD: Chung Chang Soon, Lee Kwan Woo, Lee Yo Sup, Kim Hai Do, Oh Kwang Hyung, Lee Jeung Seok, Huh Hong, Choi Dong Yeol, Chang Ki Pal, Shin Dong Hyuck, Kim Seong Ho   115

Hanover Acceptances Ltd
16 Hans Road, London, SW3 1RS
Tel: 0171 581 1477
Fax: 0171 589 3542
CH: M.S. Gorvy   59

Hanson PLC
1 Grosvenor Place, London, SW1X 7JH
Tel: 0171 245 1245
Fax: 0171 235 3455
CH: Lord Hanson, FD: A. Dougal   14, 16, 40, 42, 70, 88, 89, 90

Hanwa Co. Ltd
New Hanwa Building, 13-10 Tsukiji 1-chome, Chuo-ku, Osaka 541, Japan
Tel: +81 3 544 2171
Fax: +81 3 544 2093
P: Shuji Kita, JMD: Kenji Numata, Nobuyasu Iwahashi, Kenzo Hatoko, Masami Inoue, Takeyuki Okaue, Hiroshi Shintani, Minoru Kifuku, Shinji Takabayashi, Mitsuyuki Nakabayashi   113

Hanwha Chemical Corpn
1 Changgyo-Dong, Chung-Gu, Seoul, Korea
Tel: +82 2 729 2000
Fax: +82 2 270 2999
P: Park Won Bae, JMD: Ohu Soo Yong, Jin Sung Ik, Kim Taek Yong, Oh Whi Myung, Lee Kwan Yong, Hong Dae Sik, Kang Jun Seon, Choi Dong Kyu, Choi Nam Chul, Lee Eun Woo, Park Yong Woo, Jung Kwang Hong   115

Hapag-Lloyd AG
Ballindamm 25, 20095 Hamburg, Germany
Tel: +49 40 30 01-0
CH: Dr hc A. Leysen, B. Wrede   103

Hardy Oil & Gas PLC
2 Chalkhill Road, London, W6 8DW
Tel: 0181 741 7373
Fax: 0181 741 7172
CH: D.R.P. Baker, CE: J.A. Walmsley,
MD: Dr R.J.R. Cairns,
FD: A.S. Whyatt   48, 109

Hardys & Hansons PLC
Kimberley Brewery, Nottingham, NG16 2NS
Tel: 0115 938 3611
Fax: 0115 945 9055
CH: R.W.D. Hanson   58

Harrisons & Crosfield PLC
One Great Tower Street, London, EC3R 5AH
Tel: 0171 711 1400
Fax: 0171 711 1401
CH: G.W. Paul, CE: W.J. Turcan,
FD: M.H.F. Anderson   45, 100

Hartstone Group PLC (The)
1 Saint Andrew's Court, Wellington Street, Thame, Oxfordshire, OX9 3GG
Tel: 01844 261544
Fax: 01844 261560
CH: S.C. Dowling, CE: J. Hunter,
FD: S.E. Oakley   54

Hartwell Holdings Ltd
1st Floor, Seacourt Tower, West Way, Botley, Oxford, OX2 OJG
Tel: 01865 204300
Fax: 01264 204500
No officers designated   52

Harwanne- Cie de participations industrielles et financieres SA
25 boulevard Helvetique, 1207 Geneva, Switzerland
Tel: +41 22 786 98 60
Fax: +41 22 786 98 70
CH: B. Siret   109

Haslemere Estates PLC
4 Carlos Place, Mayfair, London, W1Y 5AE
Tel: 0171 629 1105
Fax: 0171 493 5419
CH: P.R. van Romunde   48

Havas
136 avenue Charles-de-Gaulle, 92552 Neuilly-sur-Seine, France
Tel: +33 1 47 47 30 00
Fax: +33 1 47 47 32 23
CH: P. Dauzier   96

Hays PLC
Hays House, Millmead, Guildford, Surrey, GU2 5HJ
Tel: 01483 302203
Fax: 01483 300388
CH: R.E. Frost, MD: J.A. Napier   51

Hazlewood Foods PLC
Rowditch, Derby, DE1 1NB
Tel: 01332 295295
Fax: 01332 292300
CH: P.E. Barr, CE: J. Simons,
FD: K.M. Higginson   48, 109

127

Heath [C.E.] PLC
133 Houndsditch, London, EC3A 7AH
Tel: 0171 234 4000
Fax: 0171 234 4111
CH: M. Kier, *CE:* P.E. Presland,
MD: J.G. Mackenzie Green,
FD: P.J. Hughes 53

Heidelberger Druckmaschinen AG
Kurfursten-Anlage 52-60, 69115
Heidelberg, Germany
Tel: +49 62 21 92-0
Fax: +49 62 21 92 69 99
CH: F.J. Schmitt, Dr H. Dosch 98

Heidelberger Zement AG
Berliner Strasse 6, 69120 Heidelberg,
Germany
Tel: +49 62 21 4 81-0
Fax: +49 62 21 481 554
CH: Dr rer pol W. Roller,
Dipl-Kfm P. Schuhmacher 98

Heineken Holding
2e Weteringplantsoen 5, 1017 ZD
Amsterdam, The Netherlands
Tel: +31 20 622 1152
Fax: +31 20 625 2213
No officers designated 29, 94

Heinz [H.J.] Co Ltd
Hayes Park, Hayes, Middlesex, UB4 8AL
Tel: 0181 573 7757
Fax: 0181 848 2325
No officers designated 49

Helical Bar PLC
11-15 Farm Street, London, W1X 7RD
Tel: 0171 629 0113
Fax: 0171 408 1666
CH: J.P. Southwell, *MD:* M.E. Slade ,
FD: N.G. McNair Scott 56

Hemingway Properties PLC
21 Devonshire Street, London, WIN 2EP
Tel: 0171 487 3737
Fax: 0171 935 1460
CH: S. Yassukovich, *CE:* M.L. Goldhill,
FD: A.S. Browne 56

Henderson Investment Ltd
6th Floor, World-Wide House, 19 Des
Voeux Road Central, Hong Kong
Tel: +852 5-251033
CH: Dr Lee Shau Kee 115

Henderson Land Development Co. Ltd
6th Floor, World-Wide House,
19 Des Voeux Road Central, Hong Kong
Tel: +852 5-251033
CH: Dr Lee Shau Kee 114

Henkel KGaA
Postfach 11 00, Henkelstrasse 67,
40589 Dusseldorf, Germany
Tel: +49 211 7 97-0
Fax: +49 211 7 98-40 08
CH: A. Woeste, Dr H.-D. Winkhaus 94

Henlys Group PLC
53 Theobald Street, Borehamwood,
Hertfordshire, WD6 4RT
Tel: 0181 207 3664
Fax: 0181 905 1769
CH: M.E. Doherty, *CE:* R.W. Wood,
MD: C.W. Prarfitt, *FD:* B.A.C. Chivers 57

Hennes & Mauritz [H & M] AB
Jakobsbergsgatan 17, PO Box 1421,
111 84 Stockholm, Sweden
Tel: +46 8 796 55 00
CH: S. Wikander, *CE:* S. Persson 108

Hepworth PLC
Tapton Park Road, Sheffield, S10 3FS
Tel: 0114 230 6599
Fax: 0114 230 8642
CH: Prof Sir Roland Smith,
CE: J.D. Carter, *FD:* R.E. Lambourne 49

Heraeus Holding GmbH
Postfach 1561, 63405 Hanau, Germany
Tel: +49 61 81 351
Fax: +49 61 81 33591
CH: Dr G. Sassmannshausen,
Dr J. Heraeus 103

Herald Investment Trust PLC
99 Charterhouse Street, London,
EC1M 6HR
CH: M. Boase 60

Herlitz AG
Berliner Strasse 27, 13507 Berlin,
Germany
Tel: +49 30 4393-0
CH: G. Herlitz, Dr P. Herlitz 106

Hero
Niederlenzer Kirchweg 3,
5600 Lenzburg, Switzerland
Tel: +41 64 505 204
Fax: +41 64 505 529
CH: R. Stump 108

Hertie Waren-Und Kaufhaus GmbH
Herriotstrasse 4, 60528 Frankfurt am
Main, Germany
Tel: +49 69 66 81 1
Fax: +49 69 66 81 2545
CH: Dr G. Sandler, J. Kruger

Hertz (U.K.) Ltd
Radnor House, 1272 London Road,
Norbury, London, SW16 4XW
Tel: 0181 679 1777
Fax: 0181 679 0181
CH: J.G. Astrand 53

Hewden Stuart PLC
135 Buchanan Street, Glasgow, G1 2JA
Tel: 0141 221 7331
Fax: 0141 248 5104
CH: A.F. Findlay 52

Hewlett-Packard Co.
3000 Hanover Street, Palo Alto,
California, 94304, USA
Tel: +1 415 857-1501
CH: L.E. Platt 111

Hewlett-Packard Ltd
Cain Road, Bracknell, Berkshire,
RG12 1HN
Tel: 01344 360000
Fax: 01344 363344
CH: D.A. Baldwin, *MD:* J.T. Golding 48, 109,

Heywood Williams Group PLC
Waverley, Edgerton Road,
Huddersfield, West Yorkshire, HD3 3AR
Tel: 01484 435477
Fax: 01484 547511
CH: R.E. Hinchliffe, *FD:* T. Martin 53

Hickson International PLC
Wheldon Road, Castleford, West
Yorkshire, WF10 2JT
Tel: 01977 556565
Fax: 01977 550910
CH: J. Hann, *CE:* D.J. Kerrison,
FD: J. Court 50

Hidroelectrica del Cantabrico SA
Plaza de la Gesta 2, 33007 Oviedo, Spain
Tel: +34 85 230300
Fax: +34 85 253787
CH: I. Herrero Garralda,
M. Gonzalez del Valle y Herrero 102

Higgs and Hill PLC
Crown House, Kingston Road,
New Malden, Surrey, KT3 3ST
Tel: 0181 942 8921
Fax: 0181 949 9280
CH: G. Duncan, *CE:* J.A. Theakston,
FD: C.R.H. Archer 60

Hillsdown Holdings PLC
Hillsdown House, 32 Hampstead High
Street, London, NW3 1QD
Tel: 0171 794 0677
Fax: 0171 435 1355
CH: Sir John Nott, *CE:* D.A. Newton,
FD: R.J. Mackie 44, 97

Hilti AG
9494 Schaan, Liechtenstein
Tel: +41 75 236 27 10
Fax: +41 75 236 29 65
CH: M. Hilti, Dr P. Baschera 99

Hitachi Europe Ltd
Whitebrook Park, Lower Cookham
Road, Maidenhead, Berkshire, SL6 8YA
Tel: 01628 585000
Fax: 01628 778322
No officers designated 50

Hitachi Ltd
6, Kanda-Suragadai 4-chome,
Chiyoda-ku, Tokyo 101, Japan
Tel: +81 3 3258 1111
Fax: +81 3 3258 5480
P: Tsutomu Kanai, *CH:* Katsushige
Mita, *JMD:* Yasutsugu Takeda,
Asahiko Isobe, Takashi Nonouchi,
Tadahiko Shinohara, Tsuneo Tanaka,
Hiroshi Kuwahara, Takashi Kashiwagi,
Shiro Kawate, Masao Hamada, Takeo
Takemoto, Kunio Hamada, Yukio
Kawamoto, Etsuhiko Shoyama, Tsugio
Makimoto, Yoshiki Yagi, Shigemichi
Matsuka 13, 112

Hoare Govett Smaller Companies Index Investment Trust PLC (The)
4 Broadgate, London, EC2M 7LE
Tel: 0171-374 1666
Fax: 0171-374 4397
CH: P.R. Meinertzhagen 57

Hobson PLC
James Hse, 1 Babmaes Street, London,
SW1Y 6HD
Tel: 0171 839 3355
Fax: 0171 539 4424
CH: D.C. Wigglesworth,
CE: A.J. Regan, *FD:* P.J. Hallett 59

Hochtief AG vorm. Gebr. Helfmann
Rellinghauser Strasse 53-57,
45128 Essen, Germany
Tel: +49 201 824-0
Fax: +49 201 824-27 77
CH: Dr D. Kuhnt,
Dr-Ing H.-P. Keitel 96

Hoechst AG
PO Box 80 03 20, 65926 Frankfurt am
Main, Germany
Tel: +49 69 3051
Fax: +49 69 30 36 65
CH: R. Sammet, E. Bouillon,
J. Dormann 72, 88, 90

Hoegh [Leif] & Co. AS
Wergelandsveien 7, PO Box 2596-Solli,
0203 Oslo, Norway
Tel: +47 22 86 97 00
Fax: +47 22 20 14 08
P: T.J. Guttormsen, *CH:* W. Hoegh 108

Hogg Robinson PLC
Concorde House, 165 Church Street
East, Woking, Surrey, GU21 1HF
Tel: 01483 730311
Fax: 01483 769099
CH: B.R. Perry, *FD:* C.C. Brown 59

Hokkaido Electric Power Co. Inc.
2, Higashi 1-chome, Ohdori, Chou-ku,
Sapporo 060, Japan
Tel: +81 11 251 1111
P: Kazuo Toda, *CH:* Tomoo Nakano,
JMD: Masayoshi Annen, Fumio Murata,
Shoichi Murai, Michio Nakayama,
Makoto Higuchi, Kazuo Yoshida,
Yoshio Kajiyama, Kan Tsuneta 113

Hokuriku Electric Power Co. Inc.
15-1 Ushijima, Toyama, 930 Japan
Tel: +81 764 41 2511
P: Keizo Yamada, *CH:* Masao Tani,
JMD: Muneyuki Azuma, Teruo
Nakashima, Katsutoshi Shinmyo,
Hiroto Yoshino 112

Holderbank Financiere Glaris SA
8750 Glaris, Switzerland
Tel: +41 58 61 34 94
Fax: +41 55 23 86 99/87 1
CH: T. Schmidheiny,
MD: Dr M.D. Amstutz 92

Hollandsche Beton Groep NV [HBG]
Generaal Spoorlaan 489,
2285 TA Rijswijk, The Netherlands
Tel: +31 70 3153911
Fax: +31 70 3152408
CH: J.P. Erbe, N. de Ronde Bresser 108

Holliday Chemical Holdings PLC
Deighton Works, Leeds Road,
Huddersfield, HD2 1UH
Tel: 01484 421841
Fax: 01484 515328
CH: M.J. Peagram, *CE:* H. Donaldson,
FD: J.A. Harnett 58

Holzmann [Philipp] AG
Taunusanlage 1, 60299 Frankfurt am
Main, Germany
Tel: +49 69 262-1
Fax: +49 69 262 433
CH: H. Becker, L. Mayer 96

Home Housing Association Ltd
Ridley House, Regent Centre, Gosforth,
Newcastle Upon Tyne, NE3 3JE
Tel: 0191 285 0311
Fax: 0191 284 0634
CH: J.H.V. Sutcliffe 46, 105

Honda Motor Co. Ltd
1-1 Minami-Aoyama 2-chome,
Minato-ku, Tokyo 107, Japan
Tel: +81 3 3423 1111
Fax: +81 3 3423 0511
P: Nobuhiko Kawamoto, *JMD:*
Nobuyuki Otsuka, Masaru Miyata,
Koichi Amemiya, Masaki Iwai,
Hiroyuki Shimojima, Takashi Matsuda,
Koji Nagata, Takeshi Yamada,
Tomohiko Nakano, Makoto Shino,
Riku Iwai 112

Honda Motor Europe Ltd
Caversham Bridge House, Waterman
Place, Berkshire, RG1 8DN
Tel: 01734 566399
Fax: 01734 554772
CH: K. Ito (Japan) 47, 106

Honeywell Ltd
Honeywell House, Charles Square,
Bracknell, Berkshire, RG12 1EB
Tel: 01344 826000
Fax: 01344 416240
CH: D.A. Kennedy 56

Hong Kong Telecommunications Ltd
39th Floor, Hongkong Telecom Tower,
Taikoo Place, 979 King's Road,
Quarry Bay, Hong Kong
Tel: +852 888 2888
Fax: +852 877 8877
CH: The Rt Hon Lord Young of
Graffham, *CE:* Linus W L Cheung,
FD: David N Prince 115

Hongkong Electric Holdings Ltd
Electric House, 44 Kennedy Road,
Hong Kong
Tel: +852 5-8433111
CH: George Collin Magnus,
MD: Ewan Yee Lup-yuen 115

Hongkong and Shanghai Hotels Ltd (The)
8th Floor, St George's Building,
2 Ice House Street, Hong Kong
Tel: +852 5-249391
CH: The Hon Michael D. Kadoorie 115

Hoogovens - Koninklijke Nederlandsche Hoogovens en Staalfabrieken
PO Box 10000, 1970 CA IJmuiden,
The Netherlands
Tel: +31 2514 99111
Fax: +31 2510 97475
CH: J.H. Choufoer, M.C. van Veen 95

Hoops Ltd
3D Dundee Road, Slough, Berkshire,
SL1 4LG
Tel: 01753 693000
Fax: 01753 533172
No officers designated 49

Hopewell Holdings Ltd
64th Floor, Hopewell Centre,
183 Queen's Road East, Hong Kong
Tel: +852 5-284975
Fax: +852 5-8612068/86562
CH: Dr James Man-Hon Wu,
MD: Gordon Ying Sheung Wu 114

Horten AG
Am Albertussee 1, 40549 Dusseldorf,
Germany
Tel: +49 211 9570
Fax: +49 211 957 60
CH: W. Urban, L. Mandac 109

House of Fraser PLC
1 Howick Place, London, SW1 1BH
Tel: 0171 834 1515
Fax: 0171 828 2660
CH: B.D. McGowan,
MD: A.R. Jennings, *FD:* R.J. Scott 48, 108

Household International (U.K.) Ltd
North Street, Winkfield, Windsor,
Berkshire, SL4 4TD
Tel: 01344 890000
Fax: 01344 890014
No officers designated 47, 108

Houston Industries Inc.
Five Post Oak Park, 4400 Post Oak
Parkway, PO Box 4567, Houston,
Texas, 77210, USA
Tel: +1 713 629 3000
Fax: +1 713 629-3129
CH: D.D. Jordan 111

Howden Group PLC
Old Govan Road, Renfrew, PA4 8XJ
Tel: 0141 886 6711
CH: J.B.H. Jackson, *FD:* J. Hume 53

Huhtamaki Oy
Etelaranta 8, 00130 Helsinki, Finland
Tel: +358 0 708 8100
Fax: +358 0 660 622
P: T. Peltola, *CH:* A. Tarkka 93

Hunter Douglas NV
Blenchiweg 59, Curacao,
Netherlands Antilles
P: R. Sonnenberg 102

Hunting PLC
3 Cockspur Street, London, SW1Y 5BQ
Tel: 0171 321 0123
Fax: 0171 839 2072
CH: R.H. Hunting, *CE:* K.W. Miller,
FD: D.L. Clark 49

Huntingdon International Holdings PLC
Woolley Road, Alconbury, Huntingdon,
Cambridgeshire, PE18 6ES
Tel: 01480 890431
Fax: 01480 890693
CH: R.A. Pinnington, *CE:* C.F. Cliffe,
FD: C.F. Cliffe 55

Hurlimann Holding AG
Brandschenkestrasse 150, 8002 Zurich,
Switzerland
Tel: +41 1 288 26 26
Fax: +41 1 288 21 88
CH: Dr W. Hefti, T. Fehr,
MD: T. Fehr 108

Hutchison Whampoa Ltd
Hutchison House, 22nd Floor, Hong Kong
Tel: +852 25230161
Fax: +852 28100705
CH: Li Ka-shing,
MD: Canning K.N. Fok 114

Hydro-Quebec
75 Boulevard Rene-Levesque ouest,
Montreal, Quebec, H2Z 1A4, Canada
Tel: +1 800 363-7443
Fax: +1 514 289-3674
P: A. Couture, *CH:* R. Drouin 12, 13, 110

Hysan Development Co. Ltd
23rd Floor, Caroline Centre,
28 Yun Ping Road, Hong Kong
CH: Hon Chiu Lee 114

Hyundai Engineering & Construction
140-2 Kye Dong, Chongno-Gu,
Seoul, Korea
Tel: +82 2 746 1114
Fax: +82 2 743 8963
P: Lee Rai So, Kim Kwang Myung,
CH: Kim Jung Kook, *JMD:* Kim Jae
Young, Lee Eun Bang, Cha Dong Yel,
Rhim Gun Woo, Kim Choong Won,
Hong Woong Sun, Kim Chong Tae 115

Hyundai Motor Co.
140-2 Kye-Dong, Chongno-Gu,
Seoul, Korea
Tel: +82 2 764 1114
Fax: +82 2 741 0470
P: Chun Seong Won, *CH:* Chung Se
Young, *JMD:* Lee Seung Bok, Han
Sang Jun, Kwon Soo Muk, Lee Yoo Il,
Koo Hoi Moon, Hong Du Pyo, Jeong
Dal Ok, Chu Sin Il, Park Kwang Nam,
Kim Hyung Jun, Lee Bang Joo, Kim
Yang Soo, Kim Sang Chul, Weon
Jeong Nam, Kim Jong Il, Kim Won Il,
Tae Young Sik, Kim Dong Woo, Kim
Choe Won, Har Moon Young, Kim
Joong Sung, Jang Ji Suk, Kim Se Gil,
Kim Chung Yong 114

I&S Optimum Income Trust PLC
One Charlotte Square, Edinburgh,
EH2 4DZ
Tel: 0131 225 1357
Fax: 0131 225 2375
No officers designated 61

IBC Vehicles Ltd
PO Box 163, Kimpton Road, Luton,
Beds, LU2 0TY
Tel: 01582 422266
Fax: 01582 409123
No officers designated 58

IBM - KBB

IBM Deutschland GmbH
Ernst-Reuter-Platz 2, 10587 Berlin, Germany
Tel: +49 30 3115-0
Fax: +49 30 3115-14 47
CH: H-O. Henkel, E. Hug　　92

IBM United Kingdom Holdings Ltd
PO Box 41, North Harbour, Portsmouth, Hampshire, PO6 3AU
Tel: 01705 561000
Fax: 01705 388914
CH: N.J. Temple　　44, 97

ICA Handlarnas AB
Odengatan 69, PO Box 6187, 102 33 Stockholm, Sweden
Tel: +46 8 728 40 00
Fax: +46 8 34 31 74
P: R. Fahlin, *CH:* R.-E. Hjertberg　　101

ICB Shipping AB
Kungsgatan 17, PO Box 7007, 103 86 Stockholm, Sweden
Tel: +46 8 613 30 30
Fax: +46 8 613 99 09
P: O. Lorentzon, *CH:* C. Dybeck　　107

ICL PLC
ICL House, 1 High Street, Putney, London, SW15 1SW
Tel: 0181 788 7272
Fax: 0181 785 3936
CH: P.L. Bonfield,
FD: T.K. Todd　　47, 105

IFI-Istituto Finanziario Industriale SpA
Via Carlo Marenco 25, Turin, Italy
Tel: +39 11 65 67
CH: G. Agnelli,
MD: G. Galateri di Genola　　96

IKB Deutsche Industriebank AG
Karl-Theodor-Strasse 6, 40213 Dusseldorf, Germany
Tel: +49 211-8221-0
Fax: +49 211-8221-559
CH: D. Spethmann　　99

IKEA Ltd
21 Holborn Viaduct, London, EC1A 2DY
No officers designated　　58

IMI PLC
PO Box 216, Witton, Birmingham, B6 7BA
Tel: 0121 356 4848
Fax: 0121 356 3526
CH: Sir Eric Pountain, *CE:* G.J. Allen,
FD: A.L. Emson　　46, 104

INI - Instituto Nacional de Industria
Plaza del Marques de Salamanca 8, 28071 Madrid, Spain
Tel: +34 1 396 10 00
Fax: +34 1 564 18 77
CH: F.J. Salas Collantes　　70, 90

INVESCO PLC
11 Devonshire Square, London, EC2M 4YR
Tel: 0171 626 3434
Fax: 0171 623 3339
CH: C.W. Brady, *CE:* The Hon Michael Benson, N.M.M. Riddell,
FD: H.L. Harris Jr　　54

IRI-Istituto per la Ricostruzione Industriale
Via V.Veneto 89, 00187 Rome, Italy
Tel: +39 6 47271
Fax: +39 6 47272308
JMD: M. Tedeschi, R. Prodi,
JMD: E. Micheli, F. Simeoni　　12, 13, 62, 69, 90

ISS-International Service System AS
Kongevejen 195, 2840 Holte, Denmark
Tel: +45 45 41 08 11
Fax: +45 45 41 08 88
P: Andreassen, *CH:* A. Madsen,
JMD: P. Andreassen, S. Ipsen, W. Schmidt,
FD: J.W. Andersen, Lise Friis　　109

ITOCHU Corpn
5-1 Kita-Aoyama 2-chome, Minato-ku, Tokyo 107-77, Japan
Tel: +81 3 3497 2121
P: Minoru Murofushi, *CH:* Isao Yonekura, *JMD:* Toshio Shimada, Takashi Yamamura, Hideo Matsumura, Takeshi Ogata, Kanji Morisawa, Ichizo Kobayashi, Akihito Mori, Naohiko Takano, Masayoshi Fujiwara, Hiroyasu Tanaka, Joji Akizawa, Ichiro Kanade, Yasuhiro Miya, Uichiro Niwa, Toshio Komada, Noboru Nishikawa, Setzuzo Kasoka, Hirotsugu Maekawa, Koji Nojima, Seizo Takagi　　13, 112

ITT Corpn
1330 Avenue of the Americas, New York, New York, 10019-5490, USA
Tel: +1 212 258-1000
CH: R.V. Araskog　　68, 111

IWKA AG
Gartenstrasse 71, Postfach 34 09, 76135 Karlsruhe 1, Germany
Tel: +49 7 21 1 43-0
Fax: +49 7 21 1 43 243
CH: Dr H. Wolf, Dr W.H. Prellwitz 108

Iberdrola SA
Gardoqui 8, 48008 Bilbao, Spain
Tel: +34 4 415 08 57
CH: I. de Oriol Ybarra　　72, 90

Ibstock PLC
Lutterworth House, Lutterworth, Leicestershire, LE17 4PS
Tel: 01455 553071
Fax: 01455 553182
CH: C.F.N. Hope, *MD:* I.D. Maclellan,
FD: P.G. Aspden　　49

Iceland Group PLC
Second Avenue, Deeside Industrial Park, Deeside, Clywd, CH5 2NW
Tel: 01244 830100
Fax: 01244 814531
CH: M.C. Walker, *MD:* R.S. Kirk,
FD: J.B. Leigh　　48

Imetal SA
Tour Maine-Montparnasse, 33 avenue du Maine, 75755 Paris Cedex 15, France
Tel: +33 1 45 38 48 48
Fax: +33 1 45 38 74 78
CH: B. de Villemejane, R. Mitieus　　103

Immobiliere Phenix (La Cie)
10 rue du General Foy, 75008 Paris, France
Tel: +33 1 44 70 23 00
Fax: +33 1 44 70 26 97
CH: J.-M. Messier, *MD:* S. Richard　　97

Imperial Chemical Industries PLC
Imperial Chemical House, Millbank, London, SW1P 3JF
Tel: 0171 834 4444
Fax: 0171-834 2042
CH: Sir Ronald Hampel,
CE: C. Miller Smith, *FD:* A.G. Spall
　　14, 19, 28, 40, 42, 84, 91

Incentive AB
Hamngatan 2, 103 91 Stockholm, Sweden
Tel: +46 8 613 65 00
Fax: +46 8 611 28 30
P: M. Lilius, *CH:* A. Scharp,
MD: M. Lilius　　95

Inchcape PLC
St James's House, 23 King Street, London, SW1Y 6QY
Tel: 0171 321 0110
Fax: 0171 321 0604
CH: Sir David Plastow,
MD: P.E. Cushing,
FD: R.C. O'Donoghue　　44, 99

Inco Europe Ltd
5th Floor, Windsor House, 50 Victoria Street, London, SW1H 0XB
Tel: 0171 931 7733
Fax: 0171 931 0083
No officers designated　　51

Independent Insurance Group PLC
163 West George Street, Glasgow, G2 2JJ
Tel: 0141 2224521
Fax: 0141 2219660
CH: G.M. Ramsay, *CE:* M.J. Bright　57

Independent Newspapers PLC
1/2 Upper Hatch Street, Dublin 2, Ireland
Tel: +353 1 475 8432
Fax: +353 1 671 7863
CE: A.J.F. O'Reilly,
CE: L.P. Healy,
FD: J.J. Parkinson　　53, 106

Independent Television News Ltd
200 Grays Inn Road, London, WC1X 8XZ
Tel: 0171 833 3000
Fax: 0171 430 4028
CH: M.P. Green, *CE:* D.S. Gordon　55

Industrial Bank of Japan Ltd (The)
3-3 Marunouchi 1-chome, Chiyoda-ku, Tokyo 100, Japan
Tel: +81 3 3214 1111
Fax: +81 3 3213 6066
P: Yoh Kurosawa, *JMD:* Yasushi Kajiwara, Masaaki Sugishita, Kunio Seiki, Takayoshi Yoshinbashi, Yoshiyuki Fujisawa, Hiroshige Nishizawa, Isamu Koike, Yukio Hasegawa, Goro Higaki, Yoshiomi Matsumoto, Haruhiko Takenaka, Takeshi Kusakabe, Sadayoshi Nakamura, Kazumoto Sogo, Munekazu Samejima　　112

Industrivarden [AB]
Storgatan 10, PO Box 5403, 114 84 Stockholm, Sweden
Tel: +46 8 666 64 00
Fax: +46 8 661 46 28
P: C. Reuterskiold, *CH:* B. Rydin 104

Ingersoll-Rand Holdings Ltd
PO Box No 2, Chorley New Road, Horwich, Bolton, Lancashire, BL6 6JN
Tel: 01204 690690
Fax: 01204 690388
No officers designated　　54

Inoco PLC
St Clements House, 2-16 Colegate, Norwich, NR3 1BQ
Tel: 01603 632350
Fax: 01603 664217
CH: D.J. Rowland,
CE: G.J. Robeson　　57

Intel Corpn
2200 Mission College Boulevard, PO Box 58119, Santa Clara, California, 95052-8119, USA
P: A.S. Grove, *CH:* G.E. Moore　111

Intel Corporation (UK) Ltd
Pipers Way, Swindon, Wiltshire, SN3 1RJ
Tel: 01793 696000
Fax: 01793 641440
CH: K. Chapple　　56

Interbail [Ste Financiere]
14 rue Pergolese, 75116 Paris, France
Tel: +33 1 40 67 1808
CH: J. Martineau, J.B. Pascal　101

Intermediate Capital Group PLC
62-63 Threadneedle Street, London, EC2R 8HE
Tel: 0171 628 9898
Fax: 0171 628 2268
CH: C.M. Stuart　　53

International Business Machines Corpn
1 Old Orchard Road, Armonk, New York, 10504, USA
Tel: +1 914 765-1900
CH: L.V. Gerstner Jr　　13, 110

International General Electric (USA) Ltd
3 Shortlands, Hammersmith, London, W6 8BX
Tel: 0181 741 9900
Fax: 0181 741 9460
No officers designated　　45, 100

International Paper Co.
Two Manhattanville Road, Purchase, New York, NY, 10577, USA
Tel: +1 914 397-1500
CH: J.A. Georges　　110

International Stock Exchange of the UK and The Republic of Ireland
The Stock Exchange, London, EC2N 1HP
Tel: 0171 588 2355
CH: J. Kemp-Welch,
CE: M.J. Lawrence　　51

Internationale Nederlanden Groep NV
Strawinskylaan 2631, Amsterdam, The Netherlands
Tel: +31 20 541 5462
Fax: +31 20 541 5451
CH: J.H. Choufoer, A.G. Jacobs　73, 88, 89, 90

Interpublic Ltd
4 Golden Square, London, W1R 3AE
Tel: 0171 734 7116
CH: E.P. Beard (USA)　　56

Intershop Holding AG
Bleicherweg 33, 8002 Zurich, Switzerland
Tel: +41 1 202 86 96
Fax: +41 1 202 87 10
CH: Dr J.E. Muller,
CE: Dr J.E. Muller　　105

Investment Trust of Guernsey Ltd (The)
20 New Street, St Peter Port, Guernsey
Tel: 01481 728082
Fax: 01481 722373
CH: J.M. Le Pelley　　60

Investor AB
Arsenalgatan 8C, 103 32 Stockholm, Sweden
Tel: +46 8 614 20 00
Fax: +46 8 614 21 50
CH: P. Wallenberg, *MD:* C. Dahlback

Irish Permanent PLC
56-59 St Stephen's Green, Dublin 2
CH: J.O.P. Bourke, *CE:* P.R. Douglas,
FD: P. Fitzpatrick　　101

Isar-Amperwerke AG
Brienner Strasse 40, 80333 Munich, Germany
Tel: +49 89 52 08 1
Fax: +49 89 52 08 22 03
CH: Dr G. Obermeier, A. Bayer　　96

Isosceles PLC
11 Walker Street, Edinburgh, EH3 7NE
Tel: 0131 225 4455
Fax: 0131 225 2712
CH: E.H. Sharp, *CE:* D.M. Simons,
FD: S.M. Gatto　　45, 100

Israel Fund PLC (The)
14th Floor, One Angel Court, Throgmorton Street, London, EC2R 7HJ
Tel: 0171 600 6655
Fax: 0171 600 4371
CH: Sir James G. Littler　　59

Istituto Bancario San Paolo di Torino SpA
Piazza San Carlo 156, 10121 Turin, Italy
Tel: +39 11 5551
Fax: +39 11 555 6404
CH: G. Zandano, *MD:* G. Mazzarello　92

Istituto Mobiliare Italiano SpA - IMI
Viale dell'Arte 25, 00144 Rome, Italy
Tel: +39 6 59591
Fax: +39 6 5450 3888
CH: L. Arcuti　　90

Italcable Servizi Cablografici, Radiotelegrafici e Radioelettrici
Via Calabria 46, 00187 Rome, Italy
Tel: +39 6 5734 1
Fax: +39 6 6799858
CH: R. Jucci　　103

Italcementi SpA
Via G. Camozzi 124, 24100 Bergamo, Italy
Tel: +39 35 396 111
Fax: +39 35 244905
CH: G. Giavazzi, *MD:* G. Pesenti　94

Italgas [Sta Italiana per il Gas pA]
via XX Settembre 41, 10121 Turin, Italy
Tel: +39 11 23 951
CH: A. Moroni　　96

Italmobiliare SpA
Via Borgonuovo 20, Milan, Italy
Tel: +39 2 659 60 61
CH: G. Pesenti　　101

Ito-Yokado Co. Ltd
1-4 Shibakoen 4 chome, Minato-ku, Tokyo 105, Japan
Tel: +81 3 3459 2111
Fax: +81 3 3434 8378
P: Toshifumi Suzuki, *JMD:* Hironaka Kudo, Isao Kobayashi, Tatsuhiro Sekine, Yasuhisa Ito, Akihiko Hanawa, Isao Ide, Toshie Henmi, Junpei Mizuno, Kiyoshi Yao, Sakae Isaka　113

Iveco Ford Truck Ltd
Iveco Ford House, Station Road, Watford, Hertfordshire, WD1 1SR
Tel: 01923 246400
Fax: 01923 240574
CH: G. Boschetti (Italy),
MD: A.B. Fox　　33, 59

Ivory & Sime Enterprise Capital PLC
1 Charlotte Square, Edinburgh, EH2 4DZ
Tel: 0131 225 1357
Fax: 0131 225 2375
CH: J.M. Menzies　　58

Japan Airlines Co. Ltd
Tokyo Building, 7-3 Marunouchi 2-chome, Chiyoda-ku, Tokyo 100, Japan
Tel: +81 3 3284 2315
Fax: +81 3 3284 2316
P: Matsuo Toshimitsu, *CH:* Susumu Yamaji, *JMD:* Kunietsu Sakuraba, Hiroyuki Inagawa, Akira Kondo, Shinji Watarai, Susumu Ozawa, Yoshio Iwao, Toshiro Shinano, Mitsuo Ando, Akio Kouno, Osamu Igarashi, Shinzo Suto, Fumio Kuwano, Yoshihiko Murata 112

Japan Energy Corpn
10-1, Toranomon 2-chome, Minato-ku, Tokyo 105, Japan
Tel: +81 3 5573 6136
Fax: +81 3 5573 6782
P: Kazushige Nagashima, *CH:* Yukio Kasahara, *JMD:* Hisao Yamane, Akihiko Nomiyama, Masaaki Kageyama, Jun Asanuma, Otaro Sueki, Sueo Sakata, Yasuo Ikeda, Ken Irino, Shigenari Ishii, Shunzaburo Mizote, Tohru Aizawa, Keiji Komatsu　113

Jardine Matheson Holdings Ltd
Jardine House, 33-35 Reid Street, Hamilton, Bermuda
Tel: +1 809 292 0515
Fax: +1 809 292 4072
CH: H. Keswick, *MD:* A. Morrison,
FD: C.I. Cowan　　114

Jarvis Hotels Ltd
1a Eastbury Road, Northwood, Middlesex, HAG 2BG
CH: J.F. Jarvis　　49

Jelmoli Holding AG
St-Anna-Gasse 18, 8001 Zurich, Switzerland
Tel: +41 220 44 11
Fax: +41 211 57 40
P: C. Magri, *CH:* Dr P. Gloor　　103

Jersey Electricity Co. Ltd (The)
PO Box 45, Queen's Road, St Helier, Jersey, Channel Islands, JE4 8NY
Tel: 01534 505000
Fax: 01534 505011
CH: Senator R.R. Jeune,
MD: M.J. Liston　　58

Johnson & Firth Brown PLC
Smithfield House, Blonk Street, Sheffield, S1 2BH
Tel: 0114 275 7282
Fax: 0114 275 7457
CH: M.E. Llowarch, *CE:* D.J. Hall,
FD: N.A. MacDonald　　60

Johnson Group Cleaners PLC
Mildmay Road, Bootle, Merseyside, L20 5EW
Tel: 0151 933 6161
Fax: 0151 922 8089
CH: T.M. Greer, *CE:* R.G.F. Zerny,
FD: M.A. Sutton　　56

Johnson Matthey PLC
New Garden House, 78 Hatton Garden, London, EC1N 8JP
Tel: 0171 629 8000
Fax: 0171 269 8127
CH: D.J. Davies,
FD: J.N. Sheldrick　　46, 105

Jyske Bank AS
Vestergade 8-16, 8600 Silkeborg, Denmark
Tel: +45 89 22 22 22
Fax: +45 89 22 24 96
CH: L. Rasmussen, *CE:* K. Steenkjar 106

K Mart Corpn
3100 West Big Beaver Road, Troy, Michigan 48084-3163, USA
Tel: +1 313 643-1000
CH: F. Hall　　111

KBB-NV Koninklijke Bijenkorf Beheer
Hoekenrode 8, 1102 BR Amsterdam-Zuidoost, The Netherlands
Tel: +31 20 5630100
Fax: +31 20 6911733
CH: E.J. Verloop, T. Henselijn　105

KLM - Laird

KLM Royal Dutch Airlines
Amsterdamseweg 55, Amstelveen,
The Netherlands
Tel: +31 20 649 91 23
Fax: +31 20 648 80 69
P: P. Bouw, *CH:* C.J. Oort,
JMD: L.M. van Wijk,
R.J.M. Abrahamsen 93

KNP BT [NV Koninklijke]
Paalbergweg 2, 1100 DZ Amsterdam,
The Netherlands
Tel: +31 20 567 26 72
Fax: +31 20 567 25 67
CH: F.C. Rauwenhoff,
R.F.W. van Oordt 95

KSB AG
Johann-Klein-Strasse 9, 67225
Frankenthal, Germany
Tel: +49 62 33 86-0
Fax: +49 62 33 86 34 01
CH: Dr W. Kuhborth, W. Keller,
CE: K. von der Tann 108

Kajima Corpn
2-7 Motoakasaka 1-chome, Minato-ku,
Tokyo 107, Japan
Tel: +81 3 3404 3311
Fax: +81 3 3470 1444
P: Akira Miyazaki, *CH:* Rokuro
Ishikawa, *JMD:* Shoichi Ohori, Hajime
Honma, Muneshige Nagatomo,
Tatsujiro Kochi, Toru Murata, Yu
Kojima, Minoru Tamagawa, Yuji
Sugimoto, Hisashi Tsukamoto,
Shigefumi Yasutomi, Kinya Arai,
Takashi Yamashiro, Atsushi Kanie,
Kimio Hirai, Takehiko Uchino, Minori
Kurita, Kenji Sakamoto, Toshiyuki
Kanbe, Yoshifumi Tokunaga,
Yoshihiko Iwamatsu, Keiki Ono,
Yoichi Nojiri, Ikuzo Mori, Shoichi
Kishimoto, Yoshinori Toyoda, Masaru
Kawai, Naoyuki Tsunoda, Ryuichi
Murashima, Yuji Takada 113

Kansai Electric Power Co. Inc (The)
3-22 Nakanoshima 3-chome, Kita-ku,
Osaka 530, Japan
Tel: +81 6 441 8821
Fax: +81 6 441 8598
P: Yoshihisa Akiyama, *CH:* Shoichiro
Kobayashi, *JMD:* Masahiro Narasaki,
Hajime Miyamoto, Takashi Iwasaki,
Hiroshi Ishikawa, Yasuo Hashimoto,
Takeshi Watanabe, Hideo Kimura, Seiji
Kamiyama, Hajimu Maeda, Wataru
Kinugawa, Toshitsugu Unisuga 112

Kansallis Yhtyma
Aleksis Kiven katu 3-5, 00012 KOP
Helsinki, Finland
Tel: +358 0 1631
Fax: +358 0 163 3595
CH: T. Matomaki, P. Voutilainen 99

Karstadt AG
Theodor-Althoff-Strasse 2, 45133
Essen, Germany
Tel: +49 2 01 72 71
Fax: +49 2 01 7 27 52 16
CH: Dr U. Cartellieri, Dr W. Deuss 95

Kaufhof Holding AG
Leonhard-Tietz-Strasse 1, 50676
Cologne, Germany
Tel: +49 2 21/223-0
Fax: +49 2 21 2 23-28 00
CH: E. Conradi, W. Urban 97

Kawasaki Steel Corpn
Hibiya Kokusai Building, 2-3
Uchisaiwaicho 2-chome, Chiyoda-ku,
Tokyo 100, Japan
Tel: +81 3 3597 3111
Fax: +81 3 3597 4868-9
P: Shinobu Tosaki, *CH:* Yasuhiro Yagi,
JMD: Hidehiko Kimishima, Kanji
Emoto, Shigeru Motoyama, Takao
Nishino, Takuo Imai, Koichi Masuda,
Hidemi Akizuki, Kinya Yamaguchi,
Hisashi Orimi, Reiji Nakato, Jun
Kanazawa, Toru Kondo 112

Kellogg Co. of Great Britain Ltd
The Kellogg Building, Talbot Road,
Manchester, M16 0PU
Tel: 0161 869 2000
Fax: 0161 869 2100
CH: D.G. Fritz,
MD: T.P. Mobsby 48, 108

Kelt Energy PLC
130 Jermyn Street, London, SW1Y 4UJ
Tel: 0171 930 9861
Fax: 0171 873 0908
CH: H.F. Perrodo, *CE:* R. Fox 56

Kemira Oy
Porkkalankatu 3, PO Box 330,
00101 Helsinki, Finland
Tel: +358-0-13 211
Fax: +358-0-694 6167
CH: H. Karinen, T. Kalli 97

Kenning Motor Group PLC
40 Church Street, Staines, Middlesex,
TW18 4EP
Tel: 01784 460000
Fax: 01784 460046
CH: R.F. Heath 57

Kenwake Ltd
OOCL House, Levington Park, Bridge
Road, Levington, Suffolk, IP10 0NE
No officers designated 58

Keramik Holding AG Laufen
Postfach 432, 4242 Laufen,
Switzerland
Tel: 061 765 71 11
Fax: 061 761 36 60
CH: Dr I. Gerster,
Dr E. Stiefelmeyer 106

Kerry Group PLC
Prince's Street, Tralee, County Kerry,
Ireland
Tel: +353 66 22433
Fax: +353 66 22353
CH: M. Hanrahan,
MD: D. Brosnan 107

Kesko Oy
Satamakatu 3, PO Box 135,
00160 Helsinki, Finland
Tel: +358 10 5311
Fax: +358 0 655 473
CH: E. Kinnunen, V. Lammela 98

Kia Motors
15 Yoido-Dong, Yongdungpo-Gu,
Seoul, Korea
Tel: +82 2 788 1114
Fax: +82 2 784 0746
P: Han Seung Jun, *CH:* Kim Sun Hong,
JMD: Sin Yong Baek, Shin Dong
Young, Lee Jae Il, Yoo Young Gull,
Kim Byung Nam, Hong Un Pyo, Park
Kun Woong, Kim Sung Hoon, Lee Jong
In, Lee Moon Yong, Lee Yong Hee,
Choi Sang Chul, Seo Dai Il, Kim Sung
Yul, Woo Young Dae, Oh Min Bu 114

Kimberly-Clark Ltd
Larkfield, Aylesford, Kent, ME20 7PS
Tel: 01622 616000
Fax: 01622 718280
CH: J.A. Van Steenberg 49

Kingfisher PLC
North West House, 119 Marylebone
Road, London, NW1 5PX
Tel: 0171 724 7749
Fax: 0171 724 1160
CH: Sir Nigel Mobbs,
CE: Sir Geoffrey J. Mulcahy,
FD: A. Percival 44, 96

Kingsway Group PLC
Celcon House, 289/293 High Holborn,
London, WC1V 7HU
Tel: 0171 242 9766
Fax: 0171 831 4689
CH: P. From Petersen 59

Kirin Brewery Co. Ltd
26-1 Jingumae 6-chome, Shibuya-ku,
Tokyo 150-11, Japan
Tel: +81 3 3499 6111
Fax: +81 3 3499 6151
P: Keisaku Manabe 113

Kleinwort Benson Group PLC
20 Fenchurch Street, London, EC3P 3DB
Tel: 0171 623 8000
Fax: 0171 623 4069
CH: The Lord Rockley,
FD: R.C.H. Jeens 45, 101

Kleinwort Charter Investment Trust PLC
10 Fenchurch Street, London,
EC3M 3LB
Tel: 0171 956 6600
Fax: 0171 956 7161
CH: D.H. Benson 41, 50

Kleinwort European Privatisation Investment Trust PLC
10 Fenchurch Street, London,
EC3M 3LB
Tel: 0171 956 6600
Fax: 0171 956 7161
CH: S.P.N. Ross 41, 46, 105

Kleinwort Overseas Investment Trust PLC
10 Fenchurch Street, London,
EC3M 3LB
Tel: 0171 956 6600
Fax: 0171 956 7161
CH: C.C. Maltby 41, 50

Klockner-Humboldt-Deutz AG
Nikolaus-August-Otto-Allee 2, 51057
Cologne, Germany
Tel: +49 221 822-24 90
Fax: +49 221 822-24 55
CH: Dr M. Endres, A. Schneider 100

Klockner-Werke AG
Klocknerhaus, Klocknerstrasse 29,
47057 Duisburg, Germany
Tel: +49 2 03 39 61
Fax: +49 2 03 39 36 35 35
CH: B. Wollschlager,
Dr H.C. von Rohr 100

Klovern AB
Hammarbyvagen 37B, Hammarby Gard,
120 06 Stockholm, Sweden
Tel: +46 8 615 58 00
Fax: +46 8 643 94 00
CH: F. Johnsson, *JMD:* R. Magnusson,
L. Skold 107

Kobe Steel Ltd
Tekko Building, 8-2 Marunouchi 1-chome, Chiyoda-ku, Tokyo, 100 Japan
Tel: +81 3 3218 7111
Fax: +81 3 3218 6330
P: Sokichi Kametaka, *CH:* Yugoro
Komatsu, *JMD:* Masumi Sato,
Tsunehiko Okada, Terumasa Ando,
Akihiro Yamamoto, Takasa Negami,
Masahiko Uemura, Shigero Tanaka,
Senji Ogahara, Koshi Mizukoshi,
Osamu Takata, Hiroshi Sugimoto,
Toshiyuki Soejima, Kazuo Koyanagi,
Katsuyuki Matsumiya, Hirokatsu
Yokoyama, Yoshihiko Yamaguchi,
Hiroshi Kajiwara 112

Kodak Ltd
Kodak House, Station Road, Hemel
Hempstead, Herts, HP1 1JU
Tel: 01442 61122
Fax: 01442 240609
CH: A.J. Waterlow 47, 106, 111

Koenig & Bauer AG
Friedrich-Koenig-Strasse 4, 97080
Wurzburg, Germany
Tel: +49 9 31 9 09-0
Fax: +49 9 31 909-101
CH: P. Reimpell,
H.-B. Bolza-Schunemann 108

Kolbenschmidt AG
Postfach 1351, 74150 Neckarsulm,
Germany
Tel: +49 71 32 33-0
Fax: +49 71 32 33 27 96
CH: Dr H.-U. Plaul, H. Binder 109

Komatsu Ltd
2-3-6 Akasaka, Minato-ku, Tokyo 107,
Japan
Tel: +81 3 5561 2616
Fax: +81 3 3505 9662
P: Tetsuya Katada, *CH:* Ryoichi
Kawai, *JMD:* Akihisa Minato, Satoru
Anzaki, Toshiro Nakaya, Kenzo
Hoashi, Masanori Kojima, Tokuji
Aoyama, Masahiro Sakane 113

Kone Oy
PO Box 8, Kartanontie 1,
00331 Helsinki, Finland
Tel: +358 0 4751
Fax: +358 0 475 4309
P: A. Soila 102

Kooperativa forbundet
PO Box 15 200, 10465 Stockholm,
Sweden
Tel: +46 8 743 10 00
P: R. Svensson, *CH:* G. Axell 97

Korea Electric Power
167 Samsung-Dong, Kangnam-Gu,
Seoul, Korea
Tel: +82 2 550 3114
Fax: +82 2 550 5981
P: Lee Chong Hoon 12, 13, 114

Korea First Bank
100, Kongpyong-Dong, Chongno-Gu,
Seoul
Tel: +82 2 7330070
Fax: +82 2 7345976
P: Lee Chul Soo, *JMD:* Sheen Kwang
Shik, Kim Chong Duk, Lee Ju Chan,
Hong Tai Wan, Lee Sang Chun, Suh
Hong Bae, Lee Sang Chun, Park Yong
En, Bae Hwang, Lee Sae Sun 115

Korean Air Lines
41-3 Sosomun-Dong, Chung-Gu,
Seoul, Korea
Tel: +82 2 751 7114
Fax: +82 2 755 5220
P: Cho Yang Ho, *CH:* Cho Choong
Hoon, *JMD:* Ko Chung Sam, Hwang
Woo Hyun, Cho Sei Whan, Choi Dong
Bin, Kim Dal Hoie, Lee Soo Bu, Jeon
Hee Gyun, Cho Young Han 114

Kraft Foods Ltd
St George's House, Bayshill Road,
Cheltenham, Glos, GL50 3AE
Tel: 01242 236101
Fax: 01242 512084
No officers designated 57

Kredietbank NV
KB-Toren, Schoenmarkt 35,
2000 Antwerp, Belgium
P: M. Cockaerts, *CH:* M. Santens,
M. Cockaerts 92

Krupp [Fried.] AG Hoesch-Krupp
45117, Essen, Germany
Tel: +49 2 01 188-1
Fax: +49 2 01 188-4100
CH: B. Beitz, M. Lennings,
Dr G. Cromme 92

Kubota Corpn
2-47 Shikitsuhigashi 1-chome,
Naniwa-ku, Osaka 556, Japan
Tel: +81 6 648 2111
Fax: +81 6 648 3862
P: Kouhei Mitsui, *CH:* Shigekazu Mino,
JMD: Osamu Okamoto, Kozo Iizuka,
Fumio Nakada, Keizo Homma,
Yoshikuni Dobashi, Hiroyuki Kisaka,
Tohru Hasegawa, Kazuji Hashimoto,
Kiichiro Kawaguchi, Hiroshi Miyamoto,
Mitsuo Iwanaga, Hiroshi Wakita, Shozo
Nagao, Tadao Fujimoto, Shohei Majima,
Keizo Ohmori, Takeshi Oka 113

Kumagai Gumi Co. Ltd
2-1 Tsukudo-cho, Shinjuku-ku,
Tokyo 162, Japan
Tel: +81 3 3260 2111
Fax: +81 3 3235 3308
P: Taichiro Kumagai, *JMD:* Akira
Takayama, Kazuo Hori, Yoshitomo
Tanabe, Mikihiko Kitamura, Renichi
Yoshizaki, Minoru Aoki, Yasumi
Murata, Shinsaku Nishiyama,
Toshiyuki Isomata, Haruo Mitsui,
Hiroshi Ishikawa, Seishi Takeuchi,
Sachio Masuzawa, Masaharu Saeki,
Masaharu Nishiyama, Sadatsugu
Uesugi, Yasunori Fujii 113

Kunick PLC
Low Lane, Horsforth, Leeds, LS18 4ER
Tel: 0113 239001
Fax: 0113 259864
CH: C.T. Burnett, *FD:* J.G. Jones 59

Kvaerner AS
Hoffsveien 1, PO Box 100 Skoyen,
0212 Oslo, Norway
Tel: +47 22 96 70 00
Fax: +47 22 52 01 22
P: E. Tonseth, *CH:* K.K. Kielland 97

Kwik Save Group PLC
Warren Drive, Prestatyn, Clwyd,
LL19 7HU
Tel: 01745 887111
Fax: 01745 886494
CH: S.L. Keswick, *CE:* G.J. Bowler,
FD: D.W.M. Pretty 47, 106

Kwik-Fit Holdings PLC
St James's Court, Brown Street,
Manchester, M2 2JF
Tel: 0131 337 9200
Fax: 0131 337 0062
CH: T. Farmer, *FD:* J.M. Houston 53

Kymmene Corpn
Mikonkatu 15 A, PO Box 1079, 00101
Helsinki, Finland
Tel: +358 0 131 411
Fax: +358 0 653 884
CH: C. Ehrnrooth 94

Kyushu Electric Power Co. Inc
1-82 Watanabe-Dori 2-chome, Chuo-ku, Fukuoka 810-91, Japan
Tel: +81 92 761 3031
P: Shigeru Ohno, *CH:* Tatsuo Kawai,
JMD: Naoyuki Hashimoto, Shigeki
Kitajima, Satoshi Ohsako, Hiroshi
Kamei, Takashi Matsumura, Nobutoki
Inoue, Kuniyoshi Ishii, Hiroshi
Okamoto, Michisada Kamata 13, 112

LASMO PLC
100 Liverpool Street, London,
EC2M 2BB
Tel: 0171 945 4545
Fax: 0171 606 2893
CH: R.I.J. Agnew, *CE:* J. Darby,
FD: R.L. Smernoff 30, 43, 94

LG Chemical Ltd
20 Yoido-Dong, Yongdungpo-Gu,
Seoul, Korea
Tel: +82 2 787 5114
Fax: +82 2 787 7733
P: Choi Keun Sun, Lee Joung Soung,
CH: Koo Cha Kyung, *JMD:* Choi
Kwan Yong, Lee Jung Jae, Shim Cheon
Hwan, Yeo Sung Koo 115

LG Electronics Co
20 Yoido-Dong, Yongdungpo-Gu, Seoul
Tel: +82 2 787 5114
Fax: +82 2 787 3400
CH: Koo Cha Kyung, *JMD:* Han
Hong Kwang, Choi Soo Taek, Kim
Young Dal 114

LVMH Moet Hennessy Louis Vuitton
30 Avenue Hoche, 75008 Paris, France
Tel: +33 1 44 13 22 22
Fax: +33 1 44 13 21 19
CH: B. Arnault 20, 89, 93

Labinal
Parc d'Activites du Pas du Lac,
5 avenue Newton, Montigny-le-
Bretonneux Yvelines, France
Tel: +33 1 30 85 30 85
Fax: +33 1 30 43 41 71
CH: P. Maurin, J.-L. Cler,
A. Halna du Fretay 102

Ladbroke Group PLC
Chancel House, Neasden Lane,
London, NW10 2XE
Tel: 0181 459 8031
Fax: 0181 459 8618
CH: J.B.H. Jackson,
FD: B.G. Wallace 26, 42, 93

Lafarge SA
61 rue des Belles Feuilles, PO Box 40,
75782 Paris Cedex 16, France
Tel: +33 1 44 34 11 11
Fax: +33 1 44 34 12 00
CH: B. Collomb,
JMD: B. Kasriel, J. Lefevre 92

Lagardere Groupe
4, rue de Presbourg, 75116 Paris, France
Tel: +33 1 40 69 16 00
CH: R.H. Levy 93

Lai Sun Development Co. Ltd
11th Floor, Lai Sun Commercial
Centre, 680 Cheung Sha Wan Road,
Kowloon, Hong Kong
CH: Lim Por Yen 115

Lai Sun Garment (International) Ltd
11th Floor, Lai Sun Commercial
Centre, 680 Cheung Sha Wan Road,
Kowloon, Hong Kong
CH: Lim Por Yen 115

Laing [John] PLC
Page Street, London, NW1 2ER
Tel: 0181 959 3636
Fax: 0181 906 5297
CH: J.M.K. Laing 50

Laird Group PLC (The)
3 St James's Square, London,
SW1Y 4JU
Tel: 0171 839 6441
Fax: 0171 839 2921
CH: J.A. Gardiner, *CE:* I.M. Arnott,

Lancer - MEPC

MD: G.C.G. Wilkinson,
FD: J.C. Silver 48 108

Lancer Boss Group Ltd
Grovebury Road, Leighton Buzzard,
Bedfordshire, LU7 8SR
Tel: 01525 372031
Fax: 01525 383071
CH: Sir Neville Bowman-Shaw 60

Land Securities PLC
5 Strand, London, WC2N 5AF
Tel: 0171 413 9000
Fax: 0171 925 0202
CH: P.J. Hunt 20, 42, 92

Landis & Gyr AG
Grafenauweg 10, 6301 Zug,
Switzerland
Tel: +41 42 24 11 24
Fax: +41 42 24 40 00
CH: Dr G. Krneta, Dr W. Kissling,
MD: Dr W. Kissling 102

Laporte PLC
3 Bedford Square, London, WC1B 3RA
Tel: 0171 580 0223
Fax: 0171 580 0265
CH: R. Bexon, CE: K.J. Minton,
FD: W.J. Hoskins 46, 102

Latin American Investment Trust PLC
Exchange House, Primrose Street,
London, EC2A 2NY
Tel: 0171 628 1234
Fax: 0171 628 2281
CH: M.J. Hart 55, 72

Lauritzen [J.] Holding AS
Sankt Annae Plads 28, 1291
Copenhagen K, Denmark
Tel: +45 33 11 12 22
Fax: +45 33 15 00 90
P: S. Dyrlov Madsen,
CH: K. Laursen 99

Law Debenture Corporation PLC (The)
Princes House, 95 Gresham Street,
London, EC2V 7LY
Tel: 0171 606 5451
Fax: 0171 606 0643
CH: J.M. Kennedy,
MD: C.C.B. Duffett 53

Lawrie Group PLC
Wrotham Place, Wrotham, Sevenoaks,
Kent, TN15 7AE
Tel: 01732 884488
Fax: 01732 885724
CH: H.K. Fitzgerald 50

Lawson Mardon Packaging Ltd
50 Portland Place, London, W1N 3DG
Tel: 0171 255 1040
Fax: 0171 580 7623
No officers designated 50

Lech-Elektrizitatswerke AG
Schaezlerstrasse 3, 86150 Augsburg,
Germany
Tel: +49 821 328-0
Fax: +49 821 3 28-1170
CH: Dr D. Kuhnt 105

Leeds & Holbeck Building Society
Holbeck House, 105 Albion Street,
Leeds, LS1 5AS
Tel: 0113 245 9511
Fax: 0113 242 3296
P: C.E. Holroyd, CE: A.E. Stone 52

Leeds Permanent Building Society
Permanent House, The Headrow,
Leeds, LS1 1NS
Tel: 0113 243 8181
Fax: 0113 235 2559
CH: J.M. Barr 20, 44

Legal & General Group PLC
Temple Court, 11 Queen Victoria
Street, London, EC4N 4TP
Tel: 0171 528 6200
Fax: 0171 528 6222
CH: Sir Christopher Harding,
CE: D. Prosser, FD: A.J. Hobson 47, 106

Legrand
128 avenue de Lattre de Tassigny,
PO Box 523, 87045 Limoges Cedex,
France
Tel: +33 55 06 87 87
Fax: +33 55 06 13 41
CH: E. Decoster, F. Grappotte,
MD: P. Puy 98

Leigh Interests PLC
Dunston Hall, Dunston, Stafford,
ST18 9AB
Tel: 01785 712666
CH: P.J. Custis, CE: S. Bowden,
FD: A. Kent 54

Lend Lease Corpn Ltd
Level 46, Australia Square, George
Street, Sydney, New South Wales,
2000, Australia
Tel: +61 2 236 6111
CH: S.G. Hornery, CE: D. Higgins 115

Lenzing AG
4860 Lenzing, Austria
Tel: +43 7672 701-0
Fax: +43 7672 75 740
CH: G. Randa, H.E. Stepniczka 107

Lep Group PLC
Lep House, 87 East Street, Epsom,
Surrey, KT17 1DT
Tel: 01372 729595
Fax: 01372 744307
CH: D.N. James 47, 106

Lewis Trust Group Ltd
Chelsea House, West Gate, London,
W5 1DR
Tel: 0181 998 8822
Fax: 0181 997 3953
No officers designated 52

Lewis [John] Partnership PLC
171 Victoria Street, London, SW1E 5NN
Tel: 0171 828 1000
Fax: 0171 828 6679
CH: S. Hampson 44, 99

Lex Service PLC
Lex House, 17 Connaught Place,
London, W2 2EL
Tel: 0171 705 1212
Fax: 0171 705 5732
CH: Sir Trevor E. Chinn,
MD: R. Leigh, FD: P.R. Harris 48, 108

Liechtensteinische Landesbank AG
Stadtle 44, 9490 Vaduz, Liechtenstein
Tel: +41 75 236 88 11
Fax: +41 75 236 88 22
CH: A. Vogt, MD: K. Heeb 102

Life Sciences International PLC
Crown House, 51 Aldwych, London,
WC2B 4LS
Tel: 0171 240 3445
Fax: 0171 240 3439
CH: Sir Christopher Bland,
FD: P. Triniman 56

Lille-Bonniere et Colombes SA
157 avenue Charles-de-Gaulle,
92521 Neuilly-sur-Seine, France
Tel: +33 47 47 51 00
CH: P. Mallet, M. Ladreit de Lacharriere,
MD: Veronique Morali 104

Lilly [Eli] Group Ltd
Kingsclere Road, Basingstoke,
Hampshire, RG21 2XA
Tel: 01256 473241
Fax: 01256 485070
MD: A.S. Clark 51

Linde AG
Abraham-Lincoln-Strasse 21,
65189 Wiesbaden, Germany
Tel: +49 6 11 770-0
Fax: +49 6 11 770-269
CH: W. Schieren, H. Meinhardt 95

Lindt & Sprungli AG
Seestrasse 204, 8802 Kilchberg,
Switzerland
Tel: +41 1 716 22 33
Fax: +41 1 715 39 85
CH: E. Tanner 109

Linpac Group Ltd
Evan Cornish House, Windsor Road,
Fairfield Industrial Estate,
Louthlnshire, Lincolnshire, LN11 0LX
Tel: 01507 601601
Fax: 01507 600339
CH: M.J. Cornish 49

Linton Park PLC
Linton Park, Linton, Near Maidstone,
Kent, ME17 4AB
Tel: 01622 746655
Fax: 01622 747422
CH: H.K. FitzGerald,
MD: M.C. Perkins,
FD: G.S.G. Brown 53, 98

Lion Nathan Ltd
Level 17, Tower 2, Shortland Centre,
55-65 Shortland Street, Auckland,
New Zealand
Tel: Sir Gordon Tait,
CE: A.D. Myers 115

Littlewoods Organisation PLC (The)
100 Old Hall Street, Liverpool, L70 1AB
Tel: 0151 235 2661
Fax: 0151 235 2555
CH: L.W. van Geest 45, 100

Lloyds Abbey Life PLC
205 Brooklands Road, Weybridge,
Surrey, KT13 0PE
Tel: 01932 850888
Fax: 01932 846597
CH: Sir Simon Hornby, CE: S. Maran,
FD: Mrs Laurel Powers-Freeling 18, 44, 83, 97

Lloyds Bank PLC
71 Lombard Street, London, EC3P 3BS
Tel: 0171 626 1500
Fax: 0171 283 4819
CH: Sir Robin Ibbs,
CE: Sir Brian I. Pitman 14, 18, 30, 40, 42, 44, 83, 88, 89, 91, 98

Lloyds Chemists PLC
Britannia House, Centurion Park,
Tamworth, Staffordshire, B77 5TZ
Tel: 01827 260011
Fax: 01827 261593
CH: A.J. Lloyd, MD: M. Ward,
FD: J. Fellows 51

Logistica de Hidrocarburos CLH [Cia] SA
Capitan Haya 41, 28020 Madrid, Spain
Tel: +34 1 582 59 02
Fax: +34 1 582 59 20
CH: S. Rof,
MD: A. Tellez de Peralta 103

London & Associated Investment Trust PLC
8-10 New Fetter Lane, London,
EC4A 1NQ
Tel: 0171 236 3539
Fax: 0171 248 2850
CH: M.A. Heller 61

London & Edinburgh Insurance Group Ltd
Excess House, 13 Fenchurch Avenue,
London, EC3M 5BT
Tel: 0171 626 0555
Fax: 0171 929 2014
CH: W. Stanway 51

London & Metropolitan PLC
Buchanan House, 3 Street James's
Square, London, SW1Y 4JU
Tel: 0171 925 2383
Fax: 0171 925 2416
CH: C.I.K. Harris 51

London American Growth Trust PLC
1 Angel Court, 14th Floor,
Throgmorton Street, London, EC2R 7AE
Tel: 0171 600 6655
Fax: 0171 600 4371
CH: J. Hignett 61

London Electricity PLC
Templar House, 81-87 High Holborn,
WC1V 6NU
Tel: 0171 242 9050
Fax: 0171 242 2815
CH: Sir Bob Reid, CE: R.J. Urwin,
FD: A.V. Towers 45, 99

London Forfaiting Company PLC
International House, 1 St Katharine's
Way, London, E1 9UN
Tel: 0171 481 3410
Fax: 0171 480 7626
CH: J.A.G. Wilson, CE: S.A. Papoutes,
FD: P.P. Samani 53

London Insurance Market Investment Trust PLC
6 Alie Street, London, E1 8DD
Tel: 0171 4889000
Fax: 0171 4889001
CH: J.G.W. Agnew,
MD: M.E.A. Carpenter 41, 49

London International Group PLC
35 New Bridge Street, London,
EC4V 6BJ
Tel: 0171 489 1977

Fax: 0171 489 0962
CH: M.R.N. Moore, CE: N.R. Hodges,
FD: J.M. Tyrrell 57

London Merchant Securities PLC
Carlton House, 33 Robert Adam Street,
London, W1M 5AH
Tel: 0171 935 3555
Fax: 0171 935 3737
CH: The Lord Rayne 46, 104

London Park Hotels PLC
2 The Calls, Leeds, LS2 7JU
Tel: 0113 243 9111
Fax: 0113 244 5555
No officers designated 54

London Regional Transport
55 Broadway, London, SW1H 0BD
Tel: 0171 222 5600
Fax: 0171 222 5719
CH: Sir Wilfred Newton,
FD: A.J. Sheppeck 29, 43, 94

London and Manchester Group PLC
Winslade Park, Exeter, EX5 1DS
Tel: 01392 444888
Fax: 01392 410076
CH: R.D.C. Hubbard, CE: T.A. Pyne,
FD: D.M. Jackson 54

London and St Lawrence Investment Company PLC
111 Cannon Street, London, EC4N 5AR
Tel: 0171 283 0114
Fax: 0171 283 0979
CH: G.W. Ashfield 61

Long Island Lighting Co.
175 East Old Country Road,
Hicksville, New York, 11801, USA
CH: W.J. Catacosinos 111

Long-Term Credit Bank of Japan Ltd (The)
1-8, Uchi-Saiwaicho 2-chome,
Chiyoda-ku, Tokyo 100, Japan
Tel: +81 3 5111 5111
Fax: +81 3 5511 5505
P: Tetsuya Horie,
CH: Takao Masuzawa 112

Lonrho PLC
Cheapside House, 138 Cheapside,
London, EC2V 6BL
Tel: 0171 606 9898
Fax: 0171 606 2285
CH: Sir John Leahy, CE: D. Bock,
FD: R.E. Whitten 37, 43, 96

Lovell [Y.J.] (Holdings) PLC
Marsham House, Gerrards Cross,
Buckinghamshire, SL9 8ER
Tel: 01753 882211
Fax: 01753 880411
CH: Sir David Hardy, CE: R.H. Sellier,
FD: G. McCormack 55

Low & Bonar PLC
Bonar House, Faraday Street, Dundee,
DD1 9JA
Tel: 01382 818171
Fax: 01382 816262
CH: H.W. Laughland, CE: J.W. Leng,
FD: N.D. McLeod 52

Lowland Investment Company PLC
3 Finsbury Avenue, London, EC2M 2PA
Tel: 0171 638 5757
Fax: 0171 377 5742
CH: J. Kemp-Welch,
MD: R.W. Smith 59

Lucas Industries PLC
Brueton House, New Road, Solihull,
West Midlands, B91 3TX
Tel: 0121 627 6000
Fax: 0121 627 6171
CH: Sir Brian Pearse, CE: G. Simpson,
FD: J.A.M. Grant 44, 97

Lufthansa [Deutsche] AG
Von-Gablenz-Strasse 2-6,
50679 Cologne, Germany
Tel: +49 2 21 82 60
Fax: +49 2 21 826-3818
CH: Dr W. Roller, J. Weber 87, 91

Lundbergforetagen AB [L E]
Hovslagargatan 5B, Box 14048,
10440 Stockholm, Sweden
Tel: +46 8 463 06 00
Fax: +46 8 611 38 76/611
CH: L.E. Lundberg, K. Palsson,
F. Lundberg 101

Luzerner Kantonalbank
Pilatusstrasse 12, 6002 Lucerne,
Switzerland
Tel: +41 41 29 22 22
Fax: +41 41 29 29 01
P: Dr jur T. Fischer, F. Studer 109

Lyonnaise des Eaux
72 avenue de la Liberte, Nanterre
(Hauts de Seine), France
Tel: +33 1 46 95 50 00
CH: J. Monod, MD: R. Coulomb 84, 90

M & G Dual Trust PLC
Three Quays, Tower Hill, London,
EC3R 6BQ
Tel: 0171 626 4588
Fax: 0171 623 8615
CH: D.L. Morgan 54

M & G Group PLC
Three Quays, Tower Hill, London,
EC3R 6BQ
Tel: 0171 626 4588
Fax: 0171 623 8615
CH: Sir David Money-Coutts,
FD: D.K. Watson 52

M & G Income Investment Trust PLC
Three Quays, Tower Hill, London,
EC3R 6BQ
Tel: 0171 626 4588
Fax: 0171 623 8615
CH: D.L. Morgan 41, 49

M & G Recovery Investment Trust PLC
Three Quays, Tower Hill, London,
EC3R 6BQ
Tel: 0171 626 4588
Fax: 0171 623 8615
CH: D.L. Morgan 51

M & G Second Dual Trust PLC
Three Quays, Tower Hill, London,
EC3R 6BQ
CH: D.L. Morgan 60

M C L Group Ltd
Mount Ephraim, Tunbridge Wells,
Kent, TN4 8BS
Tel: 01892 36134
Fax: 01892 36571
MD: J.E. Ebenezer 61

M.I.M. Holdings Ltd
Level 2, MIM Plaza, 410 Ann Street,
Brisbane, Queensland, 4000, Australia
Tel: +61 7 833 8000
Fax: +61 7 832 2426
CH: R.B. Vaughan 114

MAI PLC
8 Montague Close, London Bridge,
London, SE1 9RD
Tel: 0171 407 7676
Fax: 0171 407 0002
CH: Sir James McKinnon, MD: Lord
Hollick, FD: P. Hickson 47, 106

MAN AG
Ungererstrasse 69, 80805 Munich,
Germany
Tel: +49 89 3 60 98-0
Fax: +49 89 36 09 82 50
CH: K. Kaske, K. Gotte 93

MCI Communications Corpn
1801 Pennsylvania Ave NW,
Washington DC, 20006, USA
Tel: +1 202 872-1600
P: G.H. Taylor, CH: B.C. Roberts Jr 111

MCIT PLC
Gartmore House, 16-18 Monument
Street, London, EC3R 8AJ
Tel: 0171 782 2000/623 12
Fax: 0171 782 2075
CH: J.M. Green-Armytage (Canada) 60

MD Foods PLC
Craven House, Kirkstall Road, Leeds,
LS3 1JE
Tel: 0113 2440141
Fax: 0113 2425546
CH: C.F. Hall 51

MEPC PLC
12 St James's Square, London, SW1Y 4LB
Tel: 0171 911 5300
Fax: 0171 839 2340
CH: Viscount Blakenham,
CE: J.L. Tuckey,
FD: J.A. Beveridge 25, 42, 93

131

MFI - Midland

MFI Furniture Group PLC
Southon House, 333 The Hyde,
Edgware Road, Colindale, London,
NW9 6TD
Tel: 0181 200 8000
Fax: 0181 200 8636
CH: D.S. Hunt, *MD:* J.D. Randall,
FD: Susan M. Murphy 51

Machines Bull [Cie des]
Tour Bull, 1 Place Carpeaux, 92800
Puteaux, France
Tel: +33 1 46 96 90 90
CH: J.-M. Descarpentries 62, 99

Macmillan Ltd
4 Little Essex Street, London, WC2R 3LF
Tel: 0171 836 6633
Fax: 01256 810526
CH: N.G.B. Shaw, *MD:* I.K. Burns 55

Maculan Holding AG
Annagasse 6, 1010 Vienna, Austria
Tel: +43 1 51415
Fax: +43 1 51415-64
CH: Dr W. Jakobljevich,
Dr A. Maculan 109

Maersk Co. Ltd (The)
10 Cabot Square, Canary Wharf,
London, E14 4QL
Tel: 0171 712 5000
Fax: 0171 712 5100
CH: J.H. Kelly, *MD:* F.R. Jacobs 54

Magazine zum Globus AG
Eichstrasse 27, 8045 Zurich,
Switzerland
Tel: +41 1 455 21 11
Fax: +411 463 35 02
P: M. Stopnicer 107

Magneti Marelli SpA
Corso Giulio Cesare 300, 10154 Turin,
Italy
Tel: +39 11 26831
Fax: +39 11 2422395
CH: L. Francione, *MD:* P. Maritano

Mahle GmbH
Pragstrasse 26-46, 70376 Stuttgart,
7000, Germany
Tel: +49 711 501-0
Fax: +49 711 549 0347
CH: W. Eychmuller, G. Kopp 105

Majedie Investments PLC
1 Minster Court, Mincing Lane,
London, EC3R 7ZZ
Tel: 0171-626 1243
Fax: 0171 929 0904
CH: Sir John K. Barlow,
MD: W.G. Underwood 53

Malaysian Airline System Bhd
33rd Floor Bangunan MAS, Jalan
Sultan Ismail, 50250 Kuala Lumpur,
Malaysia
Tel: +60 3 2610555
Fax: +60 3 2613472
CH: Dato' Tajudin bin Ramli 115

Malaysian International Shipping Corpn Bhd
Suite 3-8 3rd Floor Wisma MISC, 2
Jalan Conlay, 50450 Kuala Lumpur,
Malaysia
Tel: +60 3 2428088
CH: R.M. Alias, *MD:* Ariffin Alias 115

Malvern UK Index Trust PLC
Hobart House, Grosvenor Place,
London, SW1X 7AD
CH: D.L. Tucker 59

Manchester Airport PLC
Town Hall, Manchester, M60 2LA
Tel: 0161 234 5000
CH: J. Byrne, *CE:* G. Muirhead,
FD: N.J. Renfrew 24, 46, 104

Manders PLC
PO Box 186, Old Heath Road,
Wolverhampton, WV1 2QT
Tel: 01902 871028
Fax: 01902 457363
CH: R. Amos, *CE:* R.M. Akers,
FD: J.A. Farmer 61

Mannesmann AG
Mannesmannufer 2, 40213 Dusseldorf,
Germany
Tel: +49 211 820-0
Fax: +49 211 8 20 21 63
CH: H. Kopper, Dr J. Funk 83, 91

Mansfield Brewery PLC
Littleworth, Mansfield,
Nottinghamshire, NG18 1AB
Tel: 01623 25691
Fax: 01623 658620
CH: Sir David White, *MD:* W. McCosh,
FD: G.P. Handley 52

Manweb PLC
Sealand Road, Chester, CH1 4LR
Tel: 01244 377111
Fax: 01244 377269
CH: R.W. Goodall, *CE:* J.E. Roberts,
FD: S. Siddall 14, 46, 102

Marieberg [Tidnings AB]
Ralambsvagen 17, 100 26 Stockholm,
Sweden
Tel: +46 8 738 29 00
Fax: +46 8 13 78 60
P: B. Braun, *CH:* O. Maberg 103

Marine-Wendel
89 rue Taitbout, 75009 Paris, France
Tel: +33 1 42 85 30 00
Fax: +33 1 45 96 00 07
CH: P. Celier, E.-A. Seilliere 93

Maritime Transport Services Ltd
Thamesport, Isle of Grain, Kent,
ME3 0EP
CH: D.K. Newbigging, *CE:* G.J. Parker,
MD: A.R.G. MacLeod,
FD: I.M. Waddington 57

Marks and Spencer PLC
Michael House, 37-67 Baker Street,
London, W1A 1DN
Tel: 0171 935 4422
Fax: 0171 487 2679
CH: Sir Richard Greenbury,
JMD: P.G. McCracken, A.Z. Stone,
P.L. Salsbury, *FD:* R.W.C. Colvill 14,
23, 40, 42, 88, 89, 92

Marley PLC
7 Oakhill Road, Sevenoaks, Kent,
TN13 1NQ
Tel: 01732 455255
Fax: 01732 740694
CH: Sir George Russell,
CE: D.A. Trapnell,
FD: C.G. Beenham 47, 106

Marlowe Holdings Ltd
Dennis House, Marsden Street,
Manchester, M2 1JD
Tel: 0161 832 5994
Fax: 0161 832 2250
No officers designated 54

Marshalls PLC
Hall Ings, Southowram, Halifax,
HX3 9TW
Tel: 01422 364521
Fax: 01422 67093
CH: A.H. Marshall, *CE:* P.D. Marshall,
FD: D.G. Holden 52

Marston, Thompson & Evershed PLC
The Brewery, Shobnall Road, Burton-on-Trent, Staffordshire, DE14 2BW
Tel: 01283 531131
Fax: 01283 510378
CH: M.W.F. Hurdle,
MD: D.W. Gordon 49

Martin Currie Pacific Trust PLC
Saltire Court, 20 Castle Terrace,
Edinburgh, EH1 2ES
Tel: 0131 229 5252
Fax: 0131 229 5959
CH: T.R.H. Kimber 58

Marubeni Corpn
4-2 Ohtemachi 1-chome, Chiyoda-ku,
Tokyo 100-88, Japan
Tel: +81 3 3282 2111
Fax: +81 3 3282 7456
P: Iwao Toriumi, *CH:* Kazuo Haruna,
JMD: Hiromasa Yamauchi, Iwao
Mizusaki, Ryuzo Toyoda, Shigeo
Sugita, Tadashige Tsuruoka, Tetsuro
Kitaoka, Yoji Otsuka, Takayuki Nakato,
Hidesuke Murakami, Sadao Nukina,
Hiroshi Matsumura, Atsushi Akita,
Hideo Tanaka, Tetsuhiro Yamamoto,
Kanichi Ota, Ichiro Momose 13, 112

Marubeni U.K. PLC
120 Moorgate, London, EC2M 6SS
Tel: 0171 826 8600
Fax: 0171 826 8611
CH: H. Tanaka 47, 105

Marzotto & Figli SpA [Manifattura Lane Gaetano]
Largo S. Margherita 1, 36078 Valdagno (Vicenza), Italy
Tel: +39 445 429411
Fax: +39 445 402000
CH: P. Marzotto 106

Matheson & Co. Ltd
3 Lombard Street, London, EC3V 9AQ
Tel: 0171 528 4000
Fax: 0171 623 5024
CH: H. Keswick 51

Matra-Hachette
4 rue de Presbourg, 75116 Paris, France
CH: J.-L. Lagardere 93

Matsushita Electric Industrial Co. Ltd
1006 Kadoma, Osaka, Japan
Tel: +81 6 908 1121
Fax: +81 6 906 1762
P: Yoichi Morishita, *CH:* Masaharu
Matsushita, *JMD:* Hideo Takahashi,
Masayuki Matsushita, Tadakazu
Yamamoto, Kiyoshi Seki, Kazuo
Ichikawa, Tsutomu Fukuhara, Shiro
Endo, Mikio Higashi, Shiro Horiuchi,
Toshikatsu Yamawaki, Yuji Hijikata
13, 112

Matsushita Electric Works Ltd
1048, Kadoma, Osaka 571, Japan
Tel: +81 6 908 1131
Fax: +81 6 909 4694
P: Kiyosuke Imai, *CH:* Toshio Miyoshi,
JMD: Hiroaki Inada, Takamasa Arima,
Koji Harada, Takeshi Mori, Takami
Hironaka, Kiyoji Yamanaka, Takanobu
Noro, Shinzo Goto, Yasuaki Kondo,
Hiroshi Koike 113

Matthews [Bernard] PLC
Great Witchingham Hall, Norwich,
Norfolk, NR9 5QD
Tel: 01603 872611
Fax: 01603 871118
CH: B.T. Matthews, *MD:* D.J. Joll,
FD: N.C. Harrison 55

Mayflower Corporation PLC
Mayflower House, London Road,
Loudwater, High Wycombe, HP10 9RF
Tel: 01494 450145
Fax: 01494 450607
CH: R.N. Hambro,
FD: D.T. Donnelly 61

Mayne Nickless Europe PLC
Mabel Street, The Meadows,
Nottingham, NG2 3ED
Tel: 0115 986 4110
Fax: 0115 986 0572
CH: J.C. Williams (Australia) 51

Mazda Motor Corpn
3-1 Shinchi, Fuchu-cho, Aki-gun,
Hiroshima 730-91, Japan
Tel: +81 82 282 1111
Fax: +81 82 287 5190/5192
P: Yoshihiro Wada, *JMD:* Norimasa
Furata, *JMD:* David R. Gunderson,
Teruo Mitsuoka, Shohachiro
Takahashi, Mamoru Takebayashi,
Sunao Yokota, Hidekazu Yonekura,
Satoshi Yamada, Gary K. Hexter, Ross
P. Witschoneke, Seiji Tanaka, Yasuo
Tatsutomi, Yoshinori Taura, Tadahiko
Takiguchi, Toshihide Deguchi 113

McAlpine [Alfred] PLC
8 Suffolk Street, London, SW1Y 4HG
Tel: 0171 930 6255
Fax: 0171 839 6902
CH: Sir John Milne,
CE: G.O. Whitehead, *FD:* K. Lever 57

McCain Foods (GB) Ltd
Havers Road, Scarborough, Yorkshire,
YO11 3BS
Tel: 01723 584141
Fax: 01723 581230
CH: H.H. McCain 57

McCarthy & Stone PLC
Homelife House, 26-32 Oxford Road,
Bournemouth, Dorset, BH8 8EZ
Tel: 01202 292480
Fax: 01202 557261
CH: J.S. McCarthy, *CE:* K. Lovelock,
FD: W.J.M. Thorne 55

McDonald's Corpn
McDonald's Plaza, Oak Brook, Illinois
60521, USA
Tel: +1 708 575-3000
CH: M.R. Quinlan 111

McDonald's Restaurants Ltd
11-59 High Road, East Finchley,
London, N2 8AW
Tel: 0181 883 6400
Fax: 0181 883 6400
No officers designated 54

McDonnell Information Systems Group PLC
Maylands Park South, Boundary Way,
Hemel Hempstead, Hertfordshire,
HP2 7HU
Tel: 01442 232424
Fax: 01442 256454
CH: I.F.H. Davison, *CE:* J.J. Causley,
FD: R.T Barfield 60

McKay Securities PLC
20 Greyfriars Road, Reading,
Berkshire, RG1 1NL
Tel: 01734 502333
Fax: 01734 391393
CH: I.A. McKay 56

McKechnie PLC
Leighswood Road, Aldridge, Walsall,
West Midlands, WS9 8DS
Tel: 01922 743887
Fax: 01922 51045
CH: V.E. Treves, *CE:* M.S. Ost,
FD: S.G. Moberley 51

Medeva PLC
10 St James's Street, London, SW1A 1EF
Tel: 0171 839 3888
Fax: 0171 930 1514
CH: B.D. Taylor, *CE:* Dr W. Bogie,
FD: D. Millard 53

Meggitt PLC
Farrs House, Cowgrove, Wimborne,
Dorset, BH21 4EL
Tel: 01202 841141
Fax: 01202 842478
CH: K.H. Coates,
MD: H.N.P. McCorkell 55

Melton Medes Ltd
Environment House, 6 Union Road,
Nottingham, NG3 1FH
Tel: 0115 958 2277
Fax: 0115 958 2332/483898
CH: N.R. Puri, *CE:* J.E. Philpotts 61

Menzies [John] PLC
Hanover Buildings, Rose Street,
Edinburgh, EH2 2YQ
Tel: 0131 225 8555
Fax: 0131 226 3752
CH: J.M. Menzies, *MD:* The Hon F.R.
Noel-Paton, *FD:* J.D.S. Bennett 54

Merchants Trust PLC (The)
10 Fenchurch Street, London, EC3M 3LB
Tel: 0171 956 6600
Fax: 0171 956 7161
CH: C.H. Black 41, 48

Merck & Co., Inc.
PO Box 100, One Merck Drive,
Whitehouse Station, New Jersey,
08889-0100, USA
P: R.V. Gilmartin,
CH: R.V. Gilmartin 111

Merck Sharp & Dohme (Holdings) Ltd
West Hill, Hertford Road, Hoddesdon,
Hertfordshire, EN11 9BU
Tel: 01992 467272
Fax: 01992 467270
No officers designated 49

Merck [E.]
Frankfurter Strasse 250, 64271
Darmstadt, Germany
Tel: +49 6151 720
Fax: +49 6151 72-20 00
CH: Prof Dr H.J. Langmann 97

Mercury Asset Management Group PLC
33 King William Street, London,
EC4R 9AS
Tel: 0171 280 2800
Fax: 0171 280 2820
CH: H.A. Stevenson,
FD: D.J. Causer 36, 50, 69

Mercury Keystone Investment Trust PLC
33 King William Street, London,
EC4R 9AS
Tel: 0171 280 2222
Fax: 0171 280 2820
CH: J.C.G. Stancliffe 56

Mercury World Mining Trust PLC
33 King William Street, London,
EC4R 9AS
Tel: 0171 280 2800
Fax: 0171 280 2820
CH: P.S. Wilmot-Sitwell 41, 47, 106

Merkur Holding AG
Fellerstrasse 15, 3027 Bern, Switzerland
Tel: +41 31 990 20 20
Fax: +41 31 990 28 01
CH: G. Krneta, *MD:* F. Frohofer 101

Merrill Lynch & Co. Inc.
World Financial Center, North Tower,
New York, NY, 10281-1332, USA
P: D.H. Komansky,
CH: D.P. Tully 14, 110

Mersey Docks and Harbour Company (The)
Maritime Centre, Port of Liverpool,
Liverpool, L21 1LA
Tel: 0151 949 6000
Fax: 0151 949 6199
CH: G.H. Waddell, *CE:* P.T. Furlong,
FD: M.G. Hill 51

Metallgesellschaft AG
Reuterweg 14, 60323 Frankfurt am
Main, Germany
Tel: +49 69 1590
Fax: +49 69 159 21 25
CH: Dr R.H. Schmitz,
Dr K.J. Neukirchen 62, 95

Metra Corpn
John Stenbergin ranta 2, PO Box 230,
00101 Helsinki, Finland
Tel: +358 0 709 51
Fax: +358 0 762 278
P: G. Ehrnrooth,
CH: R.G. Ehrnrooth 99

Metrovacesa - Inmobiliaria Metropolitano Vasco Central
C.Trias Bertran 7, 28020 Madrid, Spain
Tel: +34 1 91 559 01 00
CH: J.A. Saenz-Azcunaga Usandizaga,
MD: F. Vara Herrero 108

Metsa-Serla Oy
Revontulentie 6, 02100 Espoo, Finland
Tel: +358 0 469 431
Fax: +358 0 469 4355
P: T. Poranen, *CH:* J. Ahava 97

Meyer International PLC
Aldwych House, 81 Aldwych, London,
WC2B 4HQ
Tel: 0171 400 88 88
Fax: 0171 400 87 00
CH: H. Langman, *CE:* J.M. Dobby,
FD: B. Wright 47, 107

Michelin [Cie Generale des Etablissements]
12 Cours Sablon, Clermont-Ferrand
(Puy-de-Dome), France
Tel: +33 73 92 41 95
Fax: +33 73 90 28 94
No officers designated 62, 92

Micro Focus Group PLC
Speen Court, 7 Oxford Road, Newbury,
Berkshire, RG14 1PB
Tel: 01635 32646
Fax: 01635 33966
CH: B. Reynolds, *P.A.* O'Grady,
CE: P. O'Grady 58

Mid Kent Holdings PLC
High Street, Snodland, Kent, ME6 5AH
Tel: 01634 240313
Fax: 01634 242764
CH: J.L. Pemberton,
CE: G.L. Baldwin, *FD:* R.C. Atwood 58

Midland & Scottish Resources PLC
King's House, 36-37 King Street,
London, EC2V 8BE
Tel: 0171 522 0220
Fax: 0171 600 0733
CH: Dr J. Birks,
MD: J.P.W. Hawksley 55

Midland Independent Newspapers PLC
28 Colmore Circus, Queensway,
Birmingham, B4 6AX
Tel: 0121 2363566
Fax: 0121 2330173

CH: Rt Hon Sir P. Norman Fowler, CE: C.J. Oakley, FD: J. Whitehouse 53

Midlands Electricity PLC
Mucklow Hill, Halesowen, West Midlands, B62 8BP
Tel: 0121 423 2345
Fax: 0121 422 3311
CH: B.S. Townsend, *CE:* M.A. Hughes, *FD:* P.L. Chapman 45, 100

Migros-Genossenschafts-Bund
Limmatstrasse 152, 8005 Zurich, Switzerland
Tel: +41 1 277 21 11
Fax: +41 1 277 25 25
P: E. Hunziker, *CH:* J. Kyburz 92

Milano Assicurazioni SpA
Via del Lauro 7, 20121 Milan, Italy
Tel: +39 2 88401
Fax: +39 2 884 02 389
CH: L.A. Molinari 106

Milk Products Holdings (Europe) Ltd
Bancroft Place, 10 Bancroft Road, Reigate, Surrey, RH2 7RP
Tel: 01737 221616
Fax: 01737 241288
CH: A.J. Pollock 60

Miller Group Ltd (The)
Miller House, 18 South Groathill Avenue, Edinburgh, EH4 2LW
Tel: 0131 332 2585
Fax: 0131 332 3426
CH: J. Miller, *CE:* D.W. Cawthra 58

Minerva PLC
25 Harley Street, London, W1N 2BR
CH: D.E. Garrard 48, 109

Minet Group
Minet House, 66 Prescot Street, London, E1 8BU
Tel: 0171 481 0707
Fax: 0171 488 9786
CH: P.S. Christie 50

Minnesota Mining & Manufacturing Co.
3M Center, St Paul, Minnesota, 55144-1000, USA
Tel: +1 612 733-1110
CH: L.D. DeSimone 111

Minorco SA
9 rue Sainte Zithe, L-2763 Luxembourg City, Grand Duchy of Luxembourg
Tel: + 352 404 110-1
Fax: + 352 404 110-20
P: H.R. Slack, *CH:* J. Ogilvie Thompson, *FD:* D.E. Fisher 93

Miramar Hotel & Investment Co. Ltd
118-130 Nathan Road, Kowloon, Hong Kong
Tel: +852 3-681111
CH: Dr Ho Tim 115

Mirror Group PLC
1 Canada Square, Canary Wharf, London, E14 5AP
Tel: 0171 510 3000
Fax: 0171 293 3360
CH: Sir Robert Clark, *CE:* D.J. Montgomery, *MD:* C.M. Wilson, *FD:* C.J. Allwood 44, 99

Mitsubishi Bank Ltd (The)
7-1 Marunouchi 2-chome, Chiyoda-ku, Tokyo 100, Japan
Tel: +81 3 3240 1111
Fax: +81 3 3240 4197
P: Tsuneo Wakai, *CH:* Kazuo Ibuki, *JMD:* Atsuo Hirano, Yoji Onoe, Tadashi Serizawa, Shigemitsu Miki, Kazuya Okamoto, Seiitsu Chino, Takeshi Yano, Kenji Enya, Takeshi Tange, Akihiro Uno, Hideaki Fujioka, Yutaka Hasegawa, Yasuyuki Hirai, Norio Yasunaga, Masatoshi Shimada 112

Mitsubishi Chemical Corpn
5-2 Marunouchi 2-chome, Chiyoda-ku, Tokyo 100, Japan
Tel: +81 3 3283 6274
P: Masahiko Furukawa, *JMD:* Hideo Fukutani, Yosuke Ariyoshi, Takashi Saito, Takeo Okunishi, Yasuo Harada, Hiroyoshi Hata, Kanji Shono, Takeru Onoda, Morishisa Takano, Tsuyoshi Yamamoto, Shoei Yokoyama, Hideo Watanabe, Yoshihisa Narukawa 113

Mitsubishi Corpn
6-3 Marunouchi 2-chome, Chiyoda-ku, Tokyo 100-86, Japan
Tel: +81 3 3210 2121
Fax: +81 3 3210 8841
P: Minoru Makihara, *CH:* Shinroku Morohashi, *JMD:* Makoto Kuroda, Nobuyuki Kondo, Tetsuo Kamimura, Mitsutake Okano, Tsuneaki Kaku, Ichiro Yokose, Toshiharu Iino, Toshio Kawachi, Takeshi Kobayashi, Hiroshi Zaizen, Izuru Nagasawa, Kaname Shimazaki, Takuya Shitara, Kazuaki Kawasumi, Naoyoshi Uehara, Motohiko Numaguchi, Koichi Kuwahara, Hiroshi Kawamura, Hitoshi Ariwaka, Takeshi Sakurai, Mikio Sasaki, Hironori Aihara 13, 112

Mitsubishi Electric Corpn
Mitsubishi Denki Building, 2-3 Marunouchi 2-chome, Chiyoda-ku, Tokyo 100, Japan
Tel: +81 3 3218 2111
P: Takashi Kitaoka, *JMD:* Sozaburo Ihara, Toshio Ito, Shinzaburo Amano, Eiichi Ohno, Kazuya Nagasawa, Yoshito Yamaguchi, Yoshiharu Yamawaki, Mamoru Eto, Shoji Hirabayashi, Kazuya Yabu, Masatoshi Umeda, Takuji Shinmura, Susumu Ohnishi 112

Mitsubishi Electric UK Ltd
18th Floor, Centrepoint, 103 New Oxford Street, London, WC1A 1AB
Tel: 0171 379 7160
Fax: 0171 836 0699
CH: Sir Peter Parker, *MD:* T. Nitta 53

Mitsubishi Estate Co Ltd
Marunouchi Building, 4-1 Marunouchi 2-chome, Chiyoda-ku, Tokyo 100, Japan
Tel: +81 3 3287 5100
Fax: +81 3 3214 7036
P: Takeshi Fukuzawa, *CH:* Jotaro Takagi, *JMD:* Yoneichiro Baba, Takuji Suzuki, Takuji Yamashita, Mitsuo Sugimori, Kiyoaki Hara, Shigeru Takagi, Toshiro Okamoto, Kiyoshi Hirata, Shigeru Aoki, Hiroshi Baba, Hirofumi Okuizumi, Tadataka Uchida 112

Mitsubishi Heavy Industries Ltd
5-1 Marunouchi 2-chome, Chiyoda-ku, Tokyo 100, Japan
Tel: +81 3 3212 3111
Fax: +81 3 3284 1927
P: Kentaro Aikawa, *CH:* Yotaro Iida, *JMD:* Michiaki Kono, Yoshihisa Tsuda, Hiroshi Akita, Kiyokazu Kawai, Yutaka Hineno, Nobuyuki Masuda, Tsuneo Uebayashi, Yasuo Nagai, Hiromi Hirata, Takeshi Nakajima 112

Mitsubishi Motors Corpn
33-8, Shiba 5-chome, Minato-ku, Tokyo 108, Japan
Tel: +81 3 3456 111
P: Hirokazu Nakamura, *JMD:* Reijiro Kuromizu, Shigeru Nakagawa, Taizo Yokoyama, Nobuhisa Tsukahara, Motoo Suzuki, Yorio Kyono, Mitsuo Hattori, Minoru Wada, Tadashi Kobayashi 113

Mitsubishi Trust and Banking Corpn (The)
4-5 Marunouchi 1-chome, Chiyoda-ku, Tokyo 100, Japan
Tel: +81 3 3212 1211
Fax: +81 3 3284 1326
P: Hiroshi Hayashi, *CH:* Takuji Shidachi, *JMD:* Yukio Ebina, Masami Hinata, Shigeru Kobayashi, Kunio Inasaki, Norihisa Sasaki, Sadao Takahashi, Masanao Kato, Akio Utsumi, Noriyoshi Yamaguchi, Katsutoshi Yamada, Takahiko Suzuki 113

Mitsui & Co. Ltd
2-1 Ohtemachi 1-chome, Chiyoda-ku, Tokyo 100, Japan
Tel: +81 3 3285 1111
P: Naohiko Kumagai, *CH:* Koichiro Ejiri, *JMD:* Kyoichi Suzuki, Junichi Amano, Mutsubu Uchida, Taizo Kiyomine, Takeo Tsuchikawa, Kazuo Sato, Goro Watanabe, Naoyuki Kondo, Seiko Marumo, Masayuki Ikeda, Masayoshi Furuhata, Kazumasa Suzuki, Yoshimasa Nakano, Naomichi Suzuki, Fumio Otsuka, Shosaburo Yamanaka, Shigeru Endo, Yasuo Kurosawa, Toshikatsu Fukuma 112

Mitsui Fudosan Co. Ltd
Mitsui Nigokan, 1-1 Nihonbashi-Muromachi 2-chome, Chuo-ku, Tokyo 103, Japan
Tel: +81 3 3246 3065
Fax: +81 3 3275 2273
P: Jun-Ichiro Tanaka, *CH:* Hajime Tsuboi, *JMD:* Keiichi Minokawa, Shiro Ishizu, Kazuo Sato, Tadashi Yamada, Shinya Taira, Kunio Takahashi, Takao Shimizu, Tsutomu Manabe, Moriya Saito 112

Mitsui O.S.K. Lines Ltd
6-32 Nakanoshima 3 chome, Kita-Ku, Osaka 530, Japan
P: Masahuru Ikuta, *CH:* Susumu Temporin, *JMD:* Takane Sugimoto, Masahuru Ikuta, Masanori Shono, Shozo Hoshino, Takatoshi Wakasugi, Shigeo Tanaka, Toshitaka Hamamoto, Toshishige Yamana, Hironori Nishimaki, Makoto Ishii 113

Mitsui Trust & Banking Co. Ltd (The)
1-1 Nihonbashi-Muromachi 2-chome, Chuo-ku, Tokyo 103, Japan
Tel: +81 3 3270 9511
P: Ken Fujii, *JMD:* Keiu Nishida, Yoshio Yamashita, Hiroshi Nishiki, Hirokazu Hirachi, Kiichiro Furusawa, Nobuo Kinya, Yasuo Yamazaki, Hiroyuki Saba, Hisao Tanaka 113

Mo och Domsjo AB
Strandvagen 1, PO Box 5407, 114 84 Stockholm, Sweden
Tel: +46 8 666 21 00
Fax: +46 8 666 21 35
P: B. Pettersson 97

Mobil Corpn
3225 Gallows Road, Fairfax, Virginia, 22037-0001, USA
Tel: +1 703 846-3000
P: L.A. Noto, *CH:* L.A. Noto 13, 110

Mobil Oil AG
Steinstr 5, 20095 Hamburg, Germany
CH: Dr J. Krumnow 100

Mobil Oil Co. Ltd
Mobil House, 54/60 Victoria Street, London, SW1E 6QB
Tel: 0171 828 9777
CH: J.M. Banfield 47, 107

Moeara Enim Petroleum Mij
Heemraadssingel 56, 3021 DC Rotterdam, The Netherlands
Tel: +31 10-476 7222
Fax: +31 10-477 1840
CH: Mr Drs H. Langman 99

Molins PLC
11 Tanners Drive, Blakelands, Milton Keynes, MK14 5LU
Tel: 01908 216511
Fax: 01908 216499
CH: J.C. Orr, *MD:* P.W. Greenwood, *FD:* I.A.H. McPhie 52

Molyneux Estates PLC
Catherine House, 76 Gloucester Place, London, W1H 4DQ
Tel: 0171 487 3401
Fax: 0171 487 4211
CH: D.J. Lewis 60

Monarch Holdings PLC
66 Broomfield Road, Chelmsford, Essex, CM1 1SW
No officers designated 53

Monks Investment Trust, PLC (The)
67 Lombard Street, London, EC3P 3DL
Tel: 0171 623 4356
Fax: 0171 726 2342
CH: M. Hamilton 41, 46, 104

Montedison SpA
Foro Buonaparte 31, 20121 Milan, Italy
Tel: +39 2 6270 5519
CH: L. Lucchini, *MD:* E. Bondi 92

Monument Oil and Gas PLC
80 Petty France, London, SW1H 9EX
Tel: 0171 233 1966
Fax: 0171 233 3476
CH: A.R.G. McGibbon, *CE:* A. Craven Walker, *FD:* Liz P. Airey 48

Moorfield Estates PLC
2 Deanery Street, London, W1Y 5LH
Tel: 0171 495 0025
CH: R. Redmayne, *JMD:* D. Lucie-Smith, G. Stout 60

Moorgate Smaller Companies Income Trust PLC
49 Hay's Mews, London, W1X 7RT
Tel: 0171 409 3419
Fax: 0171 493 7229
CH: Sir Michael Richardson 56

Morgan Crucible Company PLC (The)
Morgan House, Madeira Walk, Windsor, Berkshire, SL4 1EP
Tel: 01753 837000
Fax: 01753 850872
CH: Sir James Spooner, *MD:* Dr E.B. Farmer, *FD:* G.D. Swetman 47, 106

Morgan Stanley Group Inc.
1251 Avenue of the Americas, New York, New York, 10020, USA
Tel: +1 212 703-4000
P: J.J. Mack, *CH:* R.B. Fisher, *JMD:* B.M. Biggs, P.F. Karches, R.W. Matschullat 111

Morgan [J.P.] & Co. Inc.
60 Wall Street, New York, NY, 10260-0060, USA
Tel: +1 212 483-2323
CH: D.A. Warner III 110

Morland & Co. PLC
PO Box 5, The Brewery, Ock Street, Abingdon, Oxon, OX14 5DD
Tel: 01235 553377
Fax: 01235 529484
CH: J.M. Clutterbuck, *MD:* M.S.T. Watts, *FD:* P.E. Rivers 53

Morris [Philip] Cos Inc.
120 Park Avenue, New York, NY, 10017, USA
Tel: +1 212 880 5000
CH: G.C. Bibie 110

Morrison [Wm.] Supermarkets PLC
Hilmore House, Thornton Road, Bradford, BD8 9AX
Tel: 01274 494166
Fax: 01274 494831
CH: K.D. Morrison, *FD:* M. Ackroyd 46, 104

Motor-Columbus AG
Parkstrasse 27, 5401 Baden, Switzerland
Tel: +41 56 30 11 11
Fax: +41 56 21 13 29
CH: H. Steinmann 95

Motorola Inc.
1303 East Algonquin Road, Schaumburg, Illinois, 60196, USA
Tel: +1 708 576 5000
P: C.B. Galvin, *CH:* W.J. Weisz 111

Mount Isa Holdings (UK) Ltd
Botany Road, Northfleet, Gravesend, Kent, DA11 9BG
Tel: 01474 351188
Fax: 01474 334013
CH: R.H.Y. Mills 54

Mowlem [John] & Company PLC
White Lion Court, Swan Street, Isleworth, Middlesex, TW7 6RN
Tel: 0181 568 9111
Fax: 0181 847 4802
CH: K.J. Minton, *CE:* J.R. Marshall, *FD:* C.R. Barton 50

Mucklow [A. & J.] Group PLC
Haden Cross, Haden Cross Drive, Cradley Heath, Warley, West Midlands, B64 7JB
Tel: 0121 550 1841
Fax: 0121 550 7532
CH: Albert J. Mucklow 50

Munchener Ruckversicherungs-Ges AG
Koniginstrasse 107, 80802 Munich, Germany
Tel: +49 89 38 91-0
Fax: +49 89 39 90 56
CH: D. Spethmann, H.-J. Schinzler 89, 94

Murray Income Trust PLC
7 West Nile Street, Glasgow, G1 2PX
Tel: 0141 226 3131
Fax: 0141 248 5420
CH: Rt Hon Lord Younger of Prestwick 41, 49

Murray International Trust PLC
7 West Nile Street, Glasgow, G1 2PX
Tel: 0141 226 3131
Fax: 0141 248 5420
CH: The Rt Hon Lord Younger of Prestwick 41, 46, 104

Murray Smaller Markets Trust PLC
7 West Nile Street, Glasgow, G1 2PX
Tel: 0141 226 3131
Fax: 0141 248 5420
CH: The Rt Hon Lord Younger of Prestwick 41, 49

Murray Ventures PLC
7 West Nile Street, Glasgow, G1 2PX
Tel: 0141 226 3131
Fax: 0141 248 5420
CH: The Rt Hon Lord Younger of Prestwick 56

Murray International Holdings Ltd
Murray House, 4 Redheughs Rigg, South Gyle, Edinburgh, EH12 9DQ
CH: D.E. Murray, *MD:* J. MacDonald, *FD:* G.K. Freeland 41, 46, 104

NCC AB
171 80 Solna, Sweden
Tel: +46 8 655 20 00
Fax: +46 8 83 15 70
P: J. Sjoqvist, *CH:* B. Magnusson 100

NEC Corpn
7-1 Shiba 5-chome, Minato-Ku, Tokyo 108-01, Japan
Tel: +81 3 3454 1111
Fax: +81 3 3798 1510
P: Hisashi Kaneko, *CH:* Tadahiro Sekimoto 112

NEC Technologies (UK) Ltd
Castle Farm Campus, Priorslee, Telford, Shropshire, TF2 9SA
Tel: 01952 620440
Fax: 01952 620441
MD: Y. Matsuo 59

NFC PLC
The Merton Centre, 45 St Peters Street, Bedford, MK40 2UB
Tel: 01234 272222
Fax: 01234 270900
CH: Sir Christopher Bland, *FD:* T.G. Larman 45, 100

NKK Corpn
1-1-2 Marunouchi, Chiyoda-ku, Tokyo 100, Japan
Tel: +81 3 212 7111
P: Shunkichi Miyoshi, *CH:* Yoshinari Yamashiro, *JMD:* Yoshiharu Miyawaki, Teiji Shibuya, Kazuo Kunioka, Korekiyo Iwabe, Kiyoshi Kishi, Yoshimichi Jibiki, Akira Tajimi, Yutaka Tanaka, Akihiko Nagasawa, Takayuki Koyano, Cho Otani, Shigeharu Dote 112

NKT Holding AS
NKT Alle 1, 2605 Brondby, Denmark
Tel: +45 43 48 20 00
Fax: +45 42 96 18 20
CH: C. Kjaer, *MD:* G. Albrechtsen 109

NORWEB PLC
Talbot Road, Manchester, M16 0HQ
Tel: 0161 873 8000
Fax: 0161 875 7360
CH: K.G. Harvey, *FD:* B.J. Wilson 45, 100

NPM-Nederlandse Participatie Mij NV
Breitnerstraat 1-3, Amsterdam, The Netherlands
Tel: +31 20 570 5555
Fax: +31 20 671 0855
CH: Drs J.D. Hooglandt, *MD:* J. Keyzer 109

NSM PLC
Mansfield Road, Hasland, Chesterfield, Derbyshire, S41 0JW
Tel: 01246 558558
Fax: 01246 559090
CH: J.G. Jermine, *MD:* C.J. Phoenix 56

NYNEX CableComms Group
The Tolworth Tower, Ewell Road,
Surbiton, Surrey, KT6 7ED
Tel: 01932 884 400
P: E.P. Connell,
CH: R.W. Blackburn 12, 48, 109

NYNEX Corpn
1095 Avenue of the Americas,
New York, New York, 10036, USA
Tel: +1 212 395-2121
P: I.G. Seidenberg,
CH: I.G. Seidenberg 110

Nacanco (Holdings) Ltd
100 Capability Green, Luton, Beds,
LU1 3LG
Tel: 01582 400822
CH: M.D. Herdman 53

National & Provincial Building Society
Provincial House, Bradford, BD1 1NL
Tel: 01274 733444
CH: The Lord Shuttleworth,
CE: A.D. Lyons 16, 68

National Australia Bank Ltd
24th Floor, 500 Bourke Street,
Melbourne, Victoria, 3000, Australia
Tel: +61 3 641 3500
CH: W.R.M. Irvine,
CE: D.R. Argus 114

National Express Group PLC
Ensign Court, 4 Vicarage Road,
Edgbaston, Birmingham, B15 3ES
Tel: 0121 625 1122
Fax: 0121 625 1284
CH: A.M. Davies, *CE:* P.R. McEnhill,
FD: C. Child 60

National Farmers Union Mutual Insurance Society Ltd (The)
Tiddington Road, Stratford-upon-Avon,
CV37 7BJ
Tel: 01789 204211
Fax: 01789 298992
CH: A. Evans, *MD:* A.S. Young 45, 101

National Grid Holding PLC (The)
185 Park Street, London, SE1 9DY
Tel: 0171 620 9000
CH: K.G. Harvey 30, 40, 43, 94

National Home Loans Holdings PLC
St Catherine's Court, Herbert Road,
Solihull, West Midlands, B91 3QE
Tel: 0121 711 3333
Fax: 0121 711 1330
CH: J.P.L. Perry, *CE:* N. Terrington,
FD: N. Keen 37, 43, 96

National Parking Corporation Ltd
21 Bryanston Street, London, W1A 4NH
Tel: 0171 499 7050
Fax: 0171 491 3577
CH: R.F. Hobson, Sir Donald Gosling,
CE: R.D. Mackenzie 49

National Power PLC
Windmill Hill Business Park, Whitehill
Way, Swindon, Wiltshire, SN5 6PB
Tel: 01793 892066
CH: J.W. Baker, *CE:* K. Henry,
FD: S.B. Birkenhead 23, 40, 42, 92

National Semiconductor (U.K.) Ltd
The Maple, Kembrey Park, Swindon,
Wilts, SN2 6YX
Tel: 01793 614141
Fax: 01793 697650
No officers designated 55

National Westminster Bank PLC
41 Lothbury, London, EC2P 2BP
Tel: 0171 726 1000
CH: Lord Alexander of Weedon,
CE: D. Wanless, *FD:* R.K. Goeltz 14,
16, 30, 40, 42, 72, 72, 88, 90

Nationale Investeringsbank [De] NV
Carnegieplein 4, PO Box 380,
2501 BH The Hague, The Netherlands
Tel: +31 70 342 54 25
Fax: +31 70 365 10 71
CH: Drs N. Kroes,
Prof Dr M.J.L. Jonkhart,
JMD: Mr J. de Vroe, Mr J.F. Ariens 94

NationsBank Corpn
Nationsbank Corporate Center,
Charlotte, North Carolina, 28255, USA
Tel: +1 704 386-5000
CH: H.L. McColl Jr 110

Nationwide Building Society
Nationwide House, Pipers Way,
Swindon, SN38 1NW
Tel: 01793 513513
CH: Sir Colin R. Corness,
CE: Dr B.E. Davis,
FD: A.R.H. Dales 38, 43, 86, 96

Navigation Mixte [Cie de]
1 La Canebiere, 13001 Marseilles, France
CH: A. Launois, *MD:* M. Fournier 93

Neckarwerke Elektrizitatsversorgungs-AG
Kuferstrasse 2, 73728 Esslingen
(Neckar), Germany
Tel: +49 711 31 90-0
Fax: +49 711 3190-2033
CH: U. Bauer, Dr E.A. Wein 99

Nederlandse Gasunie [NV]
Concourslaan 17, PO Box 19,
9700 MA Groningen, The Netherlands
Tel: +31 50 219111
Fax: +31 50 267248
CH: H.J.L. Vonhoff,
MD: Drs G.H.B. Verberg 101

Nederlandse Spoorwegen NV
Moreelsepark, 3511 EP Utrecht,
The Netherlands
Tel: +31 30 359 111
CH: E.J. Verloop, Drs R. den Besten 93

Nedlloyd NV [Koninklijke]
Boompjes 40, 3011 XB Rotterdam,
The Netherlands
Tel: +31 10 400 69 11
CH: O.H.A. van Royen,
L.J.M. Berndsen 98

Neptune Orient Lines Ltd
456 Alexandra Road, NOL Building
#06-00, Singapore 0511
Tel: +65 2789000
Fax: +65 2785900
CH: Herman Ronald Hochstadt 115

Neste Oy
PO Box 20, 02151 Espoo, Finland
Tel: +358-0-4501
Fax: +358-0-450 4447
CH: J. Ihamuotila, A. Kalliomaki 93

Nestle SA
Avenue Nestle 55, 1800 Vevey,
Switzerland
Tel: +41 21 924 21 11
CH: H.O. Maucher 62, 71, 88, 90

New Throgmorton Trust (1983) PLC (The)
155 Bishopsgate, London, EC2M 3XJ
Tel: 0171 374 4100
CH: J.A. Morrell 57

New World Development Co. Ltd
30th Floor, New World Tower, 18
Queen's Road Central, Hong Kong
CH: Dato' Dr Cheng Yu-Tung,
MD: Cheng Kar-Shun, Henry 114

Newarthill PLC
40 Bernard Street, London, WC1N 1LG
Tel: 0171 837 3377
Fax: 0171 833 4102
CH: Sir Christopher Harding 54

Newcastle Building Society
Portland House, New Bridge Street,
Newcastle upon Tyne, NE1 8AL
Tel: 0191 232 6676
P: K.J. Hilton, *CH:* A.A.E. Glenton,
CE: D.W. Midgley,
FD: R.J. Holinshead 57

Newman Tonks Group PLC
The Crescent, Birmingham Business
Park, Birmingham, B37 7YX
Tel: 0121 717 7777
Fax: 0121 717 7776
CH: D.E. Rogers, *CE:* G.D. Gahan,
FD: N.F. Keegan 58

News Corpn Ltd (The)
121 King William Street, Adelaide,
SA, 5000, Australia
Tel: +61 218 9218
CH: Keith Rupert Murdoch,
FD: David Francis DeVoe 114

News International PLC
PO Box 495, Virginia Street, London,
E1 9XY
Tel: 0171 782 6000
Fax: 0171 895 9020
CH: L. Hinton, *CE:* W. O'Neill 17, 42,
79, 91

Next PLC
Desford Road, Enderby, Leicester,
LE9 5AT
Tel: 0116 286 6411
Fax: 0116 284 8998
CH: Lord Wolfson of Sunningdale,
CE: D.C. Jones 48

Nichii Co. Ltd
2-9 Awajimachi 2-chome, Chuo-ku,
Osaka 541, Japan
Tel: +81 6 203 5072
P: Toshimine Kobayashi, *JMD:* Hiroshi
Ohta, Yoshimasa Kobayashi, Kotaro
Utsunomiya, Kikuo Nagase, Kazuyuki
Saitou, Keizou Mori, Nobuyoshi
Kobayashi, Takuya Hoda, Sueo
Taguchi, Toshihiko Miyasaka, Tatsuo
Shinozaki, Shigetaka Hamai 113

Nichimen Corpn
13-1 Kyobashi 1-chome, Chuo-ku,
Tokyo 104, Japan
Tel: +81 3 3277 5111
Fax: +81 3 3277 5901
P: Akira Watari, *CH:* Yoshimi Tanaka,
JMD: Shuichi Nagayama, Shunro Itoh,
Yasunori Ogata, Yutaro Hirota, Teiji
Hiraoka, Tadashi Nakano, Masao
Kasai, Mikio Hirooka, Masahiro Tajiri,
Yoshihisa Sugimoto, Tsutomu Tanaka,
Toru Hambayashi, Hiroyuki Tabuchi,
Yukuo Maeda 113

Nikko Securities Co. Ltd (The)
3-1, Marunouchi 3-chome, Chiyoda-ku,
Tokyo 100, Japan
Tel: +81 3 3283 2211
Fax: +81 3 3283 2470
CH: Shoji Umemura 113

Nippon Oil Co. Ltd
3-12 Nishi Shimbashi 1-chome,
Minato-ku, Tokyo 105, Japan
Tel: +81 3 3502 1111
P: Hidejiro Ohsawa, *CH:* Yasuoki
Takeuchi, *JMD:* Kazumasa Tanaka,
Takashi Nogaki, Yasushi Ebihara,
Yusuke Ishimura 112

Nippon Shinpan Co. Ltd
33-5 3-chome, Hongo, Bunkyo-ku,
Tokyo 113-91, Japan
Tel: +81 3 3817 1060
Fax: +81 3 3817 0810
CH: Yoji Yamada, *JMD:* Hideharu
Matsumoto, Kimihisa Suzuki, Kazuo
Ikeda, Yuzo Furuya, Kunio Takagi,
Makoto Tanabe, Hiroshi Ichimura,
Terifumi Maruyama, Ichita Satoji, Shuji
Ogawa, Takehiko Abe, Kinji Nakamura,
Hiroshi Minato, Tadaomi Ito 112

Nippon Steel Corpn
6-3 Otemachi 2-chome, Chiyoda-ku,
Tokyo 100-71, Japan
Tel: +81 3 3242 4111
Fax: +81 3 3275 5607-9
P: Takashi Imai, *CH:* Hiroshi Saito,
JMD: Toshiro Fujiwara, Azusa Tomiura,
Rokuro Suehiro, Akira Chihaya, Teiken
Akizuki, Tokio Mitamura, Kichi
Nakazawa, Kazuhiko Fukuda, Yoshiro
Kamata, Susumu Fukagai, Takashi
Asamura, Sumio Takemoto, Kunihiko
Bando, Takaki Yamatoya 13, 112

Nippon Telegraph & Telephone Corpn
1-6 Uchisaiwaicho 1-chome, Chiyoda-ku,
Tokyo 100, Japan
Tel: +81 3 3509 5111
Fax: +81 3 3580 9104
P: Masashi Kojima,
CH: Haruo Yamaguchi 12, 13, 112

Nippon Yusen K.K.
3-2, Marunouchi 2-chome, Chiyoda-ku,
Tokyo 100, Japan
Tel: +81 3 3284 5151
Fax: +81 3 3284 6361
P: Jiro Nemoto, *CH:* Kimio Miyaoka,
JMD: Tsuneyoshi Imai, Noboru
Sakata, Takeo Shimada, Toru Inada,
Michio Tanaka, Kohei Morioka, Yasuo
Shimotamari, Toru Ichikawa, Koichi
Suzumura, Saburo Terashima, Kuniaki
Shirakuma 113

Nippondenso Co. Ltd
1-1 Showa-cho, Kariya, Aichi 448, Japan
Tel: +81 566 25 5858
Fax: +81 566 25 4537
P: Tsuneo Ishimaru, *CH:* Teikichiro
Toyoda, *JMD:* Taro Asahi, Hiroomi
Amano, Yoshimi Kumazawa, Takaaki
Ochi, Michio Ohiwa, Takashi Okabe,
Mineo Kawai, Hisanori Kobayashi,
Kinya Ito, Hiromu Okabe, Takashi
Kusunoki 113

Nissan Motor Co. Ltd
17-1 Ginza 6-chome, Chuo-ku, Tokyo
104-23, Japan
Tel: +81 3 3543 5523
P: Yoshifumi Tsuji, *CH:* Yutaka Kume,
JMD: Yoshio Arakawa, Heiichi
Hamaoka, Noboru Miura, Tadao Takei,
Kosei Minami, Yoshiyuki Miyakawa,
Shuji Miyake, Koichi Takagi, Shoji
Yoshinaga, Kenichi Sasaki, Yasuo
Nakajima, Kyoji Kasai, Tsutomu
Sawada, Tadahiro Shirai, Tetsuo
Tabata, Toshihiko Sekine, Hiroshi
Moriyama, Kouichiro Tohda 13, 112

Nissan Motor Manufacturing (UK) Ltd
Washington Road, Sunderland, Tyne &
Wear, SR5 3NS
Tel: 0191 415 0000
Fax: 0191 415 1077
CH: Tadahiro Shirai, *MD:* I. Gibson 45

Nissho Iwai Corpn
4-5 Akasaka 2-chome, Minato-ku,
Tokyo 107, Japan
Tel: +81 3 3588 2111
P: Akira Nishio, *JMD:* Susumu
Yoshida, Tatsuro Okada, Tsunemitsu
Kitayama, Matamitsu Goto, Hisataka
Ohno, Masatake Kusamichi, Hiroshi
Tomomori, Masayoshi Toriumi, Yasuo
Nakata, Nobutoshi Gonda, Masamitsu
Hiroumi, Yasuo Kato, Katsumi
Yoshioka, Saburo Sakakibara, Akira
Yokouchi, Toshihiro Tamura, Toshihisa
Kajiwara, Sukeji Ishino, Takeshi
Chiba, Mitsuo Ijuin, Tadao Miyase,
Yoshinori Takeda 112

Nokia Corpn
Etelaesplanadi 12, 00101 Helsinki,
Finland
Tel: +358 0 180 71
Fax: +358 0 656 388
CH: C. Ehrnrooth, J. Ollila 95

Nomura Securities Co. Ltd (The)
Urbannet Otemachi Building 5F, 2-2-2
Otemachi, Chiyoda-ku, Tokyo 100,
Japan
Tel: +81 3 3211 1811
P: Hideo Sakamaki, *CH:* Masashi
Suzuki, *JMD:* Atsushi Saito, Ken
Tamura, Katsuya Takanashi, Akira
Tsuda, Masahiro Aozono, Nobuo
Nakazawa, Akira Ogino, Yasuhiko
Sato, Yasuo Annaka, Koichi Kane,
Hironobu Goto 112

Norcros PLC
Norcros House, Bagshot Road,
Bracknell, Berkshire, RG12 3SW
Tel: 01344 861878
Fax: 01344 861642
CH: M.E. Doherty, *MD:* R.H. Alcock,
FD: G.M. Morris 50

Nord Est
10 rue d'Athenes, 75009 Paris, France
Tel: +33 1 44 53 42 42
Fax: +33 1 42 81 10 81
CH: G. Rambaud, M. Jacquet 107

Nordbanken
Smalandsgatan 17, 105 71 Stockholm,
Sweden
Tel: +46 8 614 70 00
Fax: +46 8 20 08 46
P: H. Dalborg, *CH:* J. Palmstierna 97

Norfolk Southern Corpn
Three Commercial Place, Norfolk,
Virginia, 23510-2191, USA
Tel: +1 804 629-2600
CH: D.R. Goode 111

Norsk Hydro (UK) Ltd
Bridge House, 69 London Road,
Twickenham, Middlesex, TW1 1EE
Tel: 0181 891 1366
Fax: 0181 892 1686
CH: J.M. Clay, *MD:* J.G. Speirs 48, 109

Norsk Hydro AS
Bygdoy alle 2, Oslo, Norway
Tel: +47 22 43 21 00
Fax: +47 22 43 27 25
P: E. Myklebust, *CH:* T. Aakvaag 87, 91

Norske Skogindustrier AS
7620 Skogn, Norway
Tel: +47 74 08 70 00
Fax: +47 74 08 71 00
CH: L. Westerbo 100

Nortel Ltd
Stafferton Way, Maidenhead,
Berkshire, SL6 1AY
Tel: 01628 812000
No officers designated 44, 99

North Atlantic Smaller Companies Investment Trust PLC
30 Queen Anne's Gate, London,
SW1H 9AL
Tel: 0171 222 2020
CH: R.D.C. Brooke,
CE: C.H.B. Mills 61

North Ltd
6th Floor, 476 St Kilda Road,
Melbourne, Victoria, 3004, Australia
Tel: +61 03 829 0000
Fax: + 61 03 867 4351
CH: Christopher Michael Deeley,
MD: Campbell McCheyne Anderson,
FD: Harold Arthur Julian Vear 110

North West Water Group PLC
Dawson House, Great Sankey,
Warrington, WA5 3LW
Tel: 01925 234000
Fax: 01925 233361
CH: Sir Desmond H. Pitcher,
CE: B.L. Staples,
FD: R.J. Ferguson 27, 43, 94

Northern Electric PLC
Carliol House, Market Street,
Newcastle upon Tyne, NE1 6NE
Tel: 0191 221 2000
Fax: 0191 235 2109
CH: D.R. Morris, *CE:* A. Hadfield,
FD: J. Edwards 14, 46, 103

Northern Foods PLC
Beverley House, St Stephen's Square,
Hull, HU1 3XG
Tel: 01482 25432
Fax: 01482 226136
CH: C.R. Haskins, *FD:* M. Clark 46, 103

Northern Ireland Electricity PLC
120 Malone Road, Belfast, BT9 5HT
Tel: 01232 661100
Fax: 01232 663579
CH: D.G. Jefferies, *CE:* Dr P.H. Haren,
FD: P.G. Woodworth 48, 108

Northern Rock Building Society
Northern Rock House, Gosforth,
Newcastle upon Tyne, NE3 4PL
Tel: 0191 285 7191
Fax: 0191 284 8470
CH: R.H. Dickinson, *MD:* J.C. Sharp,
FD: R.F. Bennett 44, 99

Northington Group Ltd (The)
77 St John Street, London, EC1M 4AN
CH: G. Black 59

Northumbrian Water Group PLC
Northumbria House, Regent Centre,
Gosforth, Newcastle upon Tyne,
NE3 3PX
Tel: 0191 284 3151
Fax: 0191 284 0378
CH: Prof Sir Frederick G. Holliday,
CE: D.G. Cranston,
FD: J.M. Taylor 44, 99

Novo Nordisk AS
Novo Alle, 2880 Bagsvaerd, Denmark
Tel: +45 4444 8888
Fax: +45 4449 0555
P: M. Ovlisen, *CH:* V. Andersen,
CE: G. Almind 96

Nuclear Electric PLC
Barnett Way, Barnwood, Gloucester,
GL4 7RS
Tel: 01452 652222
CH: J.G. Collier, *CE:* Dr R. Hawley,
FD: M.R. Kirwan 18, 35, 40, 42,
79, 91

Nurdin & Peacock PLC
Bushey Road, Raynes Park, London,
SW20 0JJ

O.C.S. - Pillar

Tel: 0181 946 9111
Fax: 0181 879 1744
CH: R.D. Fulford, *CE:* D. Sims,
FD: H.N. Hall 53

O.C.S. Group Ltd
79 Limpsfield Road, Sanderstead,
Surrey, CR2 9LB
Tel: 0181 651 3211
Fax: 0181 651 4832
CH: D.H.G. Goodliffe,
MD: F.D. Cracknell 61

OMV AG
Otto-Wagner-Platz 5, Postfach 15,
1091 Vienna, Austria
Tel: +43 222 404 40 0
Fax: +43 222 404 40 91
CH: Dkfm Dr O. Grunwald,
Dr R. Schenz 94

ORIX Corpn
World Trade Center Building,
2-4-1 Hamamatsu-cho, Minato-ku,
Tokyo 105, Japan
Tel: + 81 3 3435 6641
Fax: +81 3 3434 6042
P: Yoshihiko Miyauchi, *CH:* Tsuneo Inui, *JMD:* Koichi Maki, Komao Hirose, Etsuo Hashimoto, Shozo Uchida, Shunji Sasaki, Yoshiaki Ishida 112

Occidental Petroleum Corpn
10889 Wilshire Boulevard, Los
Angeles, California, 90024-4201, USA
Tel: +1 310 208-8800
CH: Dr R.R. Irani 111

Oce-van der Grinten NV
St Urbanusweg 43, Venlo,
The Netherlands
Tel: +31 77 592222
Fax: +31 77 544700
CH: H.B. van Liemt,
J.V.H. Pennings 102

Ocean Group PLC
Ocean House, The Ring, Bracknell,
Berkshire, RG12 1AN
Tel: 01344 302000
Fax: 01344 710031
CH: P.I. Marshall,
CE: J.M. Allan 48, 108

Oerlikon-Buhrle Holding AG
Hofwiesenstrasse 135, 8021 Zurich,
Switzerland
Tel: +41 1 363 40 60
Fax: +41 1 363 72 60
CH: Dr H. Widmer 96

Okobank Osuuspankkien Keskuspankki Oy
Arkadiankatu 23, 001000 Helsinki,
Finland
Tel: +358 0 4041
Fax: +358 0 404 2624
CH: A. Tanskanen, P. Komi,
MD: S. Klymanen 105

Olivetti & C. [Ing C.], SpA
Via G. Jervis 77, 10015 Ivrea,
Turin, Italy
Tel: +39 125 522 428
Fax: +39 125 522 067
CH: B. Visentini, C. de Benedetti,
MD: C. Passera 93

Opel [Adam] AG
Bahnhofsplatz 1, 65423 Russelsheim,
Germany
Tel: +49 61 42 6 61
Fax: +49 61 42 66 48 59
CH: F. Schwenger, D.J. Herman,
MD: C. Grupe 93

Oreal (L')
14 rue Royale, 75008 Paris, France
CH: L. Owen-Jones 89, 94

Orient Corpn
Sunshine 60 Building, 1-1 Higashi-
Ikebukuro 3-chome, Toshima-ku,
Tokyo 170, Japan
Tel: +81 3 3989 6111
Fax: +81 3 3985 5365
P: Hiroshi Arai, *JMD:* Kazuya Sagara, Takao Matsushita, Takashi Naganuma, Hiromichi Tateishi, Hiroyuki Ozaki, Haruo Kuratani, Hajime Nishiuchi, Haruo Asai, Kinya Takahashi, Iwao Iijima, Ryujiro Saegusa, Kazuo Sugiyama 112

Orkla AS
PO Box 162, 1701 Sarpsborg, Norway
Tel: +47 69 11 80 00
Fax: +47 69 11 87 70
P: J.P. Heyerdahl,
CH: S. Ribe-Anderssen 97

Osaka Gas Co. Ltd
1-2 Hiranomachi 4-chome, Chuo-ku,
Osaka 541, Japan
Tel: +81 6 202 2221
Fax: +81 6 202 4637
P: Shin-ichiro Ryoki, *CH:* Masafumi Ohnishi, *JMD:* Masaji Yamamoto, Hisashi Miyakoshi, Nobuhiro Kanatsuji, Toshinori Sagashima, Choji Miyano, Takemi Arimoto, Suzuo Dan, Tohru Nomura, Shozo Endo, Motozo Yoshikawa 113

Ostasiatiske Kompagni AS (Det)
7 Midtermolen, 2100 Copenhagen O,
Denmark
Tel: +45 35 27 27 27
Fax: +45 31 42 12 34
CH: J. Erlund, *JMD:* M. Fiorini,
C. Dencker Nielsen 102

Osterreichische Brau-Beteiligungs-AG
Poschacherstrasse 35, 4020 Linz, Austria
Tel: +43 732 69 51-0
Fax: +43 732 65 51-150
CH: Dr-Ing F. Kretz 108

Osterreichische Elektrizitatswirtschafts-AG (Verbundgesellschaft)
Am Hof 6a, 1010 Vienna, Austria
CH: Prof H. Krejci 93

Osterreichische Industrieholding AG-OIAG
Kantgasse 1, 1015 Vienna, Austria
Tel: +43 1 711 14
Fax: +43 1 245 711 14
CH: Dr J. Staribacher,
K. Hollweger 87, 91

Otto Versand (GmbH & Co.)
Wandsbeker Strasse 3-7, 22179
Hamburg, Germany
Tel: +49 40 64 61-0
Fax: +49 40 64 61-85 71
CH: W. Otto, K.-A. Hopmann,
Dr M. Otto 96

Outokumpu Oy
PO Box 280, Lansituulentie 7 A, 02101
Espoo, Finland
Tel: +358 0 4211
Fax: +358 0 421 3888
CH: M. Puhakka, *CE:* J. Juusela 96

Oversea-Chinese Banking Corpn Ltd
65 Chulia Street 08-00, OCBC Centre,
Singapore 0104
Tel: +65 530 1515
Fax: +65 533 7955
CH: Tan Keng Yam, Tony 114

Overseas Investment Trust PLC (The)
20 Finsbury Circus, London, EC2M 1NB
Tel: 0171 256 7500
Fax: 0171 826 0331
CH: Lord Wakehurst 41, 47, 50, 52, 106

Overseas Union Bank Ltd
OUB Centre, 1 Raffles Place,
Singapore, 0104
Tel: +65 5338686
Fax: +65 5332293
P: Peter Seah Lim Huat,
CH: Lee Hee Seng 115

Oxford Instruments PLC
Old Station Way, Eynsham, Witney,
Oxon, OX8 1TL
Tel: 01865 881437
Fax: 01865 881944
CH: P.M. Williams, *FD:* M. Lamaison 60

PHH Europe PLC
PHH Centre, Windmill Hill, Whitehill
Way, Swindon, Wiltshire, SN5 9YT
Tel: 01793 887000
Fax: 01793 886688
No officers designated 51

PORTUCEL - Empresa de Celulose e Papel de Portugal SA
Rua Jaoquim Antonio de Aguiar 32/8,
1100 Lisbon, Portugal
Tel: +351 1 9150197
Fax: +351 1 530016
CH: J. Manuel de Oliveira Godinho 102

PSIT PLC
1 Love Lane, London, EC2V 7JJ
Tel: 0171 606 8744
Fax: 0171 606 4057
CH: A.R. Perry, *MD:* G.H. Caines 49

PT Indocement Tunggal Prakarsa
Wisma Indocement, 13/F, Jalan Jendral
Sudirman Kav. 70-71, Jakarta 12910,
Indonesia
Tel: +62 21 251 2121
Fax: +62 21 251 0066
P: Sudwikatmono 115

PWA Papierwerke Waldhof-Aschaffenburg AG
Postfach 11 00, 83060 Raubling,
Germany
Tel: +49 80 35 80 0
Fax: +49 80 35 80 598
CH: Dr Klaus Gotte, A. Heinzel 100

Pacific Assets Trust PLC
One Charlotte Square, Edinburgh,
EH2 4DZ
Tel: 0131 225 1357
Fax: 0131 225 2375
CH: I.F.H. Grant 54

Pacific Dunlop Ltd
Level 41, 101 Collins street,
Melbourne, Victoria, 3000, Australia
Tel: +61 3 270 7270
Fax: +61 3 270 7300
CH: John B. Gough,
MD: Philip Brass 115

Pacific Gas & Electric Co.
77 Beale Street, San Francisco,
California, 94177, USA
Tel: +1 415 973-2880
P: R.D. Glynn Jr, S.T. Skinner, *CH:* S.T. Skinner, *MD:* D.M. Lawerence, *FD:* G.R. Smith 110

Pacific Telesis Group
130 Kearny Street, San Francisco,
California, 94108, USA
Tel: +1 415 394-3000
CH: P.J. Quigley 110

Pacificorp
700 NE Multnomah, Suite 1600,
Portland, Oregon, 97232-4116, USA
Tel: +1 503 731-2000
P: F.W. Buckman,
CH: K.R. McKennon 111

Pakhoed NV [Koninklijke]
Blaak 333, 3011 GB Rotterdam,
The Netherlands
Tel: +31 10 400 29 11
Fax: +31 10 413 98 29
CH: J.H. Choufoer, N.J. Westdijk 102

Pall Europe Ltd
Europa House, Havant Street,
Portsmouth, Hants, PO1 3PD
Tel: 01705 753545
Fax: 01705 831324
CH: D.T.D. Williams 57

Panasonic U.K. Ltd
Willoughby Road, Bracknell,
Berkshire, RG12 8FP
Tel: 01344 862444
Fax: 01344 861656
No officers designated 50

Pantheon International Participations PLC
Alban Gate, 14th Floor, 125 London
Wall, London, EC2Y 5AS
Tel: 0171 710 4567
Fax: 0171 696 0966
CH: W.T.J. Griffin 60

Pargesa Holding SA
11 Grand-Rue, 1204 Geneva,
Switzerland
Tel: +41 22 311 89 25
Fax: +41 22 310 83 84
CH: P. Desmarais Sr 97

Paribas [Cie Financiere de]
5 rue d'Antin, 75078 Paris, France
Tel: +33 1 42 98 12 34
Fax: +33 1 42 98 11 42
CH: M. Francois-Poncet,
A. Levy-Lang 68, 86, 90

Parmalat Finanziaria
15 Corso Italia, Milan, Italy
Tel: +39 2 72 01 01 64
Fax: +39 2 869 3863
CH: C. Tanzi 100

Partek AB [Oy]
Sornaisten rantantie 23, PO Box 61,
00501 Helsinki, Finland
Tel: +358 0 39441
Fax: +358 0 3944 222
P: C. Taxell, *CH:* C.O. Tallgren 104

Paterson Zochonis PLC
Bridgewater House, 60 Whitworth
Street, Manchester, M1 6LU
Tel: 0161 236 7111
Fax: 0161 228 6719
CH: A.J. Green, *MD:* G.A. Loupos 49

Pavilion Services Group Ltd
Armstrong House, 38 Market Square,
Uxbridge, Middlesex, UB8 1NG
Tel: 01895 233333
Fax: 01525 878291
CE: J.P.W. Long 58

Pearson PLC
3 Burlington Gardens, London, W1X 1LE
Tel: 0171 411 2000
Fax: 0171 411 2390
CH: Viscount Blakenham,
MD: F. Barlow, *FD:* J.A.B. Joll 39, 43, 96

Pechiney
Immeuble Balzac, 10 place des Vosges,
La Defense 5, 92400 Courbevoie, France
Tel: +33 1 46 91 46 91
Fax: +33 1 46 91 51 42
CH: J.-P. Rodier 79, 86, 91

Peco Energy Co.
2301 Market Street, PO Box 8699,
Philadelphia, Pennsylvania, 19101, USA
Tel: +1 215 841-4000
P: C.A. McNeill Jr,
CH: J.F. Paquette Jr 110

Peel Holdings PLC
Quay West, Trafford Wharf Road,
Manchester, M17 1HH
Tel: 0161 877 4714
Fax: 0161 877 4720
CH: J. Whittaker, *MD:* P.A. Scott,
FD: P.P. Wainscott 46, 102

Pendragon PLC
Pendragon House, Sir Frank Whittle
Road, Derby, DE21 4EE
Tel: 01332 292777
Fax: 01332 292224
CH: A.N.R. Rudd, *CE:* T.G. Finn,
FD: I. Wheeler 60

Peninsular and Oriental Steam Navigation Company (The)
79 Pall Mall, London, SW1Y 5EJ
Tel: 0171 930 4343
Fax: 0171 930 8572
CH: The Lord Sterling of Plaistow,
MD: Sir Bruce MacPhail 22, 42, 92

Penney [J C] Co. Inc.
6501 Legacy Drive, Plano, Texas,
75024-3698, USA
P: W.B. Tygart, *CH:* W.R. Howell 111

Pepe Group PLC
34 Bridge Road, London, NW10 9BX
Tel: 0171 836 8666
Fax: 0171 568 4111
CH: S.K.F. Chou, *CE:* L.S. Stroll,
FD: S.R. Neil 61

Pepsico Finance (UK) Ltd
21 Holborn Viaduct, London, EC1A 2DY
No officers designated 45, 100

Pepsico Inc.
Purchase, New York, 10577, USA
Tel: +1 914 253 3055
CH: W. Calloway 110

Perkins Foods PLC
Trinity Court, Trinity Street,
Peterborough, PE1 1DA
Tel: 01733 555706
Fax: 01733 558499
CH: A.M. Davies, *CE:* H.G. Phillips,
FD: I.M. Blackburn 58

Pernod Ricard
142 bd Haussmann, 75008 Paris, France
Tel: +33 1 40 76 77 78
Fax: +33 1 42 25 95 66
CH: Patrick Ricard 97

Persimmon PLC
Persimmon House, Fulford, York, YO1 4RE
Tel: 01904 642199
Fax: 01904 610014
CH: D.H. Davidson, *CE:* J. White,
FD: B.D. Taylor 50

Perstorp AB
284 80 Perstorp, Sweden
Tel: +46 435 380 00
Fax: +46 435 381 00
P: G. Wiking, *CH:* K.-E. Sahlberg 104

Petrofina SA
52 rue de l'Industrie, 1040 Brussels,
Belgium
Tel: +32 2 288 91 11
Fax: +32 2 288 34 45
CH: J.-P. Amory, A. Frere 92

Petroleos de Venezuela SA
Edif Petroleos de Venezuela, Torre Este,
Av Liberatador, La Campina, Caracas,
Venezuela
Tel: +58 2 708 4111
Fax: +58 2 708 4661
CH: L.E. Guisti 12, 13, 98

Peugeot SA
75 avenue de la Grande Armee,
75116 Paris, France
Tel: +33 1 40 66 55 11
Fax: +33 1 40 66 41 85
CH: R. Peugeot, J. Calvet,
JMD: P. Peugeot, J. Blondeau 79, 91

Pfalzwerke AG
Kurfurstenstrasse 29, 67061
Ludwigshafen am Rhein, Germany
Tel: +49 6 21 56 11-0
Fax: +49 6 21 56 11-22 57
CH: Dr jur W. Ludwig 109

Pfizer Group Ltd
Ramsgate Road, Sandwich, Kent,
CT13 9NJ
Tel: 01304 616161
Fax: 01304 616221
CH: W.H. O'Connor 49

Pharma Vision 2000 AG
Spielhof 3, 8750 Glarus, Switzerland
Tel: +41 58 61 77 70
Fax: +41 58 61 77 73
CH: C. Blocher 101

Pharmacia AB
Frosundaviks alle 15, 171 97 Stockholm,
Sweden
Tel: +46 8 624 50 00
Fax: +46 8 655 80 10
P: J. Ekberg, *CH:* S. Gyll 96

Philips Electronics NV
Groenewoudseweg 1, 5621 BA
Eindhoven, The Netherlands
Tel: +31 40 786022
Fax: +31 40 785486
P: J.D. Timmer, *CH:* F.A. Maljers 75, 88, 91

Phillips Petroleum Co. UK Ltd
Phillips Quadrant, 35 Guildford Road,
Woking, Surrey, GU22 7QT
Tel: 01483 756666
Fax: 01483 752309
CH: B.Z. Parker 50

Phillips-Imperial Petroleum Ltd
The Heath, Runcorn, Cheshire, WA7 4QF
Tel: 01928 514444
No officers designated 59

Photo-Me International PLC
Church Road, Bookham, Surrey, KT23 3EU
Tel: 01372 453399
Fax: 01372 459064
CH: D. David, *JMD:* P.D. Berridge,
S. Crasnianski, D.W. Miller 54

Pilkington PLC
Prescot Road, St Helens, Merseyside,
WA10 3TT
Tel: 01744 28882
Fax: 01744 692660
CH: N. Rudd, *CE:* R. Leverton,
FD: A.M. Robb 32, 43, 95

Pillar Property Investments PLC
4th Floor, The Economist Building,
Economist Plaza, 25 St James's Street,
London, SW1A 1HG
Tel: 0171 915 8000
Fax: 0171 915 8001
CH: H.R. Mould, *CE:* P.L. Vaughan,
FD: H.J.M. Price 49

Pinault - Rieter

Pinault-Printemps-La Redoute
102 rue de Provence, 75009 Paris, France
Tel: + 33 1 42 82 50 00
CH: A. Roux, S. Weinberg 95

Pioneer Concrete Holdings PLC
Pioneer House, 56-60 Northolt Road, South Harrow, Middlesex, HA2 0EY
Tel: 0181 423 3066
Fax: 0181 864 1975
CH: Sir Peter Reynolds,
MD: J.W. Leevers 55

Pioneer International Ltd
Level 46, Governor Phillip Tower, 1 Farrer Place, Sydney, New South Wales, 2000, Australia
Tel: +61 2 323 4000
Fax: +61 2 323 4009
P: Sir Tristan Antico, *CH:* D.M. Hoare, *CE:* J.M. Schubert, R.F. Crocker, *FD:* G.R. Kleemann 115

Pirelli & C - Accomandita per Azioni
Piazzale Cadorna 5, Milan, Italy
Tel: +39 2 85 351
Fax: +39 2 853 54 099
No officers designated 107

Pirelli SpA
Viale Sarca 222, 20126 Milan, Italy
Tel: +39 2 64421
Fax: 64423300
CH: L. Pirelli 94, 103

Pitney Bowes Holdings Ltd
The Pinnacles, Harlow, Essex, CM19 5BD
Tel: 01279 26731
Fax: 01279 449276
CH: G.B. Harvey 55

Plysu PLC
120 Station Road, Woburn Sands, Milton Keynes, Buckinghamshire, MK17 8SE
Tel: 01908 582311
Fax: 01908 585450
CH: D.H. O'Shaughnessy,
MD: M.V.S. Macintyre 60

Polar Corpn
Pakkalankuja 6, 01510 Vantaa, Finland
Tel: +358 0 82 591
Fax: +358 0 8259 2000
CH: H. Hakala, J. Lahti 104

Polaroid (U.K.) Ltd
Ashley Road, St Albans, Hertfordshire, AL1 5PR
CH: L.C. Brewer 58

Polypipe PLC
Broomhouse Lane, Edlington, Doncaster, South Yorkshire, DN12 1ES
Tel: 01709 770000
Fax: 01709 869000
CH: K. McDonald, *FD:* B. Stock 58

Porsche [Dr Ing H.C.F.] AG
Porschestrasse 42, 70435 Stuttgart - Zuffenhausen, Germany
Tel: +49 7 11 827-0
Fax: +49 7 11 8 27-57 77
CH: Prof Dr H. Sihler,
CE: W. Wiedeking 104

Portland Valderrivas SA
Jose Abascal 59, 28003 Madrid, Spain
Tel: +34 1 396 01 00
Fax: +34 1 396 01 70
CH: A. Cortina de Alcocer,
MD: R. Martinez-Ynzenga Canovas del Castillo 108

Portman Building Society
Portman House, Richmond Hill, Bournemouth, Dorset, BH2 6EP
Tel: 01202 292444
Fax: 01202 292503
CH: D.R.P. Baker, *CE:* K. Culley,
FD: D. Gibson 48, 109

Post Office (The)
30 St James's Square, London, SW1Y 4PY
Tel: 0171 490 2888
CH: M. Heron, *CE:* W. Cockburn,
FD: R. Close 14, 16, 26, 33, 43, 69, 95

Powell Duffryn PLC
Powell Duffryn House, London Road, Bracknell, Berkshire, RG12 2AQ
Tel: 01344 53101
Fax: 01344 50599
CH: R.D.C. Hubbard,
CE: B.S. Hartiss, *FD:* A.E. Darling 50

PowerGen PLC
53 New Broad Street, London, EC2M 1JJ
Tel: 0171 826 2826
Fax: 0171 826 2890
CH: Sir Colin Southgate,
CE: E.A. Wallis,
FD: J.L. Rennocks 31, 40, 43, 94

Powerscreen International PLC
Foley Industrial Park, Stourport Road, Kidderminster, Worcestershire, DY11 7QG
Tel: 01562 820373
Fax: 01562 820374
CH: J.E. Craig 58

Premafin Finanziaria SpA
Via Guido D'Arezzo 7, 00198 Rome, Italy
Tel: +39 6 841 2629
Fax: +39 6 841 2631
CH: S. Ligresti 104

Premier Land PLC
Marcol House, 293 Regent Street, London, W1R 7PD
Tel: 0171 631 4048
Fax: 0171 636 2306
CH: D.L. Bloom, *FD:* R. Coe 61

Premier Oil PLC
4th Floor, Saltire Court, 20 Castle Terrace, Edinburgh, EH1 2EN
CH: B. Stephens, *CE:* C.J.A. Jamieson, *FD:* J.A. Heath 50

Preussag AG
Karl-Wiechert-Allee 4, 30625 Hanover, Germany
Tel: +49 511 566 00
Fax: +49 511 566 1901
CH: F. Neuber, Dr M. Frenzel 92

Preussag Stahl AG
Eisenhuttenstrasse 99, 38223 Salzgitter, Germany
Tel: +49 53 41/21-01
Fax: +49 53 41/21-27 27
CH: Dr M. Frenzel, Dr H-J. Selenz 97

Primagaz [Cie des Gaz de Petrole]
64 avenue Hoche, PO Box 335-08, 75365 Paris Cedex 08, France
Tel: +33 1 40 55 25 00
Fax: +33 1 40 55 26 90
CH: J.-C. Inglessi 106

Principality Building Society (The)
PO Box 89, Principality Buildings, Queen Street, Cardiff, CF1 1UA
Tel: 01222 344188
CH: Sir Peter J. Phillips,
CE: J.D. Mitchell, *FD:* J.W. Jamieson 56

Procter & Gamble Co (The)
One Procter & Gamble Plaza, Cincinnati, Ohio, 45202, USA
CH: J.E. Pepper 110

Procter & Gamble Ltd
Hedley House, St Nicholas Avenue, Gosforth, Newcastle upon Tyne, NE99 1EE
Tel: 0191 279 2000
CH: J.E. Pepper,
MD: M. Clasper 47, 107

Promodes
Zone Industrielle, Route de Paris, 14120 Mondeville Cedex, France
Tel: +33 31 70 60 00
Fax: +33 31 83 56 19
CH: P.-L. Halley 97

Provident Financial PLC
Colonnade, Sunbridge Road, Bradford, West Yorks, BD1 2LQ
Tel: 01274 733321
Fax: 01274 722715
CH: W.G.A. Warde-Norbury,
MD: H.J. Bell, *FD:* R.J. Ashton 48, 108

Prowting PLC
Breakspear House, Bury Street, Ruislip, Middlesex, HA4 7SY
Tel: 01895 633344
Fax: 01895 677190
CH: P.B. Prowting, *MD:* D.E. Brill, *FD:* R. Templeman 57

Prudential Corporation PLC
142 Holborn Bars, London, EC1N 2NH
Tel: 0171 405 9222
CH: Sir Martin Jacomb, *CE:* P. Davis, *FD:* J. Bloomer 40, 44, 97

Public Service Enterprise Group Inc.
80 Park Plaza, PO Box 1171, Newark, New Jersey, 07101 1171, USA
Tel: +1 201 430 7000
CH: E.J. Ferland, *CE:* E.J. Ferland 110

Publicitas Holding SA
Avenue des Toises 12, PO Box 3493, 1002 Lausanne, Switzerland
Tel: +41 21 317 71 11
Fax: +41 21 317 75 55
CH: F. Milliet 109

Qantas Airways Ltd
Qantas Centre, 203 Coward Street, Mascot, New South Wales, 2020, Australia
CH: G. M. Pemberton,
MD: J.A. Strong, *FD:* G.K. Toomey 19, 87, 114

REXAM PLC
Bowater House, Knightsbridge, London, SW1X 7NN
Tel: 0171 584 7070
Fax: 0171 581 1149
CH: R.M. Woodhouse,
CE: J.D.R. Lyon,
FD: M.J. Hartnall 44, 99

RHP Bearings Ltd
P.O. Box 18, Northern Road, Newark, Notts, NG24 2JF
Tel: 01636 605123
Fax: 01636 605000
CH: Toshio Arata 61

RIT Capital Partners PLC
27 St James's Place, London, SW1A 1NR
Tel: 0171 493 8111
Fax: 0171 493 5765
CH: The Lord Rothschild 41, 46, 105

RJR Nabisco Holdings Corpn
1301 Avenue Of The Americas, New York, New York, 10019, USA
Tel: +1 212 258-5600
P: L.R. Ricciardi, *CH:* C.M. Harper 110

RMC Group PLC
RMC House, Coldharbour Lane, Thorpe, Egham, Surrey, TW20 8TD
Tel: 01932 568833
Fax: 01932 568933
P: J. Camden, *CH:* P.J. Owen,
MD: P.L. Young 35, 43, 95

RTZ Corporation PLC (The)
6 St James's Square, London, SW1Y 4LD
Tel: 0171 930 2399
Fax: 0171 930 3249
CH: Sir Derek Birkin,
CE: R.P. Wilson, *FD:* C.R.H. Bull 21, 40, 42, 88, 89, 92

RWE AG
Kruppstrasse 5, 45128 Essen, Germany
Tel: +49 201 185-0
Fax: +49 201 185 51 99
CH: Dr W. Roller, Dr jur D. Kuhnt 13, 62, 66, 88, 90

RWE-DEA AG fur Mineraloel und Chemie
PO Box 60 04 49, Uberseering 40, 22297 Hamburg, Germany
Tel: +49 40 63 75-0
Fax: +49 40 63 75 34 96
CH: Dr F. Gieseke, Dr P. Koch 96

Racal Electronics PLC
Western Road, Bracknell, Berkshire, RG12 1RG
Tel: 01344 481222
Fax: 01344 54119
CH: Sir Ernest Harrison,
CE: D.C. Elsbury, *FD:* A.R. Wood 46, 104

Radex-Heraklith Industriebeteiligungs AG
Opernring 1, 1010 Vienna, Austria
Tel: +43 222 587 76 71-0
Fax: +43 222 587 33 80
CH: H. Longin, Dr W. Ressler 107

Raglan Estates PLC
243 Knightsbridge, London, SW7 1DH
Tel: 0171 581 1322
Fax: 0171 584 2297
No officers designated 55

Raine PLC
Raine House, Ashbourne Road, Mackworth, Derby, DE22 4NB
Tel: 01332 824000
Fax: 01332 824824
CH: R. Barber, *MD:* D.S. Vincent, *FD:* N. Fitzsimmons 52

Rallye
171 avenue Charles De Gaulle, 92200 Neuilly sur Seine, France
Tel: +33 1 40 88 92 92
Fax: +33 1 40 88 92 86
CH: A. Crestey 103

Rank Organisation PLC (The)
6 Connaught Place, London, W2 2EZ
Tel: 0171 706 1111
Fax: 0171 262 9886
CH: Sir Denys Henderson,
CE: M.B. Gifford,
FD: N.V. Turnbull 28, 31, 43, 94

Rank Xerox Ltd
Parkway, Marlow, Buckinghamshire, SL7 1YL
Tel: 01628 890000
Fax: 01628 892001
CH: P.A. Allaire,
MD: B.D. Fournier 28, 31, 43, 94

Ratos [Forvaltnings AB]
Box 1661, Drottninggatan 2, 111 96 Stockholm, Sweden
Tel: +46 8 700 17 00
Fax: +46 8 10 25 59
CH: S. Soderberg, *MD:* U. Jansson 109

Rautaruukki Oy
Kiilakientie 1, PO Box 217, 90101 Oulu, Finland
Tel: +358 81 327 711
Fax: +358 81 327 506
CH: M. Kivimaki, P. Vayrynen 98

Reader's Digest Association Ltd (The)
Berkeley Square House, Berkeley Square, London, W1X 6AB
Tel: 0171 629 8144
Fax: 0171 499 9751
No officers designated 59

Readicut International PLC
Clifton Mills, Brighouse, West Yorkshire, HD6 4ET
Tel: 01484 721223
Fax: 01484 716135
CH: Professor Sir Roland Smith,
MD: C.M. Shaw, *FD:* D.J. Lenham 57

Reckitt & Colman PLC
One Burlington Lane, London, W4 2RW
Tel: 0181 994 6464
Fax: 0181 994 8920
CH: Sir Michael J. Colman,
CE: V.L. Sankey, *FD:* I.G. Dobbie 44, 97

Redland PLC
Redland House, Reigate, Surrey, RH2 0SJ
Tel: 01737 242488
Fax: 01737 221938
CH: R.I.J. Agnew, *CE:* R.S. Napier, *FD:* P.W. Hewitt 30, 40, 43, 94

Redrow Group PLC
Redrow House, St David's Park, Clwyd, CH5 3PW
Tel: 01244 520044
Fax: 01244 520580
CH: S.P. Morgan, *MD:* P.L. Pedley, *FD:* J.M.T. Dawson 54

Reed International PLC
6 Chesterfield Gardens, London, W1A 1EJ
Tel: 0171 499 4020
Fax: 0171 491 8212
CH: I.A. N. Irvine 44

Reed/Elsevier Group
Van de Sande Bakhuyzenstraat 4, 1061 AG Amsterdam, The Netherlands
Tel: +31 20 515 23 68
Fax: +31 20 683 26 17
CH: P.J.Vinken, H.J. Bruggink 89, 95

Reemtsma Cigarettenfabriken GmbH
Parkstrasse 51, 22605 Hamburg, Germany
Tel: +49 40 82 200
Fax: +49 40 82 20 645
CH: G. Herz, L.W. Staby 100

Regal Hotels International Holdings Ltd
Rosebank Centre, 14 Bermudiana Road, Pembroke, Bermuda
Tel: +1 809 29 1111
CH: Lo Yuk Sui 115

Remploy Ltd
Remploy House, 415 Edgware Road, Cricklewood, London, NW2 6LR
Tel: 0181 235 0500
Fax: 0181 452 6898
CH: D.G. Heywood,
CE: A.G.H. Withey, *FD:* K. Taylor 58

Remy Cointreau
Rue Joseph Pataa, Ancienne rue de la Champagne, 16100 Cognac, France
CH: A. Heriard Dubreuil,
JMD: F. Heriard Dubreuil,
M. Heriard Dubreuil 98

Renault [Regie Nationale des Usines] SA
34 quai du Point-du-Jour, PO Box 103, 92109 Boulogne-Billancourt Cedex, France
Tel: +33 1 41 04 50 50
CH: L. Schweitzer 73, 86, 90

Renold PLC
Renold House, Styal Road, Wythenshawe, Manchester, M22 5WL
Tel: 0161 437 5221
Fax: 0161 437 7782
CH: J.P. Frost, *CE:* D. Cotterill,
FD: J.H.B. Allan 58

Rentokil Group PLC
Felcourt, East Grinstead, West Sussex, RH19 2JY
Tel: 01342 833022
Fax: 01342 326229
CH: H.E. St L. King,
CE: C.M. Thompson, *FD:* C.T. Pearce 51

Repola PLC
Snellmaninkatu 13, 00171 Helsinki, Finland
Tel: +358 0 182 81
Fax: +358 0 182 8219/608
CH: Y. Niskanen, T. Lepisto 93

Repsol SA
Paseo de la Castellana 278, 28046 Madrid, Spain
Tel: +34 1 348 81 00
Fax: +34 1 314 28 21
CH: O. Fanjul 92

Reuters Holdings PLC
85 Fleet Street, London, EC4P 4AJ
Tel: 0171 250 1122
Fax: 0171 353 1379
CH: Sir Christopher Hogg, *CE:* P. Job,
FD: R.O. Rowley 40, 45, 89, 101\

Rheinmetall Berlin AG
Kennedydamm 15-17, Postfach 10 42 61, 40033 Dusseldorf, Germany
Tel: +49 211 4 73-04
Fax: +49 211 4 73-29 00
CH: W. Freiherr von Salmuth, H.U. Brauner 101

Rhone-Poulenc SA
25 quai Paul-Doumer, 92408 Courbevoie Cedex, France
Tel: +33 1 47 68 12 34
Fax: +33 1 47 68 19 11
CH: J.-R. Fourtou 79, 91

Ricoh Co. Ltd
15-5 Minami-Aoyama 1-chome, Minato-ku, Tokyo 107, Japan
Tel: +81 3 3479 3111
Fax: +81 3 3403 1578
P: Hiroshi Hamada, *JMD:* Takao Nawate, Kazuhiro Sakai, Haruo Kamimoto, Tatsuo Hirakawa, Ryuji Anraku, Kijuu Itoh, Akira Suzuki, Koji Inoue, Masamitsu Sakurai 113

Rieter Holding AG
Klosterstrasse 20, 8406 Winterthur, Switzerland
Tel: +41 52 208 71 71

Rinascente - Sara

Fax: +41 52 208 70 60
P: K. Feller, *CH:* H. Steinmann   103
Rinascente [La] SpA
Strada 5 - Palazzo Z, 20089 Rozzano
(MI), Milanofiori, Italy
Tel: +39 2 57581
Fax: +39 2 8245 866
CH: F. Grande-Stevens,
CE: G. Cobolli Gigli   103
River & Mercantile Extra Income Trust PLC
7 Lincoln's Inn Fields, London,
WC2A 3BP
Tel: 0171 405 7722
Fax: 0171 404 5394
CH: M.G. Smith   59
River Plate & General Investment Trust
Knightsbridge House,
197 Knightsbridge, London, SW7 1RB
Tel: 0171 412 0703
Fax: 0171 581 3857
CH: P.D. Hill-Wood   55
River and Mercantile Trust PLC
7 Lincoln's Inn Fields, London,
WC2A 3BP
Tel: 0171 405 7722
Fax: 0171 404 5394
CH: A.E. Foucar   51
Roadchef Holdings Ltd
Imperial Chambers, 41-47 Longsmith
Street, Gloucester, GL1 2HJ
Tel: 01452 303373
Fax: 01452 529320
CH: T. Ingram-Hill,
FD: N.M. Mansley   59
Robeco NV
Coolsingel 120, Postbus 973, 3000 AZ
Rotterdam, The Netherlands
Tel: +31 10-224 1 224
CH: C.J Oort, P. Korteweg   93
Roche Holding AG
4002 Basle, Switzerland
Tel: +41 61 688 88 88
CH: F. Gerber,
FD: Dr H.B. Meier   62, 73, 88, 89, 90
Roche Products Ltd
40 Broadwater Road, Welwyn Garden
City, Herts, AL7 3AY
Tel: 01707 328128
Fax: 01707 338297
CH: Dr A.F. Leuenberger   50
Rochette [La]
2 rue Louis-David,
75792 Paris Cedex 16, France
Tel: +33 1 44 34 75 00
Fax: +33 1 44 34 75 42
CH: J.-M. Tine, H. Kreitmann   109
Rodamco NV
Coolsingel 120, Postbus 973, 3000 AZ
Rotterdam, The Netherlands
Tel: +31 10 224 1 224
CH: C.J. Oort, P. Korteweg   93
Rohm and Haas (UK) Ltd
Lennig House, 2 Mason's Avenue,
Croydon, Surrey, CR9 3NB
Tel: 0181 686 8844
Fax: 0181 686 8329
CH: S.J. Rauscher   53
Rolinco NV
Coolsingel 120, Postbus 973, 3000 AZ
Rotterdam, The Netherlands
Tel: +31 10 224 1 224
CH: Prof Dr C.J. Oort,
Prof Dr P. Korteweg   95
Rolls-Royce PLC
65 Buckingham Gate, London,
SW1E 6AT
Tel: 0171 222 9020
Fax: 0171 233 1733
CH: Sir Ralph Robins,
CE: Dr T. Harrison,
FD: M. Townsend   36, 43, 76, 96
Rolls-Royce Power Engineering PLC
NEI House, Regent Centre, Newcastle
upon Tyne, NE3 3SB
Tel: 0191 284 3191
Fax: 0191 285 6654
CH: T. Harrison   51
Rothschilds Continuation Ltd
PO Box 185, New Court, St Swithin's
Lane, London, EC4P 4DU
Tel: 0171 280 5000
Fax: 0171 929 1643
CH: Sir Evelyn de Rothschild   46, 104
Royal Bank of Scotland Group PLC (The)
36 St Andrew Square, Edinburgh,
EH2 2YB
Tel: 0131 556 8555
Fax: 0131 557 6565
CH: The Rt Hon Lord Younger of
Prestwick, *CE:* Dr G.R. Mathewson,
FD: R. Speirs   22, 30, 40, 42, 77, 92
Royal Doulton PLC
Minton House, London Road, Stoke-
on-Trent, Staffordshire, ST4 7QD
Tel: 01782 292292
CH: M.W. Burrell, *CE:* S.R. Lyons   54
Royal Dutch/Shell
Carel van Bylandtlaan 30, 2596 HR
The Hague, The Netherlands
Tel: +31 70 377 4540
Fax: +31 70 377 3115
P: C.A.J. Herkstroter,
CH: L.C. van Wachem 5, 6, 12, 13, 14,
15, 42, 62, 63, 88, 89
Royal Insurance Holdings PLC
1 Cornhill, London, EC3V 3QR
Tel: 0171 283 4300
Fax: 0171 623 2602
CH: A.G. Gormly, *CE:* R.A. Gamble,
FD: M.J. Dowdy   32, 40, 43, 95
Royale Belge SA
Boulevard du Souverain 25,
1170 Brussels, Belgium
Tel: +32 2 678 61 11
Fax: +32 2 678 93 40
CH: Count J.-P. de Launoit,
J.-P. Gerard, *JMD:* J.-M. de Munter,
P. Labadie   99
Rue Imperiale de Lyon
49 Rue de la Republique, 69002 Lyon,
France
Tel: +33 78 37 31 83
Fax: +33 72 40 29 56
CH: J. Sourd de Villodon   106
Rugby Group PLC (The)
Crown House, Rugby, Warwickshire,
CV21 2DT
Tel: 01788 542666
Fax: 01788 540256
CH: G.A. Higham, *MD:* P.J. Carr,
FD: A.M. Thomson   46, 105
Ruhrgas AG
Huttropstrasse 60, 45138 Essen 1,
Germany
Tel: +49 2 01 1 84-00
Fax: +49 2 01 1 84 37 66
CH: D. Spethmann, K. Liesen   94
Ruhrkohle AG
Rellinghauser Strasse 1, 45128 Essen,
Germany
Tel: +49 2 01 177-1
Fax: +49 2 01 177-34 75
CH: U.Hartmann,
Dr rer pol H. Horn   76, 91
Rutland Trust PLC
Rutland House, Rutland Gardens,
London, SW7 1BX
Tel: 0171 225 3391
Fax: 0171 225 1364
CH: Admiral Sir Raymond Lygo   57
Ryan Group Ltd
Alexander Gate, Fford Pengham,
Cardiff, CF2 2XR
Tel: 01222 454123
Fax: 01222 454777
CH: G.H. Waddell, *CE:* C.J. Hotson   60
Ryder System Holdings (UK) Ltd
Ryder House, 16 Bath Road, Slough,
Berkshire, SL1 3SA
Tel: 01753 821363
Fax: 01753 77870
No officers designated   55
SAGEM - Ste d'Applications Generales d'Electricite et de Mecaniqu
6, avenue d'Iena,
75783 Paris Cedex 16, France
Tel: +33 1 40 70 63 63
Fax: +33 1 47 20 39 46
CH: R. Labarre, P. Faurre   103
SAS - Scandinavian Airlines System
Frosundaviks Alle 1, Solna,
Stockholm, Sweden
Tel: +46 8 797 00 00
Fax: +46 8 797 12 10
P: J. Stenberg, *CH:* B. Berggren   95
SBC Communications Inc.
175 East Houston, Po Box 2933, San
Antonio, Texas, 78299-2933, USA
Tel: +1 210 821-4105
CH: E.E. Whitacre Jr   110
SCA - Svenska Cellulosa AB
Stureplan 3, PO Box 7827, 10397
Stockholm, Sweden
Tel: +46 8 788 51 00
Fax: +46 8 660 74 30
P: S. Martin-Lof,
CH: B. Rydin   94, 108
SCECorp
2244 Walnut Grove Ave, Rosemead,
California, 91770, USA
Tel: +1 818 302-2222
CH: J.E. Bryson   110
SEEBOARD PLC
Forest Gate, Brighton Road, Crawley,
West Sussex, RH11 9BH
Tel: 01293 565888
Fax: 01293 657327
CH: Sir Keith Stuart, *CE:* T.J. Ellis,
FD: M.J. Pavia   46, 102
SEITA (Ste Nationale d'Exploitation Industrielle des Tabacs et Al
53 Quai d'Orsay, 75347 Paris Cedex
07, France
Tel: +33 1 45 56 61 50
CH: J.-D. Comolli   104
SEP - Samenwerkende Elektriciteits-Produktiebedrijven
Utrechtseweg 310, 6812 AR Arnhem,
The Netherlands
Tel: +31 85 72 11 11
CH: H. Wiegel, N.G. Ketting,
MD: G.J.L. Zijl   104
SGS Holding SA
8 rue des Alpes, 1211 Geneva 1,
Switzerland
Tel: +41 22 739 94 98
Fax: +41 22 732 35 22
CH: Elisabeth Salina Amorini   100
SHV Holdings NV
Marshall Square 4, Frontstreet 16,
Philipsburg, Sint Maarten,
Netherlands Antilles
Tel: +599 5 22977
Fax: +599 5 23572
CH: A. Leysen,
P. Fentener van Vlissingen   94
SIG Schweizerische Industrie-Ges Holding AG
8212 Neuhausen am Rheinfall,
Switzerland
Tel: +41 53 21 61 11
Fax: +41 53 21 66 05
CH: Dr H.U. Baumberger,
CE: Dr U. Datwyler   102
SIMCO
34 rue de la Federation, 75737 Paris
Cedex 15, France
Tel: +33 1 40 61 66 20
Fax: +33 1 40 61 65 06
CH: G. Mazaud,
MD: J-P. Sorand   82, 105
SITA - Ste Industrielle de Transports Automobiles
7 rue de Logelbach, 75017 Paris,
France
Tel: +33 1 48 88 20 20
Fax: +33 1 47 63 77 55
CH: J.-J. Prompsy,
JMD: A. Lambert, D. Pin   109
SKF [AB]
415 50 Gothenburg, Sweden
Tel: +46 31 37 10 00
Fax: +46 31 37 28 32
P: M. Sahlin, P. Augustsson,
CH: A. Scharp   95
SMH-Schweizerische Gesellschaft fur Mikroelektronik und Uhrenindu
Seevorstadt 6, 2502 Biel, Switzerland
Tel: +41 32 286 811
Fax: +41 32 286 911
CH: N.G. Hayek   98
SNECMA - Ste Nationale d'Etude et de Construction de Moteurs d'Av
2 boulevard du General Martial Valin,
75724 Paris Cedex 15, France
Tel: +33 1 40 60 80 80
Fax: +33 1 40 60 81 02
CH: J. Benichou, B. Dufour   98
SOPAF- Sta Partecipazioni Finanziarie SpA
Largo Richini 6, Milan, Italy
Tel: +39 2 58 37 41
CH: L. Guatri, *JMD:* G. Daveri,
Jody G. Vender   106
SOVAC
19/21 rue de la Bienfaisance,
75008 Paris, France
Tel: +33 1 44 08 28 28
Fax: +33 42 93 15 76
CH: M. David-Weill, A. Wormser,
MD: G. Fabry   94
SP Tyres UK Ltd
Fort Dunlop, Birmingham, B24 9QT
Tel: 0121 384 4444
Fax: 0121 384 2855
CH: G.D. Radford   55
SSAB Svenskt Stal AB
Box 16344, 103 26 Stockholm, Sweden
Tel: +46 8 789 25 00
Fax: +46 8 10 79 74
P: L. Gustafsson, *CH:* B. Wahlstrom,
R. Andersson   99
Saarbergwerke AG
Trierer Strasse 1, 66111 Saarbrucken,
Germany
Tel: +49 6 81 4 05-00
Fax: +49 6 81 4 05-42 05
CH: Dr W. Lamby, H.-R. Biehl   98
Saffa SpA
Via dei Bossi 4, 20121 Milan, Italy
Tel: +39 2 979601
Fax: +39 2 97960555
CH: C.C. Bonomi   107
Saga Petroleum AS
Kjorboveien 16, PO Box 490, 1301
Sandvika, Norway
Tel: +47 67 12 66 00
Fax: +47 67 12 66 66
P: A. Larsen, *CH:* W. Wilhelmsen   97
Sainsbury [J] PLC
Stamford House, Stamford Street,
London, SE1 9LL
Tel: 0171 921 6000
Fax: 0171 921 6413
CH: D.J. Sainsbury, *MD:* D.A. Quarmby,
FD: R.P. Thorne   14, 24, 26, 40, 42, 89, 93
Saint Louis
23-25 ave Franklin-D.-Roosevelt,
75008 Paris, France
Tel: +33 1 40 76 74 72
Fax: +33 1 45 63 46 33
CH: N. Clive-Worms   38, 94
Saint-Gobain (Cie de)
Les Miroirs, 18 avenue d'Alsace,
92400 Courbevoie, France
Tel: +33 1 47 62 30 00
CH: J.-L. Beffa,
JMD: M. de Nadaillac, M. Besson,
R. Pistre   79, 80, 88, 91
Saipem SpA
Via Martiri di Cefalonia 67, San
Donato Milanese, Milan, Italy
Tel: +2 5205498
CH: L. Sgubini, *MD:* F. Nanotti   104
Sakura Bank Ltd (The)
3-1 Kudan Minami 1-chome, Chiyoda-
ku, Tokyo 100-91, Japan
Tel: +81 3 3230 3111
P: Shunsaku Hashimoto, *CH:* Ken-ichi
Suematsu, Kazuyuki Kohno, Goro
Koyama, Shinichi Ishino, *JMD:* Mitsuo
Ishida, Hiroshi Miura, Takeyoshi
Ohno, Hirofumi Tokunaga, Ken-o
Yamamoto, Masahiro Takasaki,
Katsuhiko Shimizu, Shigeru Takano,
Keiichiro Yano, Takafumi Abe,
Hirokazu Hyoudou, Nagayoshi Kudoh,
Sadao Sasaki, Tomio Fuchu, Yuji
Yamashita, Haruhisa Kawasaki,
Yasuhiro Uehara, Hiroyasu Ichikawa,
Tadayoshi Nishimura   112
Salomon Brothers Europe Ltd
Victoria Plaza, 111 Buckingham Palace
Road, London, SW1W 0SB
Tel: 0171 721 4000
No officers designated   14, 17, 40, 42, 74, 90
Salomon Inc.
7 World Trade Center, New York, New
York, 10048, USA
Tel: +1 212 783-7000
CH: R.E. Denham   17, 74, 110
Salvesen [Christian] PLC
50 East Fettes Avenue, Edinburgh,
EH4 1EQ
Tel: 0131 559 3600
Fax: 0131 552 5809
CH: Sir Alick Rankin,
CE: Dr C. Masters,
FD: I.C. Adam   47, 106
Sampo Insurance Co. Ltd
Yliopistonkatu 27, Turku, Finand
Tel:+358 21 266 3311
Fax: +358 21 266 5811
CH: J. Harmala,
MD: J.K. Leskinen   109
Samsung Electronics Co. Ltd
250 2-Ga Taepyongno, Chung-Gu,
Seoul, Korea
Tel: +82 331 727 7114
Fax: +82 2 753 0967
P: Kim Kwang Ho, Jung Yong Moon,
CH: Kang Jin Ku, *JMD:* Lee Joo
Hyung, Moon Byung Dae, Ha Sung
Han, Choi Jae Jun, Kim Chang Heon,
Kim Soon, Ahn Kweng Soo, Lee Sang
Hyun, Lee Sae Yang, Kang Young
Moon, Lee Yong Bok, Lee Sung Whan,
Kim Hong In, Oh Jeong Hwan, Oh
Jeung Keun   114
Sand Aire Investments PLC
Stramongate, Kendal, Cumbria,
LA9 4BE
Tel: 01539 723415
Fax: 01539 724965
CH: C.F.E. Shakerley   47, 108
Sandoz AG
Lichtstrasse 35, 4002 Basle, Switzerland
Tel: +41 61 324 11 11
Fax: +41 61 324 80 01
CH: M. Moret,
CE: Dr R.W. Schweizer,
Dr R.W. Schweizer,
FD: Dr R. Breu   88, 89, 92
Sandvik AB
811 81 Sandviken, Sweden
Tel: +46 26-26 00 00
Fax: +46 26-26 13 50
P: C.A. Hedstrom, *CH:* P. Barnevik   96
Santos Ltd
Santos House, 39 Grenfell Street,
Adelaide, South Australia, 5000, Australia
Tel: +61 8 218 5111
Fax: +61 8 212 5476
CH: J.A. Uhrig, *MD:* N.R. Adler   115
Sanyo Electric Co. Ltd
5-5, Keihan-Hondori 2-chome,
Moriguchi City, Osaka 570, Japan
Tel: +81 6 991 1181
Fax: +81 6 991 6566
P: Yasuaki Takano, *CH:* Satoshi Iue,
JMD: Hironobu Yagata, Yoshio Sekido,
Masaho Sugimoto, Yuji Miyake, Hiroshi
Yoshie, Tsuneo Take, Mitsuru Ozawa,
Tsutomu Odaka, Yoshio Shimoda,
Isamu Nakagawa, Tetsuo Fukumura,
Yasusuke Tanaka, Kennosuke
Matsumura, Sadao Kondo   113
Sap AG Systeme Anwendungen Produkte in der Datenverarbeitung
Neurottstrasse 16, 69190 Walldorf,
Germany
Tel: +49 62 27 340
Fax: +49 62 27 34 12 82
CH: B. Thiemann, D. Hopp   103
Sara Lee/DE NV
Vleutensevaart 100, 3532 AD Utrecht,
The Netherlands
Tel: +31 30 92 73 11
Fax: +31 30 93 76 46
CH: H van Liemt   98

137

Saur - Sidlaw

Saur (UK) Ltd
22-30 Sturt Road, Frimley Green,
Camberley, Surrey, GU16 6HZ
Tel: 01252 837639
Fax: 01252 838370
CH: B. Devalan,
MD: J-F. Talbot   45, 102

Save & Prosper Linked Investment Trust PLC
1 Finsbury Avenue, London, EC2M 2QY
Tel: 0171 588 1717
Fax: 0171 247 5006
CH: J.G. Tregoning   60

Saville [J.] Gordon Group PLC
Cranford House, Kenilworth Road,
Blackdown, Leamington Spa,
Warwickshire, CV32 6RG
Tel: 01926 426526
Fax: 01926 426026
CH: J.D. Saville   57

Savoy Hotel PLC (The)
1 Savoy Hill, London, WC2R 0BP
Tel: 0171 836 1533
CH: Sir Ewen Fergusson,
MD: R. Pajares   23, 56

Scac-Delmas-Vieljeux (SDV)
31-32 quai de Dion-Bouton, 92800
Puteaux, France
Tel: +33 1 46 96 44 33
Fax: +33 1 46 96 44 22
CH: V. Bollore   101

Scancem Group Ltd
10th Floor West, Bowater House,
68-114 Knightsbridge, London,
SW1X 7LT
Tel: 0171 823 9060
No officers designated   51

Scania (Great Britain) Ltd
Delaware Drive, Tongwell, Milton
Keynes, Bucks, MK15 8HB
Tel: 01908 210210
Fax: 01908 210186
CH: K.E. Palmgren   61

Scapa Group PLC
Oakfield House, 93 Preston New Road,
Blackburn, Lancashire, BB2 6AY
Tel: 01254 580123
Fax: 01254 51764
CH: H. Tuley, *CE:* D.M. Dunn,
FD: D.E.P. Walter   48, 109

Schering AG
Mullerstrasse 170-178, 13353 Berlin,
Germany
Tel: +49 30 468-0
Fax: +49 30 468-53 05
CH: K. Subjetzki, Dr G. Vita   94

Schindler Holding AG
Seestrasse 55, 6052 Hergiswil,
Switzerland
Tel: +41 4195 85 50
Fax: +41 4139 31 34
CH: F. Muheim, Dr B. Donni   99

Schlumberger PLC
1 Kingsway, London, WC2B 6XH
No officers designated   50

Schneider SA
64-70 Avenue Jean-Baptiste Clement,
92100 Boulogne Billancourt, France
Tel: +33 1 46 05 38 20
CH: D. Pineau-Valencienne,
MD: R. Jeanteur   105

Scholl PLC
Rutland House, Rutland Gardens,
London, SW7 1BX
Tel: 0171-225 3391
Fax: 0171-225 1364
CH: G.K.G. Stevens,
CE: N.A. Franchino,
FD: Judy P. Stammers   54

Schroder Split Fund PLC
33 Gutter Lane, London, EC2V 8AS
Tel: 0171 382 6000
Fax: 0171 382 6965
CH: C.J. Govett   54

Schroders PLC
120 Cheapside, London, EC2V 6DS
Tel: 0171 382 6000
Tel: 0171 382 3950
CH: W.F.W. Bischoff,
CE: W.F.W. Bischoff,
FD: N.R. MacAndrew   45, 100

Schweizerische Lebensversicherungs- und Rentenanstalt
General Guisan-Quai 40, 8022 Zurich,
Switzerland
Tel: +41 1 284 33 11
Fax: +41 1 281 20 80
P: M. Zobl, *CH:* F. Honegger,
E. Ruesch   102

Schweizerische Nationalbank
Bundesplatz 1, 3003 Berne, Switzerland
Tel: +41 31 21 02 11
Fax: +41 31 21 19 53
CH: J. Schonenberger,
M. Lusser   73, 90

Scor SA
1 avenue du President Wilson, Puteaux
(Hauts-de-Seine), France
P: S. Osouf, *CH:* J. Blondeau,
J. Blondeau   98

Scott Paper (U.K.) Ltd
Thames House, Crete Hall Road,
Northfleet, Kent, DA11 9AD
Tel: 01474 336000
Fax: 01474 336172
No officers designated   51

Scottish & Newcastle PLC
Abbey Brewery, 111 Holyrood Road,
Edinburgh, EH8 8YS
Tel: 0131 556 2591
CH: Sir Alick Rankin,
CE: B.J. Stewart,
FD: D.M. Wilkinson   34, 43, 57, 95

Scottish American Investment Company PLC (The)
45 Charlotte Square, Edinburgh,
EH2 4HW
Tel: 0131 226 3271
Fax: 0131 226 5120
CH: J.C. Shaw   41, 46, 105

Scottish Asian Investment Co. Ltd (The)
Le Gallais Chambers, 54 Bath Street,
St Helier, Jersey, Channel Islands
Tel: 01534 501000
CH: N. McAndrew   61

Scottish Eastern Investment Trust PLC (The)
Saltire Court, 20 Castle Terrace,
Edinburgh, EH1 2ES
Tel: 0131 229 5252
Fax: 0131 228 5959
CH: J. Kemp-Welch   41, 46, 102

Scottish Hydro-Electric PLC
10 Dunkeld Road, Perth, PH1 5WA
Tel: 01738 455040
Fax: 01738 455045
CH: Lord Wilson of Tillyorn,
CE: R. Young, *FD:* J. Gray   45, 100

Scottish Investment Trust PLC (The)
6 Albyn Place, Edinburgh, EH2 4NL
Tel: 0131 225 7781
Fax: 0131 226 3663
CH: A.M.M. Grossart   41, 45, 101

Scottish Metropolitan Property PLC (The)
Royal Exchange House, 100 Queen
Street, Glasgow, G1 3DL
Tel: 0141 248 7333
Fax: 0141 221 1196
CH: D. Walton, *MD:* J.S. Cairns,
FD: A.H. Thomson   51

Scottish Mortgage & Trust PLC (The)
1 Rutland Court, Edinburgh, EH3 8EY
Tel: 0131 222 4000
CH: Lord Sanderson of Bowden   41, 44, 99

Scottish National Trust PLC (The)
Charles Oakley House, 125 West
Regent Street, Glasgow, G2 2SG
Tel: 0141 248 3972
Fax: 0141 226 4390
CH: A.J. Struthers   41, 48, 108

Scottish Nuclear Ltd
3 Redwood Crescent, Peel Park, East
Kilbride, Glasgow, G74 5PR
Tel: 01355 262000
Fax: 01355 262626
CH: J. Hann, *CE:* Dr R. Jeffrey   18, 35, 43, 79, 95

Scottish Power PLC
1 Atlantic Quay, Glasgow, G2 8SP
Tel: 0141 637 7177
Fax: 0141 637 5317
CH: M. Stuart, *CE:* I. Robinson,
FD: I. Russell   14, 44, 98

Scottish Value Trust PLC
2 Canning Street Lane, Edinburgh,
EH3 8ER
Tel: 0131 229 1100
Fax: 0131 228 6002
CH: R.C. Borthwick   61

Seagram Co. Ltd (The)
1430 Peel Street, Montreal, Quebec,
H3A 1S9, Canada
P: E. Bronfman Jr, *CH:* E.M. Bronfman,
C.R. Bronfman   111

Seagram Holdings Ltd
Seagram House, 5-7 Mandeville Place,
London, W1M 5LB
Tel: 0171 408 4477
No officers designated   46, 104

Searle [G.D.] & Co. Ltd
PO Box 53, Lane End Road, High
Wycombe, Buckinghamshire,
HP12 4HL
Tel: 01494 521124
Fax: 01494 447872
No officers designated   57

Sears PLC
40 Duke Street, London, W1A 2HP
Tel: 0171 200 5999
Fax: 0171 200 5820
CH: Sir Bob Reid, *CE:* L.G. Strong,
FD: D.A. Defty   44, 97

Sears Roebuck and Co
Sears Tower, Chicago, Illinois,
60684, USA
Tel: +1 312 875-2500
CH: A.C. Martinez   12, 13, 110

Seb SA
Selongy (Cote d'Or), France
CH: J. Gairard, *JMD:* B. Dupont,
P. Rivier, P. Eymery   107

Second Alliance Trust PLC (The)
Meadow House, 64 Reform Street,
Dundee, DD1 1TJ
Tel: 01382 201700
Fax: 01382 225133
CH: Sir Robert Smith,
MD: G.R. Suggett   41, 48, 109

Securicor Group PLC
Sutton Park House, 15 Carshalton
Road, Sutton, Surrey, SM1 4LD
Tel: 0181 770 7000
CH: Sir Neil Macfarlane,
CE: R.S.W.H. Wiggs,
FD: C.C. Shirtcliffe   48, 109

Securities Trust of Scotland PLC
Saltire Court, 20 Castle Terrace,
Edinburgh, EH1 2ES
Tel: 0131 229 5252
Fax: 0131 228 5959
CH: D.A. Whitaker   41, 48

Security Services PLC
Sutton Park House, 15 Carshalton
Road, Sutton, Surrey, SM1 4LE
Tel: 0181 770 7000
Fax: 0181 643 1059
CH: Sir Neil Macfarlane,
CE: R.S.W.H. Wiggs,
FD: C.C. Shirtcliffe   49

Securum Industrial Holdings Ltd
One St Paul's Churchyard, London,
EC4M 8AJ
CH: J.A. Kvarnstrom   57

Sedgwick Group PLC
Sedgwick House, The Sedgwick
Centre, London, E1 8DX
Tel: 0171 377 3456
Fax: 0171 377 3199
CH: The Rt Hon Lord Fanshawe of
Richmond, *CE:* S. Riley   46, 105

Sefimeg-Ste Francaise d'Investissements Immobiliers et de Gestion
4 Place de Rio-de-Janeiro, 75008 Paris,
France
CH: M. Ladreit de Lacharriere,
MD: B. Sechet   103

Seiyu Ltd (The)
Sunshine 60 Building, 1-1 Higashi-
Ikebukuro 3-chome, Toshima-ku,
Tokyo 170, Japan
Tel: +81 3 3989 5069
Fax: +81 3 3983 7061
P: Katsuhiro Fujiseki, *CH:* Sueaki
Takaoka, *JMD:* Noriyuki Watanabe,
Shoji Usami, Hiroshi Ota, Harumi
Sakamoto, Ryuichi Takagi, Hiroshi Yura,
Masakatsu Ebine, Masaru Saito   113

Sekisui House Ltd
Tower East Umeda Sky Building, 1-88
Oyodonaka 1-chome, Kita-ku, Osaka
531, Japan
Tel: +81 6 440 3111
Fax: +81 6 440 3331
P: Isao Okui, *CH:* Hiromu Ohashi,
JMD: Katsura Chujo, Yasuhiko Fujino,
Teruhiko Tanaka, Nobuhiro Aotani,
Hironobu Ohta, Kaichi Kato, Rohri
Honda, Atsuhiko Chikahisa, Yasushi
Urushindani, Kunikazu Teraoka, Yasushi
Sakata, Tsuneo Izui, Isami Wada   113

Selective Assets Trust PLC
One Charlotte Square, Edinburgh,
EH2 4DZ
Tel: 0131 225 1357
Fax: 0131 225 2375
CH: Sir Charles Fraser   58

Sema Group PLC
Regal House, 14 James Street, London,
WC2E 8BT
Tel: 0171 830 4444
Fax: 0171 497 2155
CH: A. Barrera de Irimo,
CE: P.S.E. Bonelli   53

Senior Engineering Group PLC
Senior House, 59/61 High Street,
Rickmansworth, Hertfordshire,
WD3 1RH
Tel: 01923 775547
Fax: 01923 896027
CH: D.D. McFarlane, *CE:* A.J. Bell,
FD: T.B. Garthwaite   52

Seoul Bank
10-1, 2-Ga Namaemunno, Chung-Gu,
Seoul, Korea
Tel: +82 2 7716000
Fax: +82 2 7566489
JMD: Kim Yong Yo, Chang Man Wha,
Koo Sun Hoi, Kim Yong Suk, Kim Young
Hwi, Kim In Chul, Park Yong Ho   115

Severn Trent PLC
2308 Coventry Road, Birmingham, B26 3JZ
Tel: 0121 722 6000
Fax: 0121 722 6150
CH: R. Ireland, *CE:* V. Cocker,
FD: R.A.S. Costin   27, 43, 94

Sevillana de Electricidad [Cia] SA
Avenida de la Borbolla 5, 41004
Seville, Spain
Tel: +34 5 441 73 11
Fax: +34 5 441 21 28
CH: F. de Ybarra y Lopez-Doriga   93

Shaftesbury PLC
Pegasus House, 37/43 Sackville Street,
London, W1X 2DL
Tel: 0171 333 8118
CH: P.L. Levy, *CE:* J.S. Lane,
FD: B. Bickell   58

Shanks & McEwan Group PLC
22 Woodside Place, Glasgow, G3 7QY
Tel: 0141 331 2614
Fax: 0141 331 2071
CH: G.H. Waddell,
CE: M.C.E. Averill, *FD:* D.J. Downes   56

Sharp Corpn
22-22 Nagaike-cho, Abeno-ku,
Osaka 545, Japan
Tel: +81 6 625 3259
Fax: +81 6 627 1752
P: Haruo Tsuji   113

Sharp Electronics (U.K.) Ltd
Sharp House, Thorp Road, Manchester,
M4O 5BE
Tel: 0161 205 2333
Fax: 0161 205 7076
CH: S. Mikuni   55

Sheffield Forgemasters Ltd
PO Box 108, The Old Rectory, School
Hill, Whiston, Rotherham, S60 4JB
Tel: 01709 828233
Fax: 01709 367765
CH: D. Secker Walker,
CE: P.M. Wright, *FD:* M.A. Brand   59

Shell Transport and Trading Company PLC (The)
Shell Centre, London, SE1 7NA
Tel: 0171 934 1234
Fax: 0171 934 5252
CH: J.S. Jennings,
MD: M. Moody-Stuart   14, 15, 40, 42, 63

Shepherd Building Group Ltd
Blue Bridge Lane, York, YO1 4AS
Tel: 01904 653040
Fax: 01904 611501
CH: C.S. Shepherd   54

Shepherd Neame Ltd
17 Court Street, Faversham, Kent,
ME13 7AX
Tel: 01795 532206
Fax: 01795 538907
CH: R.H.B. Neame   59

Sherwood Group PLC
Nottingham Road, Long Eaton,
Nottingham, NG10 2BQ
Tel: 0115 946 1070
Fax: 0115 946 2720
CH: D.C. Parker, *MD:* J.J.N. Telfer,
FD: P. Newbold   58

Shikoku Electric Power Co. Inc.
2-5 Marunouchi, Takamatsu 760-91,
Japan
Tel: +81 878 21 5061
P: Kozo Kondo, *CH:* Hiroshi Yamamoto,
JMD: Akira Nada, Tsuneo Nagano, Jiro
Shinagawa, Mitsunao Sakami, Tatsuro
Amano, Nobuyuki Takahashi, Yoshio
Konishi, Mitsuo Saito   113

Shimizu Corpn
2-3 Shibaura 1-chome, Minato-ku,
Tokyo 105, Japan
Tel: +81 3 5441 1111
Fax: +81 3 5441 0439
P: Harusuke Imamura, *JMD:* Makoto
Watabe, Tsuyoshi Tanabe, Kazuyoshi
Tsuda, Takeo Shimoda, Toshio Furuta,
Keiji Ishikawa, Hisao Yokoyama,
Kazuhiko Kondoh, Takashi Kuroda,
Yasuyuki Sasaki, Norio Doi, Masami
Kikura, Masafuni Konishi, Koji
Takeshita, Shoji Shimizu, Mitsuhiro
Kishimoto, Shigeru Kageyama,
Kenichiro Murakami, Tetsuya Nomura,
Hiroshi Yamahara, Mitsuaki Shimizu   113

Shinan Bank
120, 2-Ga, Taepyongno, Chung-Gu,
Seoul, Korea
Tel: +82 2 7560505
Fax: +82 2 7571024
P: Ra Eung Chan, *CH:* Lee Heui Keon,
JMD: Ryu Yang Sang, Kang Shin
Joung, Hong Young Hoe, Lee In Ho,
Koh Young Sun, Ahn Kwang Woo   115

Shires Investment PLC
165 Queen Victoria Street, London,
EC4V 4DD
Tel: 0171 236 8000
CH: M.S. Hardie   56

Shoprite Group PLC
Centre House, Little Switzerland,
Douglas, Isle of Man, IN2 4RE
Tel: 01624 624511
Fax: 01624 624558
CH: D.K.B. Nicholson,
MD: I.A.R. Nicholson,
FD: M.W. Poole   61

Siab AB
Tegeluddsvagen 21, 115 86 Stockholm,
Sweden
Tel: +46 8 782 00 00
Fax: +46 8 660 53 48
CH: F. Lundberg, *CE:* L. Wuopio   106

Siam Cement Public Co. Ltd (The)
1 Siam Cement Road, Bangsue,
Bangkok 10800, Malaysia
Tel: +66 2 586 3333/4444
Fax: +66 2 5863454/587-21
CH: Chumpol NaLamlieng,
CE: Sanya Dharmasakti   115

Sidlaw Group PLC
Plumtree Court, London, EC4A 4HT
CH: M.G.N. Walker, *CE:* D.W. Morrow,
FD: I.R. Bodie   55

Sidmar NV
John Kennedylaan 51, 9042 Gent, Belgium
Tel: +32 91 42 31 11
CH: M. Nokin, R. Bruck,
MD: N. von Kunitzki 95

Siebe PLC
Saxon House, 2/4 Victoria Street, Windsor, Berks, SL4 1EN
Tel: 01753 855411
Fax: 01753 831176
CH: E.B. Stephens, *CE:* A.M. Yurko,
FD: R. Mann 37, 43, 96

Siemens AG
Wittelsbacherplatz 2, 80333 Munich, Germany
Tel: +49 89 234-28 12
Fax: +49 89 234-28 25
P: H. von Pierer,
CH: H. Franz 12, 13, 62, 64, 88, 89, 90

Signet Group PLC
Zenith House, The Hyde, London, NW9 6EW
Tel: 0181 905 9000
Fax: 0181 905 9895
CH: J. McAdam, *FD:* W. Boyd 45, 101

Sika Finanz AG
Zugerstrasse 50, 6341 Baar 1, Switzerland
Tel: +41 42 330 800
Fax: +41 42 330 850
P: Dr H.P. Ming, *CH:* Dr. R. Burkard, Dr K. Furgler, *MD:* Dr H.P. Ming 107

Sime Darby Bhd
21st Floor, Wisma Sime Darby, Jalan Raja Laut, 50350 Kuala Lumpur, Malaysia
Tel: +60 3 2914122
Fax: +60 3 2987398
CH: Tun Ismail bin Mohamed Ali,
CE: Nik Mohamed bin Nik Yaacob,
FD: Syed Fahkri Barakbah 115

Simon Engineering PLC
Simon House, 6 Eaton Gate, London, SW1W 9BJ
Tel: 0171 730 0777
Fax: 0171 881 2200
CH: A.M. Davies,
CE: Dr M.C.S. Dixon,
FD: T.J. Redburn 59

Singapore Airlines Ltd
25 Airline House, Airline Road, Singapore 1781
CH: J.Y. Pillay,
MD: Dr Cheong Choong Kong 114

Singer & Friedlander Group PLC
21 New Street, Bishopsgate, London, EC2M 4HR
Tel: 0171 623 3000
Fax: 0171 623 2122
CH: A.N. Solomons, *CE:* J. Hodson 52

Sino Land Co. Ltd
12th Floor, Tsim Sha Tsui Centre, Salisbury Road, Tsim Sha Tsui, Kowloon, Hong Kong
Tel: +852 3-7218388
Fax: +852 3-7235901
CH: Robert Ng Chee Siong 114

Sirti SpA
Via G.B. Pirelli 20, 20124 Milan, Italy
Tel: +39 2 67 741
CH: F. Gelfi, *MD:* L. Montella 101

Skandia Insurance Co. Ltd
Sveavagen 44, 103 50 Stockholm, Sweden
Tel: +46 8 788 10 00
Fax: +46 8 788 30 80
P: B. Wolrath, *CH:* S. Soderberg 97

Skanska AB
182 25 Danderyd, Sweden
Tel: +46 8-753 88 00
Fax: +46 8-755 12 56
P: M. Schorling, *CH:* P. Barnevik 96

Skipton Building Society
The Bailey, Skipton, North Yorkshire, BD23 1DN
Tel: 01756 700500
Fax: 01756 700400
CH: J.P. Rycroft, *CE:* J.G. Goodfellow 51

Slough Estates PLC
234 Bath Road, Slough, SL1 4EE
Tel: 01753 537171
Fax: 01753 820585
CH: Sir Nigel Mobbs,
JMD: R.W. Carey, D.R. Wilson 35, 43, 95

Smaller Companies Investment Trust PLC
99 Charterhouse Street, London, EC1M 6AB
Tel: 0171 490 4466
Fax: 0171 490 4436
CH: P.W. Darwin 41, 47, 59, 60, 61, 107

Smith & Nephew PLC
2 Temple Place, Victoria Embankment, London, WC2R 3BP
Tel: 0171 836 7922
Fax: 0171 240 7088
CH: E. Kinder, *CE:* J.H. Robinson,
FD: P. Hooley 46, 104

Smith New Court PLC
Smith New Court House, 20 Farringdon Road, London, EC1M 3NH
Tel: 0171 772 1000
Fax: 0171 772 2929
CH: M.J.P. Marks, *CE:* P.D. Roy 14, 50

Smith [David S.] (Holdings) PLC
16 Great Peter Street, London, SW1P 2BX
Tel: 0171 222 8855
Fax: 0171 222 8856
CH: A.W. Clements, *CE:* J.P. Williams,
FD: D. Butterfield 46, 105

Smith [W H] Group PLC
Strand House, 7 Holbein Place, London, SW1W 8NR
Tel: 0171 730 1200
Fax: 0171 259 9075
CH: C.J.M. Hardie,
CE: Sir Malcolm Field,
FD: J.A. Napier 46, 103

SmithKline Beecham PLC
One New Horizons Court, Brentford, Middlesex, TW8 9EP
Tel: 0181 975 2000
CH: Sir Peter Walters, *CE:* J. Leschly,
FD: H.R. Collum 27, 40, 42, 93

Smiths Industries PLC
765 Finchley Road, London, NW11 8DS
Tel: 0181 458 3232
Fax: 0181 458 4380
CH: F.R. Hurn, *FD:* C.S. Taylor 48, 109

Smurfit Corrugated (UK) Ltd
Great Braitch Lane, Hatfield, Hertfordshire, AL10 9PX
Fax: 01923 241704
CH: H.E. Kilroy 60

Smurfit Ltd
Mercer House, Thames Side, Windsor, Berkshire, SL4 1QN
No officers designated 61

Snia BPD SpA
Via Turati 16/18, 20121 Milan, Italy
Tel: +39 2 63 321
Fax: +39 63 321-384
CH: A. Coppi, *MD:* U. Rosa 101

Societe Generale
29 boulevard Haussmann, 75009 Paris, France
CH: M. Vienot, *MD:* D. Bouton 62, 63, 90

Societe Internationale Pirelli SA
St Jakobs-Strasse 54, 4052 Basle, Switzerland
Tel: +41 61 316 41 11
Fax: +41 61 316 43 55
CH: A.E. Sarasin, *MD:* V. Sozzani 103

Sodexho SA
3 avenue Newton, 78180 Montigny-le-Bretonneux, France
Tel: +33 1 30 85 75 00
Fax: +33 1 30 43 09 58
CH: P. Bellon 107

Solvac
rue Keyenveld 58, 1050 Brussels, Belgium
Tel: +32 2 509 63 09
CH: J. Solvay, P. Washer, Countess P. de Laguiche,
MD: Baron D. Janssen 105

Solvay SA
Rue du Prince Albert 33, Ixelles, 1050 Brussels, Belgium
Tel: +32 2 509 61 11
Fax: +32 2 509 66 17
CH: M. Solvay, Y. Boel, Baron D. Janssen 93

Sommer Allibert
2 Rue de L'Egalite, 92748 Nanterre Cedex, France
Tel: +33 1 41 20 40 40
Fax: +33 1 47 21 49 09
CH: P. Sommer, B. Deconinck, M. Assa 104

Sony Corpn
7-35 Kitashinagawa 6-chome, Shinagawa-ku, Tokyo 141, Japan
Tel: +81 3 5448 2111
Fax: +81 3 5448 2244
P: Norio Ohga, *CH:* Masaru Ibuka, Akio Morita, *JMD:* Fumio Kohno, Kiyoshi Yamakawa, Junichi Kodera, Jiro Aiko, Kenji Tamiya, Masahiro Takahashi, Akira Nagano, Senri Miyaoka, Shiro Koriyama 13, 112

Sony Music Entertainment (UK) Group Ltd
17-19 Soho Square, London, WIV 6HE
Tel: 0171 734 8181
Fax: 0171 734 4321
CH: N. Ohga 48, 108

Sony United Kingdom Ltd
Sony House, South Street, Staines, Middlesex, TW18 4PF
Tel: 01784 467000
No officers designated 47, 106

Soporcel - Sociedade Portuguesa de Celulose SA
Mill Lavos, PO BOX 5, 3081 Figueira da Foz, Portugal
Tel: +33 94 04 11
Fax: +33 94 05 02
CH: A. Roque de Pinho Bissaia Barreto 104

South Staffordshire Water Holdings PLC
Green Lane, Walsall, West Midlands, WS2 7PD
Tel: 01922 38282
Fax: 01922 21968
CH: L.C.N. Bury, *MD:* J.R. Harris,
FD: B. Whitty 61, 75

South Wales Electricity PLC
Newport Road, St Mellons, Cardiff, CF3 9XW
Tel: 01222 792111
Fax: 01222 777759
CH: J.W. Evans, *CE:* A. Walker,
FD: D. Myring 47, 106

South West Water PLC
Peninsula House, Rydon Lane, Exeter, EX2 7HR
Tel: 01392 219666
Fax: 01392 434966
CH: K.W. Court, *FD:* K.L. Hill 44, 97

South Western Electricity PLC
800 Park Avenue, Aztec West, Almondsbury, Bristol, BS12 4SE
Tel: 01454 201101
Fax: 01454 616369
CH: M. Warren, *CE:* J.J. Seed,
FD: J.E. Sellers 14, 46, 102

Southend Property Holdings PLC
1 Dancastle Court, Arcadia Avenue, London, N3 2JU
Tel: 0181 458 8833
Fax: 0181 458 1138
CH: M. Dagul 49

Southern Co. (The)
64 Perimeter Center East, Atlanta, Georgia, 30346, USA
Tel: +1 404 393-0650
P: A.W. Dahlberg,
CH: A.W. Dahlberg 110

Southern Electric PLC
Southern Electric House, Westacott Way, Littlewick Green, Maidenhead, Berkshire, SL6 3QB
Tel: 01628 822166
Fax: 01628 584400
CH: The Hon G.H. Wilson,
CE: H.R. Casley, *FD:* J.W. Deane 44, 99

Southern Water PLC
Southern House, Yeoman Road, Worthing, West Sussex, BN13 3NX
Tel: 01903 264444
Fax: 01903 62185
CH: W.J.W. Courtney,
MD: M.R. Webster, *FD:* R. King 44, 98

Sparekassen Bikuben A/S
Silkegade 8, 1113 Kobenhavn K, Denmark
Tel: +45 33 12 01 33
Fax: +45 33 15 11 33
CH: A. Spang-Hansen, *CE:* M. Munk Rasmussen, H. Thufason 98

Sphere Investment Trust PLC
Dragon Court, 27-29 Macklin Street, London, WC2B 5LX
Tel: 0171 404 6364
Fax: 0171 404 6329
CH: D.L. Donne 52

Spie-Batignolles
10 avenue de l'Entreprise, 95863 Cergy-Pontoise, France
Tel: +33 1 34 24 30 00
Fax: +33 1 34 24 33 20
CH: R. Berthon, A. Chadeau 92, 105

Spirax-Sarco Engineering PLC
Charlton House, Cirencester Road, Cheltenham, Gloucestershire, GL53 8ER
Tel: 01242 521361
Fax: 01242 581470
CH: C.J. Tappin, *CE:* T.B. Fortune,
FD: D.J. Meredith 53

Spring Ram Corporation PLC (The)
PO Box 11, Spring Bank Industrial Estate, Sowerby Bridge, Halifax, West Yorks, HX6 3DA
Tel: 01422 839955
Fax: 01422 831353
CH: B.R. Regan, *FD:* M.G. Towers 52

Springer [Axel] Verlag AG
Kochstrasse 50, 10969 Berlin, Germany
Tel: +49 30 25 91-0
Fax: +49 30 2 51 60 71
CH: Prof Dr B. Servatius, Dr J. Richter 103

Sprint Corpn
2330 Shawnee Mission Parkway, Westwood, Kansas, Missouri, 66205, USA
Tel: +1 913 676-3000
CH: W.T. Esrey 111

Ssangyong Cement
24-1, 2-Ga Cho-Dong, Chung-Gu, Seoul, Korea
Tel: +82 2 270 5151
Fax: +82 2 275 7040
P: Woo Duk Chang, Kim Tae Moon,
CH: Kim Suk Won, *JMD:* Yang Jae Kyun, Kwon Tae Youn, Kim Bo Ung, Byu Keun Hak, Choi Tan, Lee Tae Seon, Choi Seung Hwan, Park In Soon, Yang Jae Kyun, Choi Tan, Kim Young Bok, Lyu Sang Kyu, Kim Kwan Hyung, Oh Hee Kap, Hong Sa Seung 115

St James's Place Capital PLC
27 St James's Place, London, SW1A 1NR
Tel: 0171 493 8111
CH: The Lord Rothschild, Sir Mark Weinberg 50

Street Ives PLC
St Ives House, Lavington Street, London, SE1 0NX
Tel: 0171 928 8844
Fax: 0171 928 0617
CH: M. Emley, *MD:* B.C. Edwards 54

Street Modwen Properties PLC
Lyndon House, Hagley Road, Edgbaston, Birmingham, B16 8PE
Tel: 0121 456 2800
Fax: 0121 456 1829
CH: S.W. Clarke ,
CE: C.C.A. Glossop, *FD:* P.E. Doona 58

Stadtwerke Koln GmbH
Parkgurtel 24, 50823 Cologne (Ehrenfeld), Germany
Tel: +49 2 21 178-0
Fax: +49 178 22 22
CH: N. Burger, H. Soenius 102

Stagecoach Holdings PLC
Charlotte House, 20 Charlotte Street, Perth, PH1 5LL
Tel: 01738 442111
Fax: 01738 643648
CH: B. Souter, *MD:* Ann H. Gloag,
FD: D. Scott 56

Stakis PLC
3 Atlantic Quay, York Street, Glasgow, G2 8JH
Tel: 0141 204 4321
Fax: 0141 204 3366
P: Sir Reo Stakis, *CE:* D. Michels,
FD: N. Chisman 47, 106

Standa SpA
Strada 4, Palazzo Q1, Milanofiori, 20089 Rozzano (MI), Italy
Tel: + 39 2 89212
Fax: +39 2 892 123 20
CH: G. Foscale, *MD:* N. Pellizzari 108

Standard Chartered PLC
1 Aldermanbury Square, London, EC2V 7SB
Tel: 0171 280 7500
Fax: 0171 280 7791
CH: P.J. Gillam, *CE:* G.M. Williamson,
FD: P.A. Wood 24, 40, 42, 93

Stanley Leisure Organisation PLC
Stanley House, 4/12 Marybone, Liverpool, L3 2BY
Tel: 0151 236 4291
Fax: 0151 227 5068
CH: L. Steinberg 53

State Bank of New South Wales Ltd
Level 35, State Bank Centre, 52 Martin Place, Sydney, 2000, Australia
Tel: +61 2 226 8000
CH: R. John Lamble,
MD: John O'Neill 114

Statoil-Den Norske Stats Oljeselskap AS
4035 Stavanger, Norway
Tel: +47 51 80 80 80
Fax: +47 51 80 70 42
CH: H. Kvamme, H. Norvik 88, 92

Staveley Industries PLC
Staveley House, 11 Dingwall Road, Croydon, Surrey, CR9 3DB
Tel: 0181 688 4404
Fax: 0181 760 0563
CH: H. Tuley, *CE:* R.A. Hitchens,
FD: J.P.R Brown 53

Ste Nationale de Credit a l'Industrie - SNCI
avenue de l'Astronomie 14, 1030 Brussels, Belgium
Tel: +32 2 214 12 11
Fax: +32 2 218 04 78
P: W. Coumans, R. Tollet 92

Ste Nationale des Chemins de Fer Francais (SNCF)
88 rue Saint-Lazare, 75436 Paris Cedex 09, France
Tel: +33 1 42 85 63 13
Fax: +33 1 42 85 63 16
CH: J. Bergougnoux,
MD: J.-F. Benard 12, 13, 62, 65, 90

Ste Suisse de Ciment Portland SA
23 faubourg de l'Hopital, 2000 Neuchatel, Switzerland
Tel: +41 38 25 75 30
Fax: +41 38 25 93 90
CH: T. Schmidheiny 94, 108

Stena Line AB
Forsta Langgatan 26, 405 19 Gothenburg, Sweden
Tel: +46 31 85 80 00
Fax: +46 31 24 10 38
P: B. Lerenius, *CH:* D.S. Olsson 103

Stena Offshore Ltd
Greybrook Hse, 28 Brook Street, London, W1Y 1AG
Tel: 0171 495 4585
CH: C.E.M.J. Marbach,
MD: T.M. Ehret 53

Stephen [Robert] Holdings Ltd
The Pentland Centre Lakeside, Squires Lane, Finchley, London, N3 2QL
Tel: 0181 346 2600
Fax: 0181 346 2700
No officers designated 47, 107

Sterling-Winthrop Group Ltd
Sterling-Winthrop House, Onslow Street, Guildford, Surrey, GU1 4YS
Tel: 01483 505515
Fax: 01483 35432
No officers designated 55

Steyr - Telefonica

Steyr-Daimler-Puch AG
Franz-Josefs-Kai 51, 1010 Vienna, Austria
Tel: +43 1 531 44 0
Fax: +43 1 535 63 83
CH: Dr G. Schmidt-Chiari, Dr R. Streicher   109

Steyrermuhl Papierfabriks- und Verlags-AG
Fabriksplatz 1, 4662 Steyrermuhl, Austria
Tel: +43 7613 2436-0
Fax: +43 7613 2174
CH: W. Flottl, Mag W. Pillwein   108

Stockholm & Edinburgh Investments Ltd
243 Knightsbridge, London, SW7 1DH
Tel: 0171 581 1322
CH: P.A. Ek   45, 100

Stora Kopparbergs Bergslags AB
Asgatan 22, 791 80 Falun, Sweden
Tel: +46 23 78 00 00
Fax: +46 23 138 58
P: L.-A. Helgesson,
CH: B. Berggren   92

Storehouse PLC
Marylebone House, 129-137 Marylebone Road, London, NW1 5QD
Tel: 0171 262 3456
Fax: 0171 262 4740
CH: I.H. Davison, *CE:* K. Edelman, *FD:* D. Steele   46, 105

Stork NV
Amersfoortsestraatweg 7, 1412 KA Naarden, The Netherlands
Tel: +31 2159 57411
Fax: +31 2159 41184
CH: Mr R. Hazelhoff, Dr J.C.M. Hovers   105

Storli [Skibsaksjeselskapet]
Conrad Mohrs veg 29, 5032 Minde, Norway
Tel: +47 55 27 00 00
Fax: +47 55 28 47 41
CH: B.D. Odfjell, *MD:* B. Sjaastad 108

Strabag AG
Siegburger Strasse 241, 50679 Koeln, Germany
Tel: +49 2 21 824-01
Fax: +49 2 21 824-29 36
CH: Dr jur J. Gerhard, Dr O. Franz 104

Strafor Facom
56 rue Jean Giraudoux, 67200 Strasbourg, France
Tel: +33 88 28 88 88
Fax: +33 88 28 88 02
CH: R. Winocour, H. Lachmann,
MD: N. Talagrand   103

Stylo PLC
Harrogate Road, Apperley Bridge, Bradford, West Yorkshire, BD10 0NW
Tel: 01274 617761
Fax: 01274 616111
CH: I.A. Ziff, *CE:* M.A. Ziff   55

Sudzucker AG
Maximilianstrasse 10, 68165 Mannheim, Germany
Tel: +49 6 21 4 21-0
CH: S. Freiherr Zobel von Giebelstadt zu Darstadt, H.-G. Andreae   96

Suez [Cie de]
1 rue d'Astorg, 75008 Paris, France
Tel: +33 1 40 06 64 00
Fax: +33 1 40 06 66 88
CH: G. Mestrallet, G. Worms,
CE: P. Liotier, *MD:* P. Liotier 62, 64, 90

Sulzer AG
8401 Winterthur, Switzerland
Tel: +41 52 262 11 22
Fax: +41 52 262 01 01
CH: P. Borgeaud   95

Sumitomo Chemical Co. Ltd
Sumitomo Building, 5-33 Kitahama 4-chome, Chuo-ku, Osaka 541, Japan
Tel: +81 6 220 3272
Fax: +81 6 220 3345
No officers designated   113

Sumitomo Corpn
2-2 Hitotsubashi 1-chome, Chiyoda-ku, Tokyo 100, Japan
Tel: +81 3 3217 5082
Fax: +81 3 3217 5128

P: Tomiichi Akiyama, *CH:* Tadashi Itoh, *JMD:* Takehiko Yonezu, Yasuo Kimura, Kenji Miyahara, Takashi Tsuura, Kunihiko Matsuoka, Tsuneo Iwasaki, Ryo Yamakawa, Iwao Nishiumi, Kunihiro Ashida, Mitsuharu Ishii, Tatsuo Nishida, Michio Tsuda, Masahiro Kawata, Michiyasu Karashima, Takashi Nomura, Fumio Wada, Eizo Morioka   112

Sumitomo Corporation (UK) PLC
Vintners' PLace, 68 Upper Thames Street, London, EC4V 3BJ
No officers designated   55

Sumitomo Electric Industries Ltd
5-33 Kitahama 4-chome, chuo-ku, Osaka 541, Japan
Tel: +81 6 220 4141
Fax: +81 6 222 3380
P: Noritaka Kurauchi, *CH:* Tetsuro Kawakami, *JMD:* Makoto Sugiyama, Kozo Tanaka, Shoji Nagasaki, Nobuo Furukawa, Akira Ohashi, Shinichiro Ito, Nobuo Yumoto, Michio Moriya, Akira Shiotani, Chihiro Kimata, Yasuo Kita 113

Sumitomo Metal Industries Ltd
5-33 Kitahama 4-chome, Chuo-ku, Osaka, Japan
Tel: +81 6 220 5111
Fax: +81 6 223 0305
P: Tameaki Nakamura, *CH:* Yasuo Shingu, *JMD:* Hiroshi Sugita, Kazuaki Tsuda, Hiroshi Shimozuma, Yoshisuke Misaka, Keiichi Matsumoto, Hiroshi Nishimura, Motoo Yagi, Masaru Utakoji, Noboru Hase, Mikio Kato 112

Sumitomo Realty & Development Co. Ltd
Shinjuku NS Building, 4-1 Nishi-Shinjuku 2-chome,Shinjuku-ku, Tokyo 163-08, Japan
Tel: +81 3 346 1011
Fax: +81 3 33461149
P: Shinichiro Takag,
CH: Taro Ando   113

Sumitomo Trust & Banking Co. Ltd (The)
5-33, Kitahama 4-chome, Chuo-ku, Osaka 541, Japan
Tel: +81 6 220 2121
Fax: +81 6 220 2043
P: Atsushi Niira, *CH:* Hiroshi Hayasaki, *JMD:* Hidehiko Hattori, Hiroshi Ohashi, Akira Nishioka, Tosei Takenaka, Hitoshi Murakami, Takehiko Watanabe, Takenori Osakabe, Eiji Tokunaga, Atsushi Takahashi, Isao Nagata, Kiichi Kondo, Masayuki Tsubonoya, Yoshihiko Oda   113

Summit Group PLC (The)
2 Clerkenwell Green, London, EC1R 0DH
Tel: 0171 867 8400
CH: Sir Raymond Johnstone,
MD: C.N. Hunter Gordon   48

Sun Alliance Group PLC
1 Bartholomew Lane, London, EC2N 2AB
Tel: 0171 588 2345
Fax: 0171 588 1159
CH: Sir Christopher Benson,
CE: R.J. Taylor,
FD: T.S. Nelson   32, 43, 95

Sun Hung Kai Properties Ltd
45th Floor, Sun Hung Kai Centre, 30 Harbour Road, Wanchai, Hong Kong
Tel: +852 5-8912111
CH: Kwok Ping-sheung   114

Sun Life Corporation PLC
107 Cheapside, London, EC2V 6DU
Tel: 0171 606 7788
Fax: 0171 796 3813
CH: P.J. Grant, *MD:* J. Reeve 35, 54

Superior Oil (U.K.) Ltd
Mobil Court, 3 Clements Inn, London, WC2A 2EB
Tel: 0171 831 7171
No officers designated   51

Suter PLC
St Vincent's, Grantham, Lincolnshire, NG31 9EJ
Tel: 01476 76767
Fax: 01476 70470

CH: J.D. Abell, *JMD:* R.R. Morris, A.G.V. Owen, *FD:* A. Hewitt   59

Svedala Industri AB
PO Box 4004, 203 11 Malmo, Sweden
Tel: +46 40 24 58 00
Fax: +46 40 97 92 80
P: Th. Older, *CH:* R. Andersson 109

Svensk Interkontinental Lufttrafik AB - SILA
Stureplan 19, 103 96 Stockholm, Sweden
Tel: +46 8 797 12 93
CH: B. Berggren   103

Svenska Handelsbanken
Kungstradgardsgatan 2, 106 70 Stockholm, Sweden
Tel: +46 8 701 10 00
P: A. Martensson, *CH:* T. Browaldh, J. Wallander, T. Hedelius   82, 91

Swire Pacific Ltd
4th Floor, Swire House, 9 Connaught Road, Central, Hong Kong
CH: P. D. A. Sutch   114

Swiss Bank Corpn
Aeschenplatz 6, 4002 Basle, Switzerland
Tel: +41 61 288 20 20
CH: Dr W.G. Fehner, Dr G. Blum 14, 36, 69, 90

Swiss Reinsurance Co
Mythenquai 50/60, 8022 Zurich, Switzerland
Tel: +41 1 285 21 21
Fax: +41 1 285 29 99
CH: U. Bremi, L. Muehlemann   94

Swissair
Hirschengraben 84, 8001 Zurich, Switzerland
Tel: +41 1 812 12 12
Fax: +41 810 80 46
CH: A. Baltensweiler, H. Goetz 93

Sydkraft AB
Carl Gustafs Vag 1, 205 09 Malmo, Sweden
Tel: +46 40 25 50 00
Fax: +46 40 97 60 69
P: G. Ahlstrom, *CH:* J. Ollen 94

Synthelabo
22 avenue Galilee, 92350 Le Plessis-Robinson, France
CH: H. Guerin   103

3i Group PLC
91 Waterloo Road, London, SE1 8XP
Tel: 0171 928 3131
Fax: 0171 928 0058
CH: Sir George Russell,
CE: E.C.S. Macpherson,
FD: B.P. Larcombe   30, 43, 94

3M UK Holdings PLC
3M House, PO Box 1, Bracknell, Berkshire, RG12 1JU
Tel: 01344 858000
CH: J.W. Benson (USA)   49

T & N PLC
Bowdon House, Ashburton Road West, Trafford Park, Manchester, M17 1RA
Tel: 0161 872 0155
Fax: 0161 872 8884
CH: C.F.N. Hope, *CE:* I. Much,
MD: W.H. Everitt,
FD: D.A. Harding   44, 98

TBI PLC
31 St George Street, Hanover Square, London, W1R 9FA
Tel: 0171 355 2345
Fax: 0171 491 2378
CH: G.S. Thomas, *CE:* K. Brooks, *FD:* I.B. Creber   58

THORN EMI PLC
4 Tenterden Street, Hanover Square, London, W1A 2AY
Tel: 0171 355 4848
Fax: 0171 495 1424
CH: Sir Colin Southgate,
FD: S. Duffy   44, 97

TI Group PLC
50 Curzon Street, London, W1Y 7PN
Tel: 0171 499 9131
Fax: 0171 493 6533
CH: Sir Christopher Lewinton,
FD: B.A. Walsh   45, 101

TLG PLC
Elstree Way, Borehamwood,

Hertfordshire, WD6 1HZ
Tel: 0181 905 1313
Fax: 0181 967 6347
CH: R.D.H. Bryce, *JMD:* P.B. Rhodes, T. Vayssette, *FD:* M.M. Robertson 58

TNT Europe Ltd
Aquis Court, 31 Fishpool Street, St Albans, Herts, AL3 4RF
Tel: 01582 573666
CH: Admiral Sir Raymond Lygo 50

TOTAL
Tour TOTAL, 24 Cours Michelet, 92800 Puteaux, France
Tel: +33 1 41 35 40 00
CH: F.-X. Ortoli   75, 89, 90

TR City of London Trust PLC
3 Finsbury Avenue, London, EC2M 2PA
Tel: 0171 638 5757
Fax: 0171 377 5742
CH: S.J. Titcomb   41, 48

TR European Growth Trust PLC
3 Finsbury Avenue, London, EC2M 2PA
Tel: 0171 638 5757
Fax: 0171 377 5742
CH: Sir Geoffery Littler   56

TR Far East Income Trust PLC
3 Finsbury Avenue, London, EC2M 2PA
Tel: 0171 638 5757
Fax: 0171 377 5742
CH: Hon Sir Victor Garland   56

TR Pacific Investment Trust PLC
3 Finsbury Avenue, London, EC2M 2PA
Tel: 0171 638 5757
Fax: 0171 377 5742
CH: I. Dale   53

TR Property Investment Trust PLC
3 Finsbury Avenue, London, EC2M 2PA
Tel: 0171 638 5757
Fax: 0171 377 5742
CH: P.C. Hyde-Thomson   53

TR Smaller Companies Investment Trust PLC
3 Finsbury Avenue, London, EC2M 2PA
Tel: 0171 638 5757
Fax: 0171 377 5742
CH: P.H.G. Cadbury   41, 47, 107

TR Technology PLC
3 Finsbury Avenue, London, EC2M 2PA
Tel: 0171 638 5757
Fax: 0171 377 5742
CH: The Rt Hon Sir Peter Hordern 41, 49

TSB Group PLC
16 Hope Street, Charlotte Square, Edinburgh, EH2 4DD
Tel: 0131 225 4555
CH: Sir Nicholas Goodison,
CE: P.B. Ellwood, *FD:* J.A. Burns 27, 40, 42, 93

TT Group PLC
Clive House, 12-18 Queens Road, Weybridge, Surrey, KT13 9XB
Tel: 01932 841310
Fax: 01932 846724
CH: J.W. Newman,
CE: S.W.A. Comonte, M.R. Eke,
FD: M.R. Eke   51

TVS Entertainment PLC
Fairways House, Mount Pleasant, Southampton, SO9 5HZ
Tel: 01703 338888
Fax: 01703 335533
CH: T.B. Robertson   60

Tabacalera SA
Calle de Alcala 47, Madrid, Spain
Tel: +34 1 5228487
CH: P.P. Perez   104

Taisei Corpn
Shinjuku Center Building, 25-1 Nishishinjuku 1-chome, Shinjuku-ku, Tokyo 163-06, Japan
Tel: +81 3 3348 1111
Fax: +81 3 3345 0481/0482
P: Hyozo Yamamoto,
CH: Yoshimasa Ohgo   113

Tait [Thomas] and Sons Ltd
Inverurie Mills, Inverurie, Aberdeenshire, Scotland, AB5 9NR
Tel: 01467 627000
Fax: 01467 627102
CH: J.R. Kennedy, *MD:* T.J. Tait 57

Taittinger [SA]
9 place Saint-Nicaise, Reims, France
CH: C. Taittinger   101

Takare PLC
Takare House, Whitechapel Way, Priorslee, Telford, Shropshire, TF2 9SP
Tel: 01952 292392
Fax: 01952 292393
CH: K.G. Bradshaw,
MD: H.D. Anstead, *FD:* R.J. Reid 50

Takeda Chemical Industries Ltd
1-1 Doshomachi 4-chome, Chuo-ku, Osaka 541, Japan
Tel: +81 6 204 2111
Fax: +81 6 204 2880
P: Kunio Takeda, *CH:* Katsura Morita,
JMD: Masao Uchibayashi, Masao Imai, Tai Matsuzawa, Masahiko Fujino, Keiji Okada   113

Tampella Oy
Kelloportinkatu 1B, PO Box 256, 33101 Tampere, Finland
Tel: +358 31 241 8511
Fax: +358 31 212 3219
P: T. Summa, *CH:* V. Korpi,
MD: S.-O. Hansen   109

Tandem Computers Ltd
Tandem House, 7 Roundwood Avenue, Stockley Park, Uxbridge, Middlesex, UB11 1AU
CH: Sir Campbell Fraser   58

Tanjong PLC
Broseley House, Newlands Drive, Witham, Essex, CM8 2UL
Tel: 01376 515755
Fax: 01376 510609
CH: Khoo Teik Chooi,
CE: Tan Poh Ching   56

Tarmac PLC
Hilton Hall, Essington, Wolverhampton, WV11 2BQ
Tel: 01902 307407
Fax: 01902 307408
CH: Sir John Banham,
FD: T.H. Mason   44, 96

Tate & Lyle PLC
Sugar Quay, Lower Thames Street, London, EC3R 6DQ
Tel: 0171 626 6525
Fax: 0171 623 5213
CH: Sir Neil Shaw   38, 43, 96

Tay Homes PLC
Tay House, 55 Call Lane, Leeds, LS1 7BT
Tel: 0113 242 6262
Fax: 0113 242 1921
CH: D.T. Spencer, *FD:* S.G. Evans 61

Taylor Clark PLC
32 Haymarket, London, SW1Y 4TP
Tel: 0171 9308494
Fax: 0171 9305575
CH: R. Clark   55

Taylor Woodrow PLC
4 Dunraven Street, London, W1Y 3FG
Tel: 0171 629 1201
Fax: 0171 493 1066
CH: C.J. Parsons, *CE:* H.A. Palmer,
FD: D.A. Green   45, 101

TeleWest Communications PLC
Unit 1, Genesis Business Park, Albert Drive, Woking, Surrey, GU21 5RW
Tel: 01483 750900
Fax: 01483 75091
CH: F.A. Vierra, *CE:* A. Michels,
FD: S.J. Davidson   48, 109

Telecom Corpn of New Zealand Ltd
13-27 Manners Street, P O Box 570, Wellington, New Zealand
Tel: +64 4 823 333
CH: Peter Shirtcliffe,
MD: Dr Roderick Deane   115

Teledanmark
Kannikegade 16, 8000 Aarhus C, Denmark
Tel: +45 89 33 77 77
Fax: +45 89 33 77 19
CH: K. Heinesen, *CE:* H. Wurtzen 94

Telefonica de Espana SA
Gran Via 28, 28013 Madrid, Spain
CH: C. Velazquez-Gaztelu Ruiz,
MD: G. Ancochea Soto 12, 13, 68, 88, 90

Telegraph - USM

Telegraph PLC (The)
1 Canada Square, Canary Wharf,
London, E14 5DT
Tel: 0171 538 5000
Fax: 0171 538 6242
CH: The Hon C.M. Black,
MD: S. Grabiner,
FD: A.R. Hughes 47, 106

Telekom Malaysia Bhd
2nd Floor, Ibupejabat Telekom
Malaysia, Jalan Pantai Baharu, 59200
Kuala Lumpur, Malaysia
Tel: +60 3 208 2103/2664
Fax: +60 3 283 2415
CH: Tan Sri Dato' Dr Mohd Rashdan
bin Haji Baba 114

Telia AB
123 86 Farsta, Sweden
Tel: +46 8 713 10 00
Fax: +46 8 713 22 07
P: L. Berg, *CH:* B. Westerberg 93

Temple Bar Investment Trust PLC
Lighterman's Court, 5 Gainsborough
St, Tower Bridge, London, SE1 2NE
Tel: 0171 5222100
Fax: 0171 5222105
CH: Prof Sir R. Smith 41, 50

Templeton Emerging Markets Investment Trust PLC
Saltire Court, 20 Castle Terrace,
Edinburgh, EH1 2EH
Tel: 0131 228 3932
CH: N. Brady 41, 47, 105

Tenaga Nasional Bhd
129 Jalan Bangsar, 59200 Kuala
Lumpur, Malaysia
CH: Tan Sri Dato'
Haji (Dr) Ani bin Arope 114

Tennants Consolidated Ltd
69 Grosvenor Street, London, W1X 0BP
Tel: 0171 493 5451
Fax: 0171 495 1269
CH: K.A. Alexander 56

Tenneco Inc.
1010 Milam, Houston, Texas,
77252-2511, USA
Tel: +1 713 757-2131
CH: D.G. Mead 111

Tesco PLC
Tesco House, Delamare Road,
Cheshunt, Hertfordshire, EN8 9SL
Tel: 01992 632222
Fax: 01992 644481
CH: Sir Ian MacLaurin,
MD: A.D. Malpas, *FD:* D.E. Reid 14, 22, 24, 40, 42, 92

Tessenderlo Chemie SA
Stationsstraat, 3980 Tessenderlo, Belgium
Tel: +32 13 61 22 11
Fax: +32 3 66 81 40
CH: G. Marchand,
FD: C. Vrebosch 107

Texaco Inc.
2000 Westchester Avenue, White
Plains, New York, 10650, USA
Tel: +1 914 253-4000
CH: A.C. DeCrane Jr 110

Texaco Ltd
1 Westferry Circus, Canary Wharf,
London, E14 4HA
Tel: 0171 719 3000
CH: G.F. Tilton, *JMD:* D.A. Bennet,
L.W. Berry Jr 45, 99

Texas Utilities Co.
Energy Plaza, 1601 Bryan Street,
Dallas, Texas, 75201-3411, USA
Tel: +1 214 812 4600
P: E. Nye, *CH:* J. Farrington 110

Textron Inc.
40 Westminster Street, Providence,
Rhode Island, 02903, USA
Tel: +1 401 421-2800
P: L.B. Campbell,
CH: J.F. Hardymon 111

Thai Farmers Bank Public Co. Ltd (The)
400 Phahlyothin Road, Phythai,
Bangkok, 10400, Malaysia
Tel: +66 2 270 1122
Fax: +66 2 270-1144-5
P: Banthoon Lamsam, *CH:* Banyong
Lamsam 115

Thames Water PLC
14 Cavendish Place, London, W1M 0NU
Tel: 0171 636 8686
Fax: 0171 436 6755
CH: Sir Robert Clarke,
FD: D.J. Luffrum 29, 43, 94

Thomson Corporation PLC (The)
First Floor, The Quadrangle, PO Box
4YG, 180 Wardour Street, London,
W1A 4YG
Tel: 0171 437 9787
Fax: 0171 734 0561
No officers designated 45, 100

Thomson SA
175, boulevard Haussman, 75800 Paris,
France
CH: A. Gomez 62, 93,

Thomson [D.C.] & Co. Ltd
Courier Building, Albert Square,
Dundee, DD1 9QJ
Tel: 01382 23131
No officers designated 49

Thornton Asian Emerging Markets Investment Trust PLC
Swan House, 33 Queen Street, London,
EC4R 1AX
Tel: +81 3 246 3000
Fax: 0171 246 3003
CH: Rt Hon The Lord Walker of
Worcester 52

Thorntons PLC
Thornton Park, Somercotes, Derby,
DE55 4XJ
Tel: 01773 824181
Fax: 01773 540757
CH: C.J. Thornton,
FD: A.D. Goodwin 61

Throgmorton Trust PLC (The)
155 Bishopsgate, London, EC2M 3XJ
Tel: 0171 374 4100
Fax: 0171 628 3731
CH: The Rt Hon Lord Stewartby 41, 49, 57

Thwaites [Daniel] PLC
PO Box 50 Star Brewery, Blackburn,
Lancashire, BB1 5BU
Tel: 01254 54431
Fax: 01254 681439
CH: D.A. Robson 53

Thyssen AG
Postfach, 47161 Duisburg
CH: Dr G. Vogelsang,
Dr D.H. Vogel 82, 91

Thyssen Industrie AG
Am Thyssenhaus 1, 45128 Essen, Germany
Tel: +49 2 01 106 0
Fax: +49 2 01 23 84 75
CH: Dr H. Kriwet,
Dr-Ing E. Rohkamm 96

Tibbett & Britten Group PLC
Ross House, 1 Shirley Road, Windmill
Hill, Enfield, Middx, EN2 6SB
Tel: 0181 366 9595
Fax: 0181 366 7042
CH: J.A. Harvey, *FD:* M.R. Stalbow 53

Tilbury Douglas PLC
Tilbury House, Ruscombe Park,
Twyford, Reading, Berks, RG10 9JU
Tel: 01734 320123
Fax: 01734 320206
CH: J.R.T. Douglas, *CE:* M.C. Bottjer,
FD: M.S. Lee 58

Time Warner Inc.
75 Rockefeller Plaza, New York, NY,
10019, USA
Tel: +1 212 484-8000
CH: G.M. Levin 111

Titaghur PLC
41 Reform Street, Dundee, DD1 1SH
Tel: 01382 24107
Fax: 01382 20643
CH: R.J. Brealey 60

Tohoku Electric Power Co. Inc.
7-1, Ichibancho 3-chome, Aoba-ku,
Sendai, Miyagi 980, Japan
Tel: +81 22 225 2111
Fax: +81 22 222 2881
P: Toshiaki Yashima, *CH:* Teruyuki
Akema, *JMD:* Yoshio Kamimura,
Yoshietsu Suto, Shigeya Higa, Kozo
Arita, Keiichi Makuta, Yuzuru Aoki,
Kozo Aratame, Hisashi Abe 13, 112

Tokyo Electric Power Co. Inc. (The)
1-3 Uchisaiwai-cho 1-chome,
Chiyoda-ku, Tokyo 100, Japan
Tel: +81 3 3501 8111
Fax: +81 3 3592 1795
P: Hiroshi Araki, *CH:* Shoh Nasu,
JMD: Kazunao Tomon, Yasuro Kawaji,
Hiroshi Kawasaki, Nobuya Minami,
Akinori Miyata, Shoji Hanawa, Tetsuo
Takeuchi, Kiyoshi Ishii 12, 13, 112

Tokyo Gas Co. Ltd
5-20 Kaigan 1-chome, Minato-ku,
Tokyo 105, Japan
Tel: +81 3 3433 2111
Fax: +81 3 5472 5385
P: Kunio Anzai, *CH:* Hiroshi
Watanabe, *JMD:* Osamu Takeuchi,
Yoshihisa Ohno, Yohei Yamamoto,
Akira Takeda, Nobumasa Hirao,
Takakazu Kobayashi, Reiji Fujii, Ichiro
Kagiyama, Toru Masuko, Hideharu
Uehara, Fumitake Yoshida 112

Tokyu Corpn
5-6 Nanpeidai-cho, Shibuya-ku,
Tokyo 150, Japan
Tel: +81 3 3477 6181
Fax: +81 3 3496 2965
CH: Jiro Yokota, *JMD:* Shinobu
Shimizu, Hisashi Nagatoshi, Kunihiko
Endoh, Kuniyoshi Ihara, Tadao Endoh,
Hisashi Akiyama, Kiyofumi Kamijo 113

Tomen Corpn
6-7 Kawaramachi 1-chome, Chuo-ku,
Osaka 530-91, Japan
Tel: +81 6 208 2211
P: Yasuo Matsukawa, *CH:* Tsuneo
Kitamura, *JMD:* Hideo Hirata, Masaru
Takemura, Yoshihiro Shito, Akihiro
Tsuji, Shiro Tamakoshi, Haruya
Koyama, Satoshi Miwa, Kazuo
Miyaoka, Keiji Kuwata, Kichibe Ozaki,
Takeshi Emi, Susumu Matsui, Tsutomu
Nishiwaki, Yoshiaki Ueki, Katsuhiko
Mizutani, Nobutane Edayoshi 113

Tomkins PLC
Tameway Tower, Bridge Street,
Walsall, West Midlands, WS1 1JZ
Tel: 01922 723372
Fax: 01922 644495
CH: G.F. Hutchings 44, 98

Topdanmark AS
Borupvang 4, 2750 Ballerup, Denmark
Tel: +45 44 68 33 11
Fax: +45 44 68 28 05
CH: K. Bonde Larsen, *CE:* K.G. Schou,
MD: L. Larsen 106

Toppan Printing Co. Ltd
1 Kanda Izumi-cho, Chiyoda-ku,
Tokyo 101, Japan
Tel: +81 3 3835 5741
Fax: +81 3 3835 0674
P: Hiromichi Fujita, *JMD:* Michio
Kodaira, Toru Kono, Kenji Ejima, Ikuo
Seki, Hisanobu Ono, Masahiro Fujii,
Shinpei Hasegawa, Yasuhiro Fukuda,
Hiroshi Kidokoro, Mikio Nakano 113

Tops Estates PLC
77 South Audley Street, London,
W1Y 6EE
Tel: 0171 486 4684
CH: E.N. Goodman 50

Toray Industries Inc.
2-1, Nihonbashi Muromachi 2-chome,
Chuo-ku, Tokyo 103, Japan
Tel: +81 3 3245-5111
Fax: +81 3 3245-5555
P: Katsunosuke Maeda, *CH:*
Yoshikazu Ito, *JMD:* Minoru Oda,
Susumu Iima, Yoshihiro Harada,
Hiroshi Kiuchi, Takayu Takayama,
Takashi Hara, Kozo Susami, Hiroshi
Maeda, Tsuneshiro Hosono, Takasuke
Chiyonobu, Hidetane Iijima, Hisao
Nakayama, Masatoshi Nakazama,
Akira Sawamura 113

Toro Assicurazioni
Via Arcivescovado 16, 10121 Turin, Italy
Tel: +39 11 516 3 111
Fax: +39 11 543 587
CH: B. Salaroli, *MD:* F. Torri 101

Toshiba (U.K.) Ltd
Toshiba House, Frimley Road, Frimley,
Camberley, Surrey, GU16 5JJ
Tel: 01276 62222

Fax: 01276 682256
No officers designated 61

Toshiba Corpn
1-1 Shibaura 1-chome, Minato-ku,
Tokyo 105, Japan
Tel: +81 3 3457 2105
Fax: +81 3 3456 4776
P: Fumio Sato, *CH:* Joichi Aoi 13, 112

Tosi [Franco] SpA
Via Brisa 3, 20123 Milan, Italy
Tel: +39 2 72 42 81
Fax: +39 2 876 259
CH: J. Conseil 109

Town Centre Securities PLC
Town Centre House, The Merrion
Centre, Leeds, LS2 8LY
Tel: 0113 245 9172
Fax: 0113 242 1026
CH: I.A. Ziff, *MD:* E.M. Ziff,
FD: D.S. Syers 50

Toyota Motor Corpn
1 Toyota-cho, Toyota City, Aichi
Prefecture 471, Japan
Tel: +81 565 28 2121
Fax: +81 565 23 5800
P: Tatsuro Toyoda, *CH:* Shoichiro
Toyoda, *JMD:* Akira Takahashi, Kenzo
Tamai, Iwao Okijima, Shigeji Tsuji,
Tadashi Ohnishi, Kenichi Kato,
Terukazu Inoue, Kosuke Yamamoto,
Akira Yokoi, Kanji Kurioka, Masanao
Shiomi, Hiroshi Chiwa, Masami
Konishi, Fujio Cho, Kosuke Ikebuchi,
Shinichi Kato, Tadaaki Jagawa 13, 112

Toys R Us Holdings PLC
Mitre House, 160 Aldersgate Street,
London, EC1A 4DD
Tel: 0171 606 9000
Fax: 0171 606 9100
CH: D. Rurka 49

Tractebel SA
1 place du Trone, 1000 Brussels, Belgium
Tel: +32 2 510 71 11
Fax: +32 2 510 73 88
CH: G. Mestrallet, Baron Bodson,
R. Neirynck, J. van der Schueren 77, 88, 91

Trade Indemnity Group PLC
Trade Indemnity House, 12-34 Great
Eastern Street, London, EC2A 3AX
Tel: 0171 739 4311
Fax: 0171 729 7682
CH: A.L. Brend, *MD:* V.C. Jacob 61

Trafalgar House PLC
1 Berkeley Street, London, W1A 1BY
Tel: 0171 499 9020
Fax: 0171 493 5484
CH: S. Keswick, *CE:* N. Rich,
FD: D. Gawler 14, 44, 97

Trafford Park Estates PLC
Neil House, Twining Road, Trafford
Park, Manchester, M17 1AT
Tel: 0161 872 5426
Fax: 0161 872 7644
CH: Sir Neil Westbrook 55

Transatlantic Holdings PLC
40 Broadway, London, SW1H 0BT
Tel: 0171 222 5496
Fax: 0171 222 5840
CH: D. Gordon, *MD:* D.A. Fischel 35, 43, 95

Transport Development Group PLC
Windsor House, 50 Victoria Street,
London, SW1H 0NR
Tel: 0171 222 7411
Fax: 0171 222 2806
CH: M.E. Llowarch, *CE:* A.J. Cole,
FD: S.G. Bentley 48

Travelers Group
65 East 55th Street, New York, NY,
10022, USA
Tel: +1 212 891 8900
P: J. Dimon, *CH:* S.I. Weill 110

Travis Perkins PLC
Lodge Way House, Harlestone Road,
Northampton, NN5 7UG
Tel: 01604 752424
Fax: 01604 587244
CH: T. Travis, *MD:* T. Adams,
FD: T. Best 52

Trelleborg AB
Box 153, Nygatan 102, 231 22

Trelleborg, Sweden
Tel: +46 410 670 00
Fax: +46 410 427 63
CH: R. Andersson, *JMD:* K. Nilsson,
K. Nilsson 98

Trinity International Holdings PLC
6 Heritage Court, Lower Bridge Street,
Chester, CH1 1RD
Tel: 01244 350555
Fax: 01244 341677
CH: D.K. Snedden, *CE:* P. Graf,
FD: M. Masters 53

Triplex Lloyd PLC
Quayside House, Rounds Green Road,
Oldbury, Warley, West Midlands,
B69 2DH
Tel: 0121 544 1000
Fax: 0121 544 3400
CH: C.I. Cooke, *CE:* G.W.S. Lockyer,
FD: R.W. Mitchell 58

Trygg-Hansa AB
Flemminggatan 18, 106 26 Stockholm,
Sweden
Tel: +46 8 693 10 00
Fax: +46 8 650 93 67
CH: L. Hallden, *CE:* L.H. Thunell 103

Tsim Sha Tsui Properties Ltd
12th Floor, Tsim Sha Tsui Centre,
Salisbury Road, Tsim Sha Tsui,
Kowloon, Hong Kong
Tel: +852 3-7218388
Fax: +852 3-7235901
CH: Robert Ng Chee Siong 114

Tullett & Tokyo Forex International Ltd
Cable House, 54-62 New Broad Street,
London, EC2M 1JJ
Tel: 0171 895 9595
Fax: 0171 867 0536
P: D. Tullett, *CH:* R.W. Magee,
JMD: T.J.R. Sanders, A.J. Styant,
FD: D.L. Lowe 57

U S West Inc.
7800 East Orchard Road, PO Box
6508, Englewood, Colorado,
80155-6508, USA
Tel: +1 303 793-6500
CH: R.D. McCormick 110

UAP [Cie]
9 place Vendome,
75052 Paris Cedex 01, France
Tel: +33 1 42 86 71 71
CH: J. Friedmann 69, 82, 91

UCB SA
Avenue Louise 326, 1050 Brussels,
Belgium
Tel: +32 2 641 14 14
Fax: +32 2 641 15 71
CH: Baron Jaumotte, W. de Clercq,
P.E. Maes, G. Jacobs 86, 103

UGC Ltd
Unipart House, Cowley, Oxford,
OX4 2PG
Tel: 01865 778966
Fax: 01865 713763
CH: R.W. Perry 55

UK Paper PLC
UK Paper House, Kemsley,
Sittingbourne, Kent, ME10 2SG
Tel: 01795 24488
CH: G.D. Mace 52

US Smaller Companies Investment Trust PLC
14 Melville Street, Edinburgh, EH3 7NS
Tel: 0131 220 0733
Fax: 0131 220 0735
CH: Prof J.C. Shaw 59

USDC Investment Trust PLC
Alban Gate, 14th Floor, 125 London
Wall, London, EC2Y 5AS
Tel: 0171 710 4567
Fax: 0171 710 4555
CH: Prof Sir Roland Smith 56

USM Texon Ltd
100 Ross Walk, Belgrave, Leicester,
LE4 5BX
Tel: 0116 2610111
Fax: 0116 2610423
CH: Sir John Collyear,
MD: J.C. Foster, *FD:* R.M. Bates 60

USX - Wassall

USX Corpn
600 Grant Street, Pittsburgh,
Pennsylvania, 15219-4776, USA
Tel: +1 412 433-1121
CH: C.A. Corry   110

Ugine SA
4 place de la Pyramide, La Defense 9,
Puteaux (Hauts-de-Seine), Cedex 33,
92070 Paris-La Defense, France
Tel: +33 1 49 00 60 20
Fax: +33 1 49 00 60 07
CH: P. Choppin de Janvry   100

UniChem PLC
UniChem House, Cox Lane,
Chessington, Surrey, KT9 1SN
Tel: 0181 391 2323
Fax: 0181 974 1707
CH: The Rt Hon The Lord Rippon of
Hexham, *CE:* J.F. Harris,
FD: G.I. Cooper   52

Unibail SA
108 rue de Richelieu, 75002 Paris, France
Tel: +33 1 40 15 21 21
Fax: +33 1 40 15 00 03
CH: L. Bressler, *MD:* A. Benon   106

Unicem SpA
Viale Ottavio Marchino 10, 15033
Casale Monferrato (AL), Italy
CH: G. Nasi, *MD:* P. Mantegazza   104

Unicom Corpn
One First National Plaza, P O Box
A-3005, Chicago, Illinois,
60690-3005, USA
P: S.K. Skinner,
CH: J.J. O'Connor   110

Unidanmark
2 Torvegade,, 1786 Copenhagen V,
Denmark
Tel: +45 33 33 33 33
Fax: +45 33 33 63 63
CH: J. Hoeg Pedersen   93

Unigate PLC
Unigate House, Wood Lane, London,
W12 7RP
Tel: 0181 749 8888
Fax: 0181 749 7166
CH: I.A. Martin, *CE:* R. Buckland,
FD: J.G. Worby   46, 105

Unilever Group
Weena 455, Rotterdam,
The Netherlands
Tel: +31 10 217 40 00
Fax: +31 217 4798
CH: M. Tabaksblat   75, 88, 89

Unilever PLC
Port Sunlight, Wirral, Merseyside,
L62 4ZA
Tel: 0151 644 8211
CH: Sir Michael Perry,
FD: H. Eggerstedt   20, 26, 40, 42, 91

Union Bank of Switzerland
Bahnhofstrasse 45, 8021 Zurich,
Switzerland
Tel: +41 1 234 11 11
Fax: +41 1 236 51 11
P: R. Studer, *CH:* Dr R. Holzach,
Dr N. Senn   67, 88, 89, 90

Union Electrica-Fenosa, SA
Capitan Haya 53, 28020 Madrid, Spain
Tel: +34 1 571 37 00
Fax: +34 1 571 82 46
CH: Carmela Arias y Diaz de Rabago,
J. Trincado Settier,
J.-M. Amusategui de la Cierva   92

Union Pacific Corpn
Martin Tower, Eighth & Eaton
Avenues, Bethlehem, Pennsylvania,
18018, USA
Tel: +1 610 861 3200
P: R.K. Davidson, *CH:* D. Lewis   111

Union Texas Petroleum Ltd
5th Floor, Bowater House, 68-114
Knightsbridge, London, SW1X 7LR
Tel: 0171 581 5122
CH: J.W.J. Hardy   50

Unipol SpA [Cia Assicuratrice]
Via Stalingrado 45, 40128 Bologna,
Italy
Tel: +39 51 507111
Fax: +39 51 375349
CH: E. Mazzoli, *MD:* I. Sacchetti   108

Unitas Ltd
Aleksanterinkatu 30, Helsinki, Finland
Tel: +358 0 1651
Fax: +358 0 165 2648
P: V. Vainio, *CH:* A. Hirvonen,
E.J. Toivanen   98

Unitech PLC
Apex Plaza, Forbury Road, Reading,
Berkshire, RG1 1AX
Tel: 01734 507075
Fax: 01734 588554
CH: P.A.M. Curry, *FD:* J.L. Hewitt   50

United Biscuits (Holdings) PLC
12 Hope Street, Edinburgh, EH2 4DD
CH: C.M. Short, *CE:* E.L. Nicoli,
FD: J.A. Warren   44, 98

United Friendly Group PLC
42 Southwark Bridge Road, London,
SE1 9HE
Tel: 0171 928 5644
Fax: 0171 261 9077
CH: A.J.S. Ewen, *CE:* R.E. Balding,
FD: G.P.R. Mack   55

United Glass Group Ltd
Porters Wood, Valley Road, St Albans,
Hertfordshire, AL3 6NY
Tel: 01727 59261
Fax: 01727 42661
No officers designated   56

United Industrial Corpn Ltd
5 Shenton Way, 02-16 UIC Building,
Singapore 0106
Tel: +65 2201352
Fax: +65 2240278
P: Lim Hock San,
CH: Wee Cho Yaw   115

United News & Media PLC
Ludgate House, 245 Blackfriars Road,
London, SE1 9UY
Tel: 0171 921 5000
Fax: 0171 928 2728
CH: The Lord Stevens of Ludgate,
MD: G.J.S. Wilson,
FD: C.R. Stern   46, 105

United Technologies Corpn
United Technologies Building, One
Financial Plaza, Hartford, Connecticut,
06101, USA
Tel: +1 203 728-7000
P: G. David, *CH:* R.F. Daniell   111

United Technologies Holdings PLC
Goldvale House, Church Street West,
Woking, Surrey, GU21 1DH
Tel: 01483 769222
CH: J.T. Leingang (USA)   52

Uralita SA
Mejia Lequerica 10, 28004 Madrid, Spain
Tel: +34 1 448 10 00
Fax: +34 1 447 11 26
CH: J.A. Garcia Diez   105

VIAG AG
Georg-von-Boeselager-Strasse 25,
53117 Bonn, Germany
Tel: +49 228 552-01
Fax: +49 228 5 52 21 22
CH: Dr J. Holzer, Dr G. Obermeier   74,
84, 90

VIB NV
Slotlaan 20, 3701 GK Zeist,
The Netherlands
Tel: +31 3404 28300
Fax: +31 3404 12041
CH: Mr W. Groenendijk   100

VNU (NV Verenigd Bezit)
Ceylonpoort 5-25, 2037 AA Haarlem,
The Netherlands
Tel: +31 23-304 304
Fax: +31 23-304 754
CH: Ir J.J. Kaptein, Drs J.L. Brentjens   107

VSEL PLC
Barrow-in-Furness, Cumbria, LA14 1AF
Tel: 01229 823366
Fax: 01229 873399
CH: The Rt Hon The Lord Chalfont,
CE: C.N. Davies,
FD: R.D. Holden   48, 108

Valenciana de Cementos Portland [Cia] SA
c/ Colon 68, 46004 Valencia, Spain
Tel: +34 6 352 64 26
Fax: +34 6 351 91 93
CH: L.H. Zambrano Trevino   101

Valeo
43, rue Bayen, 75017 Paris, France
Tel: +33 1 40 55 20 20
Fax: +33 1 40 55 21 71
CH: N. Goutard   98

Vallehermoso SA
Paseo de la Castellana 83-85, 28046
Madrid, Spain
Tel: +34 1 556 10 64
Fax: +34 1 597 01 90
CH: M. Eyries Valmaseda   103

Vallourec
130 rue de Silly, PO Box 414,
92103 Boulogne cedex, France
Tel: +33 1 49 09 38 24
CH: A. Leenhardt, J.-C. Cabre,
MD: J.-C. Verdiere   105

Valmet Oy
Panuntie 6, PO Box 27, 00621
Helsinki, Finland
Tel: +358 0 777 051
Fax: +358 0 7770 5580
CH: M. Sundberg, P. Maki-Hakola   102

Value and Income Trust PLC
45 Charlotte Square, Edinburgh,
EH2 4HW
Tel: 0131 226 3271
Fax: 0131 226 5120
CH: The Rt Hon Lord Thomson of
Monifieth   59, 61

Van Ommeren [Koninklijke] NV
Westerlaan 10, 3016 CK Rotterdam,
The Netherlands
Tel: +31 10 464 91 11
Fax: +31 10 464 23 16
CH: L.M. Kretzers,
C.J.van den Driest   104

Vard AS
Munkedamsveien 45 C, PO Box 1811
Vika, 0123 Oslo, Norway
Tel: +47 22 83 03 10
Fax: +47 22 83 04 18
P: B.S. Karlsen, *CH:* K. Siem   103

Varta AG
Seedammweg 55, 61352 Bad
Homburg, Germany
Tel: +49 61 72 4 04-0
Fax: +49 61 72 4 04-338
CH: H. Meinhardt, E. Schipporeit   105

Vattenfall AB
Jamtlandsgatan 99, Vallingby,
162 87 Stockholm, Sweden
Tel: +46 8 739 5000
Fax: +46 8 370 170
P: C-E. Nyquist, *CH:* K-E. Sahlberg   92

Vaux Group PLC
The Brewery, Sunderland, SR1 3AN
Tel: 0191 567 6277
Fax: 0191 514 2488
CH: Sir Paul Nicholson,
MD: F. Nicholson,
FD: T.G. Walker   46, 103

Vauxhall Motors Ltd
Griffin House, Osborne Road, Luton,
Bedfordshire, LU1 3YT
Tel: 01582 21122
Fax: 01582 426351
CH: C.E. Golden   45, 100

Veba AG
Bennigsensplatz 1, 40474 Dusseldorf,
Germany
Tel: +49 211 45 79-1
Fax: +49 211 45 79-5 01
CH: H.J. Strenger,
U. Hartmann   12, 13, 62, 67, 76, 85,
88, 89, 90

Vereinigte Elektrizitatswerke Westfalen AG
Rheinlanddamm 24, 44139 Dortmund,
Germany
Tel: +49 231 438-0
Fax: +49 231 438-2147
CH: G. Samtlebe, F. Ziegler   93

Vibroplant PLC
Prospect Road, Starbeck, Harrogate,
North Yorkshire, HG2 7PW
Tel: 01423 885911
Fax: 01423 887231
CH: J.F.G. Pilkington,
FD: E. Woolley   60

Vicat SA
Tour GAN, Cedex 13,

92082 Paris La Defense, France
Tel: +33 1 41 26 48 48
Fax: +33 1 41 26 48 88
CH: A. Merceron-Vicat,
J. Merceron-Vicat   106

Vickers PLC
Vickers House, Millbank Tower,
Millbank, London, SW1P 4RA
Tel: 0171 828 7777
Fax: 0171 828 6585
CH: Sir Richard Lloyd,
CE: Sir Colin Chandler,
MD: R.B. Head   47, 76, 107

Victoria Holding AG
40198 Dusseldorf, Germany
CH: Prof Dr W. Hilger,
Dr E. Jannott   101

Videotron Holdings PLC
Videotron House, 76 Hammersmith
Road, London, W14 8UD
Tel: 0181 244 2444
CH: Sir G.R. Jefferson,
MD: N.J. Kane   47, 108

Villeroy & Boch AG
Postfach 1120, Saarruferstrasse,
66688 Mettlach, Germany
Tel: +49 68 64 8 11
Fax: +49 68 64 81 86 92
CH: K.G. Ratjen,
L.G. von Boch-Galhau   104

Vinten Group PLC
Western Way, Bury St Edmunds,
Suffolk, IP33 3TB
Tel: 01284 752121
Fax: 01284 750567
CH: J.H.A. Wood,
CE: M.A.W. Baggott,
FD: R.A. Green   59

Virgin Retail Group Ltd
120 Campden Hill Road, London,
W8 7AR
Tel: 0171 229 1282
Fax: 0171 727 8200
No officers designated   58

Vodafone Group PLC
The Courtyard, 2-4 London Road,
Newbury, Berkshire, RG13 1JL
Tel: 01635 33251
Fax: 01635 45713
CH: Sir Ernest Harrison,
CE: G.A. Whent   40, 45, 102

Volkswagen AG
38436 Wolfsburg, Germany
Tel: +49 53 61 9-0
Fax: +49 53 61 9-2 82 82
CH: K. Liesen, F. Piech   12, 13, 62,
66, 90

Volvo [AB]
405 08 Gothenburg, Sweden
Tel: +46 31 59 00 00
CH: B-O. Svanholm, *CE:* S. Gyll,   73,
86, 88, 91

Von Roll AG
4563 Gerlafingen, Switzerland
Tel: +41 65 34 22 34
Fax: +41 65 35 14 84
CH: Dr M.D. Amstutz,
M. Amstutz   105

Vorarlberger Kraftwerke AG
Weidachstrasse 6, 6900 Bregenz,
Austria
Tel: +43 55 74/601 0
CH: Dr R. Mandl   109

Vorwerk & Co.
Muhlenweg 17-37, 42270 Wuppertal,
Germany
Tel: +49 2 02 5 64-12 21
Fax: +49 2 02 5 64-12 54
P: G. Busch   107

Vosper Thornycroft Holdings PLC
Victoria Road, Woolston,
Southampton, SO19 9RR
Tel: 01703 445144
Fax: 01703 421539
CH: Lord Wakenham, *CE:* M. Jay,
FD: C.F.G. Girling   59

WMX Technologies Inc.
3003 Butterfield Road, Oak Brook,
Illinois, 60521, USA
Tel: +1 708 572 8000
P: P.B. Rooney, *CH:* D.L. Buntrock   111

WPP Group PLC
Pennypot Industrial Estate, Hythe,
Kent, CT21 6PE
CH: G.K.G. Stevens, *CE:* M.S. Sorrell,
FD: R.E. Lerwill   49

Wace Group PLC
Wace House, Shepherdess Walk,
London, N1 7LH
Tel: 0171 250 3055
Fax: 0171 608 3337
CH: F.H. ten Bos, *CE:* T.C. Grice,
MD: D. Ashley, *FD:* S.R. Puckett   56

Wacker-Chemie GmbH
Hanns-Seidel-Platz 4, 81737 Munich,
Germany
Tel: +49 89 62 79-01
Fax: +49 89 62 79-17 70
CH: Prof Dr W. Hilger, Dr J. Kohl   101

Waddington [John] PLC
Wakefield Road, Leeds, LS10 1DU
Tel: 0113 277 0202
Fax: 0113 271 3553
CH: D.G. Perry, *CE:* M.H. Buckley,
FD: G. Gibson   56

Wagon Industrial Holdings PLC
Haldane House, Halesfield, Telford,
Shropshire, TF7 4PB
Tel: 01952 680111
Fax: 01952 587811
CH: P.D. Taylor, *CE:* J.L. Hudson,
MD: K. Wilson, *FD:* I.R. Fox   56

Wainhomes PLC
The Beeches, Chester, CH2 1PE
Tel: 01244 310421
Fax: 01244 341924
CH: G.B. Reed, *CE:* R. Smith,
FD: S.J. Owen   61

Wal-Mart Stores Inc.
Bentonville, Arkansas, 72716-8611,
USA
Tel: +1 501 273-4000
P: D.D. Glass, *CE:* S.R. Walton   110

Walker [James] Group Ltd
Lion Works, Woking, Surrey,
GU22 8AP
Tel: 01483 757575
Fax: 01483 755711
CH: C.J. Higgins, *MD:* M.J. Kelly   59

Walkers Smiths Snack Foods Ltd
Feature Road, Thurmaston, Leicester,
LE4 8BS
Tel: 0116 269 1691
No officers designated   47, 105

Walter Bau AG
Boheimstrasse 8, 86153 Augsburg,
Germany
Tel: +49 8 21 55 82-00
Fax: +49 8 21 55 82 320
CH: R. Eberhard, I. Walter   107

Warburg [S.G.] Group PLC
1 Finsbury Avenue, London, EC2M 2PA
Tel: 0171 606 1066
Fax: 0171 382 4800
CH: C.B. Gough,
CE: Sir David Scholey   14, 36, 43,
69, 96

Warburtons Ltd
Back o' th' Bank House, Blackburn
Road, Bolton, Lancashire, BL1 8HJ
Tel: 01204 23551
Fax: 01204 28883
CH: W.R. Warburton   61

Warner Estate Holdings PLC
3 Vere Street, London, W1M 0JZ
Tel: 0171 493 6480
Fax: 0171 493 0979
CH: P.C.T. Warner, *FD:* D.J. Veaser   52

Warner Lambert (UK) Ltd
Lambert Court, Chestnut Avenue,
Eastleigh, Hampshire, S05 3ZQ
Tel: 01703 620500
Fax: 01703 629812
No officers designated   54

Warnford Investments PLC
465 Salisbury House, London Wall,
London, EC2M 5RQ
Tel: 0171 588 6856
Fax: 0171 638 2381
CH: M. Ross, *MD:* L. Sebba   55

Wassall PLC
39 Victoria Street, London, SW1H 0EE

Waste - Zurich

Tel: 0171 333 0303
Fax: 0171 333 0304
CH: J.D. Miller, *CE:* J.C. Miller,
FD: F.I. Watt 47, 107

Waste Management International PLC
3 Shortlands, Hammersmith International Centre, London, W6 8RX
Tel: 0181 563 7000
Fax: 0181 563 6300
CH: E.G. Falkman (USA),
CE: J.M. Holsten, *MD:* I. Wakelin,
FD: B. Gabrielson 44, 99

Waterford Wedgwood U.K. PLC
Barlaston, Stoke-on-Trent,
Staffordshire, ST12 9ES
Tel: 01782 204141
Fax: 01782 204402
CH: R.H. Niehaus 52

Wates Building Group Ltd
1260 London Road, Norbury, London, SW16 4EG
Tel: 0181 764 5000
Fax: 0181 764 0939
CH: M.E. Wates,
CE: Sir Christopher Wates 60

Wates City of London Properties PLC
Level 21, City Tower, 40 Basinghall Street, London, EC2V 5DE
Tel: 0171 588 2888
Fax: 0171 588 3799
CH: P.C.R. Wates, *MD:* R. Clutton,
FD: J.D. Nettleton 60

Watmoughs (Holdings) PLC
Jason House, Hillam Road, Bradford, West Yorkshire, BD2 1QN
Tel: 01274 735663
Fax: 01274 734206
CH: P.G. Walker, *FD:* J.H. Newman 54

Watson & Philip PLC
Strathtay House, Dundee, DD2 1TP
Tel: 01382 592000
Fax: 01382 561450
CH: J.K. Watson, *CE:* D.M. Bremner,
FD: G.A. Leckie 59

Watts, Blake, Bearne & Co. PLC
Park House, Courtenay Park, Newton Abbot, Devon, TQ12 4PS
Tel: 01626 332345
Fax: 01626 332344
CH: M.E. Beckett, *CE:* G. Lawson,
MD: J.D. Pike, *FD:* D.B. Bowden 57

Weetabix Ltd
Weetabix Mills, Burton Latimer, Kettering, Northamptonshire, NN15 5JR
Tel: 01536 722181
Fax: 01536 726148
CH: R.W. George 55

Weir Group PLC (The)
149 Newlands Road, Cathcart, Glasgow, G44 4EX
Tel: 0141 637 7111
Fax: 0141 637 2221
CH: The Rt Hon The Viscount Weir,
CE: R. Garrick, *FD:* I.M. Boyd 51

Weir [Andrew] & Co. Ltd
Dexter House, 2 Royal Mint Court, London, EC3N 4XX
Tel: 0171 265 0808
Fax: 0171 481 4784
CH: Viscount Runciman,
CE: A.R.C.B. Cooke 56

Wella AG
Berliner Allee 65, 64274 Darmstadt, Germany
Tel: +49 6151 34 0
Fax: +49 6151 34 33 19
CH: K.H. Krutzki, P. Zuhlsdorff 104

Wells [Charles] Ltd
The Brewery, Havelock Street, Bedford, Bedfordshire, MK40 1QA
Tel: 01234 65100
Fax: 01234 40815
CH: J.H. Wells 61

Welsh Water PLC
Plas y Ffynnon, Cambrian Way, Brecon, Powys, LD3 7HP
Tel: 01874 623181
Fax: 01874 4167
CH: I.R. Evans, *CE:* G.A. Hawker,
FD: P.J. Twamley 44, 97

Wembley PLC
Wembley Stadium, Wembley, HA9 0DW
Tel: 0181 902 8833
Fax: 0181 900 1055
CH: C.A. Hultman, *CE:* A.C. Coppin,
FD: N. Potter 52

Wereldhave NV
Nassaulaan 23, 2514 JT The Hague, The Netherlands
Tel: +31 70 3469325
Fax: +31 70 3638990
CH: J.F. Visser, G.C.J. Verweij 52, 100

Wereldhave Property Corporation PLC
19 Sloane Street, London, SW1X 9NE
Tel: 0171 235 2080
Fax: 0171 245 9962
No officers designated 52, 100

Wessel & Vett [AS Th.], Magasin du Nord AS
Vingardstraede 6, 1095 Copenhagen K, Denmark
Tel: +45 33 11 44 33
Fax: +45 33 93 39 14
CH: Baron E. Wedell-Wedellsborg,
CE: S. Gulmann, H. Werdelin,
JMD: I. Jessen, I. Jessen (Acting) 60

Wessex Water PLC
Wessex House, Passage Street, Bristol, BS2 0JQ
Tel: 0117 929 0611
Fax: 0117 929 3137
CH: W.N. Hood, *CE:* C.F. Skellett,
FD: N.A.W. Wheatley 44, 99

West Bromwich Building Society
374 High Street, West Bromwich, West Midlands, B70 8LR
Tel: 0121 525 7070
Fax: 0121 500 5961
CH: J.D. Baker, *CE:* G.W. Elliot 56

Westbury PLC
Westbury House, Lansdown Road, Cheltenham, Gloucestershire, GL50 2JA
Tel: 01242 236191
Fax: 01242 584281
CH: G.K. Maddrell, *CE:* R.L. Fraser,
FD: J.H. Bennett 56

Western Mining Corpn Holdings Ltd
31st Floor, 360 Collins Street, Melbourne, Victoria 3000, Australia
Tel: +61 3 685 6000
Fax: +61 3 670 9591
CH: Sir A. Parbo,
MD: H.M. Morgan 114

Western United Investment Co. Ltd
16 St John's Lane, London, EC1M 4BS
Tel: 0171 248 1212
Fax: 0171 236 7627
No officers designated 52

Westminster Health Care Holdings PLC
48 Leicester Square, London, WC2H 7FB
Tel: 0171 839 9302
Fax: 0171 930 2673
CH: J.W. Lockhart, *CE:* P.R. Carter,
FD: K.W. Phippen 54

Westpac Banking Corpn
60 Martine Place, Sydney, New South Wales, 2000, Australia
Tel: +61 2 226 3311
Fax: +61 2 226 4128
CH: J.A. Uhrig, *MD:* R.L. Joss 114

Wetherspoon [J D] PLC
735 High Road, North Finchley, London, N12 0BP
Tel: 0181 446 9099
CH: T.R. Martin, *MD:* M. McQuater,
FD: R. Pennycook 56

Weyerhaeuser Co.
Tacoma, Washington, 98477, USA
Tel: +1 206 924-2345
P: J.W. Creighton Jr,
CH: G.H. Weyerhaeuser 111

Wharf (Holdings) Ltd (The)
26th Floor, World-Wide House, 19 Des Voeux Road, Central, Hong Kong
CH: Gonzaga W.J. Li 114

Whatman PLC
Whatman House, St Leonard's Road, Maidstone, Kent, ME16 0LS
Tel: 01622 676670

Fax: 01622 677011
CH: A.R.W. Smithers,
CE: C.S. Knight, *FD:* H.R.I. Perrott 61

Wheelock and Co. Ltd
23rd Floor, Wheelock House, 20 Pedder Street, Hong Kong
CH: Peter Kwong-Ching Woo,
FD: K.H. Leung 114

Whitbread PLC
Brewery, Chiswell Street, London, EC1Y 4SD
Tel: 0171 606 4455
Fax: 0171 374 8421
CH: Sir Michael Angus, *CE:* P.J. Jarvis,
FD: A.S. Perelman 29, 43, 94

Wickes PLC
19/21 Mortimer Street, London, W1N 7RJ
Tel: 0171 631 1018
Fax: 0171 637 1784
CH: H.A. Sweetbaum,
FD: S.R. Stradling 51

Wienerberger Baustoffindustrie AG
Wienerbergstrasse 11, 1102 Vienna, Austria
Tel: +43 1 60 192/0
Fax: +43 1 60 192/473
CH: G. Schmidt-Chiari, E. Schaschl 103

Wilhelmsen [Wilh.] Ltd AS
Strandveien 20, PO Box 33, 1324 Lysaker, Norway
Tel: +47 67 58 40 00
Fax: +47 67 58 40 80
CH: W. Wilhelmsen,
MD: L.T. Loddesol 107

Williams Holdings PLC
Pentagon House, Sir Frank Whittle Road, Derby, DE2 4XA
Tel: 01332 202020
Fax: 01332 384402
CH: A.N.R. Rudd,
CE: R.M. Carr 45, 100

Williamson [George] & Co. Ltd
5 West Mills, Newbury, Berkshire, RG14 5HG
Tel: 01635 522088
Fax: 01635 551992
CH: R.B. Magor, *MD:* P. Magor 58

Willis Corroon Group PLC
Ten Trinity Square, London, EC3P 3AX
Tel: 0171 488 8111
Fax: 0171 488 8223
CH: R.J. Elliott,
FD: R.A. Dalzell 46, 105

Wilson (Connolly) Holdings PLC
Thomas Wilson House, Tenter Road, Moulton Park, Northampton, NN3 1QJ
Tel: 01604 790909
Fax: 01604 492387
CH: L.A. Wilson, *MD:* I.C. Black,
FD: S.D. Lawther 49

Wilson Bowden PLC
Wilson Bowden House, 207 Leicester Road, Ibstock, Leicester, LE67 6HP
Tel: 01530 260777
Fax: 01530 262805
CH: D.W. Wilson, *FD:* I. Robertson 49

Wimpey [George] PLC
27 Hammersmith Grove, London, W6 7EN
Tel: 0181 748 2000
Fax: 0181 748 0076
CH: Sir John Quinton,
CE: J.A. Dwyer,
FD: R.C.C. Saville 45, 101

Winterthur Ste Suisse d'Assurances
General Guisan-Strasse 40, 8401 Winterthur, Switzerland
Tel: +41 52 261 11 11
Fax: +41 52 213 66 20
CH: P. Spalti 67

Witan Investment Company PLC
3 Finsbury Avenue, London, EC2M 2PA
Tel: 0171 638 5757
Fax: 0171 377 5742
CH: The Lord Faringdon,
MD: C.G. Clarke 41, 44, 99

Wolseley PLC
PO Box 18, Vines Lane, Droitwich, Worcestershire, WR9 8ND
Tel: 01905 794444
Fax: 01905 776704

CH: J. Lancaster,
FD: S.P. Webster 45, 100

Wolverhampton & Dudley Breweries, PLC
PO Box 26, Park Brewery, Wolverhampton, WV1 4NY
Tel: 01902 711811
Fax: 01902 29136
CH: J.D.F. Miller,
MD: D.G.F. Thompson 47, 107

Wood [John] Group PLC
John Wood House, Greenwell Road, East Tullos, Aberdeen, AB1 4AX
Tel: 01224 851000
Fax: 01224 871997
CH: Sir I.C. Wood 57

Woodside Petroleum Ltd
Level 40, 385 Bourke Street, Melbourne, 3000, Australia
Tel: +61 3 252 2000
Fax: +61 3 602 5621
CH: D.W. Rogers, *MD:* D.C.K. Allen,
FD: D.B. Larke 115

Woolwich Building Society
Corporate Headquarters, Watling Street, Bexleyheath, Kent, DA6 7RR
Tel: 0181 298 5000
CH: C.A. McLintock,
CE: D.H. Kirkham, *FD:* M.E. Tuke 25, 42, 93

Worms & Cie
77 rue la Boetie, 75008 Paris, France
Tel: +33 1 44 13 38 00
Fax: +33 1 44 13 38 77
CH: J. Legrand, F. Essig 82, 97

Wunsche AG
Palmaille 75, 22767 Hamburg, Germany
Tel: +49 40 3 80 31-0
Fax: +49 40 3 80 31-341
CH: Dr H. Erichsen 107

Wyeth [John] & Brother Ltd
Huntercombe Lane South, Taplow, Maidenhead, Berks, SL6 0PH
Tel: 01628 604377
Fax: 01628 66368
No officers designated 58

Wyevale Garden Centres PLC
Kings Acre Road, Hereford, HR4 0SE
Tel: 01432 276568
Fax: 01432 263289
CH: J. Rudgard, *CE:* B.A. Evans,
FD: S. Murfin 61

Wyn-Ro Properties Ltd
Leconfield House, Curzon Street, London, W1Y 7FB
Tel: 0171 409 1055
No officers designated 51

Xerox Corpn
PO Box 1600, 800 Long Ridge Road, Stamford, Connecticut, 06904, USA
Tel: +1 203 968-3000
CH: P.A. Allaire 110

Yamaichi Securities Co. Ltd
4-1 Yaesu 2-chome, Chuo-ku, Tokyo 104, Japan
Tel: +81 3 3276 3181
Fax: +81 3 3276 2947/8
P: Atsuo Miki, *CH:* Yoshio Yokota, Tsugio Yukihira, *JMD:* Hidekuni Iyama, Tsuneo Nakamura, Haruo Sato, Tohru Kimoto, Kiyoaki Sato, Hiromichi Ishikawa, Shoji Saotome, Tatsuhiko Kutsuzawa, Shohei Nozawa, Morio Iso, Nobuo Kawazoe, Masahiro Hiromatsu, Shigeyuki Wakabayashi 113

Yattendon Investment Trust PLC
Harborne Court, 67 Harborne Road, Edgbaston, Birmingham, B15 3BU
Tel: 0121 643 1300
CH: R.P.R. Iliffe 50

Yeoman Investment Trust PLC
23 Cathedral Yard, Exeter, Devon, EX1 1HB
Tel: 01392 412122
Fax: 01392 53282
CH: N.W. Berry 57

Yorkshire Bank PLC
20 Merrion Way, Leeds, LS2 8NZ
Tel: 0113 247 2000
Fax: 0113 242 0733
CH: The Rt Hon Lord Clitheroe,
CE: D.T. Gallagher 47, 106

Yorkshire Building Society
Yorkshire House, Yorkshire Drive, Bradford, BD5 8LJ
Tel: 01274 740740
CH: P.H. Courtney, *CE:* D.F. Roberts,
FD: T.A. Smith 47, 107

Yorkshire Chemicals PLC
Kirkstall Road, Leeds, LS3 1LL
Tel: 0113 2443111
Fax: 0113 2421670
CH: P.A. Lowe, *JMD:* M. Greenhalgh, A. Holt, J. Walker, *FD:* M.J. Wilson 57

Yorkshire Electricity Group PLC
Wetherby Road, Scarcroft, Leeds, LS14 3HS
Tel: 0113 289 2123
Fax: 0113 289 5611
CH: C. Hampson, *CE:* J.M. Chatwin,
FD: A.W.J. Coleman 45, 100

Yorkshire Food Group PLC
Carter Mills, 146 Cleckheaton Road, Bradford, West Yorkshire, BD12 0HF
Tel: 01274 691285
Fax: 01274 604971
CH: M.R. Firth, *FD:* D.E. Morgan 60

Yorkshire Water PLC
2 The Embankment, Sovereign Street, Leeds, LS1 4BG
Tel: 0113 234 3234
Fax: 0113 234 2322
CH: Sir Gordon Jones,
FD: M.C. Batty 39, 43, 96

Yorkshire-Tyne Tees Television Holdings PLC
The Television Centre, Leeds, LS3 1JS
Tel: 0113 243 8283
Fax: 0113 244 5107
CH: G.E. Ward Thomas,
CE: B. Gyngell, *FD:* N. Castro 60

Young and Co's Brewery PLC
The Ram Brewery, Wandsworth, London, SW18 4JD
Tel: 0181 870 0141
Fax: 0181 870 9444
CH: J.A. Young, *MD:* C.P.W. Read,
FD: C. Clitherow 53

Yule Catto & Co. PLC
Temple Fields, Harlow, Essex, CM20 2BH
Tel: 01279 442791
Fax: 01279 641360
CH: Lord Catto, *CE:* A. Walker,
FD: A.P. McLeish 57

ZENECA Group PLC
15 Stanhope Gate, London, W1Y 6LN
Tel: 0171 304 5000
CH: Sir Sydney Lipworth,
CE: J.D.F. Barnes 28, 40, 43, 89, 94

ZF Friedrichshafen AG
88038 Friedrichshafen, Germany
Tel: +49 75 41 77-0
Fax: +49 75 41 77-21 58
CH: Dr B. Wiedmann, Dr K.P. Bleyer 97

Zanders Feinpapiere AG
An der Gohrsmuhle, 51439 Bergisch Gladbach, Germany
Tel: +49 22 02 15-0
Fax: +49 22 02 15-28 06
CH: J-P. Montel, Dr H. Geginat 108

Zellweger Luwa AG
8610 Uster, Switzerland
Tel: +41 1 943 22 11
Fax: +41 1 940 70 79
CH: T.W. Bechtler, *MD:* K. Peter 109

Zuger Kantonalbank
Bahnhofstrasse 1, 6301 Zug, Switzerland
Tel: +41 42 25 55 11
Fax: +41 42 25 55 55
CH: Dr R. Oswald,
J.M. Auf der Maur 102

Zurcher Ziegeleien Holding
Giesshubelstrasse 45, 8045 Zurich, Switzerland
Tel: +41 1 468 24 00
Fax: +41 1 468 23 09
CH: J. Schmidheiny 107

Zurich Insurance Co.
Mythenquai 2, 8002 Zurich, Switzerland
Tel: +41 1 205 21 21
Fax: +41 1 201 33 97
CH: R. Huppi 83, 91

Are you battling against a tidal wave of financial information?

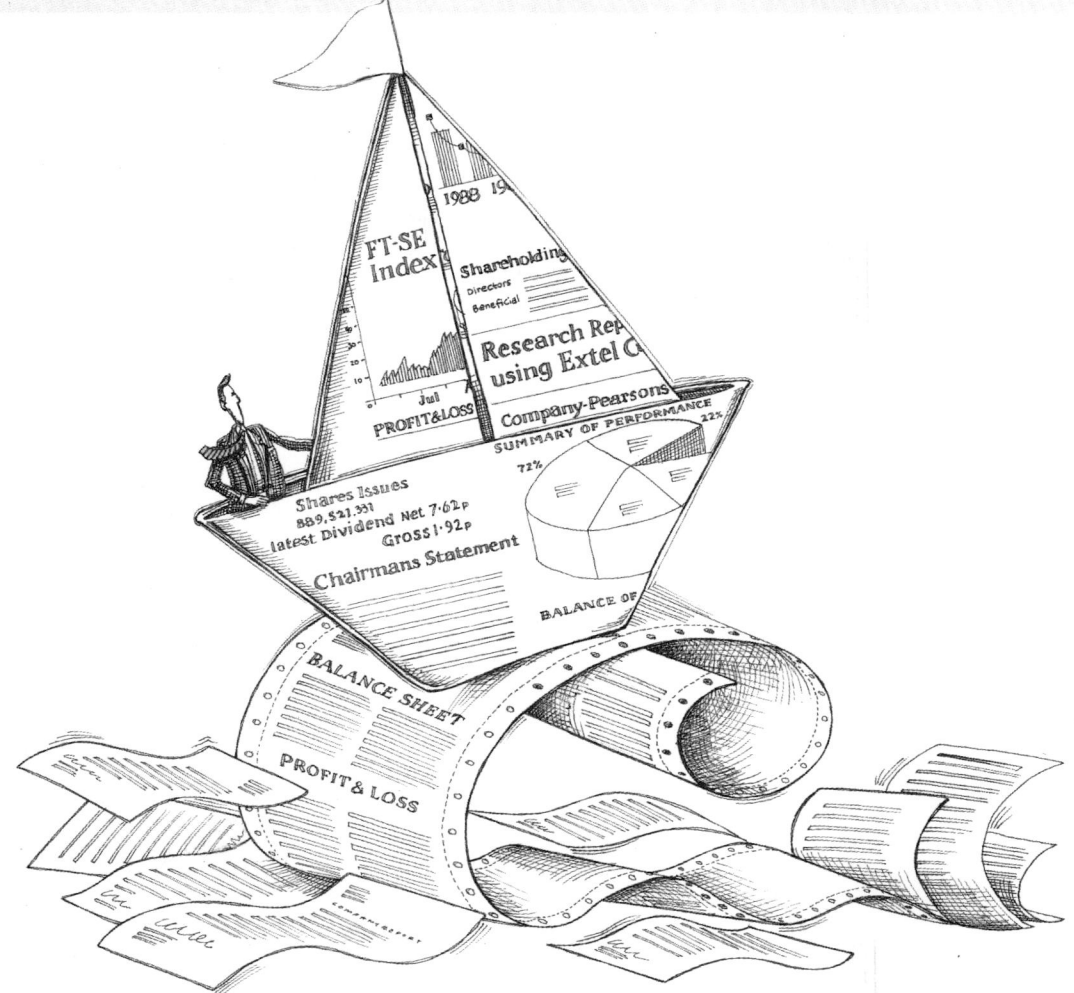

With FT Extel's publications, it's plain sailing.

Covering UK and International markets, FT Extel's publications and **NEW** CD-ROM services provide reliable and accurate information essential for researching new business and investment opportunities.

From company financial handbooks and securities taxation annuals to corporate news summaries and registrars books, FT Extel has the solution to suit your needs.

For further information and a FREE catalogue call Amelia Power on
Tel: +44 (0)171 825 8000, Fax: +44 (0)171 608 2032
or write to Amelia Power, FT Extel, Fitzroy House, 13-17 Epworth Street,
London EC2A 4DL, England.

FT EXTEL

FT
FINANCIAL TIMES
Information